HOW TO BE A DIRT-SMART BUYER

OF COUNTRY PROPERTY

Volume II

Curtis Seltzer

Copyright © 2014 by Curtis Seltzer

All rights reserved. No part of this book shall be reproduced or transmitted in any form or by any means, electronic, mechanical, magnetic, photographic including photocopying, recording or by any information storage and retrieval system, without prior written permission of the publisher. No patent liability is assumed with respect to the use of the information contained herein. Although every precaution has been taken in the preparation of this book, the publisher and author assume no responsibility for errors or omissions. Neither is any liability assumed for damages resulting from the use of the information contained herein.

The author is not a lawyer, logger, accountant, truck mechanic, real-estate broker, ditch-digger, tax consultant, wildlife biologist, agricultural economist, architect, forester, tractor salesperson, surveyor, minerals geologist, builder, Internet wiz, soils scientist, house inspector, marital-arts consultant, civil engineer, financial planner, cesspool guru or literary critic. Therefore, the views he expresses herein on these matters and all others should be taken by readers as opinions rather than professional advice. Neither the publisher nor author can assume responsibility or liability for how any individual reader applies the author's opinions.

Printed in the United States of America
Printed on Recycled Paper
Published October 2014

To Molly, a wonderful daughter and a good writer

ACKNOWLEDGMENTS

I've needed help and was fortunate to have gotten it.

Clif Rexrode, Appalachian Forestry Services of Waynesboro, Virginia, has been a boots-on-the-ground consulting forester for 30 years. His knowledge of forestry issues and his willingness to share it with me were invaluable. I cannot thank him adequately. I hope that I, at least, amused him with my questions as I wasted his time looking at one high-graded tract after another. He's been a true friend over the years.

Tom Arbogast, who heads the tax practice at Schnader Harrison Segal & Lewis, LLP in Pittsburgh, is both a lawyer and a CPA. His generous offer to review what I wrote on tax issues was a brilliant beacon in what always looks to me like impenetrable, unfathomable darkness.

Susan McCray, my CPA in Staunton, Virginia, reviewed drafts of Chapters 6 and 24, both dealing with tax issues. She saved me from myself many times. She prevented me from reaping in final form what I had sown in draft.

Les LaPrade, Jr., of McDowell, Virginia, rescued me from my computer ignorance. With patience and good humor, he reformatted the entire manuscript, taking out my "hard returns" line by line and justifying my right margins. Since I'm just a typewriter guy transplanted to a keyboard, I feel that Bill Gates treated me and all other old manuals pretty shabbily by ensnaring us in this hand-work booby trap. Les has a more sensible attitude toward computers than I have. He wants to understand why they do things: I just want them not to hurt me. I could not have submitted this manuscript without Les and his wife, Laura, who showed him a thing or two when he needed to be shown a thing or two.

Tom Atkeson, a retired engineer in Monterey, Virginia, drew several drawings that required a clear and steady hand, not my scritch-scratch penmanship. And even though Tom's hand is not as clear and steady as it was when he was at VMI and in Vietnam, it's still clear and steady enough to get the job done.

All errors of fact and misjudgments are mine.

I've picked up land knowledge over the years from many individuals, including Harrison Elkins, David R. Underhill, Portia and Tom Weiskel, Mike and Joy Brenneman, Charlie Taylor, Jim Loesel, Gibby Crummett, Harry Haney, Robert Barrett, Stephen W. Dorris, Sam Vansickle, M.C. Davis, Pete Johnson, Tim Linstrom, Joe Leininger, John Crites, Julia Elbon, Darrell V. McGraw, Robert W. Tufts, Robert Guerrant, Angela Blythe, John Alexander Williams, Nancy Debevoise, Thomas Taylor, John Lindsey, Mark Yanoski, Carey Dowd, Stephen J. Small, Willie Anderson, Barbara E. Smith, Helen Steele, Ann Swartz, Robert Payne, John David, Beverly Medgaus Jones and Melissa Ann Dowd.

I've also learned from Billy Shepherd, Alan Gourley, Mike McEver, Dan Girouard, Dave Mayo, Murray Gibson, Jim Woltz, Chris Bland, Huel Wheeler and Daniel McKittrick.

The first book I read about investing in real estate was formative—George Bockl, <u>How to Use Leverage to Make Money in Local Real Estate</u> (Englewood Cliffs, NJ: Prentice-Hall, 1965). I bought it for $1 at our library's annual book auction. It led to my first purchase of land—400 acres—with no money in the deal.

I have used masculine pronouns for lack of a gender-neutral alternative. I found using he to refer to a seller or buyer was less offensive to my ear than using she or the brain-jarring, they. My ear, of course, is now 61 years old; younger ears may find the old-fashioned masculine objectionable. For what it's worth, whenever I wrote he and him, my thoughts included she and her.

My mother, Rena C. Seltzer, helped me buy my first piece of land, and the estate of my father, Robert Seltzer, helped buy our farm. My aunt, Lucy Katz, helps me keep their memories.

My wife, Melissa Ann Dowd, didn't ask, didn't tell and didn't wonder out loud why I never seemed to be finished writing.

TABLE OF CONTENTS – VOLUME 2

Introduction……………………………………………………………………………………….i

Chapter 1:	Three Writers Show How Not to Do It………………………………………………...1

Chapter 2:	What Am I Looking for and Why Am I Looking for It ………………………………15
	Know Thyself
	Make a Revocable List
	Types of Properties

Chapter 3:	Farmland and Farm Dirt ……………………………………………………………...32
	Dirt
	Farms and Money
	Subsidies
	Rent with an Option to Operate
	Farm Leases and Crop Genetics

Chapter 4:	First-Time Farmers…………………………………………………………………...56
	Conventional Farming

Chapter 5:	Non-Conventional Farming ………………………………………………………….63
	Organics

Chapter 6:	Farming The Tax Code, Sowing and Reaping………………………………………..73
	Business and Hobbies
	Basis
	Severable Assets
	Estate Taxes

Chapter 7:	Manure Belongs on Your Boots, Not in Your Rap…………………………………..101
	"Is there anybody left to wal*k that muddy mile?"
	Buying and Selling to Your Friends and Neighbors
	Start New Things Slowly; Make Small Mistakes

Chapter 8:	Farm Equipment: Stuff is Us 112	
	Tractors: New and Used	

Chapter 9: Undeveloped Property for Hunting...130
　　　　　Hunting Hunting Land

Chapter 10: Infrastructure-Land, Property and Site...140
　　　　　Infrastructure Packages
　　　　　Property and Site Infrastructure
　　　　　Infrastructure Costs
　　　　　Property and Site Infrastructure Check List
　　　　　Flip, Flippers and Flipping

Chapter 11: Second Homes: Developers and Developments..165
　　　　　Building a Second Home Out Here
　　　　　Buying a Second Home in a Full-Package Development
　　　　　Building a Home with a General Contractor
　　　　　Your Contract with Your Contractor
　　　　　Architects, Contractors and You
　　　　　Owner-Built Second Homes

Chapter 12: Country Houses and the Second Home..189
　　　　　Wrecks
　　　　　Keepers
　　　　　House Inspection Check List Choices

Chapter 13: Environmental Issues...211
　　　　　Overview
　　　　　Common Problems, Broadly Construed
　　　　　Common Issues
　　　　　Water Hazards

Chapter 14:	Resources-Minerals and Water	249
	Discrete Assets	
	Minerals	
	Water as a Financial Resource	
Chapter 15:	Matchmaking	278
	Finding	
	Real-Estate Brokers: The Seller's Agent	
	Alternatives: Buyer's Broker	
	Disclosures, Puffing and Fraud	
	Auction Buying	
	Been-heres and Come-heres	
Chapter 16:	Negotiating	307
	Communication Channels	
	Non-Price Issues	
	Price	
	Horse-trading	
	Mushy Bottoms and Hard Frameworks	
Chapter 17:	Property Location-Surveys and Such	339
	Location Surveys 101	
	Surveys 102	

VOLUME 2

Chapter 18:	Thinking about Woodland	1
	Overview	
	Forest Planning	
Chapter 19:	One Patch of Woods	10
	Getting Oriented Toward Timber	
	Woods Work	

Chapter 20: Thinking about Timber..27
    Landowner's Objectives for Woodland
    Consulting Foresters
    Self-Help

Chapter 21: Scoping Timber Value..53
    Vocabulary
    Timbering the Jones Farm

Chapter 22: Beware The Seller's Cruise...74
    There's No Bogus Like Show Bogus Tricks

Chapter 23: Selling Timber, Tools of the Trade...94
    FSBO-A Bad Idea
    Consultant-managed Sale-Sample Consultant Contract
    Timber-sale Contract

Chapter 24: Timber Taxation...124
    Set Up
    Basis and Income
    Conservation Easements and Taxes
    State and Local Timber Taxes

Chapter 25: Country Lawyers and Country Real-Estate Law............................149
    Finding a County Lawyer
    The Legal Frameworki
    Helping Hands: Buyer-Broker, Finder, Land Consultant

Chapter 26: Common Messes..166
    Buyers Want 100 Percent of Everything
    Legal Descriptions
    Acreage Discrepancies
    Acreage Verification Contingencies
    The Special Case of Leases

Chapter 27:   Tricks of the Seller's Trade: Legal, Not Legal and Otherwise............................187

Chapter 28:   Bargaining Cultures and Resolving Property Disputes....................................208

Chapter 29:   Writing a Purchase-Offer Contract: Strategies and Tactics..............................216
               Make the Most of Your Contract Offer Information
               Contingencies
               All-Cash Offer With No Financing Contingency
               Seller Contingency
               Equitable Title
               Longer Rather Than Shorter Escrow
               Warranties to Survive the Contract
               Security Deposits: Their Uses
               Deposits: Size Should Not Matter
               Time 1: Time is Not of the Essence
               Time 2: First Response
               Negotiating Within the Contract
               A Non-Deal Deal: Seller's Remorse
               Lease-Purchase Option
               Buy a Lawsuit

Chapter 30:   Some Ideas Organized as a Purchase-Offer Contract......................................252

Chapter 31:   Thinking about Dirt Money...266
               Research and Futures Analysis
               How About a Trial Rental?
               Country Money is Different From City Money

Chapter 32:   Borrowing Money...284
               System Overview
               Costs of Borrowing
               Interest Rates
               Pitching and Hitting

	Appraisals and Borrowing	
	Mortgage Interest Deductibility	
Chapter 33:	Sources of Dirt-Smart Money 332
	13 Places to Start	
Chapter 34:	A Final Plea..367
Chapter 35:	Afterword...369

MONEY-BACK GUARANTEE...370

CHAPTER 18: THINKING ABOUT WOODLAND

OVERVIEW

I'm a guy who believes that you can't beat tree shade. Life is good in a hammock stretched between two broad-limbed maples, looking up into an Impressionist's hundred shades of shimmering green. The grass is cut. The dog's asleep in the Saturday sun, paws twitching. Such moments are often worth a three-hour Long March through Friday-evening traffic.

I know these house trees. I've had them trimmed twice, the first time badly. I rake their leaves each fall. I worry that their roots will invade my water line. I lost one of their kind in the back yard. They're family.

People like me tend to anthropomorphize trees in relationship, I think, to how scarce they are in our everyday lives. Work in a city-canyon office building 50 hours a week, and it's easy to see trees at home as friends, children or Zen pillars of serenity. The affection felt for the individual trees around our houses is readily expanded to trees *en masse*, to all woods.

A lot of people feel a kinship with a young woman's vigil to spare all redwoods from logging by nesting in the top of one magnificent tree for more than a year. Her appeal would not have had the same resonance had she camped in a coal mine (to protect miners), or "squattered" at the top of an off-shore oil rig (to protect clams) or perched at the top of a 40-foot-tall loblolly pine in the middle of a 1,000-acre, even-aged plantation destined for newsprint. As a buyer and then owner of woodland, you may find it useful to examine your use of wood products and your attitudes toward trees. This chapter and the next discuss ways to think about woods and trees, as well as your objectives in relation to them.

Trees, unlike hydrocarbon fuels, are living creatures, big living creatures with crowns/heads, branches/limbs, roots/feet, bark/skin, blood/sap and even children—as in, "Giant oaks from little acorns grow." Felling a tree usually kills it, though its roots may shoot up sprouts from the stump. A chainsaw is noisy, smelly and dangerous. It is yang, not yin. The felling process is risky—the cutter can be hurt by his own tools or have the score evened by his victim. Each tree falls with a great cracking, rush and thump. A large opening appears, like a Soviet-style erasure of a liquidated Politburo member or the disappearance of the World Trade Center towers from the Manhattan skyline. Stumps bleed. When we limit cutting in the woodlot to the culls, there is an uneasy eugenic queasiness about eliminating only those that are diseased and deformed. Some feel there exists an absolute right to life across all species. Others object to the taking of tree lives for financial benefit. Each of us can agree, I think, that human life would be very different, very diminished, were all of us to stop using forest products—newsprint, paper, cardboard, flooring, kitchen cabinets, salad bowls, toilet paper. I admit, however, that the bundle of issues and viewpoints about trees, habitat and use is a prism, not a pane.

For whatever reasons, some of us don't see cut trees as we see cut flowers, cut grass or harvested corn. When we weed our garden and thin the lettuce, most of us don't consider that as killing some to allow others to grow more efficiently. If there is a moral difference between cutting ten acres of suburban grass, ten acres of hay and ten acres of planted woods, it is not large enough for me to appreciate. All regenerate after being cut. If we carve out an exception for crops we plant—the exception being, it's ethically okay to take the life we give—then there should be no difference between harvesting peanuts on a Georgia peanut plantation and harvesting loblolly pine on a Georgia pine plantation.

A distinction can be drawn between cutting wild trees in a natural forest and planted trees in a "man-made" forest. Most of us probably feel that a crop of plants has a lesser claim on life than a redwood forest, though both are fated to die because both are living. I feel this way. My reason to allow some trees to live and die naturally while taking others, both domesticated and wild, is that those I would spare have value beyond their human utility. These can include values related to environmental health, aesthetics, genetics, wildlife preservation and endangered species. While I can see cutting some redwoods for commercial gain, I certainly wouldn't cut all redwoods for that reason. Mine is not a philosophy of stewardship that imposes preservation of what is as a trump value. I favor preserving some and using others of the same kind.

Killing and using species other than our own is necessary to our lives, just as the killing of species other than their own and using resources is necessary to the life of all other species. Trees themselves engage in a no-quarter-given struggle for life, each trying its selfish best to crowd out all others from sunlight and nutrients. So much the better when a close-at-hand neighbor is starved to death. The ethical aspect of our necessity to use other life forms requires that we be prudent and conservative, that we balance our needs against those of other life forms, that we husband our resources and theirs, and use what we take efficiently and for good reason. While nature tends to balance itself, we must enforce balance on ourselves. The alternative to self-imposed balance is a level of consumption that leads to catastrophe.

Trees in a "wild" forest can have a trump value when the forest as a system has an overriding value to itself and many species, including our own. Reasonable individuals can disagree as to what "old growth" forest is. "Old growth" has come to mean much more than virgin forest, of which very little remains in the continental United States. Land buyers reading this book are not likely to find virgin forest despite what the real-estate ad says. And those patches of woods that I've seen that have "never been cut" are almost always located on dirt so poor that the trees are stunted and barely able to survive, thus explaining their pristine condition. In my experience of actively looking at eastern timberland, I've not seen a *tract* of privately-owned woodland that's much older than 100 years, though I've seen plenty of trees with more age than that. These older trees are either singles that are off by themselves or unwanted culls left standing in woods that have been timbered a couple of times. Protecting virgin forest and not cutting old-growth forests are choices not likely to face most land buyers. If you find a wooded tract with merchantable timber, it's likely to have been cut at least once, twice or three times within the last 100 years, depending on where it is and which tree species grow there.

If you're looking at hardwood forests, it's quite probable that you will find the tract has been **high-graded** more than once. High-grading is a timbering practice in which the logger cuts only the large-diameter, high-value **sawtimber** and leaves standing low-value species and all culls. Sawtimber is good-quality wood that's used for lumber; high-value species—walnut, cherry, sugar maple, certain oaks—bring premium prices. (Veneer-quality trees are even more valuable than sawtimber, and I know several smart investors who, when they can, take only veneer to pay for a timberland purchase, leaving the sawtimber for future profit.) The result of repeated sawtimber high-grading is the long-term degradation of a forest's commercial value as the low-value tree species and culls mature and reproduce at the expense of the high-value species. A tract of cherry, sugar maple and northern red oak might be transformed by high-grading over 100 years into a tract of striped maple, black birch, hickory and low-value oaks. Had the tract been timbered with the future in mind (taking out the culls along with the sawtimber), it would be worth today five times or more its current value. Hardwood tracts are high-graded, because it takes less time, costs the logger less and is the most productive use of the logger's resources. High-grading's future economic loss is shifted to the landowner who usually is happy to see big trees—culls and low-value species—still standing.

A recently timbered tract is called a **cutover**; the term can refer to an intensity scale ranging from very selective harvesting (where, for example, just the veneer-quality trees are removed) to a **clearcut** that removes every tree no matter how small. The tell-tale signs of recent timbering are fresh-looking stumps, treetops (**slash**) scattered on the ground, roughed-up roads, dense and weedy underbrush (blackberries, ferns and sunlight-loving weeds like stinging nettle) and a landing (or deck) where logs were trimmed and loaded. A recently high-graded tract will "look" better than one where low-value species and culls have been taken for pulp or just dropped. High-grading takes fewer trees and, therefore, leaves less residual mess. A properly conceived logging job on a hardwood tract should leave some large trees, including several high-value seed trees and old den trees.

When looking at woods that have not been recently cut, you may see a lot of large-diameter trees that have no commercial—**merchantable**—value, because they are the survivors of several earlier high-grading jobs. High-graded woods will still embody the non-commercial values of forests—wildlife habitat, recreation and aesthetics—that land buyers seek. If you want to preserve "as is" a high-graded tract that is certainly your right as a private landowner, but it's not in your financial interest to do so. That decision will benefit the existing mix of species. It will not benefit species that would take advantage of a different mix of trees. There is always both a value in and an opportunity cost of doing nothing. Do not be fooled by a seller or his real-estate agent assuring you that the tract's only been "**select cut**." High-grading is the most common type of selective cut. A high-graded tract will have little, if any, present merchantable value, and its future merchantable value will have been reduced. In any case, it's advisable to hire a **consulting forester** to evaluate any significant patch of woods that you're thinking of buying. You will be helped in your price negotiations if you know the current value of the property's timber. If your forester's **timber cruise**—an estimated inventory of species, volumes and commercial value—shows little merchantable timber value, give that report to the seller, "Your woods are nice to look at, but they have little commercial value. Here's the cruise that shows that." If the cruise shows a great deal of value, you can keep that fact to yourself. A buyer is in a stronger negotiating position if he has a neutral forester showing that the seller's high-graded woods are worth little than if he offers that opinion on his own say-so.

All privately-owned woodland I've seen has been timbered several times or more. Much aboriginal woodland was converted into open farms and then allowed to grow back into forest when the farms could no longer support the farmers. You can find these woods all over New England and the mountainous sections of the mid-Atlantic states. The charming rock fences that I found in north-central Massachusetts in the late 1960s told me that the woods I was standing in had once been cleared pasture. And that land had been timbered at least once since being allowed to revert to trees. Repeated high-grading and heavy cutting can leave woodland dominated by low-value species and scrubby-looking trees. In the trade, heavy timbering is referred to as "hammering." Trees that pioneer newly open spots in hardwood forests are often the less commercially desirable species, such as striped maple, locust and birch. If you are interested in woods for their non-commercial values and don't care about their economic value, none of this matters with one exception: don't pay a timberland price for woods that have no timber value.

In my part of western Virginia, American chestnut was the dominant species in the hardwood forests colonials explored. The huge chestnuts resisted rot, which made them good for split-rail fences. The wood was easy to mill and work, which made it valuable for timber-framing and construction. The chestnuts were cut along with everything else to transform the forest into cropland and pasture. They thrived until the 1930s when a blight killed them. Chestnut saplings will still grow to a three- or four-inch diameter, occasionally more, and then die. Oaks and maples have taken chestnut's place. Most tree species are subject to diseases and insects. About 60 percent of my hemlock died in 2003 and 2004 from a tiny white creature, the woolly adelgid. I have timbered my woods twice between 1994 and 2004, taking non-sugar maple species and culls the first time and then the large sugar maples. The woods in my area that have been successively high-graded tend toward a mix of low-value pine, oaks, maples and assorted low-value hardwoods. This mix is good wildlife habitat. I try to manage my woods to encourage high-value species, such as sugar maple, red oak, black cherry and ash. I cut culls for firewood. While the species composition of this type of woodland has changed significantly since the 1700s, deer, bear and coyotes have adapted.

Woodland, of course, varies with region, topography and climate. Mixed hardwood forests of different types are common in the upper South, Mississippi Valley, upper Midwest, Appalachia and

Northeast. Conifers may or not be mixed in. Land buyers will find these types of woodlands as well as land that has been converted to tree plantations, usually a species of fast-growing pine.

Where a pine plantation has been recently clearcut and not replanted, the buyer will be able to buy the property for its true **bare-dirt value**, the cheapest it's likely to be. It will naturally regenerate into native hardwoods and conifers. It will be thick with underbrush until trees become large enough to provide shade. Buying planted pine land gives the owner cash from a thinning cut and then from the final clearcut. Buying land that's just been selectively cut can also be a cost-effective purchase strategy, because, presumably, the owner has captured all of the present merchantable timber value and is selling the land in its least attractive condition.

Controversy over forestry practices focuses on four issues: 1) clearcutting, which removes all trees; 2) establishing even-age, one-species plantations, which are very efficient at growing trees but lack diversity; 3) cutting "old-growth" forests; and 4) timbering publicly owned land. Aside from possibly buying and clearcutting land, readers of this book are not likely to face these issues with respect to the purchase of woodland.

About one third—728 million acres—of America's 2.271 billion acres is forested land. About 483 million acres of that 728 million is commercial forest; the rest is considered noncommercial woods. Of the commercial forest land (483 million acres), federal agencies (principally the U.S. Forest Service) own 97 million acres; states, 26.7 million acres; other public jurisdictions, 7.0 million acres; and Native Americans 5.6 million acres—a total of 28 percent. Private farmers own about 97 million acres, and other private, non-industrial owners—like you, potentially—own 179.4 million acres—57 percent. Most of these private, non-industrial holdings are smaller than 500 acres. The remaining 70.6 million acres is considered private, industrial forest land. The four issues of controversy mainly center on the 28 percent of commercial forest land in public ownership and the 15 percent in private industrial (corporate) ownership. The interesting fact, however, is that about half the wood harvested comes from private non-industrial land like mine. As more public land is backed out of timbering through roadless areas, wilderness designation and environmental restrictions, an increasing share of production will fall on private U.S. landowners and foreign suppliers.

Federal forest land is managed through elaborate systems of planning, public comment, regulation and pressure politics. Each national forest has its own publicly available **management plan** that describes the activities that may occur in each geographic forest sub-area. The first-time reader may have difficulty deciphering a forest plan, but it will provide a newcomer with a useful set of concepts and vocabulary for thinking about managing different types of land.

If you are interested in national and industrial forest issues, you might read the following, which include a range of perspectives: Alston Chase, In a Dark Wood: The Fight over Forests and the Rising Tyranny of Ecology (New York: Houghton Mifflin, 1995); Bill Devall, ed., Clearcut: The Tragedy of Industrial Forestry (San Francisco: Sierra Club Books and Earth Island Press, 1993); Alan Drengson and Duncan Taylor, Ecoforestry: The Art and Science of Sustainable Forest Use (New Haven: New Society Publishers, 1997); Charles E. Little, The Dying of the Trees: The Pandemic in America's Forests (New York: Viking, 1995); Richard N. Jordan, Trees & People: Forestland Ecosystems and Our Future (Washington, D.C.: Regnery Publishing, Inc., 1994); Ray Raphael, Tree Talk: The People and Politics of Timber (Washington, D.C.: Island Press, 1981); Gordon Robinson, The Forest and the Trees: A Guide to Excellent Forestry (Washington, D.C.: Island Press, 1988); Laurence C. Walker, The North American Forests: Geography, Ecology, and Silviculture (Boca Raton, Florida: CRC Press, 1998); and Jerry Mander, Eco-Forestry: The Art and Science of Sustainable Forest Use (New Haven: New Society Publishers, 1997).

Forestry-management publications can be found at www.ForestryIndex.net, which provides links to a wide range of websites and extension publications related to management, estate planning, timber taxation, environmental/conservation regulations and so on. Many periodicals are available, including: American Forests, American Tree Farmer, Canadian Journal of Forestry, Conservation Biology, European Journal of Forest Pathology, Forest Farmer, Forest Land Review, Forest Science, Forest Products Journal, Journal of Forest History, Journal of Forestry, Journal of Wildlife Management, Natural Areas Journal, Northern Journal of Applied Forestry, Oecologia and Southern Lumberman.

Forestry is a subject that is extensively researched at the U.S. Department of Agriculture's Forest Service and state land-grant universities. This literature is usually free or nominally priced. As a result of the Resources Planning Act, USDA is required to publish an assessment of America's renewable resources every ten years. The 2000 RPA Timber Assessment was published in December, 2001 and is available at www.fs.fed.us/pnw/sev/rpa/haynes_files. (e-mail: rhaynes@fs.fed.us or 503-808-2002.) The Assessment sets forth aggregated data and trends on timber inventory, harvesting, products, prices and an implication analysis

Industrial owners control about 15 percent of the forestland total. G-P (Georgia-Pacific) and Weyerhaeuser are the two largest owners, followed by Kimberly Clark, Stone Container, Mead/Westvaco, Scott, Champion, James River, Boise Cascade, Willamette, L-P (Louisiana-Pacific), Bowater and Potlatch. These forest owners have traditionally managed their large holdings to serve their needs for sawtimber and/or fiber. As a group, they are increasingly selling their land base to raise cash. International Paper sold all of its seven million acres in 2006. Most of this collective land base continues to be managed for timber production after being sold, but the maintenance costs and taxes are shifted to the new owners. These land sales can be packaged in parcels as small as 20 acres up to more than one million. If you are looking to buy woodland, these sales can be a good opportunity, especially if you are looking for hunting properties.

Timber Investment Management Organizations (TIMOS) are private companies—GMO, Pope & Talbot, and The Forestland Group, among others—that manage production from about $7 billion worth of woodland on behalf of pension funds, endowments and private investors. TIMOs provide their individual and institutional clients with financial evaluations of forestland and property-management services for millions of acres. **Real Estate Investment Trusts (REITs)**, like Rayonier and Plum Creek, also manage timberland.

FOREST PLANNING

Since each wooded property you investigate will have different features, you will inevitably find yourself thinking about what you might want to do and not do with each possible property. These thoughts are the precursor of a **management plan**, which, of course, may be nothing more than to walk through the woods three or four times a year admiring what you experience. The two basic questions that you need to answer as you think about the appropriate management plan are:

Which objective (s) do I want to promote through my management plan?

Common objectives include financial return (immediate, mid-term, long-term); wildlife enhancement (birds; non-game wildlife; game by species); biological diversity (more than currently exists or less); no human intervention/do nothing; improve property's interior accessibility with foot trails, horse trails or roads; control erosion; non-hunting recreation; etc.

Which management methods do I feel comfortable using and which do I reject?

Depending on your values and objectives, available methods can include cutting trees (all, some or a few; removing some species; removing trees larger than a certain diameter); using fire ("prescribed burns") to clear underbrush and promote wildlife;

using chemicals and/or introduced species to suppress invasive vegetation or combat insects; allowing naturally occurring fire to burn or not burn; opening the woods to engines (chainsaws) and/or vehicles; hunting; making habitat more hospitable to some wildlife and less to others; building or maintaining roads for vehicles; planting trees; among others.

Consider such questions with an open mind.

You may find that your set of answers to these questions varies with the unique characteristics of each property you screen even as some answers to each question are consistent across the board.

If you see yourself as a card-carrying tree-hugger, ask yourself whether absolute non-intervention leads to your objectives. It may or may not. Leaving woods—as you now find them—uncut in perpetuity is not a zero-change guarantee for the property or a zero-cost choice for you. (You can achieve either absolute or less-than-absolute non-intervention by placing a conservation easement on the property that spells out how you want the woods managed forever.) Non-intervention may not benefit the health of your trees, biological diversity or the conservation of the land's soil resources. Tree-hugging may get in the way of your other objectives, such as fire control, usability or promotion of a particular species. Leaving (cutover) woods uncut in perpetuity is often not the best approach even for the ecology of a specific site. Remember the ecology that you find in today's woodland is not untouched by human beings. What you see is the ecology left after the most recent human intervention, which, itself, is the successor to earlier interventions. If your objective is to manage the woods back to some earlier ecology, you probably will have to remove and suppress some of what's there so that your preferred species can become dominant. It's not uncommon to find that you have to intervene with a saw to alter the consequences of earlier interventions with saws. If you want to let what is evolve however what is evolves, there's really no telling how your woods will look and function at any particular point in the future. Woods can be significantly damaged—even decimated—by fire, hurricane, ice storm, drought, windstorm, flooding, disease and insects—all of which change what is.

Land buyers are usually appalled at what a clearcut looks like on the day the logger leaves. I am, too. I'm also disturbed at seeing the residue of selective cutting—huge tree crowns left in the woods, heads decapitated at the neck. It's easy to make the connection that if something in man-affected nature "looks bad," it is bad—morally and environmentally. It's hard for an individual who's not familiar with forestry ecology and logging practices to distinguish among timbering that increases future timber value, timbering that promotes game, timbering that encourages both game and other wildlife, timbering that was done to remove scrub and allow the woods to regenerate naturally, timbering that was done to squeeze every penny out of the woods, timbering that high-graded a site, timbering that has done environmental harm and timbering that has done environmental good.

A site that "looks good" in the sense that only a few trees have been cut on each acre could be nothing more than the most recent round of serial high-grading.This site will keep its recreation and aesthetic values, but have little future timber value. If you do not know what to look for, your eyes may trick your brain by focusing on what *looks* bad at the expense of what really *is* bad from an environmental or timber-management perspective. A patch of woods that is too clean, can lack the old snags, downed trees, rotting logs and standing dead trees that are necessary for wildlife and a healthy forest. A clean look at ground level often comes from cattle grazing, a practice that reduces the nutrient cycling on which trees depend, compacts soil and limits the ability of seedlings to establish themselves. Cattle also rub the bark off saplings and trample out grass around the trees they prefer for shade, exposing and damaging roots. But they *do* keep the woods cleaner-looking.

A last word about logging and its look: the worst every logging job looks occurs on the day timbering ends. Time improves visual aesthetics, slowly at first and then more quickly. Even the most severe clearcut looks entirely different and better ten years later. In 20 years, dominant trees will have appeared, shading the ground beneath them. Shade clears out the thickets and brush, which look bad but are good for wildlife.

Timbering can be destructive to many values, particularly in the short term. When woods are hammered, it means that too many small-diameter trees were removed in an effort to squeeze the last dollar out of the current timber sale. This leaves a tract with a much-elongated timber-cutting cycle and a more roughed-up appearance. Cutting smaller diameter hardwoods can double the time required needed until the next cycle of selective timbering can begin—from 25 years or so to 50. The marginal dollar gain that the current owner captures from cutting the smaller-diameter trees is overshadowed by the amount of future lost income. Hammered tracts are often put up for sale. Timbering to maximize current dollars can also harm wildlife and reduce game species. For example, a cut that takes out all the acorn-producing oaks and other nut-bearing trees leaves poor habitat for deer and won't provide squirrels the food that, in part, reseeds these species.

Much harm can befall land when badly conceived and implemented timbering decisions aggregate over time. No better proof of this is our own land-use history that leveled forest after forest without much thought toward the future. Injury was added by overgrazing, deep tilling and plowing, repeated burnings and introducing non-native pests and diseases. Badly timbered land erodes and returns less productively than before. The legacy of our past mistakes and ignorance can be remedied today by applying knowledge and management techniques sensibly.

Some readers undoubtedly feel that the only proper response to past abuse of forestland is to do nothing to the patch they own. I don't oppose that position if hands-off preservation is your only objective. If, on the other hand, you have multiple objectives and a time frame that's longer than today, cutting trees in one way or another can help you get there. A personal no-cut policy should be coupled by a no-wood-use policy. Otherwise, you are simply shifting the environmental costs of your consumption to some other landowner. I don't think that's a defensible position, especially if the shift involves timbering Third World forests in Third World ways for our benefit.

I advise caution, patience and conservative decisions. Don't make big decisions until you've been on the property for at least three or four years. It's far easier to live with bad consequences from a small decision. If you're unsure about cutting timber, try it out on five or ten acres, not 300. Then wait five or six years. By then, you'll have an idea of what you get from timbering and how long the logged-over look lasts.

It goes without saying that our species has a responsibility to conserve other species and do what we can to maintain enough habitat for healthy, viable populations. The elimination of any species weakens an ecosystem that has evolved with it. Successor ecosystems may or may not be better environmentally, but they will be different. That timber cutting reduces the population of some species and increases those of others in an ecosystem does not mean, in my opinion, that we should refrain from every logging activity that can be judged to adversely affect the current species mix. If you cut 15 large red oaks on 100 acres—that is, every red oak on the property larger than 20 inches in diameter, you will adversely affect the red oak population while benefiting both other trees standing close to those now-removed oaks as well as those species that pioneer the new patch of sunlight on the forest floor. While Nature advances and eliminates species, we should be properly reluctant to step into that role. We have changed ecosystems quickly, profoundly and unalterably—and we do not know all the ways those losses of habitat and species affect everything else, including us. Might the dodo have been the source of a generic cancer cure? Might the snail darter yet be that source? Might the loss of either lead to the loss of another species that is the source? The line I'm drawing is one between an absolutist position that says no harm to any species anywhere at any time for any reason and a position that allows some harm to most species in most places at most times for defensible reasons. Fortunately, you will not have to make decisions about how many spotted owls or red-cockaded woodpeckers there should be. If you have endangered species on your property, they and their habitat are currently protected.

Where one draws the line that balances the needs of some species against the needs of others should always be a matter of debate. If your position is that all logging is harmful because it harms some species and therefore no tree should ever be cut, then you have excluded the reasonable and careful use of a renewable, sustainable resource. If your position accepts that resources, such as trees, can be used in an ethically and environmentally defensible manner, then consider the commercial timber potential of whatever woods you may purchase.

My feeling is simple: as long as I use wood products, such as newspapers, plywood and paper products, I should be prepared to cut my own trees to provide in a theoretical and ethical sense some of that supply. If you won't allow some of your trees to be cut, how much of a moral right do you have to continue using these products at will? And if you want to back out wood products, what materials might replace them—oil-based plastics, genetically modified crops? Every material we produce comes with a cost, and each has a net environmental balance.

Some environmentalists are undoubtedly appalled at the notion of landowners cutting their trees, let alone cutting them to make money. If I saw something wrong with cutting trees properly, I would agree with that position. Since I don't, I have no problem making money from doing something that I feel alright about.

Much effort has been devoted to reconciling forest welfare and economic interests. No forester or logger I know, no forest products company I know, would admit that they do not have the welfare of forests foremost in mind. I do not doubt the sincerity of those expressions, but some practices, even when done properly, can have harmful consequences when scaled up. Environmental advocates claim the same interest in forest welfare when they oppose all interventions. Neither side has a monopoly on truth. Both have valid arguments—as well as some that aren't so valid. **Sustainable forestry** is the term that now refers to the idea of using forests—and the timber they produce—in an environmentally sound manner that balances various interests. It can be taken to mean cutting no more wood than the cutover land can regenerate over a certain period of time. Sustainable forestry can be stretched to cover opposite viewpoints.

If you're interested in sustainable forestry in its various meanings, start with the National Network of Forest Practitioners, 305 Main Street, Providence, Rhode Island, 02903; 401-273-6507; 401-273-6508 FAX; www.nnfp.org. The NNFP website provides links to state and individual contacts and other providers of services, information and technical assistance. These contacts can refer you to foresters in your area who can help you manage your woodland according to your own definition of sustainable forestry. You can do a www.google.com search for "sustainable forestry" by state and find additional organizations and contacts. Forest-related databases are available at www.forestworld.com; Forestworld, POB 426, 161 Austin Drive, #7, Burlington, Vermont, 05402; 802-865-1111; 802-863-4344 FAX. Other contacts related to a broad view of sustainability are the Forest Stewards Guild, POB 519 Santa Fe, New Mexico, 87504; 505-983-8992; 505-986-0798 FAX; www.foreststewardsguild.com; and Forest Stewardship Council, POB 10, Waterbury, Vermont, 05676; 802-244-6257; 802-244-6258 FAX; www.certifiedproducts.org.

This has been a long-winded way of encouraging new landowners to keep an open and inquiring mind about cutting trees in your new woods. Certain types of cutting can make your woods healthier, more productive in terms of supporting more species, more interesting and more useful. Timbering need not be done harmfully. If you have a steep slope that's easily eroded, cut somewhere else. You can improve the look of timbered land with time and a chainsaw. It's hard and dangerous work, but it's doable with time and diligence. Timbering has many facets—getting the best money from the trees you sell, enhancing your woodlot for future timber value, improving wildlife habitat, creating access where access is wanted, handling the visual mess and protecting the land and its waterways. Each facet can be done well, badly and at all stops in between.

CHAPTER 19: ONE PATCH OF WOODS

GETTING ORIENTED TOWARD TIMBER

The more time I spend on 95 acres of mixed Appalachian hardwoods where I live the more I understand how they change on their own and how I've changed them.

Seasonal change with **deciduous** trees—broad-leaf species that lose their leaves in the fall and are called **hardwoods**—is easy to track. Green switches to bright autumn colors within a few weeks; sight lines through the woods lengthen; leaf mass moves from overhead to underfoot; and the relative quiet of walking through a summer woods is replaced by the crash of dry leaves and the crunch of snow.

More profound—but far less noticeable—is the change in the trees themselves, which, in turn, alters the nature of the woods. The trees grow in height and width each year. As they do, some species crowd out others—the site-specific process is called **succession**. Cutting (or not cutting) trees shapes what the woods become as a community according to which trees are cut, their age, location and species. Succession occurs naturally and all the time. I can see succession in its various stages. Where a large tree has fallen, ferns, weeds and blackberries take hold. A few maple and locust saplings lay their claim. If mature sugar maples stand close to a new opening that's still shaded, I'll find a couple of one-inch-thick sugar saplings in a year or two; they grow fast and desperately straight. All of this new patch occurs among many others, each in various stages, each a bit different, depending on soil, sunlight, water and **aspect** (the compass direction of the slope). I have to make myself look hard at different spots to notice the dimensions of slow, cumulative change.

Before I bought this land, I hired a self-employed, **consulting forester** to **cruise** the tract to estimate the volume of merchantable timber and its dollar value. **Merchantable** refers to the dollars that I, as a landowner, would be likely to receive from, in my case, a **marked sale**, in which my forester marks with paint every tree that I'm selling. That inventory is then sent to local sawmills and loggers in a competitive bid. His inventory disaggregated the hardwood sawtimber by species and two-inch diameter classes. He expressed the estimated sawtimber volume in **board feet (bf)**. (One board foot equals a volume of wood that is 12" x 12" x 1".) **Sawtimber** is a tree of sufficient diameter, length and quality to be milled into lumber. Poor quality trees of the same size do not have lumber potential. They and low-value species have value as **pulp** or firewood. Sometimes, trees—even though they're large—have no value at all. Better timbering jobs drop these unmerchantable trees, whether or not, they are removed. A high-value species, such as a 22-inch-diameter cherry, may have no merchantable value if stout branches are found in its butt log.

I was selling **timber on the stump**, or selling **stumpage**. Buyers confined their bids to the marked trees. Prior to the bid, the forester gave me his cruise inventory along with his best estimate of what local buyers were paying for each species of hardwood sawtimber, expressed as **dollars per thousand board feet ($/mbf)**. The dollar number at the bottom of his inventory told me what he thought the marked stumpage was currently worth. Once he marked the sale, he gave me and the bidders a tree-by-tree (actually a log by log tally) count of the volume that I was selling organized by species. He only counted and painted trees 16 inches in diameter and larger.

Put crassly, I needed to know how much money I could net from the sale of the land's merchantable timber immediately after purchase. That number would figure into whether I could swing the deal. I also needed to limit the amount of mortgage debt I was going to assume. I had in mind cutting and selling the non-sugar-maple species and leaving the sugars in place to develop a sugar bush. Beyond that, I didn't know enough about woods to think knowledgeably about other woods-related objectives. Nor did I have the ability to think very much about how this timbering decision would change the appearance of the woods or its internal dynamics. Fortunately, I had stumbled into a consulting forester who knew what he was doing.

At that time, the woods consisted of 135 acres of northwest-facing slope at between 2,800 and 4,000 feet elevation. The soils were primarily limestone-based, with some patches of a poorer quality shale. The ground was rocky, mostly limestone cobble from the size of a coffee cup to that of a big-screen television. The trees were big—that much I knew—and the forest floor was pretty clean, owing to the presence of cattle who wandered in and out from adjacent pasture that also came with the purchase. A few old logging roads were in place, the main one wound up the mountain with three level spurs branching off and dead-ending at the property line. The woods had not been logged since the early 1960s. That high-grading harvest probably concentrated on red oak, cherry and sugar maple—the money trees—16 or 18 inches and larger. I figured that at least four inches of diameter had been added to trees left standing in the ensuing 32 years. That last harvest also felled the owner's ancient Reo flatbed logging truck, which sat at an intersection growing saplings out of its cab. Shed parts lay next to the carcass, along with an abandoned wood stove and miscellany of the type known as, *dumpus trashus*. Huge, waist-high chestnut stumps were scattered through the woods. The chestnuts had been cut in the 1920s and 1930s. Neighbors said that 40 timber rattlers had been killed the last time loggers ventured in. The woods were pretty.

From the cruise, I learned that the lower 55-acres had an estimated 1,200 sugar maple trees 10"+ **DBH**, each of which was capable of handling at least one tap. DBH is **diameter at breast height**, about 4.5 feet above the ground. The sugar maple 16"+ DBH had about $30,000 in sawtimber value as of that time, 1994. This acreage also had stumpage value in non-sugar species and several hundred pulp trees, both of which I wanted to remove to allow the sugars to develop. On the higher and steeper acreage, the cruise estimated about $47,000 in hardwood sawtimber stumpage, mainly oaks, cherry and sugar maple. More than 95 percent of the value in both tracts lay in the sawtimber. We decided to cut the sawtimber stumpage 16" DBH and larger, except for the sugars on the lower end. This was a **selective cut** in the sense that we were taking out trees that exceeded a diameter threshold as well as trees of certain species. The forester also marked for cutting a lot of pulp culls.

My objectives, then, were to raise cash from the sale of the non-sugar-maple sawtimber stumpage, remove culls and leave the site clean enough to install plastic tubing lines that would carry liquid sugar water from individual trees to a central collection tank at the lowest spot on the property. Some would call this type of cutting a **timber stand improvement (TSI)**, even though I was not trying to upgrade the species mix for future timber sales. What I was trying to do was to turn the woods into a source of both quick cash and annual income. The highest bid was right where the forester had predicted. After I built a collection house and invested in equipment, the sap-collection idea did not pan out for reasons having nothing to do with either the idea or the trees themselves.

This first intervention left the woods with a valuable stand of large, sawtimber-quality sugar maples along with some uncut culls and smaller diameter trees. The logger dragged most of the tops into big **slash piles** so that tubing could be run from tree to tree and then into the main lines that led downhill. Loggers leave slash in place as a rule, because dragging it into piles takes time. The logger left about 100 marked culls in place, because the cost of cutting and hauling them wasn't worth the effort. They were the logger's trees at that point, having paid for them. I wanted them cut and taken, and, if not that, dropped for firewood or forest nutrition. While most of the large-diameter, non-sugars had been cut, all of the large diameter sugars on the lower end remained along with all trees of high-value species smaller than 16" DBH. After the logging, the woods looked thinned, but not spare. The sugar maples spread their crowns into the canopy openings during the next few years. The woods did not look all that much different since we left a lot of standing volume—the 16s and smaller and most of the large sugars. I dressed up the logging roads—clearing them of rock, filling in holes—so that they were safe for trucks, tractor, horses and foot traffic. I left slash undisturbed on the steep upper half of the property where it offended my eye for the next four or five years until it decomposed. I mowed the skid roads a couple of times each summer. My wife and I walked them about eight months a year. The woods provided firewood and good company. I noticed more deer, who liked the new openings and the thick underbrush that came in during the first year.

Eight years later, in August, 2001, I faced a desperate need to pay down debt from a housing project that had crashed, miserably and overwhelmingly. Hard decisions insisted on being made. We sold 40 acres at the top of the mountain to a neighbor. I asked our forester to mark a sale on our remaining 95 acres. His cruise estimated about 231,000 bf of hardwood sawtimber 16" + DBH. Of that, about 151,000 bf, 65 percent, was the sugar maple we had left in place. Other volumes included about 27,500 bf of red oak, 21,500 bf of red maple, 13,000 bf of ash, 9,500 bf of cherry and 8,000 bf of chestnut oak. He estimated about 53,500 bf of the total of 231,000 bf were trees in the 16-18" DBH class with a stumpage value at that time of about $19,000. He recommended leaving these trees in place and cutting only sawtimber 18" DBH and larger. He also suggested focusing the sale on sugar maple and limiting it to the lower 55 acres. We included a little cherry but no white ash owing to its low price at the time. He was trying to maximize sale dollars while conserving about 100,000 bf of our timber base 16" + for the future. He estimated a sale value on the entire 231,000 bf of about $89,000, using conservative species-price multipliers.

We agreed with this strategy. He then marked for sale about 136,500 bf, confined to the lower 55 acres. About 90 percent, 123,500 bf, of that sale inventory was sugar maple, some of it veneer quality. The 1994 cutting had released them from competition. They had gained in diameter and gross volume. Some of the 14s and 16s had moved up in diameter class, which foresters call, **ingrowth**. The change from 14 to 16" diameter is significant, because mills in my area and, probably many others, pay a higher price for stumpage 16"+ than for stumpage less than 16" in diameter. The eight or ten years it takes a sugar maple to increase from the 14" DBH category (which means diameters between 14 inches through not quite 16 inches) to the 16" DBH category (which means diameters between 16 inches and not quite 18 inches) can mean a doubling, or more, of its board-foot stumpage price. The smaller diameter logs don't mill into lumber as efficiently as 16s and larger. Twelves and 14s in cherry and walnut might be cut and milled without a price discount because of their very high value, but other species in smaller diameters would generally be left or, if taken, discounted. It's far more sensible economically to let the 12s and 14s grow into 16"+ stumpage and sell them for sawtimber than sell them at a discount or at a pulp price. Our forester focused the sale on sugar maple sawtimber, because it was fetching a high price and a good portion of that was **veneer quality**, which brings an even higher price per board foot than sawtimber.

About 400 trees were painted stump and butt, and their volumes grouped by species and two-inch diameter class. The sale notice was sent out to every potential buyer within a three-hour truck haul. This is the format for a **competitively bid sale**; the alternative is a **negotiated sale**, between the forester and one buyer. Competition among buyers almost always produces a higher price for the landowner. We sweated the month-long wait.

Ten buyers submitted bids, the highest of which was a sawmill at $79,900. Two other sawmills made offers in the $70s while the independent loggers bid in the low $40s. Three bids were tightly clustered around $65,000. Owing to our forester's skill in designing a buyer-friendly, market-oriented sale, we received about $650 mbf for the sugar maple rather than the $400 mbf he had used as his cruise multiplier. And we still had 100,000 bf of 16-18s left untouched in our woodland savings account. Our forester charged 10 percent of the gross sale revenue for painting the 400 trees, marketing and managing the sale, preparing the contract and checking the actual timbering. Had we done **50-50 shares** with an independent logger, my guess is that we would have netted $30,000 to $40,000 instead of almost $72,000.

At the end of October 2002, I blew out my right knee a few weeks before the logging was to start. Following Halloween surgery, I spent the next two months on my back. While I knew that logging was going on, that was about all I knew in my drug-befuddled daze. When I hobbled into the woods in the spring, the first thing I noticed was how changed the logged areas appeared and how unchanged was the rest. This cut was far more noticeable than the first since the sugar maples were clustered in five or six areas of about five to eight acres each. These areas were now open, with a scattering of smaller-diameter sugars and a few ash and hemlock. The ground was piled high with slash; the logger had not been asked or paid to drag the slash into piles. The roads were rough, though I expected that. I was surprised, however, by the amount of slash left on the roads themselves, despite contract language that required them to be left free of slash and in good repair. I spent a lot of time that summer clearing the roads of rock and slash. I spent the next two years cutting up the slash from about 400 tree tops, two or three tops at a time, which I describe below. Photograph 19-1 shows one tree top dropped on top of another, making for dangerous footing and a tangled cutting environment.

PHOTOGRAPH 19-1

Slash

Photograph 19-2 shows one top on the ground, a much easier and safer lopping environment.

PHOTOGRAPH 19-2

Slash

Over the last decade, I've found my woods-related objectives changing as my needs changed and as the woods themselves changed. The two timber sales provided money when that was needed. As important, the woods provided quiet and tranquility, even when they looked their post-logging worst. I got two years of hard exercise lopping slash and cutting firewood, which I came to view as the penance of hard labor for making a debt-ballooning business investment based on emotion rather than analysis. The deer prospered from the flush of fresh undergrowth, and their presence may be the reason why only two rattlesnakes have been spotted in more than ten years. The deer are now acclimated to my truck and tractor. They run from our Labs, Lucy and Sophie, but both chase and flight seem perfunctory. The deer don't seem to mind a short, monotony-breaking sprint a couple of afternoons a week. They never ran from the late Briggs who, I think, wisely realized, that pursuing the uncatchable was beneath him. Two years after this second timbering, deer became so numerous that I let a neighbor hunt our woods in hope of giving the maple sprouts a chance to establish themselves.

After several months of work, the roads were clear. I then hired a bulldozer to cut in some new roads, and I've added others by hand, clearing slash, digging out rocks and filling holes. The dozer is faster; the hand-work is harder but leaves a lighter touch. The roads are kept safe for walking, horseback riding and driving. The slash is lopped to within two feet of the ground, as shown in Photograph 19-3. It is invisible in the summer and inoffensive when it is visible. I've pulled out three years of firewood—about 20 cords—and will probably be able to take one more year's worth before the downed wood loses its firewood quality. Since the woods are only a five-minute drive from our house, I spend a lot of late afternoons up there—working, thinking, arguing, revisiting life mistakes, wincing over stupid things I've done and said, what-ifing and watching the forest's paint dry.

PHOTOGRAPH 19-3

Lopped Slash

One recurring item on my agenda is asking myself whether I would have cut the timber had I not needed the money. A point comes in the life of every tree when its quality for lumber begins to decline with increasing age. If trees are to be cut, they should be taken before that point. The sawtimber trees I cut were between 75 and 100 years old. They would have gained a great deal of value had I let them alone for 20 to 40 more years, $500,000 or more. The woods would have had during that time a park-like appearance—big shady trees, not much underbrush. Had I let them be forever, they would have succumbed to breakage, blowdown, insects and disease. Had I cut them 40 years down the road, the woods would have been left with even more extensive openings. My answer, I think, is that I would have cut them later, perhaps 20 years after I bought the land to help with retirement. But the longer you know your woods, the harder it is to cut the trees. Necessity, both fortunately and unfortunately, trumps choice.

When rain softens the ground, wind—especially when it blows in opposite from its prevailing direction—will topple large, shallow-rooted hardwoods. These trees are especially vulnerable to **windthrow** after logging has thinned the stand around them. Breakage from wind and ice tends to affect older, crown-heavy trees too. Several large-diameter hickories—more than 30 inches—either broke at about 40 feet or blew over in the winter of 2004-2005. Then our little share of Hurricane Frances toppled a gun-barrel-straight 30-inch ash, which took down three smaller maples standing like a row of dominoes. Blowdowns are a major mess to clean up. When several are involved, their tops get tangled. The crown at one end and the root ball at the other creates a bind on the underside of the tree being cut that locks up the chainsaw's bar even when you know what's going to happen and try to prevent it. Wading into a mass of green, tangled tops is as hazardous a cutting job as I've done. Apart from the satisfaction of surviving these chores, the only pleasure in cleaning up blowdowns occurs when you cut an uprooted tree at the stump and the freed root pad plops right back into its hole, perfectly.

The more I know this forest, the more trees I know. Like a college class, what started as hundreds in an audience are now individuals, many of whom I've encountered personally. There's one black birch, for example, that grows on the edge of a road; if I'm not paying attention, I'll side-swipe it with my truck mirror. There are stumps with stories. One reminds me of the time I hung a big locust in the branches of a neighbor, requiring a heroic effort to get it down safely. Another I cut flush to the ground to improve a road. There's one maple with a big, exposed root on which the tractor always slips in the spring. Two maples and one huge chestnut oak have structural problems, so I try to remember to eye them carefully before I pass under. They're too hinky for me to drop. I don't know why our wind storms have taken healthy trees and not these weakened ones.

When my wife and I walk the trails, I carry a whippy, green locust branch. I use this "**flickstick**" to fillip small branches to the side without bending. It's the size and stoutness of a light-weight walking stick, but it needs to be springy to flick properly. My wife feels no compulsion to flick trails, though she and her horse like that I do it. Clear roads make walking safer and protect the soft underbellies of my vehicles. When the roads are flicked, I have a base line that alerts me to the extent of routine twig-and-branch shedding from adjacent trees. I now tend to look both up and down when woods-walking, up for **widowmakers**—broken limbs that will eventually fall—and down so that I don't trip over the fallen. I also try to be mindful of loose rock, uneven ground, holes and concealed limbs. Spend enough time tramping over rough, wooded ground, and these snares will eventually put you on your face or butt.

I try to understand what I see. A few years ago, gypsy moth infestation was in our area. I learned to recognized their egg sacs on trees and know them in flight. Before then, moths were moths to me. This species defoliated and killed oaks in the mid-Atlantic region, but we survived without loss. Three years later, I noticed that the hemlock were losing their needles. The white crud on the underside of their needles was the woolly adelgid. I note new woodpecker holes in trees I thought were sound, and fungus growing on big locust indicates internal rot. I cheer on every wiry little cherry sapling and boo the striped maples that seem to pop up overnight. For every one small thing I've come to understand, I assume there are another 100 still to learn.

I now see the familiar woods not as a forest, but as distinct patches with their own micro-communities of vegetation, trees and maybe creatures. One, for example, is a dark hemlock grove that surrounded the wreck of the Reo, whose steady disintegration I consider performance art. That area is now filled with sunlight and dead hemlock. I'm waiting to see who falls first and then who springs up. Another is a small spot where several weak-looking butternuts hang on in the middle of some huge, decrepit yellow locust. Another is an oak stand on a shaley South-facing slope where deer and turkey generally find food in the shadow of a rotting tree stand about 25 feet up. Ever observant, I noticed the stand a couple of years after I noticed the oaks. Sugar maple saplings grab space where dense slash shielded them from browsing deer and rampaging ferns. But to be honest about it, I mainly notice these triumphant maples when they're an inch-thick and ten feet tall. I do notice when a familiar view or roadway is reduced by **heliotropic** branches racing as fast as they can toward sunlight. I trim them away from the roads every couple of years. I look for evidence of bears—overturned rocks that concealed insects, grubbed out stumps, scat in the trails, a scratching tree. I even see bears themselves once in a while. I like the idea that black bears can make part of their living off me. We share the blackberries in August. (A good bear book is, Benjamin Kilham and Ed Gray, Among the Bears: Raising Orphan Cubs in the Wild [New York: Henry Holt, 2002].) I also patrol for **multiflora rose** clumps, which I spray with herbicide to keep them from taking over. I search maple stumps for sprouts, but the deer have gotten every one. I used to cheer for the deer, now I root for the stumps.

While logging creates a volume of openness in the woods, it also creates a visual and aesthetic mess on the ground. The visitor may notice freshly cut stumps after a logging job. They are low to the ground and not offensive to my eye. You will notice the thick clump of **stump sprouts** sent up the year after cutting if deer don't browse them. Most of the visual offense comes from the crowns left after the usable logs have been cut and removed. Collectively, the crowns are referred to as, **tops** or **slash**. (See

Photographs 19-1 and 19-2.)

I've seen crowns on the ground 20 feet high, even with one side mashed down by the force of the fall. Weeds and brambles thrive in the slash. By the sixth or seventh summer in my four-season area, slash is still noticeable but no longer visually offensive. Each year that it lies on the ground, gravity and hungry bugs work it down. You can accelerate the rotting and measurably improve post-logging aesthetics by lopping the slash so that as much of it as possible is on the ground. (See Photograph 19-3.) This clean-up cutting shortens the time that precipitation, vegetation and creatures need to decompose the wood. Slash makes good firewood for several years, but after that it becomes punky.

While slash is unsightly, it is environmentally beneficial, providing good wildlife habitat, fodder and nutrients for remaining trees and saplings. It looks bad, but it isn't. From an environmental view, it's probably better to let Nature rot slash slowly. Wildlife benefits from the prolonged thick cover, and the tangle allows new trees to take root. It is, however, more aesthetically disturbing than I can stand. So I cut it up. With slash lopped to three feet above the ground, there's still enough mess to protect seedlings from deer looking for an easy meal. You want to protect seedlings by leaving slash where it is. This leads to the subject of chainsaws. If you buy country property with trees on it, you will around to chainsaws pretty quick.

WOODS WORK

I ran my first chainsaw more than 35 years ago. It was a McCulloch that refused to start most of the time. The next was a Homelite that quit running without good reason half-way into every job. I now use a Stihl MS 390 with an 18" bar and a 3/8-inch chain pitch. This is a level of saw that is more than you will need for weekend work in trees with diameters smaller than 16 inches. It has been the right saw for **lopping** (cutting limbs from main stems) and **bucking** (cutting stems into logs and 20-inch-long firewood) the slash from 400 trees. For this work, I moved up from a Stihl 025C, which I found adequate for lighter use. I use the chainsaw to make length-wise cuts about two-thirds through in thick or gnarly firewood rounds, which makes splitting easy. If you do a lot of this length-wise cutting, you'll need a saw with adequate power, a bar that's long enough and a sharp chain. The dealer who sold me the Stihl said Husqvarnas were better. He had sold and repaired both, and I trust his judgment. But I've had good luck with recent Stihls and Consumer Reports likes them. I'd also consider the Husqvarna 350 and the 55 Rancher. (See http://forestry.about.com/library/reviews/aabyb-chainsaws.htm for reviews.)

Whatever brand and size you use, you must understand that you are working with a tool that can hurt you in the blink of an eye in an environment where a dozen things can go wrong even faster. I would not buy an older chainsaw that lacked an anti-kickback brake and other safety features of the newer ones. I would also suggest reading about safe chainsaw use before ever using one. (See http://forestry.about.com/od/chainsaws/.)

DO NOT USE A CHAINSAW WITHOUT WEARING: 1) HARDHAT WITH 2) ATTACHED HEARING-PROTECTION MUFFS AND 3) SCREEN FACE SHIELD ALONG WITH 4) KEVLAR-TYPE FULL-LEG CHAPS, 5) STEEL-TOED LOGGER'S BOOTS AND 6) NON-SLIP WORK GLOVES. One chip in your eye will convince you of the value of full-face protection; one was enough to convince me. I have nicks in my chaps to show where my chainsaw would have bitten me. When I was younger and more stupid, I would cut without chaps, without eye-protection other than my eyeglasses and without heavy boots. No more. A good book on this subject is Frank Philbrick and Stephen Philbrick, The Backyard Lumberjack: The Ultimate Guide to Felling, Bucking, Splitting & Stacking (North Adams, MA: Storey Publishing, 2006.)

The most dangerous cutting I've done is cleaning up slash right after a logging job. While felling trees causes the most logging injuries, lopping slash feels to me to be even more hazardous owing to the uncertain footing, tight quarters, impaired vision from high ground vegetation and the tangle of the material. Loggers don't like to do this work, because it's unprofitable, unsafe and goes slowly. DO NOT DO THIS WORK UNLESS YOU ARE OUTFITTED PROPERLY AND EXPERIENCED WITH A CHAINSAW. I advise waiting at least a year before moving into slash. That gives the compressed branches time to lose most of their spring. Bent branches can break your leg when cutting releases them. You will get into situations where the slash is on all sides, above you and under your feet. Stop, take stock. Take your time. Don't try to buzz your way out. Make sure your feet are on something firm and you're squared up to the cut. Don't straddle limbs that are still connected. It's easy to lose your balance with a running saw in slash jumbles. It's also easy to get the saw bound up in a cut. (Keep an extra blade and chain with you. Unbolt the saw from the stuck blade and attach the extra bar and chain. Then free the original blade and chain without getting bound up again. My rule is: anyone can get stuck in a cut once, but only a fool allows himself to be caught twice in the same jam.) When you get tired cutting, quit. You will hurt yourself if you continue. Take frequent rest breaks and drink water. Beer is not water. Keep your chain sharp. It takes me about 90 minutes—or one load of gas—to lop three or four tops. If I'm feeling frisky, I'll do two loads. But at 61, I'm okay with one. Don't take chances with a chainsaw; injury is too easy to come by.

Since we walk the roads and Melissa rides her horse over them, I try to keep them free of loose stones and pointy, embedded rocks. I pitch them downhill; if I toss them on the uphill side, they end up back in the road. Roly-poly stones are a danger to ankles and hooves; the pointy ones ruin tires. The dirt in these old skid roads is wet and soft enough in the spring to dig out the new crop of offenders. I can kick free the smaller ones with the sole, toe or heel of my logger boots. On the bigger ones, I use a heavy **mattock**, which has a curved blade on one side of its head and a point on the other. The big, buried stones require a **rock bar**, a solid steel shaft about six-feet long with a narrow blade, to pry them out. Some, of course, are so big and deep that I can't budge them. I may batter down an offending point or ledge with a short-handled sledge hammer or fill around them with dirt. I bash down any sharp edges. These big guys are now as familiar to me as the street corners I avoided in the seventh grade where the big-kid bullies gathered. Whenever I remove a rock from a foot trail or road, I *always* fill in the hole to make a safe, level surface. Where the road passes over a section of rock cobble, I'll remove the loose stuff and throw dirt over the surface. I don't like the feel of walking on ball-bearings. The **foot test**—how it feels to walk on a road's surface—is what I use to determine whether or not I need to do more. I don't try to groom these roads like the horse trails at expensive resorts. That level of investment and maintenance is unnecessary. I aim for safe use by people, horses and vehicles.

The roads you find in woods are usually old logging roads, or **skid trails**. Older roads of this sort were not designed to protect streams and control erosion. They tend to run in straight lines, often straight up a slope. They also run too close to streams, or even in stream beds. Newer logging roads are expected to meet environmental-protection standards called, **Best Management Practices (BMPs)**. If you're bulldozing roads from scratch, you should conform to the state's forestry BMPs. If you're working on a road by hand, try to gain elevation gradually and wind the road upslope. Where a slope is too steep to drive across, you'll need to bulldoze a level bench-road into it. This involves pushing the dirt and rock from the L-shaped cut downslope. Make these cuts a couple of feet wider than your widest vehicle for safety, even though more dirt will be dug out. Throw grass seed on both the road and downslope to stabilize the dirt. Loggers should grass-seed skid roads before they leave a site, presumably after they clear the roads of major slash and rocks. Some states require such work; others recommend it. You might find it useful to throw out some seed in the spring following logging, particularly shade-tolerant grass where trees arch over an uphill straight-away. Steep, shady, dry, bad-dirt spots on roads are likely to erode.

Logging is rough work, and you should expect a roughed up appearance—slash and roads primarily. The other anti-aesthetic legacy loggers leave are broken branches in standing trees and **leaners**, trees that have been knocked partially over by falling timber. In dense stands, it may be impossible to prevent this. Your forester can minimize this by anticipating how a logger will cut a tree. Rather than leave trees broken or leaning, the logger should take them down. This will leave a safer and more pleasing woodlot. Careful loggers try to minimize this type of damage and take pride in leaving a clean site. Bad loggers don't give a flip how they leave your land. Provisions can be written into your **timber-sale contract** to encourage loggers to minimize this type of collateral damage. (A sample contract—between a landowner and a timber buyer/logger—is found in Chapter 23.) On the 55 acres I timbered in 2002, I've since had to drop no more than ten top-broke saplings and a couple of leaners.

Small-woodlot logging involves heavy motorized equipment and the dragging—**skidding**—of hundreds of large, heavy logs over make-shift roads through the woods. (Logging on level ground disturbs the ground less than on slopes, and some types of logging use less skidding than others.) Skidders and bulldozers churn up rocks and debris. They also can leave roads with deep ruts if not smoothed up once the logging is complete. That last touch up work must be done when the ground is relatively dry to be effective. Erosion-control measures are graded in at that time.

The damage I find most offensive from skidding are the bark-skinned trees left along the edges of the skid roads. These wounds are caused by a bundle of long logs fishtailing as the skidder or dozer drags them from the woods to the landing where they are sorted and loaded. The skinning wound is found on the first four or five feet of tree trunk. This is the butt log, the most commercially valuable part of the tree. Apart from lost future value, these wounds are unsightly and take a long time to heal, if ever. My eye is drawn to them. I'm offended by the waste and carelessness. I'd guess that on my three miles of skid roads, there might be 100 bark-skinned trees. Most have been bumped twice in 12 years. None of these trees have died, though I've noticed peeling bark above the wounds in some. A number of trees have tried to close their wound, but none have totally succeeded.

A logger could minimize tree skinning by skidding out fewer logs in each gang or cutting them shorter. This would minimize the fishtailing and its impact. But these practices would increase the logger's investment of time and expense, so don't plan on having him skid logs one at a time in eight-foot lengths unless you pay him dearly. And even then, it would slow him down to the point of driving him nuts. I've thought of cutting old tires and stacking them like bangle bracelets five or six deep around a vulnerable trunk. Loggers and foresters will laugh at this idea. It might work; it also might be more work than it's worth. Getting a sufficient number of tires to a logging site and placing them on each skid-road tree is a big, dirty, sweaty job. But it might be practical to protect one or two trees when I do my own little back-yard logging.

Horse-logging skids out only a few logs at a time and is a much slower and softer process than conventional logging using dozers and skidders. Horses create much less collateral environmental damage, because they require less road-building and pull fewer logs in each hitch and at a slower speed. But a landowner will receive less money from his timber sale from a horse logger, because it is a more costly method per unit of timber removed. It obviously costs a lot less to maintain a team of draft horses than a $75,000 skidder, but it takes the horse-logger many times longer to do the same work. A horse logger may have to forgo cutting good timber on slopes where his horses would have difficulty. Still, horse logging on small tracts or where fewer than 100 trees are involved might be a competitive option, particularly if financial return is not your sole objective. (Horse logging leaves the same amount of slash as conventional methods, but the roads will be less disturbed.) The cost economics look even better if you're limiting the logging to a small number of high-value, dispersed, veneer-quality and sawtimber logs. It's arguable that horse-skidding will better protect their value than the rough and tumble of high-speed skidding. On such jobs, you might seek out a horse logger or an old-timer who logs single-handed with a smaller-than-typical skidder and dozer. With such timber, you don't want an outfit that rolls in with a million dollars in new-from-the-factory machines cowboyed around by 20 year olds wearing NASCAR caps.

After the first logging, I put in connecting trails to turn a tree-and-branch road design into a very rough grid with the outside loop tracking the property's perimeter. The connector trails link the ends of the level branch spurs. I wiggled the connectors through openings that offered the fewest trees, rocks and wet places. Most connectors run between spurs at different elevations. I try to use serpentine lines on slopes, because they're less noticeable, easier on the environment and more interesting. Making roads by hand is a matter of sawing out debris and dragging it out of the way. I also had to dig rocks and fill holes with dirt hauled by truck in five-gallon buckets. A dozer cut in the steeper sections. These connectors are mainly for Melissa's trail riding and getting around in my small pick-up truck. They're not wide and straight enough for skidding logs. (See MAP 17-3.)

I don't find woods roads offensive, but I know people who do. If you don't like the idea of vehicle-capable roads in your woods, you might consider threading in a system of hiking trails. Take a look at Robert C. Birkby, Lightly on the Land: The SCA Trail Building and Maintenance Manual (Seattle: Mountaineer Books, 1996) for information.

Vegetation will eventually become established on dirt roads whether or not they are grass seeded. Opportunistic weeds and brambles come in first, then trees. If the roadway is not mowed, it will soon become impassable. To prevent this, roads should be mowed twice a year at least if you want to use them safely. The easiest way to do this is to hire a neighbor who has a tractor and a bushhog. This can be a tax-deductible expense for woodland set up as a farm, business or investment. Hiring out this work is a sensible approach, particularly if you don't have the money to buy a tractor or are skittish around big things that smoke and roar. Your land may allow you to buy a mowing rig smaller than a tractor. Four-wheel ATVs can have drag-behind mowing attachments. You'll probably need a 4WD ATV with a good bit of horsepower—not a cheap mowing option. Self-propelled, heavy-duty sitting or walk-behind mowers might work, but I think they would be unwieldy on steep or rocky trails. Suburban-type riding mowers can be used if the trails are reasonably rock-free. But these mowers are not rugged enough for woods trails in my opinion. Finally, you could keep a road clear with a weed-whacker, though this would prove increasingly less appealing with increasing road length. If you decide to apply herbicide to the grassed road, you will lose the benefit of grass holding dirt in place. If that's your choice, it's better to hire your neighbor.

You may find yourself thinking about buying a tractor and a bushhog. (I've discussed tractors in Chapter 8.) For trail mowing, you can get by with a small tractor—called a "compact"—and a four-foot-wide bushhog, though a bigger tractor and a wider bushhog will make the work easier and faster. The tractor should have a hydraulic **three-point hitch** that will allow you to raise and lower the bushhog over rocks. You won't need 4WD, a front-end loader, quick couplers, elaborate hydraulics or a lot of horsepower—all of which are handy, of course. Power steering is always useful on uneven ground. You can still find an older 20-30 hp tractor and bushhog for $3,000 to $4,000. The new ones cost three to five times that amount.

Most of my woods roads are just wide enough to accommodate my 1957 Ford 8N tractor with its 60-inch-wide bushhog mower. I need to make two passes to mow the main roads, while one does fine on the connectors where the rear wheels mash down another 12 inches on each side. The Ford's rear wheels are reversed on the axle to set them wider for extra stability. This set up prevents me from mowing the full width of the tires. A wider bushhog would, I fear, be too much for my tractor.

Mowing woods roads requires a basic **utility tractor** (not a general purpose tractor, which is generally bigger, designed for row crops, and generally carries its implements under its belly between front and rear wheels) with at least the following features, which are explained in detail in Chapter 8:

- **20 to 30 horsepower**

- **Power Take-Off (PTO).** This is a shaft that sticks out of the rear of the tractor, which can be engaged to the engine. When engaged, it turns. Through a coupling, shaft and differential, the PTO shaft turns the bushhog blade. **Live PTO** allows you to control the engagement of the tractor's engine to the bushhog. You want live PTO because it lets you run attachments while the tractor is standing still. When checking PTO operation, make sure that the engaging gears are not worn; otherwise, you will find your bushhog slipping out of gear when it hits a clump of dirt. Replacing this gear mechanism is expensive. This will make you angry. ALWAYS DISENGAGE YOUR BUSHHOG WHEN YOU ARE DISMOUNTING THE TRACTOR.

- **Three-point hitch.** This is a hydraulic arrangement at the back of your tractor that lets you raise and lower whatever is attached. When mowing trails or anything else, you will have a frequent need to raise and lower the bushhog to adapt to the contours of the ground and avoid protruding rocks. A fixed-position mower would take a beating with each use. Tractors come in various sizes and have different-sized hitch arrangements. Make sure that you know which hitch Category (O, 1 or 2) your tractor features so that you match your PTO equipment with your hitch. Category 1 is big enough for this type of mowing.

- **Bushhog (aka, brushog or rotary cutter).** This is a mower that is either driven by your tractor's PTO or its own engine. It will have a "crazy wheel" (or tailwheel) made of segmented rubber to support its outby end. This wheel rotates 360 degrees and supports the bushhog. Make sure that your tractor size (horsepower) is sufficient to operate and lift the bushhog you get. You will want to get a bushhog that's between four and six feet wide for trail mowing with a Category 1 hitch. You want a heavy-duty bushhog with a steel deck at least 3/16-inch thick.

  Some bushhogs use a clutch to protect their blades when they hit an immovable object. The clutch disengages the PTO motion from the blade when the object is hit, thus sparing various shafts and mechanical parts. Older bushhogs use a three-piece blade, with the two end pieces attached to the center piece by pin pivots. This bat-wing blade allows the end pieces to hit a rock without transferring the force to the bushhog's mechanics. If you have a clutch bushhog, you won't need a three-piece blade. Most bushhogs come with a shearpin in the power train, which is supposed to break before a differential or shaft when the blade whacks the unseen Gibraltar. Carry an extra shearpin or appropriately sized bolt in your tractor's toolbox or tape it to the bushhog itself.

  The bushhog's gearbox changes the PTO shaft rotation from horizontal to vertical and turns the blade horizontally. Its differential is concealed in the gearbox's metal housing on top of the bushhog. The housing should have a little screw-in plug where you put in gearbox lubricant (not motor oil). Gearboxes are sized according to your tractor's horsepower. A mismatch between tractor size and bushhog size will eventually harm the smaller component. A bushhog is not a finish mower, which is appropriate for big lawns. Blades should be sharpened, advice that I don't follow very much. A sharp blade cuts neatly, a dull blade cuts raggedy. On a woods road, where the blade gets nicked a little every time you mow, you don't care that the grass is not like a putting green. Your bushhog will last longer if you don't run it over saplings, multiflora rose, embedded rocks, old fence posts and odd pieces of metal that your farm truck has decided it no longer needs.

- **Rollbar.** Tractors roll over, both sideways and end over end. Sideways rollovers are the most common. They occur when the tractor is being driven across a slope and the pitch steepens; or, when you are driving across a slope and your uphill rear tire rides up on a rock or stump. Rollovers happen in a split-second so your best protection is to avoid getting yourself into these dicey situations. Nothing is worth a rollover—no last log that you want to pull out, no last section of trail mowing, no step you want to avoid walking. You should wear a seatbelt with a rollbar.

  You can also adapt your tractor for protection. You can protect yourself, first, by extending your wheel-base width-wise. Various ways exist to do this, including reversing the rear wheel rims on the axle hubs so that the wheel wells stick out rather than in, thus widening the wheelbase by the width of your rims. You can also extend the front axle on each side to widen the wheelbase. A tractor mechanic should do this work because the wheel adjustments front and back must be kept proportional to each other. The front wheel toe in also needs to be adjusted when extending the front axles. This is a cheap way to make your tractor safer.

  You can also install a roll-over protection system (ROPS) and seatbelt. These have been standard for several years. Most smaller tractors prior to the 1980s don't have them. A ROPS can be a roll bar or a bar with a steel canopy that provides shade.

- **Ear Protection.** I always wear hearing protectors, muffs rather than plugs. You may be the only "fool" in the neighborhood who wears them, and a new fool in the neighborhood to boot, but you will be the one fool who will be able to hear the snide comments.

Aside from trail mowing, you may play with the idea of **using your farm tractor for logging your woods**, occasionally or otherwise. I pull out about ten logs a year, which is plenty for me. I use my 50-year-old 2WD Ford, even though it is not suited for this work inasmuch as it lacks power steering, front weights (for traction) and 4WD. I drag logs out of the woods to a spot where I can saw and split them into firewood and load them into a truck. I look for a place in a road that's shaded, where the footing is good, and the ground is level and open. The more rocks underfoot, the more dancing with a chainsaw, and the higher your risk of getting hurt. If you're cutting wood on stony ground, sooner or later you will "**rock your saw**." This precipitates serious self-cursing and an extensive amount of chain sharpening. If you're splitting with an ax or a maul, you want enough clearance so that you can swing through vertically with an overhead, straight-down shot. I pick a place where I can park my truck immediately parallel to the firewood to make loading easy. I load the firewood with a **tie-pick**, an ax-like tool with a sharpened point instead of a blade. A tie-pick spares my back from bending over and lifting. If the truck is hitched to a haulage cart or hydraulic splitter, I make sure that I can either drive out going straight ahead or get turned around without a problem.

Before taking my tractor off a maintained woods road, I clear a "roadway" back to the tree, making it as straight and clean as I can. I'll remove downed limbs, rocks and sticks protruding from the ground. I try to avoid or remove impediments like stumps that will catch a dragged log and imperil me and the tractor. When a stump stops a dragged log, the tractor's front end lifts up and back. In that event, you need to cut the power damn quickly or the tractor can pull itself over backwards. The 30 minutes I devote to clearing the temporary roadway usually prevents getting stuck, hung up or broke down. The idea is to baby the tractor and eliminate opportunities for things going wrong.

Before hitching a chain or cable to a log, I trim all of its branches flush to prevent snagging. Skidding is easier and safer if the log is dragged butt-end first. The closer you can chain up the log to the back of the tractor, the better. I usually hitch the log onto a grab hook welded to the bushhog or scraper blade. I use the hitch hydraulics to lift the butt off the ground, which decreases the log's drag by reducing the amount of log surface touching the ground. A log hitched this way changes the tractor's balance, however. The heavier the log, the less weight there will be on the front wheels. This reduces the traction available for turning and makes dragging uphill riskier. A tractor can pull a lot more log weight on level ground than on an uphill slope. If the ground is wet or soft from earlier rain, the tractor's woods work just waits. Safety requires dry, level, clear and slow. Though I usually do this work myself, it's always safer when there's a helper around.

Farm tractors lack the **armor** for woods work. If you want to use a farm tractor for this type of work more than very occasionally, you will do well to weld a skid plate along its underside, along with metal guards in front of the radiator, headlights, exhaust stack (if possible) and engine's sides. You should also put metal protection on the four tire rims to protect valve stems. I'd also recommend a canopy-type roll-over protection system and wheel weights all around. Woods work is hard on tires when the ground is rocky, stumpy and thick with slash. Power steering, 4WD, three-point hitch and a front-end loader (outfitted with forks, not a bucket) are very handy in this environment. Farm tractors should be used sparingly for dragging logs in the woods.

I advise against doing daily logging with a farm tractor. However, I have seen large tractors—60 hp+ with 4WD, armored and outfitted with either a **logging winch** or a **grapple loader**—used this way. The winch mounts on the three-point hitch and runs off the PTO. It lifts the butt ends of a gang of logs off the ground and puts heavy steel plate between the logs and the back end of the tractor. A grapple loader grabs, then lifts a log onto a truck or trailer. You might find this loader referred to as a **knuckle boom**, and see one on a logging truck. A tractor logging winch costs up to $5,000 and a loader can be twice that. An excellent article, complete with information on manufacturers and techniques, is Robert M. Shaffer, "Farm Tractor Logging for Woodlot Owners" Virginia Cooperative Extension, Publication Number 420-090, April, 1998; also at www.ext.vt.edu/pubs/forestry/420-090.html. Every state's extension service publishes state-specific articles that are available at a nominal price, or free on the website of the coordinating land-grant university. Since logging techniques differ from region to region, the extension service and forestry agency are good starting places for acquiring information. Logging is hard, dangerous, skilled work. Logging is not cutting up six-inch-diameter firewood on a couple of sunny fall afternoons. I advise inexperienced landowners to leave serious logging to the pros.

Tractors are dangerous helpmates in woods. You can do without tractor logging. Not so, without a **woods truck**. Well, you actually can live without a woods truck, but they are incredibly handy. Where land is set up as a business, investment or farm, its cost is deductible or depreciable.

Every rural landowner has **truck stories**. You, too, will acquire yours. (But first, you need the hero.) Generally, they are getting-stuck sagas, exotic breakdowns, ingenious field repairs using spit and electrician's tape, wild rides resulting from brake failures, runaways dragging owners (who didn't set the emergency brake), downhill slides through mud as slick as snot (as the saying goes) and legendary loads—of which songs should be sung. Many truck stories involve innocent others.

One morning years ago up a holler remote by even West Virginia's standards, a young, good-looking, recently divorced woman of my casual-and-completely-innocent acquaintance nursed her extremely expensive, extremely low-slung Italian sports car up my muddy, pot-holed road. This car no more belonged on my farm dirt than the Hope Diamond belonged in a pig wallow. My best friend—young, single and charming—and I admired this mile-long feat of determined off-road driving in silence. The convertible, we sensed, was highly motivated. It stopped in front of my run-down, sheet-tin barn, a refuge that it would refuse to enter in a hurricane. Mud dripped from its polished flanks. Its beast-like motor wheezed. The driver slowly unlimbered her limbs and other charms from behind the hand-rubbed, walnut steering wheel. Real jewels flashed, danced and jangled. Legs shimmered in pants from Paris. She wasn't wearing sunglasses. "I need some work on my tailpipe," she announced with no visible distress, looking

David square in his eye. Not wanting to be churlish, I did not point out that between her fancy house in fancy South Hills and the mud hole in which her Papagallos were now standing, 50 miles away, there were at least 25 auto-repair shops capable of fixing any exhaust system built since 1903. Nor did I mention that David and I had been about to start work. It occurred to me that I was not even present for all of her intents and purposes. So we jacked up the rear end, and I left, as the two of them wiggled under for a look. David appeared several days later, saying only that "additional alignment" had been needed. I know this is not a truck story, but it does involve a vehicle…in the country. It was the 70s, after all.

Woods truck. You will use one to get around the property and haul stuff/people in and out. It will carry you, other humans, dogs, firewood, tree seedlings, gravel (called "gravels" around here), game, water, culverts, five-gallon cans of gasoline, fencing materials, leaves, grass seed, lumber, building supplies, tree branches, dirt, posted signs, wood-cutting paraphernalia, tools, picnic supplies, guns and a pup tent with hot dogs for your kid's first sleep out.

My preference is a **farm-use truck** that does not require a license and inspection, but should be good enough to pass inspection if it were inspected which it will not be. (Check local standards before assuming the truth of my preceding statement.) A farm-use truck should be dinged up and more at home on a logging road than an Interstate. It may be necessary, however, to find a truck that is both fully licensed as well as being suitable for working in the woods and around the farm. The newer and more expensive your truck, the more slowly you want to drive it in the woods and the better you want your dirt roads to be.

Although I've driven a number of pick-ups over the years, only two were notable, and only one of these was truly woods-worthy. The unworthy was a red 1946 International with steel as thick as tank plates. Although it was a conventional 2WD, it had enough weight and balance to move through light mud and rough ground. I bought it for $100 in the early 1970s from a fellow who claimed it would "do a hunderd," and did I want to see? I doubt that I ever drove it over 40 mph, and that was pushing its engine. It proved to be feeble and spent a lot of time in the hospital getting transplants. (I had a 1972 International Scout at that time, which soured me on American cars. Its only reliable feature was that it could not be counted on, ever.) Getting parts for a truck pushing 30 was sometimes like securing an organ donation from my enemies. Yet, it had a simple, WWII-era straight-forwardness that I loved. The front window cranked out. It had overhead wipers and a couple of white stripes running from its hood back across its doors. It smelled trucky—old parts under the seat, oily rags, a hint of hay and candy bars from the late 1940s. I named him, "Phillip, Da Truck."

Phillip could carry a lot of weight very slowly. I mainly asked him to bring firewood home over pretty good dirt roads. But he and I once met a Ringling Brothers train in Charleston, West Virginia so that I could shovel out a load of fresh elephant manure for our garden. I drove him home, reeking, through the unsuspecting down-town lunch crowd of bored lawyers and bankers in what passed for his "bulldog first." Phillip's presence was not universally applauded by those to whom I waved. (I was young and unemployed at the time, which may explain, but does not excuse, my behavior. It was the 70s, after all.) I think Phillip was embarrassed and felt used. He was always willing though only intermittently able. I treasure those few crisp, fall afternoons when I gently drove him home loaded above his gunwales with sour-smelling split oak as I puffed on a cigar. Phillip was a self-indulgence. If you need a working truck, don't buy an antique no matter how cool.

For ten years now, I've had "The Cheetah," a 4WD truck both notable and woodsy as a fox. It has no style, no nostalgia, no cool. Some of the body is yellow—hence its name—but most of it is rust. It runs, but it has no jump. It could chase down a parked Impala. Its windows bear stickers from Brown and Harvard. In any context other than mine, it would be buried in the woods like the Reo. But it suits me perfectly. It's cheap, reliable and forgiving. I expect it will survive me.

Officially, the Cheetah is a short-wheelbase, 1980 Toyota 4WD pick-up with a four-speed manual transmission whose clutch survived my daughter's first driving lessons. It has no power anything, and is the opposite of "loaded." The engine is simple, something an Australopithecine or even a Ph.D. like me can work on. It's been a farm-use truck since 1993 and now shows about 260,000 miles. The Cheetah has about 12 inches of ground clearance and a functioning 4WD system. Newer 4WDs are better, because they shift power to wheels having traction. The Cheetah's first gear in Low Range is what I prefer to use in the woods, because it allows me to crawl down slopes without much brake. It's well balanced, and I've never gotten it stuck. It's good enough in mud, but won't go uphill through deep snow over ice. The bed is small, which means I can only haul small loads, which means I don't strain my back. No Cheetah was ever meant to be a beast of burden.

The Cheetah is beat to hell. It sheds parts like an overheated winter hiker—so far, mud flaps, a molded plastic thing, the rubber foot plate on its gas pedal, rear-view mirror, side mirror, a front wheel, exhaust system components, leaf spring and unidentifiable miscellany. The bed contains a number of ground-viewing holes—like a glass-bottomed boat—that make cleaning a breeze. The Cheetah is not an antique—and never will be. It can't be restored. I do maintain it, because it's a working truck.

I've rigged the Cheetah for work in the woods and around the farm. I've strengthened the frame, which was about to rust in half. I carry the spare tire above the cab's roof so that I have extra room in the bed. It's mounted on a horizontal V that is welded to the rollbar. This black beret sets him apart from other big cats in the neighborhood. There's a tow hook bolted onto the front frame and a very heavy-duty, shop-made bumper that can handle either a ball hitch or towing pin. (This was accomplished by welding to the four-inch diameter, steel-pipe bumper a half-moon plate of 1/2-inch-thick steel with a hole drilled through it to accommodate either one.) Two grab hooks are welded at either end of the bumper for dragging or pulling with chains. A welder fabricated a roll bar out of tube steel. Then he welded onto the top bar a series of paired horseshoes to carry an ax, cant hook, shovel, sledge hammer, tie-pick, maul and mattock. Also welded to the rollbar are four steel rectangles, about one inch in height. They are slots for carrying splitting wedges. I throw the rock bar and chainsaw into the bed, along with the dogs. On the passenger side's floor, I keep an extra cutting bar and chains, spark plug, safety chaps, gloves and a helmet with face mask/muffs.

The Cheetah, because of its condition, is the kind of truck you want for woodsying around, though its not good enough for much highway driving. It's easy to maneuver despite the lack of power steering, doesn't get stuck, can pull a cart or a log, could care less about dings and scrapes and forgives a mechanical nincompoop like me. It's dependable on inclines, both up and down, and doesn't overheat with a load. It features an operational horn and headlights; functioning heater and wipers; and a radio that has been known to pick up oldies when the stars are right. It has an occasional sense of humor. One time both doors jammed with me inside. I was forced to squeeze out through the driver's-side window. A neighbor was amused. A truck like The Cheetah would be good to have at your place in the country, but it could not be used for commuting between home and there. For that job, you can stick with your day car.

I'm no expert on pick-ups, but I have no trouble recommending the stubby 4WD Toyotas from 1978-1985 as a knock-about, all-purpose vehicle for your country property. They're cheap to buy and cheap to maintain. They're reliable even with a lot of miles and are known for their lack of temperament. They start; this is important. If you're looking for a farm/woods truck, avoid buying a fully-loaded anything as well as all trucks owned by teenage boys, defined as males under 50.

A fellow could, of course, plop down $35,000 for a new truck so that he can bring home half a cord of wood at Thanksgiving that he cut from his newly purchased land. Some portion of our Nation's economy depends on men making such decisions. You may think your new truck will be "like a rock" no matter how many tons of steel are dumped on it. If you treat a truck like the New York advertising agencies do, you will be looking for a replacement vehicle in short order.

If you're a first-timer with trucks and land, look for a well-used, light-weight, short-bed 4WD with power steering and a stick shift. Larger trucks can haul more, but they are less nimble and the older ones tend to swamp around in mud and snow. My neighbors like big, sprawly Fords and Chevys from the 1970s, but they won't get in an out of the tight spots the Cheetah slips through without a trace. You don't need a flatbed or a dump truck for most work. A friend from West Virginia, Claude Pauley, once described his late 1960s full-size GMC pick-up as the "haulin'est truck" he ever saw, which it was. But it was so wide, long and low that it would have run aground under load in the woods or, at least, dropped a few undergarments. Resist the old Dodge power wagons despite their neat looks. They are very heavy and are more truck than you will need in almost every situation. They're also very expensive to maintain. Hummers may be able to go anywhere, but they don't go through trees. They're too wide for scooting along most woods roads. Why spend $50,000 to $100,000 to haul home $50 worth of firewood? Hummers are fun to watch—at a curb, and on paper where they depreciate rapidly for tax purposes. Still, it will take applied intelligence, not just simple negligence, to get one stuck.

If I had a very large place that required a lot of work and if I had a lot of money, I would buy a Mercedes-Benz Unimog with a lot of attachments. A Unimog starts out as a combination tractor and truck, which can then be rigged to do almost anything, including, perhaps, bearing children.

Every so often, you will ask your truck to do more than it's supposed to do under fair-use rules. Things like: getting you off a steep slope with a full load; or getting you home with half its cylinders firing; or getting you out of a jam created by your own bad judgment. When you find yourself asking your truck for a favor, it's good to be on a first-name basis. You get there by paying attention to its needs on a regular basis so it will feel just slightly indebted to you. Laugh all you want. Spend enough time in the field with a truck, and I promise you will find yourself in a relationship.

The main lesson I think I've learned from all this road work and sawing is that trees can take care of much of themselves over time even with my mucking around. The logging and my other interventions will fade. Slash and stumps rot. New trees come up. The old chestnut stumps from the 1930s will undoubtedly be there when I'm gone. About four-feet high—the comfortable working height for a two-man crosscut saw—they are soft red rot inside hard grey shells. Ax marks are still visible on some, forgotten the day they were made. I honor both the stump and the unknown axman. Some of these stumps are more than five-feet wide. But even they will disappear into the woods in time. And that is the lesson, I guess: forested land works with what it has, changing some but staying forested. It's forgiving and adaptive. It can be used without being hurt, but it can be hurt.

This chapter describes my own approach to **small woodlot management**. I recommend James R. Fazio, The Woodland Steward: A Practical Guide to the Management of Small Private Forests, 2nd ed., (Moscow, Idaho: The Woodland Press, 1987) and Richard M. Brett, The Country Journal Woodlot Primer: The Right Way to Manage Your Woodland (Brattleboro, Vermont: Country Journal Publishing Company, 1983) for further reading. Fazio is especially helpful.

CHAPTER 20: THINKING ABOUT TIMBER

LANDOWNER'S OBJECTIVES FOR WOODLAND

In looking at woodland for possible purchase, it is critical for you to view each target with an eye toward a property-specific **set of objectives**, one of which may be selling (and cutting) its timber. Your starting objectives will lead to a **forest-management plan**, even if you want to do nothing at all. A plan can be as simple as a mental note to never do anything, but most plans involve active intervention to promote owner objectives.

I urge buyers to think about multiple objectives and how they interact. Setting objectives involves determining the scope and type of things you think you might do with the woods if you purchase them as well as ranking these objectives in terms of their importance. It's likely that you will find yourself listing multiple objectives, some of which conflict with each other. A **consulting forester**, discussed below, can help you think through a plan's objectives. Your objectives and plan may also need to involve a civil engineer (if major road and bridges are anticipated) and environmental specialists. TABLE 20-1 gets an inexperienced land buyer started in thinking about common woodland-management objectives over three time periods.

TABLE 20-1

Buyer's Woodland-Management Objectives

	Immediate	1-10 Years	10 + Years
Possible Objectives			
1. Money			
a. Maximize immediate timber-sale income (TSI)			
b. Some immediate TSI; Maximize TSI for __ years forward			
c. No immediate TSI; Improve stand for __ years forward			
d. Annual revenue			
1. Firewood/chips from culls			
2. Tap sugar maples			
3. Christmas trees			
4. Ginseng			
5. Nuts, mushrooms, berries—other food and/or seedling stock			
6. Other			
e. Rental lease for			
1. Hunting/fishing			
2. Birding			
3. Hiking/camping			
4. ATVs/snowmobiles			
5. Horses—trail riding			

    6. Cross-country skiing
    7. Mountain biking
    8. Other
  f. Mineral/energy leases
    1. Oil & gas
    2. Non-Energy minerals
      a. Surface
      b. Underground
    3. Energy resources (coal, oil shale, biomass)
      a. Surface
      b. Underground
    4. Geothermal
    5. Wind
    6. Hydro

2. Aesthetics
  a. Preserve—untouched
  b. Management for specific aesthetic goals, e.g.
    1. Visual neatness
    2. Quiet
    3. Unmanaged look
    4. Other

3. Flora and fauna
  a. Enhance habitat for particular game species
  b. Enhance habitat for non-game species
    1. Birds
    2. Flora
    3. Fish
    4. Other
  c. Protect ETS species
  d. Emphasize diversity of flora and/or fauna

4. Water Resources
  a. Preserve existing watercourses/wetlands
    1. Improve fish habitat
    2. Minimize erosion
  b. Add ponds
    1. Improve wildlife habitat
    2. Fire protection
  c. Protect/create wetlands
  d. Sell/use water
  e. Improve water quality

5. Recreation
  a. Non-hunting
    1. No roads/trails
    2. Improve roads/trails

        b. Hunting
        c. Vehicle recreation—develop roads
        d. Horseback riding

6. Timber stand
        a. Up-grade mix of tree
                species to improve
                long-term financial value
        b. Change species mix
                to help particular wildlife
                species
        c. Change species mix
                for aesthetics/recreation
                objectives
        d. Remove diseased/dead
                standing trees
        e. Reduce fire potential
        f. Plant seedlings to increase
                future value
        g. Other

7. Fire protection
        a. Develop road network
        b. Remove standing deadwood
        c. Develop ponds
        d. Lop slash to hasten
                decomposition

8. Develop second home/camp
        a. Pick site; coordinate building
                plans with other objectives

TABLE 20-1 can also be used to reflect the **intensity** with which you think you want to pursue each objective. With "0" representing no interest and "5" representing an objective that you are most interested in achieving, you can rank their importance within each time period.

The objectives I've included above are a typical range, but your objectives will be specific to you and your site. The ones I've included are illustrative, not exhaustive. A consulting forester can help you develop objectives and alert you to conflicts between and among them. You can't, for example, maximize immediate TSI and also maximize TSI ten years down the road, though you may be able to produce timber income at both points. (In this case, you might reframe the objective to be, produce maximum timber-sale income over ten years, with so many dollars immediately.)

The management plan you draft as a buyer is likely to change if you become the property's owner. Dirt-level experience will lead to some new objectives and some re-ranking. While you should understand that change is part of every plan, some decisions in forestry have long-term consequences. Once your land has been clearcut, you can't change your mind and decide, instead, on a selective cut. Unless you need to sell timber immediately upon purchase, I'd advise to not make any significant cutting decisions until you've owned the property for at least several years. Your management plan may never amount to anything more than an immutable decision to never do anything. (In this case, you may want to investigate the tax benefits of a conservation easement based on no surface disturbance, no development and no logging.)

Your plan may involve a few general ideas, or take formal shape as a highly detailed, time-sequenced written document that guides you for many years and even takes the form of a legal covenant. To receive state tax benefits for managing your wooded property as timberland, you will need a management plan drawn up by a state-approved forester.

Woodland provides many benefits that need to be considered when thinking about your specific objectives. Forested land absorbs water, which controls the runoff that leads to flooding, erosion and sediment build up in waterways. Woodland is a sponge, bare land is much less so. As water percolates through forest duff, soil and rock, it is cleaned. Trees build dirt as leaves are shed and fallen wood decomposes. Woods provide habitat for plants and animals. Trees remove carbon dioxide from the air and give off oxygen, a process on which all of us depend. They affect surface temperature. They provide the feedstock for every wood product we use—from paper and telephone poles to furniture and ice-cream sticks. Woodlands provide high aesthetic values and diverse recreation opportunities. They can also supply food and medicine. These functions are connected and depend on each other. A major change in one function reverberates with the others. Accordingly, the landowner's objectives should be broader than finding the fastest dollar in his woods. And if that is your only objective, a consulting forester can help you get that dollar with the least harm done to everything else.

If you involve a consulting forester in your scoping, discuss your preliminary forest objectives with him. He can help you evaluate them in terms of **feasibility, time-frame, interdependence, compatibility, financial costs and benefits, opportunity costs (things you can't do because of what you do) and environmental benefits and impacts.** Some objectives may be unsuited to the type of land or soil on the target property. Certain financial objectives for the timber may not be very compatible with your preferred recreational and environmental goals. A clearcut does not fit well with scenic Sunday horseback rides, at least for the ten or 15 years after the logging. Foresters are trained to think in terms of forest-management plans over time so yours will know how to identify incompatibilities and objectives that are dependent on others.

You should do some reading and investigation to develop your thoughts about ranking objectives. The books below will help you know what you know, what you want to know and some of the things you don't know. I would not, however, advise developing objectives and a plan based on books alone. Your forester's insight and experience will produce a plan that brings benefits and prevents errors far into the future. Among the books you might consult, are Mollie Beattie, Charles Thompson and Lynn Levine, Working With Your Woodland: A Landowner's Guide (Hanover and London: University Press of New England, 1983); Country Journal Woodlot Primer: The Right Way to Manage Your Woodland (New York: W.W. Norton & Company, 1983); Stewart Hilts, et al., The Woodlot Management Handbook: Making the Most of Your Wooded Property for Conservation, Income or Both (Buffalo, New York: Firefly Books, 1999); Dave Johnson, The Good Woodcutter's Guide: Chain Saws, Woodlots and Sawmills (White River Junction, Vermont: Chelsea Green Publishing Company, 1998); Thom J. McEvoy, Legal Aspects of Owning and Managing Woodlands (Washington, D.C.: Island Press, 1998); Leon S. Minckler, Woodland Ecology: Environmental Forestry for the Small Owner, 2nd ed., (Syracuse, New York: Syracuse University Press, 1980); Laurence C. Walker, Farming the Small Forest: A Guide for the Landowner (San Francisco: Miller Freeman Publications, 1988); and Rick A. Hamilton, Forest*A*Syst: A Self-Assessment Guide for Managing Your Forest for Timber Production, Wildlife, Recreation, Aesthetics and Water Quality (Raleigh, NC: North Carolina State University, undated) and A Family Forest: A Planning Guide to Protect, Enhance and Manage Private Forestland (Raleigh, North Carolina: NC Division of Forest Resources, 2002), both available from Rick A. Hamilton, Extension Forestry Specialist, Department of Forestry, North Carolina State University, Campus Box 8003, Room 3028D Biltmore Hall, Raleigh, North Carolina, 27695-8003; 919-515-5574; e-mail at: rick_hamilton@ncsu.edu.

Valuing timber in the field involves estimating both the volume of **merchantable** trees—those which a timber buyer will pay for—and its likely price. Some experienced individuals can do these calculations as they walk through a wooded property. The systematic way of determining volume and value is to have a consulting forester undertake a **timber cruise**, which is a field-based sampling of standing timber volume that he couples with his estimate of current stumpage prices. Cruises generally limit themselves to inventorying the merchantable timber. I'll introduce you to the basic vocabulary and concepts and then take you through an analysis of a sample cruise in Chapter 21.

Broadly speaking, American timber is divided into **hardwood (HW)** species, which are **broadleaf deciduous** trees such as oak, cherry, maple, hickory, birch, beech and walnut, and **needleleaf evergreen (softwood or coniferous)** species, such as pine, spruce, cedar and hemlock. American deciduous trees lose their leaves in the fall; evergreens retain their needles.

With exceptions, hardwood species grow more slowly than evergreens. Most HW species in average natural conditions take at least 50 years to reach a diameter of 16 inches; this growth time can double on poor sites with weak soils and not much precipitation. Hardwoods are generally harvested from naturally-growing, rather than planted, stands. In the East and Midwest, a natural stand of mixed hardwood species is what a land buyer is likely to encounter. In the South and New England, you will find natural stands of mixed hardwoods and evergreens.

Conifers are cut both in the wild and from managed even-age, one-species plantations. Fast-growing pine species, such as loblolly, have been planted throughout the South. They are cultivated for both sawtimber and pulp. The initial planting is usually thinned after about a dozen years and then clearcut about ten to 15 years later. This strategy maximizes volume production and financial return.

Commercially valuable trees have two different markets, speaking broadly. Both HW and conifers of sufficient size and quality are sold for **sawtimber**, which is milled into lumber, flooring and the like. A specialty sub-market for some species of sawtimber is veneer. **Veneer-quality** logs are the best grade of sawtimber, because they are free of imperfections. Veneer is a thin sheet of wood that is used to face furniture and cabinetry. It is glued over a cheaper wood. Cherry, oak, walnut, birch and maple are the hardwood species that are used for veneer. The second major market for both hardwoods and conifers values them as a source of fiber, either as a **pulp** feedstock for making paper or as **chips** for composition products. The fiber market puts no value on a tree's suitability for lumber. Sawtimber is generally more valuable on the stump than **pulpwood**, which I will use generically to mean bulk wood that is not milled for lumber. Merchantable timber also includes trees that are used for telephone and utility poles, railroad ties, pallets and other products. Pine, not hardwood, is used for poles that are treated with preservative. Pole-size or pole timber refers to either hardwood or softwood of eight to ten-inches DBH. Low-quality hardwood sawtimber is used for ties and pallets. You may find a reference to chip-and-saw timber, or C&S. This refers to small-diameter pine sawtimber that is first run through a chipping head that squares off two sides of a log and then goes through a gang saw for ripping into products, like 2x4s. For simplicity, I have grouped all non-sawtimber wood as "pulp." Every region will show a hierarchy of pulp prices, depending on what products local buyers produce. Hardwood pulp and pine pulp have different prices. Hardwood is sold for both sawtimber and pulp, as is softwood.

My experience mainly involves Appalachian hardwoods, with some knowledge of New England forests and southern pine plantations. This discussion, accordingly, is based on my experience. Be prepared for different terms and methods in other parts of the country, even though the basic approach should be similar to the one I describe. I'll focus on valuing hardwood sawtimber **stumpage**, which is merchantable trees standing in the field. A **merchantable tree** is one that a stumpage buyer will pay a landowner for; there will be many trees on a landowner's property that are not merchantable because they are too small, or defective in one way or another, or of little commercial value, or located where they can't be cut profitably. Hardwood sawtimber is trickier to value than planted evergreen, because quality and size figure into HW value, and each HW species is priced individually. It's much easier to determine the stumpage value of 100 acres of 17-year-old loblolly pine than 100 acres of mixed hardwoods with volume distributed among two dozen species of different ages, sizes and quality.

Sawtimber is cut into logs that are milled into dimensioned boards for flooring, furniture and construction. These logs are graded according to their quality. Sawtimber stumpage (volume or weight) is estimated in the field. Sawtimber stumpage should only include those trees that are merchantable, i.e., that is, only those that a stumpage buyer will pay for. It is not uncommon, however, for a land seller to provide a buyer with a stumpage cruise that includes non-merchantable volume and, hence, unrealizable value. These bogus cruises are discussed in Chapter 22.

Sawtimber stumpage is expressed either in volume—**board feet (bf)**, usually in units of **1,000 board feet (mbf)** or in green weight—tons. Better-quality sawtimber is shown in board feet. You may see a cruise where better sawtimber is expressed in board feet and the remainder in tons.

To determine the amount of merchantable stumpage and its dollar value, a forester conducts a representative sampling of the land's merchantable trees. This is called a **timber cruise**. A sawtimber cruise should not count as sawtimber any trees that are not of sawtimber quality and diameter, as determined by the local market. Such trees should be counted as pulp or firewood, if at all. A sawtimber cruise should also not include good trees that are located on **inoperable acreage**, such as inaccessible steep slopes or impenetrable swamp. While those trees qualify as sawtimber, they cannot be logged in a cost-effective way. Therefore, a stumpage buyer would place no value on them in his bid; they are not merchantable.

The forester superimposes a grid on the hardwood property. He walks into each cell in this grid. Cell size varies with the size of the property being cruised. The larger the property, the larger each cell. A 100-acre HW tract might use cells that are five acres each, or smaller. A 50,000-acre tract might use cells of 50 or 100 acres, depending on the consistency of the timber stand. In each cell, the forester takes a sample—called a **plot**—of the standing trees. Plots are typically $1/10^{th}$ to $1/5^{th}$ of an acre. The forester counts the merchantable trees in each plot, and groups them by species and diameter class. Typically, HW sawtimber is grouped into two-inch diameter classes, e.g., all merchantable trees in the plot between ten and 12 inches DBH are grouped into one class, usually referred to as 10s; between 12 and 14 inches DBH are 12s and so on. Trees in the plot that are smaller in diameter than the cruise's operating definition of merchantability are not counted. In the case of a deformed or damaged tree that meets the diameter threshold, the forester counts only that volume that is log-length and of acceptable quality.

The forester then estimates the board feet (or tons) in each of the merchantable trees—and the merchantable portion of defective trees—in the plot. He starts by determining diameter, which he measures as **diameter at breast height (DBH), or 4.5 feet above the ground's surface**. Definitions of diameter merchantability vary, according to the type of timber being cruised, its likely market and the owner's objectives. For a HW clearcut, merchantability might be defined as all trees 4" DBH and larger. A **selective cut** in a HW stand might define the diameter threshold as everything larger (wider) than 18" DBH. On trees of sufficient diameter in the plot, the forester estimates the number of eight- to 16-foot-long logs in each merchantable tree. The stumpage volume for each tree is found by consulting a chart, called a **log scale**, which provides the number of board feet in each log length for a given diameter. Tonnage is calculated similarly. Methods can vary from region to region, depending on species and market factors.

Stumpage prices change over time with market conditions. Lumber markets have cycles that tend to track new home construction. Each HW species has its own price range in every local market. These prices rise and fall with supply and demand for that species. As species go in and out of consumer favor, their prices—both as finished lumber and on the stump—rise and fall. Appalachian green/air-dried 4/4 (one-inch thick) red oak lumber, for example, fell from almost $600/mbf in 2004 to about $450 in mid-

2005 as furniture buyers swung to sugar (hard) maple and red (soft) maple, whose prices rose. Stumpage prices shadow retail lumber prices.

In addition, each stumpage buyer determines his bid price for each species in light of the supply he has and the demand for his milled product. One stumpage buyer, for instance, might bid $450 mbf for northern red oak because his log yard is empty and he has orders that he can't fill, while the mill buyer down the road bids only $300 mbf because his yard is stacked with red oak logs and he has few orders. Within a species, stumpage price bids will vary according to quality. The difference between published stumpage prices and those that pertain to a particular tract are discussed below.

The forester tries to determine a representative current stumpage price for each species by talking with likely stumpage buyers. He uses the most likely price for the landowner's timber, given location and quality, as his **price multiplier**. If, for example, a property contains a cruise-estimated 100,000 bf of sugar maple with a price multiplier of $.75/bf, the forester would project the stumpage value of the merchantable timber for the landowner at $75,000. (This can be expressed as 100 mbf of HM @ $75/mbf = $75,000, with HM meaning hard [sugar] maple.) Most sawtimber stumpage is fully priced in the 16" DBH and larger diameter classes, though a few high-value species will fetch the full price even for 12s and 14s. Smaller-diameter sawtimber stumpage usually carries a discounted price. The smaller diameters are not discounted in a sale going for pulp or chips.

A board foot on the stump is fully dimensioned at 12" x 12" x 1". A rough-sawn board foot as it comes green directly from a saw blade is also fully dimensioned. But a board foot of lumber that is sold retail after being kiln-dried and surfaced (dressed) is only 12" (L) x 11 1/4" (W) x 3/4" (T). Milled lumber is expressed in its **nominal—not actual—dimensions**. When you buy an eight-foot-long 2 x 4, it is eight feet long but only 1 1/2" wide and 3/4" thick.

Pulpwood stumpage is counted in green tons, cubic feet or cords. (A cord is a measure of volume, not weight, that is 8' L x 4' H x 4' W. One cord equals 128 cubic feet, or 1,536 board feet. A cord's weight varies according to the species and its water content.)

Wood weight is greatly affected by moisture content, diameter size and tree species. A forester's cruise of a tract's tonnage is based on just-cut **green wood**, which contains a great deal of water weight. A cubic foot of green oak at 85 percent moisture content, for example, contains about 3.5 gallons of water (about 28 pounds), about half its total weight. The same cubic foot dried to a 12 percent moisture content contains about .5 gallons, or about four pounds of water. Smaller-diameter trees weigh more per cubic foot than larger-diameter trees because less of their mass is found in the dry, non-living heartwood and more of it is the outside sapwood that transports sap (water) from roots to leaves. Outside wood is heavier than heartwood, and the smaller diameter trees have proportionally more sapwood to heartwood than the larger diameter trees. Ten cubic feet of 8" DBH red oak may weigh 25 percent more than ten cubic feet of 22" DBH red oak.

Each tree species has its own green weight per unit of volume. One cubic foot of generic oak can weigh 50 pounds. A 2,000-pound ton of this oak, therefore, would equal 20 cubic feet, about 16 percent of one cord. One of these cords would equal 3.2 tons, or 6,400 pounds. The next time you order a cord of green oak for the fireplace, you now know about what it weighs. Your back should instruct your brain to pay the firewood vendor for the trouble of stacking it where you want. Dried, or seasoned, firewood, of course, weighs less than green. It is also considerably easier to burn, more efficient and produces less creosote. It also costs more, as it should.

A forester's cruise may show a tract containing both merchantable sawtimber and pulpwood. The sawtimber is found in the sawtimber logs. Pulp is found in the smaller diameters, cull trees that don't qualify as sawtimber and in the tops of the sawtimber trees. The heart of a sawtimber cruise is to disaggregate the sampled volume by species and diameter class to determine its fair market value. In contrast, a pulpwood tract is cruised to include and aggregate as much merchantable fiber as possible. With pulp, all trees are pitched into the same pot. Volume matters, not quality.

When the forester completes his fieldwork, he tallies all the plot volumes for sawtimber by species and in diameter classes at and exceeding his merchantability definition. He then multiplies each merchantable volume by the appropriate species price. When totaled, this provides a projected dollar value of the merchantable sawtimber volume for the landowner from a competitive sale.

The forester might also value separately the smaller-diameter sawtimber, which is called **premerchantable timber**, or just "**premerch**." Stumpage buyers are not interested in premerch unless a clearcut is planned, in which case, the forester would typically estimate the volume of everything that can be sold. The forester can project the volumes of merchantable timber by species currently in the premerch at various future points. This helps the landowner figure what timber he will have available for sale down the road. The cruise may also separately estimate the market value of pulp or firewood.

For tax purposes, the value of the merchantable timber (of all types) at the time a buyer like you acquires the property is referred to as the **timber base**. This value shapes the taxpayer's **basis in the timber**. If the merchantable timber value equals the purchase price of the property, you still have to allocate your basis between land and timber. Total basis will equal the buyer's gross purchase price plus other allowable expenses. Basis is adjusted over time in both land and timber, according to what the taxpayer does and does not do.

Merchantable timber value can also be thought of as the property's **present timber value (PTV)**. The tract's premerch represents its **future timber value (FTV)**. Determining PTV, also referred to as merchantable timber value, is discussed in the following chapter.

CONSULTING FORESTERS

If you are thinking about purchasing wooded property, you should hire a **consulting forester** to develop information about the timber's value, both present and future. This is a necessary part of pre-purchase scoping of timber-bearing property. The forester may need to do no more than a quick walk-through to determine whether a cruise is warranted.

Consulting foresters are independent, private-sector consultants, most of whom hold four-year forestry degrees and participate in continuing-education seminars. As independent contractors, they may provide services to both timber sellers and buyers (though not at the same time in the same deal without mutual consent). Foresters may be sole practitioners or organized into consulting practices.

There are two national professional societies in the United States: Association of Consulting Foresters (ACF) and the Society of American Foresters (SAF). SAF admits non-foresters and is the larger of the two. SAF produces several publications and can be reached at 5400 Grosvenor Lane, Bethesda, MD, 20814; 1-866-897-8720; 301-897-3690 FAX; www.safnet.org. To locate a SAF forester, go to the SAF website, click on "Certified Forester," then click on "Search Online Find a Certified Forester in Your Area." My impression is that the ACF is primarily boots-on-the-ground foresters, either self-employed or in small group practices. SAF foresters seem to handle the larger tracts and work with the larger clients. My experience with ACF foresters has been generally positive. I would advise an owner of a small tract (less than 500 acres) to look for a full-time, experienced sole practitioner with a four-year degree who has an active practice in the area of your target property. You can find an ACF forester through its website, www.acf-foresters.com, or at the Association of Consulting Foresters of America, Inc., 732 North Washington Street, Suite 4-A, Alexandria, Virginia, 22314-1921; 703-548-0990; 703-548-6395 FAX; e-mail: director@acf-foresters.com. The ACF's Code of Ethics is available on its web site. Information on selecting a consulting forester is available from A Consumer's Guide to Consulting Foresters at www.ces.ncsu.edu/nreos/forest/woodland/won-06.html; Questions About Forestry and Forestland? Ask a Consulting Forester at www.wvu.edu/~agexten/forestry/forest.htm; and Selecting the Right Professional Forester at www.wvu.edu/~exten/depts/af/ahc/select.pdf.

Finding a private consulting forester is not difficult, though finding one who is a good fit for you may be a bit harder.

Private foresters may be found in the phone book's Yellow Pages under foresters—consulting, foresters, forestry consultants or possibly timber management. You will not find forestry consultants under "tree service," because they are not tree surgeons, tree removers or stump grinders. Forestry consultants work with timber on woodlands; arborists work with individual or small groups of trees. In my area at least most working field foresters/consultants do not advertise in the phone book because they get too many calls for tree work. You can also get referrals from local real-estate agents, bankers, lawyers and surveyors. As with all other references, ask your source the context in which he has worked with the recommended forester.

Public foresters can recommend private foresters. The **National Association of State Foresters (NASF)** represents the directors of state forestry agencies from all 50 states and America's eight territories. These agencies—which call themselves "state foresters"—provide advice and financial assistance to the ten million non-industrial private forest landowners (NIPFs) who provide more than 70 percent of the country's wood supply. The NASF website (www.stateforesters.org) provides links to all the departments or divisions of state government responsible for public forestry and the regulation of private forestry. Call the forestry department/division listed in the phone book in the county where your target property is found to find out what services are available to a buyer as well as owners. Most states now have on their sites a list of approved private consulting foresters, including areas of expertise and contact information. Contact several foresters who do cruises and timber appraisals in your target county.

The NASF website provides a state-by-state directory, including a contact person, address, phone and fax. (See NASF, 444 North Capitol Street, N.W., Suite 540, Washington, D.C., 2001; 202-624-5415; 202-624-5407 FAX; e-mail: nasf@sso.org). Program information is available for NIPFs from NASF on forest health management, fire protection and cooperative forestry, such as the Forest Stewardship Program and Stewardship Incentives Program described below. Publications are available, and forestry links are provided.

The state forester in your target county—who is called the **county forester**—will talk to buyers about local stumpage prices and timber characteristics in the area of the target property. If the local forester knows the target property, he may share some of that knowledge. Buyers should not treat a state forester as a free, on-demand consulting service. But you can certainly ask timber-orientation questions without violating the privacy of the owner of the target property. If the seller has a forest-management plan with the state, you should ask the seller for a copy.

Among the points of information that would be appropriate for you to ask a county forester are those like the following:

- Provide a list of private foresters who work in the target-property's general area
- A list of local timber buyers and loggers (Perhaps you can get him to tell you which buyers and loggers to avoid.)
- Local stumpage price data for private sales. (Public sales have a different cost structure than private sales, so stumpage prices on national forest land, for instance, are not comparable to private sales.) If he has no data, ask what his sense is of local species

prices. Many states collect and tabulate stumpage prices. Type in "stumpage prices, state" in an Internet search engine.

- Local price cycles
- Forest health issues in the area
- State timber-taxation policies
- Landowner obligations under the state's Best Management Practices (BMPs)
- Public programs available to private forest landowners (see below)

Come to the county forester's office with at least a tax map, which shows very approximate boundaries and acreage. Better than a tax map is an aerial photo and/or topographical map with inscribed boundaries. The aerial photo with boundaries should be available through the local office of the USDA's Farm Service Agency. If you don't have a professionally done topo with boundaries, you can work up a very rough approximation using the deed's legal description, tax map and a downloaded topo from www.topozone.com or a USGS topo map. Remember you're a buyer, not a landowner; don't wear out your welcome. I have found that four of five county foresters whom I've called as an out-of-state buyer have been reasonably helpful; two of five have provided me with sufficient information to let me screen out properties; one of five was uncooperative.

I would add one cautionary note about advice. Be aware that a recommendation for a private consulting forester coming from a county (state) forester in your target area may be biased toward those of his colleagues who have recently retired from the state forestry agency, particularly the office shared with the person with whom you're now talking. I have encountered this pattern three times in three states. This doesn't mean that the recommended forester is bad. It does usually mean that he has less experience as a private consultant in the rough and tumble of getting his clients the best price for their timber. I resist "steering" of this sort. My preference would be a consultant who has made his living for a number of years in the private sector doing walk-throughs, cruises, forest-management plans and sales for individual landowners. I would favor a consultant with this profile over a retired public forester because the latter will have less hands-on experience with actual timber markets and local players. I also appreciate a forester who is knowledgeable about timber taxation. You can ask the county forester for referrals to consultants whose careers have been principally spent with private clients.

In Virginia, the Department of Forestry (VADOF) provides the following services to *landowners* (not buyers) at no charge:

- prepares a forest-management plan (includes a resource inventory—a cruise plus—of tree species, composition, age, merchantability, growth rate and wildlife habitat conditions)
- prepares map showing location of various timber types (**stands**), land uses and natural features
- advises on what timber to sell and when to sell it
- provides list of consulting (fee-for-service) private foresters
- provides list of timber buyers
- advises on timber-sale contracts
- assists on tree planting
- advises on erosion-control practices

- recommends Best Management Practices to landowner (and loggers) related to preserving streamside buffer zones, skid-road layout, wetlands protection and the like
- advises on Seed Tree Law requirements (Virginia law requires leaving uncut a certain number of cone-bearing trees when certain conifers comprise ten percent or more of an acre's trees; other provisions as well)
- advises and coordinates with public cost-share/assistance programs
- provides technical assistance on managing natural resources—fish and wildlife habitat, soil and water, recreation and forestry

This is the official scope of the VADOF's "free" advice to forest landowners. The agency does not provide timber cruises for sales purposes or manage timber sales for private landowners.

As a buyer, I've asked my state forester for price information from time to time as well as his opinion about timber quality in a particular area where a target property was located. As a forest landowner, I've asked him to visit my property for the purpose of giving me advice about controlling ferns that were preventing hardwood regeneration and controlling road erosion.

Apart from these county foresters, you can check with the county extension agent or an **extension forester** who is employed in the forestry department at the state's land-grant university. Call the county extension agent—often listed in the phone book as (state name) Cooperative Extension—to obtain a recommendation and further leads. Extension foresters may be familiar with private consulting foresters in your area. The forestry professors who teach in these universities often conduct seminars and produce research that is of interest to private timberland owners.

Your local public/county forester will not give you, a buyer, a written evaluation of the target property's timber or do a cruise. If a management plan is in place for the property as part of a conservation or tax-relief program, he may provide that document to a buyer with the owner's permission. These plans generally include a base-line cruise at the time the property is enrolled. In my case, a phone chat with the county forester is a good, free first stop for a buyer. If you buy the land without having done a cruise, the county forester will do a walk-through of your property and give you a rough sense of its stumpage and current value.

Virginia has begun the Forest Mentor Network, which is a state-wide listing of experienced forest landowners who are willing to provide less-experienced owners with information and advice (www.cnr.vt.edu/forestupdate). Other states may have similar networks that a buyer/landowner can access. Faculty in the forestry department in the land-grant university are also available to the general public for short consultations and question-asking.

More than 30 states have a privately organized association of non-industrial, private forestland owners, which provides information and represents the group's interests on landowner rights, forestry practices, taxation, environmental policies and related policy concerns. A state's **forest landowner association** (which works with the state's cooperative extension service) might provide a reference for a private consultant, among other services. The national umbrella group for these state associations is the **National Woodland Owners Association** (374 Maple Ave. East, Suite 310, Vienna, Virginia, 22180; 703-255-2700; www.nationalwoodlands.org). In aggregate, the roughly eight million small private forestland owners account for almost 60 percent (about 288 million acres) of U.S. timberland, according to NWOA President Keith Argow. NWOA membership entitles a landowner to an "introductory visit from a consulting forester through the **National Forestry Association (NFA)**, a national professional forester referral program for private forestland owners. The NWOA's consulting assistance would not be available to you as a buyer when you are scoping a target property, but referrals would be.

A buyer needs to be aware that there are two other types of foresters who are available to provide opinions about the value of a property's timber. Both the **independent timber buyer** and the **industrial forester** are always looking for timberlands.

The independent timber buyer has been buying and selling timber and timberland for a long time. He's probably been a logger and may have run a sawmill at some point. These individuals are **skilled eyeballers**, and they have often made a living by being able to walk through a parcel of land, estimate its merchantable timber value and negotiate a purchase for a price that allows them to sell the timber and some or all of the cutover land for a profit. You can learn an enormous amount of dirt knowledge from them, but you must keep in mind that they are as a rule looking to make their own deals, not helping you make yours. Do not take one of these guys on a target property to help you scope its timber. The reason not to do walk-throughs with local eyeballers is not for their lack of expertise but because of it. If the deal is good, they will have a purchase offer in front of the seller before you arrive home on Sunday evening. For the same reason, I would advise against hiring a friendly, independent logger to help you evaluate your target property. The temptation to **"backdoor you"** is too great.

You may also encounter an **industrial forester** who is employed by a sawmill or wood-products corporation. The sawmill forester will be looking to buy timberland or just timber on the stump. Don't fold him into your scoping. The wood-products forester is looking to enroll timberland in his company's stewardship program. Most large wood-products companies will provide a landowner with a complete, updated forestry plan for his property according to the owner's objectives. In return for doing periodic cruises and other management services, the corporation has first rights—sometimes exclusive rights—over a long term to cut that portion of the timber scheduled for cutting in line with the plan. The company may have a "matching clause" in the landowner's contract that allows it to take the timber as long as it equals any other genuine offer. (Your sister, a student of 1960s' pharmacology in the East Village, the one with the purple hair, can give you a bid of $100,000 for your $25,000 timber tract, but don't expect the Georgia-Pacific crewcuts to match it.) If you're interested in working with a private company on a stewardship plan, I would approach them as a landowner, not as a buyer. You will get "free" management services and a guaranteed market from the industrial forester, but you may find yourself locked into a plan that does not suit your objectives and does not get you the most money for your timber. If you decide as a landowner to enroll in an industrial forestry program, read the discussion of the pros and cons in Beattie *et al.*, <u>Working with Your Woodland</u>, pp. 88-92, which includes a sample contract.

In addition to providing a market for his timber, a landowner should expect an industrial program to perform most, if not all, of the following tasks: timber cruise every ten to 20 years, periodic plan revisions, help with obtaining cost-share assistance from public agencies, boundary identification (which may include a survey and on-the-ground marking), plantings, timber stand improvements, road development (including culverts/bridge if warranted), stand protection (spraying), thinning to enhance future timber value, tax advice, etc. If you, as a buyer, become interested in land that is enrolled in an industrial forestry program, make sure to review the owner's contract. If the contract "runs with the land" for a certain number of years, you, as the new owner, will be stuck with it until it expires.

Independent consulting foresters travel, so don't be afraid to cast your net within a three- or four-hour drive of the property. On large tracts, foresters will drive a day each way—on your nickel. With three or four names in hand, interview each forester, preferably in person. (This is not wasted time; this is "quality" time. You will learn an enormous amount. You're looking to establish a long-term relationship with a forester who will help you manage your woodland.)

As a buyer, you will want a forester to do either a **walk-through** or a **timber cruise** of a target property that looks to you as if it has big trees and is ten acres or more. The forester you're interviewing may already know the property that you're scoping and can give you a thumbnail sketch of its timbering history and current prospects. A walk-through will give you the forester's informed impression of timber volume, species mix and quality. A walk-through will determine whether the expense of a cruise is justified.

In screening foresters to help you scope a target property, I would ask questions of the following type:

- Education—four-year forestry degree, two-year forestry degree; continuing education seminars on timber taxation?
- Experience
    - how long on his own as a consultant? before that?
    - types of work he does (cruises for owners/buyers; negotiated sales; competitively bid sales; plan development; management)
    - types of timber he usually sells (hardwood sawtimber; pine sawtimber; veneer; hardwood pulp; pine pulp; other)
    - has he worked with private owners who had objectives like yours?
    - how many (roughly) timber sales has he managed for private clients during the last year, last five years?
    - smallest, biggest, average dollar value of these sales?
    - how often does he manage timber sales in the area (county) of the target property
- Conflicts—does he have any personal or professional conflicts with conducting a cruise for you on this particular target property?
- Fees—how much does he charge for a walk-through; a cruise?
- References—references of several clients like you with whom he has worked during the last three years

It is very important for you to get a fix on the **forester's ethics**. The forester that you hire must be loyal to you and your interests. He must "ride for your brand." While he will have continuing relations with stumpage buyers, he must put your interests above his own. The forester you want will have forthright and familiar relations with buyers, but not "sweetheart" arrangements or anything that smacks of "steering" sales to a particular stumpage buyer. Do not agree to any arrangement where your consultant will also be paid by the stumpage buyer, particularly when a consultant says that it will "save you money on my fee." Stumpage (or timber) buyers are permanent members of your consultant's professional community while you may be a one-time visitor. Any arrangement that dilutes your consultant's loyalty to you will, in my opinion, work against you.

Ask the forester whether he has any conflicts of interest in working for you on this particular job. Don't be shy about this. He may have worked for the land seller in the past; he may even have done a cruise on the target property for the land seller. You must have complete confidence in the forester's ethics and loyalty to you. Scratch a name if you sense a forester sliding around. Ask his references whether his cruise value was roughly what they received from the sale. (When a sale occurs within a couple of months of a cruise, the cruise prices should be about the same as the actual sales prices, allowing for changes in market conditions.) If a significant divergence occurred, ask both the reference and the forester for an explanation. Avoid foresters who consistently value stumpage higher than their sales bring; this can bruise a buyer badly. I know several foresters whose cruises overestimate actual merchantable value fairly consistently. Sellers like to hand their cruises to gullible buyers.

Your forester's job for your scoping is to give you an accurate estimate of the merchantable timber value on a target property and alert you to issues that might complicate either a quick timber sale or longer-term management plan. This means that he has to think like a timber buyer, evaluating the standing timber as buyers will when they cruise the tract. When you retain him to manage your timber sale for you, his job is to package the timber in a way that gets the most money for you consistent with your other management objectives. No other interest should be allowed to confuse that simple obligation. When a consultant is helping you scope a property in advance of submitting a purchase offer, he should give you a good-faith and reasonably accurate estimate of the tract's timber volumes, species mix and likely (current) stumpage prices. Don't nickel-and-dime the consultant on his travel time or hourly rate. Don't cloud his fidelity to your interests. Authorize him to "put in enough plots" to give him full confidence in his sample-based estimates. Make sure that he understands that you don't want his choice of methods to inflate his estimates of volumes and prices. If anything, you want his timber cruise to be conservative about volumes and values so that your offer for the property is in line with the money you would net from a quick sale of the merchantable timber. Surprise in timber sales should always fall on the upside.

Tell your forester to cruise the target property using the same **log scale and cruise methodology** that are used by the stumpage buyers he will be contacting on your behalf. A log scale, or log rule, is a matrix that provides an estimate of the number of board feet (volume) in trees of various diameters (DBH) and heights (length of sawtimber logs that can be cut from each tree). Similar formulas are used to estimate green tonnage by species. You want to avoid a situation where your forester prepares a cruise for you prior to purchase that applies the International Scale (which finds more volume in certain diameter classes) while local stumpage buyers cruise with either the Doyle Scale (which finds less volume) or a local/regional scale. A tract that scales out $100,000 in stumpage value on the International Scale may sell $75,000 worth of stumpage, or less, to buyers using the Doyle Scale.

Ask the foresters you interview for their hourly rates and fee schedules. These will apply to time spent on your behalf—providing telephone consultations, walk-throughs, cruises, courthouse research, marking boundaries and the like. You should also expect to pay a mileage charge and reimburse for food and lodging expenses. Hourly rates vary by region and by consultant, with the larger firms charging higher rates. In my area, hourly rates are in the $50 range. On large jobs—say, more than 1,000 acres—an individual consultant will often team up with one or more subcontractors to get the work done in a timely manner. Since cruising is a highly site-specific process—where the time involved depends on the number of plots put in, difficulty of the terrain and reliability of the boundaries—you will probably not find consultants offering a flat cruise fee or one based on the number of acres. You might, however, find a consultant who bases his cruise fee on the number of plots he puts in. In general, it's reasonable to assume that a forester can cruise 100-200 acres in eight hours on the site. (That generalization is tossed out if he has to spend three or four hours trying to establish boundary lines.) He will also spend several hours in advance of the field cruise, plotting boundaries on a topographical map using the calls from a survey or deed and, if needed, checking boundary descriptions in the deedwork. The forester must make sure that he is not cruising—and selling—trees on neighboring property. This requires that he has confidence in the written description of the property's boundaries and that he is able to establish these boundaries on the ground. (As part of a timber sale, the consultant will flag the boundaries so that the logger does not take trees from the neighbors.) He will also spend several more hours after the field work tallying his volumes, determining current prices, drawing a map of the property that locates different stands and preparing his report. A 100-200-acre cruise on moderate topography with unambiguous boundaries would typically involve about two to four consultant days. (See, also, Fees and Services of Consulting Foresters in Mississippi at www.ext.msstate.edu/anr/forestry/forestinfo/mtn13c.html. Check with the county extension service in your state for state or regional publications on consultant fees.)

A walk-through and a cruise are paid on an hourly basis with expenses. If you choose to have the forester manage a timber sale for you, he will typically charge a percentage of your gross sale income. The percentage fluctuates according to the type of sale he conducts. A **marked sale**—where every tree to be sold is painted and its merchantable volume tallied tree by tree, not estimated—involves a timber-owner-paid fee of ten percent in my region. An unmarked sale where, for example, all trees 18" DBH and larger are being sold (but they're not marked) should cost the landowner less, because the forester has much less time involved. Your forester will recommend a timber-sale strategy based on the type of timber you have and local market practices. I've seen foresters paid so many cents per ton and so many cents per cord as well. I've always done well paying my forester a ten percent fee to conduct a competitively bid marked sale for hardwood sawtimber.

If you have little experience with forestry and logging and you're looking at tracts with substantial timber, you might want to hire a forester for a day to show you some of his recent jobs as well as ones that were cut five and ten years ago. You'll want to get an idea of what's involved during a logging job as well as the look of one that has some age on it. Ask to see a job whose objectives were similar to yours. If you're willing to spend $75,000 or more on rural property, you will be well-served to spend a small amount on a consulting forester in advance of making an offer. You will learn an enormous amount by walking through woods with a forester.

A cruise, in my unprofessional opinion, must be done on the ground when dealing with HW tracts smaller than 2,000 acres. Estimates based on aerial or satellite photos may be able to give you a general estimate of timber volume, but neither can provide a reasonable idea of the quality of the volume, which is what determines financial value of HW sawtimber. Global Positioning System (GPS) technology is now capable of generating volume estimates by species. In some circumstances—winter conditions in a deciduous forest, for example—a buyer might feel comfortable borrowing a large sum based on the results of this technology. I'm not there yet for two reasons: first, I want a forester's on-the-ground, site-specific judgment, the more specific and detailed the better; and second, I don't see any cost advantage at this time (early 2000s) on tracts of 1,000 acres or less. A third reason I suppose is that I am old enough to be suspicious of labor-saving technology. While satellite photography can produce photographs that accurately display things no bigger than a wastebasket, I don't feel confident that it can reveal the **quality indicators** that would be immediately apparent to a forester. Quality indicators are often tiny—an egg mass of the gypsy moth is the size of a finger joint; a vertical structural flaw in a tree's bole can halve the value of a butt log; a small opening at the base of a large chestnut oak is often a sign of hollowness. I doubt that current technology can distinguish among a 20" DBH veneer-quality black cherry worth $4 per board foot, a 20" DBH cherry that is sawtimber quality at $1.50 per board foot and a 20" DBH cherry with black sap disease, which in serious cases may make the tree not worth the expense to cut it. Foresters on the ground are trained to catch these differences. Given the relative inexpensiveness of getting a highly qualified and experienced forester to cruise a property, I see no reason at the present time to substitute technological wizardry for human judgment. The satellite techniques are more suited to tracts of several thousand acres and more, particularly one-species tracts.

As a buyer, you may or may not have a written contract with a consultant you've hired to provide advice and a cruise as part of your scoping. If you become the owner and decide that you want the forester to work up a management plan and/or conduct a timber sale as your agent, you'll need a written consultant contract, a sample of which appears in Chapter 23.

You will want the consultant contract to spell out the tasks you want him to do, the work products (if any) that he produces at the end of each task, method of payment and schedule, time-frame and deadlines. Another sample contract between owner and consultant is found in Beattie *et al.*, Working With Your Woodland, pp. 84-88. This owner-consultant contract is not a **timber-sale contract**, which is the contract between you, the owner of the land, and the buyer of your stumpage. (When screening consultants, ask to see the timber-sale contract he will want you to sign as a timber-selling client. Compare it with the sample timber-sale contract in Chapter 23.)

The buyer who is employing a consulting forester to scope the timber value of a target property should discuss with him the tasks that they agree will be needed to accomplish his objectives. The consultant will have a good idea of what you need even if you, as an inexperienced timberland buyer, are a little vague. Working together, develop a set of tasks that are appropriate for the particular property you're researching. These may include some or all of the following:

- **confirm to the extent possible the tract's boundaries in the deedwork and on the ground.** In the best case, you will have the owner's deed with an accurate boundary description, recorded survey and marked boundary lines. Often, you will have none of these. The forester should be able to dig out of the deedwork enough of a usable deed description to do a cruise. If he finds a big uncertainty, he'll tell you; you may have to get a surveyor involved. Once the forester has the deed description, often referred to as "the calls," he can put them into his computer program and print them out as boundary lines on a topographical map. Using that map, he should be able to locate with reasonable certainty the boundary lines on the ground.

- **alert the buyer to any problem (s) found in the boundary research**, such as lack of usable description; vague calls (a line running "from here to the top of Jones's hill"); nonexistent corners (the big red oak has disappeared), or corners that can't be found; lack of congruence between the deed descriptions and what is found on the ground (this can mean your target property is encroaching on a neighbor, or vice versa); a "bad" call (e.g., a directional call that is clearly wrong, often due to a typographical error such as NE written in the deed as SE, or a numerical transposition such as 1,345.56 feet written as 1,453.56 feet).

- **alert the buyer when boundary lines cannot be imposed on a topographical map because the deed's calls fail to close (see below)**

- **provide the buyer with a timber cruise** that disaggregates volumes by two-inch DBH classes and species on tracts where hardwood sawtimber is present, and by tons or cords where those measures are appropriate for the local market. (The forester will tell you the most appropriate way for organizing the cruise.) The forester may advise a walk-through to determine whether a cruise is warranted.

- **alert the buyer to any problems affecting health and quality of the timber stand**, such as infestations, disease and damage from fire, ice or wind, that will discount selling price

- **use the log scale that is used by likely timber buyers** (The consultant will know which log scale is most appropriate for the timber on the target property.)

- **put in a sufficient number of plots to provide a reasonably accurate sampling of the tract's timber**

- **separate sawtimber volume from pulp volume** if that separation is appropriate for the tract and/or the local market

- **exclude** from his estimates of timber volumes and calculation of values all timber that is found on **inoperable acreage**, such as steep slopes, wetlands, streamside buffer zones and other acreage that is inaccessible, economically unfeasible or limited by law.

- **prepare a topographical map** showing tract boundaries and areas within the tract (stands) where he's cruised merchantable timber.

- **gather sufficient information on local timber prices** to allow the consultant to make reasonably accurate projections of likely timber-sale revenue as of the cruise date.

- **identify any problems** that an owner should anticipate in marketing his timber (such as, no deeded right of way; need to cross a stream; need to build bridge; need to improve access road; overlapping claims to a portion of the property; environmentally sensitive areas, and so on
- **suggest a time-frame** for selling the tract's timber
- **provide a general opinion about future timber value**, based on the forester's projections of volume growth, ingrowth and price trends
- **alert buyer to any administrative or regulatory factors** that would constrain timbering or prohibit it from occurring in certain places on the property
- **inform buyer if he's expected to secure timbering-related permits**
- **write summary report of findings and recommendations**

I've worked up this generic list of tasks to help the reader understand what a forester will be doing rather than to help a consulting forester do his job. Your forester will know what to do for you even if you're not quite sure. You may want to formalize your understanding with your forester in a contract, but that may not be necessary. You should, however, have a reasonable idea of the level of detail and amount of work you will get for your money.

Consulting foresters need to be able to establish the **boundaries** of your target property on the ground. If boundary lines cannot be established with reasonable certainty, the forester may cruise acreage that the seller does not own or exclude valuable wooded acreage that he does. Foresters know how to do basic deed research and then apply a deed description to a topographical map. With that done, they should be able to locate boundaries in the field, whether they are well marked or not. Foresters now use a computer program, such as, Forest and Resource Management System Software (Farms), to draw deed boundaries on a topographical map. Older foresters can do this by hand. If you are inclined, you can obtain a topographical map and, using the deed's calls, mark boundaries with a transparent mapping compass and a set of engineering scales in feet, rods (1 rod = 16.5 feet) and chains (1 surveyor or Gunter's chain = 66 feet; 1 engineer's chain = 100 feet). Linear boundary measurements are usually given in feet, but old deeds often used rods, perches and chains. (The compass and scales together cost less than $50. You will want to use this compass in the woods if you're locating boundaries with the map.)

The forester's program will also reveal whether the property's **calls close**, that is, the deed's compass directions and linear measurements begin and end at the same point. If the calls close, the program can then easily determine the acreage within them. When calls don't close, you may or may not be facing a major problem. Sometimes the error is simply typographical, and the boundaries on the ground are correct as they stand. The error may be so minor that it falls within the acceptable margin of error. In other cases, a failure to close can mean the property is short of the advertised acreage. These surveying issues are discussed fully in Chapter 17.

If your forester identifies a boundary problem that works against your interest and is too much for him to resolve, you could hire a surveyor to give you an opinion as part of your scoping. Alternatively, you could put a **boundary contingency** in your purchase offer. This can take several forms. One version looks like this:

> **Buyer's offer is contingent on having a licensed surveyor or other qualified professional acceptable to Buyer confirm though methods accepted in the surveying profession Seller's acreage to be conveyed. Buyer shall arrange and pay for this work.**
>
> **Buyer will have _____ calendar/business days to complete this work. If the**

acreage cannot be confirmed, or is less than than the acreage referred to in this purchase offer, or is in any other way unacceptable to Buyer, he may withdraw his offer without penalty and his deposit shall be returned in full within five calendar days.

This contingency can involve the expense of a survey in the worst case, so I would insert it as a last resort. The surveyor is often able to narrow the problem to a particular line or even a particular part of a line, so his field work is limited to that section. If you have not had a forester or surveyor run the calls through his program prior to your offer, use this contingency to allow this to be done after the contract has been signed. It protects you from your lack of due diligence. The better practice, of course, is get the acreage figured out prior to submitting an offer. A boundary contingency is usually paid by the buyer. You can, of course, propose cost-sharing. Sellers are, as a rule, reluctant to help pay for this work. In most cases, I've found that a survey is not needed to reach the level of certainty, or lack thereof, sufficient for me to decide whether or not to proceed with a purchase.

A word or two about **stumpage prices**. A buyer depends on his consulting forester to estimate both the merchantable timber volume on the target tract and the current prices stumpage buyers are paying for these species. The forester's estimate of current stumpage prices for a target tract are shaped by factors unique to the timber there as well as market conditions operating on each stumpage buyer, locally and beyond. You should be aware that stumpages prices also are adjusted seasonally for hardwoods, so that a price that was good in September may be lower in March, even with demand and interest rates unchanged. Price bids will also be affected by any restrictions you impose on the logging. If, for instance, you insist that the logger lop all slash to minimize visual impact, you can expect steeply discounted bids. Most timber sales are entirely local, but certain types of timber fetch a higher price if marketed to exporters. Veneer logs often find their best price in the export market as does a specialty wood, paulowinia (or princess tree), used in Japan. In such cases, the forester may segregate export-oriented trees and market them separately.

A forester's **price multiplier** for each species is an amalgam of the prices he's been able to gather through a telephone survey of likely buyers. Some mills are more forthcoming about their price list than others. In his research, the forester may discover that a particular species is bringing record highs while another is markedly below a fair price. This information may shape his sale strategy: the high-priced species will be sold, but the other will be withheld for a future sale. He needs to package enough volume to encourage competitive bids. He may or may not decide to include low-value species in his high-value sale. The alternative might be to have sequential sales: the first for the high-value species, the second for everything else that you want cut. His strategy depends on what his research reveals. And that research is based on years of developing contacts and conducting sales. Track record means a lot when a forester calls a stumpage-buying mill and asks about prices. You can get a feel for recent stumpage prices from your forester before he starts his research, but he should update his price information when he calculates stumpage values for your cruise.

Thirty-six states report stumpage prices, and some of this information is free to the public. Information on stumpage prices is available at www.rtp.srs.fs.fed.us/econ/data/prices/sources.htm, a site that has links to the individual in each state who tracks these prices. (Contacts for this website are: Dr. Barry N. Rosen, Zicklin School of Business, Baruch College, The City University of New York, New York, New York, 10010, 212-802-6493; and Dr. H. Fred Kaiser, Staff Director, Resource Valuation and Use Research, USDA-Forest Service, 201 14th St., N.W., Washington, D.C., 20250, 202-205-1032.) Private services also offer stumpage prices, which are generally regional. In the South/Southeast, for example, you can buy reports from Timber Mart-South, The University of Georgia's Daniel B. Warnell School of Forest Resources, Athens, Georgia, 30602-2152; 706-542-4756; FAX 706-542-1670; e-mail: tmart@uga.cc.uga.edu; and Forest2Market, 15720 John J. Delaney Drive, Suite 300, Charlotte, North Carolina, 28277; 704-357-0110; www.forest2market.com. Timber Mart-South posts its recent newsletters and stumpage prices on its website, www.tmart-south.com. Forest2Market provides some price data on its website. In the South, for example, Timber Mart-South reported that Second Quarter, 2004 stumpage prices averaged $37.04 p/ton for pine sawtimber, $22.69 p/ton for pine chip-n-saw, $6.35 p/ton for pine pulpwood, $18.91 p/ton for hardwood sawtimber, and $5.43 p/ton for hardwood pulpwood.

Stumpage price data are aggregated for states and sub-state regions. For that reason, this information will get you in the right ballpark but will not zero in on the likely bid prices for your target property's package of merchantable timber in its local market. Published stumpage prices are an average, which reflect a range of quality. The New York state "Stumpage Price Report" for Summer, 2005 in area F, one of 12 price-and-reporting areas in the state, showed an average price for black cherry sawtimber (including veneer) on the International 1/4" Scale of $770/mbf, with reported prices ranging from $100/mbf to $1,400/mbf. The 1/4" in this scale refers to the presumed width, or kerf, of the saw blade; a thinner blade yields more lumber.

The forester's job is to determine the likeliest price species by species for the target property's merchantable timber, given that local buyers can vary by 50 percent or more on their prices and bids. Aggregated-and-averaged published stumpage-price data are useful as recent background, but neither you nor your forester should use this average price in scoping the value of a tract's HW sawtimber. You can use published state or sub-regional data with more confidence when valuing HW pulp and pine pulp, because the price of these feedstocks are not dependent on individual species and variations in quality. Prices for pulp stumpage rise and fall with the mix of supply and demand for the products for which they are used. Your consultant is your best source of current local prices in relation to a specific target property's timber.

Pricing stumpage is not a do-it-yourself job; stumpage buyers may or may not tell a landowner their current prices, may or may not tell them their true prices and may or may not give prices that fit the timber on the target property. It's easy for a buyer to quote you a high price on the phone and then offer you a low price when you bring your logs to his mill, because of "quality issues." If you call out of the blue, stumpage buyers will try to work their own deal for any timber you have in your sights.

You may find reference to prices for "**logs [by species] on the landing**." This is what a log buyer will pay once the trees are cut, skidded and sorted on the landowner's landing—a place where logging trucks can be safely loaded. It may or may not include loading onto the log buyer's trucks. Landing price is higher than stumpage price, because it must cover the logger's expenses. A landing price assumes that the landowner will work a deal with a logger whereby the logger is paid a percentage of the landing sales, or on a time basis, or so much per ton or one thousand board feet sold. Loggers will be far smarter than you about how to work such deals to favor their pocketbook. Don't sell stumpage this way, unless you have a consulting forester managing the process for you. It's possible to make more money selling timber as logs on a landing (grouped by species and quality) than from a lump-sum sale, but an inexperienced landowner will not have the resources and the knowledge necessary to organize the cutting and marketing to make this work.

You may find data that refers to **delivered price**. Stumpage price is the amount a timber buyer pays a landowner (timber seller) for standing trees. Delivered price is the amount a timber buyer/consumer (sawmill, paper plant, log yard) pays an independent timber-cutting logger for logs delivered to his facility. Delivered price will always be higher than stumpage price. You can roughly approximate stumpage price from delivered price by subtracting the approximate cost of cutting, hauling and profit from the latter. A state forester can estimate an average local cut-and-haul cost for this calculation. In late 2004, my local cut-and-haul cost ran about $22-$25 p/ton, including profit. But that figure varies with each logger according to his individual expenses, profit rate, equipment efficiency, fuel and labor costs, haulage distance (from logging site to mill), among other factors. If all else fails, cut the delivered price in half and that should get you in the stumpage-price ballpark for a mill.

Where an independent logger is buying stumpage, he may suggest to the timber seller—you—that his payment to you be based on **shares** (a percentage) of the price he obtains on delivery of your logs to the customer of his choosing. If his delivered price is $1,000, a 60-40 (him-you) shares format would give you $400, which, according to my ballpark rule of thumb is $100 less than the likely stumpage payment if sold to a sawmill. As general rules, I advise against working shares with a logger and also allowing timber-sale income to be based on delivered price. Avoid these arrangements. Too many things can work against the landowner in these formats.

The research done to date as well as my own experience suggest that a HW sawtimber seller like you or me nets the most through a **consultant-managed, competitively bid marked sale**, even after paying his fee. Your consultant could market your sale by sending out his cruise inventory, which, as you will recall, is a projected volume *estimate* based on systematic, impartial sampling. With HW sawtimber in a selective cut, the better method I've found is to conduct a **marked sale**, which is a tree-by-tree (actually a log-by-log tally, tree by tree) inventory of sale volume. A marked sale does not estimate volume as a forester does in a cruise. A marked sale's tally is as accurate a count of timber volume on the stump as there is. With a marked sale, the landowner knows exactly what he is selling. In a marked sale, the forester paints stump and butt every tree that is being sold. When a stumpage buyer goes through your property during the inspection period prior to bidding, he may do a simple walk-through, or a cruise, or a tree-by-tree tally to confirm your forester's numbers. The buyer's tally should be very close to your forester's.

A competitively bid marked sale on HW sawtimber should generate the most money for timber sellers sale in and sale out, though it is impossible to know how the results of a **sole-source negotiated sale** or **splitting revenue (shares) from delivered logs with a logger** would net from the same tract. If you believe that competition among buyers usually pushes price up, have your consultant conduct a competitively bid marked sale for hardwoods. The skill your forester brings to marking your timber—what he excludes and includes—into a sale package is well worth his fee. (See Ian A. Munn and E.C. Franklin, "Do Consultants Really Generate Higher Timber Prices," Research Notes Series, 1995, Number 84, Woodlot Forestry R&D Program, N.C. State University.) The National Woodland Owners Association states that "less than a quarter of all landowners use a forester when selling their timber." These non-users are in my opinion netting less as a group than they would had they used a forestry consultant to manage their sales. (See NationalForestry.Net, "Top Ten Issues," October 1, 2001; www.nationalwoodlands.org/nwoa/topten.asp.)

When you're scoping a target property with timber, a forester's **walk-through** is enough to determine whether the expense of a cruise is justified. A walk-through will give him a quick impression of the tract's timber resources in the context of what he already knows of the area and its markets. His walk-through should be more involved than a quick look from an ATV, though I've seen a forester do an accurate job on 3,000 acres of mixed hardwoods in one day from an ATV. The forester needs to get off the property's roads every so often to see the timber between the roads, hidden in coves or beyond eyeball range. The best timber on a tract is often furthest in and hardest to get to. Foresters see more than you will, because they know what to look for. They'll note the age, size and species of stumps to determine when the last cutting was done. They will know the timber-growing productivity of the soils. The mix of species and the size and condition of the large-diameter trees will give them an idea of how much high-grading, if any, has occurred. Foresters tend to spend their careers in one area and tend to specialize in certain types of timber. One forester, for example, works primarily in mixed Appalachian hardwoods; another works mainly in pine. The forester you hire is likely to know a good bit about the timber characteristics of your property based on his experience conducting similar sales in the area. A forester's walk-through usually involves a day of his time and some expense money. It's a cost-effective scoping investment.

SELF-HELP

You will do a walk-through before your forester does. It's your judgment of the timber that will determine whether you ask him to do his walk-through.

You should have a topographical map with boundaries if at all possible. This will allow you to find the boundary lines. Carry a compass and learn how to use it. Carry a **tree (dendrology) book** with you so that you can identify the dominant species. Train yourself to be able to eyeball a 16" DBH. (I took my wife's sewing tape into the woods so that I could measure diameters. After a while, your eye can tell the difference between four-inch diameter classes, and later down to two inches.) Or measure 16" from the tip of your middle finger toward your elbow: most trees that are 16" and wider at chest height will have timber value, unless they are the culls left from earlier high-grading. Trees 16" and larger in the local high-value hardwood species are what you are looking for. If you find yourself noting a lot of large-diameter trees that are poorly formed (crooked/bent stems; big branches in the butt log) or otherwise defective, you are looking at timber that's been high-graded at least once. These big trees don't have merchantable value. Don't hire a forester to do a walk-through if what you see are high-value species 14" DBH and smaller and large cull trees of all species. That good timber isn't ready to cut. Pay particular attention to the first 12 to 16 feet of tree stem up from the stump. This **butt log** should be straight and free of big branches, rot, holes, barbed wire, nicks and other damage. Every so often stop and count the high-value species 16" DBH and larger trees within a a 100-foot-diameter circle. If you count five or more of these merchantable trees each time, it's worth calling in a forester for a walk-through. Wooded property with at least 2,500 bf per acre in merchantable HW sawtimber 16" DBH and larger can be cut immediately, and that, for the roughest of estimates, is about 12 to 25 merchantable trees per acre. (The actual number of board feet will depend on diameter, defect and the number of logs that can be cut from each tree. The more board feet per acre in merchantable sawtimber in high-value species, the more timber value.)

The **county soil's survey** should be part of your timber scoping kit. It's a free publication from the county's USDA's Farm Service Agency (FSA) and provides accurate information on what the county's soils are best suited for. If no copies are available, photocopy the **soils map** for your target property from the survey in the FSA's office or local library. Take the soils map with you onto the target property, because you will be able to see how the soils change from type to type on the ground. You should also copy the table—it's called something like Woodland Management and Productivity—that explains tree productivity for each soil type.

Tree productivity is expressed in a **site index (SI)** for each soil type and location. This number indicates the predicted height of a particular species, referred to as a "common tree," after a fixed number of growth years given its soil, topography and **aspect**. The last of these, "aspect," refers to the compass direction toward which a slope faces. Aspect is an important determinant of tree productivity. In HW stands, the highest SIs are found on north aspects because they are typically the coolest and wettest. The SI time period used for Appalachian hardwoods is usually 50 years; for pine, 20 years. A site index of 60 means that the marker hardwood species on that type of soil and location would be 60 feet tall in 50 years. This is a so-so site for hardwood; an SI of 85 is much better and represents a 25-foot taller tree for the same 50-year growing period. If you find an 85-foot-tall red oak on an SI of 85 when you do your walk-through, you could anticipate three mature cuts from its root system during the next 100 years, beginning immediately and assuming a stump sprout grows after each timbering. A site like this would provide money to pay down the cost of acquisition in your 30s, retirement income in your early 80s and income to your children when they're nearing retirement.

Each species will have its own SI for each soil type and location. The soil survey provides the SIs for three to five commonly found trees on each one. These are marker trees you should look for and find on each soil type. Since most properties are a patchwork of soil types, you will find the same species growing at different rates in different spots. A valuable species like northern red oak might have a site index of 45 on steep, shaley land facing south (which is the warmest and driest aspect) and an index of 85 on nearby limestone/sandstone soils in a wet cove on a north-facing slope. Two oaks of exactly the same diameter could have an age difference of 40 years. The younger tree on the SI 85 is likely to be taller, straighter and better quality. Put another way, a 50-year-old, 80-foot-tall red oak will have far more volume than its 50-foot-tall cousin, because it should have both a larger DBH and more merchantable logs in its longer stem. And, as a rule, the faster a hardwood gets to a merchantable DBH of 16 or 18, the less it's exposed to disease, insects and other natural conditions that can diminish its quality.

If you look at enough property, you'll soon develop an eye for soil types that will indicate the quality of the site for growing timber. Certain trees and plants typically grow on certain soils. Even where a county does not have a survey, you can use the soil classifications and site indices provided for a nearby county to gauge the timber-growing productivity of a target site by matching the target property's soils to the soil evaluations in the other county's survey. If you are unable to recognize a general soil type in the field by identifying aspect, common trees, stoniness and other factors, your consulting forester can do this on a walk-through. Both your consulting forester and the county (state) forester should be able to give you a general notion of SIs just by looking at a topographical map in light of their knowledge of timber-growing patterns in the area.

The information you are hiring a forester to produce is for your benefit, not the seller's. You have no obligation to share the forester's opinion or cruise numbers with the seller. There are occasions, however, when this information should be shared. If, for instance, your forester's cruise shows little merchantable timber value and the seller's opinion is the opposite, the insertion of an expert opinion may help you negotiate a mutually workable price. If the seller challenges the objectivity of your forester, you can suggest that he hire his own to do the work again. The seller's forester may be able to confirm your forester's work simply by checking the format and parameters of his cruise. If the seller's forester uses the same format and parameters as your forester, the results of his cruise should be about the same.

A different but related issue is whether or not to ask the owner for permission to have your forester do a walk-through or cruise of his property. You may not want to advertise that you are actively scoping the seller's timber, particularly if he thinks it's not worth much. The best rule, I think, is to provide notice to the seller that you want to have a more experienced person help you out; put it this way: "I'm interested in buying your property. Since a pretty good portion of it is woods, do you mind if I have someone else visit your property before I submit an offer?" I would always get permission if the seller lives near the target property. If the seller is absentee, it's probably immaterial to him. Some foresters may want explicit permission from the owner so as not to trespass, but that seems to me to be the exception. My experience has been that sellers rarely care about what buyers do on their own nickels to scope properties prior to submitting an offer. If a seller refuses permission for your forester to visit the property prior to submitting an offer, you might reasonably infer that the seller has puffed the merchantable value of his timber and doesn't want your forester to reveal it to you. If you feel that a seller is reluctant to have non-buyers on his property, you can suggest that you'd like to take another look, this time with a potential partner.

If you find a seller asking you to respect his privacy and do nothing to bring publicity to his property, be careful. A seller once insisted that I refrain from bringing attention to his property—a large tract that was not listed with a broker and which he thought might contain anywhere from about 30 to 60 million board feet of high-value stumpage. I did some poking around. The tract contained eight to nine million board feet of merchantable timber. Its quality—hence, stumpage price—was substantially less than the seller's estimate owing to quality issues. But most important, the entire tract was categorized as a "conservation zone." While timbering was a theoretical possibility in this land classification, Hawaii had not issued a permit for logging in a conservation zone for at least ten years. When I talked to the official in the state agency who issued timbering permits, he told me that a permit was unlikely to be granted even after a well-done, environmental-impact statement. There might have been $20 to $30 million worth of stumpage on the tract, but it could not be turned into a single dollar. I now knew why the seller wanted to discourage me from scoping the property on behalf of my client. The seller had not told me an untruth; he just didn't tell me the truth about the truths he told me.

Another way to handle such a seller is to offer a purchase contract that includes a **timber-cruise contingency**. This allows you to have a forester of your choice and at your expense visit and evaluate the property once a contract is in place. Your offer is contingent on cruise results that are acceptable to you. If the price you've offered is not warranted by the cruise results, withdraw your offer and then submit a replacement. The language of the contingency is simple enough:

> **Buyer's offer is contingent on being permitted to have a forester of his choice and at his expense perform a walk-through or timber cruise, and that the results of said walk-through or cruise be acceptable to the Buyer.**
>
> **Parties agree that this work will be accomplished within ____ calendar/business days of the date of Seller's signed acceptance of this offer, weather permitting. If weather or other unforeseen circumstances arise, Parties agree to extend the deadline for this work by another ____ calendar/business days.**
>
> **If the results of this work are not acceptable to Buyer, he may withdraw his offer without penalty, and his deposit shall be returned in full within five calendar days.**

Make sure to ask your forester how much time he will need to get this work done prior to submitting your offer with its time-sensitive deadline. The cruise may take only a couple of days, but the forester of your choice may not be able to schedule your work for two months.

A buyer does not want to reveal the results of his forester's cruise when it shows a substantial amount of merchantable timber value, say 50 percent or more of the seller's asking price. Disclosure may result in the seller rejecting your offer even if it's full asking price if your timber cruise shows him that he's under-priced his property. If an under-priced property is listed with a broker, your offer must be close to full price and without a lot of "drag"—contingencies, complicated language, warranties, etc.—to position the seller to accept it without reflection. Any lesser offer gives the seller an excuse to reject it without penalty. If the seller rejects a full-price offer that's free of contingencies, which is his right, he will probably owe the broker a commission. If an under-priced property is being sold by an FSBO, the seller can reject any offer you submit. There may be circumstances where a buyer finds advantage in showing the seller the buyer's cruise value of the seller's timber, but they occur infrequently.

Woodland, even trees without any present timber value, can provide certain collateral financial benefits. To qualify as an investment for tax purposes, standing trees do not have to meet rigorous criteria, much beyond standing. The same property considered as an investment is more advantageous tax-wise to the tax-paying owner than when it is considered personal recreation property. Wooded land may be eligible for certain local property-tax breaks if it is enrolled in a state management program. (These programs start with a cruise and a set of management recommendations that are, in my experience, voluntary rather than mandatory.) The state programs are implemented at the option of each county, so you may or may not be able to enroll any particular tract. Your county assessor will know whether the county participates in **land-use programs** that benefit timber owners and agriculture interests. Conservation easements can be applied to wooded land that restrict development or timbering in return for tax benefits.

You may also be able to benefit financially by managing your timber in a way that qualifies for an environmental endorsement from one or another organization through a process called, "**certification**." A growing market exists among some public agencies and private retailers, such as Home Depot, Lowe's and IKEA, for lumber that carries a "green" certification. Several organizations inspect and certify timberland properties that meet their standards, including, among others, the Forest Stewardship Council (www.fsc.org/fsc) and the American Tree Farm System (www.treefarmsystem.org/). Certified wood costs the consumer more, about $25 extra for 1,000 bf (187 8' 2x4s). It also costs the forest landowner several thousand dollars to become certified by a group like the Forest Stewardship Council. *If* stumpage buyers exist in your area who are looking for certified standing timber, the landowner can expect a premium for his efforts. If not, being a green forest landowner may cost you money. Principle, of course, takes on meaning when it comes out of your wallet.

If you intend to manage your new property as timberland, several state and federal programs provide assistance that you should have in mind during your scoping. Public programs involve **cash subsidies** (cost-share programs) to encourage certain conservation and forestry practices, **tax incentives** and **deductions**. Some of the government cost-share dollars count as ordinary income on your 1040, while you may exclude others, partially or totally, from your income. Costs can be deducted when income is not excludable. This federal money is distributed and managed through USDA and state agencies. As of the early 2000s, they included:

Forest Health Protection Program (FHP)—USDA-funded effort to survey forests for insect and disease epidemics and provide technical and financial assistance to private landowners through state agencies for management, disease prevention and intervention. Federal and Tribal lands are also covered. About 70 million acres of public and private land are at various levels of risk from 26 insects and diseases. Risk status can change quickly. www.fs.fed.us/foresthealth/risk_maps/riskmort.pdf provides maps of forest type and disease risk.

Forestry Incentives Program (FIP)—a USDA-funded, cost-share program principally directed at reforestation and timber management, such as improving existing tree stands through selective thinning of premerchantable trees. The NIPF landowner must own no less than ten or more than 1,000 acres. Reimburses up to 65 percent of approved costs, not to exceed $10,000 per year per owner. May not be available in certain geographic areas. The owner must agree to a minimum of ten years of maintenance to the practices funded. Administered through the USDA's Natural Resource Conservation Service (NRCS), which, if you're confused about government agencies, you can find through the USDA's Farm Service Agency (FSA) or the state's forestry agency. Limited federal funding. FIP money could be excluded from income.

Environmental Quality Incentive Program (EQIP)—a federally funded program of cost-share payments to reduce the cost to a forest landowner of adopting certain forest and wildlife-habitat-enhancement practices that have environmental benefit. Assistance includes education, technical help and money. Land with special environmental features, sensitivity or threat are targeted. Improvement of forest stands, natural regeneration site preparation and tree planting may be assisted. Contact local offices of NRCS or FSA.

Forest Stewardship Program (FSP)—a federally funded program between the US Forest Service and state foresters that gives assistance to a landowner to develop a detailed management plan for all natural resources. The FSP's management plan leads to a certificate that makes the landowner eligible for additional programs

Stewardship Incentive Program (SIP)—a US Forest Service cost-share program that must be preceded by the landowner's having an FSP plan and certificate. SIP provides technical assistance and money to NIPF owners to implement their FSP. SIP funds common forest-management practices, including timber stand improvement, reforestation (tree planting) of pine and hardwoods; forest improvement; enhancement of wildlife habitat; hedge row (windbreak) establishment; wetland protection; fish stream improvement; threatened and endangered species protection; forest recreation enhancement; and soil stabilization and erosion control. The idea is to keep timberland productive and healthy. Cost-share rates range from 25 to 75 percent by practice, not to exceed 100 percent of actual costs. Payments are limited to $10,000 per person per year. The landowner must own no less than ten acres or more than 1,000. Certain circumstances, however, allow a landowner with up to 5,000 acres to participate. The owner must agree to maintain the practice for ten years. SIP funding was phased out in 2000, but was revived in 2002. SIP money could be excluded from taxable income.

Conservation Reserve Program (CRP)—a Farm Service Agency program based on acreage that pays a landowner to remove highly erodible land from agricultural production and plant grass/trees as permanent vegetative cover. Reimbursement of 50 percent of tree-planting cost, plus an annual payment for ten years. NCRS administers. CRP cost-share dollars count as ordinary income for tax purposes.

Small Watershed Management (PL-566)—federally funded assistance through the state's forester to help landowners in certain watersheds develop an FSP with emphasis on erosion control and protection of critical wildlife.

Federal Income Tax Incentives—a tax credit of up to ten percent of the cost of forest regeneration up to a $1,000 credit on the first $10,000 in total reforestation expenses in the year incurred under the Reforestation Tax Credit and Amortization (RTCA). Ninety-five percent of total cost may be partially deducted or amortized over a seven-year period. Together, the package allows a landowner to get back most reforestation costs, such as planting and seeding, over eight tax years. The amortization schedule is 1/14 in the first year, 1/7 for years two through seven and 1/14 in the eighth year. If you include payments as income and include payments with unreimbursed expenses that qualify for the RTCA deductions, you may be able to maximize tax benefits. Timber taxation is discussed in Chapter 24. Tax rules change, so make sure you get current information from a CPA who regularly prepares returns for timber-owning landowners.

State programs—vary, but can include tax breaks for tree planting/growing; rental payments for eligible lands devoted to agroforestry; cost-sharing to reforest timberland with specific species; tree seedling sales; autumn nut purchases; payments to plant trees on erodible crop or pasture land in addition to benefits from other programs; industry match of seedling purchases by landowner in return for right to buy; aerial spraying and other methods of controlling pests at below-market cost. (Some states may refer to their efforts as the BMP Cost-Share Program.)

The priorities, terms and funding levels of these programs change. Those interested in them must obtain *current* program information from the USDA or state forester's office where the target property is located. Information on the Conservation Reserve Program, Forestry Incentives Program and Stewardship Incentive Program can be accessed on line at www.nrcs.usda.gov/NRCSProg.html, which also provides links to all USDA's farm-related conservation programs. The Resource Conservation and Development office of the USDA Natural Resources Conservation Service is located at 14th and Independence Avenue, SW, Room 6103-s, Washington, D.C., 20013; 202-720-2241; 202-690-4205 FAX. Additional information is at USDA Forest Service Cooperative Forestry, POB 96090, Washington, DC, 20090; 202-205-1385; and www.forestry.auburn.edu/sfnmc/class/dewitt.html.

The **Forest Stewardship Program (FSP)** is the gateway for much federal/state assistance related to forestry. The FSP's plan involves several types of expert assessment, including a forester's cruise of the land's timber. The emphasis is on developing an integrated approach to all of the property's resources in light of the owner's set of objectives and those of the agency. Some forestry practices—such as planting, conservation, and pre-commercial thinning—may be eligible for cost-share programs whether or not your property is enrolled in the FSP. Information on all of these programs can be obtained from the nearest state forester's office. If a target property is already enrolled in an FSP, you will need to ascertain whether the obligations run with the land.

Read carefully the landowner's obligations under each federal/state program that you anticipate joining. In return for advice and monetary assistance, you will be committing yourself and your land to following a set of guidelines that may constrain you in the future. When, for example, you begin a forest stewardship plan, you are asked to choose a primary and secondary resource-management objective from the following: fish and wildlife; recreation and environmental; soil and water; and forest products. If your thinking changes, you may find yourself locked into practices that you no longer want. (You will certainly be locked in to what you've promised to do and then done during the first ten years.) You may decide that public dollars and advice are not worth the bother of either doing things the government's way or the forfeiture of doing as you please when it suits you. Before enrolling in these programs, be sure that you understand exactly how the various payments will affect both your current tax obligations and your tax status if you sell or otherwise dispose of the land. Government assistance of this type is generally classified as regular income, but some cost-share payments are excludable. Tax laws and regulations are subject to change, so it's necessary to check with a farm-knowledgeable CPA to keep current.

As I write at the end of 2005, federal tax policies could change dramatically in line with the Mack Commission's recommendations that would limit or reduce mortgage-interest deductibility, eliminate mortgage-interest deductibility on second homes and eliminate many deductions, among other things. Timber-tax policy and cost-share programs may well change in the near future. Prior to buying timberland, a buyer must check with a knowledgeable CPA to gain an understanding of current state and federal tax policies and then shape his purchase strategy accordingly.

CHAPTER 21: SCOPING TIMBER VALUE

VOCABULARY

Woodland has many values—aesthetic, environmental, recreational and economic. Each of the first three has an economic value as well.

The dollar value of woodland aesthetics is found in the lay of the land, its features and how it looks, feels, smells and sits with the owner and an eventual buyer. Woodland aesthetics, including a house site with a view, are a large part of what buyers want and are willing to pay for. The environmental values in woods—wildlife, water resources and so on—can also have economic value. Hunters and fishermen, birders, off-roaders, horse riders, cross-country skiers—all place an economic value on their recreational interests that translates into possible rental income and possible sharing of road-maintenance costs. While woodland may be the source of other economically valuable products such as maple sap, nuts and ginseng, its principal economic value is as merchantable timber.

This discussion builds on the forestry concepts introduced in the preceding chapter. It shows a buyer what a typical hardwood sawtimber cruise looks like and how to think about its findings.

Whether or not you want to cut timber on the woodland that you are interested in buying, you should learn how to think about its dollar values, present and future. At one level or another, the seller has included a dollar value for his timber in his asking price. Therefore, the timber's value (or lack of it) will be part of your negotiations. The seller usually assigns a current value to the timber that can be sold immediately and none to future timber value.

One exception to that statement may be a seller who informs the buyer about the abundance of "**young timber**" on the property. Young timber has no immediate value and, depending on its age, quality and species, may not have any value for decades. Further, a tract of young, low-value hardwood species will have far less future value than the same tract of high-value hardwood species. Whenever I hear a seller start talking about his "young hardwood timber," I assume that the property has been recently timbered—and probably hard.

"Young timber" has a completely different meaning when applied to an even-age pine plantation. In this case, the young planted trees—**premerch**—have both a current value and a predictable future value. Planted trees have an identifiable value, because it costs the owner to prepare the site, plant trees and manage the tract to promote health and growth. With hardwoods, most landowners rely on natural regeneration. Very young hardwood, 15 years and younger, would in most cases not have a discrete value in a land sale. Above that, it depends on whether the young timber is located on ground with high site indices—which means faster marketability and better quality—and contains a lot of high-value species. I've looked at timberland tracts where young timber—even as large as 12 to 14" DBH—had little value, given the low site indices and species mix. Even at that size, it would take too many years for the young timber to grow to 18" DBH and once there the species involved would not bring much money. On the other hand, a tract that is heavy to cherry, sugar maple and red oak in 12 and 14s would be a great retirement investment for a 40 year old.

It is certainly fair for a seller to expect a buyer to pay for the value of his property's merchantable timber, whether or not the buyer plans to gather it for himself. Some sellers underprice their timber value in their asking price; some deliberately overprice it. This chapter discusses how to go about determining that merchantable value. I advise buyers to try to pay little, if anything, for future hardwood value. The further that value lies in the future, the more risk attends to it and the more I rail against paying for it.

How then does an inexperienced land buyer begin to evaluate timber?

The preceding chapter introduced the basic concepts and terms of timber evaluation. The object of a **timber cruise** from a buyer's perspective is to estimate **present timber value (PTV)**, which is the amount of money a timber buyer would pay for the timber being sold. PTV is the forester's estimate of fair market value for the timber he defines as **merchantable**, that is, suitable for immediate sale and saleable. PTV refers only to merchantable timber. A wooded tract may contain much volume that is not merchantable, hence, has no PTV, insofar as the volume is found in small-diameter trees or on acreage that is considered **inoperable**. If a buyer wants to have his newly purchased property clearcut, then PTV amounts to what a forester thinks all the standing timber is likely to bring in the current market. If a buyer wants to sell only certain trees in a **selective cut**, then PTV is what the stumpage buyer will pay for those trees alone. A tree that no one wants to buy is not merchantable. A selective cut is defined by its parameters: it may be trees with a DBH larger than a certain diameter, or trees of certain species that meet a diameter minimum, or trees of a certain quality and diameter, or trees on just one part of a property, among others. Merchantable timber is also referred to as **stumpage value**, or just **stumpage**. The sale process is also called, "**selling timber on the stump**."

Each timber property can have multiple **stumpage scenarios**. Your forester can estimate PTV for a total clearcut as one stumpage scenario, a selective cut that removes everything larger than, say, 6" DBH, a selective cut that removes all hardwood species 16" DBH+ and a selective cut that takes all trees 18" DBH+ plus culls down to 10" DBH (for the purpose of improving the commercial value of the future stand). Another scenario is known locally as a **residential cut** in which the forester marks a relatively small number of large-diameter, high-quality, high-value trees. This minimizes the logged-over look, but it amounts to a more refined version of high-grading. A residential cut generally anticipates conversion of a larger timberland tract into smaller parcels of second-home properties where future timber production is less expected.

Each stumpage scenario will produce a different estimate of sale income, and each involves a different set of consequences for appearance, post-logging uses, opportunity costs and the length of the next cutting cycle.

Cruise methods are similar for both hardwood and softwood (evergreens or conifers) sawtimber, whose market is lumber broadly defined. Higher-quality sawtimber tracts are usually cruised in terms of board-foot volume. Sawtimber tracts that have lower-quality trees are usually cruised in tons. Pulpwood is estimated in terms of tons, cords or cubic feet. A timber tract with timber stands of different qualities may be divided internally and cruised with different measures, depending on each stand's characteristics. Even-age pine plantations will be classified by the age of each stand; older pines, say 20 years and older, will have sawtimber value. A lumber-quality sawtimber tract should in most cases be cruised in terms of diameter classes, species and board-foot volume, not weight. That format gives both the timber seller and buyer the best sense of the wood's lumber potential. The examples that I present below involve hardwood sawtimber estimated in board feet.

A forester will cruise your target property's timber and also refer to his written report estimating volumes and values as a **cruise**. His methodology is to sample the stand systematically and without bias. A cruise has the virtues and risks of any conscientiously done sampling technique. You can assume that a properly done cruise will estimate volume by species and two-inch diameter class within a seven percent +/-range of what a 100-percent marked inventory would show. The seven percent comes from my own experience evaluating cruises; academic research might show a five to ten percent variation. Larger tracts and tracts that have dissimilar stands may have a larger margin of error. The more consistent a property's stand is, the more accurate the cruise since the forester is sampling the same age and type of tree each time he puts in a plot. Sampling accuracy can be increased by taking more plots.

The forester gathers current local stumpage prices by talking with local timber buyers in the target property's area. I have seen cruises in the $50,000 range come within a few hundred dollars of the ultimate sales price. With larger volumes and more species and quality issues, you can anticipate that selling price will vary more from the cruise's estimated value. The most rigorously done cruise should not be assumed to be a perfectly accurate predictor of sale value. But it should be close enough for a land buyer's purposes. Stumpage prices change over time and from season to season. A cruise with species prices that is more than three months old should be recalculated with current prices. A land buyer always prefers that his forester's pre-purchase cruise err on the side of underestimating value.

After confirming the boundaries, the forester superimposes a grid that creates cells of equal size. The forester uses his judgment and observation of the tract to determine how many **cells** he needs and how big the cells need to be to make his sampling representative. Cell size can range from a couple of acres to several hundred acres, depending on tract size. On tracts of 200 acres or less—small tracts to a forester— three acres might be the right cell size.

Once he has his grid laid out, the forester walks to the center of each cell and **takes a plot** by tallying all merchantable trees by species and diameter class within. Each plot is assumed to represent the merchantable timber present in each grid cell. Plot sizes vary, 1/10th acre and 1/5th acre are typical. The number of plots put in must be sufficient to represent the entire tract. The fewer the number of plots, the more chance for inaccurate extrapolations. An **even-age forest**—planted or not—might require fewer plots than a forest of trees of varying ages. Your forester will be concerned with being efficient (with his time and your money), so he will try to put in just enough plots to be representative. As a general rule, the higher the ratio of plots for every 100 acres, the more accurate the sampling. As the forester puts in his plots, he will keep his eye on the consistency of the stand. If a stand is patchy, he may need to "regrid" and increase the number of plots to pick up the stand's variability. Cruising "small" tracts does not involve more than a day, or two at the most. It is, therefore, a false economy to tell your forester to skimp on plots to save paying for a couple of hours of his time. An acre of woods can easily have $500 to $1,500 or more in merchantable timber, so you want to err on the side of more sampling rather than less.

A tract's merchantable sawtimber is derived by estimating the volume of its merchantable trees using a tree scale and the forester's judgment. Volume is based on a merchantable tree's diameter (either DBH or at the stump), quality, number of logs in its stem and its degree of taper. The forester keeps a tally of the merchantable trees in each plot, disaggregated by species and two-inch diameter class. When he has put in all of his plots, he'll total the volume for each species by diameter class. A typical hardwood sawtimber cruise might organize volumes into the following diameter classes:

<u>Diameter Classes in Inches (DBH)</u>

<10   10-12   12-14   14-16   16-18   18-20   20-22   22-24   24+

Diameter (DBH) is a major factor in determining a tree's value. For reasons having to do with milling lumber efficiently and the value that can be extracted, sawmill buyers want sawtimber logs 18"+ DBH, though they may pay the same high price for 14"+ DBH logs of a few high-value species, such as walnut and black cherry. Sixteens generally bring a full price. With exceptions, sawtimber trees smaller than 16" DBH are often considered by stumpage buyers as **pole timber**, low-quality sawtimber or pulpwood. These types of merchantable trees are valued much lower than sawtimber 16"+ DBH. It is, therefore, important for the land buyer to know how much of a target property's merchantable timber is 18"+ DBH, how much is in the 16-18" classification and how much is smaller than 16". The best money will be found in the 18"+ volumes—at least where I live. Increasingly, mills near me pay the same for 16-18s as 18s+, but you may run into a discount. In New York, I've found mills paying full price for 12+, even 10+, hardwood sawlogs of high-value species.

In addition to diameter, the second main factor in determining the value of a given volume is species. Sawtimber volume in 18"+ classifications of low-value species might bring only $.10 per board foot, or $100 mbf, while a high-value species can bring ten times that unit price.

The third factor is quality. It is not enough to find a tract of woods loaded with large-diameter, high-value species; the trees themselves have to be healthy and well-formed so that they mill into high-value, clear lumber and veneer.

A forester's full cruise analysis might have three parts: 1) estimated merchantable timber volume by species and diameter classes, along with current stumpage prices by species; 2) topographical map of tract showing location of tract boundaries and timber stands, and 3) narrative, which might include his thoughts about sale potential, likely buyers, market conditions, premerchantable volumes, wildlife, erosion potential, boundary problems that he discovered, timber-quality issues and suggestions for his client to consider.

TIMBERING THE JONES FARM

The examples that I show in the following tables illustrate the forester's approach to hardwood sawtimber. TABLE 21-1 shows a tract's volumes, by species and diameter class, based on his plot samples. It presents the forester's aggregation of timber volumes.

Much information is contained in this inventory, and more can be inferred. The cruise involved the Jones farm, which has a few older buildings and an asking price of $189,900. The forester cruised merchantable timber on 100 of the 130 acres in the property. He determined that only 100 acres should be considered **operable acreage**—land having merchantable timber that can be accessed economically and practically. The 30 **inoperable** acres included pasture, crop land, buildings, ponds, wetlands and a steep section that had a few scattered high-value trees but the cost of building a skid road to get them was prohibitive. The topographical map the forester attached to the inventory showed the boundaries of the entire property and the location of the operable acreage.

The forester put in 34 plots, each of which represents a grid cell of about three acres. This ratio of plots to acreage should provide the client with a fairly high degree of confidence in the sampling's accuracy and its representativeness. If the tract's timber is not consistent, he should note that in his narrative.

TABLE 21-1

Timber Cruise Inventory

100 acres/130-acres Jones Farm in Appalachia County

34 plots, Doyle Scale FC 78
10" break

	Diameter Class (inches DBH)						*Volume* (MBF)
	12-14	*14-16*	*16-18*	*18-20*	*20-22*	*22+*	
HW SPECIES							
Northern Red Oak (RO)	10	20	30	27	10	5	102
White Oak (WO)	7	3		1	1		12
Chestnut Oak (CO)	4	4	5	12	20	4	50
Scarlet Oak (SO)	1	1	3	2			7
Hickory (H)		3	2	1			6
Cherry (CH)		5	7	10	6	2	30
Hard Maple (HM)	2	12	12	10	5		41
Red Maple (RM)	3	2	4	6	2	3	20
Misc HW	9	8	10	15	14	10	66
total	**36**	**58**	**74**	**84**	**58**	**24**	**334**
SW SPECIES							
Hemlock (HEM)	7	10	10	7	10	9	53
Spruce (S)	4	6	4	5	8	6	33
total	**11**	**16**	**14**	**12**	**18**	**15**	**86**

Date: August 1, 2005

Total: 420,000 bf.; 4,200 bf/A
100 acres operable of 130 acres in total tract
Culls: 167 trees, tallied from field notes counted in plots.
MBF = 1,000 board feet or 1000/bf

The forester used the Doyle (tree) Scale, the volume estimator that local timber buyers use. He applied an FC 78 to all trees. This is a taper formula that is used in volume estimates. An FC 100 would indicate no taper from stump to the top of the highest log in the tree. The forester used a "**10" break**." This means that in calculating a tree's volume and log lengths, he stopped where the stem narrowed either to a ten-inch diameter or the first crotch, whichever came first. Had the forester "broken" at a six-inch top diameter, he would be inflating the tract's timber volume by including the small-diameter top logs. Local buyers, the forester knows, don't value logs ten inches in diameter at one end and six inches at the other.

The 100 acres was cruised as one **stand**. A stand is typically an area in which the timber's characteristics—age, species mix, size and quality—are reasonably consistent. A stand need not be a single species. A stand need not be contiguous. A 100-acre tract might have three non-contiguous stands of one timber profile, two stands of a different profile and one stand of a third profile. Had all the softwood been located in one or two spots, the forester would have probably separated the inventory by stands. As it was, the softwoods were scattered throughout the 100 acres. When stands appeal to different markets, the forester may sell the stands in separate sales.

The cruise suggests the stand's **age range** without stating it. Given that so little hardwood volume is larger than 22" DBH, your forester might infer that the land was cut heavily about 75 years earlier. At that time, smaller diameters were left in place. Stump remains give clues as to recent cutting. By knowing the **site index** for this acreage, he will know how tall a northern red oak (NRO)—one of the common species—should be at 50 years. The dominant species on the Jones land is northern red oak with a site index of 85, which would be its predicted height at age 50. Since the forester found large diameter red oaks substantially taller than that, he would guess that the age of the merchantable trees in the stand are between 75 and 100 years. The lack of significant volume in the 22"+ DBH classification confirms this age range. Site index data are found in the **county's soil survey**, available from the local USDA office of the Natural Resources Conservation Service (formerly, the Soil Conservation Service). The county (state) forester and your consultant should be able to estimate a site index even in counties where a soil survey has not been published.

Jones's 100 acres of woodland is more densely forested than many Appalachian tracts on the market. The cruise projects a total of 420,000 bf, or 4,200 bf per operable acre (bf/A) of merchantable timber 12" DBH+. This combines 334,000 bf of hardwoods and 86,000 bf of softwoods. While Douglas fir acreage in the West can easily have 50,000 bf/A, a very respectable volume in the Appalachians is 4,200 bf/A. An Appalachian tract is generally not worth cutting if it cruises out to less than 2,500 bf/A. The exception to that statement would be a tract where most of the volume in a lightly forested tract is found in high-value species. This would be an unusual discovery.

The forester should not have included as merchantable timber in TABLE 21-1 any tree in his plots that he saw being used for dens and certain nests. **Den trees** may contain good sawtimber volume, but they are needed for wildlife habitat. State and/or federal law may require leaving certain trees in which certain species are denning or nesting. With species classified as endangered, both the nest tree and the acreage around it must be left uncut and undisturbed. **Snags** are dead, or mostly dead trees, that provide food and shelter to various creatures. Though unsightly, they should be left standing for that reason. **Seed trees** are healthy, mature well-formed trees of desired (e.g., high-value) species that should be left to reseed a cut area. The forester might decide to leave a particularly well-formed cherry that's 22" DBH even though a buyer will pay a lot for it in hope that its seeds will be the ones to regenerate the newly cut woodland.

PTV is mainly determined on a mixed-hardwood tract, such as the Jones tract, by the way five factors combine:

- volume of merchantable timber (stumpage) across the tract
- amount of volume in sawtimber diameter classes 16-18" DBH and larger
- proportion of sawtimber volume that is found in high-value species
- prices by species that the local market will pay
- quality of stumpage, especially the high-value species

The more volume tract-wide, the more volume that is 16-18" DBH+, the more volume in high-value species, the higher the species price and the better the quality—the more money stumpage buyers will pay the timber owner.

Sawtimber volume is determined by a tree's diameter and the number of logs eight- to 16-feet long that can be cut from its main stem. Sawtimber volume is estimated using a sawtimber **tree scale**, such as the Doyle scale or the International ¼ scale. (You may also hear reference to a "log scale" or a "milling scale." These are used to calculate board feet of lumber from logs before they are milled. The scales that concern a buyer of timberland are sawtimber tree scales that estimate tree volume in the field, not the milling scales.) Smaller-diameter trees in the 8" to 14" DBH classes may or may not have stumpage value, depending on the products that local mills produce. If a sawtimber buyer cannot mill valuable product out of log from a small-diameter tree, it's likely to be left standing or cut for pulp. Whether the smaller-diameter trees have value is a matter of local demand. In Southeast Missouri and northwestern New York, hardwood stumpage is often cut to 8" DBH for milling; along the Virginia-West Virginia border where I live, it's generally not cut below 12 inches. The 47,000 board feet of Jones sawtimber in the 12-14" classification will probably be priced at a discount to the sawtimber that is larger than 14" DBH, because that reflects the local market. The discount may even extend to the volume that is smaller than 16" DBH. Timber near me that is less than 14" DBH is generally either valued as pulpwood or not valued at all by stumpage buyers in their bids, though they may cut and haul it off. For that reason, the forester may tell his client not to include the 12-14s, 14-16s and some of the 16-18s in the sale. Better to leave them in place for the future.

A single 16" DBH 16-foot-long log from a low-value species like black gum on the stump might be valued at $.40 cents as pulp and $10 as size-discounted sawtimber. Once it grows to 18" DBH in, say, eight years, it would bring $20, at its current price and likely more given inflation. This stem has both increased in volume, and the value of the volume is now fully priced. The increase in stumpage value from ingrowth is more dramatic in the higher-value species. So size matters, particularly the growth that shifts a tree from price-discounted sawtimber to fully priced sawtimber.

The stumpage price the landowner receives is also dependent on the species prices at the time of sale. Price depends on the demand and supply for each species; these change according to consumer preferences and other factors. There is a general upward-trending but cyclical pattern to hardwood prices, but within that trend individual species rise and fall in stumpage price. In the mid-1990s, red oak in my area was bringing $600 and more per 1000/bf on the stump; that fell to about $400 per 1000/bf in 2006. Sugar maple rose during the same period from about $400 to as much as $800 per 1000/bf, and then tailed off in 2006-07. Consumers of flooring, cabinetry and furniture preferred sugar maple's white wood for a time. Then the inventory of sugar maple lumber exceeded demand, which softened the price. Stumpage prices track lumber prices for each species.

If you assume that a generic hardwood tree grows in diameter at one-quarter of an inch per year, it would only take 16 years for the discounted 14" log to grow into a fully priced 18" log. A one-log volume that would bring less than 50 cents as pulp would bring $20 to $200 16 years later, depending on species prices. That rate of investment appreciation is spectacular. If you can find a tract with high-value hardwoods in the 12-16" range and can buy it cheaply and can wait, you will make a lot of money on the timber sale 15 to 25 years later. The common investment tactic would be to sell the merchantable trees 16" and larger immediately after purchase to pay off as much of the acquisition cost as possible, then take your long-term profit from the ingrowth in the trees you've left.

When cruise volume is concentrated in smaller diameter classes (say, less than 14" DBH), the forester is probably working with a very young stand that regenerated after a heavy cut, or a poor site index and/or a high degree of crowding. If crowding is an issue, the forester might recommend an immediate **thinning** to remove the small-diameter, low-value hardwood species in order to benefit the remaining high-value hardwood species. Thinning will allow the remaining trees to use the newly freed light, water and soil resources to reach the 16-18" DBH classifications as quickly as possible. The thinning produces a small amount of immediate income for the owner and a greater amount of future income than would be there otherwise. This type of thinning is also called, **timber stand improvement (TSI)**, and may qualify for federal/state cost-share assistance.

In the Jones example, the timber distribution finds the largest hardwood volumes in the 16-18" and 18-20" DBH classes, which are immediately merchantable sawtimber. The 16-18s could either be removed or left for future cutting, depending on the owner's objectives and needs. Good volumes are also found in the 12-16" classifications. These smaller diameters are merchantable in the sense that they could be sold for pulp or as discounted sawtimber. The forester might recommend cutting the low-value species that are less than 16" DBH and leaving the mid-value and high-value species for the future. This would bring in some current income and release the remaining high-value trees from competition. Foresters can work up comparative estimates of what the owner might receive for the 12-16" volume in the current market against what might be gotten at various future dates.

TABLE 21-2, which includes the **price multipliers** for each species that the forester believes reflect the current market, sets out the volume data and values in a format that is typical of a forester's cruise for a landowner (or buyer). If you were to ask a forester to cruise the Jones tract, his report would look something like TABLE 21-2

TABLE 21-2 is a **value analysis** for the type of cutting and sale the forester envisions for this property. The PTV of each species volume is found by multiplying the total volume of that species by its current market price, as determined by the forester.

TABLE 21-2 shows that the Jones tract has 240,000 board feet of 16" DBH and larger hardwood sawtimber worth a projected $79,600 and 59,000 board feet of 16" DBH and larger softwood sawtimber worth a projected $6,475. The two total $86,075. Most merchantable value on the Jones tract is found in cherry and red oak sawtimber.

Most foresters, I think, would recommend a **selective cut** on the Jones farm that removes two types of timber. The forester would first propose to include in the sale all sawtimber 16" DBH and larger, both hardwood and softwood. No sawtimber smaller than 16" would be included in the sale. The small sawtimber has some value, but the forester is recommending that it be left for future harvesting. His price research showed that 16s are not price-discounted as sawtimber, so he includes them in the sale because the buyer wants to pay down the cost of acquisition. All high-value hardwoods smaller than 16" DBH will be left. This can be considered a **sawtimber cut**.

TABLE 21-2

Timber Cruise Valuation

100 acres/130-acres Jones Farm in Appalachia County
34 plots, Doyle Scale FC 78
10" break
Date: August 1, 2005

Large Sawtimber

	DBH 1,000/bf				Total Volume (mbf)	$ per mbf	Estimated Total Value ($)
	16-18	*18-20*	*20-22*	*22+*			
HW SPECIES							
Northern Red Oak (RO)	30	27	10	5	72	400	28,800
White Oak (WO)		1	1		2	250	500
Chestnut Oak (CO)	6	12	20	4	42	150	6,300
Scarlet Oak (SO)	3	2			5	175	875
Hickory (H)	2	1			3	150	450
Cherry (CH)	7	10	6	2	25	950	23,750
Hard Maple (HM)	12	10	5		27	450	12,150
Red Maple (RM)	4	6	2	3	15	125	1875
Misc HW	10	15	14	10	49	100	4,900
total	**74**	**84**	**58**	**24**	**240**		**$79,600**
SW SPECIES							
Hemlock (HEM)	10	7	10	9	36	100	3,600
Spruce (S)	4	5	8	6	23	125	2,875
total	**14**	**12**	**18**	**15**	**59**		**$6,475**

MBF = 1,000 bf
Total Value: $86,075
   HW = $796.00 p/A   Average species price: HW $331.67 /mbf
   SW = $64.75 p/A   SW $109.75 /mbf

Estimated 3 cords per acre @ $5 per cord. Cordage value equals $1,500 (3 x $5 = $15p/A x 100 = $1,500)

The second type of recommended timbering would be a pulp cut, which removes all low-value, small-diameter trees both hardwood and softwood that are large enough for a logger to cut economically. The pulp cut would take all of the volume assigned to cord wood, estimated at three cords per acre. This represents about 1,200 bf/A of pulp wood, using a common rule of thumb that 1,000 board feet equals about 2.5 cords. This 1,200 bf/A would be cut from the low-value trees smaller than 16" DBH and from the tops of the sawtimber trees. The pulp cut would leave the low-value species smaller than 6" DBH in place, because no logger wants to bother dropping them, particularly when this chore amounts to free work for the landowner. Loggers may choose to leave all pulp trees standing, regardless of diameter, if market conditions are such that it does not make economic sense for them to spend the time and money to cut them. Similarly, the pulp wood contained in the tops of the sawtimber trees may be left as slash rather than lopped and bucked into pulp lengths, cord wood or firewood.

The pulp estimate of three cords per acre does not include the volume of the cruise's 167 **culls**, which have limited economic value due to disease, breakage, deformities, hollowness and the like. Photographs 21-1, 21-2 and 21-3 show three different culls, each of which is more than 18" DBH but has no commercial value as sawtimber due to poor form (big branches on the butt log or rot). Photograph 21-1 shows a tree with poor form—a large branch coming out of its butt log. The young sawtimber next to it is long, straight and without significant branches.

PHOTOGRAPH 21-1

Cull and Sawtimber

Photograph 21-2 shows a large sugar maple that is made worthless for sawtimber owing to the hydra of big branches low to the ground. The forked cull in Photograph 21-1 could be cut for pulp; the cull in Photograph 21-2 is probably too branchy and time-intensive to cut for pulp.

PHOTOGRAPH 21-2

Sugar Maple Cull

Photograph 21-3 shows a large-diameter tree with extensive rot about 12 feet above the ground. The rot probably extends lower in the stem where it is invisible. Owing to weakness in the upper stem, this tree should be allowed to fall. Although it has pulp value, it is too dangerous to cut, so it has been left. Sometimes, culls can be marketed as pulp or firewood, but a stumpage buyer is not likely to pay anything for them. The trees in Photographs 21-2 and 21-3 have no commercial value despite their diameters.

PHOTOGRAPH 21-3

Large-diameter Cull

On a tract like the Jones's, stumpage buyers would typically bid the value of the sawtimber, bid nothing for the culls and, depending on market conditions, bid either nothing or just a little for the pulp. If the stumpage buyer ultimately decides to remove culls, he will reap a small profit without having had to pay for these trees. If a stumpage seller (landowner) can get the stumpage buyer to have his logger cut the culls, his remaining timber benefits.

The purpose of the two cuts taken together is to leave the new owner with all of the high-value sawtimber smaller than 16" DBH in place for future timbering. All of the small-diameter, *high-value* hardwoods—pole timber (4.6 to 9.5" DBH), small sawtimber (9.6 to 14.5" DBH) and marginal sawtimber between 14.5 and 16" DBH—would be left. The sawtimber cut and the pulp cut remove much of their competition.

If the landowner wants the 167 culls to be cut—which I recommend doing—he should put notice of that in the bid package his forester sends to stumpage buyers and place language in his contract that the stumpage buyer is required to cut the culls. Cutting the culls is uncompensated time from the logger's perspective, so the stumpage buyer may discount his bid a little to account for that expense. The logger working for the stumpage buyer will probably not cut them unless the contract between landowner and stumpage buyer requires it. The landowner may do better to not require the stumpage buyer to drop the culls (given the bid discount) and simply give them to a local fire-wood cutter after the timbering is over. The forester can recommend which approach makes the most sense.

Cutting the pulp and culls is a strategy that will free resources for the high-value sawtimber trees and make it easier for them to establish their seedlings. This promotes the upgrading of the commercial value of the forest's timber over time. Releasing the high-value hardwoods from competition also increases their annual diameter growth rate on the order of moving from 1/4-inch per year to three eighths. Release works best when the beneficiaries are young, 40 to 70 years old; it does not produce substantially higher growth rates in older trees. The fact that the most prevalent merchantable species by volume on this tract are high-value cherry and red oak indicates that the ground is well-suited to these species. Increasing their presence over time appears to be a feasible strategy.

The forester's sawtimber/pulp-cut strategy is a selective harvest that takes the largest (16" DBH plus) sawtimber trees and the pulp/culls. This approach is the opposite of **high-grading**, which only takes the largest, most valuable sawtimber—the **money trees**—and leaves all pulp and culls standing. The forester's approach of combining a 16"+ sawtimber cut with a pulp cut is likely to produce the most present income as possible consistent with preserving future value. Had the forester found that sawtimber in the 12-14 and 14-16 classifications was also fetching the same prices as the 16s and larger, he might have recommended that they be included in the timber sale if the landowner needed the cash.

The forester's cutting strategy for the Jones woods will affect the land's post-timbering appearance. Left will be all the high-value species smaller than 16" DBH, including cherry, sugar maple, red oak and white oak. Gone will be most of the lower-value trees—hemlock, spruce, chestnut oak, red maple, scarlet oak, hickory and the miscellaneous hardwoods (such as basswood, black birch and hophornbeam). Following the timbering, the woods will look more open, given that about 4,200 bf in sawtimber and pulp was removed from each of the 100 operable acres. You will see no tree with a diameter of 16" or more. The top of the forest canopy will be lower since the oldest trees have been cut, but you may not notice that change. A great deal of slash will litter the ground. Deer will flourish in woods cut this way. The slash provides cover. This habitat will usually provide more food for them—and other wildlife—than mature forest. While the Jones woods will look rough owing to the slash and skid roads, the tract's future timber-production value has been greatly improved. The owner can cut the 16" DBH+ trees every 20 to 25 years, and each time he can upgrade the stand for the next cut by dropping the low-value species. The environment has been changed on this tract, but it's not degraded or harmed. The distinction between change and harm is important.

The forester who cruised this property may recommend that the timber be sold in two or even three separate sales—for HW sawtimber, SW sawtimber and pulp. The landowner might benefit financially from dividing the stumpage, but local markets will determine whether that's the best approach. Some stumpage buyers interested only in the sawtimber may subcontract the pulp to a logger who specializes in that. If the timber is sold to more than one buyer, you will have to schedule their **logging windows** (typically 18 months to two years) to avoid two logging outfits working the same tract at the same time. This will stretch the time the Jones property will be tied up in logging activity and delay any reclamation work that you want to do involving cutting slash and dressing roads. While the window runs for a long time, it only takes a few weeks to cut and remove 100,000 board feet. Other things being equal, it's usually best for your woodlot to schedule timber cutting for the late fall and winter months when the sap is down and ground conditions are comparatively firm. Mill prices tend to rise in the winter as well.

As soon as a logger is done, he should release his interest in your timber. This release is a legal document that relinquishes his interest in any remaining sale timber that he bought but chose not to cut. Releases are often recorded. Once the landowner has a release of interest, he can alert the next logger in line. Sequenced logging of this sort is tricky and not common. I think it's better to sell all the timber to one buyer and let him decide whether he wants to subcontract portions. Once the landowner has a release from the stumpage buyer, the remaining trees are once again his to do with as he pleases.

Some foresters include an estimate of the **number of trees per acre** in their cruises. This is useful information if you're considering developing a sugarbush to tap sugar water. In that event, you want to know the number of sugar maples at least 10" DBH, which is the diameter at which one shallow tap can be drilled without harming the tree. As sugar maple gains in diameter, additional and deeper taps, up to four in the largest trees, can be installed. Knowing the number of trees alone, however, does not tell you much about the value of the timber or even the stand's **density**. Two hundred small, junky oak trees per acre are worth little, if anything. Density is a measure of the number of trees per acre. But density has to be considered in terms of average tree size too. Six hundred planted pine saplings at one year old are not dense in the layman's sense. At 20 years old, these 600 trees represent a very dense growth. One hundred HW trees, each 3" DBH, per acre, are far less crowded in terms of competing for available nutrients than are 100 22" DBH trees. When a trees-per-acre calculation is included in a cruise, it is generally limited to trees larger than a certain DBH. Fewer than ten merchantable trees per acre is a sparse stocking rate, and such a tract may have relatively little timber value unless they are large and high-value.

Density, or crowdedness, can be expressed in terms of **percent of crown cover**, that is, the percent of shaded ground beneath the canopy. Or, it can be expressed as **basal area per acre**. If you were to cut all trees on an acre at 4.5 feet above the ground (breast height), the surface area of the stumps taken together represents basal area. As a rule, basal area increases with the stand's average diameter even as the number of trees declines. When stands are crowded—too much basal area—diameter growth will slow and the quality of the timber will be affected. If you are trying to maximize the production of timber value, crowded stands should be thinned—a practice of **timber stand improvement**. Consider an example. A fully stocked stand of northern hardwood all 14" DBH would have 90-95 square feet in basal area per acre. Each 14" DBH tree would contain a little more than one square foot of basal area; a 22" DBH tree would contain 2.6 square feet. For a basal area of 90-95 square feet per acre, 95 14s are needed, but only 37 22s. In terms of stumpage value, the acre of 37 22s is far more valuable than the 95 14s.

A "cruise" that only shows number of trees per acre or basal area per acre does not provide sufficient information to determine the stumpage value of the woodland. Do not buy timberland based on these measures alone.

The Jones cruise provides no information about number of trees, average tree diameter or basal area, so it's difficult to determine the stand's density. Given, however, that there's 4,200 bf/A—a good sawlog volume for the area—you can deduce that the tract is crowded and is ready for some type of cutting. In crowded situations, trees will grow tall without gaining much diameter. Such trees will have very narrow crowns. Woods like this can contain a respectable volume but most of it may be in small DBH classes, say 14" and smaller.

As the forester cruises timber, he will keep his eye open for **quality factors, both bad and good**. He will inform you whether he observed quality discounts in the trees from disease and insects, and damage from wind, ice, frost, lightning, flooding or fire. Other defects that might discount your timber above the norm include excessive crookedness in stems, rot, splitting, crotches, fungus (stains logs), tap holes from maple sap production, skinned off bark from earlier logging, and nails and wire fencing in butt logs.

Disease and insects can kill a tree or a stand of a particular species and/or degrade timber quality to one degree or another. Both conifers and hardwoods are susceptible to various defoliators (e.g., gypsy moth, leafminers, sawflies), bark beetles, wood borers, terminal feeders (which eat buds or roots), sucking insects (aphids, woolly adelgid) as well as diseases—viruses, mistletoe, nematodes, bacteria and parasitic fungi (such as, wilts, e.g., Dutch elm disease), rusts, (e.g., white pine blister) and cankers (e.g., chestnut blight). It's easy for an inexperienced person to see mortality in a forest—you will see dead standing trees. But it's difficult for someone like me to see the first signs and stages of processes whose consequences can range from negligible to catastrophic.

You should have a specific discussion with your forester about long-term risks on a target tract, particularly from insects and diseases that are likely to appear. The southern pine beetle is a scourge of southern pine forests. Gypsy moth has ruined large portions of oak-heavy woods in the east, but it seems to come and go. In California and Oregon, a pathogen, *Phytophthora ramorum*, or "sudden oak death syndrome," has spread to 17 species, including oaks, big leaf maples, redwood and Douglas fir. Hemlock is being lost to the woolly adelgid, and beech and sugar maple are also under attack. Bark beetles are damaging western forests, particularly lodgepole, ponderosa, Douglas fir, and pines, such as sugar and western. These beetles seem to be increasing their range and numbers as winters have grown milder. (Paul R. Epstein and Gary M. Tabor, "Climate Change is Really Bugging Our Forests," Washington Post, September 7, 2003.) Your forester should have a feel for the threats that can occur over the next three to five years. Ask him about the quality negatives that he's observed on the tract. If there's a blinking yellow light in his discussion, your risk of loss is too high to accept. Don't buy, unless you're looking to flip the timber in an immediate lump-sum sale and then the land.

On the positive side, he will look for veneer-quality logs in the high-value sawtimber. Veneer logs are straight, thick and nearly flawless. Hardwood veneer logs are generally sliced into thin sheets the length and width of the log. Logs of softer woods, like pine and poplar, are peeled into long, wide sheets-like unfurling a roll of paper towels. The hardwood veneer is used for surfacing furniture and cabinetry, among other uses. Veneer logs fetch the highest price per unit of measure. Cherry, for example, might bring $5 a log as pulp, $250 a log as sawtimber and $2,000 as veneer. If your forester finds a significant volume of veneer, he may value it separately from the sawtimber of the same species. I've known tracts whose buyers have paid for the acquisition of the land through the immediate sale of just the veneer trees.

A timber cruise is a snapshot estimate of volume and value on a particular day, with current prices. No **risk analysis** is included. A buyer should not forget that all investments can either appreciate or depreciate over time. The years required to allow timber to mature and benefit from ingrowth also involve risks from disease, damage and price variability. Your forester can help you evaluate these natural and market risks. He should also be able to project an appreciated value and then apply a discount formula that fits the type of timber, location and number of years before a projected harvest. In a simple version, a discount formula knocks off a percentage of appreciated value in each future time interval to account for risk. The projected appreciated value might be discounted for the purpose of illustration at 8 percent ten years out, 12 percent at 15 years and 16 percent at 20 years. This method accounts statistically for routine factors that damage trees as well as the total disaster, such as an ice storm that breaks every tree, leaving nothing but a low-income salvage job. A routine cruise would show *merchantable* volumes and projected values, formatted something similar to TABLE 21-2.

TABLE 21-3 estimates the values of the small sawtimber, 12-16" DBH, and the "swing group," 16-18" DBH. A typical cruise would probably not provide this level of detail about the marginally merchantable smaller timber, but it's worth illustrating how these dollars play out.

TABLE 21-3

Small Timber Values

100 acres/130-acres Jones Farm in Appalachia County
34 plots, Doyle Scale FC 78
10" break

Date: August 1, 2005

Marginally Sized Sawtimber DBH

	1					2			1 + 2
	12-14	14-16	12-16 Vol.	12-16 $ mbf	12-16 $ Value	16-18 Vol.	16-18 $ mbf	16-18 $ Value	12-18 Total $ Value
HW SPECIES					10				
Northern Red Oak (RO)	7	20	30	$75	$2,250	30	$400	$12,000	$14,250
White Oak (WO)	4	3	10	30	300		250		300
Chestnut Oak (CO)	1	4	8	30	240	6	150	900	1,140
Scarlet Oak (SO)		1	2	70	140	3	175	525	665
Hickory (H)		3	3	50	150	2	150	300	450
Cherry (CH)		5	5	200	1,000	7	950	6,650	7,650
Hard Maple (HM)	2	12	14	90	1,260	12	450	5,400	6,660
Red Maple (RM)	3	2	5	50	250	4	125	500	750
Misc HW	9	8	17	40	680	10	100	1,000	1,680
total	36	58	94		$6,270	74		$27,275	$33,545
SW SPECIES					7				
Hemlock (HEM)	4	10	17	30	510	10	100	1,000	1,510
Spruce (S)	11	6	10	30	300	4	125	500	800
total			27		$810	14		$1,500	$2,310

Total Value of 12-18" DBH HW and SW: $35,855

HW $335.45 p/A   Average $/mbf: $199.67   ($33,545 / 168,000 bf)
SW $23.10 p/A $56.34   ($2,310 / 41,000 bf)

TABLE 21-3 shows that the 16-18" DBH sawtimber volume, both hardwood and softwood, is 88,000 board feet, or 37 percent of the tract's 240,000 bf total. In terms of value, the 16-18s amount to $28,775, or 33 percent of the $79,600 HW total. The 16-18s would be sold at the same price as stumpage 18" DBH+. That is why this diameter class was included in the sale.

The forester has discovered that local stumpage buyers would not pay the full sawtimber price for the 12-16" DBH trees, even for the cherry. Using discounted prices, he estimates that the 94,000 bf in the 12-16" DBH hardwood to be worth only $6,270, and the 27,000 bf in the 12-16" DBH softwood to be worth $810. Together, the 12-16s sawtimber totals $7,080 for 94,000 bf compared with the projected value of $28,775 for the 88,000 bf of 16-18" DBH sawtimber. The huge difference in price for roughly equivalent volumes demonstrates the **Bingo! effect** that occurs from ingrowth, when the next higher diameter classification shifts unit price out of its (small diameter) discount.

If the 16-18s, the swing group, will bring a full sawtimber price, why not include that volume in the sawtimber sale? First, the owner may not need or want that income increment right away. Second, he may have an anticipated need for it in the future that outweighs any immediate need. Third, trees in this diameter class will gain volume and are a rapidly appreciating asset. Fourth, if they are cut now, the timber's next cut will be extended by another 16 years or more, to wait for the 14s to move up to the 18" class. Finally, the site will look a lot more "logged over" if the trees in the 16-18" class are removed along with all those 18" DBH and larger.

Foresters often use two value measures—**timber value per acre ($/A) and average value per 1,000 board feet ($/mbf)**—that are useful in quick calculations and comparisons. In this example, these value expressions are figured on the tract's 100 operable acres, not straight-through on the 130 acres. Value per acre can be shown as either (or both) timber dollars per tract acre (that is, including all the acreage that's for sale) or timber dollars per operable acre. Value per tract acre (not operable acre) is the more common measure; value per operable acre can confuse an inexperienced buyer to the seller's advantage. When evaluating different timber properties, make sure that your calculations are figured against the same acreage base in all cases.

With HW sawtimber timber 50 years and older, value per tract acre is a quick way of getting a sense of the woodlands' productivity for timber. A high $p/A value usually suggests good site productivity and a favorable concentration of high-value species. The other measure—$/mbf—situates the market value of the tract's timber in the range of species prices. If, for instance, the lowest value sawtimber species are bringing $100/mbf on the stump with the highest at $950/mbf, a tract average of $200/mbf usually indicates that most of its volume is concentrated in low-value species. In the Jones example, the hardwood sawtimber 16" DBH and larger averages out to $796 p/A and $331.67/mbf, indicating a pretty good dollar value per acre and a mid-range average of species value.

A forester generally does not project **future timber value** in a PTV cruise. He might suggest in his narrative the implications for future timber values that follow from alternative timbering strategies involving more-or-less-aggressive immediate cuts. Projecting volume growth by species and diameter class is straight-forward when the forester knows the site indices for the operable acreage and has a timber-cruise baseline, disaggregated by species and two-inch diameter classes. Your forester can also use an **increment borer** (hand auger) to extract a small core of wood—a tree's radius—which reveals its growth rate and soundness. Borings taken from different species provide empirical data for past growth rates for each species from which future growth rates and volumes can be projected. Increment boring is usually not needed to make the rough volume-growth projections that would be useful to most land buyers.

Projecting future species stumpage prices is iffier than projecting volumes. Extension forestry faculty at the land-grant universities usually have access to models that project prices using different assumptions about demand, interest rates and other variables. Doing **future timber analysis** is a common exercise in forestry programs, because it is used so often by industrial owners, pension funds and other investors to evaluate timberland. Your forester—or you—can usually tap into these models at little or no cost. Graduate forestry students are usually happy to run your cruise through their school's model for a modest hourly rate.

Since the cruise gives you a reasonably accurate estimate of present timber value, it may suit your interests to have a future timber analysis done under four sets of assumptions: 1) no immediate timbering; first cut scheduled for a specific future year determined by existing stand characteristics; 2) immediate cut of all sawtimber 16" DBH+ plus pulpwood; 3) immediate cut of all sawtimber 18" DBH+ plus pulpwood; and 4) immediate clearcut (or semi-clearcut of all HW and SW 6" DBH+). Models will show expected returns to you at alternative time intervals out to 100 years and under three simple price assumptions—slow rate of price increase, middle rate and high rate. With this information, you can figure out which cutting strategy nets you the most income over different time frames. The same type of analysis can be done on planted pine plantations. Most modeling does not factor in catastrophic events, such as a forest fire, insect infestations or a ten-year drought. Future value models can punch in a risk discount, and discounting for risk should give you a better projection. I'd recommend doing some form of future timber analysis on the Jones farm because it has good timber dirt and a good stocking of high-value species. The two together means the owner can generate significant future income from properly sequenced HW timber sales.

A forester would charge a couple of hundred dollars to prepare a future timber analysis and forest management plan for the Jones farm once he has done the cruise. If you're either cheap or lazy, here's a knowledgeable shot-in-the-dark way to do your own future analysis. We know the HW site indices on the Jones property are good. Assume for this example that the forester has decided to leave the 16-18" classification out of the sale, because the owner needs less cash immediately and wants more down the road. We can assume that volume in the existing sawtimber classes 12-18" DBH+ will at least double in 20 years given the indices, following an immediate post-purchase sawtimber cut of all 18" DBH+ and a pulpwood cut of low-value species and culls. After release, the remaining HW sawtimber will grow at a rate of at least 1/5 inch DBH per year in all diameter classes. This is a very conservative growth rate for released 12-18" DBH trees, which, on this site, might even double this rate. Also assume a modest 25 percent rise in each species price/mbf over the 20-year period. A two or three percent annual rise might prove to be more realistic, but a conservative assumption of about 1 percent a year will keep us from being too optimistic. TABLE 21-4 projects volumes and values with these assumptions.

The PTV of the 209,000 board feet of hardwood and softwood sawtimber 12-18" DBH that was not cut when you bought the Jones place was $35,855. Under very conservative growth and price assumptions, TABLE 21-4 projects this base to double to 418,000 board feet of both hardwood and softwood in 20 years and be worth $154,001. Volume has doubled but price (unadjusted for inflation) has quadrupled as the volume moved into the preferred DBH classes.

In my layman's opinion, both volume and price could easily be more than twice the rates assumed in the above example—without a stretch. A 1/5 inch per year growth rate could easily increase to 1/4-inch or even 1/3 inch after release.

Moreover, leaving 12-18" trees produces volume faster than in the smaller diameter classes, because the same rate of growth produces comparatively more basal area growth as diameter increases. A 7" DBH tree has a basal area of 38.5 square inches (A =3.1416 x 3.5 x 3.5 = 38.4846".) If this tree's growth rate for one year is 1/4 inch in diameter, its basal area will be 3.1416 x 3.625 x 3.625 =41.2825 square inches. This is a gain of about 2.8 square inches. An 18" DBH tree has a basal area of 254.4696 square inches. When it grows by 1/4-inch in diameter, its area increases to 261.5873 square inches, a gain of 7.1177 square inches. The 1/4-inch diameter increase on a 16-foot-long 7" DBH log would amount to a gain of about two board feet; the same growth on a 16' 18" DBH log would be almost eight board feet.

Simply put, volume increases faster on the bigger trees. This growth differential is amplified by the price upgrade when the sawtimber reaches the 16 or 18" ingrowth threshold.

TABLE 21-4

Estimated Volume and Value + 20 Years
(mbf)

	12-14 become 16-18	14-16 become 18-20	16-18 become 20-22	Total Volume mbf	20-year* $/mbf plus 25%	Total value in 20 years
HW SPECIES						
Northern Red Oak (RO)	(10) 20	(20) 40	(30) 60	120	$500.00	$60,000
White Oak (WO)	(7) 14	(3) 6		20	312.50	6,250
Chestnut Oak (CO)	(4) 8	(4) 8	(6) 12	28	187.50	5,250
Scarlet Oak (SO)	(1) 2	(1) 2	(3) 6	10	218.75	2,188
Hickory (H)		(3) 6	(2) 4	10	187.50	1,875
Cherry (CH)		(5) 10	(7) 14	24	1,187.50	28,500
Hard Maple (HM)	(2) 4	(12) 24	(12) 24	52	562.50	29,250
Red Maple (RM)	(3) 6	(2) 4	(4) 8	18	156.25	6,750
Misc HW	(9) 18	(8) 16	(10) 20	54	125.00	6,750
total	**72**	**116**	**148**	**336**		**$142,876**
SW SPECIES						
Hemlock (HEM)	(7) 14	(10) 20	(10) 20	54	125.00	6,750
Spruce (S)	(4) 8	(6) 12	(4) 8	28	156.25	4,375
total	**22**	**32**	**28**	**82**		**$11,125**

Current species prices are: RO $400 mbf; WO $250/mbf; CO 150/mbf; SO $175/mbf; H $150/mbf; CH $950/mbf; HM $450/mbf; RM $125/mbf; Misc HW/$100 mbf; HEM $100/mbf; and S $125/mbf

Assuming a 20-year rise in stumpage price of only 25 percent is even more cautious if only because it falls short of the background inflation rate of two or three percent per year. Your forester can suggest an appropriate annual price inflator. The cost to you of waiting 20 years to cut your trees might be thought of in comparison with the return you would have earned had you invested the $35,855 in a stock index fund or sure-fire, can't-miss lottery numbers.

Your forester can also show you historical data that track species prices in your target area and give you an idea about the length of price cycles for locally important species. From 1960 to the mid-1990s, Appalachian HW lumber prices followed an upward trending sawtooth curve with peaks about every four or five years. Since then, however, hard (sugar) maple lumber increased from about $600 to almost $850/mbf green/air dried 4/4 while soft (red) maple went from about $500/mbf to $600/mbf with weakening in between. But red oak dropped $200/mbf, and white oak stayed more or less steady at about

$475. These are inflation-adjusted prices for milled lumber, not stumpage. This pattern suggests that hard maple prices will top out and then decline as the oaks come back into favor at their discounted prices. Exactly when that might occur, of course, is unpredictable, but I'd look for hard maple lumber price to soften at $900/mbf. Milled lumber prices determine stumpage prices.

TABLE 21-5 is the buyer's summary of all the financial values that his scoping has produced on the Jones farm, which is priced at $189,900, or $1,461 p/A. The buyer's forester has placed a *PTV* on the Jones merchantable timber of $94,655, or $728 p/A. If the buyer sold all sawtimber 12" DBH+—a hard cut—the gross sale revenue should be about 50 percent of the asking price.

TABLE 21-5

Summary of All Values

1.	12-16" sawtimber	
	Hardwood	6,270
	Softwood	810
2.	16"+ sawtimber	
	Hardwood	79,600
	Softwood	6,475
3.	Pulpwood	
	3 cords p/A @ $5 per cord	1,500
		$94,655

Merchantable timber = $94,655
   Total = $728 p/A. ($94,655 / 130)

Bare Timberland Value:	$550 p/A = $55,000 ($550 x 100 operable acreage)
Land Value of 30 open acres:	700 p/A = $21,000 est.
Value of old cabin and barn	= $25,000 est.
Timber base	= $94,655
	$195,655 Total

Assets:	Liabilities:
Cabin, marginally inhabitable	Cabin, marginally inhabitable
30 acres, good pasture	Moderate slope, no southern exposure
Good access road	No electric to property
No boundary uncertainty	Pasture fence needs to be upgraded
Calls close.	
Year-round spring	
Good timber productivity	

The buyer has also valued the other assets in the Jones property. By doing comparables analysis of recent sales of selectively cut land and small pastures, the buyer has estimated that selectively-cut woodland is worth about $550 p/A and pasture in a 30-acre parcel would bring about $700 p/A. After consulting with a couple of real-estate agents and looking at the tax-assessed values, the buyer has placed a value estimate of $25,000 on the old cabin and barn. Disaggregation shows a gross sale value of all property assets of about $195,655, almost $6,000 more than the asking price. To get there, however, the buyer would have to sell the merchantable sawtimber in the 12-18 classes, which is better left for future harvesting.

To make up this money, the buyer could sell two acres of pasture with their two buildings for about $27,000, leaving 128 acres, or sell the 30 acres including the buildings for $46,000, leaving the 100 acres of woods. If the buyer were to limit the timber sale to 18" DBH+, he would receive $57,300 and $1,500 for the pulpwood. That would be about 31 percent of the asking price. This is tax-free income until the time the new owner chooses to sell the land itself. (See timber-tax discussion in Chapter 24.) The buyer's individual circumstances will determine whether he needs to sell some or all of the timber and/or some of the acreage and improvements to make this deal work.

From an investment point of view, the buyer could consider selling the 30 acres of pasture in ten-acre lots (one of which includes the cabin and barn), the merchantable sawtimber 16 DBH+ and 50 to 60 acres of the woods. That would net out the likely purchase price of the Jones farm and leave the buyer with 40 to 50 acres of woodland (cut to a 16" threshold) for free.

CHAPTER 22: BEWARE THE SELLER'S CRUISE

THERE'S NO BOGUS LIKE SHOW BOGUS

I have discussed the elements of a cruise as a reasonably accurate method of estimating the volume and value of timber stumpage.

Cruises can be "cranked" to show more value than an owner would receive in a competitively bid sale. This is usually done by inflating the volumes above those for which a timber buyer will pay. Cruises can be deflated to show less volume as well, though I've never run across a buyer using a phony, undervalued cruise as a negotiating tool. In theory, a dozen independent foresters should cruise a tract in essentially the same way and come up with roughly the same volumes and values, allowing for a margin of error that's inherent in any extrapolation from sample data. In fact, a dozen foresters could come up with honest answers as well as several that one might rank in order of increasing creativity.

This chapter focuses on a **seller-paid timber cruise** used to help market wooded land to a buyer like you, the type of cruise that can range from dead honest to dead wrong.

Dirt-smart buyers should be alert for a **seller's bogus cruise**, which shows more stumpage volume and value than what the market will buy and pay for. Not all seller-supplied cruises are bogus. Nothing prevents a seller from handing a buyer a good-faith, accurate cruise, especially when it shows a lot of dollars. Buyers must understand, however, that sellers are motivated to invest their sale properties with assets that justify their asking price. A buyer's psychological pocketbook is clearly influenced by a cruise that shows a timber harvest will pay off 60 percent of the asking price as against one that shows only 20 percent.

I've learned that a buyer must know enough about cruising methods to protect himself from a less-than-honorable seller and his forester who inflates merchantable timber. I've seen cruises that double the merchantable timber value without exactly lying to get there. I've seen a cruise emerge from a "sophisticated" computer program that I couldn't evaluate because it provided so much information that the forest was lost for all of the trees. I've also seen a fancy forestry consulting outfit take an outdated cruise done on about 25 percent of a large tract and, without updating and verifying the information on the ground, project the same timber volumes across the entire acreage. This indefensible work resulted in a "timber analysis" given to a buyer that projected about five times the actual amount of stumpage the tract contained. Hundreds of thousands of dollars in anticipated timber value evaporated when the buyer—now owner—had a couple of honest foresters prepare a timber sale.

As you read the following observations keep in mind one simple land-buyer's rule: a scoping buyer is interested in finding out what the market will pay for the target property's (merchantable) stumpage and not a theoretical value for "standing" (merchantable and non-merchantable) timber. If stumpage buyers put no value on a tree, they will not pay anything for it. Honest cruises limit themselves to merchantable timber, that which a stumpage buyer values and will pay for. If you find reference in a seller's cruise to "liquidation value," it probably means a theoretical value based on every wood scrap on the property. Liquidation value is likely to be higher, often much higher, than the **stumpage value of the merchantable timber**, which is the value a buyer wants to know prior to submitting an offer to purchase the seller's property.

Before I begin talking about bogus seller cruises, I want to alert you to an even simpler seller trick: **the bait of big money**. Here's the way the seller works it. The seller tells the buyer that he's never done a cruise on his property, but he thinks that there's at least between "x 1000 board feet and x+y 1000 board feet." He doesn't say how he arrived at that estimate or what definitions of merchantability he used. If the seller is pressed, he'll say something like, "That's just how it looks to me." The buyer multiplies a mid-price for stumpage against the volume number between x and x+y and comes up with "big money," even using these conservative assumptions. The buyer then starts assuming that his calculation represents truth, because he wants "big money" to represent truth. This seller never hands the buyer a phony document. He never hires a less-than-scrupulous forester to inflate cruise values. He simply plants the bait in the buyer's mouth and lets the buyer's own mind direct the swallowing. Using buyer greed is an old seller trick. I've seen it worked on 500 acres as well as a deal where the seller was trawling for more than $100 million.

Hardwood (deciduous trees) and pine (coniferous) tracts are cruised with many of the same measuring and evaluation techniques, but the forester brings different standards to each type. Both types of trees produce pulp and sawtimber. Markets for pulp use more of each tree than mills that produce lumber from sawtimber. For that reason, foresters legitimately count more volume in a pine tree marketed for pulp than a hardwood tree of the same size marketed for sawtimber. Hardwood (tree) tops and low-quality trees are used for pulp as well, but the real value in hardwood timber lies in that portion of each tree—particularly the high-value species—that is good enough for sawtimber or, better yet, veneer. Pine sawtimber brings a higher price than pine pulp. While pine occurs in natural stands and mixed with hardwoods, much pine land now for sale is one-species, even-aged plantations dedicated to producing pulp (fiber) as fast and as cheaply as possible. Companies manufacturing paper and wood products, such as MeadWestvaco, International Paper and Weyerhaeuser, are divesting themselves of millions of acres of planted pine and pine-hardwood tracts.

Owing to their different growth characteristics and markets, hardwood and pine are cruised with different criteria for counting merchantable volume. **The discussion that follows focuses on valuing hardwood, not pine**. Some of the techniques I discuss that are used to overvalue hardwood can be applied for the same purpose in pine valuations. It is, of course, far simpler to estimate volume and value on an acre of even-aged trees of one species than on an acre of mixed species, ages and size. Accordingly, the opportunities for inflating the value of a varied hardwood tract are more numerous.

TRICKS

Here are some of the ways that hardwood cruises can inflate the volumes and/or projected values of timberland.

1. Basic Factors.

Every cruise report should set forth the basic parameters of its methodology and sampling, including:

- the **log scale the forester used**. (Different scales estimate log volumes differently. See below.)

- **number of plots** the forester put in.

- **number of acres** covered by the cruise. (Acres that are inoperable should not be cruised and their merchantable volume should not be counted.)

- **Form Class (FC) used**. Form Class refers to the degree of taper—from stump to top break—the forester used in estimating a tree's log volume. FC 78 is common in Appalachian hardwood.

    Yellow poplar usually merits FC 80. Less taper means more volume counted.

- **top-break diameter**. This refers to the general spot on the upper portion of each tree where the forester stops counting the length of the merchantable log (s) it contains. Foresters are taught to estimate sawtimber log volume in a standing tree up to the first major/natural stem break (e.g., crotch) or to the appropriate diameter "break." If a hardwood tree does not contain a natural break, a forester estimating sawtimber should stop where he judges the stem narrows to about ten inches in diameter. Foresters depend on their experience to tell them how a timber buyer will cut logs from a stem, hence, how he will estimate its volume and value. A forester who does not "see" a tree's volume the way timber buyers do will provide an inflated volume estimate.

    Some foresters will include a top-break diameter on their cruise report while others routinely don't. It's important for your forester to use the same top-break diameter that local timber buyers use, otherwise he will be including volume and assigning value to volume that timber buyers will never pay for. On hardwood pulp tracts, it is fair to estimate volume from the stump up to a six-inch diameter in the tree. To a sawtimber buyer, a stem's volume between ten-inches and six inches in diameter has no sawtimber value. The stem above ten inches in diameter can sometimes be sold for pulp, but the price per unit of pulp volume will be no more than a small fraction of the sawtimber price. When a sawtimber buyer bids for your hardwood tract, he may or may not assign a value to the pulp in the tops of the trees he plans to cut for sawtimber. More often than not, such a buyer will leave this "**top log**," or slash, on the ground. I've sold timber to a sawtimber mill that refused to haul these top logs to a pulp yard less than six miles from my logging site because it was an uneconomical use of the crew's time.

    The way a forester can pump sawtimber volume is to "**break the tree too high**." This has the effect of including in sawtimber volume a top log that's only six inches in diameter at its small end. The **phantom volume** in the top log can easily add ten to 20 board feet in each tree. With 1,000 trees so estimated, the seller's cruise will show a phantom 10,000 to 20,000 board feet packaged in with the genuine hardwood sawtimber volume. Timber buyers will not pay you sawtimber price for top-log volume, and often may not pay you anything at all for it. They will not include top-log volume in their own cruise on which they base their bid to you, the owner.

    Breaking too high, that is, at six inches in diameter rather than at ten, is an intentional inflation of hardwood volume and, subsequently, value.

    Pine, sold for pulp, is properly broken at six or even four inches in the top.

- **Cruise date**. Be wary if the seller's cruise is undated or more than a year or two old. You should be alert to evidence of the seller **"cherry-picking"** (removing) the high-value hardwood trees in the interim, between the cruise date and when you see it.

    If you find large, fresh-looking stumps in high-value species scattered around the property, the seller has probably pocketed the best 25 percent of the tract's volume and as much as 50 percent of the value shown on the seller's cruise. A fresh stump is usually light in color rather than a weathered grey; no sprouts will have shot up; its bark will be tight against the wood; and it may still be oozing sap. If you don't know how to identify trees from their bark, ask a knowledgeable person to walk the property with you. If leaves still cling to the top slash, you can identify stump species from them using a tree book.

With older cruises, you can assume volume growth for each year on hardwood tracts of at least two percent on below-average sites, four percent on average sites and six percent on productive sites. That assumption is subject to many field qualifications, such as drought and disease, that inhibit growth. Pine growth ranges from four to ten percent annually.

You should also be aware that five years of volume growth on a hardwood tract starting with an average diameter of five inches still has no merchantable sawtimber value. That same five years of volume growth on a tract where the trees started with an average of 17 inches in diameter can be enormously valuable.

As trees gain in diameter, each yearly increment in diameter growth increases their rate of volume gain. One inch in ring growth increases diameter by two inches. A six-inch diameter tree when it grows to eight inches, increases its cross-sectional area by 22 square inches with a corresponding volume gain. But a 16"-diameter tree when it grows to 18" increases its cross-sectional area by more than 53 square inches, more than double the smaller tree.

If you find a new cruise that projects volume growth, look carefully at the distribution of diameters in the old cruise. You may be looking at an update that shows a lot of volume growth that's concentrated in young timber for which no timber buyer will yet pay.

If a seller's forester wanted to boost volume on the seller's tract, he could manipulate these basic methodology factors to that end. I've seen, for example, a very professional-looking cruise analysis on a large, diverse tract that was based on too few plots to make accurate volume extrapolations. I've also received several older cruises that were never updated to reflect interim cutting.

2. Inflate species price multipliers.

This is easy to implement and may not be easy to catch. To inflate the value of the cruised timber, the forester need only pump the species prices ($/mbf) by five to ten percent to project more timber sales revenue than the landowner would actually receive. Since hardwood species prices vary from area to area and are determined by changing local conditions and market factors, it's easy for a forester to modestly pad the price multipliers without making the fakery obvious. A seller gave me a cruise on about 18,000 acres of Tennessee hardwood and planted pine that boosted price multipliers by about 25 percent. The difference between $100 mbf and $125 mbf might not snag your eye, but it amounted to a tract-wide valuation difference of $2 million, all of which wasn't there.

A seller's forester can limit his price research once he gets the answer he wants. For example, he may call a timber buyer who says, "I had to pay $1,700 for cherry on a sale a few months ago." The forester might end his telephoning there and use $1,700 mbf as his cherry sawtimber multiplier. Had he called the three other local timber buyers, he would have found that cherry on the stump was bringing $950-$1,000 mbf, and that tract a few months ago brought $1,700 mbf because of the unusually high number of cherry veneer logs in the stand. The odds are that the seller's forester knew $1,700 was too high, but chose to remain half-informed. You, as a non-forester, will probably not be able to access local timber buyers to ascertain price multipliers. For that reason alone, you should hire a forester to review any cruise the seller provides that puts dollar values on stumpage.

The simplest way to crank a cruise is to use stumpage price multipliers that are higher than those timber buyers will use. A little cheating—a five percent tweak on cherry, eight percent on red oak and so on—and pretty soon you have a large pile of **phantom value**. A little cheating across the board is more effective than one or two big cheats, because little price boosts are hard to detect while grossly inflated ones are not. Using above-market price multipliers is not as common as other tricks, because your forester can readily verify local stumpage prices with a few phone calls.

Price cheating is almost impossible for a land buyer inexperienced with timber valuations to detect. If a seller categorizes you as a novice, however, you may be given a price-inflated cruise. I was once sent a hand-written "cruise"—no date, no forester named, no diameter classes, no diameter threshold, no acreage definition, no narrative. It showed species, board feet and value by species. I just laughed; it looked like a kitchen-table job done by a fourth-grader. The seller promised that it was "as honest as could be." The price multipliers were double current market. Take a seller's cruise to your consulting forester and ask him to confirm price multipliers as a first step.

I've found most state-employed, county foresters are reluctant to challenge seller cruises, with some notable exceptions. Prices that state and federal agencies get for the sale of public timber are lower than those paid to private landowners, because the public sales require the logger to invest in expensive road-building and reclamation practices. Don't rely on public-sale prices; rely on your forester.

A variation on using inflated price multipliers is for a seller's cruise to include no prices and timber values at all. This forces the buyer to come up with his own price multipliers and overall values, a task that's almost impossible for a non-forester to accomplish with precision.

Mills value stumpage tract by tract, species by species. Timber quality and access vary from tract to tract, and these variations are figured into the buyer's overall bid price. Stumpage bids will vary from buyer to buyer according to the individual needs and costs of each buyer at that particular moment. A 100-acre tract of cherry might be valued by a buyer at $1,600 p/A while he might value another 100-acre tract of cherry 30 miles further from his mill (and lying on a southeast aspect that is accessed by a one-mile-long 4WD road that will require 50 hours of bulldozer work to make it suitable for log trucks) at $1,200 p/A despite having the same volume. The timber quality on the second tract will be lower than the first tract owing to its site index, and the poor access road will increase the buyer's logging cost. Each mill's current stumpage prices will reflect its current inventory of each species, demand for milled products and individual cost of cutting and hauling logs to its facility. A mill short on black cherry and long on orders will pay more for such stumpage than a mill with 500 cherry logs sitting in its yard and no orders for cherry lumber. A mill five miles from the target property can pay a bit more for stumpage than one 100 miles away. A stumpage buyer with a harvest-and-hauling cost of $300 mbf can pay more than one whose cost is $500 mbf. A mill with no market for veneer will pay less for stumpage than one that routinely ships such logs abroad for premium prices.

Stumpage buyers are reluctant to talk to and quote stumpage prices to land buyers and landowners unless it's in the context of a negotiation for a timber sale. It's also difficult for the lay person to understand exactly what a mill manager means when he says "we'd pay $700 for red oak," when his real meaning is that the mill has paid that much for the best quality red oak logs, but his more common bid price is about $500 mbf.

My guess is that the consultants who are not putting prices in their cruises for sellers are doing so to avoid lawsuits over misrepresentation and fraud. A seller's cruise lacking prices tempts the do-it-yourselfer to do it to himself. Resist! Pay a consulting forester to check the seller's cruise and determine current stumpage prices for the seller's tract.

3. Applying Large Sawtimber Price Multipliers to Small Sawtimber Volume to Produce Phantom Value.

This is a common trick. I've seen several forms.

First, the forester may apply the sawtimber price for trees 18" DBH and larger to sawtimber in diameter classes smaller than 16". (The threshold could be 16" or even 14" rather than 18", depending on local markets.) The seller's forester knows, or at least suspects, that the 12-16 sawtimber will be price-discounted in the local market. Depending on the volume in the smaller diameter classes, this calculation can significantly overestimate timber-sale revenue.

The variation on this tactic is to count small sawtimber volume into the merchantable timber base, but use no price multipliers at all in the cruise. The effect is to have the property appear to contain a huge volume of merchantable sawtimber valued at the sawtimber price, when some portion of that volume has only a discounted value.

I was sent a seller's cruise on a 6,000-acre West Virginia tract that showed 12,171,000 bf of merchantable hardwood sawtimber on the Doyle scale. Of that volume, 5,350,000 bf was in the 10-14" DBH categories, too small for a mill to pay for as sawtimber. And another 2,211,000 was in the 16" category; maybe it would be price-discounted, maybe not. High-value species like cherry in smaller sawtimber diameters will often fetch the same price as volume in larger diameters. But this tract had relatively little volume in high-value species, especially high-quality, high-value species. Sixty-two percent of the total stumpage classified as "merchantable" was smaller than 18" DBH. Most of that volume would not bring the sawtimber price bid for 18" DBH+ volume. Of the 3,420,000 bf shown for the most prevalent species, red oak (a high-value species at the time), only 1,208,000 bf was 18" DBH+. The other two thirds was in 10 to 16" diameters. The well-known consulting firm that prepared this cruise noted that timber volumes down to 10" DBH were included for "planning purposes." Fair enough, but all the volume smaller than 14" should have been pulled out of the merchantable category and put into a premerchantable analysis.

A quick reading of those numbers would encourage me to expect a much larger volume of timber than would be immediately saleable. The absence of any price multipliers for each species encouraged a buyer to apply a straight-through price to the aggregated volume of each species, regardless of quality and diameter size. A "guessed-at" straight-through multiplier for both merchantable and premerchantable volume is too gross for your purpose. It's not likely to accurately take into account the distribution of the two volumes that are priced so differently.

Second, the seller's forester can apply the large-diameter sawtimber price multiplier to that volume in the large-diameter trees found in the top log. As noted above, top-log volume has value, if any at all, only as pulp or firewood. It is too small in diameter to be milled cost-effectively for lumber. The most prudent practice in hardwood stumpage is for your forester to assign no dollar value to volume that is above the natural break or above a ten inch diameter, unless the local practice is to salvage these limbs for pulp, chips or firewood. In that event, it's fair to put the current market price on this volume sold for these products, but not as sawtimber.

I was recently handed a cruise that counted as merchantable *sawtimber* that part of the top "with a minimum of 4 inches main bole diameter." I am familiar with timber buying in the area where this property lies, and no timber buyer would pay a nickel for top volume between 10" and 4" in diameter. Any seller's forester who uses a sawtimber price multiplier for top-log volume is showing dollars that will never appear in your pocket.

A third way to produce phantom value is to count all volume in poorly formed and otherwise defective trees or the defective portions of trees, particularly high-value species. Honest foresters don't count poorly formed trees, and they deduct volume contained in the defective portions of a tree's stem. Eliminated is volume that does not meet sawtimber standards owing to severe bends, cankers, hollowness, rot, fire damage and other problems. You might hear this called, "subtracting defect." Take a stem that is 30 feet long and at least 20" in diameter along its length. The forester should include in his cruise the volume in its first 16 feet and the last eight feet, both of which are free of defect. The six feet of stem between these two lengths should not be counted because it contains a deep gash that makes it unsuitable for lumber. This 30-foot stem will cut out into a linear total of 24 feet of logs, not 30. A forester who counts in that six feet of defective stem is creating stumpage value in a log that doesn't exist in the market.

The final example I'll share comes from a tract where the seller's cruise showed $433,000 in total timber value with an asking price on the 886 acres of $350,000. Can't go wrong here, right? Don't write your check yet.

Here are the ringers in this deal. First, the $433,000 represents, the seller said, "total capital value of merchantable timber." Total capital value is the count-anything-with-bark number that a not-overly-honest landowner might use to establish his tax basis in the timber. It does not represent what the landowner would receive from the sale of his genuinely merchantable stumpage. When I read the extremely small print at the bottom of the cruise, I found a very large disclaimer about the seller's expansive notion of total capital value. Total capital value was significantly greater than merchantable stumpage value. Second, the cruise included as "sawtimber," everything 8" DBH and larger. Most of the property's volume was 14" DBH and smaller. Only 25 percent of the total sawtimber volume was 16" DBH and larger. The smaller diameters would not bring the prevailing sawtimber price. Third, the cruise offered a range of sawtimber prices by species—low, high and likely. The "likely" price was multiplied against the total species volume (which includes all the small-diameter volume). If I were to try to apply a single price to sawtimber volume that's mostly 14" DBH and smaller, I would apply a number at the low end of the range, not the middle, as this cruise did. My bottom-line guess is that this cruise showed more than twice the dollars a stumpage seller would pocket from the sale of merchantable stumpage. But it sounded like a hell of a deal when I first heard about it.

4. Inoperable Acreage.

Good timber is often found in places that for various reasons render it without commercial value. **Operable acreage** is land that is legally and physically accessible by locally available conventional logging machines and techniques. In the East, this means self-propelled vehicles with wheels and tracks; it usually does not mean overhead cable systems or helicopters. In swamps, conventional logging may mean "**shovel logging**," which requires cutting pulp-type trees and using them to make a road for a tracked cutting vehicle. These road trees are then salvaged and sold when the logging is done. This is a costlier method of logging, and the trees used for road-building need to be debarked before they are processed further.

Timber buyers will only pay for stumpage that they can cut at a profit. This means stumpage on operable acreage that can be removed with the equipment they normally use.

Inoperable acreage is land on which merchantable timber may exist but it is either legally or physically inaccessible, or uneconomical to harvest because of steep slopes, remoteness or other cost factors. Stumpage buyers will assign no value to otherwise merchantable trees that are so scattered that they're not worth the cost of getting them. A $2,000 cherry will be left standing in the woods if the logger has to spend $2,000 to build a mountainside road to get to it. Stumpage buyers will not pay landowners for trees on inoperable acreage.

Inoperable stumpage would also include merchantable trees that are fully or partially off-limits because they're located in setbacks, streamside buffer zones or designated habitat for endangered or protected species. Land that is considered high-value conservation property and is so classified by public policy may be off-limits to timbering even though it is allowed on paper. Timber on such land should be considered inoperable. The worst example of this I've encountered was a seller with about 8.5 million board feet of koa on 3,000 acres in Hawaii. All of the land was considered "conservation," which allowed timbering, though no timbering permit had been granted to anyone on conservation land for more than ten years. The state forestry official in charge of permitting said that he could not envision a permit being issued.

On one tract of almost 40,000 acres that I came to know, more than 12,000 acres were considered inoperable owing to steepness. A knowledgeable forester assigned no value to their sawtimber and pulp volumes. When a buyer asked a less knowledgeable forester to estimate the value of the tract's merchantable timber, he fully valued the volume found on these 12,000 acres. The land buyer was not pleased when he discovered that he had paid for several million board feet worth nothing to him because they were worth nothing to local stumpage buyers.

On another tract of 5,000 acres in the coastal swamps of eastern North Carolina, a seller's cruise showed about $2.3 million in timber value. Unfortunately, only about $500,000 could be captured through conventional shovel logging. The rest of the value was found in timber growing on land so wet that it could not be harvested economically. Any buyer who believed this seller's cruise was stuck with timber value on inoperable acreage.

I have seen a number of seller-supplied cruises where merchantable timber on inoperable acreage was counted to inflate volume.

5. Failure to disaggregate species by two-inch diameter classes.

Sawtimber value depends in part on diameter size. It is critical that a cruise disaggregate estimated HW sawtimber volumes by both species and one- or two-inch diameter classes, at least in the 12-and-above diameters. It's acceptable to lump large diameter classes together, as, for example, 22"+, because there's no price discount or premium above a diameter such as that. Disaggregation of volume by diameter and species is important to the land buyer, because it groups timber into readily valued components and allows the drawing of a line between price-discounted premerch and fully priced merchantable stumpage. Cruises that lump all sawtimber, particularly hardwood, into one category, such as "10" DBH and larger," are suspect, because timber buyers will usually apply a price discount on the portion of this stumpage in the smaller diameters.

Similarly, a buyer should doubt the dollar value assigned to all sawtimber volume in an aggregated diameter class of a single species, say, "all sugar maple 12" DBH and larger." It is easy for a compliant forester to help his seller by applying the large-diameter sawtimber price multiplier to the entire group, including all the 12 to 16s. This practice, in my opinion, is deliberate overstatement.

Smaller sawtimber—the premerchantable volume—should be disaggregated into two-inch diameter classes by species to give the buyer a reasonable estimate of the time needed for the volume in each diameter class to grow into a merchantable class and benefit from the associated price increase.

A "cruise" that reports a single gross timber-volume number for a tract as a whole should be suspect, except for even-age stands of one species, such as 50 acres of 25-year-old planted loblolly pine. If a seller hands you a paper showing so many board feet in something called "marketable hardwood," or "hardwood timber," or "standing timber," or "available timber," do not take this number as a valid, trustworthy cruise result. Ask for details and cruise methodology. Ask for a two-inch breakdown of all sawtimber 10" DBH and up by individual species. Don't be surprised if this information "can't" be obtained. If the seller is willing to give you the name of the forester who prepared this number, call and ask for such a breakdown. Do not be surprised if either the seller or the forester stonewalls you. A consulting forester working for you, the buyer, should provide a disaggregated timber inventory on a hardwood stand, not a single number showing gross volume or, worse, an unexplained dollar value.

On pulpwood tracts, volume need not be disaggregated into two-inch diameter classes because a pulpwood buyer is interested in aggregated fiber, not lumber potential.

I have often encountered a seller who tells me that his property contains either so many board feet or "at least" so many dollars in timber. No paper is ever available to support these statements. While it is theoretically possible that such statements are true, it is also theoretically possible for me—a 61 year old with a bum knee—to perform a reverse dunk, the very move I could not hope to do at 19 with two spry knees.

6. Combining Low-Value and High-Value Species of the Same Family.

A forester should separate hardwood sawtimber volumes into botanically distinct species, because stumpage buyers set prices for each species rather than for a tree family. The family of oaks, for example, will include northern red oak at $400-$600 mbf and chestnut oak at $100 mbf. Scarlet oak, pin oak, black oak and the others will fall somewhere in between. A sawtimber cruise that uses one price multiplier against an undifferentiated "Oaks" category where several oak species are present in significant volumes is probably overvaluing the stumpage. Most stumpage buyers in my experience do not value oak sawtimber at a straight-through price unless they're planning on turning the trees into low-value products like pulp or pallets.

A more subtle version of the same trick is to lump together closely related species within the same family, call everything the high-value species and multiply the resulting volume by that price. I've seen this used to combine chestnut oak volume at $100 mbf with white oak volume at $300 mbf, the total volume being multiplied by $300 mbf; scarlet oak at $175 mbf and black oak at $125 mbf with red oak at $400 mbf, the total volume being multiplied by $400 mbf; and soft (red) maple at $125 mbf with hard (sugar) maple at $300 mbf, the total being multiplied by $300 mbf. In each case, the value of the combined total is inflated by using the high-value species price against the lower-value species volumes. This is nothing but fraud.

7. Using the "wrong" scale.

Tree scales are formulas that foresters use to estimate the volume of wood in standing timber. These scales provide fixed volume numbers for inch-by-inch DBH categories on one axis and the number of eight to 16-foot logs in a tree on the other. Where diameter class intersects with log length, a number—volume in board feet—will be found. (Other means are used to calculate volume in tons or cords.) Stumpage buyers usually prefer—and therefore use—a particular scale for specific types of timber in each region. New York, for example, uses three different scales to estimate wood—Scribner, Doyle and International 1/4 inch—depending on the area of the state where the timber is located. Scales "count" tree volume differently, which means that 1,000 board feet under one scale will be valued differently than 1,000 board feet under the other two.

Different scales estimate volume differently because they are constructed for different timber types. One scale, for example, may be most accurate for tall, straight species of fairly uniform diameter, while another may be best suited for trees that taper with height. One scale may be the timber buyer's preference because it undercounts volumes in certain diameter classes while another scale may be the landowner's preferred alternative because it overcounts certain classes. **A forester should use the log scale in his cruise for you that is the one that stumpage buyers in that area will use on the target property's timber.**

Land sellers will sometimes cruise their stumpage with the inflating scale to give a land buyer a rosy sense of its timber value. The bogus seller cruises on hardwood sawtimber that I've seen have used the International Scale where stumpage buyers used nothing but the Doyle Scale. The Doyle is a more conservative and more appropriate scale for hardwood sawtimber. In the smaller diameter classes, the

Doyle scale will measure 30 percent less volume than the International; the two scales close toward each other in the 30"+ diameter classes. A tree 24" DBH that contains two usable 16' logs has 370 board feet by the Doyle scale and 441 bf on the International, a 19 percent increase. On tracts where the majority of merchantable sawtimber is in the 16" to 18" and 18" to 20" categories, the International Scale will seriously overestimate stumpage volume that a landowner can sell to buyers using the Doyle. A forester could prepare a "seller's cruise" using the International Scale while knowing that timber buyers will not use it. If the buyer relies on this seller's cruise, he may easily end up with 20 percent less volume for sale than the seller's cruise showed after buying the seller's property.

I've seen the "musical scales" tactic used several times. In one case, a sawmill was selling 12,500 acres of very good hardwood dirt. Most of the acreage had been selectively cut to 16" DBH. The mill's forester handed me a cruise he had prepared using the International Scale. "Do you buy for the mill on the International Scale?" I asked, knowing the answer. "No," he said. Nonetheless, he had deliberately increased the property's timber volume and value. I figured he was showing $2 million that would not be there for my client. If you find a seller using the "wrong" log scale, keep your eyes open for other tricks to pad timber value.

When scoping a seller's cruise, ask your forester to make sure that the seller's forester used the scale that local stumpage buyers use.

8. DBH vs. Point of Severance.

Most of the hardwood sawtimber cruises I've seen use a tree scale in which **diameter at breast height (DBH)** is measured at 4.5 feet above the ground. From that point up, the tree's stem loses the atypical diameter of its splayed base. Volume formulas assume the tree will be cut at about six inches above the ground, measured on the uphill side. The formulas don't force the owner to give 3.5 feet of butt log free to the timber buyer.

The height at which the tree is cut is often referred to as the "**point of severance**." A cruise whose volumes are tallied from a diameter at the point of severance may include more volume than one using DBH. A timber cruise that includes all merchantable timber 16" DBH and larger will include many fewer trees than one that takes in all trees 16" and larger at the point of severance. The 16"-DBH cruise does not include the small sawtimber trees in the 12 to 16" DBH classes, which represents the future harvest. Because the point of severance can be as close to the ground as a logger can cut, a seller's cruise based on 16" at the point of severance will count the volume in the 12-16 DBH trees that a DBH buyer will not value. Close to ground level 12-16 DBH trees widen for structural support, thus allowing a point-of-severance cruise to count their volume and price it as full-size sawtimber. A 16" cut taken at the point of severance will leave land with much less standing timber and looking far more roughed up.

I know of cases where a stumpage buyer has been known to approach landowners with an offer to buy timber on a 16" point-of-severance basis, during which he says "16 inches and larger" very loudly and "point of severance" next to inaudibly. The landowner is likely to expect that everything 16" *DBH* and larger will be left. Not so. He will find himself owning a third cousin to a clearcut. Most landowners will not know the difference between a 16" DBH cut and a 16" point-of-severance cut even when their hearing is good.

As I was finishing this book, I responded to an ad in the Wall Street Journal for about 7,500 acres in Kentucky with coal, gas and timber. When I phoned the contact person—one of the owners—she never mentioned that the timber was being cut. I went to the virtual room where documents were stored and pulled up the seller's consulting forester's report. He noted that of the 15 million board feet of merchantable sawtimber measuring ten inches and larger, all timber measuring 16 inches and larger *at stump height*—about nine million board feet—had been sold and was under contract until October, 2007.

A 16" stump cut translates to about a 12" DBH cut. The forester then goes on to break down the remaining six million board feet, in which he counted *all trees 10 to 14" DBH*. Not so fast, Louie.

If the owner has sold down to about 12" DBH, all the 12 to 14" DBH will be gone. You can't count them as there! Of the six million board feet said to be remaining after the cut, my guess is a buyer would find about one million board feet, all in 10 to 12s DBH. This seller came across as a straight-shooter; she even told me she was. Buyers are frequently disappointed.

The field vernacular for a point-of-severance harvest is a "**stump cut**." If you are handed a cruise based on point of severance or stump cut, keep in mind that small sawtimber with discounted value is being included as fully valued sawtimber. The principal purpose in my opinion for a seller-supplied cruise to use a stump parameter is to deceive an unsophisticated buyer into thinking that he will get significantly more money for the timber than he actually will. The land buyer will assume that a stumpage buyer will pay a sawtimber price straight through for all volume 16" at the stump when, in fact, the stumpage buyer will discount the volume in the trees smaller than 16" DBH. A seller-supplied stump-cruise is used to justify the seller's high asking price.

9. Using the Wrong Measure of Volume.

Cords and tons are gross measures and are almost always applied against low-value wood used for pulp, chips, or sawtimber used for industrial-type purposes such as railroad ties, pallets, mining props and fence material.

Inherent in timber measured in either cords or tons is the aggregation of the tract's merchantable trees (species, diameter class and quality) into a single volume number (in the case of cords) or a single weight (in the case of tons). That aggregation is exactly the opposite of the disaggregation analysis a forester does when he cruises hardwood sawtimber for the lumber market. A cruise expressed as tons or cords cannot capture the true value of a hardwood-sawtimber tract for lumber, because of the aggregation of high-and low-value sawtimber trees, trees with different diameters, trees with different weights per unit of volume and so on.

A tonnage cruise on a sawtimber tract that uses one, straight-through per-ton price multiplier lends itself to misinterpretation. In some tonnage cruises I've seen, the actual timber value is underestimated. This occurs because quality hardwood sawtimber is priced at the same dollar multiplier as pulp and low-value sawtimber. A forester and I bought a bottom-land hardwood tract in West Tennessee when we discovered that the seller's tonnage cruise masked the real value of the tract when looked at as sawtimber, not pulp. When my partner reworked tonnage into disaggregated sawlog volume in board feet, he found that the timber would more than pay for the purchase.

Where a tonnage cruise uses a single price multiplier, it's easy to inflate value for the gullible land buyer. A cruise that shows 1,000,000 tons on a tract can easily suggest a phantom $500,000 in timber value simply by using a price multiplier of $6 p/t rather than the $5.50 the market will pay.

While cords and tons are perfectly appropriate measures for pulpwood tracts, particularly clearcuts, readers who are scoping most hardwood sawtimber will want a cruise in board feet, organized by species and two-inch diameter class, and priced by species.

10. Volume in Big Trees on High-graded Tracts May Have Little Value.

The high-grading logger cuts only the large-diameter, high-value sawtimber trees, leaving in place most, or all, of the large low-value sawtimber trees and all of the culls. Loggers prefer high-grading because it allows them to net the most money from a timber stand with the least amount of effort in the shortest period of time. The logger removes only the "**money trees**" and leaves the junk. Thirty years after high-grading, you will find a lot of large-diameter, worthless junk. And each time a high-grading logger leaves such trees standing, they use resources that would be more profitably consumed by the small-diameter high-value trees.

When a tract has been repeatedly high-graded, it will appear to the layman's eye as a stand of large-diameter, hardwood sawtimber, and for that reason it must surely have substantial commercial value. Don't be fooled, as I was when I first started looking for timberland. Look carefully at the species of the big trees. You will find that most are the local low-values; in my area that means gum, black birch, basswood, hickory, chestnut oak and pine. Now look at the large trees again, particularly any high-value species, such as red oak, cherry, walnut, ash and sugar maple. The odds are high that you will find that these trees are culls—trees that are poorly formed; defective from lightning, fire or animals; diseased; hollow or otherwise not worth cutting. You may have to walk around the tree to find the flaw, because one side can be perfect in a worthless tree.

A truly unscrupulous seller will arrange to have his high-graded tract cruised by a not very scrupulous forester who dutifully records all volumes, regardless of quality. This cruise will show significant volumes of sawtimber in large diameter classes. The gross volumes will be accurate but buyers will bid little on this timber, because it has little value to them. An honest forester will not count volume that is defective as sawtimber. At best, it's pulp; at worst, shade.

If a seller gives you a cruise that is formatted into volumes, by species and two-inch diameter classes, see if it shows lots of volume in the large-diameter classes. It's certainly possible that you have found a genuinely valuable timber tract. It's also probable that your seller is showing large volumes in large-diameter, low-value species and culls left from high-grading. A skewed distribution by which almost all of the volume in high-value species turns up in small-diameter classes and most of the volume in large-diameter classes is low-value species tips you that the seller's property has been high-graded several times.

Your forester should be able to look at a seller-supplied cruise and give you a first impression of its reliability based on its format and who did it. (Consulting foresters know who of their peers plays straight all the time and who doesn't.) Cruises of high-graded property usually stand out to the trained eye. In my neighborhood, I'm pretty sure that a tract has been high-graded when the cruise shows disproportionately high volumes of large-diameter (low-value) chestnut oak and hickory.

With high-graded tracts, you are likely to run into either a **hearty verbal testimonial from the seller**—"Buddy, just look at the size of the timber out there; you can believe your own eyes, can't you?" or what I call **"the round-number ringer"**—an unsubstantiated timber value that is both large and suspiciously round, say $100,000, as in, "Buddy, that timber's worth a hundred grand if it's worth fifty cents." I've seen both tactics used on unsuspecting buyers. The buyer's interest lies in spending a few hundred dollars to have his forester take a look at any property with large-diameter trees and a seller's promise of instant riches.

While a high-graded tract has lost much of its timber value, it can be very good for hunting and recreation. Low-value species and culls produce food for wildlife and game. Moreover, high-graded tracts often "look good"—tall trees, big diameters, spreading crowns, clean forest floors. Such tracts can make good buys as long as you don't pay for timber value that isn't there.

11. Counting Pulp Dollars in a Sawtimber Stand.

A stumpage buyer often values a hardwood stand by limiting his estimate of worth to the hardwood sawtimber. Everything else—culls, pulp-value sawtimber, tops and the occasional conifer—are assigned no value, and his bid to the landowner will reflect that. A forester who counts the dollars in this type of volume will be inflating the tract's true market value—unless the stumpage buyers themselves will pay for it. On HW sawtimber tracts where the sawtimber is legitimately valued in the $100,000 to $200,000 range, I've seen pulp—broadly construed—valued at anywhere between $2,500 to $7,500. Sometimes that is a fair market valuation, but only if there's a market for it. Your forester will be able to tell you whether the seller's forester has padded the tract's valuation with pulp volume that stumpage buyers may cut and sell but will not pay for.

12. Data Overkill.

Foresters now have computer programs that can group and analyze field-gathered data in dozens of ways. I've seen at least once instance where the technical virtuosity of the forester's computer program buried the two or three most important bottom-line numbers under pages of printout. Cruise results should be simple and straight forward. An inexperienced land buyer needs to know two facts before making an offer on a wooded tract: 1) how much merchantable timber it contains, and 2) its estimated stumpage value when sold for a lump sum in the local market at current prices. If the seller hands you a cruise that is thick with impenetrable tables that don't lead to answers to the two basic buyer questions, it may be that the seller's forester is **playing hide the ball**. A buyer needs to see the ball whenever a seller is trying to hide it.

13. "Undering."

"**Undering**" is my word for a forester shorting a timber analysis in some way that works against a buyer. Here are some familiar examples:

a. Putting in too few plots.

The heart of a cruise is the taking of a sufficient number of samples (plots) to generate valid extrapolations for the tract as a whole. A forester must make a preliminary judgment about how many plots are sufficient to sample the tract. The more diverse a tract in age, species and quality, the more plots he might use. On tracts of a couple of hundred acres or less, he might use 20 to 40 plots per 100 acres. On larger tracts that are fairly consistent, he might put in one plot for every 15-20 acres. On very large tracts, I've seen one plot used to represent several hundred acres.

If too few plots are put in, the extrapolations can inflate volume, undercount it or get it right, depending on where the plots "land" in the field. A truly dishonest forester working for the seller would deliberately take plots where the timber was heaviest rather than in a systematic sampling pattern determined by where the lines of a neutral grid intersected. I've found cruises where I thought too few plots were put in to generate valid conclusions, but I've not yet encountered deliberate plot-rigging.

b. Under-updating.

When older cruises are "updated" to help a current sale, it's easy to make a few simple assumptions about growth rates and price multipliers, freshen the dates and present the package as a valid exercise.

Time changes trees, hence, timber values, in both positive and negative ways. An update of a 15-year-old cruise that is done in a computer and never field checked will miss the damage done by fire, insects, storms, timber poaching and a dozen other things that reduce predicted volume and lower timber quality.

There are circumstances when a quick and dirty update is all that is needed, but don't buy timberland with a seller's update as your Bible. It's too easy to **underestimate the field negatives** and, in that manner if no other, overestimate the tract's real volumes.

c. Under-refinement of the timber analysis.

Foresters must choose the level of analysis that gives their clients the truest picture of timber reality. If a forester is trying to inflate timber values for the seller, he can do so by choosing a grosser level of analysis than the one he should use. I've seen this done, for example, when foresters lump all small-diameter hardwood sawtimber into a single category, say 10-16" DBH, which is then multiplied by a single price. The far more accurate predictor is to disaggregate hardwood sawtimber volumes into diameter classes by species and then apply the appropriate multiplier for each species.

The forester finds trustworthy price multipliers through research with local stumpage buyers, which he then assesses in light of his field-based observations of the **quality of the volumes** contained in his cruise. Buyers rank hardwood sawtimber logs on the stump according to their quality. Quality on the stump affects bid price. A forester who wants to increase the value of a seller's timber need only underestimate quality issues in the stand to overvalue the seller's timber.

14. Two Sets of Books.

I have not run into a situation where a forester does an accurate cruise for a seller and a phony one for the seller to hand to a buyer. I have, however, come across properties where a **simplified summary** is given to buyers while the seller retains the more detailed cruise. The simplification uses one or more of the tricks I've described above to show more value than the stumpage warrants.

A simplified summary is an exercise in analytical statistics intended to paint an overly optimistic picture of timber value. But don't assume that every one-page analysis is a fraud. I've seen one page accurately summarize the timber on 18,000 acres. The more reliable suspicion-raiser is a handful of numbers without context, or a couple of fifth-grade multiplication equations with insufficient explanation. If, for instance, a seller's summary consists of "Timber Value: 25,000 tons x $25 per ton = $625,000."—you know nothing at all. You don't know how the tonnage was estimated, where it's located, what species are included, whether the tonnage is based on a clearcut or a diameter threshold, or where the $25-per-ton price came from. In fact, you don't even know whether the tract's "timber value" is gross sale revenue or net after expenses. The seller-supplied timber value may, in other words, be based on delivered price to the mill or logs on a landing, not the stumpage price. If delivered price is $25 p/t and the cut-and-haul cost is $21 p/t, the stumpage price—which is the money that sticks in your pocket—is only $4 p/t. The timber value, that is, stumpage value paid to the landowner, would be $100,000, not $625,000. The seller did not lie to you when he said the timber value was $625,000, he just did not tell you the relevant truth, the truth of the truth.

15. The unsubstantiated seller statement.

I once found a 4,000-acre property that was owned by an investor group, one of whom was a forester. Most of it was wooded. The forester had not cruised the property, but he told me there was "$1,500,000" in timber value. I asked how he had determined that number in the absence of a cruise. "Well," he said, "you have to assume that there's at least $400 to $500 in timber per acre." "Just because," I said. "Right," he answered. "Just because." My friend, a consulting forester, did a walk-through on the best 700 acres of these woods and allowed that a clearcut might produce about $100 per acre in stumpage. This tract had many large-diameter trees with impressive volumes, all of which were worthless because they were culls left standing by repeated high-grading.

I've also run into "deals" where the seller, a knowledgeable timber person, will walk me through the property and put a single dollar number on the timber as he shows me around. My rule in these circumstances is to cut that number in half and then, maybe, I'm in the ballpark.

16. Volume Averaging.

I was sent a cruise summary on 1,600 acres that reported 8,100,000 bf, mostly shown as hardwood sawtimber. For each of 17 species, the summary showed not the total number of trees and total board feet by species, but <u>tract-wide</u> average board feet per tree and an average tree DBH of 14". The summary did not include volumes disaggregated by species and two-inch diameter class. The summary did not state the smallest DBH that was included in the total or the diameter of the top break.

This type of summary looked good at first glance, but wasn't. Volume in an 18" DBH sawtimber tree has value; volume in a 10" DBH tree has little, if any. The average volume of the two is misleading, because all the volume in the smaller classification has value as pulp, not sawtimber. If one 20" DBH tree has 250 bf and 12 10" DBH trees have a total of 1,500 bf, the average volume in each of those 13 trees is 135 bf (1,750 bf / 13 = 135 bf per tree). That average volume number would represent real value if the size distribution was not lopsided. But there is only one tree—the 20"—that has sawtimber value of the 13. There's nothing inaccurate in volume averaging, except that it presents a totally distorted picture of the stumpage value of the tract's trees.

An inventory of a mixed-age, mixed-size stand that expresses volume and DBH as averages should be suspected of trying to pad the value of the timber. It is impossible for a buyer to put one price multiplier against an average volume and produce a reasonably accurate estimate of dollar value on such a tract. In contrast, tract-wide averages on even-age stands of planted pine should be representative and useful for estimating present timber value.

Volume averaging can mislead in another way. Some species, like chestnut oak, achieve large diameters at the expense of quality. Thirty-inch plus diameters in chestnut oak are common, but the butt log in these trees is often hollow or otherwise flawed. Such trees are culls that were left alone when the tract was high-graded. Their value is always chancy, because the timber buyer doesn't know the quality of the butt log until it's cut. Loggers will avoid taking these large trees for pulp because they are too big for the mill's machinery. Any averaging of cull volume with "good" volume inflates the total volume and value of the tract's merchantable timber.

The seller with a genuinely good tract of timber won't show a buyer volume averages and diameter averages. Good timber speaks for itself.

17. High-tech Wizardry.

Large timber tracts are now having their timber valued through high-tech methods, including **infrared aerial photography** and **satellite images**.

I'm seeing infrared used more and more on even-age stands of planted pine. An infrared aerial photograph is taken of the tract, from which tree volume is estimated by the extent and intensity of the red. This technique suggests volume only, and so it is useful on pulpwood tracts. It is not helpful on hardwood sawtimber tracts where the buyer must know volumes by species and diameter class. (An earlier technique used **aerial photographs** to show stand locations and provide a very rough picture of timber volume by extrapolating from crown characteristics. Modern inventory methods are much more accurate. An aerial photograph of woods by itself tells nothing about the property's timber value.)

Satellite photography of woods can produce about the same impressive level of ground-level knowledge that our military gets in its targeting systems. Satellite images provide more information when leaves are off. Both infrared and satellite techniques are used on tracts exceeding several thousand acres. On tracts smaller than 4,000 or 5,000 acres, I would always put a forester on the ground doing a walk-through, if not a conventional cruise. An ATV-mounted forester can get a reasonably good feel for a large tract by chugging through it with periodic walk outs. On larger tracts, I would ask him to recommend the best method of evaluation, given what he was able to see of the tract.

I don't have enough experience with either technique to know how they might be manipulated or their results exaggerated. I'm inclined to trust such techniques on even-age, planted tracts where value is measured in tons of fiber and not as much on hardwood sawtimber tracts where market value depends on volume by diameter class, species and quality.

18. Time and Liquidity.

In my area, it is almost always possible to get an **upfront, lump-sum payment** for timber stumpage when its sale involves less than $500,000. Between $500,000 and $1,000,000, the biggest mills may still be willing to pay a lump sum upfront, though they would prefer to pay in two or three "lifts" as the logging progresses. On very large tracts with timber value in excess of $1 million, the rule of thumb usually is: the larger your stumpage value, the less immediately liquid its full value sold to one buyer. The reader should keep in mind that the dollar numbers in my local "rule" will vary from region to region, but the underlying principle is likely to hold true in most places. Where a timber buyer is willing to pay a lump sum upfront for a very large timber tract, he may discount his offer in light of the time it will take him to cut the tract, carrying costs and market risk. Thus, a tract showing an honest $20 million in merchantable timber might fetch only $15 million in a lump-sum, cash-upfront sale.

Timber sales are almost always marketed to local buyers. The common exception to this statement involves tracts that contain a lot of veneer or high-quality sawtimber that appeal to high-end distant buyers or the export market. The market for most tracts does not reach beyond a three-hour, one-way truck haul. Less haulage time is preferred since it allows the logger to deliver at least two loaded trucks per eight-hour shift. Whoever buys your timber can use only so much of it at a time, and every local market taken as a whole can absorb only so much supply without depressing prices. Consequently, the value of a large tract's timber has to be estimated in terms of local mill capacity, local market factors (supply of stumpage, demand for mill products, prices) and national and international market factors over the time needed to cut it. (Even timber-sale contracts on small tracts of fewer than 200,000 board feet might give the buyer a two-year window to remove the purchased timber. This allows the mill to schedule the logging in light of its cutting crew availability, yard inventory and expected demand for specific products.)

It follows that the larger amount of timber a landowner wants to sell, the fewer buyers there are who will be able to pay a lump sum for it. Smaller stumpage buyers can't afford to tie up their capital over long periods, so they look for small jobs that can be marketed at current prices. On the larger sales, the smaller buyers drop out of the market. On very large volumes, the landowner may have to negotiate a long-term contract with a single buyer whereby he is paid the market price on a **pay-as-cut basis**. A negotiated price with a monopoly is not likely to be what the stumpage owner prefers. One frequently used approach is to market a large volume of timber divided into several small tracts. This marketing tactic gathers in the largest number of potential bidders able to pay an immediate lump sum for each sub-parcel.

Most readers of this book will be interested in land deals where the volume of stumpage timber is less than one million board feet and certainly less than $1 million in timber value. Part of your scoping responsibility with timber is to ask your consulting forester to **determine the immediate liquidity (i.e., an upfront, lump-sum sale) of the target property's timber before submitting a purchase contract for the property**. As timber value exceeds $500,000, it will be increasingly difficult to get paid the full value of the merchantable timber in an upfront cash payment. The consultant is also likely to find that the market gets increasingly less competitive as the value of the timber rises. For these reasons, you should start discounting present timber value in your purchase calculations once the value of the merchantable timber exceeds some locally determined threshold amount. You will need your consulting forester to estimate at what level of value the discounting kicks in and how much the discount factor should be. To complicate things a bit more, he will also need to factor in 1) the increasing value of the stumpage as trees grow, and 2) the increase in timber value from ingrowth.

An honest seller may truthfully tell you that his 10,000 acres contains $10 million in stumpage value. There's no trickery embedded in this seller's cruise. But whether that timber is immediately merchantable for $10 million is a different question. If your consultant's answer is not "within six months of purchase," you must start discounting the $10 million, because it won't show up in your pocket without deductions for time and costs. A buyer of a large tract needs to determine how much of the value shown on the seller's cruise is immediate and how much of it is future.

19. Timber Sales: Competitively Bid vs. Negotiated.

As a general rule, a landowner will get the most money for his timber through a competitively bid sale. In some areas, however, the local practice is to purchase stumpage through two-party negotiation rather than competitive bidding. And some tracts may realistically have no more than one bidder owing to their large volume or the timber's characteristics.

The stumpage value you see on a seller-supplied cruise rarely indicates how the forester arrived at his price multipliers. If the seller's forester assumed competitively bid prices in an area where only negotiated sales occur, the merchantable value will rise beyond what a negotiated sale is likely to bring. Therefore, ask your consulting forester the method by which the property's timber will be sold and whether the seller's cruise used price multipliers that should be discounted for lack of competitive bidding.

20. Non-local price multipliers.

Remember: timber prices are almost always set in the timber's *local* market.

Let's say that you're interested in 100 wooded acres that is situated in Midway, between Richville and Poortown. It is a tract that is "heavy to northern red oak," meaning there's more volume of that species than any other in the merchantable tally. Richville boasts ten modern saw mills and is located within a three-hour radius of excellent stands of high-value hardwoods. It is a very competitive market. Poortown lies 250 miles to the west. Local timber quality there is a bit below average due to rainfall, topography and soils. Poortown has three old mills. Richville mills will pay $600 mbf for local northern red oak on the stump because of its good quality; Poortown mills will not pay more than $400 for the same species from its local area. The Poortown timber is a lower quality, and the markets for its milled lumber reflect that well-known fact.

Your Midway target property is a bit closer to Richville as the crow flies, but driving time is about one-third less to Poortown. Timber from Midway is generally sold to Poortown mills because of its middling quality and travel time.

The seller-supplied cruise, however, uses Richville price multipliers rather than the lower ones from Poortown. The cruise says nothing about the difference in stumpage prices between the two markets. Nor does it indicate which market the seller's forester drew his price multipliers from.

In this example, the use of Richville stumpage prices for the Midway northern red oak instead of the Poortown prices overvalues the volume in this species by 50 percent. The rest of the tract's timber will be similarly overvalued.

21. Hit-a-lick timber inventories.

I don't really know a better way to describe what I've been seeing more and more of lately. On tracts of 1,000 acres and larger, I am being sent an increasing number of timber inventories that are so lacking in detail and so gross in their level of analysis that I routinely assume the real worth to the land buyer is about half the purported volume and value.

I've seen different versions of these hit-a-lick inventories. One of the most common is a cruise that shows gross volumes without any dollar values at all. The gross volumes might be labeled hardwood sawtimber, hardwood pulp, softwood sawtimber and softwood pulp. Without knowing the percentage distribution of species in the sawtimber categories, it's impossible for a buyer to project value. Since it's difficult for a land buyer to find out prices paid by stumpage buyers, he is left with some information and his own active imagination. Don't underestimate the effect of your own hopes when it comes to timber prices. And what better defense does a seller have than to create conditions for a buyer to mislead himself.

A second approach on hardwood tracts is to show volume in board feet without indicating the distribution of volume within diameter classes. This produces confusion since it's impossible to figure out how much of the board foot volume is valuable 16-18" DBH+ sawtimber and how much is in the much less valuable smaller diameters.

A third method are extrapolations of present value using old cruise data and infrared images. The old data are not updated or projected. The buyer is given two seemingly "hard" timber inventories, but neither can support a reasonably accurate estimate of present value. The buyer must get his own forester to walk the tract and provide that estimate.

Some of the most misleading hit-a-lick inventory work I've seen comes packaged in multi-color, three-ring binders that are festooned with maps, charts and tables. These are produced by highly successful TIMOS (timber investment management organizations) and large consulting forestry outfits. Fancy packages can present honest analysis or its opposite. A buyer cannot assume that big names put out work that is trustworthy for a buyer's purposes, though they may. Your own consulting forester can protect your interest in these Las Vegas-style sucker games.

22. Cheating.

A really easy way to inflate volume and value is to lie. A forester working for the seller can pad phantom trees into his plot tallies, say, one or two high-value trees per plot. This can boost tract volume by ten percent or more without leaving a clue. A greedy padding-job will be obvious to your forester, but a sneaky one of ten or 15 percent can only be caught by doing an honest cruise using the exact same grid as the seller's forester.

I've never found a forester cheating like this for a seller, but I have suspected a few seller cruises of benefiting from this practice.

23. "The Combo."

The most common tactic is for a forester working for the seller to employ a combination of volume/price inflating techniques.

It is hard to detect a six percent overestimate here and a five percent overestimate there. The easiest seller cruises to sniff out are those that use the wrong log scale for the timber buyers in that area, those that group the small sawtimber in with the large, and those that apply prices that are far above market. The hard ones to detect are those that cheat around the edges, things like sticking 5,000 bf of red maple in with 60,000 bf of hard maple and calling all 65,000 bf hard maple, or breaking the top at a six-inch diameter and not saying so.

A very simple trick is to project timber on more acres than the seller actually has. The seller owns 450 acres according to the tax maps. He decides to divide it and tells the buyer that he will convey 200 acres. The seller calculates the acreage in the parcel to be sold from the tax maps. His forester—or yours—does a walk-through and determines that there's 3,000 bf per acre of hardwood sawlogs 16" DBH and larger. Multiplication then occurs: 3,000 bf/A x 200 acres = 600,000 bf of hardwood sawlogs. Fortunately, the buyer double checks the acreage using a scaled map and a planimeter or using a computer program with metes and bounds. The actual acreage that the seller will convey is 175 acres, which means 75,000 fewer board feet than anticipated. At an average of $400/1000bf, that's $30,000 in timber-sale income the seller led the buyer to think he was acquiring which he wasn't.

No reason exists for a land buyer to become a forestry detective, dedicated to uncovering bogus cruises. You simply need to follow my advice: hire a consulting forester you like and trust, then pay him to give you his honest opinion about a seller's cruise. It doesn't hurt, of course, for you to have read this book.

Almost all of this discussion is based on my experience with hardwood sawtimber tracts in about 15 states east of the Mississippi River. Other places use different log scales. Other places have planted pine plantations rather than natural hardwood stands, or stands of Douglas fir with 40,000 bf or more to each acre, or tree species, such as cherry bark oak and cypress, with which I have no experience. Foresters working for sellers in each area and in each type of timber will undoubtedly have other ways of inflating cruises. Readers should consider my discussion as anecdotal and reflective of my experience. There are tricks that I have yet to see.

Most of those I've mentioned manipulate reality or fudge the truth without engaging in outright lies. Cruises that fabricate volume are rare, though I've seen a couple of doozies. Many seller-supplied cruises include timber volumes—hence, dollar value—that a timber buyer will not pay for. These are intended to induce the buyer to pay the seller his high asking price.

A lot of tricks used to inflate a cruise's volume and value falls between what is sort of ethical and what is sort of not. A forester who slants a cruise toward the interest of his client, the seller, can always wrap himself in plausibility: "Yes, my species price multipliers might be a little high, but those are the prices I was told when I called around. Prices change daily. Mine were in the ballpark at the time." Buyers should remember that ballparks are big places.

Whether or not a particular bag of tricks amounts to fraud in the legal sense would depend on the specifics of what is presented to a buyer and how it is represented. Real-estate law allows for a certain amount of seller "puffing." My opinion, for what it's worth, is that inflating timber volume and value is intended to defraud a buyer. If it's intended to defraud and does so, it's fraud.

Ralph Keyes's, The Post-Truth Era: Dishonesty and Deception in Contemporary Life (New York: St. Martin's Press, 2004) makes the point that members of an in-group have an easier time lying to members of an out-group than to each other. Lying within the group may, in fact, be unacceptable. That is a plausible explanation for the puffing and other deceptions that sellers employ against buyers, particularly buyers they don't know. That is not to say that every local seller tries to deceive every non-local buyer. The facts in my experience do not show that. It is, however, worth a non-local buyer's time to rigorously test statements of fact provided by a local seller, especially with respect to timber values. When your testing confirms a seller's honesty, you have the makings of a purchase.

The best advice I can give an inexperienced buyer is to find a consulting forester whom you like and trust, give him your business and rely on his professional loyalty to you to protect your interests. A consultant working on your behalf can make you a lot of money and prevent you from spending your money unwisely. It's always worth a couple of hundred dollars to have your forester review the work of the seller's forester, and, if necessary, do a walk-through. Your forester will protect your back from consulting foresters working for the seller. Don't cut this corner.

CHAPTER 23: SELLING TIMBER, TOOLS OF THE TRADE

TIMBER FSBO—A BAD IDEA

This book is about how to buy rural property; selling timber occurs after one has bought the land. Still, a land buyer should know a bit in advance about the selling of merchantable timber.

After you take possession of your new property, you should have in hand a timber cruise that your forester has prepared for you as part of your scoping regimen. That cruise establishes the value for tax purposes of the merchantable timber on your land. It is your **timber basis** for the IRS. Chapter 24 discusses timber taxation and the need to establish timber basis and choose a form of ownership at the time of purchase.

As the new landowner, you can sell your **timber as a FSBO (For Sale By Owner)** in one of several ways. I'll explain the steps that a FSBO needs to take, but I don't recommend this route. In any case, I think it's useful to lay out what a FSBO needs to do if only to convince hardcore FSBOs that this is one do-it-yourself deal that should be avoided.

First, you can contact local sawmills and loggers and take out an ad in local papers, announcing that you have timber for sale. You can send your cruise to those who contact you along with a very precise definition of that portion of your timber that you want to sell: let's say, all hardwood and softwood sawtimber 18" DBH and larger and all pulpwood 6" DBH and larger, excluding all cherry, red oak, white oak and hard maple smaller than 18" DBH. Such a cut will produce a more valuable harvest in the future to the degree that high-value species are encouraged and their competition removed.

In choosing this option, you will need to decide on and/or prepare the following for the **timber-sale packet** you send out to interested buyers:

1. **Contract** between you and the timber buyer. A discussion of a timber sale contract appears below.

2. **Establish title to the timber** that you are selling. (Usually done in the contract by the seller [you] warranting that you have clear title to the timber.) By buying the property on which the timber stands, you have title to the timber. You would not have title to the timber if it had been reserved by the seller or locked out by a no-timbering conservation easement.

3. **Mark boundaries on the ground** to reflect your legal ownership. This may be as easy as tying new ribbons on existing fence and marked boundaries. You may need to ask a forester or even a surveyor to "ribbon" the boundaries if they are ambiguous. Boundary marking has to be finished before buyers look at your timber. Do not "ribbon in" land and timber that you do not own. That is called stealing; neighbors frown on it.

4. **Define the timber you are selling and the timber you are not selling. Paint all trees you want to cut.** Spray a dot of bright paint on each tree you are selling at about five feet above the ground and another on its stump at ground level. If you find unpainted stumps during the logging, talk it over with the logger and insist on an end to this practice as well as payment for the timber involved. Honest loggers don't cut unpainted trees. Put your "cease-and-desist notice" to him in writing.

A true rapscallion will buy the same type and color of paint you've used, remove the tree and then paint the stump that you've not painted. This is intentional theft by any definition. A logger who is a wealth of practical and probably first-hand knowledge about such things told me about this one.

Spray paint for tree marking is available from Forestry Suppliers and similar vendors.

Don't high-grade your own land. Paint pulpwood and low-value species and ask the stumpage buyer to drop them if you don't want to do this yourself. If the stumpage buyer does not cut them, you can sell or give them to local folks who will cut them for firewood.

DO NOT say: "Timber to be sold includes all trees 18" DBH and larger." and assume that is all you need to do. Once a tree is removed, you cannot determine its diameter at what would have been breast height (4.5 feet above the ground). Absent painting, an 18" DBH threshold parameter on paper gives a less-than-honest logger the opportunity to cut trees that are 16 and 17" DBH, even though he has not paid you for them. You will not be able to tell from an unpainted stump whether the DBH was at least 18".

Photograph 23-1 shows the location of two blue dots on a double stump two years after cutting.

PHOTOGRAPH 23-1

Double Painted Stump

You might consider saying, "Timber to be sold includes all trees at least 20" at the stump." This formula, however, still gives a logger some leeway to cheat if he is so disposed since trees at the stump are rarely perfectly round. If such a logger wanted to cut down to 17 or 18" at the stump, the only way you would catch the theft is by identifying each and every undersized tree that he took. This involves hiring a forester to do a **stump cruise**, which provides an estimate of the volume (by species) and value of the undersized timber the logger took. Rather than fight in court over the findings of a stump cruise, you will do better to paint only the trees you want cut. If you find a stump without a paint dot on its stump, the logger removed that tree without paying you for it.

5. **Decide where you want landings and skid roads to be located**, or leave this to the discretion of the logger, acting within the state's recommended Best Management Practices (BMPs). Since road-building is a major time-and-cost factor to a logger, you need to supply a sketch of your road plan on a topographical map so that buyers will be able to factor the expense of your plan into their bid for your timber. Don't try to work up a road plan on your own. Involve the county forester. If you leave the design of landings and skid roads to the logger, your roads will be built to minimize logging time and cost. This usually means straight and steep. In terms of erosion control and aesthetics, your land benefits from roads that are less steep and less straight. The degree of less straightness needs to be balanced against safety and accessibility. If you're planning to use these roads for 4WD vehicles after the logging, keep in mind that loggers will "design" roads for their bulldozers and skidders that will be too difficult for your type of traffic. Work with the logger to construct roads that meet both his purposes and yours. Once the logging is done, you will value gradual climbs, wide turns and roadbeds that promote drainage by being graded slightly to pitch to the downhill side. It may take a logger a little extra time to build roads this way, and, if so, it's fair to pay him by the hour for the effort he spends on your behalf.

Stream crossings should be put in where banks are shallow to minimize erosion. It's better environmentally to have log trucks crossing a stream than skidders dragging logs through it. The county forester can help you design stream crossings, culvert placement and the landings where logs are stockpiled, sorted, trimmed and loaded onto trucks.

Your road plan should be distributed as part of your sale packet. It should show where you want landings, stream crossings, culverts (including length, diameter and pipe material), turnarounds and any additional grading and excavation.

Be forewarned. Timber buyers and loggers like simplicity, freedom of operation and the absence of landowner interference. If you load them down with a lot of extras, you won't get the best money for your timber, or you will get fewer bidders than you expected.

Most loggers will be familiar with road-building BMPs and do not want to knock heads with the state forestry agency over violations. Your plan is valid to the extent that it is your idea about what you want, but you should be open and willing to negotiate with the stumpage buyer who is likely to know more than you do. Include your plan as a suggestion rather than a requirement.

6. **Identify and mark any trees that you want to save**, particularly those that fit into your cutting criteria. Paint them stump and butt with a different color paint and wrap a plastic ribbon around them. If those signs are ambiguous, spray paint, "No" on the tree and the stump.

In the Contract you provide in the sales packet, make sure to include the following provisions:

7. **Establish that the buyer agrees to follow all local, state and federal laws, and that he will comply with all Best Management Practices (BMPs)**. Some states require BMP compliance; others recommend compliance. Your contract can require compliance in states that don't, but you may trigger grumbling and discounted bids. The logger may have a valid quarrel on particular points in light of the

specifics of your property. If you require BMP compliance and then agree to a couple of exceptions, note them in writing and attach the amendment to your timber-sale contract.

8. **Establish who will pay for certain expenses** attendant to logging, e.g., culverts, permits and gravel/rock at entrance and stream crossings.

9. **Set forth liabilities**. The logger should be responsible for any injury (to people and livestock) and property damage that arises from his logging operations. He should repair at his expense any damage to your fences and your neighbors' fences, buildings, roads, public property, utility lines, etc. If you clearcut a very steep hillside and flooding occurs, the landowner is likely to be found the guilty party, not the logger.

10. **Set forth payment schedule**. All money upfront, before any logging begins, is what you want. Include in your contract a provision: "Full payment is due seller when this contract takes effect." The effective date should be the day when the last required signature is added to the contract. If you are doing **shares with the logger**, you will be paid as he delivers your logs to a mill. Do not do shares; see discussion below. If you are being paid in installments, set forth the amount of and date due for each one. If there is a penalty for late payment, make sure to spell out the details in writing.

11. **No partnership.** Make sure to include a provision that the logger's work on your land for your mutual benefit creates neither a partnership nor a joint liability between you and him.

12. **Establish length of logging "window."** Loggers prefer to have more time to log rather than less. Winter logging is preferred because the sap is down, making for a better quality log and easier skidding. A two-or three-year window gives the timber buyer a chance to time the market and catch an upswing in prices. A 12- to 18-month window is standard for jobs involving less than 200,000 bf or so.

13. **Slash height**. Your woodland will shed its cutover look if you require the logger to cut slash to lay within four feet of the ground. Loggers, however, want to leave slash as is because cutting it green is hard, dangerous, time-consuming, unproductive and costly work. Many loggers will refuse to bid a tract that requires them to lop the slash. Others will lower their bid—by a lot. I recommend that you let the logger leave the slash as is. After the timbering is done hire a couple of guys to lop it down on an hourly basis or in return for the firewood if it offends your eye. Sometimes a chipper company will come in after logging and clean up the property.

14. **Subcontractors and assigns**. Ask the stumpage buyer or logger to whom you sell your timber whether he is planning to subcontract the logging. If so, you want to make sure that the subcontractor has a copy of the timber-sale contract and follows whatever prescriptions you've included. Generally, your interests will be best served if you prohibit subcontracting.

15. **Cut all painted culls**. The stumpage buyer will remove all painted trees of value to him. If your contract provides that painted culls are to be cut, the stumpage buyer may or may not remove them, depending on whether it's profitable. The logger doesn't have to remove the culls for your remaining trees to get the benefit of reduced competition. You do need, however, to make sure that the logger understands that he is expected to cut all painted trees, including culls. A logger can drop trees faster than you can; even so, you should expect a small discount for the time he spends on this job if he's not removing them.

16. **Clean up**. You want to make sure the logger seeds all skid roads and landings with the appropriate grass mixture. BMPs will suggest other practices that should be applied to reduce environmental impacts after logging. The county forester can tell you what the standard grass mix is and the proper spreading ratio in pounds per acre. If you need a shade-tolerant grass on some roads, you can pay the logger for the difference in seed price. The logger should be expected to remove logging-related trash—oil cans, garbage, etc.—and not drain machine fluids on your ground.

Loggers will leave stubs from logs they've trimmed for length or quality. These will be left in a pile on the landing where the logs were loaded. You can give them away for firewood or burn the pile where it's safe to do so. Loggers don't want to involve themselves in burning stubs or slash.

Photograph 23-2 shows stubs left on a graded and seeded log landing.

PHOTOGRAPH 23-2

Log Landing

17. **Right to Reject**. Include a clear statement in your package that the seller reserves the right to reject any and all bids.

The discussion above assumes that you are a landowner who is selling his timber directly to a stumpage buyer or logger without the assistance of a consulting forester. I advise against selling timber this way, because the buyer, who does such deals on a daily basis, is far smarter about timber deal-making that you and I are together. The **Owner-Buyer Contract** that I've provided at the end of this chapter assumes the involvement of a consulting forester. If you insist on acting as a timber FSBO, the points that I've discussed are basic to a timber-sale contract. I would advise having a local lawyer help draft the contract. Don't sign a contract provided by the stumpage buyer without review by your lawyer.

I advise against being a timber FSBO, because you will be expected to know more than you can know and do things that you've probably never done before. Too many opportunities exist for mistakes. Managing and marketing a timber sale are business activities that require a combination of local experience, personal contacts, a track record that buyers trust and specialized knowledge. Even knowing something about this process, I would not take on this job. Stumpage buyers will be reluctant to bid competitively in a FSBO-orchestrated sale. They will, however, try to negotiate bilaterally for your timber. The odds are high that you will not get the best money for your timber acting as your own agent.

The second way of selling timber *that I advise against* is **working shares with an independent logger**. These deals use different payment formulas. The most common is for the logger to split what he gets as his delivered income with you, 60-40, or 50-50. Another is to guarantee you a certain price per thousand board feet for each species with your share of income depending on the volume he sells. Another is to propose a split of sales revenue after deducting his costs. In theory, working shares appears to be a reasonable approach since you are dividing revenues according to a fixed formula. Working shares involves no work on your part, and you save paying a consulting forester his commission.

If your logger is honorable, as a number are, he will cut exactly what you want, deliver every board foot that he cuts, tally every cent that is received, provide accurate records to you of every transaction and pay you on a timely basis with checks that don't bounce. However, the incentives for a logger working shares to short the landowner are as substantial as the opportunities are numerous. The logger necessarily gathers all sales receipts from the mill, which are typically stuck in his front shirt pocket. Obviously, if he does not report all sales or all sales revenue to you, you will be receiving your rightful share of a wrongful total. It is easy to toss a few receipt tickets into the woodstove at night; you'll never know. If this logger cut and sold 100,000 board feet of cherry from your land but only reports selling 95,000, at $1,000 mbf, he pockets $5,000 that he would otherwise have had to split. If you wave your cruise in his face showing 100,000 bf, he will simply say that a cruise is an estimate and the timber "just didn't cut out that good." Don't count on getting his mill buyers to confirm his sales. Sawmills are very reluctant to get between a logger—with whom they regularly work—and a landowner, particularly a newcomer. You should not expect to be able to get the sawmill to send you copies of the sales tickets your logger hauls from your land. When your logger is selling your timber to more than one mill, which is typical, it's impossible for you to track sales.

A variation on the burned-ticket tactic is even simpler. Instead of hauling all your logs to a mill, he dumps a load or two at the back of his own property or, slyer yet, on the landing of his next job. A few weeks after he's finished your job, he sells your logs for his own account. Even if you were to find his stash, it would be next to impossible for you to prove these logs came from your land.

There's always the possibility of a **piggy-back payment scam** between an unscrupulous mill and an unscrupulous logger. You'll never see the pea in this shell game. It can work like this: The mill is paying about $450 mbf for hard maple, but the mill cuts a receipt to your logger for your maple logs using $375 mbf. That income is then split with you according to your contract. The logger provides you with copies of all scale tickets showing volume (or weight) and receipts. The mill also slips your logger $50 mbf off the books. Two of the three parties win: the mill has bought your maple volume for $25 mbf less than it would otherwise pay. Your logger is now getting as his share $237.50 mbf ($375/2 = $187.50 + $50 = $237.50) rather than $225 ($450/2 = $225). The $50 he gets off the books will not be declared on his taxes. But you have lost $37.50 mbf. Why would the logger cheat for $37.50? Because over many thousands of board feet, a little cheating adds up to a lot of money, undeclared for taxes. If you get wind of this collusion—a very unlikely possibility—the mill will tell you that it paid $375 mbf for your maple because it found "quality problems" in the logs that were apparent only when they were graded at the mill on delivery. The mill had no choice but to discount the price they paid to your logger. How prevalent is this type of collusion? I can't say.

A third reason to avoid working shares is that it encourages the logger to high-grade your timber. Assume the logger is completely honest. He will do best for himself on your job if he cuts only your most valuable timber. This will not gross the most money, but it will be the most profitable approach from his perspective because he will invest the least amount of time and effort, and incur the least cost. For example, it is clearly in his interest to gross $100,000 by high-grading 100,000 bf of hardwood sawtimber at $1,000 mbf than to gross $105,000 on the sale of 200,000 bf priced at an average of $525 mbf. He and you will get $50,000 each in the first instance, and $52,500 in the second. But the logger will have spent the same amount of time to cut the last $5,000 on 200,000 bf as he did to cut the first $100,000 on the high-graded

100,000 bf. From his perspective, the extra income ($2,500) is gained only by doubling his investment in work, time and expense. From your perspective, you gain $2,500 from the trees you want cut so as to improve your remaining high-value trees by eliminating competition. You might get the logger to drop the trees, but don't expect that he will haul them out for sale.

Don't fall for the line: "I'll just do a selective cut and split the money with you 50-50." That's a high-grading proposition.

Doing shares never gives the landowner a guaranteed amount of money. You are being promised only a fixed percentage of whatever the logger reports as revenue in the sale of your timber to buyers of his choosing. Prices fluctuate at mills, and different mills scale the quality and board feet of arriving timber a little differently. An independent logger faced with the choice of hauling to three mills—the first pays a bit more per 1,000 bf but scales board feet short; the second pays a bit less per 1,000 bf but scales higher; and the third does a little of both—may choose wrong and end up with $500 less per load than had he chosen better. Independent loggers tend to have firm opinions and long memories about timber buyers and mills. The logger you pick may simply like the people at the lower-price mill better than those at the higher-price mill and persist in selling there even though he—and you—make less money.

Even when you have a cruise showing, say, $100,000 worth of hardwood sawtimber 18" DBH, you won't be able to hold a shares logger to guaranteeing you a fixed sum. The logger won't know what your logs are actually worth until he sells them. Uncertainty is always a factor in timber sales—prices fluctuate, standing timber that looks solid may be hollow or have invisible insect damage, the highest-priced mill may be overstocked with the species that you're selling. Working shares is always a roll-of-the-dice arrangement. You're gambling on the logger's integrity, his judgment in marketing your logs, local prices, local inventory surpluses and a dozen other factors. All you have is a fixed percent of some number to be determined by several others, at least one of whom may want to short you every so often.

I am not anti-logger. They work hard at a necessary and dangerous job. I don't begrudge them a living. I understand that every forest product I use first requires a logger to cut a tree. I've done enough woods work to appreciate what that means. The position I assume in this book is to be pro-landowner. And my best advice to landowners is to hire a consulting forester to manage a timber sale rather than work directly on your own with an independent logger.

James Fazio, author of an excellent how-to guide for managing a small woodlot, wrote: "Many people entrust the welfare of their woodlot to a logger on the basis of a handshake. This is as absurd as selling a crop without measuring it. Even with a solid contract there is rarely a perfect marriage between logger and landowner." (James R. Fazio, <u>The Woodland Steward: A Practical Guide to the Management of Small Private Forests</u>, 2nd ed. [Moscow, Idaho, The Woodland Press, 1987], pp. 93-94.)

For these reasons, I advise against both any do-it-yourself, FSBO timber-selling strategy and working shares with a logger. The dirt-smart timber owner tries to strip risk and uncertainty out of the sale of his timber. Direct marketing and working shares is heavy with both. The "savings" you project on a timber sale by not paying a consulting forester is likely to be entirely theoretical. Let me work through the numbers for several ways of selling timber to make my point:

1. Consultant-Managed, Competitively Bid Lump-Sum Sale.

You've paid for a pre-purchase cruise that shows 100,000 bf at $100,000 in stumpage on a $300,000 property. Your forester charges ten percent to manage a **competitively bid marked (painted) sale**. Depending on weather and ground conditions, it can take three to four days for an experienced forester to paint and tally 100,000 bf on the stump. Price research and preparing the bid package (map, inventory, bid form, contract) will take another couple of days. The inventory he distributes is based on the volume he estimates in every tree that he marks for sale, grouped by species and two-inch diameter class.

Let's say the highest bid is exactly $100,000. From this gross of $100,000, you pay your forester ten percent—$10,000. Your pre-tax net income is $90,000. His fee is tax-deductible. Since your pre-purchase cruise valued the stumpage at $100,000, you had no taxable event when you sold it for what you paid for it. The $100,000 is paid to you in a lump sum before any logging starts.

2. 50-50 Split with an Independent Logger.

For you to make $90,000 on a 50-50 split with a logger, he will have to sell your 100,000 bf of stumpage, cut and hauled to a mill as logs, for $180,000. Stumpage price as a percentage of delivered price at the mill varies over time according to species, market conditions, inventories and other factors. Delivered price for hardwood sawtimber is rarely twice stumpage value. (On pulp cuts, however, delivered price can easily exceed stumpage price.) Delivered price in this example might be $130,000 to $160,000, with your share at $65,000 to $80,000 tops. Less than $80,000 is more likely.

3. Negotiated Unilateral Sale to Mill.

If you negotiate unilaterally with a single buyer for this stumpage, my guess is you will be offered $80,000 to $85,000 tops. That's $5,000 to $10,000 less than what the consultant is likely to net for you in a competitive sealed-bid sale. A negotiated sale with an independent logger will net you even less than that, perhaps $70,000 to $75,000.

4. **FSBO-Managed Competitively Bid Sale**.

This one is hard to estimate, because so many variables are in play. I see no upside on the $90,000. I anticipate buyers reluctant to get involved with an amateur, discounted bids, misunderstandings and contract disputes. Maybe, $60,000 in your pocket.

5. **Negotiated Sale with a Custom or "Alternative" Logger.**

If you are not interested in getting the best money for your timber, you can research the "alternative-logging" options available in your area.

I've found three types of alternative loggers that you might consider.

There is, first, the **"piddler."** He is a fellow in his 50s or 60s who's been around logging all his life, has some basic equipment and wants to make enough to get by. Left to his own devices, he will generally high-grade a tract, but very slowly. He usually works shares and is happy to have freed himself from the pressure to make as much as possible from each job. He might work by himself or with one other person. I've seen a couple of husband-wife teams make a living working four or five hours a day in good weather.

Second, there are the **loggers with portable sawmills**. One buyer I know buys stumpage and then subs logging and sawing to independent Amish crews. I've also seen a portable mill outfit buy a tract and sub the logging. From an owner's perspective, this amounts to a unilateral negotiated sale.

The third "alternative" I've seen is **horse-logging**, which has environmental benefits. Horse-logging works best financially where the landowner wants to cut a small number of scattered high-value trees rather than large volumes. On 100,000 bf of stumpage, I don't think a horse-logger could submit a competitive bid against a conventional machine logger.

CONSULTANT-MANAGED SALE—SAMPLE CONSULTANT CONTRACT

In almost all circumstances, I would recommend selling timber through a consulting forester who works in the area. It's my experience that a good forester will increase the gross revenue of your timber sale by more than enough to cover the cost of his commission. Your sale expenses—his commission—are tax-deductible, but your time in arranging a sale is not. Moreover, his counsel and presence should leave your property in as good as shape as can be expected at the end of the cutting. The butchered cutover tracts I've seen are almost always done on shares and without a forester helping a buyer.

The key to getting the best money from your sale is competition among buyers. Your sale has to be packaged to make it attractive to at least two or three buyers who want to do essentially the same thing with your logs. Packaging involves including trees that will be valued and excluding some trees that will lead buyers to discount their bids. Your consultant can cover his fee simply by packaging your sale correctly to the local market. Stumpage sales, with the exception of certain high-value logs for the export market, always follow local marketing and contract mores. You will not know these practices, and you probably won't be able to learn them on your own. If you package your timber incorrectly and include unusual or complex language in your contract, you will scare off buyers. Local knowledge and local buyer contacts that are built up over time are your forester's key to maximizing your sale's revenue. If you live four states away from your rural property and hire a forester from where you live to handle your timber sale, he may come in with methods and ideas that are unfamiliar in your timber's local market. You need not hire the forester who lives closest to your property or even one who lives in the same county or state. But you do need to hire a forester who is actively working in your local market with your property's timber types. Stumpage buyers prefer negotiated bilateral sales with landowners, but they will participate in a competitively bid sale managed by a forester whose inventory methods they've come to trust and who manages the sale honestly. A forester who opens bids privately will not be trusted by buyers. Too much incentive exists for the forester to work a sweetheart deal with a preferred buyer. Bids should be opened at the job site, publicly, with bidders in attendance.

Your forester cannot guarantee that your timber will sell for the value he estimates after doing a cruise or even a marked inventory. The buyer he thinks is most likely to bid the highest may not bid at all owing to an unexpected surplus of logs at his mill of the species you're selling. While any particular sale can be depressed by factors operating on individual buyers, your forester should have a track record that shows his pre-sale valuations for landowners are pretty close to the winning sale bids.

Wherever your property is, the steps that a consulting forester will follow in handling your timber sale are linear and familiar to stumpage buyers of all sizes:

1. **Sum up the timber stand**. You should have this done before submitting a purchase offer. If you didn't, you need to decide with your forester's help whether you want to market the sale using a cruise (an estimate), marked inventory (tree-by-tree tally, which is more accurate than a cruise) or as is, letting each buyer submit a bid without any landowner-supplied framework. I advise against the last of these alternatives in almost all circumstances, because it leaves you without any sense of the value of what you're marketing. Where an as-it-is approach can work is with an even-age, one-species tract, all of which would be sold for a single purpose. A forester does not need to cruise or mark a 50-acre tract of 23-year-old loblolly pine (with 500 trees to the acre and an average diameter of 16 inches) whose only market is pulp. He can estimate volume and sales value with a paper and pencil in about five minutes.

2. **Sign a contract with the forester authorizing him to sell your timber for you.** This occurs after you purchase the property, not before. The contract specifies what the forester will do, his compensation and the approximate time-frame. The forester will be acting as your agent in this sale, which means he should have no interest higher than getting you the best money from the most responsible buyer.

3. **Establish the boundaries of the property and flag them on the ground.**

4. **Mark and inventory the sale timber.** If you decide to market the timber through a marked sale (instead of using a cruise), your forester will paint each sale tree stump and butt. As he marks the sawtimber according to your sale criteria, he will tally the number of trees he's painting and group their volumes by species and diameter class.

5. **Prepare a sale packet/bid package/prospectus**, including:

    - **Topographical map** with property boundaries; access to property will be shown or described;

    - **Inventory of sale timber** to be sold. Volumes will be disaggregated by species and diameter class;

    - **Forester's Road plan**, if needed;

    - **Schedule**, indicating when the forester is inviting buyers to view the property with him, along with the date and location of the public bid opening. Other visiting arrangements can be made.

    - **Bid Format and Submission Date.** Sealed bids are the usual format. The forester will include a bid sheet that requires a buyer's signature. The bid should be put in a sealed envelope. Bids received after the forester's stated deadline will not be accepted. Bids can be mailed to your forester, faxed or submitted in person in a sealed envelope at the bid opening. Bids should always be opened in public where every buyer can see the bids of his competitors.

    - **Timber-Sale Contract**, which is the legal document that establishes the terms of the sale between you, the owner of the timber, and the buyer.

    - **Notice to all bidders** of the consequences of submitting a bid that the seller accepts which the winner then fails to perfect by not paying his bid amount and/or signing the timber-sale contract.

6. **Coordinate signing of the timber-sale contract and delivery of payment.** Questions and uncertainties will be cleared up at this meeting.

7. **Inspect logging in progress as landowner's representative.** Your forester doesn't oversee or manage the logging, but he should visit every so often. Problems can be worked out on the ground. Your forester will protect you from unpainted trees being cut and BMPs not being followed.

8. **Perform a final inspection just before logger leaves.** Final grading and reseeding should be confirmed, if not already in progress.

Selling through a consulting forester will involve a forest landowner in two separate contracts, one between you and your forester which precedes the other between you and the timber buyer.

The contract between you and your forester that appears below assumes that he has completed a cruise for you, which you relied on in purchasing your property. Your timber-sale contract with him should look something like this:

CONTRACT WITH CONSULTING FORESTER

This Contract is made between John Smith, 111 Universal Drive, Bigcity, New York, 20005, Owner, and William Green, Mountain Forestry Consultants, P.C., 345 Beta St., Woodland, PA, 15555, Agent, for the following professional services with respect to the Owner's property and timber, located on the west side of Rt. 600, three miles north of Woodland, Pa, and more particularly described as 100.00 acres conveyed to Owner by Deed of April 1, 2002, recorded in the Blake County (PA) Courthouse, DB 66, PN 578, whose boundaries are shown on the recorded survey appended as Attachment 1, and more particularly that 96.52 acres of the Owner's 100.00 acres that lie north of Clear Creek and which contain the stand of timber from which its merchantable portion will be sold for a lump sum:

1. Agent affirms that he is a professional forester licensed in Pennsylvania and agrees to the following:

A. That in return for ten (10) percent of the gross selling price of the Owner's Timber-Sale Inventory, payable on the date the Owner receives payment for his Sale Inventory, the Agent will represent the Owner and his interests in performing the following tasks:

1.) Mark with orange ribbon the boundaries of the Owner's stand that is being sold;

2.) Paint stump and butt all trees that Agent and Owner agree are included in the Sale Inventory, according to these criteria:

    a. All hardwood sawtimber 18" DBH and larger for the following species: _____

    b. All softwood sawtimber 16" DBH and larger;

    c. All hardwood pulp defined as _____; and

    d. All softwood pulp defined as _____.

    e. All log scales and other parameters used to tally volume shall be those most likely to be used by local timber buyers.

    f. Culls shall ___ shall not ___ be marked for cutting.

3.) Tally and group the sawtimber volume in board feet by species and two-inch diameter class; by cords for all pulpwood.

4.) Prepare a Sale Inventory that aggregates sawtimber volumes by species and two-inch diameter class; by cords for pulpwood.

5.) Prepare a Bid Packet for Owner's Sale, which includes:

    a. Contract between Owner and Timber Buyer; [This may or may not be included in Bid Packet; see below for one version. Follow the forester's advice on whether or not to include it.]

    b. Timber Sale Inventory;

    c. Survey of Owner's Property if available;

d. Topographical map of Owner's Property, showing boundary lines, sale stand areas (shaded in blue), Buyer's access point (s) and any no-logging areas (shaded in red);

e. Directions to and road map showing location of property;

f. Schedule of time and dates for property inspection when Agent will be on site;

g. Sealed-bid Schedule—setting forth time/date deadline for receipt of sealed bids; time and location of public opening of all timely bids by Agent;

h. Description of Sealed Bid procedure;

    (1.) Date and location of signing of timber-sale contract;

    (2.) Forms of acceptable bidding;

    (3.) Forms of acceptable payment;

    (4.) Time and place of signing of Owner's Contract with Timber Buyer;

    (5.) Buyer's payment shall be made directly to Owner at time of signing, unless otherwise provided herein_____.

i. Road Plan, needed____ not needed_____. If needed, Road Plan to be laid out with Owner and implemented with Timber Buyer.

6.) Market Owner's Timber-Sale Inventory to all likely buyers;

7.) Show property on at least one scheduled viewing date and, if necessary, by arrangement;

8.) Conduct sealed-bid auction for Owner's Sale;

9.) Provide Owner with results of sealed-bid auction. If Owner does not accept high bid, Owner and Agent will jointly determine their next steps. If Owner decides that he no longer wants to sell his Sale Inventory through Agent, Owner agrees to pay Agent for his receipted expenses, mileage at $.__ per mile, and time, at the rate of $__ per hour, spent in preparing and marketing Owner's sale through the last consultation with Owner.

10.) Provide periodic inspections of Buyer's logging of Owner's timber, exercising such authority as Agent is provided under Owner's contract with Buyer.

11.) Advise and consult with Owner throughout the process of selling and removing his timber, as needed;

12.) Prepare __ not prepare __ Management Plan for Owner that incorporates Owner's objectives for the Timber Sale and future uses of property.

2. Owner warrants that he has clear title to said property and an unencumbered right to sell any and all of its timber to a Buyer procured by the Agent. Owner further warrants that no liens, easements, claims, reservations or encumbrances, financial or otherwise, restrict his ability to sell this timber through the Agent.

3. Owner agrees to the terms of compensation for the Agent as set forth above.

4. Owner warrants that the boundary lines as set forth on the survey (Attachment 1) are accurate to the best of his knowledge.

5. Owner warrants that he knows of no dispute over the location of any boundary line. [If a dispute does exist that cannot be resolved, the Owner should inform the Agent of that fact and

instruct him not to paint trees in the disputed area.]

6. Owner agrees that Agent bears no liability for trees Agent paints in any area the Owner falsely or mistakenly represents as his. Agent bears no liability for the accuracy of deed calls or survey measurements, but does bear responsibility for accurately marking these lines on the ground.

7. Owner agrees to allow Agent access free access to his property during the term of this Contract.

8. Agent may not sign a Timber-Sale Contract on behalf of the Owner, except in the following circumstances:_____.

9. No partnership is created by this Agency agreement. Agent is not liable for: 1) fulfilling the obligations of the Owner's Contract with the timber Buyer, 2) failing to fulfill these obligations or 3) satisfying any debts Owner incurs during the Agent's work for him.

10. Owner agrees that Agent is held harmless for any damage or injury to any property or party that occurs during work on the Owner's property during the term of this Contract, except for those caused by negligent or reckless acts of Agent. Agent agrees that Owner is held harmless for any damage or injury to any property or party of the Agent's during the course of his work for the Owner.

11. The Contract shall come into effect on the date of the signature of the second signing Party.

12. The term of this Contract shall run from the date of effect through the date on which the Buyer of the Owner's timber finishes his work, or on any other mutually agreeable date herein set forth _____ .

13. This Contract is binding on both parties, their heirs, executors and administrators during its term. If the Agent dies or is incapacitated, the Owner may employ another Agent and pay the first Agent, or his estate, and the second Agent in proportion to the work each did.

14. This Contract may be amended only in writing.

15. The laws of the Commonwealth of Pennsylvania shall govern this Contract.

16. Owner and Agent agree to try to resolve any dispute arising between them during the term of this Contract without resort to litigation.

17. Parties agree ____ not agree ___ to submit any dispute they cannot themselves resolve to binding arbitration by an arbitrator they select from a panel made available through XYZ Association of Arbitrators. Arbitration expenses and fees shall be divided equally.

18. Notarized signatures are___ are not ____ required.

19. Facsimile copies with signature and date are____ are not____ acceptable to both Parties.

_____ (Owner) _____ (Agent)
Address   Address
Phone   Phone
Fax   Fax
Date _____   Date _____

Contract language differs from region to region, state to state, timber type to timber type and consultant to consultant. The contract your consultant hands you will not read exactly like the one above, but it should cover most of the same issues. My sample contract is likely to be more detailed and more "lawyered up" than the one your consultant uses. A simpler version may be all that you need. The layers of detail that I added are there if you think you need them. This contract language is owner-oriented. Your consultant may have a contract that is skewed more toward his protection. In that event, you will have to hammer out any differences you think are important. Some owners, perhaps you, prefer language that leaves areas of potential conflict vague or unaddressed. I find security in writing solutions in advance of their emergence as problems. If, however, you insist on a soup-to-nuts contract drafted by the guy who teaches contracts at Yale Law School (who happens to be your old college roommate), you may find that no consultant wants to sign it. Sample consultant contracts are available from forestry departments at land-grant universities, professional forestry societies, forest landowner groups, county foresters and in Beattie *et al.*, Working With Your Woodland, Chapter 3.

The premise of this sample Owner-Consultant contract is that the sale of your timber will result in a lump-sum, full-price payment in advance of any cutting. This is almost always the best method from the landowner's point of view. You may, however, find yourself in a situation where the timber's revenue will be paid in several stages. In that case, you may need to ask your consultant to become more involved in the sale. If you are being paid a percentage of what is being sold at a mill, you may want to ask your forester to monitor the cutting-hauling to assure full payment.

TIMBER-SALE CONTRACT

With your consultant contract in place, you and (mostly) he will jointly prepare a second contract that sets forth the terms of the timber sale between you and the timber buyer, with your forester acting as your agent. I advise against a landowner using a **timber-sale contract** supplied by the stumpage buyer. Your consultant will have a generic contract that he uses, which may or may not be adequate for your purposes. Do not assume that because you earn a living merging and acquiring billion-dollar businesses, that your innate savvy will protect you in a timber sale. In the absence of a carefully thought through contract prepared with the help of a consulting forester, you are likely to be plucked by a logger who thinks an M&A is the almond version of an M&M.

In addition to your consultant's standard timber-sale contract, you can get samples from your county forester, forest landowner groups, forestry extension faculty and in two books, Beattie *et al.*, Working with Your Woodland and Minckler, Woodland Ecology: Environmental Forestry for the Small Owner, 2nd ed. Another publication with much useful contract information is The Forestry Conservation Circular, Vol. 21, No. 5, most recent edition, "Woodlandowner's Guide to Selling Timber and Timber Sale Contracts," prepared by the Department of Natural Resources, Cornell University, Ithaca, NY. See also the Virginia Department of Forestry's, "Selling Timber," at www.dof.state.va.us/mgt/saletimb.htm.

These sample contracts, as well as the one I've drafted, are helpful in orienting you to the contract issues you should consider, but the particulars of your sale—timber type, species mix, volume mix, topography, access, stand density, haulage distance to mill and any post-logging uses you envision—will determine contract language beyond the generic. It may be necessary for you to work with both your consultant and a local lawyer, though the latter will probably be needed more for a final reading and less for a start-from-scratch drafting.

Your forester and your timber-sale contract should protect you against harmful timber-harvesting practices, but not against timber harvesting itself—which is the point of the sale. You cannot expect your land to look the same after logging as before. If you load a contract with restrictions and extras, the best buyer money may not bid at all. You need to find a balance in your thinking and then in the contract between what is fair to ask a stumpage buyer to do (consistent with him making a profit) and what is not. In the contracts I've signed, I've usually wanted the buyer either to remove the "top log" or lop the slash to a four-foot height for aesthetics. Several buyers have refused to do this, though a couple were willing "to work with me" on the slash nearest the roads. These stumpage buyers did not want to cut and haul anything other than the sawtimber logs. The pulp/slash work would have cost them time and probably money. I was persuaded to not include a slash-lopping provision in my contracts.

I now think it's better from a landowner's perspective to not write a top log/lop slash provision into your contract because of the bidding discount you will suffer. The slash will rot down in seven to ten years. You can sell or give it away for firewood. I advise getting the best money from your sale and then dealing with the slash separately if it annoys you.

Every timber-sale contract is a legal document that involves payment, mutual expectations, and issues of liability and responsibility. It should contain the language necessary to protect the interests of the landowner/seller. In the contract I've drafted below, I've placed an * in front of those contract clauses that are more law than forestry. Your local lawyer should pay them particular scrutiny.

This sample timber-sale contract is not one that I suggest you rip and use. Consider it as an exercise to raise issues that you may face in the context of a contract.

A consulting forester with whom I've worked for a number of years reviewed my language and suggested changes that I've placed in italics. He thought some of my language was unnecessary or duplicative of state BMP requirements, or harmful, or so restrictive that stumpage buyers would boycott/bid down the sale. I have placed in brackets my commentary on the language in a particular section and my friend's thoughts. His general point: every ounce of restriction that a contract places on a timber buyer may produce a pound of bid discount. Enough ounces will produce no bids and an aborted sale. This sample contract, then, is a way for you, a landowner, to think about what's important to you and how much it's worth.

TIMBER-SALE CONTRACT

This Contract is made between John Smith, 111 Universal Drive, Bigcity, New York, 20005, herein, Seller, and Big Tree Sawmill, Rt 1, Woodland, PA, 15555, herein, Buyer, for the purchase and sale of the following timber:

1. Seller agrees to sell all trees painted or otherwise marked for sale by William Green, Mountain Forestry Consultants, P.C., 345 Beta St., Woodland, PA, 15555, Agent for the Seller, on the Seller's property located on the west side of Rt. 600, three miles north of Woodland, PA.

The sale property is further defined as a portion of the tract of 100.00 acres conveyed to the Seller by Deed of April 1, 2002, recorded in the Blake County (PA) Court House, DB 66, PN 578, whose boundaries are shown on the recorded survey appended as Attachment 1 and further shown on the topographical map prepared by Agent, appended as Attachment 2.

Of the Seller's 100 acres, 96.52 acres are included in this sale. The sale area is colored blue on the topographical map (Attachment 2), and represents the land of the Seller that lies north of Clear Creek.

Buyer's access to the Seller's property is restricted to the gated road that joins Rt. 600 at the large white oak and which is further identified by three orange ribbons on said oak. No other access to Seller's property is permitted.

Buyer may use that portion of Seller's land that he needs to construct roads, landing areas and the like, subject to state reclamation provisions and this Contract. Agent must approve the design of Buyer-constructed roads and landings before Buyer

installs them.

2. "Sale Inventory" represents all merchantable timber to be sold as set forth, a total of 120,685 bf hardwood sawtimber (18" DBH and larger) and 49,940 bf softwood sawtimber (16" DBH and larger) in the following volumes as shown below and on the Seller's Sale Inventory (Attachment 3):

    a. Hardwood sawtimber, 18" DBH and larger

Red Oak	43,565 bf
White Oak	15,610 bf
Scarlet Oak	10,250 bf
Black Oak	5,240 bf
Bear Oak	4,355 bf
Chestnut Oak	3,225 bf
Pin Oak	2,785 bf
Black Cherry	10,475 bf
White Ash	7,995 bf
Hickory	3,445 bf
Hard Maple	6,260 bf
Soft Maple	5,780 bf
Misc.	1,700 bf (includes Cucumber, Basswood, Black Birch)
Total	120,685 bf hardwood sawtimber

    b. Softwood sawtimber 16" DBH and larger, including

White Pine	32,250 bf
E. Hemlock	17,690 bf
Total	49,940 bf

c. Hardwood pulp:	1,150 cords
d. Softwood pulp:	687 cords

[COMMENT: Most contracts specify what is being sold. In this case, my forester believes that it would be a mistake to specify the volumes by species being sold—despite selling the tract as a marked sale—because the owner/seller would be vulnerable to a lawsuit if, for whatever reason, the buyer came to believe that the specified volumes were either not present or not harvestable. Prior to the contract being signed, each buyer will have made his own on-site determination about stumpage volumes and values. The landowner's consultant will have marketed the sale with the disclaimer that no guarantees were being offered by the seller to the buyers, and that each buyer was responsible for his own evaluation of the tract's timber. I agree with the forester on this point. Don't include inventory numbers in your Contract.

"Sale inventory" in Section 2 would be better described simply as "All painted trees with no guarantee of volume, quality or value."

3. All sawtimber and pulpwood trees included in the sale are painted twice with orange dots, one on the stump and one at about 4.5 feet above the ground.

The Buyer shall remove all painted trees during the Contract's term.

[COMMENT: This language requires the removal of all pulpwood logs from trees the

forester has painted. A buyer may refuse to bid on the sale because of this requirement. Alternatively, you can require that all painted trees be felled, and leave it to the buyer as to whether or not their logs are removed. You can, of course, say nothing about removal and felling, which is the buyer's preference. If there are 50 pulpwood/cull trees on a tract where, for instance, more than 200 sawtimber trees are being sold, having the buyer cut them is not a deal-killer or much of a discount factor. Having him remove the cull logs, however, could be. Your forester can suggest the best approach. You may do best by removing the pulp/cull cutting requirement and simply pay a neighbor to drop the unwanted trees after the timbering is done.]

No unpainted tree shall be cut, except for trees felled in the building of skid roads *and landings and those inadvertently damaged in the felling of painted trees. Buyer shall pay Seller the stumpage value of all non-painted trees 10"DBH and larger felled as liquidated damages. Agent and Buyer shall jointly determine the value of such trees. Buyer is not liable for any trees that are damaged as a result of his normal work practices that are customary in the industry. Buyer shall make a good-faith effort to protect Seller's unpainted trees during logging activities.

4. Seller does not guarantee sawtimber or pulpwood volumes and quality. Buyer acknowledges that he has had sufficient opportunity prior to signing this Contract to evaluate Seller's timber using his own methods and personnel.

Seller and his Agent bear no liability for any discrepancy between the volumes represented and the volumes cut by Buyer.

* 5. Seller warrants that he has good title to this Sale Inventory and has the right to sell it to the Buyer under the terms of this Contract.

* Seller further warrants that no liens or encumbrances exist that limit Seller's ability to sell this Inventory. Seller is permitted by the terms of his mortgage on this property with Kountrybanc of Woodland, PA to sell this timber without limitation or reserve.

[COMMENT: It is important for the seller to make whatever arrangements are necessary with his mortgage lender to allow the sale of the timber. A bank might insist that some or all of the timber-sale income be applied to the mortgage principal since the sale of the timber reduces the value of the property that secures the note. A bank might also insist that the timber not be sold unless a minimum price—a reserve— is met.]

* 6. Seller warrants that he will do nothing to restrict Buyer's rights under this Contract during its term.

7. Seller grants to Buyer permission to enter the property at any time during the term of this Contract for the purpose of inspection, assessment, tree removal, clean up, reclamation and any other such work connected to the purposes of this Contract.

* 8. The term of this Contract shall be eighteen (18) ____ twenty-four (24) ____ months from the date on which this Contract becomes effective, which is the date of the last required signature on this document.

* 9. Buyer shall reserve no rights or profit in Seller's timber at the end of this Contract or when he has finished his work, whichever comes first. Upon Contract expiration or the completion of Buyer's work, Buyer's rights under this Contract shall terminate and revert to Seller. Buyer shall then provide Seller with his signed Release of Interest,

which includes all standing timber and all logs remaining on the property.

10. Buyer shall pay Seller the lump sum of $_____ upon signing this Contract. Payment shall be made by certified funds or other method designated by Seller. This payment represents the full purchase price, unless otherwise provided in an Addendum to this Contract, mutually agreed to.

11. No tree on the Seller's property shall be cut before full payment payment is made to Seller.

12. Seller's Agent shall represent the Seller in managing this Sale, including inspecting the Buyer's timbering and reclamation work.

Agent shall have the right to suspend Buyer's timbering and/or reclamation work without penalty to Seller if, in his opinion, Buyer is failing to perform said work in accordance with the terms of this Contract and/or applicable law and regulation, and/or logging operations are damaging Seller's property beyond reasonable wear and tear. All Parties shall make a good-faith effort to resolve any such stoppage as quickly as possible.

Buyer shall not skid timber, haul logs or perform reclamation work when weather or ground conditions will result in severe rutting, erosion or similarly adverse environmental impact.

[COMMENT: Each forestry consultant will have developed his own timber-sale contract with language that spells out his duties and responsibilities as the seller's agent. Consultants and loggers try to get along, and generally do. A timber buyer who doesn't like the forester representing you is not likely to bid on your sale. I've known foresters who refuse to send sale notices to certain timber buyers because of past difficulties. Your contract should include language of this type, including the right to suspend the logger's operation.

Operating in wet, soft conditions, especially on slopes, will severely disturb your ground. Your consultant can recommend language that is generally accepted in the area to address this concern.]

13. Buyer shall remove each painted sawtimber tree to its lowest merchantable diameter for the products appropriate to each tree.

[COMMENT: The landowner's property will look better and be safer for vehicles if stumps are cut low.]

14. Buyer shall provide phone call ___ written notice ___ to Seller's Agent at least 24____ 48 ____ hours in advance of commencing logging on Seller's property.

[COMMENT: A phone call, rather than written notice, is usually sufficient.]

15. Buyer shall locate and construct skid roads and haulage roads under Agent's direction if no Road Plan is attached to this Contract. Existing roads shall be used wherever possible, unless Agent provides different instructions as part of this bidding process. New roads shall follow contours where possible. All roads—old and new— shall be left at least eight (8) feet wide and no more than twelve (12) feet wide where possible, except in curves and turnouts. Where possible, new roads shall be built in dry areas and avoid wet spots and mud holes.

[COMMENT: My forester thinks I'm crazy. He objects to these guidelines because they are uncommon and subjective. I agree. On the other hand, the landowner's property will be protected from road-building-caused erosion and the roads will be safe for vehicle traffic. On mountain land, you want to avoid to the extent possible straight up-and-down roads and roads dozed through wet spots. An alternative way to handle this would be to have your forester walk the property with the successful buyer and agree on a road plan.]

Seller shall leave roads in condition suitable for a 4WD vehicle. All waterbars and dips left when the logging is completed shall accommodate 4WD traffic, except where BMPs and/or Agent specifically designates otherwise. Buyer shall install waterbars and dips in accordance with BMP standards for road grade.

[COMMENT: Waterbars are one of my favorite hobby horses. I hate them. A waterbar is a trench two or three feet deep and about three feet wide that is excavated at an angle across a skid road to prevent erosion by catching water running down the road's surface and channeling it to the outslope side. A proper waterbar has steep sides, which prevent vehicle traffic. They last a long time, which is their virtue from an erosion-control point of view. A dip is a broad, shallow swag graded into a road that performs the same erosion-control function. I love dips. Your state BMPs may require waterbarring a road that need only be dipped. This is usually one of those cases where a good idea—erosion control—is implemented mindlessly. Your choices are then to 1) live with permanent inaccessibility created by the waterbars; 2) construct detours around the waterbars; or 3) convert the waterbars into dips after the inspector leaves and the logging is done. On ground that I don't want to travel, I've left the waterbars in place. Where I want to use the roads, I've taken the third option. My dipped forest roads are friendly to feet, hooves and tires. If a fire occurs, the local VFD can get to it. Had I not reclaimed the waterbars, my woods would be unusable. In a timber-sale contract, I would ask the logger to put dips in roads that I plan to use and deal with the authorities if they pick a fight. If you convert waterbars to dips, you should have a dozer touch them up every four or five years to maintain their water-carrying capacity.]

Buyer shall leave roads free of rocks and logging debris, including slash. Roads shall be left in a general condition equal to or better than their condition prior to logging.

Buyer shall rough-grade logging roads and landings before seeding with mixture approved by Agent. Areas of road prone to water collection shall be ditched and graded to facilitate drainage. Roads on hillsides shall be graded to the outslope to drain water to the downhill side. Buyer is responsible for installing ditches, culverts and gravel where needed to control erosion in consultation with Agent. No new road shall exceed a gradient of more than ten degrees without the Agent's prior approval. All trees of three (3) inches or more diameter that must be taken down in the construction of roads and landings shall be cut at the stump rather than pushed over.

[COMMENT: My forester objects to the last sentence. Loggers prefer to push trees down rather than cut them when building roads because it's faster. If you don't put this language in your contract, you are likely to find some substantial trees pushed over next to a road or left in a heap. I find pushed-over trees, with their exposed root balls, unsightly and annoying. Since this language could affect a bid, consult with your forester about whether he thinks it's necessary.

I would insist that the logger remove logging slash (tree tops) from roads. This may involve nothing more than dozing them over to the side. If slash is left on your roads, it will make them impassable. You will have to cut and remove the slash by hand or hire a bulldozer to push it away. I've done this work; it is dangerous and miserable. In most cases, loggers can fell trees away from a road or if necessary clean up after themselves. Requiring loggers to leave your roads free of slash and large rocks—and even in as good a condition as they found them—are not unreasonable measures.

Skidding logs kicks up rocks (big) and stones (smaller). The logger's final dressing of the skid roads prior to seeding should remove all of the former and many of the latter. Expect to find stones the size of large grapefruit here and there.

Some states allow loggers to comply with erosion-control BMPs by positioning slash across sloped skid roads. The branches are supposed to trap dirt, diffuse runoff and prevent rutting. This is a cheaper and quicker way of complying than excavating water bars and dips The technique, in my opinion, doesn't work very well over time because slash rots, leaving roads with no erosion control. The immediate downside is that the landowner's roads cannot be used as long as the slash remains. I learned this lesson the hard way.]

16. Agent shall designate where Buyer is to cross Clear Creek and any other watercourses, and design such crossings with Buyer. Agent and Buyer may___ shall____ consult with the appropriate state forestry official in locating and designing such crossings. If temporary bridges are erected, Buyer shall___ shall not ____ remove them when he is done with logging.

* 17. Buyer shall comply with all state Best Management Practices (BMPs) and logging laws and regulations in effect during the term of this Contract. Buyer bears responsibility for said compliance. Where this Contract requires a higher standard than the BMPs, this Contract shall be followed.

Buyer holds harmless Seller for any failure by Buyer to comply with applicable laws and regulations.

[COMMENT: BMPs vary from state to state. In some states, they're mandatory, and in others they're not. BMP compliance affects a logger's profit, so requiring compliance will increase logging costs in non-mandatory states. The seller should consult with his forester about the pros and cons of requiring compliance in such states.]

18. Buyer is responsible for filing all forms required by law to carry out this Contract and obtaining all permits except those the Owner chooses to obtain, including _____.

Buyer __ Owner __ will notify the local state forestry office prior to commencing any logging activity where such notification is required.

[COMMENT: Some states now require that the local state forestry office—the county forester—be notified prior to logging. Virginia requires the landowner to provide notification; the logger may be the notifying party in other states. Failure to notify results in a penalty. My language places notification responsibility on the logger, but that language may be wrong for your particular state.]

19. Buyer will fulfill his reclamation obligations under the BMPs and this Contract as soon after finishing his timbering as is feasible in light of weather and field conditions, but in no case longer than 180 calendar days from the date his logging crew leaves the property. This obligation remains in effect until it is fulfilled, including beyond the termination date of this agreement.

[COMMENT: The sections that follow spell out specific practices a landowner might want a logger to follow where BMPs are voluntary. The landowner should check with the state forestry department to determine where the language below differs from the state's voluntary BMPs. A far simpler alternative than writing your own BMPs is to require the buyer to follow the state's voluntary BMPs. But occasions can arise where that's not agreeable. The landowner should expect to have his timber discounted for either approach. Certain timber buyers may boycott a stumpage sale where BMP-compliance is required in a non-mandatory voluntary state. If your forester forecasts dire bid results, you may want to opt for having him talk informally with buyers.]

20. Buyer shall incorporate the following practices:

    a.) Buyer shall engage in no logging operation of any kind, including use of existing roads and construction of new roads within 50 feet of a pond, lake, wetland or stream without prior authorization of Agent. Agent has designated all no-operation zones on topographical map (Attachment 2).

    b.) Buyer may___ may not ____ skid logs through Clear Creek. Slash may not be left in Clear Creek.

    c.) Buyer shall __ shall not __ lop all slash to within __ feet of the ground.

[Comment: I recommend against including a slash-lopping requirement in a stumpage contract. Lopping adds cost to the logger without economic benefit. The closer to the ground slash is lopped, the more cost to the logger. If you have no alternative, you might consider a requirement that the logger lop all slash lying within 50 feet of your roads down to five or six feet. If the logger objects to that provision, you might propose that all slash within this corridor be dragged beyond the 50-foot boundary. It takes less time to hook a skidder to a top and drag it off than to work it down with a chainsaw. In any event, do not spring a slash-lopping requirement on the high bidder without advance notice.]

    d.) Slash and organic material may not be used as fill for roads and landings, except where permitted by state law and Agent.

    e.) Tree tops falling on the property of adjoining landowners shall be pulled back to Seller's property or lopped in place.

    f.) Buyer shall leave all landings and roads graded to remove ruts, with 4WD-vehicle-capable waterbars __ dips __, and culverts clean and functioning. All landings and roads shall be seeded with a grass mixture of _____ at a rate determined by the Agent, but not to exceed ____ pounds per acre. Surface area to be seeded shall___ shall not___ be prepared by discing in ____ pounds of lime and _____ pounds of _____ fertilizer per acre. If Seller desires a different mix or a more intensive application rate, he shall provide the necessary materials at his expense or make up the cost difference.

    After seeding, Buyer shall ___ shall not___ mulch all landings disturbed by logging.

[COMMENT: Seeding roads and landings is a common practice; mulching is a BMP in some states and not others. Seed selection is site specific. Kentucky 31 fescue is often used on steep slopes in my area, but alternatives are available. I've tried shade-tolerant seed on shady roads with little success. The grass doesn't stand up well to vehicle traffic.]

g.) Buyer shall install and maintain all necessary culverts, bridges and areas where he's applied stone, such as entrances and stream crossings, at his expense, unless otherwise agreed as an appendix to this Contract. Buyer shall leave all such improvements in place upon finishing the job, unless otherwise agreed as an appendix to this Contract.

h.) Buyer shall burn _____, leave _____ all log stubs, trims and unmerchantable logs at landings.

[COMMENT: Buyers and loggers will want to leave in place all stub trimmings and waste logs. Burning is time-consuming and potentially disastrous in dry conditions. Efficient loggers will leave most of their waste in the woods. The landings where logs are gathered and loaded onto trucks often accumulate piles of trimmings. Loggers will object to moving or burning this waste pile. Give the pile away for firewood. Photograph 23-2 shows a stub pile next to a seeded landing about 18 months after logging ended. I gave away this pile for firewood.]

i.) Buyer shall remove all man-made trash generated during the logging operation from Seller's property. Buyer shall remove any temporary structures and all equipment and supplies, unless otherwise provided.

j.) Buyer shall not dump or otherwise leave petroleum products on Seller's property. If a spill occurs, Buyer shall clean up the spillage and reclaim the affected portion of Seller's property.

k.) Buyer shall provide for all erosion-control and reclamation work required by applicable law or this Contract, unless other arrangements are approved by Agent.

l.) Buyer shall maintain adequate drainage on all roads during logging.

m.) Buyer shall leave stumps no higher than 12" from the ground, except where impractical. Buyer shall cut each tree in such a way so as to leave paint mark visible on the stump.

n.) Buyer shall take down and, at his choice, remove any unpainted tree that is broken, badly damaged, bent or leaning as a result of his work. Hung trees shall be felled. Any such tree the Buyer removes shall be paid for at its fair stumpage price, as determined by Agent and Buyer. Buyer shall leave no tree standing that he has partially cut.

o.) Buyer is responsible for repair or replacement of Seller's property (such as fences, gates, bridges, structures) and utility lines/pipes that Buyer damages during his work. Buyer is also responsible for repair or replacement of the property of the Seller's neighbors that Buyer damages during his work.

[COMMENT: If the buyer/logger is not held responsible for such damage, the landowner will be. "Damage" does not mean the normal wear and tear that logging produces. It refers to crushed culverts, broken fences, mashed gates, collapsed bridges and the like. If there is a particularly vulnerable item on your property—such as a low-hanging utility line or a bridge that might weaken under logging traffic—work out in advance who pays for what level of damage. It's normal for the logger to pay for damage he does to a neighbor's fence, trees and other property. You can also establish a no-logging buffer around farm buildings.]

* 21. Buyer agrees to indemnify, defend, and hold harmless Seller from all claims, damages and actions of any kind resulting from the operations of the Buyer, his agents, employees, associates, assigns, subcontractors and third parties associated with his timbering and hauling operation.

Buyer agrees that Seller bears no liability for any property damage experienced by Buyer, his agents, employees, associates, assigns, subcontractors and third parties associated with his timbering and hauling operation.

[COMMENT: You should anticipate resistance to this provision. Your buyer/logger would prefer to have the contract be silent on your potential liability for problems he causes. Accidents and mistakes happen. A motorist who runs into a log spilled on the road in front of your entrance, a real-estate agent visiting your land whose SUV is crushed by a top left hanging in a tree, an equipment fire that starts on your land but burns your neighbor's barn—all can lead to a lawsuit that ensnares you.]

* 22. Buyer agrees to indemnify, defend and hold harmless Seller for any accidents and/or injury to Buyer, his agents, employees, associates, assigns, subcontractors and third parties arising in any way from Buyer's work under this Contract.

[COMMENT: Workers' compensation generally exempts employers from employee personal-injury suits arising from workplace accidents. Some states, however, allow employee suits against employers who have been willfully negligent about working conditions or equipment safety. Language of this sort protects you against a suit brought by an equipment salesman visiting your logger on your property who steps in a naturally occurring hole and ruins his back. The salesman is a third-party within the meeting of this section. The Buyer should have accident and property insurance to cover these situations, but injured parties often look for a second pocket, such as the landowner's.

Your local lawyer can suggest language to cover 21 and 22 to replace my efforts. See also 28.]

23. Buyer is responsible for the security, safety and maintenance of his equipment and the daily supervision of his employees, associates and subcontractors (if permitted) while working on Seller's property. All Buyer agents, employees, associates, assigns, subcontractors and third parties are bound by the terms of this Contract.

* 24. Buyer shall not sell, assign, subcontract or otherwise convey his interests or rights under this Contract without Seller's written authorization.

[COMMENT: A sawmill that buys your stumpage may use its own employees to timber your land or subcontract the work to an independent. I've also seen occasions where a buyer will sell his interest in a timber tract. It is, therefore, important for the landowner to have yes-or-no control over such actions, and, further, that all parties understand that the terms of this Contract bind everyone in the buyer's chain. There will be certain logging crews that you do not want on your property; your consulting forester should know who they are. A landowner cannot tell the stumpage buyer not to use his own crew, but he should have the right to review and reject, if necessary subcontractors. Talk to your stumpage buyer about the crew he will put on your land.]

* 25. Buyer agrees to supervise his logging crew and assumes responsibility for the crew's compliance with the terms of this Contract.

[Comment: Logging crews—whether employees of the stumpage buyer or subcontractors—may or may not be adequately supervised. I've seen both ends of that spectrum. I have had mostly bad experiences with unsupervised crews. You want to work

through one point of contact with the buyer—the person who signs your contract. If the logging crew is not complying with the contract, you need to work it out with the signatory, not the guys running the chainsaws.]

* 26. Buyer agrees to provide his logging crew with a copy of this Contract, or the relevant portions thereof, to facilitate compliance with its terms.

[COMMENT: Loggers rarely see timber-sale contracts. The mill's supervisor or forester should explain its terms to the logging crew. This may or may not be done. I see no harm in asking your timber buyer to show his crew those parts of your contract that affect their behavior. If the buyer refuses to accept this provision, photocopy your contract and hand copies to every logger the first day the crew appears on your land. Explain important provisions in person The contract is notice of what you have a right to expect. Logging crews differ in how they do their jobs and the condition in which they leave the property. Some take great pride in leaving a "clean job." Others leave more than their share of broken and bent trees, tops hung in standing trees, trees needlessly damaged by skidding and equipment, severe ruts and so forth (which "so" can cover a world of unpalatable "forth").]

* 27. Buyer bears risk of loss to all painted trees during the term of this Contract.

[COMMENT: The landowner should not bear any risk of loss once the timber is sold. You are selling your timber "as is" as of the day your timber-sale contract is signed. Once sold, any damage and loss from natural causes fall on the buyer. The buyer may or may not accept risk of loss from vandalism to, or theft of, his painted trees. The language in 26 puts all risk of loss of any kind on the Buyer. If you have agreed to a pay-as-the-cutting-goes arrangement with a logger rather than an all-money-upfront contract, you would bear the cost of such loss because each tree is yours until it is delivered and sold to the mill.]

* 28. Buyer agrees to maintain both workers' compensation insurance and liability insurance to cover this work. Buyer shall provide Seller with a certificate (or copy) of his public-liability insurance policy with minimum limits of $100,000 in the event of death or injury for one individual and $300,000 for more than one individual; and property damage insurance with minimum limits of $25,000 and an aggregate of $50,000 before this Contract takes effect. Buyer shall comply with all applicable *workers' compensation laws, regulations and coverages.

Seller bears no liability and is held harmless for any insurance insufficiency by Buyer during the term of this Contract.

* Buyer shall ___ shall not___ furnish the Seller with a performance bond of $_____ that guarantees his performance of the terms of this Contract.

[COMMENT: Every buyer/logger I've worked with had no problem in providing his workers' compensation and other insurance information. His insurance is your first line of defense. I've never used a performance bond on a timber sale, but you may have circumstances where one would make sense. You should anticipate resistance to a performance bond; in most situations, it won't be necessary.]

* 29. Buyer shall ___ shall not ____ place the sum of $500.00 with the Agent to meet, in whole or part, the cost of damage that Seller's property sustains as a result of any violation of this Contract. Agent shall decide whether damage has occurred and arrange for repair. This sum shall be placed in the Agent's escrow account and returned to Buyer when he completes his work, less any deductions.

[Comment: This is alternative language to the performance bond. It implies that a $500 cap exists on logger liability, though it doesn't include the words, "as liquidated damages," which would cap exposure legally. If you have a routine logging job, neither a performance bond nor a $500 damage escrow is probably necessary. If, on the other hand, a field situation exists that requires delicacy and careful equipment maneuvering, these provisions may be appropriate. Before you include either one, make sure that you, your consultant and the buyer have a common understanding of what constitutes the type of damage that merits compensating you.]

30. Buyer shall notify Seller ___ days in advance before commencing logging operations. Seller shall remove any personal property that might interfere with Buyer's work prior to commencement.

31. The laws of the Commonwealth of Pennsylvania shall govern any dispute arising from this Contract.

* 32. The Parties do ____ do not____ agree to attempt to resolve any dispute through binding arbitration____, non-binding mediation _____ or binding mediation_____. If the Parties agree to use any of these methods, they will select an arbitrator/mediator from a panel of three supplied by _____ and agree to divide his costs and fees equally regardless of outcome.

[Comment: I have done arbitration work for more than 20 years. Most arbitrators are quick studies and experienced in understanding unfamiliar work processes. The parties may want to select an arbitrator at the time they are negotiating a contract since that costs nothing except some time. The panel of arbitrators could be supplied by a consulting foresters' association. These individuals will understand the nuances of timber sales, but may have no experience running an arbitration and interpreting a contract in semi-judicial fashion. Arbitration awards should be binding and enforceable. You might do better by selecting a local lawyer who's had some experience as a mediator in domestic-relations or personal-injury cases; experience in contract law is, of course, helpful. If you want a written opinion, I'd limit the writing to ten pages. In most commercial arbitrations, the arbitrator issues an award without explanation.]

33. Parties may amend this Contract at any time by mutual agreement. All amendments shall be in writing.

[COMMENT: Timber buyers and loggers are businessmen who are usually more comfortable with oral understandings than legal writing. If you're working with someone with whom you are comfortable—and you should not be working with someone with whom you are not—don't be surprised if you work out an amendment on the fly and never put it in writing. Oral agreements are binding in a contract such as this, but it's always better to put things, especially changes, on paper.]

* 34. In the event of default by Seller, Buyer is entitled to the prompt return of his full purchase price, plus a twenty (20) percent penalty as liquidated damages. If Buyer defaults, Seller is entitled to his full purchase price, plus a twenty (20) percent penalty as liquidated damages.

[COMMENT: This is a standard liquidated-damages clause that is intended to bind the parties to their contract and cap the penalty if either backs out. You need to be careful that you do not set up an incentive for a timber buyer/logger to frighten you into a

default, from which he walks away with all his cash plus 20 percent for his effort. If you allow both parties to walk from the contract with no loss other than a 20 percent penalty, you may be embedding an incentive for the buyer to default if the lumber market takes a nose dive. On the other hand, a landowner can get out of his contract if a last-minute buyer comes up with a price that's more than 20 percent better than the original agreement. A "breach" of contract is a violation of one or more of its agreed terms; a "default" is a failure to perform, a backing out of the agreement altogether. Ask your local lawyer for his opinion on this section.]

* 35. This Contract is binding on the heirs, executors, administrators, successors and assigns of both Parties.

* 36. This Contract comes into effect on the date when the last required signature is affixed.

* 37. Notarized signatures are___ are not ____ required. Facsimile copies with signature and date are ___ are not ___ acceptable to both Parties.

_____ (Seller)	_____ (Buyer)
Address	Address
Phone	Phone
FAX	FAX
Date_____	Date_____

Timber-sale contracts are necessarily specific both to the landowner's tract and to the geographical area where it's located. Your consulting forester will know the contract mores that will help your sale fit the form and content of what local buyers expect. Remember that the sample contract I've presented above *should be customized.* Your consulting forester and local lawyer will make useful suggestions from their different perspectives.

If the practice in your area is rigged against using upfront, lump-sum competitive bidding, you will have to work within that system. Where bilateral negotiation is the norm, you want to explore whether more than one buyer exists for your stumpage. In that way, you can, at least, pick the buyer who you think will pay you the best money. Where you are forced to be locked into a deal with an independent logger working on pay-as-he-sells shares, you are most exposed to being cheated. In that situation, have your consultant pick the logger and then paint and inventory your timber prior to logging. That work will give you a reasonably accurate idea of what the logger will be cutting and selling. Your consultant may be able to work out a reporting system at local mills where the logger is selling your logs to keep tabs on deliveries and prices. But my experience has been that mills and yards are very reluctant to do this. They do not want to get into the middle of a squabble between landowner and logger.

I've flagged the provisions in the contract that will complicate logging and increase the buyer's cost; these, as I've noted, will discourage bidding and discount bid price. You and your forester need to determine which, if any, of these practices is important enough to you to pay such penalties.

Consultants disagree over whether or not to send out an owner's timber-sale contract with the sale notice. If your contract is loaded with scary, costly provisions, I advise that you include your contract as a matter of fully disclosing the terms of a purchase. If you have some ideas that you might want to include, I wouldn't send out a contract with the sale notice. You will probably be able to work out a satisfactory contract with the high bidder as long as you're willing to be reasonable.

Timber buyers won't hang around physically and legally once they're through logging your property. To avoid situations where you are trying to get them to fix something after they've moved on, ask your consultant to do a walk-through a few days before logging is likely to be finished. He may be able to reach an oral understanding with the crew as to what needs to be done. This may involve highlighting a few sentences in the contract. On more contentious issues, your forester may write up a **punch list** of end-of-the-job things to complete. Where a job is finished in the winter, you and the logger will want to wait until spring to do the final grass seeding. Put any deferred work in writing: **"Final grading and seeding will be completed no later than June 1, 200_."** In wet, muddy conditions, the logger will not be able to dress your roads and landings; that work, too, may have to wait until drier months.

A final point to be made is one regarding which state's laws will govern your timber-sale contract. "Governance" can be an issue when the owner's timber straddles two states; or where the timber tract lies in one state, and the owner is in a second; or where the property lies in one state, the owner is in a second and the buyer operates his business in a third. If you don't specify which state governs, you will probably find yourself following the laws of the state in which the bulk of the property lies. Other thing being equal, it's in your interest to apply the laws of the owner's state of residence.

I've mentioned the idea of an owner having his timber receive **certification** from an independent third-party, which is an endorsement attesting that the harvesting and reclamation methods used comply with one or another set of environmental protocols. If a landowner insists that a stumpage buyer/logger operate within one of these protocols, he must include notice to that effect in his sales package and contract. Three of the prominent certification programs are: 1) Forest Stewardship Council, whose program is Smartwood in the United States; 2) American Forest and Paper Association, the Sustainable Forestry Initiative; and 3) National Forestry Association's Green Tag Forestry Program for non-industrial private landowners. The owner should limit bidding to buyers and loggers who are either qualified or are willing to become certified prior to starting the owner's job. Your buyer needs to be connected into the markets for certified logs in order to bid appropriately for your stumpage. You want to avoid a situation where your good environmental intentions cost you thousands of dollars.

States regulate logging practices on privately-owned land. Many states now require loggers to pass a certifying exam and have at least one certified individual on site. Logger certification involves first aid, safety equipment and practices, and knowledge of certain legal, commercial and environmental matters. **Best Management Practices (BMPs)** are mainly concerned with controlling erosion and reclaiming logged sites. They concentrate on: 1) road/landing construction; 2) timbering activities; 3) preparing the site for replanting, which can involve mechanical work such as chipping or discing, applications of herbicides and fertilizer, or burning; 4) reclamation of roads, landings and other excavations; and 5) protection of streamside management zones (SMZs).

Where a state requires compliance with its BMPs, the USEPA will have approved them before voluntary compliance was shifted to mandatory. A timber-selling landowner should become familiar with his state's BMPs, whether voluntary or mandatory. They are available from the state's forestry department in print or on the department's website. To get a sense of mandatory BMPs, Virginia's are available at http://state.vipnet.org/dof/wq/bmpguide.htm#intro.htm. Federally mandated BMPs are included there as an appendix. If you want a look at a beefed-up version of one state's BMPs, go to www.wvhighlands.org/Tree Draft.2.htm, which was drafted by the West Virginia Highlands Conservancy.

I've heard a range of stories concerning BMP enforcement in the field: the range goes from "not much" to "too much." Environmentalists may be inclined toward the first opinion and loggers, the second. State inspectors can "write up" a logger for a violation they observe, or a citizen can report a situation to the state forestry department that he believes is either causing a problem or is a violation. Trout Unlimited, for example, often monitors water quality below mining and logging jobs on trout streams. "Trout quarrels" arise over siltation from stream crossings, adequacy of erosion-control measures on logging roads both during and after the cutting, and timbering practices in SMZs. Enforcement is usually an order to the logger to fix the problem; an occasional fine is imposed. Reasonable individuals can reach different conclusions as to whether the enforcement of a particular BMP is reasonable or not. As a forest landowner, you have a right in a mandatory state to have your buyer/logger comply with current BMPs. The effect of BMPs in mandatory states is to have driven out of business or, at least to the commercial margins, the rogue loggers who took a perverse pride in leaving a mess in their wake. In non-mandatory states, the landowner gets to choose the level of protective expectations he wants the logger to apply.

Each state employs foresters—the county forester—who, as part of their duties, inspect logging jobs, usually at least once during the work and then soon after the logger has left. Larger, more complicated jobs and problem loggers may get several in-progress inspections. The inspector has no authority to enforce the landowner's contract with the logger, so do not expect him to. It is next to impossible for an absentee, inexperienced landowner to oversee BMP compliance. Your consulting forester should keep his eye on the timbering and try to resolve BMP issues in the field where possible. Both the landowner and the consulting forester should have a frank conversation early on with the buyer and the logger, if possible, about their expectations. Aim for practical, realistic expectations, and a cooperative, problem-solving relationship with the logging crew. Be as clear as you can about what you want and how you want the site to look when he leaves. But be prepared to compromise with the crew on your ideas. Assume that anything unstated or implied is subject to misunderstanding. Your logger will be far more inclined to help you if you treat him respectfully rather than as a necessary evil.

The visual appearance of woods following logging may or may not indicate harmful environmental impacts. A perfect logging job, with no adverse impacts, may look dreadful. Many logging jobs look bad at first even when they comply with applicable BMPs. Remember that logging changes a woodland's environment, but that change is not necessarily adverse to promoting environmental objectives. Don't judge your land's environmental book by its post-logging cover. Since post-logging visual aesthetics constitute so much of a landowner's objection to logging, you should talk with your forester about which practices you want the logger to follow and to what degree.

The eleven issues/practices that you want to think about are:

1. Lopping of slash
2. Leaving tree tops hanging in standing trees
3. Leaving broken and bent trees standing
4. Leaving a pile of log trimmings at landing
5. Leaving slash in roadways and waterways
6. Ditching uphill side of roads where necessary
7. Grading road with slight pitch to down side to promote water drainage
8. Installing culverts and gravel fords where necessary
9. Leaving roads rutted and subject to erosion
10. Leaving roads ungraded and rocky
11. Waterbars vs. dips.

As noted before, I would not require the stumpage buyer/logger to lop slash, because of the price discount you will suffer on your timber sale. Keep in mind that slash rots. Immediate visual improvement can be achieved by hiring two or three chainsaw operators to do this work *after* the logging is completed.

You can pay them by the hour or exchange their labor for the firewood they remove. It should not cost you anything to require that hanging tops be pulled out of standing trees. Leaners and bent trees can be dropped without much work. Log trimmings can be given away for firewood, burned or left alone.

I would, however, insist that the logger remove slash and other debris from roadways and waterways. And in that connection I would ask the logger to not drop trees in skid roads to the extent feasible, because he will then clear the road by bulldozing the slash into large and very unsightly roadside piles.

Logging obviously changes a physical environment, but even clearcutting's changes need not create environmental harm. Logging's principal environmental threat involves siltation of waterways and erosion. The risk of these adverse impacts increases as slopes become steeper and as the logging approaches a total harvest. Clearcuts on steep slopes in wet conditions create the most problems. Clearcuts on flat or gently rolling land are generally managed with little soil loss and erosion.

A great deal of logging can be done with minimal, if any, stream siltation. This is generally accomplished by leaving **buffer zones** on either side of a waterway where no cutting or only reduced cutting is permitted. The specifications for these streamside management zones (SMZs) are state-specific. Zone width should increase with the steepness of the zone's slope toward the stream. Virginia, as one example, recommends a minimum zone of 50 feet on each stream bank; with a 60 percent slope, a 290-foot width is recommended. A zone might be 250 feet wide on one bank and only 75 feet wide on the other, varying with slope. Within an SMZ, Virginia currently allows the removal of no more than 50 percent of its canopy in a given timbering, but the BMPs are not clear as to how much time must pass before 50 percent of that new canopy may be removed.

SMZs used undisturbed buffer ground and vegetation to catch soil and rock before they enter waterways. Proper design of skid roads above a zone should minimize the amount of potential silt the zone has to trap. After logging is done, the skid roads—which are generally the biggest source of siltation problems—should be slightly pitched (3 percent) across their width to allow water to run off to the immediate downhill side. If a road is not graded to slope slightly to the outboard side, water will run down the road itself, eventually cutting in an erosion channel. Flat, level roads collect water. The logger should also be expected to excavate **dips** across the road's width where the grade steepens. These in-road diagonal swales channel water from the road's surface into the forest where it is absorbed.

I object to waterbars as one-size-fits-all, erosion-control devices because they make the roads permanently impassable and unusable. If you are planning to run vehicles, horses, bikes or foot traffic over your woods roads, you want the logger to install dips, not waterbars. This may, however, run afoul of the BMP standards in a mandatory state. If the state forestry inspector insists on waterbars, the logger will have to put them in. At that point, you either lose access to your property or regrade the waterbars with a dozer or by hand.

Crossing streams with logs, logging equipment and trucks can deposit dirt and debris in the waterway. This happens more when ground conditions are muddy and/or ramps must be cut into high stream banks. In most cases, adequately sized culverts and/or **well-graveled fords** minimize the amount of dirt deposited in flowing streams. Crossings should be made at a right angle with the stream's flow, preferably where the channel is narrow and the banks are low. I have seen a small headwaters stream— home to native brook trout—forded with stone and gravel without siltation or harmful effect.

BMPs usually specify how fords are to be designed and constructed. They should not be made of either small logs or "scabs," which are the four bark-bearing sides left after squaring a log. Where possible, it's better to drive trucks through streams than to skid logs through them because less mud and disturbance is created. Logging in wetlands, swamps, floodplains and coastal areas should be done, if at all, with protection of wildlife habitat, plant species and environmental hydrology in mind. Similarly, logging done around high-country lakes and headwater streams must control siltation. Your consulting forester will know what loggers should do to protect your waterways.

You will need one final document to complete your timber sale. The purpose of a **release** is to establish that the stumpage buyer has finished his work whereupon he abandons (releases) his legal interest in your trees and property created by the sale. The release terminates your timber-sale contract and may indicate that both sides complied with its terms to each other's satisfaction.

AGREEMENT AND RELEASE OF INTEREST

This AGREEMENT AND RELEASE made this ___ day of _____, _____ between John Smith of Bigcity, New York, Seller, and Big Tree Sawmill of Woodland, Pennsylvania, Buyer.

WITNESSETH

In accord with the Timber-Sale Contract of _____, 2005 between the Seller and the Buyer, regarding the sale of the Seller's timber located on the west side of Rt. 600, three miles north of Woodland, PA, the Parties agree to the following terms of release.

1. Buyer has completed his harvest of Seller's timber and releases all interest in Seller's trees, logs and property that arose from the Timber-Sale Contract.
2. The Buyer has completed all work required under BMPs, if applicable, and the Timber-Sale Contract to the satisfaction of Seller and his Agent.
3. Seller agrees to release Buyer from all further obligations under their Timber-Sale Contract.

In Witness whereof, the Parties hereto have executed this AGREEMENT AND RELEASE as of the ____ day of _____, _____.

_____   _____
Seller   **Buyer**

CHAPTER 24: TIMBER TAXATION

Let me start with the truth. I am totally witless about federal and state tax laws, regulations, court rulings, agency directives and opinions, let alone the idiosyncrasies of individual IRS agents. I have no advice about taxes other than to pay what your tax-smart CPA tells you to. I am wise enough not to follow my own advice on tax matters were I so foolish as to have any. I am also outraged that Americans are expected to pay their taxes under a system that most of us have no reasonable hope of comprehending.

Diligent readers of this book will recall that Chapter 6 is full of my tax-related opinions, souped up a bit to the level of advice. Now that I have had time to reflect on that indiscretion, I feel obliged to confess my ignorance—before jumping into the same shark-infested pool.

The federal tax code is so massive (60,000+pages), impenetrable, loop-holed, dynamic and arbitrary that the ordinary citizen is less likely to get bitten walking over starving crocodiles every morning than stepping through the jaws of the IRS once a year. The more complicated your return, the more you should not do it yourself. If you call the IRS with a tax question, they often won't answer it. It's the nightmare of being expected to provide the correct answer on a final exam when your teacher refuses to teach you the correct answer during the term. And much of the interpretive information that is provided is incorrect. Every year, I pay the taxes my CPA tells me I owe with only the barest understanding of how these sums are calculated from the receipts and documents I dutifully assemble. For reasons that I can't understand, Americans put up with this bipartisan insult. Americans vote for politicians promising tax breaks and lower tax rates, but we can't seem to mobilize around making the tax-paying process simpler, easier, fairer and less time-consuming. As it is, a taxpayer needs to know tax angles and play them, because that is how the system is organized. It's the legal angles that are threaded through the Code that benefit this organized group and that one; the illegal ones are not what I'm talking about.

Timber taxation fits into this system—if you want the embedded tax benefits available to a landowner, you have to spend time in tax planning and then jump through the hoops. Timber-owners are a special interest when it comes to taxes, a successful special interest.

Timber taxation is a specialty for CPAs, lawyers and investment advisers, not the likes of me. Consult with these professionals about your timber-taxation questions before you buy a single tree. Timber owners and timber sellers benefit from having timber-taxation issues explained to them before they become owners and sellers. Much information can be found at www.timbertax.org; "Forest Landowner's Guide to the Federal Income Tax, USDA, Handbook 718," www.soforext.net/formgnt/aghandbook.html; "Estate Planning for Forest Landowners," www.southernregion.fs.fed.us/spf/coop/taxation/default.htm or www.soforext.net/pdfs/estate.pdf.

An especially helpful booklet appeared in 2005 by Harry L. Haney, Jr., William C. Siegel and Larry M. Bishop, <u>Federal Income Tax on Timber: A Key to Your Most Frequently Asked Questions</u>, R8-TP34, Rev. December, 2005 (USDA, Forest Service Southern Region, 2005); www.srs.usda.gov/pubs/7124. It organizes answers to each timber-tax issue by type (personal use, investment, trade or business), then shows the best tax treatment and exactly which forms and lines you should use.

This chapter is a humble effort—and I know more than any reader how humble it is—to introduce my understanding of the main timber-tax issues, using IRS words where they are comprehensible and my own where they are less so.

SET UP

Timber-taxation issues only affect **timberland.** Timberland is wooded land whose trees have current or future commercial value. Woodland may or may not be timberland, but it's usually in a landowner's interest to consider his woods as having present commercial value as well as future commercial value for IRS purposes. Of course, not every patch of natural woods should qualify as timberland with commercial value, present or future. Ten stunted oaks behind the old farm house shouldn't qualify as a timberland investment or business. But even small patches of land can be established and managed to produce—or anticipated to produce in the future—some type of commercial wood product—nuts, Christmas trees, seed stock, mistletoe, maple sap, sawtimber, pulp, chips, firewood and so on. And there are non-wood-product uses that fit the woodland environment that can generate income, such as hunting leases, recreational fees for trail usage and camping, among others. Part of your process of considering the value of your new woods is to think through the best way to set up your woodland on paper and on the ground in the most tax-advantaged way.

Let's assume that you have at least a couple of acres of woods; more, of course, is better. If income is never produced or intended to be produced from these woods, you will be able to deduct a proportional share of your mortgage interest and property taxes. That's about it. If you consider these woods primarily for your **personal use**, you may want to cut some timber at some point. You will have additional deductions. If you set up the woods as a noncorporate **investment**, you will get more tax benefits, including itemized deductions that can be taken against any source of income, but only to the extent that the total of these deductions exceeds two percent of your adjusted gross income that year. If you set up the woods as a **trade or business**, you will determine whether this is an activity in which you materially participate or one in which you do not materially participate.

A trade or business is supposed to make money in addition to having a profit motive. It's hard to show gross income from managed timberland each year and even harder to show a profit. Fortunately, you don't have to. **The IRS defines profit to also mean the appreciation in the value of the asset.** As trees grow, their value increases. And in this fashion, you show a non-taxable profit in your timber business each year through the growth of your timber.

There are six tests the IRS uses to determine whether a taxpayer materially participates in a timber trade or business—and you only have to meet one of them. The easiest to meet in my opinion is the one that requires personal participation in the activity to substantially constitute all material participation during the tax year wherein material participation is defined as regular, continuous and substantial involvement. If you find that you devote at least 100 hours during the tax year to your timber business—hours spent traveling to and from the woods, walking through the woods inspecting the trees (for growth, insects, disease, theft), clearing the roads of rocks and tree branches to enhance fire protection, improving the timber stand by cutting low-value species, attending forestry conferences, reading forestry books, keeping forestry accounts, enrolling your woods in the state's managed-timberland, tax-savings program, talking with the county forester, talking with loggers about prices, pruning small branches off high-value saplings to improve their future butt logs, etc.—you should be able to qualify as a material participant. It's arguable—though I've not tried this—that the two weeks you spend deer hunting in your woods should go toward material participation since the purpose of your hunting is to increase natural regeneration by reducing the amount of sapling production lost to winter deer browse. I've asked my neighbor to hunt my woods for that very reason. You lose nothing by making this argument. Your best position tax-wise is to be a material participant in a timber business.

One of your first tax decisions with respect to woodland is to establish your motives and purposes. If you want to make a profit in some way from the trees themselves or their woodland environment during your ownership, then you should consider establishing your woodland as some form of either business or investment. If you don't want to use your trees to try to make money, then you are giving up certain tax benefits. You may still make a profit on your trees without managing them as a business or investment. If, for instance, you sell $100 of firewood from your five-acres of woods, that should be reported as taxable income. And any net profit that you get on the sale of your woodland is likely to be taxable. The National Timber Tax Website organizes a forest landowner's choice of purposes in the following way (see www.timbertax.org):

- **Personal Use**. Timberland is titled in taxpayer's name. Timber is a capital asset. Taxable gain from sale of stumpage qualifies for capital-gains treatment when held for more than one year; reported on 1040, Schedule D. Timber-management expenses are not deductible and must be capitalized.

- **Hobby**. Timberland is titled in taxpayer's name. Timber is a capital asset. Taxable gain from sale of stumpage qualifies for capital-gains treatment when held for more than one year; reported on 1040, Schedule D. Timber management expenses are deductible under "hobby loss rule," to the extent of the taxpayer's current timber-related income. Deductions are allowed and are not subject to passive-loss rules.

- **Investment.** Title in investor's name. Deductible management expenses are reported as miscellaneous itemized deductions on 1040, Schedule A and subject to a two percent floor of adjusted gross income. Stumpage sale gain or loss qualifies for capital-gains treatment when held for more than one year.

- **Activity Incidental for Farm Business**. Timberland titled with other farm business. Deductible management expenses are reported on 1040, Schedule F if a sole proprietorship. Stumpage qualifies for capital-gains treatment when held for more than one year. Passive-loss rules apply to the farm as a whole.

- **Activity Incidental to Non-Farm Business**. Timberland titled with other business property. Costs are reported on business return.

- **Active Timber-Production Business**. Titled in the name of the business. Owners are "active," materially participating in business. Occasional stumpage sales qualify for capital-gains treatment, but ordinary business sales of timber do not.

- **Passive Timber-Production Business.** Operating losses are restricted by passive-loss rules; otherwise same as Active Timber-Production Business.

- **Timber Production and Utilization Business**. Timber is produced primarily for in-house use, not outside sale. This applies to sawmills, and presumably the small, portable mills an individual buys, as long as the product is used in-house, that is, for construction of structures on the property. Timber used for fuel on the property might also fit here. (www.timbertax.org/strategies/acquisition.)

Your choice from among these options may be easy or not, depending on your circumstances. Your timber-smart CPA and lawyer should help you understand the benefits and consequences of each option. The most advantageous tax situation is one where you are allowed the maximum deductibility of current costs, fast recovery of capitalized expenditures, capital-gains treatment and active participation. (Self-employment tax does not apply to capital gains.) But these benefits come at a cost—your time, for example, as an active manager, paperwork, an itemized 1040 with schedules and upfront legal expenses. Tax benefits expand as you move from personal or hobby purposes to investment or business status. It is usually in a taxpayer's interest to set up woodland as at least an investment if circumstances permit.

In addition to determining your purpose in the new woodlands, you will need to discuss your **ownership options**—no structure (suitable for land dedicated for personal use), sole proprietorship, partnership, S corporation, limited liability company, corporation, family corporation or trust. An ownership structure of some sort helps to establish an investment or business purpose. Sole proprietors in a trade or business may be subject to self-employment tax on ordinary income, but are not subject to self-employment tax on capital gains. If you sell your timber after one year of owning it, you will get long-term capital-gains treatment and not have to pay self-employment tax. The 2005 self-employment tax was 15.3 percent, with 12.4 percent going for OASDI (old age, survivors and disability insurance) and 2.9 percent for Medicare. OASDI stops being imposed at $90,000 for 2005, but the Medicare hit has no cap.

I have decided not to discuss using timberland as a conventional business, because I don't think it fits the profile of the readers of this book. Therefore, I'm not going to go through thinking about Christmas tree farms, orchards, managed timberland that produces annual income, maple-syrup operations, seed-stock nurseries and other tree-related businesses. If this is your path, see Steven H. Bullard and Thomas J. Straka, Forest Valuation and Investment Analysis, 2nd ed. (Self-published, 1993, ISBN 0-9641291-0-8); William G. Hubbard, Robert C. Abt and Mary L. Duryea, Estimating the Profitability of Your Forestland Enterprise, Circular 836, University of Florida Extension, November, 1989 also at www.sfrc.ufl.edu/Extension/pubtxt/cir836.htm; F. Christian Zinkhan, William R. Sizemore, George H. Mason and Thomas J. Ebner, Timberland Investments: A Portfolio Perspective (Portland, Oregon: Timber Press, 1992); James M. Vardaman, How to Make Money Growing Trees (New York: John Wiley & Sons, 1989); and Laurence C. Walker, Farming the Small Forest: A Guide for the Landowner (San Francisco: Miller Freeman Publications, 1988). Bullard and Straka, Zinkhan *et al.*, and Vardaman are expensive. They can be purchased at Forestry Suppliers, Inc., 1-800-647-5368; FAX 1-800-543-4203; www.forestry-suppliers.com. Books are also available through the Forest Shop at http://forestshop.com. Another source of information on the business and taxation aspects of woodland ownership are the forestry extension professors in each state who hold public seminars on woodland management, taxation and investment strategies. Your consulting forester is a source of first-step information on these subjects.

I've oriented this discussion mainly around the idea of thinking about your woodland as either an investment or an investment-type business in which you materially participate. If you don't qualify as a material participant, you can qualify as a nonmaterial participant. But don't give up on trying to qualify for material participation in your business of managing your timberland (not woods) for profit.

To establish an active timber-investment trade or business, a taxpayer has to meet just one of the following six tests:

1. Taxpayer's participation in the activity must exceed 500 hours during the tax year.

2. Taxpayer's personal participation in the activity substantially constituted all of the material participation during the tax year.

3. Taxpayer's participation in the activity exceeded 100 hours, and no other individual participated more.

4. Taxpayer's aggregate participation in all of the "significant participation activities," including actual timber management, exceeded 500 hours during the tax year. A significant participation activity is one in which participation exceeded 100 hours during the tax year.

5. Taxpayer's material participation has occurred in the activity for any five of the preceding ten tax years.

6. Taxpayer's participation in the activity was on a regular, continuous and substantial basis for at least 100 hours during the tax year based on facts and circumstances; no other individual participated more; and a paid manager was not employed. (See Haney *et al.*, <u>Federal Income Tax</u>, p. 13.)

I think many readers who are looking at wooded properties can qualify as a material participant in a timberland-management business if they plan it out and meet the requirements of at least one of the six tests. I encourage even the most urban-centric buyers to scope wooded property with the idea of purchasing it as an investment or timber-management business rather than for personal, recreational or hobby use. If you're buying woods, it's not that hard to recast them as timberland that you actively manage. There are tax benefits for doing so.

It's not difficult to set up your newly purchased property as either an investment or a timber-management business. The former requires minimal documentation and record-keeping; the latter, which provides additional tax advantages if you qualify as a material participant in this business, requires a business structure, a business-like approach to the investment and business-type record-keeping. In the eyes of the IRS, you can operate a business as a material participant that invests in timberland with one property. That property, of course, has to be genuine timberland, though it need not have merchantable timber at the time of your purchase. To show that you are operating an active business, your CPA may ask that you keep a record of your activities related to your timberland-investment business, including a time log to prove that your participation meets at least one of the IRS's six tests for material participation. The reward for jumping through these hoops is that you can fully deduct management expenses, taxes and interest paid on your timberland business from any other source of your income. If the timber business is managed in conjunction with a farm, deductions over gross income produce a net operating loss, which allows the taxpayer to be eligible for a two-year carry-back to earlier returns or a 20-year carry-forward.

The cruise you commission as part of your scoping will also help you establish a broad commercial—rather than personal—purpose for the IRS. The cruise demonstrates that you were determining the financial value of the timber asset prior to purchase. I think a pre-purchase cruise will also help a taxpayer establish the intent of material participation in a timberland-management business. For the same IRS reason, I advise choosing an ownership structure at the time of purchase that is consistent with managing the property for gain. This can be as simple as filling out a Schedule C in your first ownership year and thereafter, but it may involve setting up a legal ownership entity, such as a limited liability company. A third start-up step for the IRS is to have your consulting forester write a **forest-management plan** that anticipates future income and demonstrates your commercial motive. You can also consider enrolling your new woodland in the state's timberland-management program, which can discount your property tax, make you eligible for various kinds of financial and non-financial benefits and, again, further substantiate for the IRS your profit-making intentions.

The pre-purchase timber cruise is the first document you will collect in your **timberland records** folder that will help establish your material participation in a timberland business. The forest-management plan is the second. Any expenses you incur related to your purchase should be retained: one copy in your long-term timberland records folder and the other in your folder of receipts for that tax year. Records and receipts help establish that your woods should be at least viewed as an investment. The more business records and documents you have, the easier it is for you to establish that you are actively engaged in the management of the timberland property for profit. Timberland management is the type of business that does not require a high level of activity to sustain itself each year.

On some properties, you can economize by asking your consulting forester to prepare a pre-purchase scoping report based on a thorough **walk-through**, rather than a timber cruise. A walk-though is less accurate than a cruise, but it's often sufficient for you to make a sensible offer. A walk-through will give you a volume break down by species and a dollar value for both sawlogs and pulp. I have had success asking a forester to do a walk-through estimate for all sawlogs 12" DBH and larger by species, using whatever scale local buyers will use. Pulp volume and value appears separately. On 250 acres, a walk-through might take a day with another couple of hours in the courthouse checking boundaries. The write up should take a day or less. A walk-through is usually not good enough to market your timber for its highest possible price or as a database for a management plan. There are circumstances, however, where a walk-through is all you need for a quick timber sale. With a walk-through timber valuation in hand, you can market merchantable timber during escrow contingent on your purchase of the property, with a minimum bid pegged to your walk-through value.

Like all other business and investments, it's necessary for a woodland owner claiming the timber and property as either an investment or business to keep business-like records. Timberland, generally, involves a minimum amount of paperwork each year. In most years, expenditures are few and timber is not sold. But the three-years-profit-out-of-five rule can be met by the IRS policy of allowing profit to be taken to mean appreciation in the value of the timber assets. As an investment, timber generates some expenditures that you can deduct in the year they occur. Other outlays will increase your **basis** in the woodland, which decreases your taxable gain when you sell the property for a profit. As a business, including a timberland-investment business, expenditures will fall into different categories—some can be deducted against income, some depreciated and some taken on the sale of the property. Make sure that you note the date and purpose of each expenditure, and then ask your CPA to sort them properly each year.

If your timber consists of several stands that you manage independently, your CPA will probably set up a **timber account** for each one. This allows you to keep separate income-expenditure records stand-by-stand. On a 100-acre tract that has one stand of merchantable timber and another that has just been clearcut, the money spent on site preparation, herbicides and planting will be allocated to the latter premerch account. Your job is to keep a record of what you do, what expenses you incur and why you are incurring them. Your CPA will take it from there. Record-keeping is discussed in William E. Schlosser, "Financial Record Keeping for Forest Landowners: Developing A Good System," February, 1999, University of Idaho, Extension Forestry; www.ets.uidaho.edu/extforest/feb99.htm.

BASIS AND INCOME

How do you handle **income received from a timber sale** for tax purposes?

If you sell your timber within your first-ownership year, any taxable gain (net sale income – adjusted basis) will be taxed at your ordinary rate. A pre-purchase cruise will establish your basis in the timber that you sold. And the sale should not show much taxable gain, considering the timber sale occurs shortly after you've closed on the property.

If you hold off selling the timber for more than a year and you are materially participating, you must dispose of your timber within the provisions of **Section 631, Gain or Loss in the Case of Timber, Coal, or Domestic Iron Ore**. Under Section 631 (a), cutting of timber is considered a sale or exchange and is eligible for long-term capital-gains treatment. The fair market value, i.e., the taxpayer's basis, of the timber is established as of the first day of the tax year in which such timber is cut. Section 631 (b) figures basis differently and applies to taxpayers who either retain an economic interest in the timber or make an outright sale. Taxable gain under Section 631 (b) for both pay-as-cut and outright sales qualifies for long-term capital-gains treatment.

In all cases, the taxpayer's CPA must calculate the taxpayer's basis in the timber sold, regardless of when the sale occurred or what type of sale it was.

To do this, he organizes your new property into two, or more, **separate accounts**, preferably in your first tax year. One account is for the **land** itself, including costs you've incurred in the purchase of the land itself, non-depreciable improvements to the land and depreciable land improvements—the difference is explained below. A second account is devoted to the costs and income involved in the **timber**. A timber account can include all merchantable timber—that is, the timber you want to sell—and both naturally generated premerchantable timber and planted premerch. Your forester and CPA will help you decide whether each type of timber should have its own timber account. Generally, undeveloped woodland will have only two accounts—land and timber. But you might have basis allocated among as many as seven sub-accounts—forested land, other unimproved land, improved land, timber, premerchantable timber, improvements and mineral rights (such as oil, gas, hard-rock, minerals, clay, sand, topsoil, stone and water). Some of the sub-accounts may be further divided into subassets, each with a separate basis.)

Wooded property used for investment/commercial purposes may come with other types of assets, each capable of having an independent basis, expenses and income. One such account could be set up for **depreciable equipment** used in the timberland investment or business, bought from the property's seller or acquired independently. An equipment account includes all depreciable machinery, tools, vehicles and equipment that have a useful life of more than one year and cost more than $100 each. Separate accounts might be created for **depreciable improvements** (structures), such as a workshop, equipment shed or farmhouse used as a business office. If you're planning to sell a severable asset, your CPA will advise you as to whether you will be better off to separate its basis from other assets or combine it.

The IRS looks at your rural property used as an investment or business as a bundle of separate assets, each of which can independently produce income and involve expenses. These accounts are sometimes referred to as **basis accounts**, but you should understand that calculating basis involves more than just totaling certain costs. Income from the sale of an asset—such as timber, or part of the land, or the minerals—decreases your basis in that account and in the property's entirety as well. So each asset account must keep track over time of both income from any sale and those expenditures that increase basis.

Each asset will also produce a gain or loss when the owner sells it. When an asset is sold, the CPA goes back through your records to determine its original acquisition cost, called **original basis**. If you've increased your investment in the asset during your ownership, you've increased your basis. If, for instance, you spend $10,000 to build woods roads and do timber stand improvements, you will have increased your basis in your timber account by $10,000. You may also have decreased your basis through sales and other activities. Your CPA will add all the allowable increases (certain costs/expenditures) to your original basis, subtract all allowable decreases, and arrive at a number—your **adjusted basis**. By subtracting your adjusted basis from sale income, he will determine whether you had a taxable gain on the sale of an asset, a loss or no taxable gain. If you had a gain, you pay tax on it; if you had no taxable gain, you have no income to pay tax on. If you had a loss, you may be able to use it to reduce your taxable income in other areas. Figuring taxable gain by subtracting adjusted basis from income is the method used when you sell property assets separately, in combination or as an entirety.

If you decide to plant trees, you should be aware that, as of 2005, you can deduct outright the first $10,000 of such expenses in that year and amortize as a deduction all reforestation expenses above $10,000 over 84 months. If you deduct the reforestation cost, it cannot be added to your basis.

Within a timber sub-account, your CPA may establish more finely disaggregated accounts depending on the types of timber on the property, such as:

   o   all merchantable timber, which you sell immediately after purchase

- merchantable sawtimber
- merchantable pulpwood
- merchantable timber by specific species, such as paulowina (a very valuable wood)
- premerchantable timber that has been naturally generated
- premerchantable timber that has been planted
- timber dedicated to maple-sap production
- timber dedicated to production of nuts, seeds or bark

Each such account will follow the same format for keeping track of how the property owner's basis in the asset is changing over time as allowable costs are added and partial sales are subtracted. Adjusted basis is a net figure, after additions to and subtractions from are made. At any given time, it is easy to figure what your adjusted basis is in each sub-account, account and the property as a whole. For simplicity, I will use **timber basis** to represent the total adjusted basis in the property's timber assets and **land basis** to represent the total adjusted basis in the property's land.

For most readers, undeveloped wooded property will be divided into a timber account (with a running adjusted timber basis) and a land account (with a running adjusted land basis). If you buy such a property and neither sell any of its assets nor add to them, your adjusted basis at the time you decide to sell the property as a whole will be your original basis at the time you bought the property. When you have a low basis and a high selling price, your taxable gain—the difference between the two—is high.

Adjusted basis should not be confused with fair market value. Adjusted basis is a number representing the running net of what the owner has put into and taken out of the property from a tax perspective. It has nothing to do with the property's current market value. Confusion can arise on timberland when a buyer uses a cruise to establish both the FMV of the merchantable timber and his original timber basis (cost) at the time of acquisition. When a CPA sets up multiple accounts for a property, he has to divide the original total purchase cost among them, a process called, **allocation**. A timber cruise or an appraisal of equipment can be used to allocate costs to their respective accounts. That allocation of value is really a process of figuring and then apportioning the new owner's cost of acquisition for tax purposes, nothing else.

A buyer should, however, remember that it is usually to his advantage to have an idea of the seller's adjusted basis in a property during negotiations. Knowing a seller's basis will reveal the approximate amount of taxable gain a given price will net for him. From that, a buyer can deduce the seller's after-tax net profit. A buyer may also be able to work down the seller's price if he's able to propose ways, or agree to seller-proposed ways, to reduce the seller's tax hit.

Original land basis is the owner's cost of acquiring the land. The owner's cost of acquisition (basis) can be increased by including certain allowable expenses associated with the acquisition.

If the new owner had an appraisal done as part of his pre-purchase scoping, his original basis is his original actual cost, not the appraisal value. However, appraisals can be used to allocate costs among different accounts. If, for example, the land has a house that the new owner later sells, an appraisal of the house itself done during, just before or just after the new owner purchased the land and house together can establish his original basis in the house alone. Such a property would have two accounts, a land account (basis) and a house account (basis).

A common buyer's strategy is to purchase a large acreage with a house/barn, and then immediately sell the house/barn with five or ten acres as a way to help pay for the retained land. The buyer should have the house/barn appraised at the time of purchase to establish his basis in these improvements and, if possible, receive payment for their sale a year after purchasing them so that he can treat any profit as a capital gain. The higher the appraisal value of the small acreage and improvements, the better it is for the buyer tax-wise. When selling an asset from a property, the more basis that can be allocated to the sale asset, the less taxable gain will result. Less taxable gain means less tax to be paid on income from the sale.

Land basis may or may not be the same as **bare land value**, which is one of the assets you try to estimate when figuring a fair-market-value purchase price. Remember that land basis is essentially a cost calculation for tax purposes. Bare land value is a market value, not a cost; it's the amount of money you think the land is worth to you, and, possibly, the amount of money you think another buyer would actually pay you for the land, severed from all other assets, were you to sell it, by itself, immediately after buying the property. Thought about in two different ways, it is likely that the first value of bare land will not be the same as the second. None of the factors that increase or decrease your estimate of the value of the bare land in either instance play a role in calculating land basis.

Where timberland is divided for tax purposes into a timber account and a land account, the IRS requires that the land be assigned some minimum value, which could be either a percentage of the purchase price or a specific number, such as $300 per acre. A tract you bought for $500 per acre, which your forester cruised out prior to purchase at $1,000 in present timber value per acre, might be allocated at $300 per acre in original land basis and $200 in original timber basis even though you sold the timber for $1,000 per acre three days after buying the tract. Your total original basis (adjusted for miscellaneous acquisition expenditures) in the property cannot exceed your original cost (adjusted for those expenditures). The forester's cruise "appraised" the value of the timber, not your cost to buy it. There always has to be a land basis in timberland, allocated as some portion of the original property cost, even where the value of the timber exceeds the property's purchase price. Your taxable gain on this timber sale—assuming no acquisition adjustments—would be $800 per acre ($1,000 income -$200 basis = $800 per acre taxable gain). **Timber basis** is what you paid for the timber in tax terms, not what you sold it for. If you're going to have a big gain on a timber sale involving recently purchased property, it's likely that you will come out ahead by selling after holding for more than one year to get the capital-gains rate.

A pre-purchase timber cruise is an estimate of value that can be used to establish your cost basis in your property's timber. Say that you buy 100 acres for $1,000 per acre, and your forester cruised the merchantable timber before purchase at $600 per acre. Your CPA will allocate your cost basis, i.e., timber basis, at $600 per acre and your land basis at $400 per acre, using the cruise to show the cost of the timber at time of purchase. If you sell the timber for $600 per acre, you've sold it for what you paid for it, hence no taxable gain was realized. If you sell the timber for less than $600 per acre, you have a loss; if you get more than $600 per acre, you have a taxable gain. If you don't have a cruise done around the time of the property's purchase, your CPA has to come up with a reasonable allocation of cost (basis) between land and timber when you do sell the timber. A consulting forester can work backward to estimate the cost of your property's stumpage at the time of purchase, but a buyer/taxpayer is advantaged by having the timber evaluated prior to submitting a purchase offer.

The timber-selling taxpayer's interest usually lies in having his timber basis calculated as high as possible when he's keeping the property from which he's selling the timber. For that reason, many buyers have a cruise done immediately *after* purchase rather than before, and ask the forester to push the timber value as high as possible to shelter timber-sale income from taxation. A buyer who cruises after purchase, however, loses the edge he would otherwise have in knowing the timber value before submitting an offer to the property seller. I suppose an individual could pay for two cruises by different foresters—one before purchase, and the other after for tax purposes. I've never heard of this being done, but I suppose someone who plays this game with the IRS would not boast about it. I doubt that you will find a consulting forester who will give you an honest cruise before purchase and an inflated one after

If you've acquired woodland through inheritance, gift or exchange, you will need to establish a property basis—both timber basis and land basis—at the time of your acquisition. A timber cruise can establish your timber basis at the time you buy woodland or inherit it. If you receive the woodland as a gift, you assume the donor's basis, not the basis at the time of the gift. The donor's basis may possibly be adjusted for gift taxes paid. With an exchange, you will carry into the new woodland your adjusted basis from the property you exchanged out of. Your CPA may be able to value the woodland property as an entirety using comparables. The timber basis can then be subtracted from the entirety appraisal to produce a land basis. Your interest at the time you acquire the property through means other than purchase is to have the timber and the land valued as high as possible to lower future taxable gain. If your intention is to sell the timber but keep the property, your interest usually lies in having as much of the property's total basis as possible allocated to timber.

Recent changes in estate taxation increased the amount a taxpayer's estate can exempt from federal estate taxes. The exempted amount rises from $1 million in 2002 to $1.5 million in 2004, to $2 million in 2006, to $3.5 million in 2009, to full exemption (no dollar cap) in 2010, then back to $1 million in 2011. This scheme is so arbitrary that it will likely be modified during the years it's in effect. Still, all of us will have to do estate planning in light of these rules as well as the high probability that they will be changed. If they are not changed, those readers who are really rich should try to die in 2010 if they like their heirs; if they hate them, die on January 1, 2011. Aside from your own estate lawyer and CPA, you might want to contact attorney Stephen J. Small at the Landowner Planning Center, 75 Federal Street, Suite 1100, Boston, MA, 02110-1911; 617-357-4012, ext. 264; FAX 617-357-1857; www.stevesmall.com. Small, a former IRS lawyer, is experienced in using conservation easements in estate planning, and he has written two helpful books: <u>Preserving Family Lands: Book I: Essential Tax Strategies for the Landowner</u>; and <u>Book II: More Planning Strategies for the Future</u>. Another resource is William C. Siegel, a lawyer and forest resource consultant, in River Ridge, Louisiana who has written widely on timber taxation and pens a column, "Taxing Matters," in <u>RMS Timber Landowner Report</u>, POB 380757, Birmingham, AL, 205-991-9516; FAX 205-991-2807; www.resourcemgt.com; e-mail: rms@resourcemgt.com. Siegel can be reached at 504-737-0583 or e-mail: wcsieg@aol.com.

Your **original timber basis** can and, usually does, change over time to the extent that you add allowable costs to the running basis balance and subtract allowable basis that you've captured from timber sales. If you've planted timber and made no sales, it's possible that you will find that your current (adjusted) timber basis exceeds your original basis. That will change once you sell timber and recalculate your running timber basis. Depending on what you've done after purchasing a property, your adjusted basis in the property may be greater than, less than or the same as your original basis.

Once you've established your original timber basis at the time you acquire the property, you will use it against the income you get from a timber sale. Take the example of a purchase of undeveloped woodland at $1,000 per acre where your CPA allocates $500 per acre to land basis and $500 per acre to timber basis. If you sell the timber for $500 per acre, your new timber basis after the sale is $0 per acre. You pay no federal income tax on that timber sale, because you sold the timber for exactly the amount of its value (and what it cost you) at the time of acquisition based on your consultant's timber cruise. Since you've used up your entire timber basis, the only basis you have remaining in the property is your $500 per acre land basis. And if you do nothing to increase your timber basis after your first timber sale, your next sale of timber will be figured against a timber basis of $0 per acre. Accordingly, all your net income from that second timber sale would be taxable.

What happens if, after selling the timber, you decide to sell the land? In the example above, you used up all of your $500 per acre timber basis, leaving you with a $500 land basis as the only remaining basis in the property. If nothing changes and you sell the property for $2,000 per acre in two years, you will have a taxable gain of $1,500 per acre ($2,000 income -$500 basis = $1,500 taxable gain), taxed at your capital-gains rate.

It should be apparent that you and your CPA should look for ways to pack in as much timber basis as possible prior to a timber sale. The cost of a pre-purchase cruise is added to the original timber basis. The cost of a survey will probably be allocated between the timber basis and the land basis, but if the survey is done solely to facilitate the timber sale, it's arguable that all of its cost should be assigned to the timber basis. (Remember that arguments that make sense to me will probably carry no weight with the IRS.)

Even woodland that is without current merchantable timber value should carry as much timber basis as your CPA feels is defensible. That timber basis, for which you've paid, is found in the property's premerchantable timber plus whatever basis you've added to the timber in allowable costs.

If you buy woodland that has no timber value, either merchantable or premerchantable and your plan is to create timber value in the future, the cost of site preparation (herbicides, cleaning up slash, road development) and planting seedlings can begin building your timber basis. Reforestation, as mentioned above, can be deducted instead of added to basis. Certain land-improvement costs, such as building a bridge to be used by the logger, will probably be divided between your timber basis and your land basis. If you are setting up timber sub-accounts, you may need a forester's help in allocating start-up costs among them.

This discussion is limited to trees used for producing timber on the stump. Other types of trees with other purposes may or will have different IRS rules. You need to establish the appropriate basis accounts for planted crop trees (fruits, citrus, nuts), Christmas tree plantations, non-planted crop trees (such as paw-paws and butternut whose fruit or seeds are sold), nursery stock and seedlings, among others.

After selling your timber, you need to figure your taxable gain or tax loss on the sale. You start by determining your **adjusted timber basis in the year of your sale**. This is your original timber basis at the time of the property's purchase plus the net of all your adjustments to that basis from that time through the sale. You increase your purchase-time timber basis primarily through capital improvements. You decrease your timber basis through depreciation of capital improvements, amortization, depletion and sales. (You can't depreciate land or timber.) You can deduct all permissible timber-selling expenses, such as the cost of a cruise and marking, your consultant's sale-management commission, legal fees, surveying fees, advertising and the like. You don't add these sale-related expenses to your basis. The **up-dated adjusted timber basis** is the number you subtract from gross timber-sale income (less permissible deductions) to determine your **taxable gain**.

If your up-dated adjusted timber basis exceeds the amount you received from your timber sale, you have a **tax loss** even though you're holding cash in your hand. If your up-dated adjusted timber basis at the time of the sale is $500 per acre and you receive $400 per acre in timber sale income, you have $400 per acre in your hand tax-free (because it is covered by your $500 per acre basis) and $100 per acre in tax loss.

Calculating and adjusting your timber resource basis over time is referred to as, **depletion**. The cruise you did at the time of purchase establishes your **timber depletion base**, which is the volume, diameter classes and species of your stumpage. Your timber base at any given time is figured in terms of a **depletion unit**, which is basis/cost (dollars) per unit of timber volume (board feet, cords, tons). If you have $15,000 in adjusted timber basis and have 3,000 merchantable cords of wood in your timber base, each depletion unit (cord) is valued at $5 ($15,000 / 3,000 = $5). As your timber depletion base changes over time through sales, so does your timber basis. When you sell your timber in certain ways, you can take a

depletion deduction, which is calculated this way: adjusted basis divided by total timber volume just before the sale multiplied by timber volume sold.

Depletion of your timber base does not produce the same level of tax benefits that depletion of oil or natural gas does. Since timber is a renewable resource, cutting it produces a time-limited depletion, not a permanent one. Still, you can claim a deduction for depletion of your timber if you cut the timber yourself for sale or have someone cut it for you, but not if you sell standing timber on the stump. You cannot claim a depletion allowance when you cut your timber for personal use. Let your CPA determine whether you're eligible for depletion benefits and what they might be.

Timber can experience **non-sale losses** as it matures. Trees grow in size and value and, at the same time, they suffer mortality from natural forces as well as diminished value from fire, wind breakage, drought, disease, insects and the like. The **normal, background-type loss** that occurs from Nature's variability—a tree falling over; woodpeckers ruining a tree—is **not deductible.** A **casualty loss** is a loss from a naturally occurring physical event that happens suddenly, unexpectedly or in an unusual manner. Such events include timber damage from windstorm, wild fire (not arson), hurricanes, volcanoes, hail, ice storms and plane crashes. The IRS seeks "suddenness" in casualty loss, which means drought and most disease and insect losses are not deductible. Casualty loss must be more than a diminution in value (such as loss from breakage); the event must eliminate the timber's value suddenly. Casualty loss deductibility is handled differently according to the type of timberland owner you are. A casualty loss may be deducted up to the amount of the lost timber's adjusted basis, and other limits apply to this type of loss.

If you own the timberland as an investment or business, you can deduct a **noncasualty loss** when the level of loss is beyond what is considered normal and the cause is out of the ordinary (i.e., unusual and unexpected). In some circumstances, you could claim that loss from drought or disease was a deductible noncasualty loss.

Loss from timber theft is also deductible in the year it is discovered. Theft loss can be deducted up to the adjusted basis in the timber stolen.

When figuring loss, you have to count in salvage proceeds, insurance payments and, in the case of theft, any money you get as reimbursement. Since the rules and forms vary, it is best to work with a CPA who is up to speed on recent IRS rulings. Determining whether a loss qualifies as a casualty loss and then calculating its value will involve a CPA and a forester. Don't try this yourself. A good discussion is found in Melvin J. Baughman's, Income Tax Guide for Woodland Owners, rev. 1999 at www.extension.umn.edu/distribution/naturalresources/DD3934.html. Since tax law and interpretations change, you have to get timely information when you have a question. The National Timber Tax Website provides up-dated information.

When your CPA divides your rural property into various accounts (and, if necessary, sub-accounts), he is setting up a plan for handling the ordinary and necessary expenses you incur in each one. Expenses, depending on their nature, can be 1) **deducted** (expensed) **against income** in the year that you incur them, 2) **capitalized** (depreciated, amortized, allocated to basis, depleted, sold, or otherwise disposed) or 3) **deducted from sale proceeds**. To be able to do each of these things when appropriate, you must have your timberland property set up as an investment or a business, which means the activity you engage in must be carried out with the intention to profit, if only eventually. Holding woodland for personal pleasure/recreation or as a hobby gives you access to many fewer tax benefits involving deductions and capitalized expenses.

IRS looks at a combination of factors to test your profit motivation, including how you carry out your timberland activity; your expertise; amount of time you devote to the activity; appreciation of assets; success in making a profit; your taxpayer history of income and loss; your overall financial status; and, finally, how much recreation or personal pleasure is involved in the "investment/business." (IRC Section 212 pertains to investment; Section 162 for business.) If questioned, you have the burden of persuasion and proof. Timberland investment/business by its nature is a very long-term venture so you will not have to show a cash profit every year or at any particular future moment. Profit in timberland is also established by appreciation in the value of the timber through growth.

Current expenses and depreciable assets may be allocated among your accounts. If, for example, you use your tractor about 60 percent for farming that is intended to make a profit, 30 percent in timberland intended to make a profit and 10 percent in personal non-profit work, such as tilling your garden, your CPA will allocate the tractor's purchase price and certain maintenance costs as 60 percent to your farm account and 30 percent to your timber account. The 10 percent of the tractor's time that you use for personal chores is lost for depreciation purposes, because that share of your tractor is not used in a trade or business.

Equipment, depreciable in whole or shared with another account, that can be related to your timberland investment/business can include a tractor with a bushhog, hydraulic log splitter (used for a business purpose, such as firewood sales), chipper, bulldozer, walk-behind trail mower, tractor winch, farm truck, chainsaw, 4WD ATV and the computer you use to manage your timberland. Such items are called **capital assets**. They have to be valued at more than $100 and have a usable life of more than one year. Once you establish the original basis of the equipment, you depreciate it on your yearly tax forms according to a specific term of years. Depreciation allows you to recover the cost of acquisition over a period of years.

You can also depreciate the cost of an existing building or the construction of a new one that you use to store/maintain timberland-related equipment, tools and supplies.

Just as you cannot operate a hobby farm and get farm-related tax benefits, so too you cannot run a **hobby woodlot** and get timber-related benefits. The stuff you buy should have some reasonable connection to your for-profit timberland activity. You might have a hard time persuading an IRS auditor that you should be allowed to fully depreciate a $75,000 bulldozer, $25,000 tractor, $30,000 pick-up truck and a $400 chainsaw for use on a three-acre "timber tract" in your backyard. To make that level of investment fly against this undersized tract, you would have to show that the work you are doing with it can arguably justify that level of investment. If you were planting Paulownia—a high-value species—you might be able to sell the IRS on it even though the time horizon before your profit may be 60 years away. You can argue that the three acres requires intensive mechanical work to prepare the site—stump and slash removal (dozer/saws), road work (dozer), environmental protection (dozer/saws), ground preparation (tractor with implements), maintenance (tractor), regular application of inputs ("inputs" is a great IRS word) such as herbicide, fertilizer, pesticide, seedlings, all of which require a truck) and so forth. You should expect that the IRS auditor will visit the three acres to see whether you've done all the work you've described. Less extreme examples will, of course, raise fewer eyebrows.

My own experience with being audited is that **paper persuades and a field trip settles any questions**. I had one of the audits from hell where an auditor sat in my dining room for two days going through every check, receipt and scrap of paper I had collected for three tax years. One question involved why I had such high expenses for fencing. I explained that I had installed a rotational grazing system for the cattle that required division of the pasture into small paddocks. By rotating a gang of cattle from fresh field to fresh field every couple of days, I could about double the number of pounds of gain my farm produced each grazing season. The auditor was stilled puzzled. So I walked her out back and through the fields and gates, through the muck and manure. No problem.

In justifying your timberland as an investment/business, you should show an auditor your cruise at the time of purchase (which establishes your timber basis and your timber-depletion base), forest-management plan and simple business plan for your timberland (showing number/species of trees planted, if any, likely year of harvest, projected revenues and costs). Then walk the auditor, if it comes to that, through the three acres, showing where you have used the dozer, tractor, truck and saw. Even though cheaper alternatives for accomplishing this work would have been available to you, the IRS does not require that you use them. The IRS does not care that you are investing your capital inefficiently, or that you could have hired the work for $5,000, or that you could have spent half the money by buying used, smaller models. The Agency mainly cares that you show them you have thought seriously about making a future profit. Your plans and your intentions, rather than your long-term success, are what will be examined for the obvious reason: you can't show long-term success (or failure) in timber until the long term arrives. In this regard, timberland can cover the purchase of machines and equipment by projecting a very large cash profit many decades in the future; timber can be better than farming in this respect.

I am not recommending that you cheat on your taxes. Your profit purpose has to be authentic, and you have to do the work. But I am also observing that timberland can expand the elasticity of your tax situation if you do the proper legal, forestry and tax planning, have the right intentions and follow through.

Remember that depreciation helps you on your annual taxes for each year of its multi-year schedule, but 25 percent of the total amount you depreciate on residential and nonresidential property is added back when you sell the depreciated asset, thus increasing your taxable gain. The recapture tax does not apply to depreciated equipment.

Land and certain land improvements, such as earthen work of a permanent character, are not depreciable. Other non-depreciable land improvements include land leveling, excavating roadbeds of permanent roads and earthen impoundments, such as berms and dikes. Land assets that are depreciable include bridges, culverts, graveling, fences, non-permanent structures, temporary roads and firebreaks. For land assets to be depreciable and for other property, such as equipment, vehicles and tools used on the timberland to be depreciable, you must hold the property as either a business or as an investment, not for pleasure, personal or hobby use.

Non-depreciable equipment (with a less than one-year usable life) might include a used chainsaw, hand tools, gas can, protective chaps and helmet with hearing protectors. Certain equipment might be depreciable or might not—like a chainsaw or gate—depending on size, number, cost, life expectancy and your CPA's judgment. Such items should be deducted.

You can depreciate certain **maintenance and repair costs** on depreciable equipment, but not all such costs. If the expense adds to the life of the equipment, or significantly increases its value, you can depreciate it. Basis in such a machine is increased when maintenance and repair costs are depreciable.

The **costs of consumables and other supplies** are not depreciable. They are deducted from your annual gross income. These timberland-related costs can include gas and oil, herbicide, nails, posted signs, chains and locks, gates, grass seed, software, books and subscriptions to forestry publications.

Payment of management and operating expenses, including overhead, related to your timberland investment or business is deductible. This can include things such as travel to a timber-taxation conference, conference fees, conference food/lodging; travel to look at potential timberland investments; certain educational expenses; travel to meet potential buyers of your stumpage; property taxes; timberland-related phone, fax, internet and postage; proportional shares of insurance, utilities, vehicle costs, rent, office maintenance and equipment; research supplies, books, timber pricing services and other-related expenses.

Your timberland investment/business may also be eligible for all or some of the **home-office** deductions if you dedicate a room of your residence to that activity. You cannot make use of the home-office benefit if you have set up your timberland as a hobby or for personal recreation. Home-office status is a big, flapping red flag to the IRS computers, but don't be scared away from taking legitimate deductions. I've had a home office for more than 20 years without a problem.

You have tax benefits from the cost of hiring **equipment time and operator** for your timber investment/business, but how your CPA handles them can depend on what the time was used for. If you hired a bulldozer to build permanent roads through your timberland, the IRS would consider that a depreciable purpose. The same dozer building ponds for fire protection might be depreciable. The dozer time devoted to maintaining or improving roads is probably a deduction. When you give $25 to your neighbor to take down a tree that's too big and tricky for you to try with the penknife-size, ring-a-ding-ding chainsaw your wife gave you for your first Christmas as a timber owner, that's a deductible rather than depreciable expense. The same is true for the neighbor you hire to mow your woods trails, with his equipment or yours. Hired spot labor is deductible, except when it's spent on depreciable assets, in which case, it's a depreciable cost.

Also deductible annually are any fees you pay to your forester, lawyer or CPA who provide timberland-related advice and services.

All costs you incur in **planting, or reforestation by natural or artificial seeding, can be amortized,** a process, like depreciation, of recovering your basis over a period of years as the asset is used up, worn out or sold. This includes all timber-establishment costs—site preparation, seedlings, equipment used in preparation and planting, hired labor and post-planting work until the trees can survive on their own. Currently, the first $10,000 of reforestation costs can be deducted outright in the year incurred and expenses above that can be amortized/deducted over 84 months.

You cannot capitalize your own labor or pay yourself a wage that you deduct. While you may feel it is unfair that you cannot pay yourself for timberland work, you will not win this fight with an auditor. You may, however, be able to set up your timberland and farm businesses as a limited liability company or other organized entity, which then pays you as an independent contractor to perform certain part-time work. In any event, you must capitalize pay to family members and in some cases your spouse.

You should keep a record of all timber-sale expenses you pay, such as forester commission, legal fees, CPA fees, purchases related to getting the timber out, such as a culvert and so on. Such one-time expenses should be deducted from timber-sale income. These sale-specific expenses are in addition to and separate from your routine timberland expenses noted above.

You may also incur some **post-sale expenses** related to extra reclamation, additional excavation, planting of seedlings, herbicide application, site preparation, fire-pond development, more erosion-control work in the roads, slash clean up and so on. Post-sale expenses are not usually added in with sale expenses, though some exceptions might exist. They should be deductible.

I've discussed in Chapters 6 and 33, the federally funded, state-administered **cost-share** programs that help a landowner pay for conservation, reforestation, timber stand improvements and environmental protections on his property. Some of this money (such as the Conservation Reserve Program) is required to be reported as part of your ordinary gross income; other money, such as that for the Forest Land Enhancement Program (FLEP), Wetlands Reserve Program (WRP), Environmental Quality Incentives Program (EQIP) and the Wildlife Habitat Incentives Program (WHIP) can be excluded from gross income, fully or partially. Different cost shares are handled differently; and the rules can change from Congressional tax bill to Congressional tax bill. Let your CPA sort this out.

Your timberland may also generate income and expenses from **non-timber-sale activities**, such as 1) annual rental income from a hunting or recreation lease; 2) income from renting your sugar maples for sap production; 3) sale of maple sap you collect; and 4) sale of occasional products like nuts, firewood, locust fence posts, mistletoe or ginseng. These would be handled as either ordinary rental income or sale income.

Form T (Timber), Forest Industries Schedules, is the attachment that you use for timberland acquisitions, sales and expenses. It has the following schedules that you may or may not need to complete, depending on your circumstances: A, Maps; B, Acquisitions; C, Profit or Loss from Land and Timber Sales; D, Losses; E. Reforestation and Timber Stand Activities; F, Capital Returnable Through Depletion; G, Land Ownership; H, Road Construction Cost; and I, Drainage Structures. If you make an isolated timber sale and are a small woodlot owner, you need to complete only Schedules C and F. Haney et al., Federal Income Tax, provides an excellent guide to how to report timber-related income and expenses and which form to use.

A lot of information is available on timber taxation. (A lot of information appears to be necessary.) Start with the USDA's, Forest Owners' Guide to Timber Investments, The Federal Income Tax, and Tax Recordkeeping, Forest Service, Agriculture Handbook 718, most recent edition. This is obtainable from the U.S. Government Printing Office or your local USDA Forest Service Office or at www.timbertax.org/research/aghndbk/aghndbk.asp?id=research&topic=aghndbk. The **National Timber Tax Website** at www.timbertax.org is a fountainhead of information on the subject, including links to all relevant federal regulations, at www.timbertax.org/research/regulations/regulations.asp?id=research&topic=regs. Visit the Purdue University website at www.fnr.purdue.edu/ttax; Baughman's, Income Tax Guide for Woodland Owners, rev. 1999, University of Minnesota Extension Service at www.extension.umn.edu/distribution/_naturalresources/DD3934.html. Good references can be found at www.nyfoa.org/NYFOACasualtyTaxIntro.html. The Journal of Agricultural Taxation & Law carries the most articles on the subject. Additional information can be obtained from the Forest Industries Council on Taxation (FICT), 1111 19th St., N.W., Suite 800, Washington, D.C. 20036; 202-463-2757; FAX, 202-463-2057. General sources for taxation and investment information include The American Agricultural Law Association's www.aglaw-assn.org/biblio/22%20%20%Forestry.htm; and www.na.fs.fed.us/pubs/_misc/ir/irtoc.htm, the USFS's "Guide to Internet Resources." Attorney William C. Siegel, who specializes in forestry taxation and was referenced above, may be contacted at 504-737-0583; e-mail: wcsieg@aol.com. The Haney et al., Federal Income Tax, is current as of 2005, comprehensive and well-organized.

All of this discussion applies to the federal tax code as of 2005. The Breaux-Mack Commission proposed a sweeping simplification of the tax system in the fall of that year. Mortgage-interest deductibility would be reduced significantly, and many deductions removed. The Bush White House did not endorse these proposals. A land buyer, particularly one considering farm and timber assets, must consult with his CPA prior to making an offer to determine the then-current tax rules that will be applied to his purchase.

CONSERVATION EASEMENTS AND TAXES

More common than the sale of a conservation easement is its **donation by the landowner to a public agency or 501 (c) (3) charitable organization,** such as a land trust, conservation group or a landowners' association of neighbors set up to hold such easements on their own land. The holder of the easement must have the capacity to enforce the easement over time. Not all rural land automatically qualifies under state laws and IRS regulations for the substantial income-tax and estate-tax benefits a donor can get for contributing one or more of his rights in his land. Among the rights often contributed, in whole or part, are the right to develop for commercial or residential purposes, right to timber, right to mine and quarry, right to install a wind farm, etc. To get the tax benefits, the conservation easement—what you are giving—has to have both an authentic market value and a clear environmental benefit. You are giving away something of value, leaving your property, theoretically, that much less valuable than before. An appraiser determines the value of the right (s) you've chosen to donate.

Your land needs to be located where some significant public or environmental benefit will be achieved by restricting one or more future uses of the property through the easement. An easement that preserves open space on an inaccessible patch of remote mountainside is not likely to qualify under the IRS rules, because the development right you're giving away has no value on that property. Similarly, a donation of a restriction that has no market value will not wash. The organizations that accept these donations, such as land trusts, should not be in the business of scamming the IRS. You should assume that the easement's valuation has to be based in reality. Timber easements, whereby the landowner donates his right to cut timber on his property, or limits this right, are often overvalued by a compliant forester who inflates the donation's value. The IRS may not pick up some inflation, but egregious inflation will probably catch their eye.

Donation of a qualifying easement brings the donor four different tax benefits. First, the donation is a charitable contribution whose value may be deducted from your income for federal and state income taxes. The full value of your donation is multiplied by your federal income tax rate and state rate combined to determine the value of your deduction. If you—an individual—have held your property for more than one year, your deduction is limited to 30 percent of what amounts to your adjusted gross income in the year you make the donation. If, on the other hand, you take your deduction in the first ownership year using your basis in the land, you can deduct up to 50 percent of your adjusted gross income. If you are inclined to place a conservation easement on your land, consider doing it soon after you purchase the property to take advantage of the extra benefit. You can carry any unused deduction forward for five years, giving you a total of six years to use the entire deduction. Second, the easement reduces your estate's value, which can help lower or even eliminate estate tax, depending on your individual circumstances. Third, the executor of your estate can exclude from your estate 40 percent of the value of the land carrying your easement after subtracting the value of the easement up to $500,000, using Section 2031 (c) of the American Farm and Ranch Protection Act. Fourth, a number of states allow land with such an easement to be assessed in light of the value of that easement being severed, which will produce lower property taxes.

The rules for using these tax benefits are more complicated than these few sentences suggest. I have relied on several publications written by attorney C. Timothy Lindstrom, who is director of The Jackson Hole Land Trust, POB 2897, 5455 East Broadway, Suite 228, Jackson, WY 83001; 307-733-4707; tim@jhlandtrust.org. My brief discussion is based on Linstrom's, <u>A Simplified Guide to the Tax Benefits of Donating A Conservation Easement</u> (available from the Jackson Hole Land Trust); "Tax Advantages of Conservation Easement Donation," November, 1998 and "Conservation Easements in Virginia," 1999; <u>The Conservation Easement Handbook, The Federal Tax Law of Conservation Easements</u> and other information published by the Land Trust Alliance, 1319 F Street, N.W., Suite 501, Washington, DC, 20004. State and sub-state land trusts are now common. They can be accessed by doing a search on www.google.com, using "land trust, state or city." The Land Trust Alliance and The Nature Conservancy (TNC) can also provide information on "qualified organizations" in your area that are set up to accept these easements. Tim Linstrom is willing to chat briefly with interested callers and takes on paying clients. Steve Small, cited above, specializes in conservation easements.

While the tax benefits of conservation easements are huge, you should approach donation or sale cautiously and with great thoughtfulness. First, a valuable right today is likely to be much more valuable in the future. The tax benefit you get is based on current value. Today's $100,000 no-cut-timber right could easily be worth ten times that in ten years. What do you need more and when do you need it: tax benefits now or cash later? Life is so uncertain that I would hesitate to sever an asset that might at some future point rescue me from my habit of shooting my own financial foot. Second, the value of any no-cut timber easement will depend on when, in the growth cycle, you grant it. A no-cut easement immediately following a clearcut would, I think, have little value. The same easement given on a stand of cherry in its 80th year, would be worth much money. A ten- or 15-year difference can multiply value many times over if the first year of that span occurs when the trees are still considered too small for sawtimber but the last year captures the **ingrowth effect**. A no-cut easement could have additional value where the timber is around, but not part of, habitat for a federally endangered species. Third, most conservation easements are donated in perpetuity, which means forever. Fourth, you may have a problem selling a valuable tract once you've peeled off a right that makes it valuable. One hundred acres of woods surrounded by suburbs has scant market value if you've donated its timber and development rights. Who, you should ask yourself, will want to buy it so that it can be kept untouched? This is not a brief against conservation easements. It is simply a few words to make you understand that these vows, unlike those of marriage, cannot be broken.

If you're considering an easement, think of ways to limit its scope while achieving your objectives. You can, for example, donate a no-development right while keeping the right to build a house or two if the acreage is sufficiently large. You might donate an easement that prohibits clearcutting, but allows cutting of mature timber at least 20 years after the previous cut. You can also put a full no-cut easement on one part of your land, but not on the rest. Do not donate an easement that allows public access to your land unless that is what you and your immediate heirs want. You might also investigate a time-limited easement, say one that runs for 20 years, or one that is in effect during the life time of the donor.

As a rule, I would advise against putting a no-cut timber easement on your property.

STATE AND LOCAL TIMBER TAXES

Timberland is subject to **local and state taxes**. The principal local tax is likely to be the county's **property tax**, which can take several forms. Some states also tax income earned on the sale of timber. The National Timber Tax Website provides information on forest property taxes each state uses, along with a general discussion of their differences. Each state adopts a property tax format, which is administered through a local jurisdiction—such as city, county, township or parish. Differences in timberland taxes—property and/or sale—can be significant from state to state. See www.timbertax.org/state_laws/quickreference.asp?id=statelaws&topic=reference. In most states, standing timber is not taxed, either by custom or law. California is one exception, imposing a 2.9 percent tax on timber every 60 years.

The Website's property-tax data, when I reviewed them, were based on a 1996 publication by Sun Joseph Chang. Sun lists **five types of state forest-property-taxation systems**: 1) *ad valorem* **property tax**, by which tax is collected on the basis of the value of the land and the trees; 2) **productivity tax**, by which the annual tax is based on the capitalized value of either the gross or net mean annual revenue from the timberland; 3) **site value tax**, by which only the land is taxed; 4) **flat property tax**, by which the same amount of money is collected per acre of timberland no matter the timber's current value; and 5) **exemption** states where some or all of the timber value is exempt from property tax, or the tax is qualified or discounted in some way. When scoping timberland property, keep in mind that some states tax timber production. That will lower income from any sale of timber immediately following purchase. The National Timber Tax website at www.timbertax.org provides the following analysis of state timber-tax systems, which differs from Sun's typography:

TABLE 24-1

STATE TAX LAWS

State Tax Laws > Quick Reference: Forest Property Taxation Systems in the United States

Ad valorem property tax (Current Use) – A tax, duty, or fee which varies based on the value of the products, services, or property on which it is levied.

Flat property tax – under this system the same amount of money per acre is collected on any acre of timberland regardless of its value.

Site Map

Yield Tax – is a tax on the value of the harvested timber. The tax is collected after the timber is harvested.

Severance Tax – is a flat tax on a specific unit of volume harvested (i.e., board feet, cubic feet, cords, tonnage etc.). The tax is collected after the timber is harvested.

State	Ad Valorem	Flat	Exemption	Severance Tax	Yield Tax
Alabama	X			X	
Alaska			X		
Arizona		X		X	
Arkansas	X			X	
California	X			X	
Colorado	X				
Connecticut	X[1]				
Delaware	X		X		
Florida	X				
Georgia	X			X	
Hawaii	X[2]				
Idaho	X				X
Illinois	X				X
Indiana	X	X			
Iowa	X		X		
Kansas	X[2]				
Kentucky	X				
Louisiana	X				
Maine	X[1]				
Maryland	X				
Massachusetts		X[4]			X
Michigan		X			X
Minnesota		X[3]			
Mississippi	X				

State					
Missouri		X			X
Montana	X			X	
Nebraska	X				
Nevada	X				
New Hampshire		X			X
New Jersey	X				
New Mexico	X				X
New York	X	X^3			X
N. Carolina	X			X	
N. Dakota		X			
Ohio	X	X^3			
Oklahoma	X^2				
Oregon	X^1				
Pennsylvania	X^1				
Rhode Island	X		X		
S. Carolina	X				
S. Dakota	X^2				
Tennessee	X				
Texas	X				
Utah	X				
Vermont	X				
Virginia	X^5			X	
Washington	X^1				
W. Virginia	X				X
Wisconsin		X			X
Wyoming	X				

X^1 Current use based on forest productivity

X^2 Current use based on agricultural productivity

X^3 Reduction in Fair Market Value (FMV)

X^4 Reduction in FMV for land classified as forestland or recreational lands; Flat tax for land classified as agricultural & horticultural land.

X^5 Current use based on site productivity

Source: http://www.timbertax.org/statetaxes/quickreference.asp   10/5/2005

The quickest way to obtain current property tax information in the jurisdiction of your target property is to visit the local (tax) **assessor's office**. Here you will find the **tax-assessed value** of the property, which comes from the jurisdiction's periodic **reassessment** of all property within its borders. The property's tax-assessed value will be divided into categories: the land itself, according to its class (e.g., residential, agricultural, timberland), improvements (structures that are permanently attached to the land, such as a house or barn), minerals and, where applicable, possibly water rights. Such assets, including standing timber, are considered **real property**. (A right, benefit or interest that runs with the land—such as a life estate—is also considered real property.) The tax-appraisal value is supposed to represent current **fair market value (FMV)**. The values you find in the county records may represent 100 percent of FMV, or something less, depending on the state's policy. West Virginia, for example, values land for tax purposes at 60 percent of FMV; some towns in New York use 94 percent. (For convenience, I will use "county" to represent the appropriate jurisdiction for the target property.) Tax-assessed values, tax rates, current taxes and related information are collected in the jurisdiction's **Land Book**, copies of which are usually available in several county offices. Your jurisdiction may have another name for this comprehensive compilation of property information. It also may be fully accessible by computer and no longer kept in hard copy. Whatever the format and name, this information is public record and should be freely available.

The quickest and easiest way of getting a ballpark sense of the fair market value—likely sale price—of a target property is to phone the tax assessor and ask a generalized question that fits your target. Don't ask, "Whadda you think the Fred Smith place is worth?" Ask, "What is unimproved timberland in the 200 to 300-acre range selling for per acre in the southeast end of the county?" If you decide to base your offer on that general opinion, don't quote the assessor to the seller. Attribute the opinion to "knowledgeable sources," if you're asked.

In the assessor's office and the Land Book, you should find the following:

- target property's **acreage** (as carried on the tax rolls; this figure may or may not be the same as the deeded acreage; it is often inaccurate)

- most recent **tax-appraisal values for its land, improvements and minerals**

- information as to **what percentage of fair market value** the tax-appraised value represents (This can be 100 percent or less.)

- **property classification** to which your property has been assigned

- whether this county has adopted **use-value taxation (land use)** and whether the target property is so classified (See below.)

- whether any **special taxes, levies, fees or charges** apply to this property

- **tax rates** that apply to the property's land, minerals and improvements

- **dollar amount of current taxes** by land, minerals and improvements

- **date** when property taxes are **due**

- **discounts**, if any, for early payment; **penalties** for late payment

- **exemptions and breaks**, e.g., seniors, resident homeowners, etc.

- information on **other taxes** the jurisdiction imposes, such as a machinery and equipment tax, farm-machinery tax, business or occupation tax, self-employment tax, special taxes/levies or fees (sewer and water districts, trash disposal, road taxes, school construction etc.) and personal property taxes (vehicles, boats, motorcycles etc., which are assets that do not fit the definition of real property). You may have to visit other offices as well to get a complete picture of the full load. Personal property, which is property other than real property, is usually taxed, though jurisdictions may be more or less inclusive as to the types of personal property they tax. Some items, such as vehicles, may be taxed both locally and at the state level.

In terms of timberland, it is important to remember that standing timber—timber on the stump—is considered real property that conveys when you buy the land, unless the owner explicitly retains ownership or reserves an interest in it. But cut timber—logs or trees on the ground—is personal property. Thus, an unscrupulous owner might take advantage of an inexperienced buyer by cutting the 50 best cherry sawtimber trees between the day the buyer submits a contract and when the owner accepts it, 15 days later. The 50+ logs are worth $35,000 and become the owner's personal property as soon as they are on the ground. The unfortunate buyer failed to include a provision in his purchase contract that linked his offer to the owner leaving the timber unchanged as of the offer's submission date, not its acceptance date. The buyer should also include language that prohibits timbering between the date of contract submission and closing. This is scummy behavior, but the owner has a breastwork of law to hide behind.

A word about **minerals**. Minerals are usually taxed both as property and as they are produced. If the property's minerals have not been severed from the surface, then the landowner owns the subsurface minerals and is responsible for their taxes. If the mineral rights have been sold outright, the owner of the target property is not responsible for any taxation on minerals. If, as is far more common, the mineral rights have been leased to another party, the owner of the minerals is responsible for the property tax. Who is responsible for payment of the production tax as the minerals are produced? The answer will depend both on state law and on the terms of the lease agreement the owner (lessor) has negotiated with the lessee, the outfit that's leased the owner's minerals. (The lessee may, in turn, assign his lease rights to a production company who will do the actual mining or drilling.) The lease may specify how the lessor (owner) and lessee will divide the tax hit. This language can be written as the parties agreeing to pay 1) the state severance/production/yield tax in equal shares, fifty-fifty; or 2) in the same proportion as they have agreed to divide (gross or net) production revenue, e.g., seven-eighths to the lessee, one-eighth to the owner. If the lease does not specify how the production tax is to be apportioned, assume that the lessor, you, are liable for the production tax until you are explicitly told differently by your CPA or tax attorney. Ask this question as part of your pre-purchase scoping so that you are not surprised by a post-purchase wake-up call.

The major property tax break in rural areas is **use-value taxation systems**, which are now in place in every state, though not in every county in every state. Commonly called **land use**, these programs allow counties to tax agricultural, open and/or timberland at the value for which the land is currently used rather than at a higher and better use which is the fair market value. Use value is the expected selling price of the property with the restriction that it can be used only for its current use or a similar use. The purpose of land use is to help owners hold their property for these lower-value uses, such as agriculture or woodland, instead of converting it to commercial or residential development. Conservation easements that sever or limit development rights are designed to keep such land in its current use. Land-use land is appraised at the FMV of its current use, not its FMV as its highest possible use, which produces a big tax savings for the owner. If a landowner decides to withdraw land-use property from the land-use program, he usually has to pay some portion of his past tax savings, plus interest, as a **rollback tax**. Not all rural counties employ land use. Where it has not been adopted, individual property may still be eligible for land-use treatment if the state provides this status for managed timberland and land in **agricultural and forestal districts**. The rules and formulas governing these calculations are complicated and state-specific. Check with the county or regional office of the state forestry agency regarding the tax break for managed timber lands; the assessor should be able to provide information on agricultural and forestall districts.

Most states extend a **use-valuation** approach to timberland that is similar to the agricultural use or land-use tax break for valuing agricultural land. The way this is handled varies. Some states classify all timberland as agricultural land, which then makes it eligible for a use valuation. Others extend use valuation to timberland that is part of an owner-occupied farm, but not to non-occupied land. In a few states, timberland can get use-valuation status if it is enrolled in the state's managed-forest program, which usually requires a forester-written plan for the owner's timber property. State policies on use-valuation for timberland is in E.B. Kelley, "Recent Developments in Forest Taxation Policy: A Comparative Overview of Selected Major Timber-Producing States," 1998 at www.cnr.umn.edu/FR/publications/proceedings/improving_forestproductivity/papers/KELLEY~1.PDF.

Do not be surprised if a county classifies wooded land in several ways, each of which has a different tax rate. Wooded land that is part of an occupied farm residence may enjoy a much lower rate than wooded land that is not. Residential status may have been established years ago, so even if you are a new absentee landowner, you may still benefit from it. In such cases, you, as the new owner, want to do nothing that provokes a review: some counties are vigilant, while others are not.

Wooded land with some version of land-use status is taxed more lightly than the same land without. Ask local officials about how agricultural, undeveloped and timberland are taxed. Ask whether there are different classifications of timberland, depending on ownership or the productivity of the land for growing timber. Ask if the tax rate is fixed, regardless of stumpage value. Ask, finally, about the current and future status of the target property. If your property is in a state that imposes a **tax on yield or timber-sale income,** you will need to figure that into your offering price.

You will also want to do a little **future analysis** when it comes to local taxes. If you think the county is a backwater, you will probably assume that the property tax burden will continue to be comparatively low, consistent with the minimum public services available. I urge caution about making such straight-line extrapolations. Demands for services can change quickly, and for different reasons. State and federal programs often do not adequately fund the new standards they impose on localities; the phrase that drives local officials nuts is "unfunded mandates." Requirements related to water supply, waste-water treatment, education, corrections and the like can force localities to raise taxes to fund worthy improvements. A low-tax community with inadequate services may be on the cusp of raising its property tax. Big projects—second-home developments, resorts and so on—can also inflate property values and taxes. You must look in the local newspaper and ask around to determine whether you are about to be blindsided. If the county has land use, you can assume it will continue to have it. If it does not have land use, I would assume that it will not adopt it in the future. Our most rural/agricultural counties often don't adopt land use because their populations are so overwhelmingly farm-based that there are too few non-farmers to carry the tax burden that land use would shift away from farmland. In this case, farmers might lower their property tax but they would have to pick up the local tax needed in some other way. If the county is developing as an outer-ring suburb, anticipate higher local taxes. Ask whether any new levies or special assessments are in the works. Check the zoning office to see whether the target property is located in a designated growth area under the local comprehensive plan. If so, you can expect residential and/or commercial development—and higher taxes. But your target property will be worth more. Finally, ask how the county treats recently sold property for taxes. If you pay far more for your property than the tax-appraised value, it's a good bet that the next county-wide reappraisal will increase your property's valuation. Make sure to ask when the next county-wide reappraisal will take place. It's actually a pretty good bet that your property's valuation will increase in every subsequent county-wide reappraisal. If you see selling prices rising, property taxes will follow.

Jurisdictions reappraise their property for tax purposes every few years, according to their state's requirements. This is referred to as the county's **reappraisal** or **reassessment**. The purpose of the reappraisal is to determine the current fair market value for every piece of real property in the jurisdiction.

You must assume that your property will be reappraised at higher value in each round, unless it's located where market prices are falling. My property value more than doubled between five-year assessments—and I think that it is still undervalued in light of the market.

Property tax is levied by a local jurisdiction according to its state's rules. The local **tax rate** is often expressed in dollars per $100 of assessed value. It may also be referred to as the **millage rate**, where so many mills, each of which is equal to $1/10^{th}$ of one cent, are levied per dollar of assessed value. If your 100 acres of undeveloped land is appraised for tax purposes at $150,000 and the tax rate is $1.65 per $100 of tax-appraised/tax-assessed value, the current annual property tax would be $2,475 ($150,000 value / 100 = 1,500 x $1.65 = $2,475). The bottom line in understanding your property tax burden is the dollar amount of the annual payment, which is the product of your tax rate and the property's tax-assessed value.

Appraisal values for similar agricultural, undeveloped and wooded properties are likely to differ within a county according to their slightly different uses, locations and possibly zoning status. Sometimes, it's impossible to figure out why pasture or woodland on one side of a fence is appraised differently than pasture or woodland on the other side. Each jurisdiction provides an appeal process by which you can challenge your reappraisal. You will need to make your case before an official board of "review and equalization." This is done by assembling information on nearby comparables the reassessment appraiser valued lower than your property. You can also present recent-sale comparables. I have seen landowners win appeals on house values, but not on land, particularly undeveloped land.

Each state has its own reappraisal system that counties follow. **Land tables** are constructed, using recent selling prices and other data, to provide values for different land types. Digital cameras are now used to build data banks on improvements. Agricultural land is usually grouped/graded into one of several classes—cropland, pasture, woodland, range and so on. Agricultural land may be valued according to rental rates rather than selling prices. Timberland, apart from that associated with agricultural land, is also subject to categorization by type, purpose, location and/or size. My experience is that tax appraisers do not try to determine the merchantable timber value on the land they classify as timberland. Instead, they use the appropriate land tables that are developed at the county level. In many counties, this results in a single appraisal value, say $400 per acre, applied to all timberland, whether it has just been clearcut or contains $2,500 per acre in merchantable timber.

Your **local tax burden** is the sum of all local taxes that you will be expected to pay as the new owner of a target property. Local tax burden is always somewhat greater than the property tax alone. You will discover much tax-burden variation among counties within a state, depending on their degree of urbanization-suburbanization, but not that much variation between like counties in the same state. Local taxes and particularly the property tax reflect each county's expenditures for local services. Counties that share a basic profile—rural, low-population, low development potential, similar topography—should be roughly comparable in spending, taxing and regulating. You should find the local tax burden, particularly property taxes, declining as you move further away from suburbs into increasingly rural, small-population counties. My experience is that rural counties provide the basic package of public services, but not much over that unless they are a hot second-home market for urban buyers. Basic services translate into a low tax burden. Rural counties also try to keep property taxes low as a way to help farmers, the elderly on fixed incomes and local families with limited earnings. When reappraisal values are announced, rural counties will often lower their tax rates to keep the tax burden about the same as before (with a little increase, of course).

Timberland owners need to be aware that some states impose a tax on the sale of timber. This may be called a **severance tax, yield tax, excise tax or production tax**. Several states—Washington, California and Louisiana—combine an *ad valorem* tax on property with what I will refer to as a production tax, which is generally calculated on gross sales revenue. However, California levies a 2.9 percent tax once every 60 years against the value of standing timber. California also extends a use-value tax break for managed timberland in timberland production zones that results in lower valuations and lower taxes. (See John W. LeBlanc, "How Much Will I Owe in State Taxes: The Yield Tax and Timber Production Zones," Working in the Woods: A Guide for California's Forest Landowners, University of California, Natural Resources Cooperative Extension, undated, at www.cnr.berkeley.edu/departments/espm/extension/YIELDTAX.HTM.) Georgia taxes timberland owned by large landowners annually at its full FMV in its highest and best use, and also taxes production. Georgia continues to be a major timber-producing state.

When comparing different target properties, it's often useful to compare their current **per-acre total tax burdens**. If similar type land is taxed differently from one to another, you might start asking why. Land carrying a higher tax burden may be, simply put, "better land" in terms of its productivity and location. You can also compare the per-acre tax-appraised value of your target property's timberland, pasture and cropland with the same types of land held by its neighbors. If your target property's lands are significantly out of whack with those of your neighbors, it may reflect some fact on the ground or, alternatively, a difference in ownership history. Properties that have been sold repeatedly and recently are likely to have higher tax-appraisal valuations than those that have not.

Kelley, *op. cit.*, estimated the **per-acre tax burden** (both land tax and production tax where imposed) on very large timberland owners in about a dozen major timber-producing states. The lowest burden was calculated for eastern Oregon, at a little more than $1 per acre. Oklahoma, Alabama, Idaho, North Carolina, Minnesota, West Virginia and Arkansas were less than $3 per acre. Mississippi, eastern Washington and inland California were between $3 and $5 per acre. Georgia and western Oregon were at $8; coastal California was at $9; and western Washington was almost $25. The West Coast rates reflect the incredibly high volumes and values that appear in these forests. The key assumption in Kelley's work was that the owner had an annual harvest requirement of 20 million board feet.

Tax considerations are always a factor when evaluating investments. But both local and federal tax policies are broadly favorable to timberland investment. I've never seen a timberland purchase fall through because of its tax burden, except in NewYork, where the local property and school taxes are very high.

CHAPTER 25: COUNTRY LAWYERS AND COUNTRY REAL-ESTATE LAW

Buying rural property always requires that the buyer have some knowledge of the legal framework in which such transactions occur, common problems of ownership and conveyance and, finally, the procedural steps he is expected to take to complete a purchase. I've touched on these points in other chapters. The discussion that follows is not meant to substitute for competent legal advice. Consider these next chapters not as a law-school text on real estate but as practical lessons learned on the campus of rural give and take. **Don't try to buy rural land without competent local counsel.**

FINDING A COUNTRY LAWYER

Every buyer needs an experienced, local dirt lawyer. He should be your advocate and source of guidance. He will know the state's code (laws), which governs land transactions, and he will have access to relevant case law (legal decisions). He will also know the local players—zoning official, real-estate agents, bankers/lenders, farmers, USDA employees, soil engineers, excavators, surveyors, consulting foresters, home inspectors, well drillers, septic-system cleaners and so on. A lawyer in your target county is local; the further away your lawyer is from local, the less he will know about the local players.

Your lawyer may know, or at least know of, the seller. Any knowledge of the seller's financial circumstances, motives for selling and negotiating personality are invaluable to you. If you have specific questions about the seller, your lawyer's network of friends and contacts can probably come up with reasonably accurate answers. Your lawyer may be able to get sensitive information for you because he works with local folks every day and knows how to approach such matters better than you do. He will know the individuals in each county office who get things done and those who can't, don't or won't. Following his advice—"Go here, not there."—will save you time and money.

The time to find local counsel is after you've chosen your target county but _before_ you approach any seller. I would even advise securing a relationship with a local lawyer before you start driving around with real-estate agents or on your own. Pay for an hour or two of his time to learn about the county's politics, economics and personalities. You may want to introduce yourself to the county through your lawyer. You want his advice regarding your buying objectives and local fair-market values. Lawyers often know about property that's coming on the market, as well as land that's not listed but is for sale privately or about to come on the market. He'll also know of property that's had a troubled legal history. He should have opinions about which properties are over-priced. Land that has been sold and resold several times within the last five years is often priced above market. He may also be able to steer you away from areas in the county that may not suit your objectives, such as places whose dirt is hard to perc, as well as spots that may be close to a planned development. Make sure that the lawyer knows from the outset that you will pay him for his time. Don't mutter and scrimp over these dollars. Consider them the cheapest degree you've ever paid for.

How do you find a dirt-smart lawyer in a place where you are walking in cold? The local bar association can provide names. The legal reference, Martindale-Hubbell, is available in larger libraries. It will give you a sense of the size of the firm and its self-professed areas of competence. Buy a copy of the local phone directory. Start your screening by eliminating lawyers who don't include "real estate" in their directory advertisements. Ask people you know and whose judgment you trust. I once found a dirt lawyer in Cody, Wyoming by asking a friend in Pennsylvania who had graduated from the University of Wyoming's law school for a contact; he called his former roommate, now a Wyoming judge, who gave him the name.

Country lawyers are usually general practitioners out of financial necessity, but some specialize more than others in real estate. You can narrow the field by walking into the county clerk's office where deeds are recorded and digging through recent land transactions. Deeds are usually prepared on a lawyer's stationery. That ten-minute research should supply the names of several lawyers who are doing most of local real-estate work. In and of itself, that information doesn't highlight the best lawyer for you, but it can introduce you to your main choices.

New, out-of-county buyers are always told to "ask around" for a lawyer. This hit-and-miss technique can work as long as you test those whose opinions you've gotten. Don't just request a lawyer's name. Ask your source why he prefers this one over the others. What's the source's personal experience with the lawyer? Are they related? You have to get a fix on the source before you can trust his opinion. It won't hurt to ask for legal references from the county's zoning officer, one or more local lenders and recent out-of-county buyers. If you know a local resident, start there. Don't ask the seller.

The danger that lurks in asking for a reference is that you may feel that you are then locked into the recommended person. Another lawyer may be a better fit for you after interviewing both. Thank the source of the recommendation for his effort and tell him that you'll be interviewing several possibilities. Try to keep your source from becoming invested in your decision.

Rural lawyers, particularly sole practitioners, have been slower to establish Internet websites than their city counterparts. Since everybody in the county knows who the local lawyers are, there's little reason to bother with a website. An out-of-county buyer can easily do an Internet search for local lawyers by typing into a search engine, "lawyer, county name, state"; or "lawyer, zipcode." Listing websites such as www.findlaw.com, will produce lawyers in larger cities and those with websites and profiles. But when I typed in "lawyer, Highland County, VA" and "lawyer, 24465," the closest hits were lawyers 45 miles distant. Three lawyers practice full-time in Highland County, one of whom is my wife. None have a website, and none showed up on the any of the legal websites I tried. If these websites don't work for you, go to the website of the state bar, which is the licensing and administrative organization for lawyers in the state, and the state's bar association, which is a due-paying organization of state lawyers. One or both should have a referral service, by which you can find a real-estate lawyer in your target county. I finally discovered a listing for two of the three Highland County lawyers on the website of the Highland County Chamber of Commerce in the Business Directory under Attorneys. The third lawyer in the county apparently chooses not to be a Chamber member.

The more rural the county, the smaller its population and the fewer its lawyers. In the smallest communities, you might find only two or three. Other things being equal, it's better to pick from the target county's lawyers rather than pull one from the next county over. Leave your Big City lawyer at home, particularly if he does nothing but appellate work before the U.S. Supreme Court, is president of the American Bar Association and teaches at Harvard Law School. He will not have the ground-truth knowledge and information of a local dirt lawyer, even a mediocre one. Two of the best land deals I ever negotiated involved very expensive, out-of-county, Big-City lawyers representing the sellers. They knew absolutely nothing about how to evaluate undeveloped rural land for their clients.

A rural county usually has a cluster of lawyers around its court house. You will find several sole practitioners and a couple of partnerships. At least one of the bigger firms will be run by an older, "connected" white male. He is likely to have his finger in a real-estate project or two and will represent some of the major local economic interests. He might sit on the board of a local bank or provide part-time counsel to the county. He's a product of one of the state's law schools and has chosen to be a big fish in a small pond. This generic guy, in my experience, places his interests before those of any new client. If, however, you look like a fat pigeon—someone who is wealthy or prominent by local standards—this fellow may be your best choice, because he will curry favor in hope of future business. If, on the other hand, you have a low profile, I'd recommend a different choice.

Lawyers, like all of us, are inclined to find formulas and stick with them. Real-estate work lends itself to using a standard contract form (each word of which has been tested), standard title-search procedure and standard way of handling buyers. The buyer's lawyer should always be responsible for checking the seller's title, and he may perform other tasks as well including handling escrow, finding financing and managing the closing. Experienced dirt lawyers do their title work the same way every time to protect themselves and their clients from errors of both omission and commission. This may be good enough, but you will go far to protect your interests if you can gently persuade your lawyer to work on your behalf beyond his customary standard. Since you are an out-of-county buyer, you will tell him that you need more advice and different advice than is his norm. For instance, you say, you would prefer to use something other than the standard purchase contract because, as he knows, it favors sellers. This is particularly true of the boiler-plate language found in contracts used by real-estate brokers (who are, as a rule, working for the seller.) You will be asking this lawyer to do a little bit more advising, both legal and non-legal, owing to your inexperience in the county. I've found that if you put your needs and expectations on the table during your first meeting, lawyers can adjust their services. I caution, however, against coming across as excessively needy or compulsively nerdy.

Finally, you need to be frank in saying to him that you intend to be a little more involved than most clients without—emphasize this—being a pest. Lawyers hate clients who call them every ten minutes with a "quick legal question," change their contract terms a dozen times and then squabble over every billed minute. You want to be helpful by researching the non-legal aspects of your target property; you don't want to do legal work for your lawyer. You can share information that has legal implications, raise points about the property of which he may or may not be aware and ask questions. You need to respect the line between being helpful and being controlling and neurotic. It's fine to provide thoughts about direction, but avoid telling your lawyer how to be a lawyer.

If you get the feeling that the local lawyer you're interviewing sees you as a nuisance, either change your approach or start fresh with your next choice. I recommend doing the former before doing the latter. If you sense that the lawyer you're interviewing is not very flexible and doesn't want to do anything different, keep looking. You're trying to find the lawyer who will work with you as well as for you.

I find that treating a lawyer as a colleague in a joint project works best for me. Some out-of-town buyers treat local lawyers as servants. This doesn't wear well. I've also seen buyers be cowed by their own lawyers. This, too, is not the right relationship. I can't offer a one-size-fits-all relationship for buyers and local lawyers, but I would encourage you to respect your lawyer's professional knowledge without kowtowing to it. Get his fee money figured out at the start, and don't quibble. If something goes haywire, you want this lawyer on your side.

I look for a well-organized, efficient lawyer with at least ten years of local experience. I look for evidence of a real-estate practice. Maps and surveys scattered around an office are good signs. I like relatively neat, organized offices with a touch of local art, but I don't trust desks that are free of paper. A bit of legal clutter indicates to me that work is being done. I avoid pretentious offices with needlessly expensive décor—the lawyer is likely to be the same. Lawyers whose hourly rates are in the middle of the local pack are best bets. They're not too fancy to work hard for you, and they're not likely to bill you for the time they "spend on your case" while taking a shower.

I like rational, analytical lawyers. I avoid the bullies and screamers. They may work for you, but their bullying and screaming are tactics they've devised to disguise their intellectual weaknesses. I also avoid any lawyer who cannot write a letter without grammatical errors.

I prefer working with women. My experience, admittedly limited, is that male country lawyers sometimes tend to be disorganized, or not very serious about being a lawyer, or not particularly conscientious about working for new clients, or a little loopy, or burned out, or fast and loose, or infected with contorted legalese, or otherwise unsuitable. I look for a female lawyer at least in her mid-30s who has run her own practice for a while and has family responsibilities. I ask about her educational background, local ties and current real-estate practice. I'm looking for thoroughness and judgment. I want someone who's analytical and protective of my interests. I ask her to tell me in advance when she might have a conflict representing me with a particular seller. I want to feel intellectually and emotionally comfortable with her as a lawyer. I have found that female country lawyers work a bit harder for their clients and, generally speaking, are at least as good if not better than their male counterparts. Exceptions to all of the above generalizations exist, and every reader should keep an open mind. Crummy lawyers exist, both male and female, both urban and rural. My experience is that the out-of-county buyer, male and female, has better odds of finding a good fit with a female attorney. (This has a little to do with the fact that my wife is a country dirt lawyer—but not that much.)

I also have decent experiences with male urban refugees who went back to the land 30 years or so ago. They have blown through their hippie days and are now semi-respectable members of the local establishment. They tend to have fancier law degrees than the home-grown lawyers, but may not be as locally smart. I've also found I like ex-student trouble makers and those who take on public-interest cases—environmental issues, indigent clients and court-appointed work—from a feeling of political ethics and professional obligation. For me, they tend to be easier to connect with than the "straight" local lawyers who are occasionally unreasonably suspicious of "outsiders," even their own clients. I've found such "marginal" lawyers more trustworthy and better suited to me than the good ole boys, though I've worked successfully with the latter. But this preference reflects who I am. If you're a Marine, look for a fellow vet. If you graduated from a certain college, look for an alumnus. If you're a Mason or a bird watcher, look for those connections.

Check out the stuff hanging on the office walls and cluttering her work space. It always gives you a clue about how the lawyer sees herself. My wife, for example, has hung the Brownie Pledge in needlepoint at the entrance to her private office and paintings of her horses inside. (She has a wallet-size photo of me that she hides behind a potted plant on an inaccessible bookshelf.)

Dirt lawyers may affect the persona of the "country lawyer." They put on this exaggerated display of being unsophisticated and "just folks" for the same reason a mother bird feigns being wounded—to draw the attention of a predator from her valuables. Certain lawyers like to be underestimated, and others may be testing you. The best way for a potential client to handle this in his own lawyer is to pretend it doesn't exist, and sooner or later it won't. I also tend to go along with it, as if the two of us are conspirators on an inside joke. The danger in the "country lawyer" routine is that your lawyer will underestimate you if you buy into his schtick. When opposing lawyers start sugaring their approach with down-home self-deprecation, it's time for Code Red: you're about to be knifed. I'm also wary of the country gentleman routine, which I've seen combine manners and pedigree for the purpose of masking piracy.

It is important that you start your lawyer's billable clock when you walk into her office. You're interviewing, that's true, but you're also soliciting advice that will help orient you. Country lawyers will begrudge giving free time to a Big-City land buyer who blows down Main Street in a $75,000 Mercedes and then whines about paying $125 for an hour's advice. Buying property is usually the least expensive piece of legal work you can get, because only a few hours of lawyer time will be involved in a routine transaction. At 2006 hourly rates in my area, such a closing costs the buyer $500. A complicated and troublesome closing might cost $1,000, but that's an exception. It can cost you about the same in legal fees to buy $500,000 in land as it would to have your lawyer represent you in a $250 dispute in small claims court. The hour or two of local legal advice you pay for before you start looking at property can help you avoid the complications that cost big dollars down the road.

You should also ask your lawyer how you will be billed. Some lawyers may charge a fixed fee for representing a real-estate buyer. Others will quote a buyer a likely cost range, say $500 to $1000. Most, I think, bill their time at an hourly rate, logged in six-minute increments. Simple purchases involve an hour or so in the courthouse, several hours at closing and time spent talking with you and others involved in the transaction, such as lenders, real-estate agents, appraisers, surveyors and inspectors. Complications and unforeseen problems will increase billed time. Coordination also consumes time. Closings now can involve as many as 100 pages of documents that your lawyer may have to assemble and present to you. While the number of billed hours in your purchase can't be predicted, your lawyer should be able to estimate its likely range of costs, especially if he knows the property. He can also give you a heads-up about factors and circumstances that might arise that will increase your bill.

Some lawyers may ask a client, especially a new one, for an upfront retainer that assures them of at least partial payment. This is more common in lawsuits than in real-estate purchases, because your lawyer will be paid from your funds at closing. You should hand your lawyer a check for the time spent with you during your first advisory conversation. This establishes a professional relationship and builds confidence. As part of your first conversation, also discuss your expectations about access and communications. It's fair to expect your calls of a general nature to be returned in a day or two and urgent calls sooner. E-mail may be a comfortable channel for both of you. Before you leave, hand your lawyer a contact sheet that lists your name, address, phone, cell, fax, e-mail, Social Security number, lender contact information, contact information for spouse and any other items that he's likely to need.

Apart from general questions and information, I would advise discussing the following with any lawyer you interview:

- Local zoning regs—get a sense of what the various zoning designations allow and what is involved in obtaining a use variance or change in zoning status for your target property if that's a necessary part of your plan;

- Procedures for new construction and remodeling—what permits are needed; will septic system need to be inspected/upgraded; which contractors are best suited for the project;

- Recommendations for local professional help, such as surveyor, home inspector, CPA who does farms and timberland, etc.;

- His local lender preferences—ask why one is preferred over the others;

- Negotiating—if you don't want to dicker with the seller or the seller's agent, ask your lawyer to help, or even do it for you;

- Navigation—lawyers are good at pointing clients in the right directions; it may be cheaper for you to track down certain information than to pay a lawyer or paralegal; in any event, self-help produces increased land literacy; but don't get too much in the middle of your lawyer's work;

- Backstopping—if you and your lawyer are comfortable with having you do certain research tasks, make sure he backstops and double checks your work; your lawyer should do your title search, though there's no reason why you can't dig out some of the deedwork as part of your scoping;

- Research—ask your lawyer to flag potential issues/problems that might not be part of a routine title search, e.g., water issues, ownership of subsurface minerals and lease status;

questionable access, etc., as well as things he recommends that you investigate on your own;

- Purchase Contract—you can use a standard purchase contract that your lawyer may have in hand or one that you and your lawyer write together. I prefer the second option, but it depends on the lawyer and the circumstances of the purchase. Ask whether he is comfortable with having you participate in writing a contract. Ask yourself, first, whether this is something that you want to do.

The danger in "helping" your lawyer is that you will wear out your welcome, even one that you're paying for. If you think you have something to offer in this regard, then propose it. But don't feel obligated simply because you've read this book. If you tend to do-it-yourself projects, try not to drive everybody nuts, including yourself.

If you are uninformed about your target county, I recommend that you ask your local lawyer—whom you've chosen before you ever start your property search—to help you. Take an ad out in the local paper that states you're a land buyer looking for a property with the features you've decided on. Have landowners send replies to a local post office box that you open for this purpose. Ask for a brief written description of the property; tax map, survey and/or topo with boundaries; photos if available; size, price and contact information. Ask your lawyer to pick up your mail and rank the responses in terms of what he thinks best fit the objectives you've discussed with him. He will weed out the problems, scams and properties priced for the out-of-town billionaire.

You may be tempted to work into your purchase a fixed-price title search outfit to save yourself a hundred bucks on legal charges. These will be found in larger cities, but they may do work in rural areas. Instead, I encourage you to use a local lawyer who will either do the work herself or use her experienced real-estate paralegal who has worked for her for a number of years. The generic title-search firms provide a generic title search, which will work in the majority of cases. What the generic title search will not pick up is the local knowledge about the property that your local lawyer is likely to have. It's the unrecorded ground truth, the word-of-mouth wisdom, that can save you.

The final step in the process of purchasing land is the **closing**, or **settlement**, where buyer money is exchanged for seller documents and possession. In some places, you'll hear about "**closing escrow**," where "**escrow**" refers to the time between when the buyer's contract takes effect—with earnest money held in escrow on behalf of the purchase—and when the purchase is completed. Most property is purchased with the involvement of an **escrow agent**, whose job is to hold money and documents as a neutral party. A third-party—other than one of the lawyers working for the seller or the buyers—is often retained to serve as the escrow agent. Experienced buyers often prefer to have their lawyer act as the escrow agent for the purchase, because they feel their deposit is safest there.

The **settlement agent**—the person who manages the closing—may be the escrow agent too, or he may be a real-estate broker, lawyer, or a representative of a title company. The settlement agent's job is to get all of the paperwork and money in order, explain the transaction, get signatures where needed to complete the transaction, then route each item to its proper destination. It's not unusual in rural areas for one of the lawyers to handle both settlement and escrow while also representing either buyer or seller**.** Closings can get complicated, and your lawyer should be present, especially if you're not.

At the heart of the closing is the **settlement statement** (also called a **HUD-1**), which is the transaction's balance sheet. It shows debits and credits for each side, a debit being an item that a buyer or seller is paying out (fees for home inspection, mortgage points, legal fees, commission) and a credit is money coming to a buyer or seller. As a buyer, you will need to refer to your settlement statement when you do your 1040 deductions for the purchase year. It also will be used to establish your original **basis** in the property when you sell it and need to calculate taxable gain. Keep one copy of your settlement statement in your tax records for the year of purchase and another copy in your property folder.

A settlement statement can make a buyer feel as if he is sitting on a carnival dunking stool with Sandy Koufax throwing at the bull's-eye. Each time you look at the document, you're getting soaked for something else. Buyers need to understand that property sales always require that a buyer pay more than the agreed purchase price. The add-ons are items such as taxes, professional fees, loan fees and sale-related charges. The time to defend yourself against garbage fees and inflated charges is when you are first negotiating with lenders and those whom you hire to provide you with advice or work. Whether you are an experienced buyer or not, have your local lawyer walk you though the expenses you are likely to owe at settlement **before** you get to closing. While exact dollars are difficult to project on all items, a buyer should not be surprised by debits and credits on his side of the settlement statement. Big, bad surprises can derail a closing. Be forewarned: A buyer can easily pay five percent or more above the purchase price, the bulk of it in financing fees.

You will also be expected to sign a number of fine-print documents at closing. It is next to impossible to read and comprehend these documents when a half-dozen stakeholders are staring at you in a pressure-packed conference room. Ask your lawyer to show you these documents well in advance. Read them! Once you've signed a document, it will be construed to mean that you have read and understood it even if you never have and wouldn't understand it even if you had. Everyone benefits from a settlement that goes without a hitch. Previewing your documents with your lawyer and anticipating your expenses will further this shared interest.

The key closing documents are the **settlement statement, deed of trust, promissory note and deed**. Both the deed of trust and the deed will be recorded in the county clerk's office: keep copies at home as well. The **deed of trust**—also called a **trust deed**—is your mortgage document. It creates a **lien** on the property you're buying for the benefit of your lender. (If you have no lender, you have no mortgage or deed of trust.)

A **lien** gives your lender the right to have your debt paid from the sale of the property. When property alone secures the borrower's debt, the arrangement is called a **purchase money mortgage**. The buyer should resist signing a personal guarantee of real-estate debt. A lien can be called even when you are current on your note payments. Lenders may define a default as breaking a promise to the lender, failure to perform promptly, false statements, the borrower's death or insolvency, an attempt by a creditor or public agency to take property on which the lender has a lien, events of this type affecting a co-signer, and whenever the lender "…in good faith believes itself insecure." The **promissory note** sets forth the terms of your borrowing with the lender, to which you will be held. This note spells out the amount financed, interest rate, repayment schedule and all the rules the lender imposes. The buyer does not own the property free and clear until all notes secured by the property are paid in full and released by the lender.

The **deed** is the document that conveys title to the property from seller to buyer. It is very important for the property's **legal description** in the deed to be accurate and be exactly the same as the legal description in the seller's chain of title. Inadvertent description errors can be corrected later on, but errors that are defects can be barbed hooks, and, once embedded, may be removable only with much pain.

Well in advance of closing, discuss with your lawyer **how you want to take title**. This decision has both legal and tax implications. An individual has the choice of taking title in his own name or through an entity the individual owns, in whole or part, such as a limited liability company (LLC) or corporation. Lenders may not lend money to an LLC. The LLC members must personally guarantee the note or take title in their names then transfer title to the LLC. Lenders may also be sticky about financing purchases for a living trust. (Robert J. Bruss, "Real Estate Mailbag," <u>Washington Post</u>, July 6, 2003.) A married couple has several options, including an entity, or as husband and wife where the surviving spouse becomes the owner of the common property (**tenancy by the entirety**), or as **tenants in common** where each has an undivided interest in the property as a whole, with or without the right of survivorship, among other rights. State law governs forms of ownership, so it is important to have clear objectives and an equally clear understanding of the implications for taxes and inheritance of each option in the state where you are holding title.

The form of ownership you choose should be consistent with your ownership goals. I've advised in other sections of this book for buyers to consider ways to organize rural property as an investment or a business if, for no other reason, than the tax advantages. Consider this: the 2003 tax law allowed small businesses—such as one set up for land investment—to expense up to $100,000 in equipment costs in the year they were incurred. Farm equipment, logging equipment, ATVs, and pick-up trucks and SUVs weighing more than 6,000 pounds used in business qualified. For equipment placed into service after May 5, 2003 and before January 1, 2005, a first-year "bonus" depreciation write-off of 50 percent existed, up from 30 percent. The buyer's form of ownership should match his objectives in buying the land, and the time to decide both is in advance of purchase with proper legal and tax-planning counsel.

A buyer should retain at least one copy of every document he signs at a property closing. Put them in a 9"x14" accordion-type folder with a tie hood so nothing slips out. You should have a similar file for your scoping documents—home inspection, termite report, survey or topographic map with boundaries, timber cruise, appraisal, field notes, permits, regulations, title report, correspondence, certificate of occupancy and the like. Put every communication with the seller, his agents and your lawyer in writing—and keep a copy. You might want to start a third file dedicated to financing and lender documents, and a fourth file for insurance documents, including house/farm, title insurance, liability and so on.

I would keep copies of your basic **start-up documents**—appraisals, timber cruises, settlement statement, communications from your lawyer, receipts for major items, loan documents, deed, etc.—forever. You will need some for tax purposes, such as calculating your original basis. While the IRS's statute of limitations for audits requires the taxpayer to keep records for only three years, no such time cap exists if the IRS accuses you of fraud. The IRS can, therefore, ask for a 20-year-old settlement statement or other documents establishing basis when they think you're cheating on capital gains arising from a property sale. Other documents—like an appraisal or timber cruise—can establish FMVs that you can show a purchaser when you want to sell. Both lenders and insurance companies change their documents from time to time, so it can be helpful to have the originals in your possession. Your estate administrator will also welcome a rudimentary level of organization and document retention.

Find a local lawyer in whom you have confidence and then understand the legal aspects of the buying process before you enter it—that's how you get started.

THE LEGAL FRAMEWORK

State law governs the purchase and sale of **real property**, which includes all the rights, interests and benefits of real-estate ownership. The law governing real property differs from state to state, sometimes significantly, as with theories of water rights. Common to all states is the idea that land is purchased and sold through a **written contract of sale** between buyer and seller in which ownership/title is conveyed in return for some type of "**consideration**," usually cash. Real estate is not governed by the **Uniform Commercial Code**, now adopted wholly or partially by all states. The UCC provides uniform laws for commercial transactions, including all **personal (chattel) property**. Each state has a supreme court that has interpreted its laws—the body of which is called "**case law**." If you find yourself in a real-estate dispute, a county judge will adjudicate your case according to his reading of the relevant state statutes and case law. Suing can be expensive and aggravating, and appealing decisions is even worse. Courtroom justice can be a crapshoot, especially if you're new to the county and come across as arrogant, greedy, a smarty pants, rich or just different. Dirt-smart buyers should try to stay out of local courts, especially as a first step into a new community.

Federal laws and regulations bear on various aspects of land buying. Your financing is shaped by the Fair Credit Reporting Act, Truth-in-Lending Act (whose Regulation Z requires lenders to tell borrowers the true cost of obtaining credit on personal loans of $25,000 or less, or when a loan is secured by a residence) and various federal mortgage loan and loan-guarantee programs. Federal law and regulation also provide a framework for environmental protection, anti-discrimination (Fair Housing Act) and myriad programs affecting farms. Apart from the federal financing programs in the Department of Housing and Urban Development, Veterans Administration and Department of Agriculture, today's rural land buyer may find himself involved with agencies of the Departments of Agriculture and Interior, Army Corps of Engineers (wetlands and streams) and the Environmental Protection Agency. State and regional agencies (e.g., inspection/enforcement offices related to animal health, water quality, logging, water impoundments, new road entrances and wildlife management; irrigation and water districts; conservation districts) may find their way into your new life. Most of this infrastructure of statute and regulation did not exist 50 years ago. You will inevitably touch it if you borrow institutional money or use a federal mortgage program. (Each touch requires that you sign something that's as long as the Bible and reproduced in half the size of unreadable fine print.) It is reasonably safe to assume that use of your land for anything other than the lowest-impact activities—such as camping and hiking—will eventually brush you against some public agency and its regulations.

Ignoring the framework of laws that surround property ownership doesn't exempt you from compliance. In addition, ignorance can be costly. Before buying rural land or a farm, you should become conversationally familiar with current Internal Revenue Service (IRS) policies on:

- capital-gains tax rates and how to qualify for this treatment when you sell rural land; as of 2005, there were three capital-gains rates, 5% and 15% depending on income level, and 25% on certain real-estate sales where depreciation was taken

- advantages of itemizing on your 1040 (mortgage interest and property taxes are currently deductible on a vacation home or personal recreation land if you itemize, but not if you don't)

- farms/rural property set up as an investment or profit-making business, rather than for lifestyle or hobby purposes

- mortgage-interest deductibility for land investments and second homes

- types of land-related expenses that can be taken in the year you incur them

- types of costs and incomes that change your **basis** in the property

- types of improvements and equipment that can and must be depreciated

- conservation easements

- timber-taxation strategies if you're buying timberland

- farm-taxation strategies if you're buying farmland

- mineral-taxation strategies if you're buying land with minerals

Each of these topics can make you money or cost you money, depending on your knowledge and actions. Current IRS policies are discussed in other chapters. Many of the most critical tax decisions you make with your new property are made at the time of purchase.

While a miasma of legal, tax and regulatory complexity can loom in front of you, the buying of land—like getting married—is usually quite simple. You need the following elements:

- A seller with **clear title** to the property. A seller with a defective title is more than willing to sell to you, but you don't need this headache.

- A <u>*written agreement*</u>—**purchase contract**—between buyer and seller that sets forth:

    What is being sold—deed description, number of acres;

    Selling price;

    Terms and conditions;

    A schedule for getting the deal done, setting out who is expected to do what by when, and how various costs are to be apportioned; and

    Signed and dated by both buyer and seller. Signature notarization is preferred, but not necessary.

- **Financial arrangement** providing the buyer with the means to pay for the property that is acceptable to the seller;

- **Closing**, or settlement, date at which time the buyer acquires the property in return for his consideration (money) and/or promises to repay a lender's note. (It is worth understanding that a buyer does not acquire the deed and unfettered ownership until he has removed all property-secured mortgage notes. During the interval, the actual deed would be held in escrow by a trustee or by the seller himself if he is financing the sale. When you own property **free and clear**, it means that it carries no mortgage debt.)

These basic elements of a real-estate deal can require the services or opinions of lawyers, lender(s), appraiser, real-estate broker(s) or agents (one to four), home inspector, surveyor, insurance agent, forester, soil engineer, termite inspector, zoning official, building inspector, government farm officials, CPA and neighbors. Most of this crowd will be bringing a framework of law and regulation to your purchase. They should know more about what they're doing for you than you do.

Each of these individuals will have a relationship to the buyer and the purchase process. These relationships are governed by laws and regulations that are mostly invisible until something goes wrong.

For instance—the home inspector visits the seller's farmhouse in May, tries the furnace and reports that it is in working order. Between that inspection and when you turn it on for the first time in November, two months after your closing, the fuel-oil pump stops functioning and the cost of repair is $1,500. Is the home inspector responsible? Was there a material defect in the pump that the seller knew but did not disclose? Can you prove the inspector missed something that he should have found? What laws might have been broken? What legal remedies are available?

Dozens of things can go screwy in buying property because buying property puts hundreds of potentially screwy things in play. Each screw up takes place within the law and gets you thinking about lawyers, lawsuits, justice and money. This is a heady brew, and I urge you to think about other ways of resolving a dispute over a fuel pump besides a lawsuit. When all is said and done, a fuel pump is a fuel pump, but a lawsuit is a protracted agony.

To simplify matters, you can group your new associates into three categories from your legal perspective:

1. Those with whom a buyer contracts for a service that they provide, such as a lawyer, buyer broker (who represents you), CPA, forester, home inspector, surveyor, soil engineer and so on.

Some of these individuals will bill you on an hourly basis for their time, plus expenses. Others will charge a fixed fee for their service, which is usually the case with home inspectors. Surveyors often bill on a cents-per-linear-foot basis. Their foot-rate for interior lines is likely to be less than their foot-rate for boundary lines, though they may have to shoot the boundaries before they can shoot lines for internal divisions. If you're asking a surveyor to research your boundary lines or check acreage and closure, he'll probably bill at an hourly rate, because it's difficult to estimate the time needed to solve a complication.

A buyer-broker is a special case. He may be paid either from the commission the seller pays the listing broker or from the buyer's funds.

Whether or not you have a written contract with these individuals, you will have an understanding and agreement with them that they will perform some service or work for you in return for which you will pay them. Unwritten understandings of this sort are usually construed as **constructive contracts**, that is, an agreement amounting to a legal contract. To avoid squabbles, make sure you understand what you are asking each vendor to do, what work he will do to meet your request and how he will bill you.

You have a right to expect that such individuals make a good-faith effort to provide you with accurate information and services that meet the standards of their profession or trade. They shouldn't miss something obvious or important, or make a careless mistake that costs you money. Lawyers carry malpractice insurance, and some other professionals carry **Errors and Omissions (E&O) insurance.**

If a mistake is made, you will have to decide whether it is worth the time, expense and emotional strain to seek a remedy. The best strategy all things considered may be to say nothing and fix the problem yourself. Sometimes you can negotiate a settlement with the individual who did the flawed work, assuming the individual either agrees with your analysis or figures its cheaper to settle than to fight.

Suing is almost always the least promising way of settling a dispute for at least three reasons: first, its outcome is unpredictable; second, it is expensive; and third, it is not much fun. Lawsuits do not necessarily produce justice. I have seen judges rule without regard to equity and justice, disregarding where the weight of the law fell. I've also seen excellent work from the same individuals. I admire folks who get into court fights over principle, but judges may not share your interest in having the system do what's right. If you can't work out something with the other side, suggest **mediation**, in which a neutral third-party helps the disputants reach a compromise settlement. Mediation can be set up either as a format by which the parties are bound to the result or not.

In the matter of the bad fuel-oil pump in the farmhouse, it's doubtful that you can get compensation from either the inspector or the seller. Both will deny knowledge of any problem, and both can be telling the absolute truth. Had you discovered the problem within a week or two of taking possession, you would have a stronger claim against both of them. Two months, however, is probably too long. Everyone has had experience with a machine that works perfectly today and is totally inoperable tomorrow. Lesson: if you don't do a walk-through just before closing during which you test all systems (which you should), do your testing within a day or two of taking possession.

If the home inspector failed to inspect the furnace, you may have a claim against him. Your position is weakened if you accepted his report as presented, which indicated by the absence of checks in appropriate boxes that he had not inspected the furnace. Often it costs more to sue and win than it does to forget about it.

2. Those with whom a buyer's relationship is essentially that of cooperative adversaries, such as with your seller and lender. In each case, the land buyer enters into an elaborate written contract, specifying what each party will do and when they will do it. You have a right to expect the seller to disclose the property's **material defects,** which can be thought of as deficiencies of various kinds that a reasonable person would consider to be of such size or seriousness that they bear on—are "material" to—the basic soundness of what the buyer is purchasing, and, therefore, are material to the sale itself.

Sellers will sometimes place language in their bid package or a purchase-offer contract they prepare that says the buyer is expected to perform his own **due diligence** on the property and its assets. Due diligence refers to a buyer's investigation and research into a property that satisfies whatever are his standards of competency and thoroughness. I've used the word, "scoping," instead.

Contract language that states the buyer is expected to perform his own due diligence is a pre-emptive effort to shift liability for future problems onto the buyer. The seller gives himself the basis for arguing that the buyer did not do adequate due diligence, otherwise he would have discovered the bad pump, which, of course, was perfectly fine the last time the seller used it. The seller could also argue that the buyer knew the pump was bad (as a result of his due diligence) when he made his offer and is now trying to force the cost of an anticipated repair onto the seller.

Buyers should always perform thorough due diligence, especially when the seller has inserted a due-diligence clause in the contract. When facing such a clause, the buyer should get in writing, if possible, what exactly the seller thinks due diligence covers and what types of liability he thinks it excludes.

If you think the seller is using due-diligence to rig up a last-minute parachute for himself, you can add your own language behind his:

> **Buyer agrees to perform due diligence on Seller's property, but his effort does not relieve Seller of his obligations to disclose all material defects of which he is aware and bear any liability arising from the warranties this Contract includes.**

While consumer law has gotten away from *Caveat emptor!*—Let the buyer beware!—due-diligence language and "**permitted title exceptions**" struggle to make it rise again. The latter is the seller's statement to the buyer in a purchase contract that he will convey good title, *except for* those items (exceptions) where he doesn't want to, or can't. Permitted exceptions give the seller a way to sell property with a defective title or other problems. I've encountered permitted exceptions a number of times. Sometimes the seller includes this language because he doesn't want to spend the time to determine whether he has a problem. Other times, however, he knows of a title problem and wants to get out of cleaning it up. Remember the seller is the one giving himself this permission; you need not agree.

I think any buyer will do well to act as if *Caveat emptor!* still rules. To protect the buyer, the buyer's side needs to inform the seller that state law requires him to disclose fully known defects and problems in his property. *Caveat vendor!* –Let the seller beware!—is much more current law: the seller will be held legally accountable for defects, significant problems and deficiencies in the property of which he is aware or about which it is reasonable to assume he should have been aware. Let your lawyer make these positions known to the seller's lawyer. Brokers are required to disclose defects that they know about. Make sure that you ask the seller's broker/agent to disclose all defects in writing well in advance of submitting an offer.

While current law appears to be more on the side of the buyer on disclosure issues, the cost of enforcing disclosure falls on the buyer. Sellers, in other words, still wiggle off the hook of their own making. For this reason, disclosure is most effectively enforced during negotiations where the threat of enforcement carries weight with the seller.

Despite the law and the buyer's best efforts, a seller may eventually fail to disclose a situation that will adversely affect the buyer's use and enjoyment of the property. In court, the aggrieved buyer must prove that the seller either knew of the problem, or that it is reasonable to suppose that he should have known of it. These standards of proof are often hard to meet. To avoid these messes with a seller you think is playing hide the ball, insert a "**disclosure clause**" in your purchase offer:

> **Seller warrants that he has disclosed all material defects of which he is aware in the property's title, improvements, assets, resources, access, boundaries, rights and interests. Such defects include, but are not limited to, conditions, situations, facts, deficiencies, uncertainties, disputes, claims and unresolved issues that would negatively affect the Buyer's use, possession and enjoyment of the property.**

This language is a big, fat Seller Beware! Lawyers will roll their eyes. Let them roll. You want this seller to do what he's supposed to do, and this is the way to get him to do it. If the seller refuses to sign, it's possible that you've smoked him out.

This language covers material defects that are both **latent** (hard to see) and **manifest** (visible but perhaps not understandable).

3. Those who seemed programmed to get in the way of making a deal. This could be anybody, including you, by your attitudes and behavior. The two usual suspects are the seller who blows up a decent deal in hope that a better one will walk through his front door the next day and the seller's real-estate agent who holds a TNT in miscommunication.

Once the seller signs a purchase contract, the purchase should go through assuming all contingencies are satisfied or voided before closing. If the seller backs out on an oral agreement to sell before he signs your written purchase contract, you have no contract, hence no remedy in court. (A few exceptions may exist in certain circumstances, but don't count on exceptions to win in the absence of a written contract.).

Purchase contracts are usually written in a way that gives the buyer several contingencies to get out of doing the deal. But, as a rule, few sellers work into their contracts similar ways to extricate themselves. While real-estate agents in my experience can muddle up a purchase and often fail to do what they are supposed to do, the buyer usually has little legal recourse for their lack of competence, laziness and poor judgment.

I was interested in a 50-acre timber tract north of Lake Placid, New York in the spring of 2006. It was priced at $30,000, a little high but in the ballpark. So I started scoping. I found the following:

> The property had no physical or legal access; it was completely landlocked;
>
> No metes and bounds were available;
>
> At least one boundary line was in dispute;
>
> The seller's deed provided for ownership of 100 acres—an error. Once the seller

took possession of the property, he came to realize that he had purchased only 50 acres. The seller did not have title clear of a defect, i.e., he lacked a merchantable title.

The seller would not draw boundaries on a topo map to orient me;

The seller's deed contained the word "warranty," but it appeared to me to be something less than a general warranty deed. Given all the title and legal problems, I wanted the seller to be held to the seller's obligations under a general warranty deed. The seller wanted to get out of this mess by pawning off the property with what amounted to not much more than a quitclaim; and

The seller would not tell me whether he had title insurance; I was reasonably sure that he did not have a policy and that none could be obtained.

I began negotiations with the one neighbor who could provide access to a public road. The neighbor and the seller did not get along. The seller's real-estate agent then told me that she had advised the seller to consider only a no-contingency contract. The seller wanted to survey the property at a cost of $8,000, thinking that it would make the property more marketable. If an access easement could be worked out with the neighbor, the survey would not be necessary because I was prepared to sell the timbered land to the neighbor at a discount in return for being allowed to haul out the timber. I told the agent to relay this information and ask the seller to wait for two weeks to let me see what I could do with the easement. She responded by telling me that she had advised her client to pay for the survey. This was the same agent who had been unable to orient herself on a tax map, insisting that north was west until I asked her to look at the directional arrow at the bottom of the tax map in the portion marked "Legend." Her sales tactic was to try to stampede me into a purchase while playing hide the ball. Her other job, I was told, was bartending.

As you scope property, you will find yourself digging a metaphorical hole. As you work, the sides of the hole should become firmer with each piece of information you strike. At some point, you will find a solid bottom. The process is one of growing more and more confident of the hole's dimensions and stability. The Lake Placid 50-acre hole kept getting mushier and mushier. The more I found out, the more I knew that none of the sides were stable. I was digging in sand. I felt like Alice in her rabbit hole, guided by the seller's real-estate agent who consistently misread both me and the facts in front of her. A brighter agent would have helped make this deal.

Buyers are usually on their own when dealing with both seller and real-estate brokers. The latter are almost always representing the seller, even when you are "working with" one who drives you around on Sunday afternoons. Such brokers/agents will be paid by the seller and are legally obliged to represent his interests, not yours. The only exceptions are where a broker/agent signs a **dual agency agreement** with both seller and buyer in which he works for both sides or where a buyer signs a **buyer-broker agreement** with a broker/agent who is then obliged to work exclusively for the buyer. A buyer can easily find himself making a written offer on a standard seller-oriented contract surrounded by two or more broker/agents, all of whom are working for the seller.

You can even up the sides by doing the following:

- **Never submit a standard seller-oriented contract without your local lawyer being there when you fill out its terms. Never!** Consult with him on language and contingencies. This is your most important hour of his time.

- **Contain the confusion**. Put everything in writing. Copy all written work to the appropriate parties. Be clear, explicit and simple in telling brokers/agents what information you want and what, if anything, you want them to do to get the deal to work. Don't let problems slide. Buying land is like tacking down a piece of linoleum that wants to curl up on all edges. You have to nail down every corner, otherwise one will trip you. Organize the process. Keep an accordion file devoted to the purchase. Separate tasks. Make a timeline, so that you know at a glance each deadline.

- **Know what you want to do before the time when you are asked to do it.** Buyers are usually expected to make a lot of decisions all at once without being able to think through the legal ramifications of the language they're signing. If you want to include contingencies, have them written out before submitting them to the buyer. Avoid situations where you have to think up "legal" language off the top of your head, under pressure. If you've prepared a contract with your lawyer ahead of time, don't change it or delete language without consulting with him in private.

HELPING HANDS: BUYER-BROKER, FINDER, LAND CONSULTANT

It is amazing—almost inconceivable—that most real estate is sold to buyers working with real-estate professionals representing sellers. Put another way, most buyers are on their own until they sign a purchase-offer contract. This is crazy. Buyers should pay for loyal professional advice from the beginning of their property search. Why? Because it will either save money or make it. The less the buyer knows about an area, the more valuable this advice is likely to be.

One way to get help is to retain a **buyer-broker** who works for the buyer's interests. This individual is a licensed real-estate professional who may choose to represent buyers exclusively or both buyers and sellers. The buyer pays his buyer-broker a percentage commission figured against the selling price from his own funds. The buyer signs a **buyer-agency agreement** with the brokerage setting forth the terms of their understanding. If the target property is listed with a cooperating broker, your buyer-broker can be paid from the seller-paid commission, depending on your agreement. If the target property is not being represented in this way or is being sold by a FSBO, the buyer pays his buyer-broker directly.

Real-estate agents/brokers are permitted to work for both buyer and seller as long as the arrangement is disclosed and approved by both parties. Dual arrangements can benefit the buyer when the seller is paying for it, but I'm generally suspicious of these work-for-both-sides deals, because I think they mainly serve the wallets of the broker/agent. But I have seen circumstances where they work without favoritism or harm. Dual agency on a purchase may produce a total commission paid to the dual agent that is higher than what the agent would receive were he to be paid by either buyer or seller, but not both.

I would trust a buyer-broker (also called, a buyer-agent) who represents buyers exclusively, or even principally. These individuals make their living by providing good service to buyers. They shouldn't let their buyer clients get into harmful legal and financial situations. They have no financial loyalty to sellers as a group, or any particular seller. If you retain a buyer-broker who will not be paid from the seller-paid commission, you will be buying his undivided loyalty. Four percent of the gross sales price is a fair fee for a buyer-broker whom the buyer is paying. In any case, try to find a buyer-broker who does nothing but work for buyers. There are now about 2,500 affiliated with the National Association of Exclusive Buyer Agents, 1-800-986-2322; www.naeba.org.

I'm wary of a generalist agent/broker who tells a buyer, something like, "I swing both ways." This individual, I fear, is mainly working for himself. Even when he signs with you as a buyer-broker, his long-term interest and the bulk of his business lies mainly with sellers.

Realtors—a real-estate agent or broker who is a member of the National Association of Realtors—can become an **Accredited Land Consultant (ALC)** by completing an education program through the

Association's Realtors Land Institute. This program provides background in land issues, including finance and marketing. An agent who is an ALC should know more about the subjects in this book than an agent who isn't. An ALC who is a buyer-broker and only works for buyers can be a great find for you.

A buyer-broker will help you find properties. He will check the Multiple Listing Service (MLS) for prospects in your target area that match your search criteria. He'll show you properties. A broker representing the seller does all this for a buyer too. A buyer-broker becomes valuable to a buyer to the extent that he helps a buyer with scoping. This can be a time-consuming task, so you will need to obtain an understanding of exactly what services and information the buyer-broker will provide for you. At the very least, ask him to help with the scoping that will be difficult for an out-of-town buyer to do. This can involve information that is not on the public record but is available through discussions with older members of the community and neighbors. It can mean asking questions in the right way. It can mean having a local person ask a question. It can mean telling a buyer where to go and how to do things.

You may be able to obtain a buyer-broker by asking a local agent to act as one for you, though I recommend focusing on agents who have a record of working for buyers. Another place to look is www.rebac.net, the website for the Real Estate Buyer's Agent Council, whose members are called Accredited Buyer's Agents.

Finders are not licensed for their work. In many cases, a finder is acting *ad hoc*. He may be a lawyer, surveyor, forester, excavator, contractor or friend of a friend who knows of a property and informs a buyer of its availability. A finder should work directly and exclusively for a buyer, not through a real-estate agent or broker. Licensed brokers/agents do not share their commissions with finders, and, in some states, may not be allowed to do so. A buyer who wants to use a finder must work out a consulting contract with him directly—and probably on the buyer's initiative. Finders are not allowed to provide brokerage services and should disclose to their clients that they are not brokers if that is the case. A finder's job is to identify target properties for a buyer, and generally nothing else. Finders are generally paid a percentage fee of the gross selling price at closing. Finders usually get one to four percent for a successful effort, depending on the particulars.

A non-resident buyer must find a local finder—a person who may not have ever thought of himself as a buyer's finder. If you take out a "Land-Wanted" ad in the local classifieds, include notice that you're willing to pay a one percent finder's fee for any property brought to you by the finder which you did not already know about and which you subsequently buy. You must be scrupulously honest about dealing with finders. If you already know about a property when the finder first starts telling you about it, stop him and say that it is known to you. Do not cheat a finder by pretending to have knowledge which, in fact, the finder is introducing to you *de novo*. On the other hand, you want to protect yourself against a seller who tells his cousin to answer your ad with reference to the seller's property. In that case, you're paying a fee for a lead that the seller would have otherwise provided on his own.

If you buy land found by a finder, you should be prepared to have your local lawyer help you with the purchase contract. Finders should not perform such tasks.

A **land consultant** may or may not be trained in real estate or investments. I am not aware of licensing requirements. I describe myself as a land consultant. Apart from having taken a real-estate course and losing money in the stock market, I have no specific training for what I do. I have background in a number of fields that I've found useful in helping buyers find and scope properties—journalism and research skills are the two that come into play most often. I'm good at seeing connections and putting things together—I don't know what field that is, but it's probably common to many professions. I'm very good at asking questions and finding out stuff. The grander term for those activities I've called, scoping, which also involves analyzing situations and writing summary memos. I am not a licensed broker or agent. I disclose this to my clients and state in writing that I do not provide brokerage services. Buyers also ask me to find property that fits their investment criteria.

A land consultant should work for the client's best interest and not his own. He should avoid becoming invested in having his client make a purchase that generates a fee but is not good for the client paying him that fee. It is essential that buyers enforce this rule with any investment consultants they interview. A land consultant will have a buyer sign a contract that holds the consultant harmless for the uses to which the client puts the consultant's work. Were it otherwise, the consultant would be forced into a position of back-stopping any loss the client might suffer after a purchase. The consultant should obviously do his best work in scoping a property. Nonetheless, nothing protects a buyer as much as his own due diligence on all aspects of a purchase, including scoping his consultants.

I work two tracks: first, I will be asked to scope a property that a client thinks is a possible acquisition. This work has taken me from a golf resort in Alabama to 600,000 acres of timberland in Ontario—and many properties in between. I charge an hourly rate.

The second track combines a preliminary screening of a property with a particular client in mind. I try to find a good fit with a client's individual objectives and financial capabilities. I will screen a target enough to think that it has possibilities. When the client wants me to investigate further, I reach an understanding about what tasks I'm expected to do. I put this understanding into a contract with the client before I start scoping. I will then research the target and write an evaluation. I will flag risks, problems, uncertainties and particularly things that a buyer can't determine prior to purchase. I will offer opinions about the value of the property's assets, profit potential and marketing strategies where that is appropriate. I often discuss strategies and tactics for buying, including the benefits of managed-timberland programs, conservation easements and other approaches that help a seller with taxes. I will frequently recommend hiring consultants where specific evaluations are needed. I'll also offer an opinion about what the client might consider paying for the property in light of the client's objectives. And not infrequently, I'll suggest that the client consult with his lawyer about specific issues and contingency language of the type found in this book. The level of due diligence the client employs beyond my work depends entirely on the assets and problems identified in the target property. I know something about minerals, timber and farms, but I don't consider myself an expert; I always note for the client where I've pushed my knowledge and expertise to its boundary. I continue to be available as the client learns more about the property. I often advise clients to not purchase a property that we've researched because of a problem turned up during the scoping. This means that I earn nothing from my work, but it protects my client. When agents/brokers are working for the seller, they are not supposed to offer such advice to a buyer because their fiduciary obligation is to the seller.

My rule of thumb is simple: I want repeat business. To that end, I try as hard as I can to make sure I find deals that work well for my clients.

CHAPTER 26: COMMON MESSES

OWNERSHIP AND ACREAGE ISSUES

In other chapters, I've touched on the many little matches that can burn a buyer. Here are the ones related to ownership and acreage that I've seen most often.

BUYERS WANT 100 PERCENT OF EVERYTHING

Rural land in the United States is usually sold by the acre, which is 43,560 square feet, or the area in a square, 208.71 feet on each side. (A "state acre" is 40,000 square feet; a football field, goal line to goal line, is 48,000 square feet.)

Acreage is determined by calculating the number of acres contained within a property's legal boundaries. Boundary lines are always measured and described as if they existed on a level plane, never as running with the land's ups and downs. Hilly land will always contain more than one square acre of land for every one square acre to be conveyed.

My concern is that a buyer not acquire less acreage than what he believes he is buying. The process of determining ownership and acreage can be easy as pie or a mess.

The initial piece of the puzzle the buyer needs to understand is **the nature of the seller's ownership in the property**. The seller may be ready to convey to you his full ownership in the property's acreage, but he may not fully own the entire property or he may not own all the rights in the property.

Ideally, the seller should own 100 percent of all rights and interests in the land he's selling. The real world is often different.

Ownership of rural land is often **fractionalized through inheritance**. Part of the **title search** that a buyer hires a lawyer to do is to make sure that the seller owns 100 percent of the property. Occasionally, a title search will turn up a long-forgotten orphan fraction, a $1/32^{nd}$ or a $1/64^{th}$, that is now several generations distant from the original division. Your seller doesn't own this orphan fraction. The seller may be able to buy this share from its rightful owner. The seller can also propose that he and the fraction owner divide the land in a mutually agreeable way, whereupon the seller sells you his somewhat diminished share. If the fractional owner refuses to sell or divide, the seller can file a **partition suit** that forces the sale of all shares in the entirety. You could then buy the property at that public auction. To the extent that the auction is competitive, you may end up paying more than the original asking price. The sellers will split the net proceeds after paying off their mortgage debt, if any, plus legal and auction expenses.

If you find yourself faced with a group of sellers each of whom owns a fractional share of the entirety, you have to be certain that the group is agreed on selling at the price you've been quoted. Insist on having one of the sellers be authorized by the others to act as their agent, so that you need to negotiate with only one individual. Be prepared for your negotiated price to be rejected by one hold out. This is often a ploy to get more money from a buyer. When you negotiate your money with the sellers' agent, tell him that it's a final offer, because you have placed your negotiating faith in his promise to you that he is the authorized agent of all the sellers. Once you say, take it or leave it, you must be prepared to walk away. Sellers in this circumstance are likely to come back to you in a week or two, "after the holdout has had time to reconsider your offer."

When the owner of the long-forgotten or disputed fraction can't be located, the seller should file a

suit to quiet title, an action that allows anyone with an ownership claim to submit it to the court or lose his right in the property forever. Such suits are often used to free the seller's title from old or bogus claims arising from distant divisions, dower's rights (a widow's claim on the real property of her deceased husband), squatting and other adverse actions against the property. Buyers should insist on the seller doing what's necessary to convey a clear title.

The other way to look at the seller's ownership is to determine whether he owns and is conveying **all the rights of ownership** in the property.

Ideally, the seller owns a **fee simple absolute estate**, which may be referred to as **ownership in fee** or **fee-simple ownership**. This type of ownership means the seller possesses all of the rights in the land that an owner can have. This means he has unrestricted control, possession, use and enjoyment of all of the property's rights and assets, limited only by public authority and recorded easements. Fee-simple ownership should mean that the property is free of all life estates, easements, leases and interests that others hold in the seller's land. Many fee-simple owners don't own their entire property in absolute. A simple road easement that allows a neighbor to use a road on the seller's property alters absolute ownership.

The buyer is interested in getting all of the rights and interests he needs, even if that bundle is something less than fee simple absolute. Sellers use the terms, fee and fee simple, to mean whatever they want it to mean. When a seller says he owns the property in fee simple, you should write a **fee-simple section** into your purchase offer, such as:

> **Seller agrees to convey said property in fee simple to Buyer, subject only to easements and other documents of record in _____ County, _____. The Parties understand and agree that fee simple includes all mineral and water rights; all solar and air rights; all timber, recreational and agricultural rights; and all other rights customarily included in fee-simple ownership.**
>
> **Seller agrees to convey the property free of all life estates, unrecorded easements and deeds, leases and reservations of interest or profit.**
>
> **Seller shall disclose to Buyer all matters, including all unrecorded easements, deeds, contracts, arrangements, permissions and understandings, that limit in any way the conveyance of this property in fee simple, or its full use and enjoyment by the Buyer, excluding only easements and other documents of record.**
>
> **Seller's disclosures shall be in writing and delivered to Buyer within ten calendar days of this Contract taking effect.**
>
> **All exceptions and disclosures must be acceptable to the Buyer. If any exception or disclosure is not acceptable, Buyer may void this Contract without penalty or further obligation. The Escrow Agent shall then return Buyer's deposit in full and in a timely manner.**

I've included specific language in this fee-simple clause that goes beyond the typical boilerplate you'll find in a standard purchase contract. Lawyers will object that a buyer does not need this elaboration; usually, you shouldn't. But where you and your lawyer suspect that a seller cannot convey his property in fee simple, you need to know what's missing, both recorded (which you should be able to find) and unrecorded (which can hit you blindside). Buyers need to discount their offers to owners who cannot convey a complete set of property rights, or move on to a less complicated purchase.

One wrinkle on fee ownership that I've seen is a **subject-to clause** that the seller insists on inserting into any buyer-submitted purchase contract. The seller in this case sends to every buyer a sample purchase contract *that he will accept*, which includes the following:

Seller shall convey an insurable title, qualified by the usual standard preprinted exceptions, to Buyer by General Warranty Deed in fee simple, free from all liens, excepting taxes not yet due and payable, but subject to all matters of public record.

The buyer can read the "preprinted exceptions," which may or may not be significant.

The reverse in this language is that the seller is promising to convey the property in fee simple, but subject to matters of public record which, in this example, meant, something quite a bit less than fee simple. When I found this language, "all matters of public record" meant that my buyer would not get the mineral rights on approximately 75,000 acres nor would he have hunting rights on approximately 10,000 acres that had been granted to a state agency. Both severances were matters of public record. If a buyer had not done a **title search prior to submitting a purchase contract**, this language would have forced him to accept the property less both severances. If I had not done the Courthouse scoping, the buyer would have made an offer assuming fee-simple ownership. He would have been forced by this contract language to buy the property less two valuable rights that he wanted. At the very least, he would have ended up paying more for the property than he should have paid.

In this instance, the seller found a way to avoid saying in his sale prospectus and in his proposed contract that mineral rights and hunting rights were not included in the sale.

In my experience, simply stating in your purchase contract that "Buyer's offer is for the Seller's land in fee simple." is insufficient protection. I've done that, only to find sellers failing to disclose missing pieces of their ownership. Their defense is that they misunderstood the meaning of fee simple. Since the time and cost of suing the seller was more than what was at stake, I accepted the drubbing with mutters. Had I used the more elaborate and redundant language of the fee-simple section above, I think I would have forced full disclosure.

A quick look at the deedwork should uncover the **recorded** limitations on the seller's rights in the property. The deed itself should make reference to these limitations. But that is not always the case. The deed into your seller may not include references to all recorded documents affecting the property—both easements and limitations that others hold against the property and easements and rights that the seller's property holds against others. I looked at a 230-acre tract in western Maryland recently whose deed made no mention of a recorded ingress-and-egress easement over an adjoining neighbor that provided the only access to the property.

The best title search will not turn up **unrecorded** deeds, leases, contracts for sale, life estates, gifts and easements; oral understandings and permissions; claims against the property by adverse possession and prescription; disputed boundary lines; unrecorded notes that use the property as security; and liens, litigation and judgments that are in the works but have yet to be recorded. Such items can short a buyer of purchased acreage, limit enjoyment and use of the property, or reduce the value of the property's assets. That is why it's important for your contract to ask the seller to disclose unrecorded items that affect ownership and acreage.

Here is one example. The seller sells the timber rights—that is, the right to cut sawtimber-sized trees for 12 months—but this sale contract is not recorded. The seller then sells the land to an absentee buyer without disclosing the timber sale. The logger appears in February, six months after the buyer has closed. The logger finishes his work in a month and leaves. The new owner appears with his family on a sunny day in May and is overcome with shock and awe. The seller, meanwhile, has retired to a 100-foot-long RV with no fixed address. The logger informs the new owner that the seller told him that he had orally disclosed the reservation and had secured the buyer's oral approval at that time. The logger makes a point of then saying that in his opinion the seller, were he ever to be located, would so testify in court while standing on something holy from each of the world's more than 600 religions. The new owner is screwed.

Even if he manages to get something for the timber, which is unlikely, he's left with a cutover tract that he no longer wants.

Had this buyer included a fee-simple clause similar to the one above (which requires seller disclosure of unrecorded contracts), he would have protected his interests. An honest seller will not take offense at this language. If the unscrupulous seller did not disclose the timber sale in writing as required by the fee-simple language, the seller could not hide behind an "I-said/you-heard" defense, which boils down to the seller's recollection of his word against the buyer's. This is a suit worth filing against the seller, because the buyer has the paper to win it. Whether the buyer can collect his money is, sadly, another question. The best reason for including fee-simple language is that it forces the marginally honest/crooked seller to disclose a quagmire before you get stuck in it. It won't help when the seller is out to scam a buyer intentionally.

Here are several other examples of complications that lack of recordation and oral understandings can cause for a buyer.

1. A buyer purchases a farm and five years later a neighbor informs him that the seller, recently deceased, had orally given him six veneer-grade cherry trees at the back of the farm in return for having built a long section of fence. The neighbor now wants to cut the trees, which are worth about $7,500. The neighbor wants the current owner to "honor" the previous owner's "contract," about which he knew nothing. The new owner loses whichever way he resolves this. He can pay the neighbor $7,500; he can allow the neighbor to cut the trees; he can ignore the neighbor's claim (which should be placed against the seller's estate, not the current owner). If he refuses to pay or give the neighbor the trees, the neighbor bears him ill will, perhaps forever. This dispute is not between the current owner and the neighbor legally, but it is practically.

I think the best way to handle this problem is to explain to the neighbor that the seller never disclosed the tree-for-fencing deal when the buyer bought the farm, either orally or in writing. Then explain that the neighbor should send the former owner's estate a bill for $7,500. The new owner should tell the neighbor that he will write a letter in support of this claim, attesting that the fence was built and that the deceased owner never informed him of the neighbor's claim on the trees. If the neighbor is being honest about his claim, he should understand your dilemma and accept your decision. If he's just trying to pick your pocket for an easy $7,500, you've avoided helping him.

2. A buyer purchases a farm that contains three or four acres of blackberry thicket. A neighbor informs the new owner that the seller always allowed him—and his very extended family—to pick berries. The seller, of course, never said anything about this permission. Not wanting to be hateful and selfish, the new owner agrees to continue this arrangement, only to find the bushes picked clean when he and his family arrive with buckets ready. This is a case of permission rather than prescriptive use: the neighbor has no legal right to use the blackberry thicket or hold the new owner to the old owner's practices. A permission ends when the owner who gave it sells the property. But once the new owner mumbles his own begrudging permission, he will incur a double dose of hard feelings if he subsequently retracts it. If the seller is available, you might first check with him about the validity of the neighbor's "claim." It may be that the seller hated blackberries and placed no value on giving them to the neighbor. It may be that the seller once gave the neighbor permission, only to find the bushes stripped. If you want your blackberries for yourself, you will need to choose from four options: 1) just say no politely and explain that you intend to strip the bushes yourself; 2) offer to make the patch available after you've taken whatever you want; 3) offer to split the patch if that suits your needs; or 4) propose a trial arrangement of some sort for one year with no promises implied after that.

3. Mr. A purchases a wooded tract with a road running through it from front to back. There's a small, second home cabin in the middle of the property that he wants to use on pretty weekends and during

hunting season. The cabin fronts this lovely road. The elderly seller had not used the cabin for many years due to poor health. At the back of the tract, the road forks: one branch enters National Forest land, the other leads to an adjoining 50 acres owned by Mr. B. Neither the National Forest nor Mr. B have a recorded easement that allows use of Mr. A's road. But Mr. B does have a recorded access easement to get to his property that crosses property owned by Mr. C.

Mr. B says that he has always used Mr. A's road, because his deeded right of way is undeveloped and the cost of constructing a road is high. Many years ago, a previous owner of Mr. A's land informed Mr. B that he didn't like Mr. B using the road and told him to stop. But no one ever put up a locked gate or took any action against Mr. B's continued use. The seller never told Mr. A anything about Mr. B's use of the road, and Mr. A never observed Mr. B using it during his visits. Mr. A wants Mr. B to stop using his road. If, however, Mr. B's practice fits that state's criteria for an **easement by prescription**, he has the legal right to use Mr. A's road though nothing was ever recorded. To establish this type of claim, Mr. B's use had to have gone on continuously for a statute-set number of years and meet the other standards, such as Mr. B's use of the road had to be open, notorious, continuous and adverse (that is, against the wishes and interests of Mr. A, the property's owner).

Since Mr. B owns an access easement over Mr. C, he can not claim continued use of Mr. A's road as an **easement by necessity**, which allows an owner of landlocked property to acquire an ingress-egress easement to a public road. (If Mr. B wanted an electric line run to his place, he would have to negotiate a utility easement with the landowners whose property the line would cross. He could not claim an electric easement by necessity.) Mr. A may or may not be able to keep Mr. B from using the road, depending on the facts of Mr. B's prescriptive-use claim.

The unfortunate Mr. A also discovers in his first ownership year that his road is inundated with 4WD pickup trucks and ATVs during hunting season. Hunters are driving from the public highway into the National Forest over his road because it is the easiest access for miles around. Mr. A places a heavy cable and lock across his road each day of the two-week November deer season, only to find it cut repeatedly. When he physically stops hunters in front of his cabin, they claim they have always used this road just like Mr. B does—and continue on. If Mr. A prevails legally, his cabin is a sitting duck for retribution. If he does nothing, he puts up with trespassers. I know of a landowner who was forced to sell his land because he could not keep hunters from crossing it to get to National Forest land. A partial solution to Mr. A's problem lies in persuading the National Forest to install a locked gate where Mr. A's road enters federal land. Excavations on each side of these stout metal gates prevent circumvention. The National Forest's network of roads would be blocked from vehicle traffic coming to it over Mr. A's road, but hunters may still choose to drive to that point over Mr. A. If the Forest is unwilling to install a gate, Mr. A will have to build something similar where his road joins the highway, post his property, take an ad out in the local paper providing notice against trespass and use of his road, excavate waterbars and, if necessary, press charges.

Every land buyer should become familiar with two legal doctrines—**adverse possession and prescription**. **Adverse possession** is the acquisition, i.e., ownership, of land through its protracted, actual, continuous and unauthorized *occupation* when its true owner knows of the occupation, opposes it, but does nothing to evict the adverse occupier during the statutory time period that varies from state to state, from five to 30 years. Some states require that the party claiming ownership by adverse possession must have paid the property tax on the disputed acreage. Virginia does not require tax payment, but it does require that the party asserting possession (ownership) by adversity must show **"color of title,"** that is, a plausible argument and facts supporting his claim.

Prescription is a method by which a party can acquire title to the land of another, i.e., ownership, by protracted and unauthorized *use* that is open, notorious, adverse to the rightful owner and continuous for the statutory period of time. The difference between them is that adverse possession requires occupation while prescription requires use but not full-time occupation. A party that uses a road on another's property against the owner's wishes can acquire a **prescriptive easement** to continued use of that road if his use meets all of the state's statutory requirements. A prescriptive easement gives its holder continued use of a road on another owner's land, but not its ownership.

4. You discover after buying a farm that a 500-foot-long fence line doesn't follow the boundary line that your surveyor just marked. Your neighbor has fenced in about five acres that your survey and deed calls indicate belong to you. Your seller says "they've been fussing about that line for years, but I never paid it any attention since they never moved the line onto me." The neighbor claims he built the new fence five years ago exactly along the run of the old fence. When you bought the farm, the acreage you bought was calculated from the deed calls, which means that you paid for five acres that you don't occupy or use, and may or may not own. You did not have the surveyor check whether the deed calls matched the functional boundary lines on the ground. The legal issue in this case is whether the neighbor can meet all the state's tests for **adverse possession**. The land is worth $20,000. The seller, of course, told you nothing about a disputed fence line. In fact, the seller thought the fence line was in the right place. So you go to court.

The neighbor gets on the stand and knows all about adverse possession. He ticks off each of the state's tests that he's met. And then to clinch the deal he testifies about his Granddad—now deceased—who "was told by the seller himself that he didn't object if we wanted to leave that old line where it was, and I was standing there 40 years ago when he said it." The neighbor's testimony undermines his adversity argument. Adverse possession must be established against the wishes of the owner, not with his consent. Further, the seller was not aware that the fence line was wrong; he thought it ran along the boundary. Therefore, he did not know of the neighbor's possession of his property, so the neighbor's adversity claims fails on a second test. And if the seller had agreed to leave the line where it was, then he gave the neighbor's granddad permission to use *his* five acres. If the neighbor had oral permission to use it, the Court should consider the arrangement to be a **license**—a personal privilege for one person to enter another's land for a particular purpose, in this case, pasturing cattle. A license can be ended at any time by the party that gave it in the first place. Licenses do not run with the land. An oral or informal license would end with the death of either party or when the land is sold. The neighbor loses the five acres that he never had a right to possess or use.

It's obviously better to discover the mismatch between the deed calls and the fence line before you submit your offer. Once you've purchased the property, you've probably acquired the seller's position in the dispute, for better or worse. If your contract asked that the seller disclose all boundary disputes and he didn't, you may be able to get your $20,000 from him if you were to lose this case.

5. To get to the seller's 100 acres, you have to cross land owned by A. Troll. A leaf-strewn road shaded by an overarching canopy of mature sugar maples takes you from the state-maintained road into the seller's property, about 1/2 mile away. Mr. Troll, the seller of the 100 acres, drives you in over this deal-clinching driveway. You check the deed and find specific reference to a 24-foot wide ingress-and-egress right of way (ROW) easement crossing Mr. Troll. You value the driveway access as being worth at least $10,000. You buy the 100 acres from a grinning Mr. Troll. The next day you find that Mr. Troll has chained off the wonderful driveway leading to your land. When you confront him, he smiles and tells you to read your deed. You finally discover that your deeded ROW is not the driveway. In fact, your ROW is no road at all. It will cost you at least $20,000 to construct a road over your ROW, which you finally locate in an inhospitable gully filled with quicksand and boulders the size of beer trucks. Though Mr. Troll now says he doesn't want the likes of you using his fine driveway, he allows, with great reluctance, that he will sell you a 24-foot-wide ROW over it for $10,000—to be neighborly. You're skewered. Mr. Troll, the seller, never said that his driveway was your deeded ROW—and you never asked. Mr. Troll has now bitten you for an extra $10,000 on top of the $10,000 extra you paid him for the driveway access that you assumed

was your ROW.

Always locate a ROW easement on the ground as part of your pre-purchase scoping. Its location will be fixed either by deed or survey. If you have to cross the land of another to get to your seller's land, always insist that the seller convey a recorded ROW easement (deeded easement) that shows and/or states its location, along with any restrictions on its use. Then locate the ROW/easement location on the ground so that you avoid being captured by Mr. Troll and his far-flung relations. Always nail down the legal basis for access if the seller's property does not have **frontage** on a public road. Insert language into your purchase contract that makes your offer contingent on having access that is legal, unambiguous, physically usable, of sufficient width for your purposes, uncontested and permissible by public authority (usually the State's Highway/Road Department issues a permit for a new entrance). If your land does not have electricity, you should make sure that you can run an electric line in this ROW.

If you are buying land where the seller tells you that you have access by prescriptive use, adverse possession, necessity, implication or permission, place a contingency in your offer that requires him to secure access to a degree acceptable to you and your lawyer. Individual circumstances will dictate the level of security you will need.

Permission from the landowner whose land your access road crosses is not good enough, because permission can be withdrawn at any time. Permission is not an easement. Be particularly careful when buying land from large paper companies, utilities and land companies. They've often acquired their holdings decades earlier and may not have good access easements. An unrestricted easement that is recorded prior to your purchase is preferred. While you have an absolute right to get to landlocked property, you don't have a right to get there by the most convenient and cheapest route. If you have to build a road from scratch over a ROW, discount your offering price.

The best position for a buyer in every purchase is to have an existing entrance on owned frontage along a maintained public road. Next best is a recorded ROW easement over an adequate access road to an existing entrance on a maintained public road.

If you are buying land with frontage but without a developed entrance on the public road, you need to make sure that you have sufficient **sight clearance** in both directions from your proposed entrance so that you can obtain a permit to install your entrance. In Virginia, for example, a new entrance now needs 100 feet of sight clearance in both directions for every ten miles per hour of speed limit: thus, a 50-mph zone requires 500 feet of clear sight in both directions from the proposed driveway's centerline. This is a safety-enhancing regulation that can catch an unknowing buyer. Existing entrances are grandfathered, regardless of their hazardousness. The local office of the state highway department will know the applicable standards and may be persuaded to measure free of charge. New entrances usually require a permit.

In sum, when submitting a purchase contract, a buyer should make sure that the seller understands that he is to convey to the buyer, subject to items of record: 1) 100 percent ownership of the property; 2) the full set of fee-simple rights in the property, unless otherwise disclosed and agreed to; 3) all that he owns in the property with nothing reserved or omitted; and 4) full disclosure or any unrecorded claim, boundary dispute, access issue and the like that might in any way negatively affect the buyer's full use, possession and enjoyment of all the rights in the property. While a title search occurs after your contract is accepted, it's in the buyer's interest to check out enough of the seller's deedwork to understand all the recorded limits on the property and the location of any easements before submitting an offer. See Chapter 27 for additional discussion of ownership issues.

LEGAL DESCRIPTIONS

Once you have determined the nature of the seller's ownership, you then must **make sure the property is described legally** in such a way that the acreage you will receive at closing is the same as that which you are paying for. Acreage to be conveyed from seller to buyer should be described in the deed that transfers the property. The same description—or a reference to its exact statement in a previously recorded document, such as an earlier deed—should be included in your purchase contract.

Don't buy land that is not legally described in a recorded document in the property's chain of title. Don't buy land that cannot be described with specificity.

It is not enough, however, to insert a reference in your purchase contract to an earlier recorded description, because such descriptions can range from erroneous and vague to Mary-Poppins practically perfect in every way. States, to my knowledge, do not require that deed descriptions be checked for closure and accurate acreage when property is sold. I know of no state that requires a survey as a condition of land sale. To make matters even more interesting, vague descriptions can be accurate in terms of acreage and precise descriptions can include an error.

A special level of acreage uncertainty is reached when the seller's deed was not recorded, recorded improperly, or an **"off-conveyance"** from the seller's property was not recorded. An "off-conveyance" refers to a piece of the whole being separated by sale, gift or exchange. An unrecorded deed binds only the parties who made it. If you buy 100 acres, of which 12 had been previously sold to a neighbor through an unrecorded deed and you had no knowledge of this transaction at the time of your purchase, your interest in and claim to the disputed 12 acres is superior to the neighbor's. You should win a lawsuit on these facts. But do not be surprised to find the seller testifying that he orally informed you of the unrecorded deed. If your purchase contract specified that you were making an offer for 100 acres, you should prevail against the seller's testimony. But if your contract includes a boundary description (that you did not check for acreage) that amounts to 88 acres, not 100, or refers only to the seller's property, you will lose. Unrecorded sales will not turn up in a title search. You increase your chances of discovering one and protecting your interests in any future lawsuit when you include something like my fee-simple language above that requires the seller to **disclose any "unrecorded easements and deeds**.**"**

Property deed descriptions can be set forth in a proper format with elaborate detail and still contain errors that add to or subtract from the actual acreage being conveyed. These problems are discussed below.

A property's deed description, even when dead-on accurate, does not mean the seller holds **clear title** to the property accurately described. Don't assume that once you confirm the seller's acreage as advertised, it means that the seller has good title to that acreage. You've simply determined that the acreage the seller claims to own is accurate. The title-search question for your lawyer is: Does the seller have good title to this acreage?

Confirming deed acreage starts with a plotting of the calls, described in Chapter 17. The title search should show that the seller has a clear chain of title for the specific number of acres described in the seller's deed. Keep in mind that the acreage in the chain of title may contain an error; and also remember that the title history may not reflect acreage in the field that the seller will convey. Again, **the buyer's job is to make sure that each layer of analysis—deeded acreage, acreage in the chain of title, acreage on the ground—all agree on the same acreage number**. And, again, it's better to do most, if not all, of this research before you submit an offer, because your offering price will reflect what you've found. If you don't do the necessary research before making an offer, place a contingency in your contract that allows you, the buyer, to void your offer without penalty if the seller is unable to convey the amount of acreage under contract, legally and physically, to your satisfaction.

A **title search** is a backtracking process in which the researcher follows the acreage's legal ownership back in time through deeds, wills and other records. Establishing **clear title** to the seller's 100 acres does not guarantee that the seller's property actually contains 100 acres. Your lawyer can certify good title to inaccurate acreage through no error of his own or lack of diligent effort. The buyer in this case has no claim—cause of action—against the lawyer who performed a competent title search. An acreage error can be passed along from title search to title search with each lawyer confirming the erroneous antecedent acreage figure. While the lawyer's title search tracks a specific acreage, he's checking for ownership of that acreage, not whether that acreage number is correct in the passed-down calls and on the ground. He will pick up gross errors in acreage, something like a sale of ten acres 30 years ago that was not deducted from the root property that he's now searching. The acreage errors that are not obvious are found only when a surveyor checks the calls for closure and acreage and then confirms the calls for closure and acreage on the ground.

Each state determines how far back title is to be searched. In Virginia, it is the custom, not the law, that the search be taken back 60 years. If you're buying property that has not been sold once or twice within the last 50 years, I'd take the title back through at least three or four sales to make sure the ownership line of the deeded acreage is, at least, consistent over a longer period. A buyer can always ask his lawyer to take the title back beyond the period set by custom or law.

Title insurance, which insures a property owner against certain adverse claims and errors, should cover a new owner from the day the property was first titled until he disposes of it. Title policies exclude certain acts from their coverage, such as public regulations affecting the use of the property, takings under eminent domain and adverse developments (defects, claims, encumbrances) that the new owner was aware of but did not disclose to the insurance company. Policies usually do not cover unrecorded easements, acreage discrepancies and boundary conflicts that a correct survey would disclose. If you buy without a survey and later discover an acreage shortage, your title insurance won't make you whole. What is protected is the policyholder's title to the property; his title free of any defect, lien or encumbrance other than those of record and listed in the policy; his right to ingress and egress; and the marketability of his title. I've bought rural property without title insurance, following the advice of local lawyers who said it wasn't necessary in their county. I would do so again only if I were confident about the items that insurance covers.

It is easy for errors in calls and acreage to creep into documents, particularly lengthy deed descriptions that were copied and recopied by hand or typewriter. I found one deed, for example, that had been properly searched for title back more than 60 years. In each change of ownership in the twentieth century, the property was described in typewritten deeds as containing, "100 acres." However, when this parcel was originally sold from a large tract in the early 19th Century, the original handwritten deed described it as "108 acres." Sometime after that, a now-long-deceased lawyer misread a handwritten "8" for an "0" and wrote the deed for "100 acres," leaving it eight acres short on paper but not on the ground. The error was not caught until a surveyor plotted the deed's calls on his software.

When deeds were transcribed as land was sold and resold, it was easy for a lawyer or secretary to drop, transpose, miswrite, miscopy and otherwise mess up numbers and compass directions. The farm where I live is divided by a state road: the deed I received when I bought it in 1983 had a 20-acre chunk on the wrong side. My lawyer, then in his late 70s, also represented the seller in our transaction—a fact I learned when I walked into his office for the closing. No one caught his mistake at closing, and I was then too stupid to take the time to read the deed before I signed all the papers. He had inadvertently written 20 acres "west of SR 640" instead of "east of SR 640." Since the error harmed no one, a simple **deed of correction** was done several years later after I took the time to read our deed. A deed of correction is also referred to as a **correction deed** and **deed of confirmation**. Its purpose is to correct spelling mistakes, typographical errors and other misstatements. The point I'm making is simple: legal descriptions should be verified, both in title and on the ground.

And, perhaps, I'm drawing an additional point from my own lack of diligence. Make sure that *you* read and understand your deed description and other documents before you sign them. By the time you get to your lawyer's office for closing, you should have read the deed several times, at least once in conjunction with a topo in the field.

If you ask your lawyer to do a complete title history back to the first records, he will prepare an **abstract of title**—a written chronology and narrative of the property's history of record showing surveys, mortgages, liens, estates, easements, court rulings and the like. Doing an abstract of title is more likely to uncover errors of the type described above than the conventional time-limited title search. Title insurance requires a lawyer to prepare an abstract of title. Since title searches are only looking at the relatively recent chain of title—and things that adverse the seller's title—the standard title-search report will usually contain a boilerplate disclaimer that neither acreage nor boundaries are confirmed by that search. Once again clear title does not validate or establish actual acreage in the field. A run-of-the-mill title search may reveal an acreage problem; an abstract of title will show you how the problem came to be.

The next step in confirming acreage on paper is to determine whether a **recorded survey** exists for the target property. **Recordation** refers to entering a drawing of the property's boundaries into the county's deed books, noting time and date. Recording a survey provides notice to the general public that the owner of the surveyed land claims certain boundaries and location. Recording, however, does not establish the validity of the survey's measurements or validate the deed's acreage claim. It does, on the other hand, place the holder of the recorded survey in an advantageous position in the event of a challenge to his boundaries or acreage. The survey's measurements have to be based on calls in a deed, presumably a deed of record.

A survey may be found, once recorded, either immediately following the deed in the deed book or in a separate book devoted to surveys and plats. In the latter case, the clerk should note on the deed the location of the survey in the survey book, by book number and page. Make sure the recorded survey carries the surveyor's signature, state license number and date of completion. The recordation date and time will also appear on the survey document. Remember recordation does not guarantee a survey's accuracy.

Property can be, and is, sold without a survey being recorded by either buyer or seller. But the calls in the seller's deed had to come from somewhere, from some earlier survey, for the seller's land to have been "deeded off." Dig back enough and you will find a first deed description and survey, though they may be primitive. Somewhere in the chain, there should be surveyed calls that constitute the current description. And that's the set on which the seller's title rests. As you backtrack the seller's deed, you will often find gifts and sales of land that reduce the original tract. Some of these off-conveyances provide a legal description of the parcel that was severed, and some provide a description less than a set of calls. When the seller's acreage is the remainder of a tract that's been whittled, hire a surveyor to check acreage and boundaries.

The seller may have, or know of, an **unrecorded survey** on his property. This is not common, but it's not unknown. Why would a landowner not record a survey that he possesses? The obvious answer is probably right: the survey shows something the seller does not want to be known. If you get wind of an unrecorded survey, make the effort to find out what that something is. You may be able to do this without seeing the unrecorded survey through diligent sleuthing with neighbors and local surveyors. If you know the seller has an unrecorded survey and you think it's necessary to see it, you can always insert an **unrecorded survey contingency** in your purchase contract:

> **Buyer's offer is contingent on the Seller providing him with a copy of any unrecorded survey of Seller's property. Buyer may modify or withdraw his offer**

without penalty if this survey reveals information that is, in Buyer's opinion, unacceptable.

If you can't figure out the problem and the seller refuses to produce the survey, I would not submit an offer.

When the seller cannot or does not provide a survey, a buyer has four other information sources to check before giving up hope. First, surveyors often collect old local surveys and documents in the course of their work. Retired surveyors may give their files to one of their occupational heirs. Ask them for help. One of the local surveyors may have the unrecorded survey of the seller's land or an unrecorded survey of adjoining land. Second, some counties employ a full- or part-time surveyor; ask him. If your seller's land is part of a larger tract with shaky calls, the county's surveyor may have had to plot out the original deed, from which your seller's land came. Third, check the neighbors' deeds to see whether they have recorded surveys that show the common boundaries with your seller's property. Their deed calls should match exactly the seller's deed calls where the two properties join and share a line. A discrepancy between your seller's calls and a neighbor's may indicate where a closure or acreage error is in your seller's deed. Lawyers and surveyors often search the deed work for adjoining landowners to clear up problems in a seller's deed. If you can find no deed calls at all for the seller's property, you will have to use the calls from the neighboring deeds and piece the target's boundaries together. Let a surveyor do this work for you. Finally, if the target property has ever been leased for minerals, the lessee—the company that's leased the minerals from the owner—may have worked up a map or survey and may share its information with you.

If you commission a survey that shows you have a questionable claim to say 25 acres of the 250 that you just bought from the seller, you can choose either to record your new survey or not. Recordation will support your claim to 225 acres within your survey boundaries if that's an issue, but it will weaken your argument for the other 25. It's obviously in your self-interest to record a survey that shows your new property contains 250 acres, especially if your neighbor is using 25 of them. Your lawyer can advise you on whether or not to record.

Different surveyors working from the same records can—and, occasionally, do—come to different conclusions about a boundary line.

One survey surprise is an **overlap**, in which the seller's survey (or your new survey) includes land that a neighbor's survey shows as his. Overlaps tend to involve an acre or two at most, but not always. Overlaps can be found on the ground, in the paperwork, or in both places. Surveyors should note on a newly drawn survey where they have found one. If the overlap is inconsequential, I'd suggest either ignoring it or, when each side has a defensible claim, working out an equitable division, swap or sale. Court victories in such disputes may cost the winner more than the contested terrain is worth. Where the overlap involves land with significant value, you have no choice but to look for resolution. Surveyors representing each party may be able to correct the error, or, failing that, suggest a compromise. If you and the neighbor can't figure it out, you have four choices: forget about it, mediation, arbitration or litigation. It's always better to discover an overlap before you submit a purchase offer. That allows you to place a contingency in your contract that requires the seller to solve the problem with the neighbor, subject to your approval.

ACREAGE DISCREPANCIES

Non-alignment situations—where the boundary lines in the deed, survey or topo don't match the boundary lines on the ground—often present themselves as an encroachment by a functioning fence line. If, for instance, your topo map (using the deed calls) shows a boundary running along a hard-to-access ridge but you find a well-maintained fence at the base of the ridge (and none at the top where it should be), either the paper boundaries are wrong or the fence is—and there's always the third option, that both are. But the likeliest explanation is that it was too hard to build the fence along the real boundary, so it was built where it was feasible, whether or not by mutual agreement.

A fence encroachment means that a buyer may be buying land that the seller may or may not own when the seller is encroaching on the neighbor. Or, the buyer may be facing a claim to the seller's land that the neighbor may or may not own. A fence encroachment, in and of itself, does *not establish* legal ownership to the fenced-in land. It does, however, give the buyer notice that he needs to determine the seriousness and source of the problem. A fence encroachment, even with a small amount of land involved, is one loose end that can quickly turn into a biting snake. People are touchy and self-righteous about their property; I know I am.

The smallest non-alignments can create large, long-lasting grievances between neighbors. If your new land is the victim of even a long-ago willful encroachment, it's hard not to think of your current neighbor as a complicit beneficiary. At the very least, you may harbor undeclared hard feelings and end up with less functional acreage than you thought you had purchased. Don't assume that a friendly approach to your new neighbor will result in quick-and-easy justice for you, the newcomer. It's far more likely to poison the well of local opinion regarding your "arrogant" demand for change. When you discover a non-alignment that benefits your seller, you will take over his position. Don't be surprised when the neighbor appears asking you for justice. Keeping silent about a non-alignment that seemingly brings you free acreage does not strengthen any legitimate claim you have to ownership. It may simply paint you as dishonest. For these reasons, the best path I think is to **disclose any non-alignment or acreage discrepancy your scoping discovers to the seller in writing and have him to sort it out as a condition of your purchase**.

Know going into this discussion that both the seller and the neighbor may be genuinely ignorant of what you have uncovered. Neither is likely to be pleased by the prospect of having to work a deal with each other because you want them to. Your seller is going to be especially miffed if the encroachment benefits him and you're asking him to give up sale money for your benefit. Your leverage with the seller is to tell him that you will alert the neighbor if he refuses. And your leverage with both the seller and the neighbor is to say that they are both under the obligation to disclose this problem to every buyer of both properties in the future. So they may as well work it out now, for you.

"Ground shrink" is a term hunters use to describe a deer that scoped out at 250 pounds standing at a distance but weighs only 150 on the ground after the shot. Ground shrink is always blamed for the loss of the other 100 pounds, which, of course, never existed, except in the hunter's excited imagination.

Land buyers want to avoid ground shrink, where the buyer has bought "x" number of acres in an impulsive, non-researched rush, only to find upon completing the purchase that he owns something less than "x."

Here's a typical ground-shrink dilemma.

More or less. The seller's deed says he owns "100 acres, more or less." You offer him $100,000, which he accepts. Just before closing, you learn that he has only 90 acres. Can you void the contract? Probably not. Can you force him to take $90,000? Probably not. In both cases, the "more or less" probably covers him. What if you can prove beyond any doubt that the seller knew the property was short ten acres, and still advertised the land as being 100 acres, more or less, which is the precise language found in his deed? Sorry, you're probably still out of luck, though you may have an argument based on failure to disclose a material defect. "More or less" allows him to sell you less than 100 acres. If you didn't turn up the ten-acre shortage before closing, most courts, I think, will find that failure was caused by the buyer's failure to perform his own due diligence,

You would, on the other hand, have a right to void your contract if the seller advertised the property to be sold as containing "100 acres," rather than "100 acres, more or less."

You would not have a right to void if the seller advertised "100 acres, tax-map acreage," which means only that the seller is paying tax on 100 acres as it appears on the county's tax rolls. Tax-map acreage does not establish that a seller either owns that amount or can convey that amount.

When a seller advertises 100 acres, more or less, the buyer can stipulate in his purchase contract that his offer is based on **"$1,000 per acre conveyed and not $100,000 in gross."** That language would allow the buyer to void his offer if the seller can't convey the full 100 acres, and, if needed, provide the basis of a post-sale lawsuit against the seller. As an alternative, the buyer could insert into his contract, **"$1,000 per acre, established by survey or other means acceptable to the Buyer, and conveyed."**

What happens in this example of a ten-acre shortfall when the buyer offers "$1,000 per acre" and the seller's deed conveys 100 acres, more or less? The buyer discovers the shortfall prior to closing and wants to pay $90,000. The seller says 100 acres, more or less, means that $1,000 should be multiplied by 100, not 90, because the buyer is buying the deeded acreage, not what's on the ground. In fact, the seller argues, the buyer is getting exactly what the deed provides, 100 acres more or less. Were this to come to court, I think judges would not be of one mind. My hope is that a judge would find that the buyer's contract language trumps the seller's deeded-acreage argument, because it is more specific and both parties agreed to it. But my record of predicting judicial behavior is abysmal. I have seen judges act arbitrarily and without regard to where the weight of both facts and law fell. The buyer in this example will do better to resolve this dispute as part of his purchase, rather than bring a lawsuit whose expenses are likely to exceed the money at issue. All things considered, the buyer would do well to settle on buying the 90 acres he wants for a split-the-difference $95,000, or $1,055 per acre.

Ground-shrink disputes often involve the "more or less" qualification in a deed. This phrase and concept, I think, was intended to cover the minor, inescapable errors that were inherent in the old survey methods and instruments. To what degree "more or less" can be stretched to cover major mistakes is, a matter of local judicial interpretation and the facts specific to each dispute. The buyer's argument is strengthened if he can prove that the seller knew of a large shortfall and failed to disclose it. The size of the shortfall may also swing a judge to one side or the other. The buyer should argue that the seller's failure to disclose and the $10,000 he wants to reap from this concealment amounts to a deliberate "unjust enrichment." The legal predisposition is to support the seller in such disputes because the buyer had the opportunity and means to verify acreage prior to purchase. The facts in this example lend themselves to a split-the-baby ruling, similar to the $95,000-for-90-acres compromise mentioned above.

I am not arguing against buying property whose deed carries the "more-or-less" qualification, because many safe-to-buy properties do. I am arguing that buyers must protect themselves by verifying acreage prior to submitting an offer.

I have been involved with two instances of 300-acre properties with "more-or-less" language that were badly off: one was 90 acres more than what the seller and his deed were conveying; the other was 100 acres less. I also bought a property with a deed providing for "447 acres, more or less" that upon a post-purchase survey at my expense turned out to be only 425 acres. The seller knew of the shortfall and did not disclose it. My preliminary scoping suggested that the property would be short 15 acres, plus or minus. This purchase turned out to be as good an investment as I ever made. Another example is a tract—sold as 30 acres, more or less—that contained only 20; the buyer, who did no scoping or deed plotting, was stuck. I've scoped at least a dozen properties during the last five years that diverged on the ground from the deed by more than five acres.

If you find yourself with a "more-or-less" deed, have a surveyor plot the acreage for you. When you face a shortage, you have to make a decision about how to proceed. You can, of course, abandon the property altogether. Or, you can submit a dollar-per-acre-conveyed offer along with a copy of your surveyor's mapping and acreage calculation. This should be accompanied by words to the effect that the seller now has an obligation to disclose the acreage shortage to any buyer following you. Or, you say nothing about the shortage and make an offer that includes a **minimum-acreage contingency**, such as:

Buyer's offer is contingent on Seller being able to convey 100 acres, legally and physically. If the Seller is unable to so convey at least 99.50 acres to the Buyer's satisfaction, Buyer may amend or void this Contract at his discretion and without penalty.

Buyer will determine acreage at his expense and within thirty (30) days of the effective date of this Contract.

This approach—not disclosing what you already know—allows the seller to become invested in a sale to you. When you show him the bad news, you've set the stage for an acceptable compromise. A fourth alternative is to include an **acreage-slide formula** in your contract by which the buyer agrees to pay increasingly more per acre as the number of acres the seller can convey falls and increasingly less per acre as the number of acres the seller can convey rises, acreage to be determined by means acceptable to both parties and jointly paid for.

Less is Not Always More. What do you do when your seller occupies less land than his deed provides because a neighbor has fenced some in?

During your pre-purchase scoping, you discover that your seller's deeded 100 acres is 25 acres short on the ground. A neighbor's fence encloses this parcel. Your seller believes that the fence line is on the deeded boundary. This is too large a matter for you to forget or forgive. If you're paying for 100 acres, you don't want to end up with 75.

You have to show the fence encroachment to the seller. You are the bearer of very bad news so be prepared for anger and rejection. His first defense is that you are wrong. Since you only have a plot of his boundaries and not a survey, he will feel justified in quarreling with you. He will argue that his land contains more than the 100 acres in the deed owing to its rolling topography. (This, as you know, is true, but irrelevant.) He'll argue that he's selling "what you can see with your own two eyes." (No, he's not.) Then he'll say that he priced the property "as it lays," so your piece of paper means nothing in terms of price. (How it lays or doesn't lay has nothing to do with how much acreage it contains legally.) He will be reluctant to open this can of worms with his neighbor, because every solution promises to cost him in time, money and aggravation. Although 25 acres is at stake, the seller's not sure that he can, if it comes down to it, prevail in a lawsuit. Let him blow off steam and then come back a week or two later after he's had a chance to check your information and talk to a lawyer. He will soon realize that he's now supposed to disclose this 25-acre "latent defect" to all buyers as long as it's not resolved. If the seller chooses to stonewall you, walk away. If you buy the property, you buy the problem. And since you are aware of it, you have no cause of action against the seller after buying it. Any solution will, therefore, cost *you* money, time and aggravation—and there's no guarantee that you will get the acreage.

Let's assume that you've raised the issue of the 25 acres before submitting an offer, and have gotten nowhere. You might consider two approaches to force the seller to respond. First, you could make an offer based on 100 acres that is contingent on the seller being able to convey 100 acres, both in deed and on the ground. The seller has the burden of resolving the shortage to your satisfaction if he wants your money. If your offer is close to full price for 100 acres, you've given him an incentive to do so. Your offer has also made the shortfall public knowledge if a broker is involved.

The second approach is to make a fair offer for 75 acres without mentioning the 25-acre problem. This assumes that you really want the land as it is. You may be able to get some or all of the 25 acres eventually, but that speculation and likely expense is not a factor in your offer. You offer less money because you're bargaining over 75 acres on the ground, not the 100 in the deed. Point out that your offer is higher on a per-acre basis, assuming that it is. You can also offer to pay the seller for the disputed 25 acres whenever a suit that he brings at his expense is successful. If your seller balks, mention that he'll never sell 75 acres at a 100-acre price unless he deliberately conceals the shortfall. Introduce the word, "fraud," into the conversation. The way you get this seller to accept the reasonableness of a price reduction is to show him gently that his alternatives are worse. Ease him into understanding that a sale to you is likely to be his best money all things considered, even though he will realize less than he expected initially. Make sure to mention that most buyers will sue a seller over acreage that is 25 percent less than promised. So it's better to sell the property as 75 acres now, than to trick another buyer into a "100-acre" purchase, which will cost the seller the expense of defending his unethical action and is likely to forfeit the amount gained to boot.

What should you do if your pre-purchase scoping shows that a seller will convey to you by deed less land than you will own on the ground? You would be getting more land than you're bargaining for and paying for. This non-alignment is not caused by a fence encroachment, but by a deed error of which you know and the seller doesn't. I've encountered this issue on a 385-acre tract on the ground that was being sold as a 295-acre tract, based on the seller's deed. This seller had inherited the property years earlier and had made no effort to check the acreage.

What to do? I would first consider who the seller is. If he is a competent, knowledgeable individual who's either too lazy or cheap to find out how much land he's selling, I see nothing wrong in taking advantage of his lack of due diligence on his own behalf. One way to proceed is to offer this seller his full asking price. That's what I did. The seller eagerly accepted, thinking that he had lucked into a fool for a buyer. A slyer alternative is to offer five or ten percent less than the asking price and make the seller work for the deal. I didn't try this, because I didn't want to jeopardize getting the land under contract. I do not think a buyer is under any obligation to a competent seller—who is capable of becoming knowledgeable—to disclose information that the buyer acquires at his expense and which benefits him at the seller's expense. Remember this is information that the seller could have and should have developed on his own.

If, on the other hand, your seller can not be reasonably expected to understand the selling process and reasonably defend his interests, I would either walk away from the property or disclose the information as I submitted an offer. P.J. Proudhon, the 19th Century French anarchist, said: "Property is theft." A buyer taking advantage of an unsophisticated or powerless seller is one such example.

An ethical line exists between taking unfair advantage and making a bargain purchase. Dirt-smart buyers should appreciate the difference and keep to the right side of the line.

I've had two clients over the years who have introduced themselves to me by saying that they were "thieves" and only interested in land that they could "steal." In both instances, I initially supplied a more generous interpretation of their intentions: "You're looking for an investment without risk, land that you can buy with the sale of the timber covering the full acquisition cost. Right?" Wrong. They *were* thieves, not investors. And they stole a lot of my time. I don't see how a person can be a thief in one area of his life without being a thief in others. Perhaps, I'm ethically dense. Thieves succeed every so often, but I've seen them get taken just as frequently. Thieves undermine themselves through greed. It's best to think of yourself as a land investor, guided by an interest in stripping risk out of a purchase and making a reasonable profit.

What should you do when you discover after a purchase that your seller occupied more acreage on the ground than he had title to?

Against my advice, you did not have the deed's calls plotted before purchasing 100 acres. You are thinking of selling a portion to pay down some of the debt, so you commission a post-purchase boundary survey. The surveyor reports that you, indeed, own 100 acres as provided in your deed. But he also found that the seller occupied and used about 25 acres of a neighbor's land that was fenced into your new property years ago without dispute. The surveyor informs you that your deed provides no right to these 25 acres.

If you pull down the surveyor's ribbons and don't record the survey, you are hiding the truth. This doesn't strengthen your claim to the land once it's discovered, because adverse possession requires that your occupation be open and notorious. But there is an interesting twist to this set of facts. Your functioning fence line is clearly open and notorious, though the neighbor is unaware that it is wrong. Must your real boundary line be marked on the ground to show the neighbor where the common line really lies? I don't know. But what is clear is that you won't win an adverse-possession claim for the 25 acres unless the neighbor knows or has public notice (via recordation) that you are occupying land that is his.

You consider not recording your survey. If your neighbor never sees it, you hope that you might avoid a dispute and continue to occupy and use the 25 acres without a legal right to do so. Then you realize you have to pull down the new ribbons that your surveyor just put up. If the neighbor sees the ribbons far inside your side of the existing fence, he's likely to figure out where your common boundary lies. Your plan to sell some of your new acreage is now squirreled up, because you can't guarantee good title to the 25 acres.

Recording your survey, however, provides public notice that you don't own the 25 acres if someone takes the time to copy your survey and match it against the presumed boundary on the ground. If no one checks—which is likely—your public notice is made, but bears no adverse consequence. You should understand, however, that you're taking a step toward establishing ownership of land that you do not own. Your case for title by adverse possession may start either from the date on which the fence was erected or the date on which you record the survey. Gaining title/ownership might be as much as 30 years in the future and require a lawsuit. If you wait six months or more after purchase before recording your survey, you've made it harder for your neighbor to find it in the records. A standard title search of *his* property will probably not dig out your recorded survey—but it could, depending on the diligence of the researcher. Since there's nothing wrong with his deeded acreage, the title search on his land will probably not reveal his fenced-out loss of 25 acres on the ground. Your occupation will reveal itself if the neighbor's land is surveyed or field-checked against the deed's calls.

Sooner or later, someone on the neighbor's side will discover your occupation. If you claim you never knew about it, the facts leaking out are likely to show that you're not telling the truth. You can argue that you did not understand the ground implications of the survey that you recorded. Landowners often do not make the connection between survey and ground truth. But a surveyor should make note of a very large discrepancy on his survey, unless you persuade him not to. I will simply note the obvious: people have different levels of tolerance for their own intentional dishonesty.

If you suspect this situation, you could instruct your surveyor not to mark the boundaries on the ground, or not to mark the boundary where the encroachment occurs. Your surveyor may or may not cooperate with you once he discovers the 25-acre encroachment. Your neighbor's chances of discovering the error are reduced, but your ability to sell that 25 acres is not enhanced. This type of deception will blow up in your face eventually.

If you leave the ribbons up and record your survey, the neighbor has nobody to blame but himself for not becoming aware of the boundary. If he sleeps on his rights after recordation, he weakens his claim to the land. Recordation provides public notice of your adverse possession of his land whether or not he ever sees the survey in the courthouse. The longer this clock runs without his alarm going off, the longer he sleeps on his rights, the stronger your claim is. The **doctrine of laches** (pronounced, "latches") is the idea in law that an individual who believes he is wronged must assert his position in a timely fashion. Failure to advance a timely claim is grounds for dismissal. But remember: you are trying to take land legally that does not belong to you legally at the time you are trying to take it.

Your choice is to reveal the problem and deal with it openly with your neighbor, or conceal it in hope that he never figures it out. Honesty may result in your "loss" in whole or part of the 25 acres. Dishonesty may result in your continued occupation of his 25 acres. It may result in your legal ownership of the land. It may have other results on the order of "What goes around, comes around."

There's another way for you to look at this problem. You did not pay your seller for the 25 extra acres; you only paid him for the deed-based 100 acres. Therefore, it costs you nothing to "give" them back to your neighbor. An act of this sort is not being an urban patsy. It's no different than returning a wallet that you find on the sidewalk. It's a good way to move in to your new community.

ACREAGE-VERIFICATION CONTINGENCIES

Placing a **deeded-acreage-verification contingency in your purchase offer** is a fast, cheap way of protecting your interest in obtaining the acreage the seller is marketing. The contingency makes your purchase depend on having a surveyor of your choice run the calls through his deed-mapping program, which will either confirm the seller's calls and acreage or identify an error or uncertainty. *The plotting does not verify the seller's acreage on the ground, however. For that, you need the surveyor to field-check the calls.* If an acreage error in the deed is explainable or small, you can accept it without haggling. This should build good will that you may have to spend on more contentious issues. If the error is substantial, this contingency allows you to either walk away from the contract without penalty or renegotiate in light of the acreage problem.

Here is generic deeded-acreage-verification contingency that you can use if you have reason to suspect the deeded acreage *exceeds* the seller's acreage on the ground:

> **Buyer's offer is contingent on receiving a satisfactory acreage-verification report within ____ calendar days of the effective date of this Contract. This report shall be prepared at Buyer's expense by a licensed land surveyor of Buyer's choice. The report shall determine the accuracy of Seller's deeded acreage.**
>
> **If these results are unacceptable to the Buyer, he may either amend or void this Contract without penalty by written notice to Seller. In the event of an amended offer, Seller is free to accept, reject or propose alternative terms.**

You can adapt the language in this contingency to provide for a verification of acreage and boundaries *on the ground*. Simply revise the last sentence in the first paragraph to read: **The report shall determine the accuracy of Seller's acreage and boundaries, both in the deed and on the ground.**

The cost of verifying deeded acreage is often no more than an hour of a surveyor's time at his computer. The cost will rise if he has to work back through the chain of titles to locate the root of an error. This is not a survey contingency; you are not obligating yourself to pay for a field survey. You can anticipate surveying costs for field-checking acreage; some errors can be found by having a surveyor walk the lines with the calls in hand.

Once you have a signed purchase contract with a seller, you have negotiating leverage in the event of an acreage issue. He now has knowledge of a material defect, which he needs to disclose to any other buyer. If he tries to finesse the problem by including a **permitted title exception** involving acreage, it's a red flag to other buyers, at least the ones who are not buying on impulse and certainly those who have read this book. Moreover, the seller has invested time and energy in working a contract with you; there's no percentage for him to repeat the process with someone new with little expectation of a better outcome.

A buyer faces a different decision when his scoping suggests that the seller's deeded acreage is less than what the seller will convey on the ground. If the cause of this windfall for the buyer is some error in the calls, I don't think I would bring it up. It's the seller's obligation to know how much acreage he's selling. If he thinks he's selling 100 acres and the deed's calls plot out to 125, pay him for the 100 acres. On the other hand, if the extra 25 acres will be conveyed by the seller's adverse occupation or use of neighboring land, I would certainly bring it to the seller's attention.

Another variation of an acreage problem is one where you suspect a discrepancy of some significance, probably requiring survey work, but you're not sure of its size. In this case, you can propose that both parties arrange for and share the costs of verifying boundaries and acreage. You can also couple that with an **acreage slide**.

> **Buyer's contingent offering price is $100,000, based on Seller's representation that the property contains 100 acres.**
>
> **The Parties agree to select a mutually acceptable surveyor to confirm acreage and boundaries, and they further agree to share equally the cost of this work.**
>
> **Buyer is offering $1,000 per acre conveyed in the deed and on the ground rather than a lump sum of $100,000. Buyer's final offering price will be determined by multiplying $1,000 per acre by the number of acres the surveyor determines to be in the property, subject to the following formula:**
>
> **The offering price of $1,000 per acre will stand for any surveyor-certified acreage within 3.000 acres of 100 acres.**
>
> **If the certified acreage is determined to be between 90.000 and 97.000 acres, the offering price will be increased to $1,050 per acre.**
>
> **If the certified acreage is determined to be between 103.000 and 110.000 acres, the offering price will be lowered to $950 per acre.**
>
> **If the certified acreage is less than 90.000 acres or more than 110.000 acres, the Buyer reserves the right to withdraw this offer and submit a replacement.**

An acreage slide is fair in concept to both sides. It will work when you are dealing with a reasonable and, preferably, motivated, seller. Whatever the findings, the Parties are obligating themselves to carry the deal through, except when a large discrepancy is found.

Acreage slides can work tricks on your pocketbook when a big dollar difference kicks in for the next increment of acreage change. For that reason, the fairest slides are those that adjust price to acreage in small increments. If, for instance, you increase your price $50 per acre for the first three acres under 100 acres and then $50 per acre more for the next three acres, you would pay $101,850 for 97 acres and $105,600 for 96 acres. You avoid these jumps by figuring a different price per acre for each total acreage.

Consider one other way an acreage slide can bite you. Take the example of a 25-acre shortfall in a 100-acre tract. You, the buyer, will be expected to increase your **per-acre price multiplier** from, say, $1,000 per acre to say, $1,100 per acre, for a total of $82,500 (75 x $1,100 = $82,500). If you gain 25 acres, you agree to drop your per-acre price to $900, a total of $112,500 (125 x $900 = $12,500). This appears at first glance to be an acreage slide that adjusts the *per-acre price* by ten percent in either direction with equitable and equivalent results. But note that you are buying the next 25 acres for $12,500, or $500 per acre, whereas you're giving up 25 acres for $17,500 at $700 per acre. A true ten-percent slide would be figured on the gross purchase price of $100,000, not the per-acre price. Figured on the gross purchase price, a ten-percent slide on the agreed purchase price would amount to a flat $10,000 for 25 acres in either direction. Each acre is now valued at $400, whether it's a gain or a loss to the buyer. This formula, however, does not reflect market reality by which larger acreages sell for fewer dollars per acres and smaller acreages sell for more per acre.

Buyers and sellers can disagree as to which slide formula is fair to both sides. I want readers to be aware that different formulas produce different results, some of which may not be obvious. Make sure that you understand the dollar arithmetic for both buyer and seller any time an acreage slide is proposed.

As a buyer, I prefer to use an acreage-certification contingency that covers both the deeded acreage and a field-check, if necessary. I pay for this work and have no obligation to share its results with the seller. If results favor the buyer, he can proceed at the price offered; if the results favor the seller, the buyer can use them to reopen negotiations or walk away. Most sellers agree to an acreage contingency that the buyer pays for; it never seems to occur to them that it's possible that they may be conveying more acreage than is shown in their deed.

The following generic acreage contingency will protect a buyer in most circumstances:

Buyer's offer is contingent on obtaining acceptable results from a surveyor's report regarding the property's boundaries and acreage, in the deed and on the ground. Buyer shall arrange for this work at his expense.

Buyer shall complete this work within 60 days of the effective date of this Contract. He must notify Seller in writing within ___ calendar days of receiving these results whether or not they are acceptable. Absent such notice, this contingency shall become void.

If results are not acceptable to Buyer, he may void this Contract without penalty and his deposit shall be promptly returned in full in a timely manner.

THE SPECIAL CASE OF LEASES

Acreage for sale, especially in the West, can involve a seller-held lease to private or public land and/or water. Seller-owned acreage is referred to as **deeded acreage**; seller-leased acreage is referred to as **lease acreage**. The seller can transfer the lease acreage to the buyer in several ways, including the assignment of the seller's interest in the lease; seller sale to the buyer of such interest; or even a risk-reward sharing arrangement by which the seller continues to pay a share of the lease's rent in return for a percentage share of future profits.

Be careful with leases. The deeded acreage you are about to buy may be **operationally dependent** either on a lease or a use easement that can be cancelled arbitrarily. Operational dependency means that the deeded land more or less requires access to, or the use of, the leased resources to function as an economically viable unit. The leased land may, for example, be the best, or only, source of livestock water in dry weather or the strongest patch of August grass which the deeded acreage must have to carry cattle through until September's last flush of growth.

Use of federal land and resources is subject to the vagaries of Congressional and Presidential policies. Buyers should not expect unfettered continued use of public land for grazing where endangered, threatened or sensitive (ETS) species exist or where grazing has caused substantial land-degradation or water-pollution problems. Leasing public land is cheap and cost-effective from the lessee's (tenant) perspective, which is why farmers and ranchers want to continue doing it. From the public's point of view, it can be environmentally expensive. Federal land leasing is, therefore, likely to be subject to future rent increases, greater regulatory constraints and uncertainty. While the profitability of a small deed and a large public lease may work well on paper, you can find yourself leaning on a lease that gets caught in a protracted regulatory fight which will, at the very least, raise your costs. Sooner or later, livestock farmers should expect federal agencies to lower allowable stocking rates, tighten regulations related to the pollution of surface waters and ETS protection, and raise leasing fees.

Leased land almost always involves different types of risk, each ranging from pretty small to very high. Risk can take the form of higher rent; new requirements for tenant-paid land improvements or different practices; and, in the worst case, loss of the lease. Risk is often expressed as the product of probability times consequences, with the highest risk being associated with a catastrophic event that's expected to happen. That's a useful way of assessing risk associated with leased land.

A common situation is a "small" farm being dependent on a large leased acreage. I would avoid buying land that needs lease acreage to function profitably, except if you are looking for a second home and have no interest in farming the lease. Your interest in the lease can be turned into cash by selling or subletting it to a new tenant. An undersized farm can also work for a buyer who is looking to change the operation to make a profit on the deeded acreage alone. Buyers like these should look for ways to cash out lease acreage.

A buyer's opportunity arises when a seller preemptively discounts his asking/selling price because he sees no use for his lease-dependent deeded land other than for that which he has used it for—and not very successfully. If a buyer has figured out a different use, he will benefit from the seller's self-inflicted price discount *as long as the new use works*. New wine in a seller's old bottle works only when the new vinter knows what he's doing. If you have no experience in the new idea to which you are committing your life, you are taking on a high risk of failure. Don't be seduced into a particular property because you are entranced with a nifty outside-the-box idea. It may be outside the box because it can't fit inside.

The first acreage considerations, then, are to determine whether the deeded acreage comes with and is dependent on leased land and/or water. As a general rule, a buyer can expect that the seller and his agent will reveal the existence of such leases. (On the other hand, I've found sellers and agents may or may not reveal that mineral rights have been either leased or severed.) If the seller owns a **water right,** make sure that it is included in what you're buying. If the seller has leased a needed water right to a neighbor prior to your purchase, don't buy his land. Do not assume that you will be able to obtain water rights in arid country. Where a target property depends on irrigation or off-site water for livestock, make sure that water supply is part of your deal.

If you want to be safe, you can insert a **lease-and-severance disclosure section** in your purchase offer:

> **Seller agrees to disclose to Buyer all leases of whatever kind affecting the property, both pending and in effect, recorded and otherwise, whether Seller is landlord (lessor) or tenant (lessee), including, but not limited to, leases related to minerals, timber, water, air, land, crops, hunting, fishing, improvements, recreational use and gathering.**
>
> **Seller agrees to disclose all severances, reservations of and limitations on interests or rights in the property, both pending and in effect, recorded and otherwise, including, but not limited to, minerals, timber, water, air, land, crops, hunting, fishing, improvements, recreational use and gathering.**
>
> **Seller shall provide Buyer with photocopies of all such leases and severances within five business days of this Contract taking effect. Buyer may withdraw this Contract**

without penalty if Seller fails to comply with this section or if the disclosures are unacceptable to Buyer.

Almost every lawyer who reads this language will tell you that it is onerous, too detailed, cumbersome and redundant. I agree. Boilerplate in the standard contract will protect a buyer, they will say.

Language, such as I've proposed, is intended both to educate the seller about your expectations and protect your interests in the event of willful or unintended failures to disclose. Since most real-estate contracts are either written by the seller's lawyer or are pre-printed forms used by real-estate brokers representing the seller's interest, they neither educate the seller about what the buyer expects nor protect the buyer's interests sufficiently.

Real-estate contracts are not "**adhesion contracts**," which are contracts that offer consumers take-it-or-leave-it terms. The buyer can add language to a pre-printed contract, but the large blocks of small print often intimidate buyers into leaving those sections alone.

Think I'm being nerdy? I found for a developer a wooded 800-acre tract with extensive river frontage. Despite the presence of an active single-track rail line through its middle, the land could be developed for second homes. A contract was offered and accepted. The buyer then happened on the fact that the seller had reserved the timber. My client tried to buy the timber reservation without success. The deal collapsed. I am now noticing that this tract is being marketed by the same broker with the notation, "Timber reserved." Stuff like this happens. An honest seller will not be put off by disclosure language on leases and severance, because it requires nothing more of him than to disclose what he's already prepared to disclose. A seller who wants to hide something from you is likely to feign offense. That's good, not bad. You want to pop every jack-in-the-box at least once before you give it to your kids.

And, finally, speaking of surprises. I once leased a farm for summer grazing during a severe drought. I put my cattle on and a few weeks later I drove up with a fresh supply of mineral salt. I noticed three or four horses that had not been there before. When I asked the owner about the horses, she said she had leased the farm to their owner after she had signed the lease with me. She saw nothing wrong with the arrangement inasmuch as "horses are not cattle." Given my circumstances, I came to the conclusion that it was best to not point out that both horses and cattle eat the same grass. I let the double lease go without comment. On the off chance that other landlords might reason that grass eaten by a steer differs in some way from grass eaten by a horse, I advise including the words **"lease the landlord's premises exclusively to the tenant"** in your contract. If the landlord wants to reserve some portion of his land for his own use, he will include that exception in the lease.

CHAPTER 27: TRICKS OF THE SELLER'S TRADE: LEGAL, NOT LEGAL AND OTHERWISE

The ingenuity of human greed, especially over small sums, is always entertaining to observe.

Sometimes, it's infuriating and occasionally it's the cause of despair for our species. The buying and selling of land is as good a stage as any on which to observe actors playing small.

Here are some scenes I've seen in the theater of the deal.

1. General Warranty Deed. A general warranty deed is what a buyer wants.

A general warranty deed binds the seller (grantor) to six types of covenants and warranties about his ownership and title that go back to the origins of the property. A **special warranty deed** limits these promises to the buyer (grantee) to the seller's period of ownership.

The six covenants are:

1. **Covenant of seisin**: Seller promises that he owns the property.

2. **Covenant of the right to convey**: Seller promises that he has the legal right to convey the property that he owns. The right to convey is often combined with, or read into, the covenant of seisin, though there are circumstances where a seller, such as a trustee, may hold title to a property but be prohibited from selling it.

3. **Covenant against encumbrance**: Seller promises that his deed at the time he conveys title to the buyer is free of all liens and encumbrances except those set forth in the deed.

One encumbrance that should be recorded is an access easement that allows the seller's neighbor to drive over the seller's property to get to his property. This easement **runs with the seller's land and is a right held by the neighbor**. The neighbor in this case holds an **appurtenant easement**, that is, a right of way annexed to his property. The seller's land over which the neighbor's easement runs is called the **servient tenement**; the neighbor's land that benefits is called the **dominant tenement**. Other common recorded easements are those held by utilities and public highway departments.

This covenant is supposed to protect the buyer from encumbrances, such as mortgages, liens, easements, restrictive covenants and reservations of interests in minerals, timber, crops and improvements. It should also protect the buyer from unrecorded encumbrances, such as a claim of adverse possession or prescriptive use. Sellers may breach this warranty in my experience, if only because they don't know what a general warranty deed requires of them. And there are sellers who know and don't give a flip. Sellers often do not disclose unrecorded claims, disputed areas and encroachments. After the sale, these sellers want nothing more than to walk away from unresolved troubles running with their recently sold property. The buyer can sue the seller for his expenses in removing an encumbrance. But it is often not worth the effort to fight both the individual claiming something against the property and the seller who won't pick up the phone.

To protect yourself, you can insert language into your purchase contract that makes this covenant explicit for the seller:

> **Seller warrants that he will convey the property to Buyer free of all encumbrances, except those that are stated in the deed. Encumbrances**

> **include, but are not limited to, liens, mortgages, leases, judgments, lack of—or restrictions on—ingress and egress, encroachments, unrecorded easements, life estates, restrictive covenants, boundary disputes, claims of prescriptive use or adverse possession, understandings, agreements, promises, permissions, licenses, allowances, reservations of profit or interest, and any other arrangement that might diminish the Property's value and Buyer's possession, use and enjoyment of it.**

While a lawyer will argue that this language is too specific and there is too much of it, take comfort in the fact that you are giving clear notice to the seller that you expect him to deliver both a clean title and a property free of surprises. If the seller objects to this language, the buyer needs to find out what specifically he objects to, because that is where the trouble lurks. The buyer's response is ask the seller's lawyer to explain the terms of a general warranty deed to the seller.

4. **Covenant of quiet enjoyment:** The seller guarantees that the title he gives to the buyer will be superior to any third-party claim of ownership. The seller is liable for damages if his title is found to be inferior.

5. **Covenant of further assurance:** The seller promises to get whatever legal instrument (deed, release, waiver) is needed to make the title good. Not all states read this covenant into a general warranty deed.

6. **Covenant of warranty forever (covenant of general warranty):** The seller promises to defend the title against "lawful claims" and compensate the buyer for any loss arising from the failure of the title.

All of these protections are embedded in the phrase, "general warranty deed," though state law determines the exact content of a general warranty deed used within its jurisdiction. It is, therefore, worth asking your local lawyer to tell you what such a deed both means and includes in your target property's state.

Equally important is the time dimension of the seller's warranties. Under a general warranty deed, the seller is making these promises to the buyer back to the property's origins. The seller is promising to defend the buyer's title against his own actions that may have clouded the title as well as any such actions taken by all of his predecessors in title. The other time consideration is that the covenants of seisin, conveyance and encumbrance are present promises; the others—general warranty (forever), quiet enjoyment and further assurances—are **future promises**. I recommend that buyers think about asking sellers for other future promises to support seller-provided disclosures and warranties.

Other types of deeds provide the buyer with less protection. A **special warranty deed,** or **limited warranty deed**, has the seller making good on the covenants only for the period of his ownership. Here's an example of a buyer needing to understand the difference between a special and a general warranty deed.

A seller offered about 12,000 acres of timberland in five separate tracts. He included a purchase contract in his bidding package that contained the following language:

Warranties of Title: Seller is the owner of the Property (exclusive of mineral interests) and will convey title to the Purchaser by Special Warranty Deed, warranting title against damages or losses resulting from claims of parties claiming by, through, or under the Seller, but not otherwise.

That's what I expected from a Special Warranty Deed. On top of the time limitation, the seller then gave himself "**Permitted Title Exceptions**," which included, among other items, the following:

Such matters as would be disclosed by a current survey or inspection of the Property including, without limitation, all encroachments, overlaps, boundary line disputes, shortages in area, cemeteries…and other similar matters not of record.

Any access related exceptions or any loss or claim due to lack of access to any portion of the Property.

Rights and claims of parties in possession of the Property.

Licenses and easements not of record.

A buyer of this property might end up owning 1,000 acres, not 12,000, and he would have no grounds to challenge the shortage in area. A general warranty deed would not be compatible with all of these permitted title exceptions; a special warranty deed can accommodate them.

Another contract I was sent in 2003 used the identical exception language and then added more exceptions related to all riparian rights, all mineral rights, all rules and regulations of any governmental authority and all "…other matters, recorded or otherwise, which would not materially affect the use of the Property for its intended purposes." This Seller was willing to convey title, but was unwilling to make it good or defend it against almost every imaginable problem. The Seller had trouble finding a buyer, for good reason.

Sellers who convey with a deed less than a general warranty along with permitted title exceptions are putting the buyer at risk in many ways. As a rule, I would advise against buying a property whose owner proposes a sale where he wants to be let off every hook that he thinks will snag his buyer.

If, however you insist on pursuing a property like this, insert into your purchase contract a **disclosure contingency** that requires the seller to inform you in writing about all that he knows or should reasonably know about each permitted title exception he demands. Thus, if the seller wants to back out matters of access from his title, your contingency will force him to reveal what is bad about his access. Disclosure does not fix the access problem and may not obligate the seller to do anything. Disclosure increases your knowledge, which increases your security to the extent that you can cost out the price of a remedy. A property discounted by title exceptions should be discounted in price. A disclosure requirement should be coupled with a provision that allows a buyer to void or amend his offer if the results of the disclosure are unacceptable.

Fiduciaries, such as trustees and executors, and corporations, often use special warranty deeds, because they can't make promises about what occurred before they came into temporary possession. Corporations use them to limit their liability. You can easily check to see whether the title going into the seller was a general or special warranty deed.

If it was a general going in and a special coming to you, you are fairly well covered, as long as you're careful about researching what happened during the seller's ownership. If the seller can't give you a reasonable explanation of why he's conveying with a special warranty deed, I'd look for a problem in the title and/or on the ground. The buyer may be able to purchase **title insurance** to supplement a special warranty deed.

A **bargain-and-sale deed** gives the buyer no express covenants or warranties against liens and encumbrances. This instrument might also be referred to as a **statutory warranty deed**. Such a deed implies that the seller holds title and possession, but it's an implication not a warranty. These deeds usually use the phrase "grant, bargain and sell" or "grant and release." They can be beefed up to a special warranty deed if the seller (grantor) adds a **covenant against grantor's acts**. Such deeds are in common use, but must be thoroughly researched because they put the buyer at risk. Be very careful with them. See if you can get title insurance. When a seller offers a bargain-and-sale deed, a buyer can counter by asking to append to the contract and deed all covenants that are typically included in a general warranty deed. This puts the seller on the spot, if only to get him to disclose what a buyer might need to know. And after all, the buyer is asking for nothing more than normal guarantees when he asks for a general warranty deed.

A **quitclaim deed** conveys whatever interest the seller possesses in the title, such as that interest is. The seller is not promising either that he owns the property or that he is conveying title to the buyer. The buyer is getting none of the covenants. Don't buy property with a quitclaim unless you and your lawyer are absolutely certain about what you are doing and why.

To prevent a seller from unloading a problem property onto an unsuspecting buyer, include the following sentence in your purchase contract: **"Seller shall convey marketable title to this property in fee simple with a General Warranty Deed."** If the seller balks at meeting these three ordinary standards, make sure that he explains why he can't. Then make sure that you and your lawyer can live with a purchase that lacks them.

2. A second trap involves two, two-letter words, **"As is."**

When the seller advertises his property "as is," what does it mean? My guess is that most *sellers* believe that "as is" means, "Buyer Beware!"—that the seller is selling what a buyer can see as well as all problems, visible or not.

I bought an "as is" 1957 tractor, in the late 1980s, which I still have. Its transmission was worn in third gear such that it slipped into neutral when the tractor was going down a hill with a load behind. The seller made no mention of this defect, and I did not discover it when I took a modest test drive around his flat barnyard. About a week after I had the tractor home, I was using it to haul two five year olds in my cart down a sloping pasture when third gear popped out. The tractor's brakes turned out to be not so good as well. We rode the runaway at increasing speed onto the flat, turning just in front of a fence line and road ditch. The kids thought I was a swell daddy for bouncing them around like exploding popcorn. My "as is" tractor brought three of us to within a few feet of death or serious injury.

Many buyers also believe that "as is" means "Buyer Beware!" and take your chances. Real-estate columnist Robert J. Bruss, however, correctly pointed out that while "as is" means the seller will not remedy any defect or condition, he still has the obligation to disclose any defect or problem known to him. (Robert J. Bruss, "'As is': Is seller absolved?," Richmond Times-Dispatch, January 26, 2003; www.bobbruss.com, or http://inman.com/bruss/. Informative reports on buying and selling property are available through Mr. Bruss's web site.)

The "as is" country property I've seen generally involves land with a handyman's special house or land with a hidden defect, such as problematic access. The "as is" condition is rarely identified. You may think the "as is" applies to the wretched farm house when the seller is really trying to unload a farm whose water system goes dry for three months every summer. The wretched farm house distracts you from looking deeper into the property. If you don't insist on the seller disclosing all defects and problems, he may not.

Auctioneers often sell rural land, **"as is, where is**," a phrase that certainly provides a buyer with another layer of warning, though I doubt it adds or subtracts anything legally from the seller's duty to disclose specific problems. When I've sold land "as is, where is" through an auction, what I meant to communicate was that I would put no money into improving the property for the buyer's benefit and would accept no contingencies on the sale.

Protect yourself from as-is sellers with a **disclosure contingency**:

> **Buyer's offer is contingent on Seller disclosing all latent or material defects in the property, its improvements, title and legal status that would in any way adversely impact or otherwise limit Buyer's possession, use and enjoyment of all of the Property and all of its rights and interests.**
>
> **Defects shall be construed to include items needing repair or replacement and conditions (including, but not limited to, physical, environmental, structural and legal), both visible and invisible.**

This language does not ask the seller to fix anything, only to disclose everything. Don't be bashful about asking in writing what "as is" specifically covers. Look the seller in the eye and say: "Before I put an offer in front of you, I want you to tell me in writing everything that needs to be repaired or replaced, everything that I need to do to make the place safe and in compliance, everything that might lead to a dispute between you and me or between me and my new neighbors." A seller who might feel alright about concealing something from you in the contract's legal briars might be incapable of lying to your face. Give the "as is" seller a chance to tell you the truth.

Most disclosure language appears to me to be limited to "*latent* material defects," which would probably be construed as significant items that are concealed, and possibly defects that are in the process of becoming either significant or manifest. I would have disclosure cover all defects, both latent (concealed) and visible, both latent (not yet at the point of a full-blown problem) and manifested as significant. Inexperienced buyers cannot be counted on to understand the visible, manifest defects their eyes see. Put the burden of explanation on the seller and don't assume that you can interpret what can be seen.

3. Seller owns less than 100 percent of property. Buyers assume that sellers own 100 percent of the property they're selling. Sometimes, this assumption is wrong. Sometimes, sellers don't know that they don't own all of their property, and sometimes they do.

What I mean by 100 percent ownership in this example is 100 percent of all of what might be called "shares" in the seller's property. If you think of the seller's property as a stock company with 100 shares, the seller should own 100 percent of every share, and the company should own 100 percent of all of the property's assets.

With real estate, those 100 shares may have been divided among several owners, often through several generations of inheritance where property is split equally among each generation of children. Your seller may own 95 shares, with the other five being divided equally among ten individuals, each of whom owns one-half of one share. A buyer does not want to pay a seller for 100 shares and wind up with 95 and ten partners. A title search is supposed to identify such situations.

In real estate, "shares" are referred to as "**ownership interests**." Mr. Smith may own a 1/8th interest in your target property while the other 7/8^{ths} belong to the seller, his brother. Such divisions are enlivened when Mr. Smith's 1/8th is divided equally and passed to his five children, each of whom now owns 1/5th of a 1/8th interest. Generational equity begets difficulties. When a lawyer finds it impossible to track down or clear up the last fractional interest, he will usually recommend a **suit to quiet title**, which asks all owners to show the court the nature of their claims.

If you find a seller who says he's willing to convey all of the **"Seller's rights, title and interest in the property**," proceed with caution. A buyer does not want that phrase used in the purchase contract or in the deed, because it can be construed to mean 100 percent of *whatever* rights, title and interest the seller has, which may be less than 100 percent. If no covenant or warranty language follows this sentence, the seller is providing title without any promise to the buyer that the title is good. Such an instrument—lacking warranties against liens and encumbrances, and clear title—is a **bargain-and-sale deed**. A deed of this type can, however, carry such warranties.

I have seen the predicament of **fractional ownership** occur in two ways. First, I've found a seller who simply did not know that he did not own all 100/100^{ths} interests. This happens with property that has been divided amongst several generations of children. This inheritance pattern is common in rural areas where land was a family's chief estate asset, and parents in each generation wanted to be fair to each of their children.

The second set of circumstances is deliberately deceptive: the seller knows he does not own 100 percent but does not disclose this to the buyer. If the buyer's lawyer finds the problem in his title search, the seller may be pushed into acquiring the outstanding interest, or the sale proceeds can be proportionately divided if the sellers agree to that, or the buyer's deal falls apart.

If the buyer completes the purchase without becoming aware of the seller's short ownership, one of several things may follow. Nothing: the minority interest never turns into a problem or claim. Or, the owner of the fractional interest appears with a demand for money from the new owner, i.e., the buyer. The new owner may be able to go back against the seller for compensation. If the fractional owner and the new owner (buyer) can't resolve the dispute, either can bring a **partition suit**, in which the court orders a public sale with the net proceeds divided proportionally. Nothing prevents one or the other owner from buying the property in full through this means. Anyone else, however, can bid more, leaving both factional owners without the property but dividing the net proceeds. Or, a **suit (action) to quiet title** can be brought by either claimant to ownership, which forces a judge to decide who owns what. Suits to quiet title are often used where a gap is found in the chain of title, or a **cloud on the title** arises from an easement, occupation (squatting) or **dower's rights** (a widow's legal interest in the real property of her deceased husband). Such suits are also used to establish the legitimacy of everyone's ownership claims, and lack thereof. Finally, a deal can be negotiated among the parties where one of the owners buys a **quitclaim deed** from the other(s), in which the latter conveys whatever his interest may be in the property.

Where a legitimate ownership interest materializes, the new owner/buyer can initiate action against the seller who can be asked to make up for damages the buyer suffers from the seller's conveyance of a defective title. This action is based on the seller having promised that he was conveying a **marketable title** and **general warranty deed** to the buyer. The buyer might also look at the malpractice insurance of the lawyer who performed his title search. The new owner's title insurance may fix some, if not all, of the problem. A good chance exists that this buyer ends up in a courtroom.

The **concept of title** in real estate covers both the bundle of rights in a property and the idea of ownership. A buyer's purchase offer that includes the words **fee simple** and **marketable title** should protect a buyer on both counts. Marketable title should be construed as meaning title to **all interests** in the property, but a seller may argue that the buyer knew he was only buying title to 17/18^{ths} interests (95 of the 100 shares) with the remaining 1/18th unaccounted for.

Prevention is cheaper than cure. Prevent a seller from hiding behind his statement of what he believed the buyer understood by including language in your contract that specifically requires the seller to convey **all interests in all the rights and assets in all the property** that are being conveyed.

> **Seller shall convey to Buyer at closing all ownership interests in all rights and assets in the entire Property, consisting of ___ acres. Seller shall convey the Property in fee simple with marketable title and a General Warranty Deed, subject only to limitations of record.**
>
> **If Seller is unable to warranty and convey anything less than a full and complete set of rights, interests, title and ownership in the Property, Buyer may void this Contract**

without penalty, and his deposit shall be returned in full within five business days.

Seller is liable for all costs and damages borne by Buyer in the event that Seller fails to comply fully with these obligations.

If you want to flush out a seller whom you suspect of knowingly trying to sell you less than 100 percent ownership interest or property with less than 100 percent of all rights and assets include language like this. See Chapter 26 for additional discussion.

These short-ownership situations are not uncommon. I know of one experienced buyer who offered $2,000 per acre for an 80-acre farm that he could see was "covered up with timber" properly estimated at about $400,000. A great buy—except that a good portion of the best timber was on an adjoining property despite a fence line that made it appear that it was included in the 80 acres. After hiring a consulting forester I recommended, the timber value on the seller's 80 acres was established at $159,000. And, then the seller, it turned out, only owned $6/7^{th}$ of the ownership interests though she let the buyer assume he was buying all interests in the property. A good lawyer—my wife—discovered the orphan $1/7^{th}$ interest in the title search, which was held by an individual in another state who had no idea that he owned an interest in West Virginia property.

Some years ago, I bought a farm from 17 fractious heirs, divided into three groups—siblings of the decedent and children of the decedent's two families. (The decedent had divorced his first wife, married his secretary and had a second family. The heirs of the first family did not care for those of the second, in part because the property of the second-family heirs had come to their father from the mother of the first family's heirs.) One sibling considered himself first among equals, and he was angry about selling the property and the share-and-share-alike division his brother-in-law's will set forth.

In such a situation, the sellers are supposed to agree on a sale price before putting their property on the market. One person—the executor of the estate or a lawyer representing all heirs—should be authorized to handle the sale and negotiate on behalf of the group. The typical procedure is that all ownership interests need to agree for the buyer's offer to be accepted. Occasionally, the group decides to allow their agent to negotiate and bind them all, as long as a predetermined minimum price is met.

Buyers need to be wary in such circumstances. I've seen the "**hold-out seller**" appear, the one who wants more money than all the others. Sometimes this is genuine, but often it's not. The seller's agent keeps blaming each new bite out of your wallet on this "unreasonable" soul who is impossible to please. My advice is: don't play the game. Make your best dollar offer, and once the agent informally accepts it, don't budge. The exception would be if you made a low-ball offer and want the property. Then expect a lot of offer-counter-offer bargaining.

Since the 17 heirs were in a precarious internal balance, I assumed that I would have to pay the minimum price they had established. I tried an offer below that, which did not fly. I wanted to make the deal as quickly as I could before stronger money showed up. Dividing these sellers was not in my interest. The time for a buyer to try to divide sellers is when their set price is unrealistically high. I paid the minimum price and have always considered myself fortunate.

On a different tract, I made a full-price offer to the family member who represented herself to me as the designated agent of nine equal interests, all of whom, she said, were agreed on a price of $1,000 per acre. I scoped the property and determined that it was under-priced. So I offered her the full price for all the shares. After placing her signature—representing her share—on my purchase contract, she informed me that one of the other heirs had just bought six of the remaining interests, leaving one outstanding. Interesting news, I thought, given that I had been told that she was representing all interests. My offer per share was about half again better than what the inside buyer had paid. I found myself with two shares under contract and a simple purchase growing more and more tangled.

The insider filed a lawsuit against my two sellers that challenged the validity of their ownership. I thought this far-fetched, since he had acknowledged their ownership when he tried to buy both shares. It struck me as legal bullying. He had money to scare them, and they didn't have enough money to not be scared. Although my contract said the sellers would defend their title, I decided to pay a lawyer to defend their ownership because they were ready to cave. I stayed in this test of wills, because I knew the real value of the property. At worst, there would be a partition suit, from which I would make a profit. I didn't see a downside; my wife thought I was nuts. The insider's suit was so weak that he eventually abandoned it. His lawyer then threatened me with a partition suit. I felt like B'rer Rabbit being threatened with the briar patch. "Fine with me," I said, "but before your client shoots himself in the foot, you might want to know what I think the property is worth." "Oh, we know all about it," he sneered. "Well, I'll just send you some information anyway and maybe we can work something out." I then faxed my timber cruise and other materials, showing the timber alone was worth twice the selling price that I had agreed to. The blowhard lawyer shut up, and the insider soon purchased my shares after I tacked on a profit. I was willing to accept the results of a partition suit, because I knew that many stumpage buyers would be interested in buying this land with its timber. But I was also willing to keep things simple and make a deal. It made sense to me to give the insider a shot at solving his problem, which, to his credit, he did.

Estate land that is gummy with intra-family squabbles may have to be approached as a problem in dysfunctional-family analysis. Fifty-year-old grievances that began when one heir was eight and another 12 often explain why the former eight year old now refuses to do the sensible thing recommended by the former 12 year old. A buyer can make the situation worse by throwing money at the sellers if resolving one holdout creates demands for more money from all the others. If the buyer can extend time to the sellers to sort it out among themselves, old patterns of dominance may once again prevail. Non-involved agents of the sellers—executor or lawyer—may be helpful. If your lawyer can work with the seller's lawyer that may prove to be the key. Try not to get in the middle of these fights and try not to gang up on the hold out. You want to acquire this property by being the solution to the sellers' chaos, not its perpetrator.

4. Acreage Tricks. I've discussed acreage booby-traps in other chapters. Apart from errors in deeds and on the ground that are unknown to the seller, there are sellers who try to take advantage of unwary buyers. There is, for example, the seller who uses a tax map to establish the acreage he's selling when he knows the tax-map acreage exceeds what his title will convey. I've also cautioned about the perils of buying acreage, **more or less**.

A similar caution should be issued regarding rural acreage to be conveyed "**in gross**," which is "more or less" in bigger clothes. "In gross" means the buyer is not buying a certain number of acres and is not making an offer of so many dollars per acre. Rather, the buyer is essentially buying what the seller has as an entirety whatever that may be. Some lawyers will argue that the buyer is better protected with "in gross" language than I have represented it. But I don't think most courts will provide a remedy to a buyer who buys 100 acres in gross, which is then surveyed after the sale at 95 acres, even if the deed states 100 acres.

A buyer will not persuade a seller to delete acreage "in gross" from sale documents when the seller is knowingly including the phrase to disguise an acreage shortage. Consider the phrase a flag to have a surveyor run the deed's calls through his mapping program.

5. Jacking Up the Price. Buyers assume that once a seller either advertises his asking price as a FSBO or establishes his listing price with a broker, that a cap has been placed on the property's price. Not so. A FSBO can reject a full-price offer at will and without explanation. When a FSBO senses a buyer is able and willing to pay more, the buyer may find even a full-price offer countered with a higher asking price. Similarly, a seller is not required by law to sell for the asking price he's set through a broker. A seller would, however, be obliged to pay the broker's commission on a full-price offer free of all contingencies. Since few full-price offers are free of all contingencies, sellers can reject most offers without penalty. I've seen prices increased by local sellers against non-local buyers who they viewed as "rich." I've never seen it used by a local seller against a local buyer.

If you sense that a seller is gaming you, stop playing. Restate your offer and without verbalizing the thought, it becomes a take-it-or-leave-it proposition.

If you are genuinely "rich" and want the property, pay the extorted difference and laugh it off over drinks. But the better tactic is to have your local lawyer negotiate on your behalf while you remain anonymous until closing.

As a general rule, I would advise buyers to stick with any offer, full-price or less, they feel is justified by the property's assets and their own finances. Price negotiations are usually controlled by buyers, even though it seldom feels that way. Be disciplined; don't offer more than it's worth and don't pay more than you can afford.

A genuinely slimy trick is for the seller to low-ball his asking price in a classic bait-and-switch move. The buyer invests emotionally and financially in preparing an offer only to have the seller bump the price up a couple of times. Since the law views an advertised price only as an invitation to buyers, you can't hold the seller to it. These sellers hope that a low-ball asking price will lure buyers into a bidding war where the switch is made as the bait is forgotten. A favorite way of doing this is for the seller to tell the buyer that he, the seller, would gladly sell for the original asking price but his spouse, or kids, or siblings, or widowed mother, or lonely Bassett Hound just can't let the place go for that little.

A seller playing low ball may be truly desperate to sell or, more commonly, just the opposite. The desperate tend to price high and come down due to the weight of their circumstances. Professional land buyers always hope to find a desperate seller who must sell fast and cheap.

A variation on the low-ball asking price is the seller who announces an increase in the asking price soon after the buyer arrives on the property. I've had this trick pulled on me twice, in both cases by wealthy sellers. I've also seen it used when the seller's real-estate agent was writing up my purchase offer after the seller and I had agreed on a price over the phone. The best counter is to stop dead in your tracks. Announce that you're going out for coffee and you'll stop by on your way home to see whether the seller has returned to the agreed price. If the seller doesn't budge, go home. Your phone is likely to ring in a few days. If you split this difference, however, the seller has won something extra from your wallet that he doesn't deserve. This lesson cost me $3,500; my professor was a grandmother, wearing an apron and brogans.

In one case, a family—a father and two sons—seemed to be selling about 40,000 acres of hardwood timberland and a sawmill. As my client and I stepped out of our car, their broker whispered to me that the price of the mill had just been raised by about $3 million. Once inside, I learned that the company owned about 12,500 acres, not 40,000 plus. The non-owned acres were subject to long-term timber leases that landowners could cancel. And then the company's forester handed me a cruise of the 12,500 acres using a tree scale that inflated the merchantable volume by about 25 percent, which he admitted when I helpfully pointed it out.

I've seen a country seller pull something out of the deal at the last minute to sweeten his own pot. This seller had about 95 percent of the sale property on one side of a road. He tried to keep the other five percent after a price agreement was reached. I've also seen sellers try to reserve a last-minute interest in timber, minerals and rental income.

In hot real-estate markets, desperate buyers will sometimes submit offers that exceed the asking price or allow themselves to be run up in price. The fortunate seller benefits from too many buyers pursuing too few properties. In the country, I've seen this market principle materialize more commonly as several buyers pursuing a particular property that has some especially value combination of assets which makes it desirable. It's the same principle that allows the owner of a certain 1955 Chevy with certain assets to price his car twice that of other 55s. Since any particular parcel of country property is almost always a discretionary purchase as either an investment or a second home, don't step onto the hot-market escalator of rising offers. Suitable alternatives are almost always available; they just have to be found.

Low interest rates tend to inflate asking prices. Buyers need to keep in mind that buying an overpriced property with a low interest rate is not generally a good deal. If a choice has to be made, I think it's better to buy a discounted property at a high interest rate and then refinance when rates drop.

6. Seller does not live up to contract. I divide this familiar situation into two groups: chips and big deals.

Chips. Some wrongs—and all insignificant ones—are best forgotten. My wife says I preach this better than I practice it. She's right, of course. I chew on slights that are decades old. But I know that chips—when everything is said and done—are just chips. Chips should not hang a good buy. Here are a few examples.

It is common practice for property taxes to be **pro rated** between buyer and seller for the sale year, using the date of closing as the dividing line for each share. I had a contract with a seller that provided for proration of property taxes in this fashion. The seller signed the purchase offer. At closing, the seller did not appear. His lawyer—the settlement agent—informed me the seller had decided that I should pay all the property tax for the year. I confidently pointed out to him the language in the contract providing for proration and even used my index finger to point to the seller's signature. The lawyer shrugged. A stick up! Fortunately, not every molecule in my brain was seeing red. The large property at stake was being bought at an excellent price, and the tax in question amounted to a couple of hundred dollars. The seller was just this kind of guy—small smart, big dumb. I could have insisted that the settlement agent apply the contract's terms exactly as they were written. Had he refused, I knew that I would win somewhere down the legal line. But the principle involved in winning this chip wasn't worth the expense and aggravation. More important, fussing would have jeopardized the entire deal. Having spent inordinate amounts of my life making grand stands for great principles over small matters, I considered benign indifference a matter of maturing wisdom. I smiled as I thought, a chip is, after all, a chip. I'm not mature enough to have forgotten about it in case you haven't noticed.

In another case, a seller had agreed to not cut any timber on his property, beginning on the date on which the contract came into effect. During the next few months, the seller's tenant on the property continued to cut trees for firewood despite being asked—then told—not to. The tenant knew he was expected to leave a few days before closing. He had stopped paying rent seven or eight months earlier and his firewood cutting was, I guessed, a juvenile show of thumbing his nose and saving face. Not much money was being burned in the tenant's woodstoves, so I pressed it just a bit. The non-rent-paying tenant accused me of depriving him and his family of winter heat. That he was a logger and could cut firewood on the job didn't count on his abacus. So I stopped after I realized that he needed to show public defiance more than I needed to win the point.

One chip that often disappears is an item of the seller's personal property the buyer expects to remain and for which he has paid when buying the property. Washers and dryers, barn refrigerators, materials—such things have a way of not being there when the buyer takes possession. Obviously, the buyer is in an unassailable position if a specific item is written into the purchase contract as conveying with the property sale. A wronged buyer can walk away from the purchase over a missing chip, but that rarely makes sense. (Sellers understand this.) I have found sellers saying that they did not understand that the item was included in the sale despite it being specifically written into the contract. Often, the choice facing the buyer is between being taken advantage of a little and being seen by the community as a legal hammer bringing in lawyers to bang the last penny out of a local seller. Sellers offer last-minute quibbles over chips when the buyer is getting a good deal on the property, and the sellers can't do much to rebalance that. A seller getting the worst of a deal feels justified in evening the score, psychologically.

The cost and time of going to court to be compensated for a chip are never worth it.

And some chips make for funny stories. Like the house purchase I once made where the seller took every light bulb.

Where the buyer has not specified in the contract those items of the seller's personal property that he has purchased, some may vanish. The seller has a powerful incentive to throw in deal sweeteners when his land is over-priced, and that incentive disappears once the contract is carried out. I've found four tactics that discourage disappearance: 1) write each item into the contract using language that describes location, amount and condition; 2) take a photo of each item and attach it to the contract, 3) take dated notes of when and where buyer and seller agreed on each item; and 4) tag the item: "Conveys to Buyer." I've seen sellers substitute bad lumber for good lumber, non-working appliances for functioning ones and cheap stuff for good stuff. I've also seen paid-for tools, farm equipment, stored hay and consumables (paint, fencing materials) wander off prior to possession. It's almost impossible to win these disputes unless you've documented each item with one or more of these four prevention measures.

It's often convenient for a non-resident buyer, particularly one who lives at a distance, to store stuff on the seller's property prior to closing. Most of the time this works without a problem. However, the buyer must realize that the seller bears no liability if the buyer's items disappear. A vacant property is an invitation to light-fingered passersby. And then there are the phantoms. A seller told me that two small antiques I had purchased and left in an obscure closet with her permission were stolen from her empty house just before closing. No neighbor could remember a house burglary ever happening in this community, certainly not in houses that have just been emptied and cleaned. No, I was told when I asked, the seller had not filed a police report. I didn't miss the put-upon air at the effrontery of my question. After a while, I blamed myself for having left them in the seller's house. Too much temptation.

I think the best rule is: don't tempt sellers with chips, theirs or yours.

Far more common than the once-in-a-blue-moon-theft story, is the failure of the seller's memory regarding your chip: "Gee, I just don't remember that as being part of our agreement." If you've done one or more of the four preventive actions, you can refresh his recollection. If he sticks to his failed memory in the face of your proof, you may have to concede the chip—but make sure to get one back in exactly the same way. Failed memory can afflict both seller and buyer.

A buyer might be interested in some of the seller's farm goods, which can be anything from a butchered hog in your new freezer to 300 bales of alfalfa in the barn. Livestock is personal, not real, property, so farm animals do not convey in a farm purchase, unless specifically included in your contract. Cattle don't run with the land.

Crops growing in the field are considered real property. Harvested crops stored on the seller's farm are his personal property and will not convey unless specifically included in the contract. Cut crops in the field—like recently mowed hay—is personal, not real property; the seller owns it. Standing timber will convey as real property, but downed timber and wood piles will not because they are personal property. I've known a seller to cut several valuable trees during escrow, so that they became his personal property…and ran with him, not the land. The buyer could not prove that these trees were cut after his purchase contract was in effect. This theft amounted to about $3,500.

Big Deals. If you think through the issues and write your purchase contract properly, the seller should not be able to snooker you out of any Big Deal.

When a big event has occurred in the escrow period between when your purchase contract came into effect and closing—fire destroys a barn, a vicious tree-killing insect takes up residence in the timber, an access problem blindsides you—you can delay closing by mutual consent. The seller should always bear the risk of loss from natural disaster and fire during the escrow period. Where the barn is insured, your goal would be to get the amount of money needed to replace it. If the insurance money is short of that amount, ask the seller to either make up the difference or lower his selling price. If you place a contract on a wooded tract in early April before the leaves are out and find that by the end of August when you are scheduled to close that something is defoliating and killing all the oaks, you should not be expected to perform since the seller is not delivering the property in essentially the same condition, less normal wear and tear, as it existed when the contract came into effect. The buyer should not bear this cost.

Often, the best way to handle last-minute problems of this sort is for the seller to put a portion of the sale revenue he gets from the buyer in a special **escrow account** until the matter is sorted out. The buyer's lawyer should hold this money in his trust account. If the seller makes the problem go away, he gets the escrowed cash. An escrow can compensate the buyer for the changed condition in the property. Depending on the final disbursement of the seller's escrowed money, recorded documents and tax computations may require amendment. Escrowing money from the sale can be used on both chips—if you really insist—and big deals, assuming the seller agrees. It lets the deal go through and provides an incentive for the seller to resolve the dispute. In the worst circumstances—say, the charming *ante-bellum* house that you had planned to convert into a B&B burns to the ground—you can void the contract, because the lost item is essentially irreplaceable. Your contract allows you to do this because it provides that the condition of the property should be the same on the day of closing as it was on the day the contract took effect.

Buyers face a difficult choice if some Big Deal disappears before closing. If the deal favors the buyer, I might go ahead with the closing after giving notice that you reserve your right to seek a remedy for the missing value. With your sales money in his pocket, the seller may see the logic of buying his way out of a scrape of his own making. Some Big Deals are obviously deal-killers.

7. Backup Contracts and Piggy-back Buyers. When a buyer has a purchase contract in place, he should be concerned when the seller accepts a backup contract for more money and/or better terms. This seller now has an incentive to find a way to scrub your contract. To avoid a buyer-initiated lawsuit, a seller has to be very crafty in contriving to entice the buyer in first position to void his contract.

I've never seen a contract where a seller inserts a contingency that allows him—the seller—to void the deal in the event that a better offer comes along. But I don't see anything "illegal" about a buyer and a seller agreeing to such language.

I have seen a seller make it difficult for a buyer to perform after he had a better offer come in. The seller may, for example, not provide information to the buyer, or he may create difficulties for the buyer in gaining access to the property. If a buyer in these circumstances fails to comply with every deadline and procedure in the contract, the seller can use technical failure to justify voiding the contract. I have not seen a case where a seller arranges for an accomplice to submit a bogus backup contract as leverage for getting the buyer to increase his already accepted offer. Anything, of course, is possible. The buyer protects his contract through full and timely compliance, and then performance. A buyer should work closely with his lawyer to make sure all deadlines and other contract breakers are satisfied.

I had a client some years ago who submitted a bid on more than 10,000 acres of timberland. The seller inserted language into the contract that allowed the seller to pay for an appraisal after the contract came into effect. If the appraisal came in at some percentage higher than the contract price, the seller reserved the right to void the purchase. I advised my client against agreeing to this provision, because it was such an obvious ploy—it was so obvious that even I could figure it out—to boost the sales price once the buyer was invested in the purchase. The appraisal, paid for by the seller, came in above the cap and the seller bumped up the buyer by almost $1 million. I advised my client to walk away. He didn't, and he lost money in the deal. Don't sign a contract with a seller-appraisal contingency.

I once faced a piggy-back-buyer situation. A large farm was being sold through sealed bids with a published minimum bid. A fellow I knew had observed me scoping the property. A week or so before the bids were due he called to scope me. His unstated thought was: If Seltzer is going to bid on it, I could bid $5,000 more and get a good deal. I certainly did not want to help my competition. Nor did I want to share the fruits of my year-long research with him. Since he had more money that I had, I knew he would be a stronger buyer. I didn't want to make him angry—leading to a bid; and I didn't want to motivate him to submit a bid by sharing the real value of the property that I had discovered. Since he trusted my research and judgment, he was playing with the idea of riding my expressed interest against me. He would know I was concealing the truth had I told him the property was without virtues. My best defense I figured was to try to freeze him in place by feeding him some good news, some bad and a lot of uncertainties. He never submitted a bid.

It is not uncommon for buyers to run into each other as they look at a property. Nor is it uncommon for buyers to determine what each other might know. If you tell another buyer something useful about the target property, you should assume that he will use it for his own interests. It's best to be cordial and as selectively informative as a President's press secretary.

There's one situation where you can profit from finding another buyer. If you've scoped a property and determined it's not for you, it might be suitable for someone you know. In this case, it's fair for you to ask for a one or two percent **finder's fee** from that buyer for introducing him to the property and giving him the benefit of your research. The fee is payable only if your buyer purchases the property. The buyer owes you the fee because he has benefited from the information that you gave him and upon which he acted. This legal principle is called, ***quantum meruit***. Acting as a finder is not acting as a real-estate broker, for which you need to be licensed. It's always best to draw up a finder's fee agreement between you and your buyer.

8. Access Maintenance. The seller has divided his property into six, 100-acre parcels, configured side by side in a line. The seller has constructed a so-so, gravel road about 12-feet wide on the longest boundary line of his original 600 acres. Access roads to each lot come off this common road, which ends at Lot Six, the one you want to buy. The seller has recorded a right-of-way (ROW) easement that gives each Lot owner access to the common access road, which, the easement states, 'the Lot Owners shall maintain." The access road is 6,000-feet long from the gate on the public road to the back boundary of the property's 600 acres where you—Lot Six—want your driveway, because that places it as far from Lot Five as possible. Everyone agrees that the cost of the improvements is $6,000.

Lot Six—you—are buying a mess, left there intentionally by the seller. Your first question involves upgrading the common road to 16 feet wide and improving its quality. Let's assume that all six lot owners agree on the benefits of upgrading and improving. Should the $6,000 estimated cost be split six ways equally? No, no, says Lot One; I only use 200 feet of the common road before my driveway turns off. I should pay $200, which represents my portion of the common road, figured on $1 of cost per linear foot. While I have 1,000 feet of frontage on the common access road, I only use 200 feet for ingress and egress. Lot Six uses all 6,000 feet for access," Lot One points out, "so maybe he should pay $6,000."

Different formulas are available to allocate these costs fairly. The seller, foreseeing the squabbling arising from six lot owners, has bailed on a solution in favor of letting the lots slug it out after he's gone. Each lot buyer would be treated better if the seller had devised an equitable formula that is disclosed when buyers visit the property.

Here is the formula I suggest:

The first $1,000 for the first 1,000 feet should be split equally among the six lot owners.

The second $1,000 for the second 1,000 feet should be split equally among Lots Two through Six.

The third $1,000 for the third 1,000 feet should be split equally among Lots Three through Six.

The fourth $1,000 for the fourth 1,000 feet should be split equally among Lots Four through Six.

The fifth $1,000 for the fifth 1,000 feet should be split equally between Lots Five and Six.

The final $1,000 for the final 1,000 feet should be paid exclusively by Lot Six.

The actual money would look like this for Lot Six's share:

1/6 of 1st $1,000 for Lot One's 1000 feet =	$ 166.67
1/5 of 2nd $1,000 for Lot Two's 1,000 feet =	200.00
1/4 of 3rd $1,000 for Lot Three's 1,000 feet =	250.00
1/3 of 4th $1,000 for Lot Four's 1,000 feet =	333.33
1/2 of 5th $1,000 for Lot Five's 1,000 feet =	500.00
1/1 of 6th $1,000 for Lot Six's 1,000 feet =	1,000.00
Lot Six Total	$2,450.00 (41%)

Lot Six is paying for remoteness. The danger to everyone in the seller's language is that it fails to specify how costs are to be allocated and maintenance decisions made. I have seen the absence of a maintenance formula spark a war among neighbors sharing a homeowners'-association road.

9. **Seller Provides False Information**. You arrange a face-to-face meeting with the seller prior to submitting an offer. During the pleasant conversation in the seller's living room, you ask the following questions:

Are there any disputed boundaries? Answer: No.

Is there an approved septic system? Answer: Yes.

Have you promised anything off the property that would otherwise convey? Answer: No.

Does the roof leak? Answer: No.

Does the flat bottomland next to the river ever flood? Answer: Not that I recollect.

Is the spring water to the house safe to drink? Answer: I've been drinking it all my life.

The seller has answered each of these questions falsely, knowingly. Can you win in court on any of them? Probably not. Let's look at each one.

Approved septic system. The seller has lied. The seller has nothing more than a four-inch-diameter pipe that empties into a large covered hole in porous ground. This cesspool was installed in the 1940s before the county required septic systems and permits. It is not an approved septic system. It is one step up from a straight pipe into the creek. While its use may be grandfathered, if you want to add a bath or a bedroom, the county health department is likely to require installing a real septic system that complies with current standards. Is the seller liable for the cost of the new system? Can you prove that he lied, and, even so, is that enough to win? The seller's defense is that he thought he was telling you the truth inasmuch as the party that he bought the farm from ten years ago told him that the house had an approved septic system. "Never had a bit of trouble with it," he said, "so I never had reason to check about approval." The cesspool functions well, and there's no record of it ever being serviced by a local plumber or septic-cleaning service.

I doubt that you can prove that the seller committed fraud, that is, a deliberate lie. Do you win the cost of an approved septic system for your extra bedroom or new bathroom? That's doubtful. As long as you keep within the grandfathered use, the grandfathered system probably won't be challenged even though it won't meet current standards. (There will be exceptions to that generalization.) Once you undertake an upgrade, like a new bedroom or a bathroom, then it's your responsibility to upgrade the support systems. Even if the seller lied when he told you that he thought the house had an approved system, the mistake doesn't harm you if you continue the use of the property as it was when you took possession. Further, if the seller erred honestly, your pre-purchase due diligence (scoping) should have included a visit to the county office where septic permits and applications are kept. Your negligence and laziness, the seller will argue, explains why you didn't find out the truth. Cost of installing a new system: $3,500 to $25,000, depending on soil conditions and local standards. You might get a judge to split the cost of a new system if you can prove beyond a reasonable doubt that the seller knew of the condition and intentionally misled you. But that is very difficult to prove.

You could have inserted a **septic-system contingency** in your purchase offer that gives you the right to inspect the system and void your offer if the findings are unsatisfactory.

Promise Off the Property. The seller's barn is serviced by a ten-ton-capacity metal, silo-style grain tank and an electric auger unloader. The tank's legs are bolted to four 55-gallon, concrete-filled drums that are completely buried in the ground. The unloader is a 100-foot-long pipe that encloses a motor-driven auger. It has drop tubes every 20 feet inside the barn for unloading the grain, which drops into feed trays. The pipe is attached to the exposed roof rafters using metal strapping and heavy bolts. The tank and auger were used to feed corn to cattle.

You don't think you'll use this equipment, because you are planning to convert the seller's Vermont dairy farm to an organic rose garden, from which you plan to sell only the inner petals of the rare albinos. You've done no marketing study, but you're sure this idea will make you as rich as Bill Gates, because you like roses. You see no use for the tank and unloader. You have no interest in climbing the tank's ladder and looking inside.

You don't do a walk-through inspection prior to closing. Upon visiting your new farm the day after closing you notice the tank and auger are missing. You make inquiries and determine to your surprise that a neighbor in the dairy business will pay you $1,800 for "that rig if you get it back in decent shape." Eighteen hundred dollars will get you started in the albino rose business.

You also learn that the seller says he had promised this equipment to his cousin who lives about 250 miles away.

The seller's tank and unloader are considered real, rather than personal, property because they are physically attached to the land and building respectively. All real property should convey, unless specifically excluded; all personal property doesn't convey unless specifically included.

Of course, the seller failed to exclude this real property from his sale to you. The cousin now claims that it had always been *his* tank and *his* auger, which he had simply loaned to the seller some years ago.

The cousin has no receipt of purchase, but does threaten to produce his pellucid 112-year-old grandfather who will recall the entire arrangement as if it were still 1960 when the deal, he says, was struck; the cousin will serve as translator because the grandfather had a stroke in the 1970s and has been unable to speak or write since. The seller, his recollections now refreshed, confirms the cousin's story. The seller, further, says he always told you the truth: that nothing that belonged to him had been promised off the purchase prior to your possession. (The seller should be splitting hairs at Yale Law School not feeding cows.)

The grain tank is considered real property, because, like a house, its foundation becomes part of the ground. The unloader was personal property until the seller attached it to the barn, which made it part of the barn, an improvement. At that point, it became a **fixture**, that is, personal property that has become real property by becoming permanently attached to real property. Both items should convey. While both can be detached, the nature of their attachment is far more permanent than temporary. Nonetheless, the seller's story about this equipment being loaned to him by the cousin is probably good enough to get a local judge to go along with it, even without the receipts or tax returns that might verify their claim.

You protect yourself from these shenanigans by being both very broad and very specific in your purchase contract concerning what you are buying. For illustration purposes, you might consider language of this type:

> **Seller shall convey to the buyer his farm of 100.00 acres, as conveyed to him on March 14, 1992, Deed Book 73, Page 106, in fee simple, including all real property, all subsurface minerals and all other interests and rights in the property, and all improvements and fixtures, including but not limited to, all buildings, structures, facilities, barns, sheds, windows, doors (including remote control to garage door), garages, woodsheds, windmills, antennae, outbuildings, grain tanks/unloaders, bridges, culverts, fences, gates, satellite dishes, roads, water resources and systems, pumps, electrical boxes and lines, standing and downed timber, and roadside mailbox and post. All fixtures and attachments convey except for:**
>
> _____
> _____
> _____
> _____
>
> **The following items of personal property shall convey:**
>
> _____
> _____
> _____
> _____
>
> **In addition, Seller, per agreement, shall convey to Buyer the pile of road gravel next to his barn, the stacked firewood next to his house and the 700 linear feet of two-inch-diameter PVC water pipe stored in his barn.**

Here are a couple of variations on the tank-and-auger story.

The weekend after closing, the cousin appears with a flatbed truck and begins to dismantle the tank and auger. He tells you the loan story. You try to reach the seller, but can't. The cousin, backed by four burly sons, continues to work. What do you do? Call the sheriff? Call your lawyer? Stop them at gunpoint?

A call to your lawyer first and then the sheriff might work. You want to halt the removal and give yourself the time and a legal venue to figure things out. If the cousin hauls off the equipment, you will have a hard time getting it back in usable condition. Perhaps you can videotape your peaceful opposition to the removal in which you make clear that you consider it your property, and it's being taken against your will. You will undoubtedly lose a fistfight with Daddy and his four big boys.

The seller appears two weeks after closing with cousin, four burly sons and truck, and begins to take down tank and auger. You say, "Stop! What's going on here?" Seller says, "What's the problem? I'm taking the tank and auger that I had orally reserved when we were negotiating four months ago." You, despite being a Mensa member and having total recall of every one of the 10,688 bridge hands you've played during the last three decades, have no recollection of this conversation. Seller produces wife from cab of truck who confirms that she heard her husband say exactly what he now says he said.

"Otherwise," she says, "why would we be here? We're not thieves." Who's not? you ask silently. "Me and…him," she adds.

Give it up. You won't win in court. Your word against theirs; one against six.

You can protect yourself by writing language into your contract that excludes all **sidebar agreements, written and oral**. This is referred to as the **Entire Agreement** section; it is usually standard:

> **This Contract, including any attachments initialed and dated by the Parties, shall constitute the entire agreement between them. It shall supersede any other written or oral agreement between them. This Contract can only be modified in writing that is initialed and dated by both Parties.**

Be careful with Entire Agreement language, since it cuts both ways. If you have made beneficial arrangements that fall within its scope, the Entire Agreement language will end them.

Roof Leaks. Three weeks after you move in, a heavy rain falls. This is the first rain since you've taken possession. You place a five-gallon bucket under a leak in the back closet. The bucket happens to be in the closet's darkest corner. You now notice old water stains on the closet's ceiling. You talk to the seller. "Wasn't leaking when I owned it. Must have just started," he says. You say, "What about all the signs of old leakage on the ceiling?" "Oh that," the seller says, "was years ago. I just never repainted the ceiling after I fixed it. Never took that old bucket out of there, I guess."

You, or the house inspector in your employ, should have noticed the water stains prior to placing a purchase contract in front of the seller. The price of being non-observant and doing inspections without a flashlight is $1,000.

Most properties have little dings like a leaky roof that hide from buyers. They're either tucked out of the way or are so out in the open that they're not noticed—leaky basement pipes, painted-shut windows, warped doors that can't close tightly, dead electrical outlets, semi-operational equipment like a basement sump pump that you look at when the basement is Sahara dry and a ten-ton-capacity access bridge that won't handle the 30-ton logging trucks that are needed to haul timber from the property.

It's hard for the buyer to prove that the roof wasn't in fine shape at closing. Usually, each nickel and dime is not worth the aggravation of a fight, even though loose change adds up to dollars. It does not make sense to spend a dollar to win a nickel.

Prevention, of course, is your most economical defense. Rural property may look simple to evaluate, far less complicated than a suburban house, but it is not. And its scoping frequently requires consultants with whom the typical suburban buyer is not familiar—forester, soils engineer, farm consultant, minerals consultant, water engineer, excavator, farm-equipment appraiser, septic-system inspector and so on. These experts are in addition to the routine home-inspection and termite report you should have in both suburb and country. And while your bug guy is poking and prodding, ask him to look for other bogies—powder post beetles, carpenter ants, fire ants, winter flies, black widow spiders and any similarly unattractive guests.

The expensive overlooked problems in rural property tend to be outside the house—water systems that go dry or need to be rebuilt, septic systems that don't function well or are undersized, old barns that cannot be cheaply adapted to your new purposes, electrical and plumbing systems that need to be totally replaced, livestock ponds that leak, fences that need to be rebuilt, outbuildings with problems (rotting floors, leaky roofs, collapsing foundations), undersized or weak bridges, pasture that can support fewer animals than before due to overgrazing or climate change and so on.

Invisible liabilities are almost always the ones that pinch the buyer of rural property the hardest. Lack of mineral ownership is an obvious one. Others include the severance of some other property right, such as, the sale of air rights on the back ridge to a wind-farm developer; a neighbor's right to deprive the target property of water; underground pollution that affects water quality; an acreage shortage or boundary dispute; insect infestation or disease in the timber; termites in the barn (which is rarely looked at in the required termite inspection of the residence); and nuisances created by neighbors that don't reveal themselves during your visits. (Remember, for example, that Laura Cunningham bought her place in the country without "seeing" that her property was situated next door to an over-lighted, noisy community college campus.) Keep your eyes open for the invisibles.

With working farms, I would hire an independent **farm consultant** for help in evaluating the property's assets in terms of your plans. This person might be a retired agricultural extension agent, a full-time consultant or just a person with a lot of experience. You may need to combine the latter with an individual who provides the latest business analysis, depending on your plans. Your local lawyer may be able to recommend a retiree with the farm and building experience you need. Dollars paid to such consultants are the most cost-effective investments you can make.

You can also protect your interests by inserting "**warranty language**" in your purchase contract, such as:

> **Seller warrants that all mechanical, electrical, plumbing (including water supply, water purifiers and septic/sewerage systems), heating and air conditioning (including attic fans, ventilators and humidifiers), and structural components of all buildings, structures and other improvements, together with all fixtures and personal property that will convey under this Contract, will be in good, safe working order and not require repair as of closing. Exceptions to this warranty include by mutual agreement of the Parties the following:**

_____

_____

_____

_____

You can specify individual systems and items for warranty to the degree you think necessary. For example, if the property has a water impoundment (lake with a man-made dam), make sure the seller has a current inspection and state permit. Swimming pools, spas, electric garage doors, working fireplaces, woodstoves, built-in appliances—one or more may deserve to be singled out. With a woodstove, for example, its installation needs to be in compliance with the current standards imposed by the fire-insurance carrier you plan to use. That means it has to be set up at least 16 or 20 inches from adjacent combustible walls, on an approved fireproof pad that extends a certain distance beyond the stove. If you're worried about the seller's roof, include no-roof-leak language.

You generally want the seller to promise good working order as of closing, not as of when the purchase contract takes effect, which might be three months earlier. Put another way, you want working order and property condition to be the same at closing as they were when the contract took effect. Stuff can happen between the two dates.

One 1,500-acre purchase I worked on involved a contract that came into effect two years before closing occurred. The buyer needed to get the property rezoned so he placed a contingency in his contract that made closing contingent on getting all necessary approvals—a complicated process that ultimately required him to spend $400,000 on archeological investigations alone. This property included a beach along a river that the buyer valued highly in his development plans. If something occurred during escrow that diminished the value of that beach—erosion from a hurricane, an oil-tanker spill—the buyer had contract language to protect his financial interest in the property as it was when he and the seller reached a meeting of the minds on their contract.

Warranty language establishes the buyer's expectations about property conditions and reflects what the parties have agreed to, insofar as the seller warrants (promises) to deliver the property at closing in the same condition, less normal wear and tear, as it existed when the contract was signed. Exceptions to warranty language can be noted in the contract by specifying items that are excluded from the seller's promise. An item in "as-is" condition means its condition at the time the contract takes effect, not "as-is" at the time of closing.

The necessary companion protection with warranties is to write in a **walk-through** provision in the purchase contract that allows you to visit the seller's property just before closing; test all systems to make sure they are in working order; confirm that whatever the seller promised to do, if anything, during escrow as part of your contract, has been done; and check that everything you are buying is still on the property and in essentially the same condition as when you signed your contract. Your walk-through, or **final inspection**, is usually scheduled for within 48 to 72 hours of closing. If you are working with a FSBO, make sure he is present for the walk-through. Otherwise, the seller's broker/agent typically accompanies the buyer.

Many, if not most, real-estate brokers advise their sellers to stay away from the buyer on his final walk-through. They want to be the communication channel between the two. Since rural property is more complicated than urban/suburban housing, I urge non-local buyers, novices in particular, to do at least one pre-purchase **walk-around with the seller** who, after all, will be far more knowledgeable about his property's assets and liabilities than even the most conscientious agent. If the seller walked you through when you were "just looking," you have a base of agreement as to what was what, then. Don't let his real-estate agent talk you out of having the seller walk you around on a final inspection. If nothing has changed, you will find nothing wrong. When a disagreement materializes, try to approach it as a joint problem with a common history to be solved rather than the first in a series of grievous wrongs inflicted on an innocent. If the seller has made a mistake, give him room to correct it. If the seller is trying to take a second bite out of your lunch, let him do it if it's small enough; resist if he's stealing your meal; or bite back.

If you determine that something is not there, not the same or not in working order during your walk-through, try to resolve it quickly. If the issue is a chip, forget about it. If it is significant, you have leverage—your willingness to void the purchase—and the seller has incentive to make it right. The seller is near enough to closing to smell your cash. This is your most advantageous negotiating moment. If you void your contract, the seller may sue you for performance, depending on the circumstances. At that point, you either work out something with the seller or convince a judge that you were justified in voiding your contract. Voiding a contract is a serious act because of its risks and potential expense. Don't do this without first consulting your lawyer. It is not worth losing a farm over a roof leak.

A familiar walk-through drama occurs when a buyer picks a number of nits to extort a price reduction from an anxious seller. I advise against taking this last bite out of the seller's apple. First, it's not honest bargaining. Second, it's a transparent tactic. News of your clumsy, cheap "cleverness" will precede you in your new community. Third, you risk losing the deal. I have seen people act against their rational economic self-interest time and again to make a point if only to themselves. In your eyes or mine, that point may be off-center or just plain counter productive. But in their eyes, a principle is being stood for by acting economically "irrationally." Push too far with nibbles and nits, and the seller might blow up the deal despite his compelling motivation to sell. My belief is that buyers "make their money on purchases" through diligent research and thoughtful planning, not through last-minute shakedowns.

Does the flat land by the river flood? Of course it does. Every water channel will overflow its banks given sufficient rainfall. Flashfloods in semi-deserts are notorious killers. Key Run, the creek behind my farmhouse, is dry nine months of every year; I've also seen this "intermittent stream" cover the entire bottom to a depth of four feet four times in 20 years. Flooding creates flat bottom land by depositing dirt eroded from ground higher in the watershed. If your target property has a creek with bottom land, assume flood potential whether or not the seller recollects any high water. Check the floodplain maps available from the Federal Emergency Management Administration (FEMA) and the U.S. Army Corps of Engineers. Avoid land that is listed as flooding more frequently than every 100 years if possible. Ask neighbors. A seller's opinion or his honest recollection doesn't bind the seller in court; neither opinion nor memory amount to warranty.

The failure of sellers to recollect adverse events may be a new field for academic research. One seller will forget that he only owned a one-third interest in the land he was selling. Another will forget an agreement on a selling price. Buyers tend to lose in these episodes, because they are trying to be accommodating and cooperative. Where you are sure that the seller is doing nothing more than trying to hurt you with his failure-to-recollect tactic, don't participate in your own wounding.

Drinkable Spring Water: That the seller and his family—all of whom drink household water drawn from a spring—say they have never been sick, proves not much about this water's **potability** (drinkability). They may blame their chronic diarrhea on the "weak stomachs" that seem to run in their family, not the bacteria-contaminated water they've drunk for three generations. People can become acclimated to some contaminants and bacteria over time, which is why, I suppose, Montezuma wreaks more gastric vengeance on tourists than natives. Your city stomach is used to chlorinated or bottled water that contains no fecal bacteria, which is associated with mammalian waste. (The level of *Escherichia coli*, or *E. coli*, is the common indicator.) In this instance, the seller suspected his water might be a little gamey, but had no evidence that it was harmful.

If farmhouse water is drawn from a well, spring, lake, stream or cistern, place a **"water-quality contingency"** in your contract:

> **Buyer's offer is contingent upon obtaining acceptable results from a water test Buyer arranges for and conducts at his own expense. Water must meet minimum safety and quality standards, as set forth by local sanitarian or other public health official. In the event that results are below these standards, Seller shall, at his expense, take steps necessary to upgrade water to meet these standards. Buyer shall take a second test at his expense. If results are still unsatisfactory, Buyer may void this contract at his choosing or reopen negotiations with Seller.**

Under no circumstances should a buyer allow the seller to take the sample (hold a sterilized bottle under a flame-sterilized kitchen tap) on his own and send it to the laboratory. It's too easy for an unscrupulous seller to mix Evian from the supermarket into the sample.

"Fixing" a spring system with a high coliform count can involve nothing more than dumping a gallon of bleach into the water source and running the house tap until the water tastes clean of chorine, at which point a sample is taken. This "fix" may produce an acceptable sample without fixing the cause of the problem, which is something like livestock being pastured too close to the spring or septic-system effluent getting into it. The real fix may require rebuilding the fence line so that animals are kept further back or relocating a drainfield. Proper fixes tend to cost more than quick ones, which is one of humanity's long-standing grievances. A usually less desirable option is to install a home-chlorination unit that mixes a bleach solution with the incoming water, and the blend is pumped through the house. Drinking clean spring water is one of life's pleasures; drinking chlorinated water in the country is one of life's grumbles.

CHAPTER 28: BARGAINING CULTURES AND RESOLVING PROPERTY DISPUTES

Every community has a bargaining culture that shapes the conduct of negotiations, suggests which tactics are acceptable and which aren't, and regulates what words and signals mean or don't mean. After more than two decades of living in a rural county with 2,500 residents, I'm just getting the hang of my **local bargaining culture**. In work that I've done in other rural areas East of the Mississippi, I've found basic similarities.

If you come from a bargaining culture where yes means yes and you propose to buy land in a culture where yes means a contingent maybe, miscommunication and fouled understandings are inevitable.

A familiar example is the fixed-price construction contract, where you and a contractor agree on a single sum in advance that is supposed to cover all contractor costs and profit. In the contractor's mind, he may come from a bargaining background that will hold to a fixed price as long as it is profitable. When his fixed price turns out to produce breakeven, or worse, he asks for an extra payment or two. Sometimes paying money above a fixed price is justified, and at other times, you're working with a contractor who bid low to get your business and figured he could wring more dollars out of you down the road. All of this is made more complicated when different individuals acting within a bargaining culture interpret its code differently, or follow it, or ignore it. Maybe the entire notion of a bargaining culture has no practical relevance. I'm willing to concede the point without much argument, because I've seen shifty individuals come out of honest and straight-up rural bargaining cultures such as the one where I live.

I try to factor into land bargaining a limited sense of how the seller's local bargaining culture shapes his perceptions and ways of communicating. I try to use words and tactics that I think the seller's heard and seen before from buyers. I listen intently for cue words that I've heard before, from which I infer movement or heels being dug in. Admittedly, this may amount to no more than hunch and guess. I can usually establish an approximate "bargaining fix" that suggests how I should approach negotiations. Having said all that, it's equally important to keep in mind that rural sellers are not a single group from a single bargaining culture. Even individuals from one group bargain differently with different people.

Let me say this in another way: I negotiate differently, and communicate differently, with an Ivy League lawyer selling land than with a local graduate of the hard-knocks school (who is likely to be the better bargainer). For that matter, I have bargained differently with a Harvard-trained lawyer than with a 1960s graduate of the University of Virginia's Law School. I bargain differently with wheeler-dealers than with small landowners. I bargain differently with environmentalists than I do with business interests. (I have found dishonorable individuals in both groups. The business guys are simply after money; the environmentalists believe their morally superior goals justify ethically inferior behavior. It's a recurrent source of disappointment.) I don't try to affect the culture of the seller by pretending I'm someone that I'm not. It's hard to say empirically whether my approach achieves better results than alternatives.

When you find yourself dealing with a seller who gives his word and would keep it even when it's against his self-interest, you have lucked out. Bargaining may be hard with such a person, but a deal struck is a deal made. You need to be the mirror image of such a seller.

Don't be surprised to find a seller whose bargaining style is to slide around like an eel in a barrel of crude oil. These individuals think they are being clever negotiators by dragging out bargaining and "revisiting" agreed-on terms. Smart they may be, but the outcome of such tactics may not produce more money or a better deal. It can just as readily produce a buyer who walks away in disgust before a contract is signed.

Then there is the seller who combines the two: you will be able to count on some of his yeses, but not others. This individual may be deliberately dishonest or simply slipshod. You have to convert this person's commitments to paper asap.

Bargaining involves testing each other's reliability. By agreeing and testing on small, preliminary points, you can get some sense of the seller's style. It's always useful to learn what you can of the bargaining culture from your local lawyer and, more importantly, get his read on the seller's bargaining history and style.

The danger in thinking of negotiating through the lens of cultural styles is to fall into the quicksand of stereotypes. Individuals who share ethnicity, or religion, or regional identification, or class, or occupation, or social status, or educational background or gender preference don't necessarily share a way of negotiating. But individuals who fit a multi-factor profile often, but not always, do. Sellers who live in the country don't fit a single multi-factor profile. They don't all bargain the same way because of one shared characteristic: rural residence. Some are honest sellers; others aren't, as is the case across the board with individuals in every group. You can use the idea of bargaining culture to sharpen your communication skills. Owing to individual variability, it's a sometimes useful predictor of behavior, but not always.

I find much negotiating insight in Peter Wink's, <u>Negotiate Your Way to Riches: How to Convince Others to Give You What You Want</u> (New York: Barnes & Noble, 2003). Despite the distasteful title, Wink presents a sensible framework for approaching negotiations based on research, effective communication, shared problem-solving and fair dealing. The principles he uses can readily be applied to negotiations over land.

I have found that rural people prefer oral agreements to written ones. When you come from a bargaining culture that always uses written documents and the seller comes from an oral bargaining culture, your document will be viewed with suspicion. A pervasive history of legal land swindling exists in America. Much of it involved paper in the form of legal documents that took advantage of the party less legally literate. Mineral buyers came into the Appalachian coalfields after the Civil War and bought billions of tons of high-quality coal reserves for pennies per ton using a deed that allowed the mineral owner and his leaseholder to use the surface in any way necessary for extraction. Often, they employed "native" lawyers as their fronts. Mining, at the time, meant underground mining. A century later it often meant surface mining where the leaseholder cut the timber and then stripped away the dirt and rock to get at the coal. The old deeds legally wrecked many a mountain farm. A communal memory exists in rural areas regarding outsiders with "lawed-up" paper and cash money. Rural populism fed on tales of carpetbaggers, land buyers, railroads and bankers acquiring resources with outside cash and the help of government.

Walking into a seller's farm kitchen with a purchase contract drawn up on 14-inch Big City law-firm stationery with 30-line-long, one-sentence paragraphs that include three "except that's," will get you nowhere. And properly so. Your goal is to have a meeting of the minds, not effect a land swindle. You should give the seller a contract as simple as you can make it while protecting your interests. Write it clearly, using short declarative sentences and familiar words. Your intent is to have both of you understand what is being signed.

While it's fine to bargain orally with a seller, you should assume that any oral agreement you reach on the sale of real estate binds neither of you and is not legally enforceable. For that reason, a buyer should submit a purchase offer in writing with all terms and contingencies included. Explain to the seller that oral agreements are not binding, which is why you're sticking paper under his nose. Once your negotiation succeeds, get it down on paper immediately, with both parties signing and dating the document. When you're working through a real-estate agent, your written offer will be presented to the seller without you being present. This format is awkward and often gets in the way of a deal, but a buyer is rarely allowed to present his contract directly to a seller when an agent representing the seller is involved.

If, as part of your pre-purchase scoping, you find yourself walking the property with the seller and agreeing on matters as you move about, write them on a legal pad attached to a clipboard that you just happen to be carrying. Both of you should initial each agreement with a date. This document might cover items such as:

> **Property definition—acreage to be determined by _____. Back fence needs repair. That fence is neighbor's section. Seller will ask neighbor to have this section replaced by next spring. No guarantees. Three 16-foot-long, 12"-diameter metal culverts next to creek convey. Seller reserves cattle scale; does not convey. Seller to remove by closing. Seller retains 100 percent interest in all crops that he's planted, but agrees to pay $25 per acre on 53 acres of planted corn for this retained interest. All crops to be harvested by December 1 of this year. Seller will seed back 20 acres with cover crop by October 15 at his expense. New barn roofing materials stored in barn to convey. 50 panels of sheet metal, nails and 10 gallons of red roof paint. Agreed on contract price: $275,000. $4,000 security deposit. 60-day due-diligence contingency, results acceptable to buyer. Closing within ten calendar days after contingency is removed.**

Have your lawyer incorporate these notes into the purchase contract he prepares. Tell him to use plain English and simple sentences wherever possible. I would append a photocopy of your original field notes to your contract. Some "boilerplate" can be translated into plain language to everyone's benefit with no loss of legal meaning. Other sections can be lifted verbatim from any standard contract. A contract drawn by a local lawyer—even the buyer's—will go much further with a local seller than one cooked up by a new associate in the 500-partner law firm you use in Big City. It will work better in most cases than the standard real-estate contract, which favors sellers. Never approach kitchen-table bargaining with a fancy brief case, tie, cufflinks and $1,000 Italian loafers. Keep your hands on the table, not in your pockets. Don't take the seller's pen.

As to eye contact. Conventional wisdom has it that the absence of constant eye contact indicates a shifty bargaining partner. I've found the opposite to be true. Swindlers and thieves, even the pettiest ones, have mastered continuous eye contact. I disregard it. I look much more toward a total package of behavior: body language, voice inflection, choice of words, how points are stated, hand movement, intentional tactics and so on.

When a buyer comes into a new place, he has no lines into the local word-of-mouth communication network on which the community depends. He can't extract information from this system, and he has no ready means of feeding it either credible information or his spin on an argument. The seller becomes the only source of community information on the stranger who's just rolled into town with a checkbook. The buyer's seller-reported behavior is fresh meat to the local lions. Your vehicle will be noted, along with accent, dress, vocabulary, restaurant orders, questions, marital status, appearance and suspected origins. The community will be trying to classify the newcomer into a sociological type with which it already has some experience. You cannot protect yourself from what the seller feeds into the local network about you. It does not matter that the seller is the sleaziest slime ball in the county, and every local knows it. Even those who distrust the seller may extend to him a presumption of credibility about a buyer of whom they know nothing at all. No independent and competing source of information is available about the buyer. If the seller spreads the word that the buyer nickel-and-dimed him, or didn't keep his word, or acted unreasonably (however defined), the buyer will move into the community burdened with bad press whether or not the specific charge is true. Some people won't talk to you on that basis alone—and you will never know why. (They may be kin to the seller, which you may or may not learn.) Others will try to get the better of you to prove some point to themselves. Still others will consider the source of the gossip and pay no attention to it, preferring to make their own judgments on their first-hand experience with you. Your goal is to have current residents deal with you on the basis of their first-hand knowledge which shows that you are decent and honest. (If you are not decent and honest, you deserve what you get.)

For these reasons, I advise buyers to establish independent communication contacts with members of your target community <u>before</u> you look at your first property. Visit the county casually before you start serious land-looking. Eat at local restaurants; tip 15 percent, neither more nor less. Buy stuff at local stores, while striking up introductory conversations. Subscribe to the local paper in person, not by mail. Chat with the paper's editor. Open an account at a local bank. Buy a county phone book. Have casual conversations with as many folks as possible, while always introducing yourself to the extent possible as having a connection to a local person or neighborhood. Include on your list the librarian, county clerk, sheriff, EMTs, firemen, county dump operator, store keepers, Chamber of Commerce director and others who work in the town nearest your target property and in the county seat. Get a haircut in the local barbershop. If you are a member of an organization or fraternal order—Lions, Elks, VFW, Ruritans, Masons, AARP, etc.—contact the local chapter and go to a meeting. If you are a church member, attend services and introduce yourself to the minister and congregation. Put something into the collection plate. You can't help but learn about a community new to you through this low-key, self-introduction process. Of equal importance, you are building a track record with information gatekeepers on your terms. It won't prevent a seller from bad-mouthing you, but it will broaden your base of support and provide others with independent assessments.

Unequal access to the local communication network puts a strain on a buyer. The buyer doesn't want to quibble over every dollar and in so doing assure himself of bad local press from the seller. On the other hand, no buyer should be a negotiating patsy by giving in on every seller demand. The best way to handle this is to make sure that the seller sees that you're willing to give on some things in return for take on others—and that you expect the same from him. Assume that you will be negotiating with your mirror image until the seller demonstrates that you aren't.

This doesn't mean you should be unskilled or naïve in bargaining. A buyer should enter land negotiations with a pile of **throwaway chips** that he can give up without much loss. Throwaways might include some (not all) warranty language in the purchase contract, or fence/buildings you'd like the seller to repair prior to closing, or farm gates that you like to have him replace, or a situation you'd like the seller to clear up that can be lived with, or an upgrade on an access ROW (from an 18-foot-wide easement to 24 feet that would be nice but isn't truly needed). Concede these chips as needed for things that are important to you. Trading is usually done on the basis of equal values, but getting something more important by giving something less important may often be a matter of perspective. You can also give a lot of chips for one big something. And you always can gain leverage in negotiations by giving away seller-perceived leverage. Tactical "giving in" can show the seller you're willing to work with him for the deal, not that you're a pushover. Keep in mind that a willing and able buyer with a reasonable attitude is the solution to a seller's need to sell. Think of yourself in this way, and you will empower yourself in negotiations.

A hard-ball, take-it-or-leave-it offer will guarantee you bad word-of-mouth, especially if it works, which I suspect it won't. Whatever the bargaining culture, such offers work mainly with sellers whose backs are against the wall, but not even then. I urge readers not to play the game the way Michael Scanlon, the conduit between crooked influence-peddler Jack Abramoff and Congressman Tom DeLay, described his advice to DeLay during the Clinton impeachment: "'This whole thing about not kicking someone when they are down is B.S.,' Mr. Scanlon once wrote to Mr. Rudy [a DeLay and Scanlon associate] in an email published in <u>The Breach</u>, a book by Peter Baker about the impeachment. 'Not only do you kick him—you kick him until he passes out—then beat him over the head with a baseball bat—then roll him up in an old rug—and throw him off a cliff into the pound surf below!!!!!'" (Brody Mullins, "Behind Unraveling of DeLay's Team, A Jilted Fiancee, <u>Wall Street Journal</u>, March 31, 2006.) I've seen land buyers act like this; I hope not to see another.

In some situations, you might benefit from asking a seller whether he'd prefer that you submit your best offer or a lower one that is negotiable. This is a simple way to establish the ground rules of your negotiations; I've found that it works. Do not, however, raise your best offer if that is what the seller chooses. If you submit a best-money offer, give the seller no more than 24 hours to respond.

The bargaining rapport and momentum that you establish on peripheral issues will provide a path for your negotiations on more substantive issues where you give up something you want for something you want more. I've found rural sellers to be comfortable with give and take in various forms. I've found that folding myself into a give-and-take bargaining system is usually acceptable to these sellers. It's a fair system when both sides are knowledgeable. In this type of give and take, buyers often can succeed more by listening harder and talking softer.

Take, for example, Yankee buyers South of the Maryland border. (The same example could be drawn from the downstate Big City buyer in the rural upstate.) Country sellers may both fear and despise such buyers. Urban Yankees, in particular, sound smarter (though they're not), act dumber (often true) and appear richer (sometimes true, sometimes not) than they are. They are usually more comfortable with a high-speed, secular, professional business culture than the rural seller. Urban anybodies—Northern or Southern—may now be lumped together by rural sellers and considered a Yankee type. Yankees are, of course, distrusted for these reasons as well as our funny accent, aggressiveness and the guilt we bear for winning the War of the Northern Aggression. Any seller who enters negotiations believing the buyer is both smart and dumb can easily get crosswise in his own assumptions. A buyer wants to avoid fitting into the seller's cultural preconceptions, especially when they're accurate. If you feel that you would not negotiate well with a seller, have your local lawyer do it for you.

I've found variations of the Yankee-Dixie dynamic in the West ("amenity buyers" vs. ranch sellers), the Northeast (city buyers vs. native Yankee sellers), West Virginia (outsider buyers vs. West Virginia sellers) and even within certain counties.

Urban buyers are also the country seller's most coveted market, because it is assumed such buyers have more money than sense. First-generation country residents—urban folks who retired to the country or younger bail outs—also prefer to sell to the "surgeon from Denver" or the prominent Manhattan editor. Me too; every seller should do better with a wealthy buyer. You may find, consequently, that if you are so categorized, negotiating with a dollar-blinded seller feels like a street shakedown with the seller's attitude summarized as, "Give it up."

What can an urban buyer who fits the country seller's preconceptions do to protect his pocketbook? First, don't be stupid. Don't look at country property no matter how expensive from the leather-clad bucket seat of a show-room-new $100,000 Hummer or a $250,000 Lamborghini. Don't flash diamonds the size of cow flops. Don't brag about your job, your important friends and the appreciation rate of your portfolio. Look and act average, while *silently* projecting the ability to make this purchase at the right price. Second, scope the property. If money is no object, your scoping is looking for the hidden legal and physical liabilities that will turn the purchase into a nightmare. Third, bargain. I don't care whether you can buy the seller's property 25 times over with your pocket change. Your willingness to bargain gives respect to the seller, which improves the buying process for you. Finally, let your local lawyer do the heavy lifting. He will carry off the purchase on your behalf better than you will.

A dispute arises with the seller: what do you, the out-of-county buyer, do?

If it's a chip, forget about it. Winning a chip from a local seller almost always costs the newcomer-buyer more over his long run than the chip is worth. The cost is paid in stories about your poor behavior if nothing else.

When the dispute is over something more substantial—involving, for example, at least two percent of your purchase price—a buyer might feel more comfortable in asking his local lawyer to negotiate with the seller's lawyer. Let lawyer haggle with lawyer, which they do all the time. At most, this task will cost you a couple of hours of your lawyer's time.

If the dispute is of such magnitude that it's a deal-breaker, I'd first try local lawyer to local lawyer negotiations. If that fails, I'd have your lawyer suggest **third-party mediation** of the dispute to the seller's lawyer. Mediation is a method of resolving disputes in which the parties hire an independent neutral to help them reach a compromise. The mediator has no power to impose a settlement. His role is to keep negotiations moving, present different ways of solving issues and help the parties write a settlement that everyone signs. Mediation fails when this process—usually a day or less—produces no acceptable settlement. Mediation works in a majority of cases. But it requires good-faith bargaining on both sides. A party who refuses to bargain stops mediation cold. The disputants' incentive to resolve their problem through mediation is their knowledge that mediation allows them to control their settlement and that litigation is always a more costly, more time-consuming and less predictable option. Since both buyer and seller want the purchase to go through, they share an interest in having mediation succeed. One of the ground rules for mediation is that both parties have at the negotiations an individual authorized to make a deal then and there.

In selecting a mediator, the parties must agree on a person who has no interest in the outcome, is not biased for or against either party and has experience in both mediation work and real-estate issues. Community mediation centers can recommend trained mediators. Dispute-resolution organizations can also provide referrals. These include the Society for the Promotion of Alternative Dispute Resolution, American Arbitration Association and several for-profit mediation vendors. The local bar association might recommend names of lawyers who do mediations. Choose someone who has been trained in mediation techniques and has experience in real estate. Mediators whose experience is with personal-injury cases or divorces may have the mediation skills, but not sufficient background in real estate. If your dispute concerns a particular area of expertise, such as the valuation of timber or a farm business, you may want to provide the mediator with a consultant who is present during the mediation session and helps the mediator propose alternative solutions. The mediator and the costs of mediation are divided equally between the parties. Some mediation issues benefit from having lawyers present for both sides, but I have seen lawyers derail mediated settlements in favor of litigation. I have also seen a lawyer use a mediation session for discovery, that is, to find out what the other side was going to present as evidence in the litigation he was planning. When the issues and resolution have tax consequences for one or both parties, share the cost of a CPA presence at the mediation.

If mediation fails, you have four choices: 1) ask the two lawyers to give it a last try between themselves; 2) concede defeat; 3) **arbitration**, in which the parties must agree to submit their dispute to a third-party neutral who has full authority to issue a binding decision; and 4) litigation. I'd always try option one, since you have little to lose and everything to gain.

I've worked as an arbitrator for 20 years, primarily dealing with workplace grievances arising within a contract between a union and employer. I've also done a few commercial mediations. Each process works, though each works best in different circumstances. When the parties are genuinely locked up, arbitration is the better choice because it guarantees a settlement. Arbitration is a cheaper, faster option than litigation. Arbitrators are not, of course, of one mind. In any given case, my guess is that 20 arbitrators would reach ten different conclusions. Fifteen would side with one party, with varying levels of agreement and award. Maybe five of the 20 would rule for the other party, with their own variations on agreement and award. The split among arbitrators is determined by how they view the facts, law and case presentation. Where one party is obviously in the right, 20 of 20 arbitrators should rule that way, but that might slip to 95 out of 100. Most cases, however, present arbitrators with degrees of rightness on each side. This explains why arbitrators would split among themselves on a particular case as well as why arbitrators split their own decisions, giving something to each party. Some arbitrators decide cases on the basis of which party made the better presentation; others look more for the truth. Arbitrators also differ in the degree of their participation in the hearing: some ask no questions; others ask questions limited to clarification; still others ask substantive questions that are intended to reveal what happened and the degree of reliability of the information presented.

Arbitrations resemble court hearings with the arbitrator as the judge. Each side presents its case with documents and witnesses. Cross-examination occurs. The arbitrator is expected to be fair and neutral. Rules of evidence are not applied, other than those consistent with basic fairness and due process. Arbitrators may be asked to make a win-lose decision in which one side totally prevails over the other. As chancy as it is, I favor letting an arbitrator reach whatever decision he thinks is best. That is neither more nor less risky than submitting the case to a judge. Where buyer and seller are in dispute before the purchase contract has been carried out, an arbitrator might be asked to devise a reasonable compromise. I recommend that buyers be represented by counsel in any arbitration. I also recommend that the parties authorize the arbitrator to write a short opinion that presents his view of the issues and the reasons for his position on each one. Otherwise, the parties are left with a legally binding award and no explanation of how the arbitrator got there.

One example will suffice. A developer bought at an "as-is" auction a 124-acre tract of undeveloped land along a Virginia creek for $2.25 million and a buyer's premium of $225,000. After signing the contract but before closing, the developer discovered an active bald eagle's nest on the property, which limited its development potential. The developer said that he had asked about the presence of bald eagles; the seller said the developer had the knowledge and means to discover the nest on his own. The arbitrator ruled the contract valid and directed the developer to perform. The developer appealed and the arbitrator's decision was upheld by a county circuit court judge in 2006. ("Arbitrator enforces sale of Stafford property," Virginia Lawyers Weekly, March 27, 2006.)

I would do everything possible to keep buyer-seller disputes out of court. While arbitration involves elements of a crapshoot, judges are no different and juries can be worse. Justice is not guaranteed in either arbitration or court. Litigation may not produce a reasonable result, and may produce a deferred result where the losing side appeals. Judges and arbitrators as individuals differ in ability, dedication and perspectives; even good ones blow decisions. I've seen excellent work from rural county judges, as well as a decision so pre-determined that it still makes me talk to myself. I've seen usually competent judges and arbitrators render decisions that are half thought through and not very defensible. Where judges are elected, the out-of-county buyer must consider the local politics of his dispute. Where judges are appointed, a buyer has to fear the arbitrary or quirky individual with a sinecure who doesn't much care any more about the reasonableness of his decisions. In some communities, local judges and local juries will be predisposed to rule in favor of the local seller they know over the Big City buyer they don't know. If you come across as arrogant, stay out of local courts because you risk getting a comeuppance based on who you are not what your case is. Rural judges and juries in my experience favor the side—client and lawyer—they like more often than not. If you are likeable, you have a chance. Your local lawyer should make the call as to whether litigation gives you a shot at fairness in the local court.

I'll add one final point. I have on occasion used something that might be called an **informative non-threat** to persuade a party to work with me. I'm not a lawyer, but I've married two and have been around legal stuff as an arbitrator and land buyer. I've had on occasion predicted how a court might rule in an effort to persuade a party to resolve a common problem with me. I was, for example, interested in buying a small timber tract that had a great deal of timber value. It had not been cut for years, because it was completely landlocked, physically and legally. The landlocked timber parcel had only one way to access a public road—all other ways were blocked by public land. I wrote to the owner of the land lying between the road and the landlocked parcel, observing that in my opinion a court would grant an easement by necessity to the landlocked parcel over him, which would cost each of us about $10,000 to fight it out were it to come to that, which, I said, I certainly hoped it wouldn't. I proposed selling him the landlocked parcel at a steep discount after I cut the timber in return for using his land to get the timber to the public road. I both wrote and said that I was not threatening him with a lawsuit, but I did want him to understand my sense of the situation. He saw it in essentially the same way. Had I threatened him with a lawsuit, I think he would have called my bluff—and won. I did not want the headache of a suit. But by laying honest cards out on an honest table, he and I could play an honest hand with each other.

CHAPTER 29: WRITING A PURCHASE-OFFER CONTRACT: STRATEGIES AND TACTICS

MAKE THE MOST OF YOUR CONTRACT OFFER

Purchase (offer) contracts on rural land present buyers with opportunities both to accomplish certain bargaining objectives and protect their interests. The contract itself should be used to further both ends.

The standard contract that real-estate agents use advantage sellers, if only to the extent that protections for buyers have to be added or written in as modifications to the boilerplate. These contracts are not neutral; they protect the seller without the seller doing anything while forcing the buyer to actively rebalance the contract. I prefer to use a contract that I write, incorporating the boilerplate protections for the seller while adding those a buyer needs. I don't try to skew the contract unfairly in my favor. I write the contract to advance objectives related to the purchase that are tangential to the basic functions of a purchase contract.

Your offer to purchase gives you a one-time opportunity to acquire both vital information about the property and warranties (promises) from the seller. Lawyers will disagree with broadening the functions of the offering contract, but I have found that my way serves a buyer better than using the standard form. One danger in following my advice is that a buyer will write a contract that is too complicated or too one-sided for the seller's taste.

Any contract a buyer—lawyer or not—writes should be done with the active assistance of the lawyer you're using in the target-property's county. Thus, writing your own contract may come down to talking out issues with your lawyer who then does the writing. Do not write a real-estate contract on your own. The harm that you might do to yourself outweighs the benefits.

I use purchase contracts to accomplish some, or all, of the following objectives, depending on the property:

Get information from the seller that he alone possesses, such as knowledge of an unrecorded easement, an erroneous fence line that benefits the seller's property, farm-business financial records, tax schedules, insurance values, participation (and obligations) in government cost-share programs and crop subsidies and so on.

Get the seller to disclose legal and physical problems with the property, which your scoping might not otherwise reveal, e.g., a covered hazardous-waste dump, an unknown archeological site that would foul up a building project, presence of an ETS species or a water supply that is based only on permission.

Have the seller do something to make the deal go through, such as repair electrical service to the barn or remove fallen trees from access road.

Allow the buyer to perform certain on-site investigations, such as sampling for water quality, radon, asbestos or mold; doing a timber cruise; having a structural engineer examine a bridge or a dam; or taking percolation tests in anticipation of a new septic system.

When these investigations are structured as contract **contingencies**, the buyer must include language in each contingency that permits him to be the sole judge as to whether or not the results are satisfactory. If **results-acceptable-to-the-buyer** language is not part of each contingency, the buyer cannot void his contract and get the return of his deposit when results are not acceptable. When results are adverse, the buyer should be able to void his contract or offer to resume negotiations with the seller based on new information. A "contingency" that simply permits the buyer to seek financing or take a water sample does not allow the buyer to get out of the deal if he fails to get financing or does not like the results of the water sample. A contract contingency that benefits the buyer is one that makes the deal's completion depend on getting satisfactory results.

Allow the buyer to perform certain work on the property in advance of closing, such as marking timber in anticipation of a sale, surveying or excavating. Seller should approve all such work as part of the contract, and the buyer needs to understand that he will not benefit from his expenditures if the purchase does not close.

Educate the seller as to what the buyer expects of him and his property. This is done through 1) **warranties that survive the contract**, 2) disclosures and 3) conditions of sale. Warranties that survive the contract are also referred to as warranties that survive escrow.

Notify the seller that he will be expected to stand behind warranties that survive the contract.

Identify and clean up loose ends that a title search is not likely to find, such as unrecorded contracts and easements, encroachments, boundary disputes, licenses (permission to use the land or its assets) and pending actions that might adversely affect the buyer's use and enjoyment (such as seller's inside knowledge that his across-the-road neighbor is planning to build the largest hog farm on the East Coast).

Provide the seller with opportunities to refuse certain language and demands as a way to secure others of more importance to buyer.

Provide sufficient complexity to allow bargaining within the framework of the contract if buyer thinks negotiating is advisable. A buyer can concede throwaways, contingencies, repairs and some disclosures for seller concessions.

Provide the buyer with time to put in place post-purchase plans for property. This usually involves doing work in advance of selling some of the land or a severable asset.

Strip risk from a purchase by making it contingent on buyer securing all approvals he deems necessary to implement a post-purchase plan. This is commonly used by buyers who want to divide a large property or turn it to some purpose that requires rezoning or a conditional-use permit.

A purchase contract should be seen as involving three sequences.

The first is an offer from the buyer to purchase property on terms he proposes. Those terms involve getting the seller to disclose information, allowing the buyer to do certain things, making the offer contingent on results acceptable to the buyer and agreeing on price and other sale conditions.

The second phase—**escrow**—begins once the contract is signed by both parties and comes into effect. Escrow is the time when all of the agreed work by both buyer and seller that was set forth in the accepted offer is done. Escrow is usually scheduled for 45 to 90 calendar days, but I've seen open-ended escrows used by buyers whose offer is contingent on getting the property rezoned.

The third phase begins after closing and the buyer takes possession. The several future warranties included in a general warranty deed and whatever warranties the buyer stipulated would survive the contract are now available for protecting the buyer. The contract offer is the one chance the buyer has to get his seller to both promise something and live up to it.

Many lawyers will look disapprovingly at my discussion of contracts and the sample language I've included. They'll say: "Too much extraneous stuff; keep it simple." Every buyer knows without having to be told that a full-price, all-cash offer free of contingencies, disclosures and title search will "win" the property of almost every seller. That level of simplicity—what the seller's real-estate agent calls a "clean contract"—can get the buyer into trouble after the deal is done. And if the seller is not on the warranty hook after closing, he's off the hook—and you've taken his place. I'm not recommending that every buyer write his own contract, and I'm certainly against readers festooning every contract with every contingency I've described in this book. You need to balance a contract with words that cover the needs your scoping has identified with fair play for the seller. The buyer needs to find that level of detail and self-protection that lies between too much and not enough—the place determined by the individual characteristics of each deal and the needs of the seller.

I do not advise inexperienced buyers either to write their own contracts or use the sample contract in this chapter *verbatim*. I advise, instead, that readers become familiar with contract concepts and the language that expresses them. In consultation with your local lawyer, lift and adapt whatever language that helps. If you have cold feet, use the standard contract *your* lawyer would use when working for a buyer and add any additional language you and he feel is appropriate. Do not, however, use your lawyer's standard contract if it's the same as the standard contract used by sellers—which is likely to be the case. That standard contract is likely to be no different than the real-estate broker's standard contract.

The following discussion focuses on ways that contract language and tactics can help a buyer get better terms, safer terms and pay less.

INFORMATION

Sellers and real-estate brokers vary in their willingness to inform buyers about items of importance. When a seller fully complies with a state's disclosure requirements, many pieces of information may still not be made available. Use your contract to ask for information from the seller.

I looked at 170 acres in 2005 that was accessed by way of a 2.5-mile-long driveway, about two miles of which were private road that crossed and served four property owners. My target property had a deeded right to use this road, but the easement said nothing as to the width of the easement, who was responsible for the road's maintenance (a not inconsiderable expense) and whether the easement was unrestricted in terms of the types and number of vehicles that could use the road. The absence of written restrictions should be interpreted as the intentional absence of restrictions, but the other property owners might complain about its use by logging trucks and cement mixers. [A buyer could put in his contract a provision that requires the seller to secure written advance approval of the buyer's easement plans from the other owners as a condition of sale.] The right to use this road was located in an antecedent deed, an owner or two back, and no reference to it was included in the seller's own deed of record. I sensed that the seller was reluctant to use this access road for anything more than an occasional safari ride in with his pick-up truck. The neighbors, I guessed, opposed any other usage and were willing to fight in court over more traffic and heavier vehicles. The seller did not say this to me outright, but I felt confident in making those inferences from the non-answer answers he provided. I never got to a contract with this seller. My pre-offer discussion of an access contingency was enough for me to learn that this deal was more headache than I wanted.

A few months later I was working on a 1,000-acre property in New York's Adirondack Park, which fronted a large reservoir and appeared to have an unrestricted, deeded, ROW easement that the owner never used. He canoes in, I was told, several miles each way when he visited, which wasn't often. The property had merchantable timber value, but I was not interested in trying to find a logger who wanted to truck logs across frozen water to a state-owned public boat landing even if the state environmental regulators approved that idea. Use of the four-mile-long ROW was the key to this property, but the key wouldn't turn the lock's tumbler. Relations between the seller and the property owners over whom his easement crossed were so hostile that any effort to use the easement—certainly by logging trucks—would initiate a legal war. The prize wasn't worth the blood. Again, the discussion of potential contract language prior to submitting a contract with an access guarantee in it led to information that forced me to scratch this one off my list.

A buyer's contract should always require that the seller deliver **marketable title** at closing. A marketable title is one that has no serious defects, does not depend on problematic questions of law or fact to prove its legitimacy, does not leave the buyer open to litigation, does not threaten the buyer's quiet enjoyment of the property and allows the new owner to sell or mortgage the property. Marketable title does not guarantee acreage; it refers to ownership of what the seller is selling. A marketable title can have certain defects that might impose limits and restrictions on ownership. These should be turned up in either the buyer's **title search**, whereby the buyer's lawyer investigates all public records for title defects for a certain number of years back, or an **abstract of title**, which is the lawyer's narrative report of all the items found in the record. A title search usually occurs after contingencies are removed. A **preliminary title search** generally takes place after the seller accepts the buyer's contract. I feel more comfortable with a preliminary title search occurring during scoping, before the offer is submitted. If a problem is turned up, the buyer can then include in his contract a provision for the seller to cure the found defect. Nothing is lost by having the buyer request that the seller disclose any defect in title.

When a seller has evidence of title, it shows proof of his ownership. But a deed, in and of itself, does not establish ownership. The seller's deed must be combined with evidence of ownership as recorded in a chain of title leading up to the seller's ownership. This is done through the buyer's lawyer (or licensed abstractor or title company) issuing a **certificate of title** (which is research-based opinion that the seller's title is marketable and no claims against the seller's ownership are found in the public record), title insurance or a Torrens certificate (a title system used in some states). A certificate of title does not guarantee the seller's ownership, however. It will not pick up unrecorded liens and claims against the property, as well as hidden defects, such as fraud, incorrect marital information and forgeries. For that reason, the buyer needs to ask the seller to disclose what he knows about defects in his ownership (title). It's one more step a buyer should take to protect his interests. If a buyer has doubts about the seller's title, he can make his offer contingent on obtaining title insurance and acceptable results from an abstract of title.

CONTINGENCIES

The tactical use of **contract contingencies** is one way of accomplishing many of the objectives I listed at the beginning of this chapter.

A contingency provides for either something to be done to the buyer's satisfaction and/or something to occur before the contract becomes binding on the parties. The buyer can use unacceptability as grounds for either voiding his offer without penalty or resuming negotiations within the existing offer. A purchase contract with a **results-acceptable-to-the-buyer contingency** gives the buyer a legal out if that need arises. The non-specific language of results acceptable to buyer is better than a contingency where, for instance, the offer is made to depend on specified financing terms, such as a 25-year mortgage at no more than seven percent with no more than three points. The buyer may find himself not wanting to do the deal even when he arranges financing that fits the specific requirements of his offer. Results-acceptable-to-buyer language gives the buyer an emergency all-purpose release if one is needed. Results-acceptable-to-the-buyer contingencies are much more useful to buyers and, therefore, may be harder to get sellers to accept. This type of contingency never incorporates specific terms. The buyer says to the seller: the results of my efforts to fulfill my obligations under this contract need to work for me; I can't anticipate what those results will be at this time because there are things I still don't know; I'll perform on the contract if I get results—financing, information, etc.—that in my opinion meet my needs. If a contingency produces unacceptable results, the buyer can terminate the contract offer without penalty or do a final round of negotiation with the seller in light of the new information.

Used judiciously and prudently, contingencies can be made a part of a buyer's negotiating strategy to:

- protect the buyer from booby-traps that he did not find in his pre-purchase scoping;
- get the property under contract quickly with a no-penalty escape;
- force disclosure of seller-controlled information;
- provide time and opportunity within an incentive-loaded framework for the parties to solve a problem within a buyer-friendly context;
- build momentum toward closing as each contingency is resolved;
- negotiate changes in price and terms when new information is uncovered;
- buy time without paying for it;
- pressure a seller into concessions by stretching his time frame and getting him invested in working with you; and
- give the buyer leverage by being able to terminate his offer without financial penalty when results of a contingency investigation don't suit him.

These are powerful points of leverage and should not be used frivolously.

Every contingency represents a loose end that needs to be either resolved to the buyer's satisfaction or withdrawn by the buyer for the sale to close. Contingencies present both parties with the possibility of additional negotiating where results are either marginally acceptable or marginally unacceptable to the buyer. This grey area of marginal acceptability/unacceptability usually takes the form of information that either increases the anticipated expense of the buyer's purchase or decreases the estimated value of a property's assets. When a buyer uses an unacceptable result to suggest reopening negotiations, the seller is no longer bound to anything in the contract. It may be fair for the seller to give something to the buyer to help him with the less-than-pleasing result while taking more of some other thing. If a seller comes to think that a buyer is gaming him with contingencies, it's likely to blow up the deal. Contingencies can be used to straighten out the smallest details as well as matters that will make the deal or break it. Buyers should not use contingencies gratuitously. They should be inserted when needed and written with great deliberateness.

While contingencies are protective, they cannot take the place of thorough pre-offer scoping. The reason, of course, is that the buyer's contract offer must include a price, which should be one the buyer can comfortably afford and is justified by the value of the property's assets. *You determine your price and calculate assets before you submit your offer, based on what you discovered during your scoping.* You can fine-tune an offer with grey-area bargaining once the results are in hand, but I would not put too many oxen loads on that burro. A seller may be willing to reopen your offer on one or possibly two items (including price), but I would assume that two items is the outside limit with all but the most desperate of sellers.

A buyer will sometimes find a seller who announces that he will consider no contract that contains any contingency. That may be a tactic to prevent a buyer from discovering what the seller is hoping to hide. Rather than confront this seller directly, a buyer can offer a **three-price contract** and a 90-day closing. During escrow, the buyer continues his scoping. If a lot of discounting factors are found, his lowest price becomes his offer; if some discounting factors appear, his offer is then his middle price; and if the property comes up clean, then he commits to his highest offering price. A three-price offer, however, does not give the buyer the opportunity to void the contract if something unacceptable is discovered. Submit such an offer only with the consent of your local lawyer—and even then be careful.

I've found that when a seller does not want to allow the buyer to thoroughly research his property, he's trying to hide something big and bad. Why else would he refuse to let you smell his cantaloupe?

A contingency can save you from disaster. One of my clients made an offer on about 1,000 acres of Virginia timberland that bordered a river. The seller was a sawmill; the buyer was a developer. The contract contained a results-acceptable-to-the-buyer timber-evaluation contingency. The timber value turned out to be just fine; the problem with it was that the owner had secretly sold it. His broker was innocently marketing the land as if the timber were part of the purchase. The seller might have argued in his court defense that he had orally informed the buyer that the timber did not convey. From what I understood of the facts, the seller simply hid the timber sale. When the buyer discovered the backdoor deal, he tried to buy out the timber contract without success. He then used the timber contingency—results acceptable to the buyer—to cancel his offer and get his deposit back without further entanglement.

The danger in learning about contract tactics and contingencies is that readers will approach every land sale over-armed for their need and, as a result, play it too clever by half. The buyer wants to buy the seller's property, not scare him away or humiliate him with contract virtuosity. **The best purchase contract is as short, clean and simple as is needed.** One results-acceptable-to-the-buyer contingency is sufficient protection; two is aiming a pistol at your foot; and three is pulling the trigger. A land buyer should not see himself as trying to trick the seller. Trickery gets you into trouble. Buyer tactics discussed here are available to block seller tactics that are adverse to the buyer's interests. Think of it as a ju-jitsu defense where the buyer turns his opponent's aggressiveness to his own ends. If you start throwing a bunch of legal bean balls at a seller, he'll take his bat and go home. As a buyer, you've become more trouble than your offer is worth.

Many real-estate contracts include a **financing contingency**, which makes the purchase depend on the buyer's arranging institutional financing, usually a specific dollar amount at no more than a specified rate and terms. If the buyer is unable to secure acceptable financing within a certain number of days, his contract offer becomes void without penalty. If he gets acceptable financing, the purchase goes through. Take my advice: don't offer a financing contingency pegged to a specific rate and term, and try to have the seller agree to give you an unspecified reasonable amount of time to arrange financing, not to exceed two or three months. You justify this open-ended language to the seller by saying that you want to maximize your chances of getting the deal done. If you are forced into using a specific rate and term, always make sure to provide a cap on points or closing costs. If your contingency simply states five percent interest, the seller may be able to find a lender who is offering a five percent rate that carries a load of points and an unfavorable adjustable term.

When institutional financing is not forthcoming, a buyer can propose **seller financing** as a replacement, which brings advantages and disadvantages to both sides. I advise against rigging an institutional-financing contingency so that it will fail in order to force a seller into financing your purchase. As soon as you miss the deadline on a single payment, the seller can get even—and more—by declaring the note in default and repossessing his property along with whatever cash of yours he has in hand.

Familiar contingencies provide for a **house inspection, termite inspection, urea-formaldehyde (found in old insulation) test, mold test, radon test and indoor-air-pollution tests**. Most termite-inspection contingencies require the seller to treat the infestation; he voids the contract by refusing. Fixing other problems found in various tests and inspections is a matter of negotiation.

Mold was the subject of some 10,000 lawsuits in 2003. It tends to be a problem in air-tight, energy-efficient houses in warm, wet climates. (Associated Press, "Mold-based lawsuits on the rise," <u>Richmond Times-Dispatch</u>, July 27, 2003.) Mold—one of many types of fungus—requires moisture and food—cellulose, wood, soap scum, dust. It's found in damp basements, bathrooms (unventilated), attics, air-conditioning ducts and around leaks in pipes or outside walls. Old farmhouses, especially those lacking basements, may be less likely to have mold, radon and indoor-air pollution, because they have leaky windows and doors and no wall insulation—all of which promote higher indoor-outdoor air-exchange rates. This leakiness, which increases heating/cooling bills, allows indoor-air pollutants to move outside. Modern housing is more heat-efficient, but the tightness created by insulation and energy-efficient windows and doors creates air-pollution sumps. These can be mitigated by installing in-line filters on forced-air heating systems. Systems using radiators and electric baseboard heaters need stand-alone room air purifiers. Dehumidifers help with mold. (See Mary Beth Breckenridge, Knight Ridder, "Mold Enters Quietly, But It Makes Its Presence Known," Washington Post, March 25, 2006.) Mold is not necessarily harmful. Whether its presence kills a purchase, depends on its type, extent and estimated cost of remediation.

Two common country contingencies involve an **acceptable water sample** and a **septic-system investigation**. The latter can make a purchase be contingent on obtaining buyer-acceptable results in locating a site for a new system or determining that the existing system is in working order and of acceptable size and design for the buyer's purpose. On old household-water systems, the buyer should make sure that the sample is tested for **lead** (in addition to bacteria, chemical pollutants, hardness, suspended solids, etc.), which can leach from old lead pipes or lead-based solder that is now banned.

On houses built before 1978, sellers are required to disclose any knowledge of **lead-based paint** and provide the buyer with a booklet, "Protect Your Family from Lead in Your Home." The buyer may have the house inspected at his expense for such paint within ten days of the contract coming into effect. Lead was used as a pigment and a drying agent in alkyd oil-based paint for home interiors and exteriors. It is estimated that about 75 percent of pre-1978 private housing has some lead-based paint. Fixes include removal, which is expensive, and repainting (i.e., painting over), which is less. Testing will determine the level of hazard, if any. Flaking and peeling lead-based paint is extremely hazardous, especially to small children. Stripping and sanding such paint elevates the likelihood of ingesting or breathing lead particulate. If you suspect a problem, insert a **lead-testing contingency** with results acceptable to buyer. The lead-disclosure statement is not a contingency that allows the buyer to void the contract; it simply discloses what the seller claims to be his knowledge of the hazard.

On rural property, a buyer should use contingencies to deepen his knowledge of a property's assets and liabilities when there's insufficient time to do the necessary scoping prior to submitting a purchase offer. Occasions arise when it's more important for a buyer to get a contract in place as soon as possible than to scope every detail to absolute certainty. A contingency protects the buyer's back in fast contracts. If, for example, you are targeting a working farm with other buyers circling, you might propose a contingency that asks the seller to show you his profit-and-loss statements, Schedule Fs and net-worth statements for the last five years, with results acceptable to the buyer. You can offer a bit more than you would otherwise and prepare to back out or renegotiate price if the seller's numbers are lower than you anticipated. When a seller balks at disclosing information required by a contingency, he's showing you more than anything he may be telling you.

You may want to use a **timber-evaluation contingency** for wooded acreage. Your offer is contingent on the seller's agreement to allow your forester to perform an evaluation (walk-through or cruise, the choice is your forester's) of the property's timber, with results acceptable to you. Budget a window of 60 calendar days for this work. Foresters can generally get to a new client within that period of time. More time should be allowed for very large properties. Consult with your forester before writing your contingency's term. Any contingency that includes a term gives you that amount of time to continue scoping other aspects of the property at no cost or risk to you. *As a rule, a smart buyer will have his forester do a walk-through or cruise before submitting a contract offer, not as a contingency within a contract where price is already agreed to.*

If you've determined the value of the seller's timber—or any other asset—prior to making an offer, you can propose a contingency with the idea of negotiating it away in return for some seller concession. A concession of this type appears to the seller as if you are giving up a lot and assuming a big financial exposure, when, in fact, you're giving up nothing and assuming no risk at all. This can be quite effective with one or two contingencies. The buyer needs to be convincing and bargain with a poker face.

A generic form of scoping contingency is one that land investors use: it's a **90-day study contingency**, with results acceptable to the buyer. Study contingencies are often used when a buyer wants to get a contract in place before other buyers submit theirs. They're also used when a buyer doesn't know enough to feel confident in his price, or he doesn't know what he doesn't know and hopes that he can find out what he doesn't know over a couple of months. From the buyer's perspective, a study contingency creates a 90-day option to buy, but it's more advantageous than a normal option because it allows the buyer, first, to reopen the contract's purchase price if the study results don't please him, and, second, to not lose any money if he fails to perform. Sellers of large tracts are accustomed to study contingencies. If you find your seller rejecting a 90-day study contingency, you can substitute a 90-day timber-evaluation contingency or a 90-day environmental-assessment contingency, both of which are the same wolves in different sheepskins. Thirty- and 60-day study periods are appropriate for small acreages.

You can propose a **clean-it-up contingency** for specific messes—e.g., where the seller's access is unclear or in active dispute, a disgruntled tenant has left after wrecking the house, or a boundary dispute exists that you do not want to inherit. You probably want to call it something other than a clean-it-up contingency, but you should be clear about its purpose with the seller who in all likelihood will be expected to do something he probably would prefer to pass on to you.

An **environmental contingency** is appropriate where the buyer suspects a problem, such as a leaking, buried fuel tank; hazardous materials (a pile of disintegrating asbestos shingles dumped out back; disintegrating metal drums of creosote or agricultural chemicals); presence of wetlands or endangered, threatened and sensitive (ETS) species; restrictions on water use and the like. Working farms often have large fuel tanks on the premises. In the past, these tanks were usually buried. Today, they are more commonly installed on the surface in cast-concrete vaults. Farms and residences have generally been exempt from federal regulation of tanks when they hold less than 1,100 gallons of fuel oil for noncommercial purposes as well as heating oil used on site. But abandoned tanks can leak residues and require some degree of remediation. If you suspect contamination, ask the seller to disclose what he knows and then write a contingency that allows an inspection with results acceptable to the buyer. On large tracts, an environmental contingency usually calls for a Phase I Environmental Analysis—sufficient scoping to alert you to the type of problems found on the property and a preliminary assessment of their hazardousness and remedies.

If you are intending to sell a portion of the target property, divide it for future sale, or do any construction, you are likely to find yourself requesting plan approval from the local zoning authority, building inspector, architectural review board or one or more environmental agencies, such as the county health department or a state office. Plans that raise zoning/rezoning issues, conditional uses and exceptions to the local plan bring public scrutiny and often opposition. Public hearings are scheduled, and plans require approval by public boards. An applicant has no guarantee that his proposal will be approved as submitted or approved at all. Whenever your immediate post-purchase plans involve a permit, rezoning, conditional-use permit (which is authorization for the applicant to engage in a use of his property that is inconsistent with existing zoning but may be allowed if the "general welfare" is advanced), it is imperative that you include in your contract a clause that makes your **purchase contingent on receiving all necessary permits and approvals in a form acceptable to buyer**. This is usually handled by having the owner/seller apply for the permits that are then conveyed with the property. Have your local lawyer work out this language.

One other type of contingency exists that a buyer may use. It is not part of the buyer's purchase contract with the seller. It is a **contingent sale contract** that the buyer negotiates with those who want to buy all or part of the seller's property once the buyer closes with the seller. A contingent contract obligates the investor-buyer to sell something to the next buyer at a certain price and terms only if he purchases the entirety.

Negotiating by manipulating contingencies should be used sparingly, if at all. Bogus contingencies will be seen as such by most sellers. When a seller reaches a certain point of unease with a buyer's genuineness and good faith, he's more likely to stop negotiating than to be backed into a deal holding his nose.

I usually write contingencies using the phrase, **"with results acceptable to the buyer**." That reserves to the buyer full control over his performance on the contract's initial terms and gives him an unchallengeable, penalty-free exit if he needs it. I resist putting fixed numbers into contingencies, with the exception of a specific number of days for its term.

However, I have employed fixed-number contingencies when my pre-offer scoping made me confident of their results. The circumstances would be an offer where I'm sure of two contingency results, but not of a third. I want the seller to become increasingly invested in my offer, so I use two contingencies whose results I know will be acceptable. The third contingency—results acceptable to buyer—may come in positive or negative. In the first case, I can close the deal. In the second, I hope the seller will help me solve the unacceptable result now that we are this far along.

You may find it advisable to insert a one-time, no-additional-deposit **time extension** on a contingency that the buyer activates through written notification. I'd cap the extension at no more than 30 calendar days. The most common rationale for writing in extension language is that certain investigations may be hard to schedule and even harder to predict their duration. Archeological and environmental studies often open new doors of investigation that take a long time to shut.

I've seen a number of inexperienced buyers insert a **non-contingent non-contingency** into their contracts. Real-estate professionals working for the seller may "help" with its wording. These non-contingencies read something like this: "Buyer reserves the right to have Seller's house inspected and a radon test performed at his expense within 30 days." Such language only gives the buyer the right to have this work performed on his nickel within that period of time. It does not make the buyer's purchase contingent on obtaining acceptable results. This buyer can't void his contract without penalty even when the inspection results are horrendous. Buyer performance is still required at the contract price. Don't use non-contingent non-contingencies, except as chips, which means you are willing to cut them from your offer to get the seller to sign.

It's sometimes beneficial for a buyer to have a **general bail-out contingency**, though it's never called that. This is a contingency that a buyer uses to get out of a purchase if he needs to. It can be related to any plausible condition on the property, as long as the words say that buyer determines the acceptability of results and no penalty is imposed for voiding the contract where results are deemed unacceptable. Don't tie a bail out to specified results or specific numbers. A general bail-out contingency should be time-capped and buyer-paid to make it palatable to the seller. Don't propose an appraisal contingency as your bail out, because sellers will resist a deal dependent on the buyer getting a satisfactory appraisal from a buyer-paid appraiser. This type of contingency protects you for the period of its term, not longer.

A timber-evaluation (not cruise—too specific, too costly) or soils-evaluation contingency can be used this way. A timber-evaluation contingency might look like this:

Buyer's offer is contingent on obtaining results acceptable to the buyer from a

timber evaluation that he arranges with a forester of his choice and at his own expense and concludes within sixty (60) calendar days of this Contract taking effect. Buyer shall perform on this Contract if he deems results acceptable, and shall provide timely written notice to Seller of such acceptability. If Buyer deems results to be unacceptable, he shall provide timely written notice to Seller of such unacceptability. In that event, Buyer's earnest money/security deposit shall be returned to him in full within five (5) calendar days of receipt of notification, and this Contract becomes void without penalty to Buyer or further obligation from Seller.

A bail-out contingency is an emergency parachute that gives you the right to walk away from your offer within its term. If you remove this contingency, you will be expected to buy the property. If you insert a bail-out contingency, you will be required to do whatever it is you say you want that time to do. You must do that work before voiding the contract. A study-period contingency is, for this reason, a good choice, since its work and costs can be negligible. Still, you have to do something. You can't bail out without at least paying for your parachute.

A results-acceptable-to-the-buyer contingency steers the buyer into a five-branch decision tree. The first is that the results are acceptable, allowing the purchase to be completed with no change to the original terms. The second is that the results are so unacceptable that the buyer immediately voids the contract and gets his full deposit back. The third is that the results are marginally unacceptable, but the buyer goes through with the deal anyway. The fourth branch is one where the results are unacceptable and the buyer approaches the buyer to reopen the negotiations based on the new information. The last of these is available to the buyer without having to write it into the contingency language itself. The fifth branch—which I advise against taking—is the case where the results are acceptable, but the buyer pretends that they are not to effect one final cut in price. Some buyers bargain this way; I don't recommend it.

Contingencies are usually assumed to disappear at the end of their term if the buyer does nothing to alert the seller that he is invoking their escape language. That means you will be expected to perform on the contract if you do not explicitly invoke the contingency's termination and escape in writing. A buyer cannot use a contingency to void his purchase offer after the contingency deadline has passed. You should consider a contingency to be self-liquidating if you do not invoke its escape protections in writing within its time limit. A self-liquidating contingency is one that removes itself, which means that your offer is no longer contingent and will proceed to closing.

Where results are unacceptable, notify the seller that you're voiding the contract at least a day in advance of the contingency's termination. You can use an e-mail or a fax as long as you also send a letter that gets there no later than the deadline date. Get a return receipt. Don't cut contingency escapes close or scrimp on postage. If you miss the deadline, you can be held to performance. Once a buyer removes all contingencies or allows them to liquidate themselves, all parties should expect the purchase to go through as set forth originally, or with whatever modifications the parties might have added during escrow. Going through with the contract is called, **performance**.

Once a buyer's contingencies expire (liquidate themselves by not being invoked), are removed or are declared satisfied, the seller expects performance. Where a buyer doesn't close, the seller may sue for **specific performance**, which means the buyer will be forced to go through with the purchase as set forth in the contract offer.

ALL-CASH OFFER WITH NO FINANCING CONTINGENCY

Sellers like brief, straight-forward, short-escrow, uncomplicated, all-cash purchase contracts. They hate contingencies, and most won't do seller-financing propositions, because they need their cash out of the property immediately. Buyers can accommodate some or all of these seller wants in certain circumstances—in return for a price discount or **boot**. (Boot is a generic term for other stuff that a buyer or seller incorporates into a deal in addition to the simple sale of property for cash. Seller boot might be agricultural equipment, materials, labor or all manner of personal property. Buyer's boot can be anything of value that the seller agrees to accept. Boot is included to even out a deal or sweeten the pot, depending on your perspective. Boot is often used to even 1031 tax-deferred exchanges.) A buyer should understand that when he has arranged financing and makes up the difference with cash, he is submitting a no-strings, all-cash offer to the seller. Every buyer should describe such a no-contingency offer—as NO STRINGS, ALL CASH—at least five times in the seller's presence as explanation for his discounted price. An all-cash, no-contingency is a bird in the hand to a seller.

Only if I've done my scoping thoroughly would I consider making an offer without a contingency of some sort. If a contract does not carry a financing contingency, the buyer will be expected to perform whether or not institutional financing is available on acceptable terms. Freeing a contract of a financing contingency and some type of bail-out contingency is needlessly risky in many cases. Sellers don't usually quibble over a financing contingency, so you're really only asking for one contingency. If you have your money worked out in advance and you've done your scoping, you might consider a contingency-free offer in return for better price or terms.

What is an all-cash offer free of financing contingency worth to a seller? It depends on the seller's circumstances, particularly his urgency to make a deal with *you*. A buyer can use the carrot of an all-cash offer free of financing contingency in negotiating. Don't toss it in as a freebie; it's worth something—maybe a lot—to the seller. I'd assume it's worth at least one or two percent off your best negotiated price. An all-cash offer free of contingencies could be worth as much as five percent off the seller's lowest price in some situations. If the seller is unwilling to budge from his low (last) position, work with his number as you start adding contingencies, complications and sweeteners you want. A seller often realizes that simplicity and certainty offset a lower price.

The best negotiating approach is to separate and individualize items conceded and sought. That approach allows you to judge how the seller values each one. You can then combine items from both sides of the table in whichever way works. Always trade something for something. An all-cash offer unencumbered with contingencies is a close-to-guaranteed, go-through offer to the seller; get its value in return. Don't offer to eliminate the financing contingency and come up with an all-cash offer as your beginning position. Approach it like this: "If I were able to make you an all-cash offer, how much of a reduction in price would that be worth to you? And if I were able to assume the risk of an offer free of a financing contingency, what would that be worth to you?" If his first response is negative, don't make your offer all cash and don't eliminate contingencies. Keep negotiating. The more tentative his stubbornness makes you, the more he will come to value the possibility of all cash and no contingency. Patience.

SELLER CONTINGENCY

I've run into a seller contingency once. The seller had agreed to the buyer's purchase contract and price, subject to an appraisal that the seller would arrange. If the appraisal value came in at more than 103 percent of the contract price, the seller reserved the right to cancel the contract. The deal, in other words, was contingent on the seller's appraiser submitting an appraisal value that worked against the seller's interest. I told my client to reject this contingency, because I figured the seller would get the appraisal he was paying for. Were the appraisal to come in at less than 103 percent, the seller could simply accept the results and go through with the deal on the agreed terms. The seller, however, sensed that he could get more out of this buyer. The appraisal came in about $1 million more than the contract price, about 105 percent of the original. Against my advice, my client agreed to pay the appraisal price—and then lost his security when he couldn't flip the property during escrow. Subsequently, another buyer came along, paid the appraisal price and struggled to resell at a profit.

Buyers should reject a seller-contingency ploy out of hand. Facing such a seller, the buyer can respond in one of two ways:

1. "Sure," the buyer says, "I (the buyer) will arrange and pay for the appraisal, and we'll go with whatever the appraisal value is as our agreed selling price." The buyer is likely to get the appraisal value he pays for, just as the seller will get what he pays for.
2. Buyer says to seller: "You know the value of your property better than any appraiser. Let's move along or forget about appraisals. Your appraiser will give you what you want, and mine will give me what I want. They're just a waste of our money."

The second response is used if the first fails. There are other responses, but they all tend to suck a buyer into playing this seller-rigged game. I see no purpose for a seller contingency in a purchase contract other than to take a second bite out of the buyer's pocketbook.

A variation on this trick is a seller who has an appraisal in hand, which he doesn't reveal, and confides to the buyer, "I'll sell it to you for the appraisal price." I ran into a Denver developer with a 9,000-acre ranch (9,000 deeded, about 40,000+ on public lease) in Wyoming who proposed this through his broker. The seller was sitting on a jacked-up appraisal, the actual value of which he would disclose only after my buyer agreed to this way of determining selling price. I didn't laugh aloud, but a ploy as clumsy as this surely deserved a Kramdenesque har-de-har-har.

A purchase contract is, in one sense, a set of seller contingencies that expect the buyer to accomplish certain tasks during escrow. These typically include arranging his financing so that the buyer can pay the price he's offered the seller, carry out whatever investigations the buyer has insisted on, waive or satisfy the buyer's own contingencies and complete the buyer's side of the legal work. The seller's sale, in other words, is contingent on the buyer getting these jobs done. I would be wary of a seller contingency that gives the seller room to reopen the buyer's contract in any way during escrow. The appraisal contingency is one such device. Others might involve an independent evaluation of timber or minerals with a reservation allowing the seller to increase the agreed purchase price or void the deal; a contingency that allows the seller to sell or remove certain assets during escrow with price revisions; a contingency that allows the seller to increase the contract price if a higher offer comes in during escrow; and, finally, a seller bail-out contingency that gives the seller the right to void the contract, with or without cause.

EQUITABLE TITLE

The buyer can make use of the escrow time, typically 30 to 90 days, to perform certain work to benefit his impending possession. This work is distinct from that which the buyer does to satisfy his contingencies. *A buyer should consider doing such work only if he is certain that he will complete the purchase.*

During the escrow period, the seller continues to hold title and ownership. Title conveys to the buyer on the day he pays the seller at which time the seller delivers the deed (which may then be held by a trustee if an institutional loan using the property as security is involved) and the buyer accepts the deed. A buyer with a mortgage acquires full ownership only upon removing the debt (lien) from the property. The day on which closing occurs is usually the day on which documents are recorded with the county clerk.

The buyer holds a legal interest in the property during escrow that is called, **equitable title**. (When a seller is fully financing a sale of his own property though an installment land contract, the buyer holds equitable title in the property he's possessing until he completes the purchase.) A buyer with equitable title has the right to obtain absolute ownership during the time the seller holds legal title by completing the purchase. In states following the **title theory of mortgages**, the buyer with a mortgage holds nothing but equitable title until the mortgage is paid. In those states, equitable title gives the borrower possession and use of the property. In states where the **lien theory** is followed, the mortgage borrower (mortgagor) holds both legal and equitable title with the mortgage lender (mortgagee) holding a lien on the property. Equitable title begins once a buyer removes all contigencies.

The set of buyer rights under equitable title during escrow varies from state to state. The buyer, for example, may be able to insure assets on the seller's property. Within these rights, work done on the property by the buyer at his expense during escrow can save him time and money once he takes possession. If escrow occurs during good weather and closing is scheduled for the beginning of bad weather, a buyer may want to do good-weather work during escrow rather than postpone those jobs for a year. Work done under equitable title should not surprise a seller, but the legal concept can be invoked when necessary to help in persuading a seller to allow the buyer to do reasonable tasks during escrow.

When a buyer wants to do work on the property during escrow, I advise him to write these tasks into the purchase offer and discuss the work directly with the seller. A buyer's purchase contract might provide for the buyer doing one or more of the following tasks during escrow:

- Cruise and paint merchantable timber; allow timber buyers to visit the property and evaluate timber. (This will allow the buyer to sell the timber shortly after closing.);

- Survey and mark lines on the ground in anticipation of selling part of the property soon after closing;

- Allow prospective buyers for the newly surveyed parcel(s) to visit the seller's property in the company of the buyer. (This doesn't work very well when the buyer is trying to sell the seller's owner-occupied house.) The buyer can then negotiate contingent contracts—contracts of sale contingent on his purchase of the property from the seller—with these buyers. Do not under any circumstances sign a contract to sell a lot from an impending purchase without making that lot sale contingent on your purchasing the property;

- Arrange for the local utility to design and cost out power access to the the property; determine whether neighbors will grant easements;

- Arrange for septic-system site tests. Both percolation and soil-color methods require digging holes with backhoes and then filling them (The number of holes dug depends on how many are required to find a spot that satisfies the standard.);

- Allow engineer and contractor access to property to design new septic system;

- Allow access to seller's property/house by buyer's architect and contractor to develop construction/remodeling plans;

- Allow testing of water quantity and quality;

- Allow farm consultants to visit the property, test soil and water, and evaluate operation;

- Where farm equipment is part of the purchase, allow access of mechanics to test and evaluate equipment;

- Allow buyer to do farm-related work, such as pruning orchard or vineyard, controlled burning of undergrowth to increase certain types of game forage, mechanical cutting of unwanted brush (e.g., multiflora rose), planting of seedlings, application of fertilizer and other season-dependent treatments to cropland or pasture;

- Allow the buyer to store materiel and equipment in designated places; and

- Conduct agreed-on excavations, such as road grading and pond construction.

Within a purchase contract, the buyer's right to possession and full use of the seller's property is deferred until closing. Equitable title does not change this. However, equitable title does provide a framework for securing the seller's consent to do tasks of minimal intrusiveness. More intrusive tasks, such as excavations and controlled burns, are probably beyond the buyer's rights under equitable title, though the seller may raise no objection as long as it costs him nothing and his property benefits.

The buyer must understand that any activity he undertakes during escrow that improves the seller's property will not be compensated if he fails to perform. Buyers should secure seller consent to any activity that alters the seller's property, rather than rely on their rights under equitable title. When I've wanted to do something during escrow, I've talked it over with the seller and, assuming he agrees, spelled it out in the contract. I don't try to use equitable title as a club to beat out permission to use the seller's land. But I do explain that I'm not asking for anything that is legally unreasonable.

In 2005, I was helping a client who was pursuing a 3,000-acre property in the Adirondack Park that was owned by a prominent record producer and his wife, an equally prominent singer. My client wanted to cut some of the merchantable hardwood sawtimber immediately after completing the purchase. The best stumpage bids for that timber would be found in the fall for winter cutting. It was, therefore, advisable to have his forester mark the timber during escrow, so that the sale could take place as early into the winter as possible. The problem was that the sellers might not do the deal if they understood the buyer wanted to cut some of *his* newly purchased trees. Rather than invoke equitable title, my client did not bring up the idea of marking trees during escrow, equitable title or not. In this case, the seller had the wherewithal to kill a deal were he offended and not worry too much about paying the penalty for doing so. Better, then, to wait and not put the purchase at risk.

Equitable title gives a buyer with an **installment land contract** the right to possess, use and alter the seller's property. But that is a different application of equitable title than its use during escrow.

Buyers of urban/suburban residential property are always told to put no money into the seller's property before closing. The logic of this advice is clear: if the buyer fails to perform, he loses the money spent on improving the seller's property. The same risk comes with buying rural property, but the context can be much more personal and less formal, depending on the rural seller.

As a seller, I would not object to most escrow work a buyer wanted as long as I bore no responsibility to compensate him if the purchase fell through. I would not go along with work that would disturb my occupation during escrow or work that would change the property in a way that I would not want to live with in case of failure to perform. That leaves a lot of room, especially with rural property that a seller does not occupy. I think you will find most rural sellers willing to "work with" a buyer on escrow work, particularly tasks that are dependent on a season or ground conditions. The rural seller will understand the reasonableness of such requests.

A buyer may be able to use an escrow investment to act as a proxy for earnest money. A buyer who puts $10,000 into improving an access road during escrow is offering the seller more security in getting performance than $7,500 escrowed as earnest money. The **investment proxy** becomes even more persuasive to the seller when he understands that a buyer's failure to perform will limit the seller's recovery to the earnest money because the buyer—as all buyers should—will package a **liquidated damages** clause with any cash security deposit. This language limits the buyer's financial exposure from a bail out to his cash deposit. A buyer can also argue to the seller that his road investment should shave a thousand or two off the purchase price, because the seller is getting an improvement he will value in the event that the buyer fails to perform. These tactics work when the buyer's proposed investments during escrow match what the seller would want to do were he keeping the property or making it more marketable. Depending on the buyer's intentions and subsequent use of the new property, tax benefits can be available for certain expenses. The buyer must remember, of course, that the $10,000 in new road will not be available to pay for the land purchase, which is the destination of escrowed earnest money.

Some escrow investments may lend themselves to a **buy-back provision** in the purchase contract. This comes into play only when the buyer is unable to complete the purchase. Here's one example where a buy-back might work. It is fairly common for access to property to involve a seller-owned bridge. No one likes to rebuild bridges, even simple ones. It's hard work, usually expensive, and may cut the road link to the outside for several days or more. If both buyer and seller agree that the access bridge needs to be replaced, the buyer might agree to pay for the construction with the proviso that if he fails to perform for any reason, the seller agrees to reimburse him for all receipted expenses, or, if not that, some percentage. The cost bears on the buyer, but the inconvenience is borne by the seller. A buyer can get favorable terms if he agrees to couple this investment with some security deposit.

LONGER RATHER THAN SHORTER ESCROW

Sellers like to close in 30 days. They want their money sooner rather than later. They don't want the buyer thinking about the purchase for longer than is necessary. They don't want "buyer's remorse" or cold feet to set in. The shorter the escrow, the more secure a seller is likely to feel.

Conversely, buyers usually benefit from a longer escrow period. They need time to carry out whatever inspections and contingency evaluations they've written into the contract. A longer closing provides the opportunity for important information to turn up and for issues to be resolved. Where a buyer is planning sell a portion of the property soon after closing, a longer escrow gives him more time to market the lot(s) without paying interest on the purchase. Buyers benefit from a late-starting mortgage clock. And there's always the "woodwork" factor, as in once a contract is in place, you just never know what's going to come out.

If a buyer has done his pre-purchase scoping, he can consider giving up a longer escrow for something taken off the purchase price. I stress the "if" in that sentence. The danger in a short escrow is that the buyer's pre-offer scoping has missed something important that would turn up in a normal escrow term. First-time rural buyers should stay away from short escrows as a price-reduction tactic. As your experience grows, keep the idea in your tool kit.

WARRANTIES TO SURVIVE THE CONTRACT

In both a General Warranty Deed and a Special Warranty Deed, the seller gives the buyer three warranties—promises—that bind the seller to him in the future. These are: 1) the covenant of warranty forever or general warranty, in which the seller promises to defend the title against lawful claims and compensate the buyer for any loss from a successful claim to superior title; 2) covenant of quiet enjoyment, in which the seller promises that no claim of superior title will disturb the buyer's possession and enjoyment of the property; and 3) covenant of further assurances, in which the seller promises to execute any additional documents needed to perfect the title conveyed. The difference between the two types of deeds is that the seller's promises under a General Warranty Deed covers the property from its origins, whereas the seller's promise under the Special Warranty Deed is limited to his time of ownership. These are the only three covenants from the seller that survive the purchase contract unless additional language is included.

A seller often makes representations about his property and promises of one sort or another to encourage a buyer to proceed with a purchase. *For these statements to bind a seller after the sale*, the buyer's contract must include language, seller's "**warranties to survive closing**." The more specific these warranties are, the more enforceable they will be.

A standard real-estate contract will include language about "warranties that survive closing." This boilerplate usually has the seller promising that he has paid in full all construction/repair expenses that were undertaken within 120 days of closing; that the information in a listing agreement, if any, regarding connection to public sewerage or septic tank is correct to the best of his knowledge; that the seller has disclosed all material latent defects on the property that are known to the seller; and that the seller has disclosed any information that he possesses that materially and adversely affects the consideration to be paid by the Buyer. The seller is only warranting his disclosure of defects he knows or information he possesses. If he doesn't know something and doesn't possess information about a defect, he has no obligation to disclose anything. This is a reasonable standard when dealing with a good-faith buyer with nothing to hide, but it's less effective with a seller who wants to avoid disclosure.

The boilerplate warranty on disclosure relies on the seller's judgment as to what he thinks a material latent defect is; what he thinks he knows about such defects; and what information he believes he possesses (however, he defines possession) about what he thinks might materially and adversely affect the Buyer's "consideration" however the seller chooses to define that term. Whatever protection the boilerplate language provides in theory will be defined in practice when the buyer has to prove that a seller-known defect was not disclosed. Nonetheless, the boilerplate is better than nothing. If a seller-written contract fails to include it, the seller's promises about disclosure terminate with the close of escrow.

SELLER DISCLOSURE AND WARRANTY SURVIVAL: GET AS MUCH AS YOU CAN

Readers who have purchased houses should be familiar with the **standard disclosure forms** now in fairly common use. These forms are state-specific and vary in the questions asked of sellers and level of detail requested. Some states use an **environmental disclosure form** that asks sellers to disclose what they know about various hazards. Institutional lenders may require an environmental review or seller disclosure. Insurance companies may perform their own review of a property—screening for asbestos, PCBs, radon, USTs, waste sites, urea, lead paint, and air and water pollutants.

A buyer should always ask a FSBO or a seller's agent to see the seller's completed state-required disclosure forms before he submits a purchase offer.

Some standard real-estate disclosure forms give the seller a choice between completing the disclosure form and signing a **disclaimer** that says the seller is making no statement about the property's condition. Disclaimer amounts to a seller offering his property "as-is" while getting out of any obligation to disclose known problems. Disclaimers are a red-flag warning to buyers.

If either the disclosure form is less than adequate for your purposes or the seller signs the disclaimer, you should consider inserting a **disclosure contingency** into your purchase offer with a warranty that survives closing. This contingency should include broad disclosure language as well as a list of items, including defects, that you want the seller to think about in terms of disclosure, rather than leaving his thoughts to his own judgment.

Defects common to houses in both rural and urban/suburban areas include:

- Wet basement
- Crawlspace—unheated, not enough headroom, uninsulated, pipes subject to freezing

- Problems with sewerage/septic system—backups, undersized
- Water problems—pressure, quality, quantity, leaky pipes
- Radon gas in basement
- Infestation of wood-destroying insects—termites, beetles, ants
- Infestations of other creatures—bats, squirrels, bugs, rodents, snakes
- Mold
- Lead hazards—lead-based paint, lead solder in water pipes
- Urea-formaldehyde-based insulation (referred to as Urea-formaldehyde Foam Insulation [UFFI], which emits a gas that irritates some individuals.)
- Cracks, deterioration or shifts in foundations and concrete slabs
- Roof problems—leaks, gutters, water getting into eaves
- Asbestos—shingles, siding, hot-pipe insulation
- Inadequate draw in chimney flue; fire hazard in fireplace or chimney
- Inadequate ventilation in garages
- Inadequate mechanical ventilation in bathrooms and kitchens, or for furnaces
- Water pipes that tend to freeze
- Inoperable windows; warped doors
- Poor quality construction materials—composition board instead of plywood; cheap windows, doors, cabinets
- Old electrical system—lack of three-hole outlets; less than 200 amp service; old/unsafe wiring; no Ground Fault Indicators (GFIs) in bathrooms, kitchens; no wired smoke detectors

Defects common in farms and undeveloped rural property and other items about which you should seek disclosure, include:

- Unrecorded easements, licenses (permissions), life estates, rental agreements, donations, leases, reservations of interest, etc.
- Severance—minerals, water, other assets
- Boundary disputes, acreage discrepancies/shortages, encroachments
- Pollution from neighbors—water, light, noise, odors, visual, etc.
- Pollution on property—water (chemicals, fertilizer, hardness, softness, acidic, iron, sulfur, petroleum), dumps; underground storage (fuel) tanks; PCBs, invasive weeds
- Unauthorized use of property—chronic trespass problem; dumping; dogs running about; hunters
- Adverse potential—any situations that might qualify as adverse possession or adverse use; prescriptive use; easement by necessity
- Environmental restrictions—floodplain, wetlands, presence of ETS species, conservation easements, earthquake, windstorm, hurricane, wind-driven rain, coastal flooding/storm

surge, drought, lightning strikes, pests/disease in crops and/or timber, land enrolled in federal conservation programs, non-native weeds (kudzu, multiflora rose, Spotted Knapweed, Leafy Spurge, etc.)

- Physical conditions in land—arid/wet, water supply/quality, sinkholes, soils unsuitable for buyer's plans, septic sites won't perc, surface subsidence from underground mining; over-grazing; erosion

- Land-use restrictions—zoning restrictions

- Access problems—physical, legal

- Fencing issues—bad sections of fence that buyer will need to repair/replace; fencing inappropriate to buyer's plans; gates need to be replaced

- Operability and safety of farm infrastructure, equipment and machinery that will convey

- Soundness of farm buildings—roofs, electrical systems and foundations

The seller and/or his broker will say that the standard contract covers disclosure of each and every item above with boilerplate language such as the following:

Seller warrants that he has disclosed to Buyer and Brokers all material latent defects concerning the Premises that are known to Seller. Seller further warrants that he has disclosed to all parties any information, excluding opinions of value, that he possesses which materially and adversely affects the consideration to be paid by Buyer. (Arizona Association of Realtors "Residential Real Estate Purchase Contract and Receipt for Deposit," included in Galaty, *et. al*, Modern Real Estate Practice, 13th ed., p. 149.)

The devil in this excerpt lies both in the details that are provided and those that are not. This language lacks specificity from the buyer's perspective. While the seller is asked to disclose all defects that he judges to be both material and latent, what about defects that the seller judges not material and/or not latent? It is arguable that a material defect that is out in the open, such as a floodplain, overgrazing, erosion or a pine stand showing pine beetle infestation, is not latent and therefore need not be disclosed. It's far better to let the buyer judge whether a defect is worthy of mention than to leave it up to the seller. This standard language will give rise to differences of opinion, both large and small. An obvious defect, such as a sound but undersized bridge or a boundary encroachment that would be revealed in a survey if the buyer pays for one, may or may not need to be disclosed. What happens if the seller claims that he did not know of a material latent defect at the time of the contract? In many situations, he'll be able to shed liability. What happens if the seller claims he disclosed something orally and the buyer claims no such disclosure occurred?

Finally, why is the seller exempted from having to disclose defects and adverse information that he should reasonably know about? As a result of the corporate scandals in the early 2000s, Stephen M. Cutler, director of the Securities and Exchange Commission's enforcement division announced: "'If you [corporations, financial/accounting firms] know or have reason to know that you are helping a company mislead its investors, you are in violation of the federal securities laws.'" (Jerry Knight, "SEC: Look Out, Aiders and Abettors," Washington Post, August 4, 2003.) If a buyer does not hold a seller to this same standard, the seller can hide behind professed ignorance of the condition. This standard is less than the covenants of warranty forever and quiet enjoyment, which protect the buyer whether or not the seller knows about them at sale time.

I would consider holding the seller responsible for conditions about which it is reasonable to expect him to know, even though he may not. The justification for such a seemingly overly rigorous standard is simple: the buyer should not be expected to bear a future burden for the seller's present ignorance, deliberate or otherwise. This is exactly the standard that sellers are held to in a General Warranty Deed. The seller's lack of knowledge about a title defect or an encroachment doesn't exempt him from future responsibility and financial liability, at least in theory. The seller will object to this language. He may be trying to conceal a defect that he knows about but is not revealing. Or he may simply be objecting to the open-endedness of this language, an understandable position. You will have to determine how important this type of warranty is to you in relation to the property and the seller's capabilities.

State law governs most aspects of the seller's obligation (and that of his real-estate agent if one is involved) to disclose *latent* problems. The law assumes the buyer can discover on his own, or with the help of those he hires, manifest problems. Rural property often contains defects and adverse conditions that are perfectly visible to an inexperienced buyer, who, for that reason, will not understand the implications, hazards and remedial costs of what he sees. This happened to Jeanne Marie Laskas in western Pennsylvania when she saw the seller's pastures loaded with multiflora rose without understanding how this infestation reduced the land available for grazing, lowered the value of the land and would cost her thousands of dollars to bulldoze them out. When I was first starting out, I saw a sinkhole without understanding what it revealed about the porous limestone beneath it. I've seen a floodplain without comprehending its danger to a barn. I've seen a pasture filled with Viper's Bugloss without knowing what it was revealing about the soil underneath my feet or the (poor) quality of the grazing it would support. My own list of defects-seen-but-not-processed is not endless, but it does go on.

I've run into my share of material, latent problems that were never disclosed. One example represents the class. I was interested in buying a 425-acre tract that a real-estate agent said contained one million board feet of hardwood sawtimber. I knew the agent was knowledgeable about timber, so I put some preliminary faith in his judgment. The land lay on the West Virginia side of the Tug Fork River opposite Kentucky, about 35 minutes south of Huntington. It was a convenient commute over a good road. West Virginia has a disclosure form; neither the seller nor the agent disclosed anything. My partner, a consulting forester, smelled a rat long before I found it. "Fire damage," he said, when I told him where the land was. "Either from the railroad traffic or people setting fires. Sometimes you can see it; sometimes not. Depends how far back it occurred. Fire damage will ruin a butt log." So I called the county forester. "Yeah, I know the place," he said laughing. "I've been in this job 24 years. That hollow has been burned at least 15 of those years. The last time was two years ago. I'm in there almost every year, putting out arsons. I wouldn't give you $30,000 for that place [the sales price in 1989]." It was priced at $215,000. Assuming, for the sake of argument, that this property contained one million board feet of hardwood sawtimber, that level of fire damage would make almost all of that volume worthless. Is fire damage not a material, latent defect? Apparently, it wasn't—in the eyes of the seller and his agent.

While many states require sellers to sign property disclosure forms, the specifics of what is expected to be disclosed may not always clear to the seller. This grey area gets bigger when dealing with rural land and rural sellers, particularly those who assume the buyer will comprehend the significance of obvious conditions, such as mortality in certain tree species in the seller's forest or a seasonally swampy field the buyer visits in the dry season that cannot be used for a residence or a septic system. Disclosure laws may not provide sufficient guidance concerning how significant a defect must be before the seller is expected to reveal it. Is the disclosure requirement limited to current problems or does it reach back for the length of the seller's ownership…and beyond? The absence of a current problem in a condition that routinely recurs every ten years should be disclosed, but may not be. What about latent problems the seller thinks could become manifest in the future? And what about conditions that exist in the neighborhood but not on the property itself, such as low-flying military jets practicing maneuvers over sparsely populated rural areas; or a mat of habitat-destroying, propeller-fouling hydrilla (*Hydrilla verticilata*, the most challenging aquatic weed in much of the U.S.) next to the seller's lakefront house; or a Saturday-only, dirt-bike race track on the neighboring farm?

Before meeting with the seller or submitting a contract, work up a list of potential defects to submit to him, first for discussion, possibly as disclosure inclusions in your contract. These would be general possibilities, as well as items that you noticed on your visits. You can append a winnowed list of disclosure items to your contract and request that the seller disclose any information he has on any of the items on the list, *and any other item*, that would adversely affect your occupation, use and enjoyment of the property. Your list, you tell the seller, is not meant to be exhaustive. It's representative and illustrative of defects, broadly conceived. You want him to disclose any problems that you have not listed that would adversely affect you. If a "reasonable person" would consider something such a defect, tell the seller to disclose it. The buyer needs to give the seller a chance to disclose **"any other condition or fact that would adversely affect the buyer's possession, use and enjoyment of the property**," both in conversation and in his contract. Work through each item with the seller. Keep a copy of your list with his responses. Note the date of your discussion on the list. Provide a copy of the list with your notes to the seller.

You need to be tactful and polite in this process. You're not trying to incriminate the seller or place him under Gestapo-like interrogation. Your tone in talking about your concerns can establish a working relationship even when your questions are pointed.

If the seller gets testy or stonewalls when you ask for full and specific disclosure, he may be concealing something that's important to your plans. Your objective is to get him to disclose prior to submitting your offer. This allows you to discuss remedies and shape your offering price. Failure of the seller to disclose defects and, more broadly, adverse items known to him, gives the buyer grounds for a post-purchase lawsuit if that becomes necessary. But post-purchase lawsuits are a buyer's least-preferred option.

When you encounter a situation where you need the type of disclosure that conventional research and standard disclosure forms are not yielding, try something different. Once you have the property under contract with at least one 45-day contingency (results acceptable to the buyer) included, take out an ad in the local newspaper for two or three weeks, such as the one below:

NOTICE OF PENDING PURCHASE

I have a contract to buy John Blow's 105 acres on Honest Eddie's Road in Highhope County. It's tax map A-1-10 in the Big Spring District, DB 98, PN 45. The property lies three miles north of Smitty's sawmill on the left.

I would appreciate learning as much about this property as possible during the next three weeks, by October 30th. Please send me any information that you think is relevant to my purchase, such as unrecorded easements or rights of way; leases or rental arrangements; boundary disputes; access problems; uncertainty over water supply or water rights; sale of any of the property's assets, such as timber or minerals; possession or use of this property without the owner's permission, and so on.

If anyone has a claim against this property, now is the time to make me aware of it. I will protect your identity and privacy.

Please send your letter to me:

Mr. Innocent Buystander
Big City, USA

I have never had to do this myself, but I would consider it in the appropriate circumstances. Make sure that you take the ad out after you have the seller's signature on your purchase offer contract. You also need to have a contingency included; otherwise, you can't void the contract without penalty. You must receive the information at least a week or so before your contingency expires, to give you time to investigate. I see nothing wrong, legally or ethically, in doing this, but I would run the idea by my local lawyer before going ahead. You should anticipate some ill-feeling from the seller, which you should weigh into your decision. You may want to show the seller your proposed ad after he signs your contract so that he's not totally blindsided. Where a seller signs a disclaimer, I would not hesitate to take out an advertisement of this sort. This ad would smoke out a **right of first refusal** held by a neighbor and properly set forth in his deed but not in the seller's. I know of one example when a seller signed a contract with an out-of-town buyer even though he knew that his neighbor held a valid right of first refusal. By chance, the neighbor ran into the seller's lawyer at a social event just in time.

The buyer wants two things from the seller. First, he wants full disclosure prior to submitting an offer, and, second, he wants every seller's promise of no problem to survive closing. This is no different from the seller's perspective than what is implied in the standard disclosure form, namely, that the buyer can sue the seller for remedy if the seller fails to disclose a problem that he was required to reveal under state law.

What I am proposing is that the buyer may need to enlarge the normal items of required disclosure, make the items specific by listing them and make the seller's post-purchase warranties explicit.

Buyers should understand that misrepresentation/disclosure suits are expensive and difficult to win. Sellers defend by saying that they did not need to disclose problems about which they did not know; or conditions they had fixed; or problems the buyer should have seen and understood on his own; or something that the seller failed to understand was a latent defect at the time of the sale; or some small defect that inexplicably became big only after the sale; or conditions that the buyer's due diligence, including a home inspection, should have revealed. To prevail, the buyer must prove that the seller had knowledge of a problem, and then intentionally misrepresented it to the buyer either by saying nothing or by saying something that was misleading. The buyer may have to prove that the seller did not orally inform him of the defect. The buyer also has to prove that he suffered monetary damages as a result of the seller's actions. If the seller signed the disclaimer, a lawsuit becomes even harder to win.

An excellent article on this subject offered a rule of thumb in the Washington metropolitan area: aggrieved buyers should forget about claims for damages of less than $20,000. (Daniela Deane, "Truth or Consequences: How Much to Tell Buyers is Tricky Terrain for Sellers," <u>Washington Post</u>, July 5, 2003.) The misrepresentation issues most frequently cited in the Washington area involved wet basements, termites, roof leaks, sewers, wells and septic tanks. Since lawyer time in the country is less expensive, the 2006 rural threshold might be that buyers pass on misrepresentation suits of less than $7,500. The deciding variable regarding to sue or not may be whether your local lawyer thinks the local court will award you attorney's fees in addition to direct damages. To win in a financial sense, the buyer has to prove fraud, then prove damages (i.e., what the seller's fraudulent behavior cost the buyer), then persuade the judge that the damages are as much as is claimed, then convince the same judge that the seller should pay the buyer's lawyer's fees as part of the award. If attorney's fees are not granted, the money you win as compensation may not break you even on the suit.

In theory, where a seller agrees that his warranties survive closing it should mean that the seller stands ready to compensate the buyer for any covered loss during the buyer's ownership without a lawsuit. The covenants included in a General Warranty Deed generally last only for the buyer's term. The succeeding owner (you) assume these liabilities for the next owner, your buyer. Warranties, outside of the deed, should have **time caps** to be fair to both parties. Appliances (personal property) that convey might carry a six-month cap; house systems, one year and so on. Some warranties and time caps on warranties can be bargaining chips. Do not time-cap any covenants and warranties in the seller's deed.

So what happens in the real world when you think a warranty covers a problem that arises a couple of years after you take possession? It depends, of course, on the facts, law and individuals. The seller may no longer be alive or accessible. The seller may not be financially able to defend his warranty to you or compensate you for damages. If the cost of fixing the problem is less than your attorney's projected fees, you might be wise to do nothing to enforce your warranty. Extended title insurance might help on some claims. Warranties, I think, are most enforceable the closer in time they are to when they were given. That's not fair, and it's not the law, but that, I think, will be the practical application in most cases. Your best chance of winning lies with a warranty dispute that happens within your first year of ownership.

Warranties, even those clad in the stoutest iron, can be unenforceable. But the minimum value of writing in warranties to survive closing is to scare the seller into dealing honestly with you and revealing problems about which he knows. And that is worth a lot to a buyer, particularly when he is able to use the anticipated cost of remedying disclosed problems to reduce the purchase price.

Here is language for a disclosure-and-warranty contingency that you might discuss with your local lawyer:

> **Buyer's offer is contingent on Seller disclosing to Buyer in writing within 20 calendar days of this Contract taking effect all conditions in the Property, latent or manifest, including, but not limited to, those involving title, ownership, rights, interests, warranties, assets, boundaries, easements, encroachments, encumbrances, access, improvements, environmental hazards and conditions, natural resources, law and regulation that could in the mind of a reasonable individual adversely affect the Buyer's occupation, use and enjoyment of the Property.**
>
> **Buyer may void this Contract without penalty if Seller either fails to comply with this disclosure requirement or if any disclosure is unacceptable to him. If the Buyer voids this Contract, his security deposit shall be returned in full within five (5) business days of providing the Seller written notice.**
>
> **Failure to disclose said conditions of which Seller knows or should reasonably know does not exempt Seller from his responsibilities after closing. Seller shall bear the responsibility and liability for those conditions that adversely affect the Buyer's possession, use and enjoyment of the property, which conditions pre-dated closing, and were either known or should have reasonably been known by the Seller. "Conditions" are to be broadly construed and would include facts, disputes, claims, defects, issues of reliability and capacity in systems, lack of service capability (cell phones, electricity, sewage, trash pick up, etc.), annoyances, trespass, restrictions on property use and so forth.**
>
> **Seller and Buyer shall discuss each disclosure and decide whether a remedy is needed and how the cost of any such remedy shall be apportioned.**
>
> **All warranties from Seller under this Contract, including, but not limited to those in the General Warranty Deed, shall survive closing.**

The question of how long any particular warranty survives is not specified. A court would apply a reasonableness rule when warranty length is a matter of judgment rather than law. The parties can establish whatever time caps or dollar caps they agree are fair and reasonable. If you find this language cumbersome, you might write a simpler section and append a list of things you want the seller to consider for possible disclosure.

In sum, the buyer protects himself against seller misrepresentations and failure to disclose by: 1) thorough pre-offer scoping; 2) understanding the strengths and weaknesses of the standard disclosure statement; 3) including contract contingencies that allow additional investigations; 4) inserting a disclosure-

and-warranty contingency in the purchase contract; and 5) providing in the purchase contract that the seller's warranties, regarding disclosure and other matters, survive closing.

SECURITY DEPOSITS: THEIR USES

The buyer normally gives an escrow agent a **security deposit** (also referred to as **earnest money, hand money, consideration** or **good-faith deposit**) at the time he submits his purchase offer to the seller.

The escrow agent should be someone on the buyer's side of the transaction, such as the local lawyer the buyer is using. Don't use the seller's lawyer as the escrow agent if you can avoid it. You may run into difficulty in retrieving your deposit if you have to void the contract in adversarial circumstances. Where the buyer is working through a real-estate broker, the deposit would routinely be held in the brokerage's escrow/trust account. The buyer can insist that the deposit be held by his lawyer instead, which may or may not succeed. The alternative is to deposit the earnest money with a neutral escrow agent—recommended by the buyer's lawyer. A real-estate broker who is working for the seller is not exactly neutral from the buyer's perspective. If you don't want the seller's broker to hold your deposit, simply submit a purchase contract through your lawyer and deposit your money in his trust account. If you are using a standard real-estate contract, you will have to do a small bit of editing in its text to accomplish this. **Never give your deposit directly to the seller, especially to a FSBO!** Never give your deposit to anyone without getting a receipt in return and/or a paper trail documenting it. Never put your deposit in anything other than an escrow, or trust, account, held by a lawyer, escrow agent or licensed broker.

The buyer's deposit is intended to show and secure his willingness to perform on the contract. It is supposed to prove to the seller that the buyer is serious. The deposit is the buyer's money that is at risk in an offer. (But this risk is minimal if the buyer uses contingencies with results acceptable to the buyer.) If the buyer fails to perform on the purchase for any reason once all contingencies are resolved, compensation to the seller should be limited in the buyer's contract to the escrowed deposit, a concept known as **liquidated damages**. The buyer gets his full deposit back if he voids the contract because the contingency results are unacceptable. The buyer's money is not at risk in any way until after the buyer removes all contingencies, that is, accepts results, resolves a contingency issue with the seller or allows the contingency to expire without invoking it.

Sellers prefer larger rather than smaller deposits, because they think it increases both the likelihood of performance and provides more compensation if the buyer fails to perform. I have my doubts. If a buyer decides that he is unable to perform after removing his contingencies, the size of the deposit won't persuade him to go through with the deal. Larger deposits do provide the seller with more compensation, but they also increase the likelihood of costly, lose-lose litigations when a deal falls apart. A shrewd seller might propose to a buyer that he will accept a one percent earnest-money deposit instead of the normal three percent if the buyer will increase his offering price by $1,000.

Real-estate agents (working for the seller) often advise a buyer to make a deposit of sufficient size to make it worth the seller's time to sign his contract—the bigger, the better. In some cases, this may help a buyer, such as when several buyers are submitting contracts at about the same time. But I'm skeptical of the argument in most cases. I think selling price and, then, terms drive sellers, not the size of a deposit. Your signed contract will discourage other buyers from coming forward with backup offers. It's that discouragement effect for which your deposit should compensate the seller, because that's his risk. The valuation of that risk depends on the specifics of the property and the local market. In a hot seller's market, there is arguably no risk to the seller. If you're proposing a shorter-than-typical escrow, give the seller a smaller-than-typical deposit.

A buyer who has done his pre-purchase scoping can feel confident in putting down a larger rather than smaller deposit if only because his contract will contain contingencies that, if exercised, void the contract and activate return of his earnest money without penalty. Buyers can negotiate concessions in price and terms in return for larger deposits. Larger deposits—even with contingencies—can bring a seller to your contract. You can always propose a large increase in your deposit in return for the seller agreeing to disclose-and-warranty language. If the seller agrees, you will have much more confidence in your purchase, which allows you to increase your deposit.

The other way to think about a security deposit is to offer it to the seller in two stages. The first deposit—a token—is made when the buyer submits his contract. The second—a larger one—is due when the buyer removes all contingencies, indicating that he will perform. The first stage of a contract may be larded with contingencies, which the buyer uses to justify a two-step deposit.

The buyer accomplishes several goals in a **two-step deposit**. First, he minimizes the amount of his money that's at risk during the early phase of the contract when the chance of a deal blowing up can be high. Contingencies protect this money in the early phase. Second, he retains his money a little longer, earning a bit of interest. Third, he gives the seller a real incentive to help him resolve problems that arise during the contingency investigations. Finally, he builds a process of working together with the seller.

Security money in escrow may earn interest for the buyer in some states. In others, escrow interest is taken and used to fund public goods, such as legal services. In states that allow the buyer to keep the interest, the amount that accrues over the two or three months of a typical escrow at passbook rates is small. Conceding this interest to the seller has psychological and negotiating value.

Earnest money goes to the seller at closing once all the buyer's contingencies are satisfied or removed and all terms have been met on both sides. Accordingly, a buyer who deposits $2,500 as earnest money in a non-interest-bearing escrow for a $100,000 purchase, has to come up with $97,500 at closing, in addition to closing costs.

Sometimes, a buyer will tag his deposit with a "subject to" condition, such as, the deposit or the purchase is subject to approval of a relative. It's hard for me to imagine why a seller would sign a contract with such an "escape clause," but some do. This is too tricky for my tool kit.

If the buyer fails to perform on the contract for reasons outside the various contingencies his contract includes, the seller can **sue for specific performance** to force the buyer to do the deal on the terms offered and accepted. Such a suit can be a disaster for the buyer. The usual reasons for a buyer's failure to perform involve an unexpected change in personal or financial circumstances, or last-minute surprise information that fundamentally alters the buyer's interest in a purchase. But the buyer is exposed to the seller's demand for performance only if he has failed to include a **liquidated-damages section** in this contract. This language limits the buyer's exposure for bailing out to his deposit:

> **The Parties agree that Buyer will relinquish his deposit to Seller as liquidated damages in the event that Buyer fails to perform on this Contract once all contingencies are satisfied or removed. This payment shall be Seller's sole remedy for Buyer's failure to perform. Any fees due real-estate brokers shall be paid from this deposit.**

Liquidated-damages language gives the seller quick and litigation-free compensation for the buyer's breach. The seller gives up a theoretical and a lot of hard-to-get money (performance) for a small but guaranteed amount of cash (deposit, possibly less some or all of a broker's fee). Liquidated damages shields both buyer and seller from having to go through a contentious and expensive lawsuit over performance. If your contract does not contain a liquidated-damages section, the seller will get your deposit and then sue you for performance.

There is one other security-money tactic that you might find an occasion to use. Most buyers try to put in as little security money as they can, because they fear its loss. As I've shown above, a properly worded contingency—with results acceptable to the buyer—will protect your deposit. Go at the seller from a different direction: if his asking price is $100,000, offer him $60,000 to $70,000 with a deposit of $25,000. Your message is that you are a serious buyer, but your scoping has proved that his asking price is demonstrably above market. Couple this with a results-acceptable-to-the-buyer contingency, of course. And then offer to increase the deposit by $10,000 once you remove all contingencies. This may help you with a seller who knowingly has inflated his asking price. This tactic is strengthened when the tax-assessed value of the property is in the $60,000 to $70,000 range, and you base your offering price on that publicly available number.

I know an investor who prefers optioning land to buying and taking title. His business is to option land and then get a significant portion resold before his option runs out. If he doesn't get a sufficient portion under contract (contingent, of course, on his purchase of the land), he loses his option money. An **option to purchase** allows its holder to buy the land at a set price for some period of time—the option period. Option agreements expire if they are not exercised. The option buyer gives his "option money" to the seller in return for this right to purchase at the agreed price during the option period. Option money may be larger than a deposit if it ties up the seller's property for a long period of time. The option period can start either before or after the buyer has done his due diligence and has removed contingencies. The seller keeps the buyer's option money if the buyer fails to exercise his option and make the purchase by a specific date. Option money is typically between two and three percent of the purchase price on smaller deals and less on large deals. This investor's game is high-stakes gambling, and I do not advise readers to try it. The longer the option period, the better are the chances to make the deal work. My acquaintance always tries to get a six-month option, or longer.

One tactic I've learned from him is that it's usually handy to include an **extension clause** in a purchase contract or an option contract that allows the buyer to lengthen the closing by another 30 to 60 days in return for increasing the amount of the deposit. Time is bought by upping the buyer's ante. If you anticipate needing extra time to complete pre-closing investigations or allow for the contingent sale of a few lots from the target property, put an extension in your contract. If you don't have a buyer-activated extension opener in the contract, the seller may not agree to give you more time. Use an extension when the odds of a deal working out for you are strongly in your favor. Don't play "in for a dime, in for a dollar" unless you're prepared to lose your dollar. If an extension will help you strip risk out of the purchase, then it's worthy of serious consideration. The cost of extending a contract that you know you're going to complete is cheaper—far cheaper—to you than closing and paying a month or two of mortgage interest.

Earnest money—your deposit—is not funny money. It's your cash, and you can lose it if your contract doesn't protect it. I've seen deposits of between $2,000 and $325,000 lost when buyers couldn't perform. However, when a contract is properly written with a results-acceptable-to-the-buyer contingency, your deposit is not at risk until you remove the contingency.

DEPOSITS: SIZE MAY OR MAY NOT MATTER

An earnest-money deposit must be at least a dollar, but its actual size is a matter of negotiation between buyer and seller. How big should it be?

Sellers generally believe that a buyer is more likely to go through with a purchase if a big deposit is escrowed. Under a liquidated-damages clause, the buyer's failure to perform brings the deposit to the seller. The deposit may or may not be reduced by broker fees, depending on contract language and circumstances. The seller's logic—larger deposit levers the buyer toward performance—only works with a buyer who has removed all contingencies or accepted their results. During the time when contingencies are operating, the size of a deposit does not work against a buyer because he can get it back without penalty. A buyer should be 100 percent committed to performance before removing the last of his contingencies.

However, even in the most carefully thought out deal, a buyer's circumstances can suddenly change for the worse. A buyer may find himself facing a choice between losing his deposit or performing on a contract that he no longer wants. Buyers in this bind are of two sorts: those who want to perform but unexpectedly find themselves unable to do so and those who can perform but no longer want do so. The seller's logic—size of deposit matters—does not apply to the unable because, by definition, the purchase is now beyond his means. His impending breach is a matter of necessity, not discretion. He will lose his deposit as liquidated damages; a larger deposit doesn't force him into performance. Buyers who can perform but no longer want to might be influenced by deposit size, but I doubt that will occur in most situations because of the seriousness of the adverse surprise that has turned around their buy decision. Accordingly, I think the seller's belief—large deposit is incentive to perform—is largely specious, because it applies to so few cases. If a seller demands a large deposit, I would walk him through this analysis in an effort to loosen his grip on a false premise. If he's not persuaded, write into your contract a provision that increases the size of your liquidated-damages obligation if you fail to perform after all contingencies are removed or satisfied.

Where a contract does not contain a liquidated-damages clause, the size of the deposit may be functionally irrelevant to getting the buyer to perform. Absent such a clause, a buyer is open to being sued for performance if he doesn't want to perform. The size of the deposit has no bearing on the buyer's behavior since he is on the hook for the entire amount. A buyer without a liquidated-damages clause must begin negotiations with the seller to buy his way out of performance, making the best deal he can.

From a buyer's perspective, I would not hesitate to increase a deposit in exchange for some seller concession as long as the buyer has at least one contingency—with results acceptable to buyer—in place. That's a smart use of deposit money.

The buyer's deposit, regardless or size, is at risk of loss only after the buyer removes all contingencies. Therefore, it's often sensible to offer a very small deposit—say $500 or $1,000—as a good-faith gesture and then agree to a substantial increase once all contingencies are resolved. At that point, the buyer should feel comfortable about performing and all of the financing will be in place. Sellers, I think, will be inclined to go along with a two-step deposit once the buyer lays out these arguments and agrees to make the second deposit larger than might be expected. In effect, this approach allows the buyer to purchase an option to buy at no cost and no risk, which the buyer converts into a binding contract with the second deposit.

Take these tactics one step further. Offer the seller a very small deposit…along with a closing within one week of your removal/satisfaction with your last contingency. The seller should understand that he has no sale until the buyer removes all contingencies, regardless of the size of escrowed deposit. On a 90-day escrow, all contingencies might be resolved in the first 45 days. While there are reasons to close at the end of 90 days, the last 45 days are risky to both parties. It should be worth something to the seller to not have to sweat out those last escrow weeks. Increase the seller's security in your purchase by giving up that time, unless, of course, you need it for some reason. A shorter escrow will cost a buyer something, because you will be starting to pay mortgage interest six weeks earlier. So you need to judge whether the concession you're getting from the seller is worth the price you'll pay.

Submitting a contract with a low-ball deposit will work only when you explain to the seller your reasons for doing so and explain that he really doesn't have much of an interest in a larger sum. If you simply submit a contract with a low-ball deposit, the seller will question your intentions and capabilities. A small deposit with a short closing should push the parties to work together to get contingency issues resolved. The seller should be helpful because he will see that his money is a lot closer to his hand in a 45-day closing than in a 90. Since the contingencies keep the buyer's deposit out of the seller's grasp for the length of the contingency period, the seller should realize that insisting on a large deposit doesn't get him real security.

In my experience, a short closing is worth something to the seller. It's far better than language that provides for a "closing within 90 days, or sooner by mutual agreement," which gives the seller nothing for certain. In practice, the buyer often has no incentive to close sooner. The "or sooner" bait simply increases the seller's crankiness as he sweats out the last half of escrow. Sellers won't concede anything for "or sooner."

As I wrote this in the spring of 2006, I was toying with submitting a purchase offer on a timber tract with a **jumbo deposit**, perhaps 30 to 50 percent of the purchase price. The seller was uncooperative and refused to supply any information about his property. His real-estate agent has announced that he will accept no contingencies, despite the property being landlocked with uncertain acreage. The only reason to be interested in this piece is that its merchantable timber value is about double the seller's asking price. If my scoping cleared up all the uncertainties, a big deposit might have squashed seller roadblocks, eliminate competition and justify a slightly lower offer. But maybe not. I wasn't quite there.

And in the end, I never got there. A neighbor got in line first.

TIME I: TIME IS NOT OF THE ESSENCE

Most standard real-estate contracts include a section: "Time is of the essence." What does that mean to the buyer?

It means the seller can void the contract if the buyer does not act on its provisions and contingencies by their specific written deadlines. Since most—and often all—such deadlines fall on the buyer, the seller wants "time is of the essence" in the contract so the buyer does not intentionally dawdle. When a buyer agrees to this language, he may ultimately face a choice: either go ahead with the purchase even if one or more of his contingencies cannot be resolved within its specified deadline or lose the contract altogether. Sellers who have an acceptable **backup contract** in hand may not or may not agree to give their first buyer an extension. A seller in that situation judges which of the two buyers is most likely to perform and at what selling price.

It's fair for a seller to expect the buyer to move forward on the contract in a timely fashion. Both parties share a common interest in performance. Buyers should assure sellers of their good-faith intention to perform while resisting, if possible, the draconian straitjacket of "time is of the essence." The buyer might propose that his contingencies be worded with some wiggle room:

> **This _____ contingency will be removed or invoked no later than 45 days from the date this Contract takes effect. Buyer may extend this deadline by five (5) business days on his own initiative and without penalty. Seller may grant Buyer additional time upon Buyer's request.**

Where a seller has bargained hard for a short closing, he will be reluctant to agree to extensions. In such circumstances, the buyer should assess the seller's options. If the seller has an equal to or better alternative than to grant the buyer's request, he's likely to refuse.

I have used "time is of the essence" and a short closing on several occasions to prevent a seller from coming down with seller's remorse. I do this only when I am absolutely sure that I have scoped the property thoroughly and negotiated favorable terms. As a rule, I would not include a "time is of the essence" provision since it rarely functions in a way that benefits buyers.

TIME II: FIRST RESPONSE

A critical consideration for the buyer is **how much response time to give to the seller** when submitting a purchase contract.

Real-estate agents working for the seller may suggest as much as two weeks. Where the seller is out of town, or hard to reach, or involves several parties, a week is fair. But I think being time-short rather than time-long is generally in the buyer's best interest, especially when other buyers are preparing offers. I have seen offers appear within a three-day window that are just slightly better than the one submitted. Sellers are not above using one buyer's offer to extract slightly better terms from a competitor.

In most circumstances, the buyer should make his offer good for no more than 24 hours. This will not prevent a cagey real-estate agent from having another client slip in his offer, but it will make it harder. A 24-hour window works well during the week, but not when it's submitted between Friday and Sunday. Submit your offer Monday through Thursday if possible.

If the reader thinks I'm paranoid about real-estate agents, I offer this anecdote. Some 1,500 acres was for sale at $1.3 million through a United Country broker in West Virginia. When I visited the property on behalf of a client, the seller's broker told me another offer was coming in. He had not mentioned that on the phone. He volunteered that it was not a full-price offer. My client quickly made a full-price offer with a couple of reasonable contingencies, but he gave the seller and his broker too much response time. The broker announced that the other buyer had suddenly submitted a full-price offer with no contingencies, which the seller had accepted. This broker, who was working for the seller, told the other buyer about the terms of our offer. One mistake we made was in giving the seller more than 24 hours. The second was in not including a **strict confidentiality provision** in the contract that prohibited both seller and his broker from revealing the terms of our offer. The other buyer, incidentally, should feel miffed too. This broker used our offer as leverage to get him to raise his and strip it of contingencies, which put him at risk. A broker working for the seller has no obligation to preserve the confidentiality of a buyer's offer from what I can determine. A buyer can, of course, insist on confidentiality and demand that the broker sign such a provision. Keeping your offer open for as short a period as possible will lessen the chance of a broker playing this game.

If you find yourself in this situation, write a confidentiality statement into your offer that prohibits the seller's broker from sharing the terms of your offer with anyone other than the seller.

> **Broker agrees to keep the price, terms and conditions of the Buyer's offer confidential and shall not disclose them—or allow them to be disclosed—to any party other than Seller.**
>
> **Broker's dated signature in the margin of this Contact indicates his acceptance of this provision.**

Anticipate that the broker will object to signing this restriction. Tell him to get the seller's approval if he thinks he needs it. If the broker continues to fidget and stonewall, you may have uncovered his plan to work you against another buyer. If that is your hunch, make your offer good for no more than a few hours. You can always extend it.

WHEN A BUYER LAYS A TRAP

A few buyers I know offer sellers contracts with a time-related, spring-loaded trap. It goes like this. The buyer gives the seller 24 or 48 hours to reject in writing the contract offer. If the seller does not do so, the buyer's contract asserts that the contract shall be deemed accepted by the seller.

This is a self-defeating approach, because it undercuts the trust and mutual problem-solving that a buyer should be promoting. Moreover, I doubt that the buyer could persuade a judge to enforce a purchase in circumstances where no meeting of the minds existed and no contract was signed.

NEGOTIATION WITHIN THE CONTRACT

Purchase contracts are not symmetrical. Buyers usually have to do more than a few things before closing while sellers may have to do nothing but sweat out the buyer's efforts. If the buyer does not obtain acceptable results in all of his contingencies, his contract should allow him to void his offer without penalty and have his earnest money returned in full.

While voiding his contract is one choice, the buyer has another option available when contingency results adversely impact the buyer's pre-offer estimate of property value. The buyer realizes that he has offered too much, now that he has the results in hand. The buyer should take the new information to the seller and ask for one of two responses—either remedy the problem if it's remediable, or, alternatively, agree to a lower purchase price to reflect the new information and the buyer's willingness to accept the property "as is." When a buyer proposes to negotiate a modification to the purchase contract arising from a contingency, the seller faces an identical choice: say no, whereupon the contract becomes void, or negotiate in an effort to salvage a deal.

Once the buyer notifies the seller in writing that results are unacceptable, he should make sure that the seller agrees that the contract's time limits are suspended until the parties decide what they want to do. When negotiations produce a resolution within the time window of the contingency, the buyer is not at risk. If, on the other hand, informal negotiations extend beyond the contingency's time frame, the seller may claim at some arbitrary point that he now expects full performance given that the contingency deadline has passed. Even though the buyer has told the seller that results are unacceptable, he has not formally voided the contract. So it can be argued that the contract is still in effect with a running clock. The seller can argue that the buyer told him that results were unacceptable, but did not notify him that he was voiding the contract on that basis. This is less than honorable behavior—and may be part of an effort to hammer the buyer into going through with the contract in some form or another. The buyer should protect himself against this tactic by having the seller sign an amendment to the contract, extending the contingency deadline to allow for additional negotiations. If the seller does not grant an extension, the buyer can agree to go ahead with the contract or immediately terminate his offer in writing.

Whether a buyer can get a seller to negotiate with him depends on the type of problem that the contingency turned up, its seriousness and cost and, finally, the other options available to the seller. A buyer who tries to hammer the seller with new information into a huge price discount will be turned down. A smaller bite can work, but not always. I've seen excessive demands push a rural seller into walking away from negotiations when his pride trumps his economic self-interest. It's one thing to horse-trade, but it's quite another for a rural seller to feel that he is being gamed by the "city" buyer. The seller must feel that the buyer is being genuine, reasonable and fair in his requests, not greedy or bullying. The buyer should approach the seller with a willingness to concede something in return for the seller's willingness to help out on the contingency results. This is a delicate time for both buyer and seller. It requires a buyer to bring reasonableness and tact to the table.

Having made the above point, I should add that a buyer who has done his pre-offer scoping should not be surprised by a contingency result. The point of scoping is to eliminate surprises and accurately value property prior to making an offer.

Good scoping gives a buyer a chance to game a seller with a non-surprise surprise result, which is used to force a price discount from a seller now invested in the buyer's offer. There may be sellers who deserve this, and there may be buyers who can bring it off without blowing up the deal. I've not tried it myself, and I don't think I would feel quite right about it.

A NON-DEAL DEAL: SELLER'S REMORSE

A type of seller exists who thinks a better offer will materialize from somewhere the moment he signs your purchase contract. He reasons that if you are willing to buy his property for $100,000, somebody "out there" will pay $110,000. A sale at $100,000 is, therefore, too cheap; I'm losing money, he thinks. This is seller's remorse, and it can occur whether the seller is right or wrong about his new intuition, and whether or not he's making a considerable profit on the $100,000 sale. The buyer has no contractual obligation to better his offer, but some circumstances may warrant a voluntary buyer concession to grease the skids even when the buyer need not do so.

Feigned seller's remorse is a tactic I've seen a seller use to create conditions within the contract that are adverse to the buyer in hope he will increase the contract price. Sellers have many ways to gum up a contract after signing it. They can be unhelpful in providing access—keys to locks on gates and house visits not being accommodated; FSBOs failing to show up at arranged meetings; a large freshly cut tree suddenly sprawls across a woods road, blocking access. They can stall and stonewall the buyer's requests for information. They can claim they can't find information they had led you to believe was available. They can refuse to discuss any contract revisions when a buyer's contingency results reveal an unexpected surprise. This seller is playing a risky game, because he may lose you—a buyer under contract—through his artifice to avoid remedying a contingency result or his interest in picking out a bit more money from the buyer's pocketbook.

When the buyer feels that the seller is faking remorse, it's best to stick with the original offer. Any willingness to negotiate is likely to harm the buyer's current position. This is a bluff worth calling. But like all called bluffs, you may lose the hand.

Signs of seller remorse, genuine or phony, are always easy to recognize. The seller starts whining about how good a deal the buyer "was given." The seller discovers new information showing one asset or another to be worth more than he previously communicated. The seller starts complaining about how the sale will work a hardship on him. He says a better offer has just come through as a backup contract and waves paper under the buyer's nose. (The buyer will not know whether this backup is genuine or a dummy submitted by the seller's third cousin, currently collecting seashells on Grand Cayman Island in lieu of making license plates under state supervision.) Some sellers like to play this kind of poker.

But most don't play a serious game with a real-estate contract, because they don't want to lose the sale, even when it's not quite what they wanted. Buyers can usually count on the seller's self-interest in making the sale overriding the inevitable second thoughts. Don't hesitate to remind the remorseful seller of the old homily: a bird in hand is worth two in the bush. And keep in mind that your contract does not require you to do anything more than fulfill the terms of your offer: you don't have to pander to the seller's insecurities. But a buyer may have to test the authenticity of the seller's remorse. If he's feigning for tactical reasons, hold your ground or give him a face-saving throwaway. If he genuinely wants to get out of the contract, meet all deadlines and perform.

If a seller stonewalls your effort to renegotiate after your house-inspection contingency reveals a latent $50,000 roof problem that your pre-offer scoping failed to detect, remind the seller that he will now have to disclose the bad roof to every buyer coming after you. Signing a disclaimer may or may not allow a seller to avoid disclosure of a now-documented defect, depending on state law. Once you put disclosure into the mix, the seller may decide that he'll net no more money from the backup contract than he would from you. You may have to exert pressure by writing a letter to both seller and his broker that discusses the hidden roof problem. Attach the inspection report. You may even have to send a copy to the state agency that handles real-estate disclosure issues. Buyer disclosure can trump seller remorse.

All this advice changes if the seller has a genuine **backup contract** in hand that's better than yours. As long as the buyer removes contingencies or accepts their results in writing within the deadlines and satisfies all other terms, the purchase should go through. But sellers may start throwing monkey wrenches into the gears. This buyer needs to recognize that this seller has no incentive to negotiate over contingency results. You may have to buy the property "as is" on the contract's terms or abandon the purchase.

ANNOYANCE, NUISANCE AND TRESPASS

I have never seen a purchase contract ask the seller to disclose problems related to annoyance, nuisance and trespass. I think it's a good idea whose time should come.

A nuisance in the law is thought of as an activity by one property owner that unreasonably annoys or seriously affects the use and enjoyment of the property of reasonable others. A public or private nuisance does not exist until a court says so. The court can then order a remedy. Absent a finding of nuisance, the condition is an annoyance that neighbors have to endure. Annoyances/nuisances can be noise, pollution, odors, wood smoke from an outdoor wood-burning furnace, safety hazards, bright lights, headlights in your window, visual obstructions (that ruin a view), commercial activities or social activities.

Rural property is often burdened with annoyances that are not obvious to the first-time visitor—a kennel of dogs next door who sleep during the day and bark at night, extra-bright "security" lights, late-night socializing, pungent but episodic odors, chemical fumes, late-night chainsaw testing, teenagers on ATVs and dirt bikes, unauthorized trash dumping (visible in winter, but not in summer), early morning wake ups, the seller's driveway that is used as the community turn-around, a colony of fighting cocks crowing their challenges 24/7, target practice with automatic weapons and unscheduled varmint shooting.

Certain buyer-perceived "nuisances" may be no more than routine life in the country. Such things are to be anticipated and accommodated. Farms, it must be remembered, are large, mechanized workplaces, not oil paintings. Farmers manure their fields in the spring. Calves bawl for three or four days when they are weaned. Rifle-firing hunters roam woods and fields. Logging trucks and tractors are inevitably noisy. Such things are normal rural background. They are to be expected. A court has to decide whether any particular activity rises to the level of nuisance. Routine, necessary rural activities won't. If you object to this "background," you might want to rethink a country purchase.

Even large properties of several hundred acres or more can be affected by neighboring noise and eyesores. As I write this paragraph, several large landowners in my county are objecting to the plans of an adjoining neighbor to lease his land for a wind farm. The neighbors object to seeing 400-foot-tall wind turbines from their front porch, among other reasons. They believe the turbines will be an eyesore and lower their property values. Each buyer has to decide what type and scale of rural activity he can and cannot put up with. Offenses that would not meet a court's test of nuisance can still drive you batty. The one thing worse in an owner's mind than an annoyance is an annoyance that a court has declared is not a nuisance.

Whether a court finds an annoyance to be a nuisance usually depends on the specifics of the case. Activities that are out of normal scale, or highly concentrated, or atypical, or abnormally burdensome, or totally unanticipated will be hardest to defend. Were I to buy a cottage on one acre surrounded by working dairy farms with nearby waste lagoons, I would have to put up with the constant smell of fresh manure. A local judge would not rule that the pre-existing dairy farms were a nuisance to me. He would say that the annoyance was obvious, and I bought the place with an open nose. In situations where an annoyance does not rise to a legal nuisance, you are stuck with it. My guess is that local judges will not find pre-existing conditions a nuisance, and I will extend that guess to say that local judges will be predisposed to favor locals over newcomers in these disputes—and properly so.

If you are a princess who is rendered sleepless by a pea under your mattress, you should be very cautious about buying property in an environment that's new to you. The occasional down-the-road shot at a garden-raiding woodchuck will set you to phoning the sheriff. If you are offended by a neighbor's level of disorderliness (which is different than your own), you will be offended each time you drive by his disconnected downspout. Parts cars drive some neighbors nuts. I try to keep in mind a distinction between (offensive) things that are normal and typical for the property's neighborhood and things that are abnormal, atypical and out of scale. That allows me to live with certain annoyances that are part and parcel of where I've chosen to buy property. Since rural areas are normally quiet and peaceful, noise and disturbances acquire more power over newcomers who think nothing of living in a downtown area roiled by sirens and a dozen other routine assaults on their senses. In the spring, my wife has occasionally shouted from the depths of her early-morning blankets: "Shut up, birds!" Each buyer needs to decide his tolerance for the target-property's rural neighborhood. If an annoyance is open to view prior to purchase, you are likely to be expected to live with it afterwards. But a princess may never learn to sleep on a pea, no matter the number of mattresses. If you decide that you are a princess, find yourself a castle in a kingdom that has outlawed peas.

Annoyances that have been declared nuisances by a court can be modified or even stopped. Annoyances that don't rise to nuisance will continue. Most annoyances never get challenged in court, which means the put-upon party learns to put up with being put upon. It's difficult for a newcomer to challenge a rural neighborhood's equilibrium by proclaiming that his long-residing neighbor's behavior is a nuisance. If everyone else has put up with the neighbor's behavior for years, why shouldn't the newcomer fit in by putting up with it too? No one likes to be told, particularly by someone just moving in, that what he's been doing for years is objectionable and should end on the newcomer's say so. The newcomer who assumes that all of his new neighbors will join him in asking the offending neighbor to change his ways is fooling himself. The in-coming buyer might win a nuisance suit against the neighbor, but it will come at a high price that will be paid repeatedly in the years ahead. If the outsider wins in court, his victory will not be seen as a community benefit even though it is. It will be seen as a city-person throwing his weight around.

Rural people tend to be more accepting of the bothersome quirks of their neighbors than city newcomers, even when they have no bothersome quirks of their own. This is consistent with their high degree of tolerance for live-and-let-live eccentricity among people they know well. They are far less tolerant of the same eccentricities occurring in remote places (like Manhattan) and among people they don't know. Newcomers with their city peculiarities benefit from this willingness to accept differences as soon as their rural community incorporates them as familiar. When a newcomer stirs up a claim of nuisance no matter how justified, it jeopardizes the *laissez-faire* ethic that tends to benefit everyone, often the newcomer himself most of all.

The buyer's best protection against annoyance and nuisance is to scope for them in every possible manifestation prior to making an offer. This means you should try to visit the property on a normal weekday, in the evening and on a weekend. The seller may or may not be helpful, given that you are asking him to reveal a condition that might dissuade you from purchasing his property. Casual conversations with neighbors may be the best source of information; ask each neighbor about the other neighbors.

Consider including an **annoyance disclosure** in your purchase contract. Don't call it a nuisance disclosure, because nuisance, legally speaking, is confined to those annoyances that a court has already ruled are nuisances. A seller could deny his property was affected by a nuisance when it was surrounded by multiple annoyances that had never been litigated. **Ask the seller to reveal any neighborhood conditions or activities that a reasonable person might consider intrusive or annoying, and which might negatively affect the buyer's possession, use and enjoyment of the property.** This should, at least, open a discussion with the seller as to what you are concerned about. I would explain the difference between annoyance and nuisance, and, further, tell him that you want to fit into the neighborhood as much as possible. If nothing else, you want to know what to expect, and what level of annoyance acceptance is likely to be expected of you.

I encourage buyers not to become their new neighborhood's self-righteous, self-appointed enforcer of correct behavior. Sooner or later, everyone around you, including you, will do something of questionable legality or taste. Temper your beliefs on these matters with patience and a strong dose of tolerance. These qualities will come around to you in return.

Trespass is a common problem with rural land. It comes in two general forms: trespass by those who have been trespassing in one way or another for years, and one-time trespass usually by strangers. The first type is more common and difficult to handle. It may be neighbors, nearby landowners, local folks or non-residents who regularly visit your property. They may be hunters, berrypickers, firewood cutters, teenagers, "cut-throughers," "mounties" (ATVs, snowmobiles, horse riders, 4WD off-roaders, dirt bikers, boaters or RV campers), swimmers, trash dumpers or fishermen. Non-local trespassers tend to be birders, hikers, hunters/fishermen, mountain bikers and ATV riders. The trespass can be seasonal or constant, blatant or sneaky, benign or amazingly invasive. Trespass by non-local parties is usually easier to control through **posting the property** with signs prohibiting trespass. Posting and newspaper ads will help with local folks, but word of mouth is best. Don't be surprised to have some trespassers proclaim a right to use your property against your wishes based on history, permission or inventive legal theories devised on the spot by instant experts in English common law.

And there is always the situationally blind trespasser. I was visiting a friend's land near Greenfield, Massachusetts many years ago when I ran into one. My friend had been having trouble with hunters coming onto her land without permission and hunting birds in her swamp. She posted her property, particularly around the beaver pond. As I was leaving one afternoon, I noticed a truck parked at the end of her swamp road. I drove down, got out and walked in about 30 feet. A fully decked out hunter was standing with shotgun ready, taking aim. I politely pointed out that he was standing next to—not under, not close to—a newly mounted yellow posted sign tacked to a tree. The sign was not more than six inches from his rear gunsight. I explained the landowner's position and asked him to turn his head about one degree to the right, toward the sign. "Never saw it," he said. Given that he was armed and I was not—except with my first wife, a passive-aggressive pacifist and Yale law student—I did not laugh. "Anyway, I'm not hunting, just looking," he allowed, as the bird flapped away. I asked this non-hunting hunter to leave…and left before he mistook me for a bear in season.

There's only one way to stop trespass: the owner must take whatever steps he needs to take in the circumstances to stop it. The landowner must be clear, firm and consistent. To the extent possible, denial of access should be business, not personal. You should not negotiate with trespassers; any negotiation comes out of your side. You can listen and then explain, but don't negotiate. If necessary call the sheriff and get a restraining order. Such measures should be taken only as a last resort.

Ask your seller to **disclose any trespass** in your purchase contract. Trespass is not likely to be construed as an "encroachment" or an "encumbrance," so you need to include a specific trespass disclosure. Neighbors will probably know of trespass patterns on the seller's property, though it may turn out you're asking them to squeal on themselves. The point of your trespass disclosure and a warranty that no trespass has occurred is not so much to get the seller on the hook if a problem turns up, but more to get him to reveal the problem before you buy it.

When the seller discloses a trespass, he and the buyer can then devise a plan to: 1) provide public notice prohibiting trespass through newspaper advertisements, posting signs and personal contact; 2) undertake prevention measures, such as stout chains with locks and locked gates; and 3) enforce the no-trespass policy by notifying the sheriff's office and the local game warden of your posting, having your lawyer send warning letters to habitual offenders, and bringing charges as a last resort. Solving trespass is likely to be easier if the seller initiates notice to chronic trespassers before closing. These situations can bruise feelings on all sides, so move with thoughtfulness rather than self-righteousness.

The buyer's purchase offer might include language on annoyance, nuisance and trespass such as the following:

> **Seller agrees to disclose situations and patterns of annoyance, nuisance and trespass on and around the Property that might adversely affect the Buyer's possession, use and enjoyment of it.**
>
> **With annoyance and nuisance, Seller agrees to discuss each situation with the Buyer within seven (7) calendar days of this Contract taking effect. Seller further agrees to implement a control plan that the Parties negotiate.**
>
> **In the event of trespass, Seller agrees to provide names of individuals known to him who are engaging in trespass. The Parties agree that they will negotiate a plan of action for each trespasser.**
>
> **If the Buyer is not satisfied with the implementation of this section or the situations as disclosed, or otherwise known to him, he may void this Contract without penalty within 30 days of its coming into effect, whereupon his deposit shall be returned to him in a timely fashion.**

A special case of "trespass" arises from animals owned by one party finding their way onto another's property. Bulls seeking cows are often the culprits. A bull with his nose open will go through the best, stoutest, highest and newest fence on my farm. If you are running pure-bred cows and the neighbor's mongrel bull comes over, you have a right to be upset. Your breeding program and farm income are diminished. Most neighbors, you will find, will try to keep their stock at home. Absentee owners may be less cooperative. You will need to take legal action if this situation becomes chronic, with demonstrable financial impacts.

LEASE-PURCHASE OPTION

The idea of a purchase contingent on buyer satisfaction with the property can be taken down a different road: the **lease-purchase option**. There's no more thorough investigation available than a year-long, on-site colonoscopy of the seller's property. It's also a low-risk, not-too-expensive way to see if country living on this piece of land fits.

A lease-purchase option may or may not establish a future selling price between the parties. The right to buy at a set price during the term of the lease, or at its end, is typically part of an option. If it isn't, your year-long rental can at least give you an inside track if your tenant-landlord relationship has been positive. The option could include a **right of first offer**, that is, the tenant/buyer has the right to submit an offer before the seller puts the property back on the market. In the absence of a fixed, future selling price, the buyer can anticipate that the seller will argue that his property has appreciated, thus justifying a price higher than a year earlier. From the buyer's perspective, you may have more money after a year's rental, and you should certainly have more knowledge about the property that may, perhaps, be used to whittle the price. If you think you're going to buy when the lease expires, propose to the seller that in lieu of all or part of your rent you put rent dollars and/or labor into property improvements. But if you do that, make sure to agree on a purchase price in advance, otherwise you will end up paying for the improvements that you made.

I would use a lease-purchase option on rural property more as a deep investigative tool than as a negotiating tactic over price. It gives you time to scope the property and experience it. It gives you a way into a property as well as a way out. If you're subject to impulse buying, a lease-purchase option satisfies your impulsiveness without permanent harm, since the most you can lose is a year's rent. Make sure that your lease-purchase contract contains a **right to assign** your interest. That gives you the option of selling your arrangement to a third-party who is bound by the terms you negotiated. With a lease-purchase contract that sets a future selling price, you may be able to sell it for more than what the seller is owed, thus producing a profit.

Your local lawyer should draft the lease-purchase option agreement. He needs to make sure the seller has clear title before you sign. The seller should be required to produce evidence of ownership or offer a warranty as part of the lease that he possesses clear title and the unencumbered right to transfer title. When the purchase is effected, it should include updated seller warranties on title. You and your lawyer should also be comfortable with language regarding missed/late rental payments, grounds for the landlord/owner terminating the lease, circumstances where you lose your option money and property maintenance responsibilities. You need to protect yourself against a landlord/owner who wants to terminate the option agreement over an insignificant issue to pocket your option money without further obligation. (See Kenneth R. Harney, "The Nation's Housing," "Danger Lurks In Lease-Option Deals," <u>Washington Post</u>, December 17, 2005.)

BUY A LAWSUIT

There are times—though not many—when you might want to get into a messy deal. If the mess can be cleaned up for a known and acceptable amount of money, over a period of time that can be reasonably estimated, and a large pot of money/value can be realized for your effort, consider buying a property that requires a lawsuit. Messes always discount sales price.

A common messy situation involves a **suit to quiet title** and a **partition suit**. The first is used when your title search reveals the fact of, or the possibility of, another ownership claim in the property (land, minerals, rights, interests) the seller will convey. In land purchases, the buyer wants fee-simple ownership of the property, which includes all ownership interests in all of the property's assets, interests and rights. In some cases, when your deedwork reveals that another party may, or does, hold an ownership interest in one of the target property's assets, a suit to quiet title gives that person an opportunity to come forward and establish his claim. This type of suit is not usually very expensive. It may result in no one coming forward to assert a claim, or someone asserting a claim that the court rejects, or someone with a claim the court upholds. Two of these three outcomes solve the mess to the buyer's benefit. Where a valid claim exists, it's usually a (small) fractional claim. Since the buyer has no standing before purchase to bring a partition suit, it's up to the seller. You can, of course, buy the property and then live with the situation as is, or try to buy the minority interest, or propose a physical division of the property, or file a **partition suit** that asks the court to order the sale of the land with the net proceeds to be divided proportionately between the owners. Bringing a partition suit is not very expensive. But the cost of implementing an auction sale can result in a ten or 15 percent whack out of the gross selling revenues. The sellers may also have to pay for other expenses, such as an appraisal, survey, consultant opinions and lawyer time. In the end, you will receive cash for your ownership interest. You get the property itself only if you are the high bidder. Partition suits are the least preferred option if you want the property, because it can significantly increase your total acquisition cost and open you to being outbid.

Landlocked properties present an investor with both risk and reward. The current owner may not be able to negotiate a ROW easement with his neighbors owing to a history of squabbling. He may also be unable to afford bringing a lawsuit. If you're scoping and review by your lawyer indicates that the seller would win a lawsuit, I would approach the neighbors. You may be able to succeed where the current owner never will. Negotiate a ROW easement that is contingent on your purchase of the seller's property. You can trade part of the seller's land for the ROW or, if it's a timber tract, sell the land after timbering at a steep discount to the neighbor who lets you "haul out over him."

I would enter a legal mess with the greatest caution. It can easily consume far more time and money than you anticipated, which is why they're messes. Lawsuits, even easy ones, are emotionally intense, and when they've passed, like Southern history, they're still not past. A court's ruling may not always decide the issue on the ground. I know one land buyer who purchased a large tract at a very good price, knowing that his legal access was muddled. He believed he had access over a particular road, but the judge disagreed. The access the judge awarded to him was on firmer legal ground, but impractical on real dirt. Eventually he had to buy a right of way over the first road. Gaining access to his property took, money, aggravation, a court suit and five years. The suit consumed the first couple of years and then negotiating with the winners consumed the rest. Had he done better scoping, he would have been better able to forecast his troubles. He assumed that the judge would grant his request for the most practical entrance, even though it was not as legally defensible as at least one of the others. Had he asked a local lawyer about this case, he would have been warned against proceeding on his hopes. He might have done better had he had his local lawyer approach the owners of the road he wanted to use. Had his original purchase price not been steeply discounted, this investment would have been a disaster. As it was, the investment worked for him despite the protracted time and considerable expense. Had he wanted the property for something other than a long-term investment, he would have been stuck for five years.

A buyer is sometimes asked by a seller holding a minority interest in a property to buy him out. Often, he fears the majority seller whose fighting capabilities exceed his. Or, he may not be sure of the validity of his own ownership. I have turned down such proposals because the effort to resolve the mess seemed large and uncertain in terms of the gain that might be realized. A minority seller must discount his asking price to make it worth your while to take his place. When work and payoff are in more favorable alignment, I would consider jumping in. But where the likely benefit is not worth at least twice the anticipated cost in terms of time, expense and aggravation, I would avoid buying a lawsuit.

And if you do buy one, keep in mind that you did so for financial gain, not principle. I advise buyers not to fight for principle alone in a land squabble. Having done it once, I found it to be a dreadful experience. Fighting over money is when all is said and done, just fighting over money. But losing on principle—when you're right—really hurts.

CHAPTER 30: SOME IDEAS ORGANIZED AS A PURCHASE-OFFER CONTRACT

The "contract" that follows is a sample of possible approaches, presented as a contract might organize them. I didn't write a model contract because one size never fits all.

State laws vary, and every purchase presents its own combination of things you need to worry about and things you don't, based on your pre-offer scoping. Even basic contract features will vary—how property is described, deed types, mortgage and trustee arrangements, etc. States may require specific provisions and specific language in real-estate contracts. It is, therefore, helpful to have a copy of the local broker's contract in front of you for purposes of comparison and adaptation. Ask a local broker for a copy of this standard contract; you certainly want to read it at your leisure before you sign one.

I advise against a buyer writing his own contract from scratch. Yet, I also think it's essential for every buyer to be conversant with contract ideas and language so that he can work with his local lawyer to craft a contract that fits his specific needs and circumstances. After scoping, you may decide to use the standard contract with only one or two changes, which you can write in on that form. If you do decide to write a contract from scratch with your lawyer, keep the language simple and clear. Lawyers often write badly, and even good lawyers tend to write in a lawyerly style that can be difficult to understand.

Your interest in a purchase will be subverted if you hand a seller a semi-comprehensible contract. Please don't toss in every contingency and provision I've included in this book. Don't include every contingency that you can think up on your own. Offer a seller a contract that protects your interests with economy of concept and language. The more incomprehensible a contract, the more legal pretzel twisting it contains, the more one-sided it is, the more reluctant your seller will be to sign.

The "contract" that follows is not meant to be a contract. Don't rip and use it.

A standard real-estate contract will follow the format I've used, more or less. I've added language for illustrative purposes that a standard contract will not contain. Think of this as an exercise in thinking through how various elements of contract ideas and language might fit together. In other chapters, I've written examples of contingencies and other contract language that you can discuss with your lawyer where they might be needed. Real-estate forms of all kinds can be obtained from Professional Publishing Co. of Novato, California at www.TrueForms.com.

I have deliberately included more language than would normally be needed for illustration purposes. This contract exercise is more elaborate than buyers will normally need. I have included different ways of getting at similar points as a way of presenting choices.

Individual circumstances will dictate when a buyer should insert specific contingencies and other protections. Remember, clear and simple is more likely to fly with a seller than convoluted and complicated.

DO NOT USE THIS CONTRACT VERBATIM. Use it to organize your thoughts about how to make an offer. Any contract that you offer a seller should be reviewed by your local lawyer prior to doing so.

REAL-ESTATE SALES CONTRACT

This Contract of Sale and Agreement, made and entered between _____ (name and address of Seller [s]), herein Seller, and _____(name and address of Buyer [s]), herein Buyer, on the ___ day of _____, 2___, provides as follows:

1. PREMISES AND DISCLOSURES.

A. Seller shall sell and convey and Buyer shall purchase on the terms and conditions herein set forth all interests, assets and rights in Seller's real property, together with all improvements thereon, including but not limited to, all standing and fallen timber; all natural resources, surface and subsurface; all water rights; all appurtenances to the property, including, but not limited to, rights of way (recorded and unrecorded), easements, prescriptions and permissions; all gates, fences, culverts, roads, bridges and stores of gravel and soil; and all other rights and privileges of ownership, lying and being situate near _____, Virginia in _____ County, more particularly described as _____ acres, conveyed to Seller by Deed of _____, [date] in Deed Book __, Page ____, in the _____ County Clerk's Office, and being the same property as shown on the _____ County Tax Maps as Parcels ___ and ___ in the _____ District, and being the same property as shown by a recorded survey of August 6, 1999, Map Book ____, Page ____, prepared by John Johnson, a surveyor licensed in the Commonwealth of Virginia.

B. Seller warrants that he is lawfully seised of this property in fee simple. Seller shall convey all assets of, and rights and interests in, the property in fee simple with marketable title free of encumbrance and limitation, except for those of record in the Clerk's office and those disclosed in writing to Buyer that are accepted by Buyer in writing prior to this Contract taking effect. Buyer retains the right to withdraw or modify this Contract in light of Seller disclosure regarding any encumbrance or limitation. This Contract shall not come into effect until Buyer accepts in writing any such disclosure.

C. Encumbrance and limitation are defined to include, but are not limited to, unrecorded rights of way and easements; claims of possession and/or use against the property; claims of prescription, implication or necessity against the property; permissions to access or otherwise use the property; retentions of profit and/or interest in the property; liens of any kind against the property; zoning and/or other regulatory restrictions on the property; any environmental condition or status (such as presence of wetlands; endangered, threatened or sensitive species; migratory bird habitat; floodplain; public conservation plan; buried fuel tank; sites or sources of ground and/or water contamination and/or pollution; sensitive or restricted surface waters; old mines and pending plans to mine or extract other minerals, including oil or gas; subsidence hazards from underground excavations; karst topography; caves; geologic faults; earthquake zone; hurricane/tornado/hailstorm belt, etc.); claims on behalf of or against the property involving water, irrigation, springs, pollution, water impoundments, surface and subsurface water, and water rights; non-compliance with local, state and/or federal laws and regulations; and any other condition or situation that would adversely affect the Buyer's possession, use and enjoyment of the property and/or its value.

D. Seller shall convey the property with a General Warranty Deed and English Covenants of Title that include the six customary warranties: seisin, conveyance, against encumbrances, quiet enjoyment, general warranty (forever) and further assurances. [*English Covenants of Title are invoked in the Commonwealth of Virginia; some General Warranty Deeds do not include all six covenants, depending on the state.*]

E. Seller warrants that the conveyance shall be without encumbrance (other than those disclosed or of record), lien, limitation, discount, lease, easement, reduction or reservation of interest or profit, excepting those of record in the Clerk's Office of _____ County or disclosed and accepted by Buyer in the manner described in 1.B., above.

F. Parties agree that the Seller is selling this property "as is, where is" as of the date that this

Contract takes effect_____ is submitted_____. Any change in the condition or status of the property beyond reasonable wear and tear as of Closing may, at Buyer's option, lead to his voiding of this Contract without penalty or its renegotiation on mutually agreeable terms.

G. Seller warrants that the property shall be free of any material defect, latent or otherwise, as of Closing that would adversely affect Buyer's possession, use and enjoyment of the Property and/or its value, except for defects disclosed by Seller in writing and accepted by Buyer in writing prior to this Contract taking effect. Buyer reserves the right to void this Contract without penalty and, at his choice, submit a revised offer or none at all when he determines that any defect is unacceptable.

H. Defect shall be construed broadly to mean a condition, status, situation, problem, complication, uncertainty and the like, including but not limited to, unrecorded rights of way and easements; claims of possession and/or use against the property; claims of prescription, implication, or necessity against the property; permissions to access or otherwise use the property; retentions of profit and/or interest in the property; unrecorded liens and estates of any kind in or against the property; zoning and/or other regulatory restrictions on the property; conditions of annoyance or nuisance around the property, such as offensive and/or unreasonable odors, noise, light, disturbance of view, activities, behavior and so forth; trespass occurring on the property; environmental condition or status (such as presence of wetlands; endangered, threatened or sensitive species; migratory bird habitat; floodplain; public conservation plan; underground storage tanks; sources of ground and/or water contamination and/or pollution; sensitive or restricted surface waters; ground or geologic faults or instability; excavations beneath the surface or otherwise concealed; reclaimed excavations and/or mines; plans to mine or extract other materials and/or minerals, including oil or gas, on or around the property; subsidence hazards from underground excavations; karst topography; caves; earthquake zone; hurricane/tornado/hailstorm belt, etc.); unrecorded claims on behalf of or against the property involving water, irrigation, springs, pollution, water impoundments, surface and subsurface water, and water rights; non-compliance with local, state and/or federal laws and regulations; and any other condition or situation that would in the judgment of a reasonable individual adversely affect the Buyer's possession, use and enjoyment of the property and/or its value.

I. The property and Seller are subject to the Seller disclosure provisions in this Contract as set forth herein and all those required by local, state and federal law.

J. Seller warrants that no timber cutting or surface-disturbing activities of any kind shall occur on the property after the date this Contract takes effect. If any such cutting or surface-disturbing activity does occur, the Buyer may void this Contract without penalty, or, alternatively at his option, resolve the matter through negotiations.

K. Seller warrants that he will not enter into any agreement for the sale, lease, option, exchange, severance, reservation or exploitation of the timber, minerals, water rights, hunting (game) rights and other wildlife rights, access rights, recreation rights and all other property rights and resources once this Contract takes effect, except with the prior written authorization of the Buyer. Buyer reserves the right to reject any such agreement without penalty and without affecting this Contract. Where an agreement is acceptable to both Seller and Buyer, they agree to pro rate income from this agreement with _____ percent to the Seller and _____ percent to Buyer from the date this Contract takes effect until the date of Closing at which time all income accrues to Buyer.

L. If any such agreement is in effect prior to the effective date of this Contract, Seller shall disclose all terms of each such agreement in writing prior to the date on which this Contract takes effect. Buyer reserves right to withdraw or modify his offer without penalty in light of any such agreement whose terms Buyer deems unacceptable. Buyer shall notify Seller of his response to such disclosure in writing.

M. Seller shall provide the Buyer with copies of all leases (including mineral leases), rental agreements, easements, estates running with the property, reservations of interest or profit and any other limiting agreement prior to accepting this Contract, excepting those documents that are of record with the Clerk of _____ County. Seller shall at the same time provide Buyer with information setting forth his understanding of any oral agreements, licenses or permissions the Seller gave to other Parties that affect the property to be conveyed.

N. Seller shall disclose in writing prior to acceptance of this Contract all boundary disputes; any boundary lines on the property that are marked and/or run differently than their presentation in Seller's Deed and/or in Seller's survey; unresolved ownership claims against the property; adverse possessions, uses and claims against the property; any easements—or claims of—easements in gross, by necessity, implication or prescription of which he is aware.

O. Seller shall disclose in writing prior to acceptance of this Contract any incidents of which he is aware of trespass whether or not declared so by a court of law; unauthorized use of the property for camping, picnicking, trash dumping, hunting, fishing, trapping, timber cutting and firewood cutting; unauthorized use of the property by private vehicles (such as motorcycles, snowmobiles, ATVs, 4WD vehicles, boats and air-borne craft), commercial vehicles and public vehicles; unauthorized use by horse riders, hikers, bird watchers, swimmers and skiers; unauthorized use of the property by livestock; unauthorized tapping, exploiting or gathering of resources (including, but not limited to, water, coal, minerals, soils, rock, oil, gas, ginseng, plants, crops, wildlife, mushrooms, nuts, roots, mistletoe, berries and the like); and incidents of theft or attempted theft, whether or not reported to law-enforcement authorities.

P. Seller shall notify in writing any individual known to him engaging in such unauthorized uses, above, that he is to cease and desist immediately, unless otherwise directed in writing by Buyer.

Seller _____ shall _____ shall not post his property prior to Closing. Buyer shall pay for the posting materials if the Parties agree to posting prior to Closing. Seller shall make good-faith effort to help Buyer end any such activities that Buyer determines are adverse to his possession, use and enjoyment of the property and/or its value.

Q. Seller shall disclose in writing prior to acceptance of this Contract any environmental condition of which he has knowledge that would adversely affect the Buyer's possession, use and enjoyment of the property and/or its value, resources and assets. Environmental "condition" is to be construed broadly, to include, but is not limited to, the presence of state and/or federal endangered, threatened or sensitive flora and fauna and/or their habitat; wetlands; protected streams and/or restricted waterways; flooding and/or floodplains; pollution of surface and/or underground waters; acid-mine drainage; surface subsidence and/or instability; landslide potential; karst topography; soil conditions unsuited to building, agriculture and septic fields; earthquake; severe weather (windstorms, hail, tornado, hurricane, ice and snow, early frost, lack of precipitation, high heat); infestations of insects (e.g., fire ants, termites, gypsy moth, wood-destroying beetles and/or ants, Africanized bees), birds, bats, snakes, and other aquatic and land fauna; infestation of nuisance flora (e.g., toxic plants, multiflora rose, kudzu); and the presence of diseases, insects and conditions that adversely affect crops and/or timber.

R. Seller shall disclose in writing prior to acceptance of this Contract information of which he is aware regarding the property's compliance status with state and federal environmental and safety regulations including, but not limited to, surface and underground mining for coal and other minerals; exploration and production for oil and natural gas; water and air quality; forest management and stewardship plans; buried fuel tanks; disposal sites for garbage and/or toxic/hazardous waste, including agricultural chemicals; water impoundments; and the installation of unapproved septic and/or wastewater systems. Copies of Seller permits, inspection reports, notices of non-compliance, and planning documents for any environmental condition or land use (including reclamation, conservation, forest-management plans and the like) shall be furnished to Buyer at such time.

S. Seller shall ___ shall not ____ provide Buyer with current tax-assessed values for the property's land, improvements, timber, minerals, water and any other assets and resources. Seller shall inform Buyer of any information he has regarding current and/or proposed reassessments and proposed local or state tax policies that would affect the property. [*This information is public record. Let the seller persuade you to delete it.*]

T. Seller shall disclose in writing prior to acceptance of this Contract any matters of land use, regulation, zoning, planning, and condemnation by public authority that affect property, whether in effect or proposed. Seller shall ____ shall not ____ provide the current zoning status of the property and its status under whatever local comprehensive plans are in effect. [*Also in public record.*]

U. Seller shall disclose in writing prior to acceptance of this Contract any instances or patterns of annoyance involving the property of which he is aware, including, but not limited to, unauthorized trash dumping; vehicles using the entrance drive for turning; bright lights, loud noise, dust/dirt, and/or offensive odors originating off the property; low-flying aircraft; and early-morning/late-night activities, among others.

V. Seller shall disclose in writing prior to acceptance of this Contract information of which he is aware regarding any Party having, exercising or claiming access to, or through, this property by right of way, easement, prescription, implication, necessity, adverse use, permission, license or otherwise. Seller need not provide information that is recorded in the Clerk's office in _____ County.

W. Buyer may void this Contract without penalty if Seller is unable to convey 100 percent of ownership interests in all of the property assets, rights and interests. Buyer, at his option, may submit an amended and revised Contract to reflect Seller's true position in the property.

X. Seller shall disclose in writing prior to acceptance of this Contract any arrangement whereby Seller, or any previous owners of this property, sold, purchased, leased, rented, optioned, granted, or been granted water or water rights for or from this property.

Z. This property has_____ has not _____ used irrigated water during the last ten years.

AA. This property has _____ has not _____ purchased water during the last ten years.

BB. If the property has needed, used, sold and/or purchased water, Seller shall provide Buyer with copies of all documents related to such activities.

CC. Seller shall provide the following:

    (1). This property is _____ is not _____ currently classified in a land-use (farm use) valuation category for tax purposes.

    (2). This property is _____ is not _____ currently enrolled in a public forest management/stewardship program.

    (3). This property is _____ is not _____ subject to a conservation easement of any kind, whether of record or not.

(4). This property is _____ is not _____ currently enrolled in a state and/or federal agricultural program. Seller shall attach information regarding each such program, including obligations running with the property, plans, payments and taxability of such payments.

DD. Failure of Seller to disclose and/or inform Buyer of such information of which he is aware in regard to the above shall be sufficient grounds for Buyer, at his option, to withdraw this Contract prior to acceptance or void this Contract once it has taken effect.

EE. Buyer may withdraw or void this Contract without penalty if either Seller fails to disclose as provided or the results of such information and disclosure are unacceptable to Buyer. Upon withdrawal or voiding of this Contract in these circumstances, Buyer shall have all security deposits returned in full and in a timely manner. Buyer shall have no further obligation to Seller.

FF. Buyer at his option may, alternatively, propose to Seller negotiations to resolve items or information and disclosure. Seller at his option may accept or reject Buyer's offer to negotiate. Depending on the results of these efforts, Buyer may submit a substitute Contract for Seller's consideration.

GG. If Seller fails to disclose a condition of the type set forth above, Seller shall bear full liability for all subsequent costs of remedy incurred by Buyer.

HH. Upon voiding of this Contract, Buyer shall have his security deposit returned in full within five business days of providing Seller written notification of the termination of this Contract. "Without penalty," as used in this Contract, shall be construed to mean full return of the Buyer's security deposit as provided in the preceding sentence.

II. All warranties to survive Closing.

2. PRICE.

A. The exact purchase price for this property shall be calculated by multiplying $_____ per acre by the number of acres and fraction thereof contained within the boundaries as established by _____ survey of record, or _____ deed description, or _____ tax maps, or _____ survey done at the expense of Buyer, or _____ other means acceptable to Buyer and Seller. Any expense incurred in establishing acreage shall ____ shall not____be divided between Seller and Buyer in the following manner: ____% Buyer; ____ % Seller.

B. Buyer shall deliver a first security deposit of 0.75 percent of the gross sales price of $_____, as calculated above, to the Buyer's attorney _____, with this Contract. Buyer's attorney shall serve as Escrow Agent for the Parties. Escrow Agent shall hold this deposit in accordance with the escrow provisions of the Commonwealth of Virginia. It shall be deposited in the Escrow Agent's escrow account at the following financial institution: _____. Buyer shall deliver his deposit in cash, wire transfer or certified check. Buyer's attorney shall provide receipt to both Parties.

C. Buyer shall deliver in the same manner a second security deposit of 5.25 percent of the gross sales price on the day he notifies Seller in writing that all disclosures and contingencies have been accepted or withdrawn.

D. Both security deposits shall be applied to the sale of the property, unless otherwise agreed.

E. The balance of the purchase price shall be paid in cash, wire transfer or certified check or other means acceptable to the Parties at Closing.

    F. Buyer's security deposits are subject to the prorations set forth in **Section 9.**

3. TERMS.

    A. Seller acknowledges that Buyer has deposited in escrow for all Parties the sum of $_____ with _____, Escrow Agent and attorney for the Buyer. This sum is the first good-faith deposit toward the purchase of the property described above.

    B. Interest shall ____ or shall not___ accrue to Seller____ or Buyer ____as provided by the law in the Commonwealth of Virginia on all deposits.

    C. In the event Seller cannot provide a marketable title in fee simple to the property described above and a General Warranty Deed with English Covenants of Title and fulfill all other terms of this Contract, this Contract shall be terminated. Buyer shall notify Seller and Escrow Agent of termination in writing. Escrow Agent shall then return all monies deposited as security deposit in full to Buyer within five calendar days and without penalty.

    D. The purchase price shall be paid as follows: The escrowed deposits together with the balance of the purchase price shall be given by Buyer, or his designated representative, to Seller, or his designated representative, at Closing.

    E. Seller agrees_____ does not agree _____ to pay _____ percentage of the financing charges incurred by Buyer to secure a mortgage on this property.

    F. Buyer's possession shall begin at settlement on the date of Closing.

    G. Recordation of the Deed shall take place in _____County, Virginia on the date of Closing, or other date agreeable to the Parties.

    H. The Closing shall take place at the office of _____, or at another location the Parties designate at a mutually agreed time.

4. EFFECT AND DURATION.

    A. This Contract shall take effect on the day the Parties agree in writing on its provisions in their entirety, as evidenced by the last required signature or dated set of initials. The Contract takes effect at 5 p.m. on that day, unless otherwise agreed.

    B. This Contract shall be in effect until Closing, which is scheduled for _____ (month, day, year), or no more than _____ calendar days from the date that Buyer notifies Seller in writing that all contingencies are withdrawn or satisfied, whichever is later.

    C. The Parties may extend their Contract escrow by mutual agreement in writing.

5. DEED.

    A. Seller shall convey the property by General Warranty Deed with English Covenants of Title, free of liens, covenants, reservations, restrictions, tenancies, estates, encumbrances and arrangements other than those recorded in the Clerk's office in _____ County, Virginia or disclosed by Seller and accepted by Buyer in writing, as provided above.

6. TITLE.

A. Buyer shall take title in the name (s) of _____.

B. Buyer may assign, transfer, convey, option, gift, or sell his interest in this Contract prior to closing at his option without penalty. Any such act shall not diminish or alter any provision in this Contract or the Buyer's obligations to fulfill its terms, including price. Buyer shall notify Seller in writing prior to invoking this provision.

7. TITLE REPORT.

A. Buyer does_____ does not_____ require a preliminary title report _____ and/or abstract of title _____. If Buyer does require such document (s), he shall make arrangements for this work at his expense, to be completed within thirty (30) calendar days of the date this Contract takes effect.

B. If the title report reveals a defect, the Buyer may void this Contract without penalty. Seller shall be provided a reasonable amount of time, not to exceed _____ calendar days from receiving written notification from Buyer, to cure his title to Buyer's satisfaction before Buyer may void this Contract.

8. TITLE INSURANCE.

A. Buyer does ____ does not ____ require a Standard _____ Extended _____ Title Insurance Policy. If Buyer requires such a policy, he shall arrange for it in a timely manner at his expense.

9. PRORATIONS AND COSTS.

A. The Parties agree to pro rate property taxes, assessments, fees and other state and local taxes for the current year from the date of Closing, with the Seller paying his proportional share through that date and the Buyer assuming all such liability as of the following day. Seller bears sole responsibility for bringing all such accounts current from prior years.

B. Rental and/or royalty income shall be pro rated in the same manner.

C. Seller agrees to pay the expense of preparing the deed and any taxes due from grantor/Seller.

D. Buyer agrees to pay for a title examination, costs associated with activities described in **Section 8**, title insurance and the fees of his attorney.

E. The Parties agree to pro rate all other settlement costs from the day of Closing, including but not limited to, homeowners-association fees, utility bills and irrigation fees.

F. Buyer agrees to purchase from Seller all heating oil, propane gas and gasoline in tanks on the Property. The supplier of each fuel shall estimate the stored quantity as of the date of Closing and Buyer shall pay the Seller for each volume multiplied by current delivered price as of the date of this estimate.

G. Parties agree that Buyer _____ Seller _____ shall pay the costs of recording the Buyer's Deed.

H. Parties agree ____ do not agree ____ to pro rate other income, such as government cost-shares, agricultural production payments, etc. If the Parties do not agree on proration, they shall attach to this Contract an Addendum setting forth their plan for dividing such income.

10. BUYER'S RIGHT OF VISITATION AND IMPROVEMENT.

A. The Buyer, his Agents, Employees, Contractors, Surveyors, Foresters, Associates and Others acting on his behalf or in the furtherance of his interests in this property and in this Contract may visit the property at any time between the effective date of this Contract and Closing. The Parties agree to work out a visitation-notification and access procedure. Seller agrees to allow the Buyer, his Agents, Employees, Contractors, Surveyors, Foresters, Associates and Others acting on his behalf or in the furtherance of his interests in this property and this Contract to perform any of the following work and tasks during this period at Buyer's expense:

(1) Survey perimeter boundaries, to be marked on the ground where needed;

(2) Survey of interior divisions for three 25-acre lots on west side of property and interior road, to be marked on the ground;

(3) Cruise of the property's timber by consulting forester; no increment boring;

(4) Painting of the property's merchantable timber inventory by consulting forester, using blue paint dots stump and butt;

(5) Improvements to existing entrance road, including widening to 16 feet with a two-foot-wide apron on either side; grading, ditching, installing rock and gravel where needed; and installing one 36"-diameter, 20-foot-long metal culvert in stream.

Merchantable trees cut in the process of making road improvements shall be gathered as logs at a landing near the gate and not sold prior to Closing. In the event of default or failure to perform, these logs remain the property of Seller; otherwise they belong to Buyer;

(6) Securing appropriate utility easement and installing underground lines to new house site by pond, located on the drawing attached to this Contract;

(7) Sampling of soil and water resources;

(8) Taking soil samples by hand auger or backhoe in anticipation of application for three (3) septic permits;

(9) Showing the property to prospective buyers; and

(10) Other_____.

Seller shall maintain existing roads in current condition during the time this Contract is in effect.

B. Seller shall provide Buyer with key (s) to locked gates for these purposes. Gates shall be left locked at the end of each visit or day, unless otherwise agreed.

C. Seller agrees to apply for ____ rezoning, ____ permit or ____ variance on behalf of Buyer. Closing shall take place within ten (10) calendar days of Seller getting appropriate approval. Buyer shall pay all costs incurred in obtaining the approval he requires. All approvals shall run with the property and convey to Buyer. Failure to obtain the necessary approvals in a form acceptable to Buyer shall be grounds for Buyer to terminate this Contract without penalty.

D. Seller bears no responsibility for or liability for any personal property, materiel, supplies, tools, equipment, machinery and the like that Buyer, and those associated with Buyer in any way, use or leave on the property, except for those instances of damage from fire, vandalism, accident and theft and the like that are covered under Seller's insurance policies. Where the Seller's policy covers such damage, Seller shall submit a claim and pay the Buyer and/or his associates the award, less the amount of the Seller-paid deductible.

E. Seller agrees to keep his current property-protection and liability insurance policies in effect until Closing. If Seller has no such insurance, he shall secure adequate coverage for the escrow period.

11. FAILURE TO PERFORM.

A. Once all contingencies are removed or deemed acceptable by Buyer and he notifies Seller of same in writing, any Buyer failure to perform on this Contract shall result in the forfeit of Buyer's deposits and all of the documents and physical improvements to property as produced under Section 10 as liquidated damages and a reasonable estimate of Seller's damages from said lack of performance. This sum, together with the documents, improvements and materials below, shall be Seller's sole remedy as to damages for any failure to perform

B. All culverts, bridges, rock, gravel, fences, gates, utilities, and other materials and supplies Buyer has on property at the time of his failure to perform become Seller's property at no cost to him as of the date of Buyer's failure to perform.

12. INSURANCE AND RISK OF LOSS.

A. Risk of loss from all naturally occurring acts, such as fire, ice, wind and flood remains with Seller until Closing.

B. Seller agrees to secure a farm homeowner's policy to cover the duration of this Contract which will provide sufficient funds to fully replace Seller's farmhouse, three major barns, machinery shed and silo.

C. Seller does ____ does not____ have an accident liability policy in place.

D. Buyer holds Seller harmless and without liability of any kind for any accidents, personal injury and/or damage, including fire damage, to property of any persons visiting, inspecting, analyzing and/or working on this property in connection with Buyer's activities permitted under this Contract, including, but not limited to, activities listed in **Section 10**. Those subject to this language are the Buyer, his Friends, Visitors, Associates, Prospective Buyers of Timber and/or Land, Representatives, Agents, Prospective Representatives and Agents, Employees, Contractors and their Subcontractors, Surveyors, Foresters, Public Officials invited to the Property by the Buyer and Others acting on his behalf or in the furtherance of his interests in this property and this Contract.

E. If any Buyer activity, or individual associated with Buyer as set forth above, causes any damage, including fire damage, to Seller's property and Buyer fails to perform, Buyer shall compensate Seller for the cost of repairing the damage or the fair market value of the loss.

13. DAMAGE.

A. If the property's natural resources are materially damaged from a naturally occurring event or activity, such as flood, casualty, fire, wind and infestation/disease during escrow, Buyer may terminate this Contract without penalty. Material damage shall be construed to mean more than $1,000 in loss, as estimated by the Parties jointly, or, if there is no agreement, by a qualified professional chosen by the Parties whose fee shall be divided equally between them. The Parties may renegotiate the terms of their Contract in light of a material loss.

B. If the property is damaged in any manner from fire or other acts related to the presence or activity of Buyer, his Friends, Visitors, Associates, Prospective Buyers of Timber and/or Land, Representatives, Agents, Prospective Representatives and Agents, Employees, Contractors and their Subcontractors, Surveyors, Foresters, Public Officials invited to the Property by Buyer and Others acting on his behalf or in the furtherance of his interests in this property and this Contract, Buyer is not relieved of his obligations to perform under this Contract, according to the terms as set forth herein.

14. CONTINGENCIES:

The Buyer's offer is contingent on the following items being resolved to his satisfaction:

A. Seller must be able to provide clear, marketable title; undivided and full ownership in fee simple, subject to easements of record and disclosures accepted by Buyer as set forth above; and a General Warranty Deed to the Property described and conveyed and all its rights, resources and assets.

B. Results of a timber evaluation, paid for by Buyer, must be acceptable to Buyer;

C. Seller shall provide Buyer a deeded right of way of at least 16 feet in width or other arrangement satisfactory to Buyer allowing vehicular access from State Route 3 over the road currently being used.

D. Buyer's offer is contingent on the Property being free of any environmental encumbrance, pollution from off-site sources and/or liability.

E. Buyer's offer is _____ is not _____ contingent on obtaining a satisfactory percolation test at a site of his choosing and at his expense. If Buyer's offer is contingent on such a test, Buyer shall have _____ calendar days from the date on which this Contract takes effect to arrange for and receive results from such a test. Buyer shall notify Seller within three (3) calendar days of receiving results whether the results are or are not acceptable. Seller shall make the property available for such testing at mutually agreeable times. Buyer shall replace and regrade excavations made on the property.

F. Buyer's offer is _____ is not _____ contingent on obtaining a septic permit at his expense for either _____ bedrooms or _____ square feet of residential area. If Buyer's offer is contingent on such a permit being obtained, Buyer shall make a good-faith effort to obtain such a permit within _____ calendar days of this Contract taking effect, or as soon thereafter as possible. The permit shall be issued to the Seller's property and convey to the Buyer at Closing.

G. Buyer's offer is _____ is not _____ contingent on performing a septic-system inspection at his expense within _____ calendar days. Buyer may void or modify this Contract if the inspection results are unsatisfactory.

H. Buyer's offer is _____ is not _____ contingent on the sale, settlement, lease or exchange of other real property owned or controlled by Buyer.

I. Buyer's offer is _____ is not _____ contingent on obtaining acceptable financing from an institutional lender.

J. Seller is_____ is not _____ asked to finance any part of this purchase. If Seller is being asked to finance a part of this purchase, the Buyer's proposal is appended to this Contract.

K. All contingency results must be acceptable to Buyer. If these contingencies are not met or resolved to Buyer's satisfaction, Buyer may terminate this offer without penalty and his security deposit shall be returned in full in a timely manner.

15. FEES.

A. A brokerage fee of _____ percent is due to _____
_____ at closing from Seller's funds. Additional terms of this brokerage fee are appended to this Contract.
A fee of ____ percent is due to _____ at closing from Buyer's funds for consulting. Additional terms of this fee are appended to this Contract. Fees owed shall be paid by the Escrow Agent at closing.

B. Broker and Seller agree to keep the price, terms and conditions of Buyer's offer completely confidential and shall not disclose them or allow them to be disclosed to any other party, including other buyers.

16. PROPERTY OWNERS' ASSOCIATION DISCLOSURE.

A. Seller represents that this property is not located within a development that is subject to the Virginia Property Owners' Association Act.

17. AMENDMENT.

A. This Contract may only be amended in writing. Signed and dated facsimile documents are____ are not ____ an acceptable means of amendment.

18. NOTICE.

A. Whenever notice is to be given under the terms of this Contract, such notice shall be deemed to have been given when enclosed in an envelope having proper postage, addressed to the receiving Party and deposited as Certified Mail at a U.S. Post Office. The date at which such notice shall be deemed to have been given shall be the date of the envelope's postmark.

B. The Parties agree____ not agree____ to substitute a private overnight mail carrier, either UPS or Federal Express, for the U.S. Post Office. Date of notice shall in this case be the pick-up date from the point of origin as evidenced by receipts.

C. The Parties agree _____ not agree _____ to substitute facsimile documents for mailed original documents under both **A.** and **B.** above. Such documents shall be signed and dated by the Party giving notice. Date of notice shall in this case be the transmission date from the point of origin. Sender shall include transmission date on his facsimile cover sheet. The receiving Party shall acknowledge time and date of receipt by signed and dated return facsimile document.

19. GOVERNANCE.

A. The laws of the Commonwealth of Virginia shall govern this Contract.

20. MECHANIC'S LIEN NOTICE.

A. The law related to Mechanic's Lien Notice in the Commonwealth of Virginia shall apply.

B. Seller shall deliver to Buyer at closing an affidavit, on a form acceptable to Buyer's lender, if applicable, signed by Seller that no labor or materials have been furnished to the property within the statutory period for the filing of mechanic's or materialmen's liens against the property. If labor or materials have been furnished during the statutory period at Seller's behest, Seller shall deliver to Buyer an affidavit signed by Seller and the person (s) furnishing the labor or materials that such costs have been paid.

C. Buyer is responsible for prompt payment to those providing labor, services, and materials at his behest on, or related to, Seller's property between the effective date of this Contract and closing. This includes, but is not limited to, those activities listed in **10. A.** Liens of any kind filed against the property for such activities during this time are the sole responsibility of Buyer. Seller is not liable for the payment or resolution of such expenses and liens.

21. RESOLUTION OF DISPUTES.

A. The Parties, Broker and consultant agree to submit any disputes or claims arising out of this Contract to non-binding mediation before binding arbitration or litigation. Non-binding mediation by a third-party neutral does not obligate either Party to agree to a settlement arising from this process unless that settlement is accepted by both Parties, in which case it becomes binding. If non-binding mediation fails to bring forth a settlement, the Parties are free to transfer their dispute to binding arbitration by mutual agreement or litigation. The Parties shall choose a mediator, and if necessary, an arbitrator, from panels of qualified commercial neutrals experienced in real estate provided by the _____. The costs of such services shall be divided equally between, or among, the Parties in dispute.

22. ENTIRE AGREEMENT.

A. This Contract, including any attachments initialed and dated by the Parties, shall constitute the entire agreement between them. It shall supersede all other written or oral agreements between them. This Contract can only be modified in writing that is initialed and dated by both Parties.

23. WALK-THROUGH.

A. Buyer shall have the right and opportunity to walk through the property within 48 hours of the scheduled Closing.

B. If the Buyer observes any change in the property's condition, apart from normal wear and tear, from the day on which this Contract took effect that he finds unacceptable, the Parties agree to attempt to resolve the issue prior to Closing. The terms of any resolution shall be appended to this Contract.

C. If the Parties are unable to resolve the issue, Buyer may void this Contract without penalty.

24. MISCELLANEOUS.

A. This Contract may be signed in one or more counterparts, each of which shall be deemed to be an original document. All such documents together shall constitute one and the same document.

B. For the purpose of computing the duration of this Contract, the first day shall be the day this Contract comes into effect by the dated signature of the last required Party. All time periods shall begin at 5 p.m. on the day specified in this Contract. Each time period shall run for the specified period of days, ending at 5 p.m. on the termination day as provided.

C. This Contract shall be binding on the Parties, and it shall bind and inure to the benefit of their heirs, agents, personal representatives, successors and assigns.

D. If handwritten or typed terms conflict with or are inconsistent with the printed terms of this Contract, the more recent shall control.

25. ACCEPTANCE.

A. This Contract shall constitute an offer to enter into a bilateral contract with Seller upon the dated signature of the Buyer.

B. Buyer's offer shall become null and void as of _____ (time) on _____ (day/month), 2____, if not accepted by Seller. Changes, counter-offers, and amendment are permitted until that time and date without a binding Contract coming into effect. Buyer at his choice may extend the offering period at his option in writing.

C. The Parties do _____ do not _____ require signature notarization on this document.

WITNESS the following duly authorized signatures.

Sellers accept this offer at 5 p.m. on _____ day of _____, 2____.

SELLER	DATE	BUYER	DATE
ADDRESS		ADDRESS	
PHONE		PHONE	
FAX		FAX	

Escrow Agent, _____, acknowledges receipt of $_____ from Buyer as security deposit.

CHAPTER 31: THINKING ABOUT DIRT MONEY

RESEARCH AND FUTURES ANALYSIS

Buying property usually involves spending your own money. This is unfortunate.

In the real-estate aisle of your local book store, you will find numerous guru books promising that you can buy property for free, and, if not that, with no money down, and, if not that, with just a little something in the deal. Each of these books—and the initially free seminars that often trail them—has some useful information. Their systems, however, may or may not work, and may or may not be unethical or illegal. (John T. Reed is the anti-guru guru whom I endorse. He evaluates all of the get-rich-quick gurus at www.johntreed.com/Reedgururating.html. His own invaluable website is www.johntreed.com/.) I recommend reading the short-cut boys with Reed in one hand and a three-bin sorter in the other: 1) information that appears useful and legal; 2) information that does not; and 3) stuff in the middle, about which you might want to learn more.

The key to making money in country real estate is research.

If your scoping has discovered a property whose purchase price is less than its break-up value, you should be able to borrow close to 100 percent of the purchase price and immediately sell enough of the property or assets to repay some, if not all, of your short-term note. This leaves you with a core holding in the property free and clear. There's no trick to this flip, other than to find a property that can be parted out quickly for more than you've paid for it. Your research has to be based on facts and analysis that a lender knows is credible. If you bring a longer term perspective than that of a flipper, your profit comes from appreciation rather than dismemberment. Your research is no less rigorous, however; it does have different questions, depending on your objectives. Research—pre-purchase scoping—allows you to buy at the right price, given your goals, which, in turn, allows you to get your investment onto a profit track. There's no trick to research, just diligence and effort applied to questions you know you need answers to.

Real-estate investment is a subject that can be learned. That is, after all, what this book is about. Like every investment, rural land carries risk. In my experience, a patient, persistent buyer can strip much, even most, risk out of a land investment. I could never write that sentence about common stocks.

I urge readers to become familiar with the vernacular literature on buying real estate. Robert J. Bruss recommends these: William Nickerson, How I Turned $1,000 into Five Million in Real Estate in My Spare Time (New York: Simon & Schuster, 1984); Robert G. Allen, Nothing Down for the 90s: How to Buy Real Estate With Little or No money Down, or latest edition (New York: Simon & Schuster, 1990); Robert Shemin, Unlimited Riches: Making Your Fortune in Real Estate Investing (New York: John Wiley & Sons, 2002); William Bronchick and Robert Dahlstrom, Flipping Properties: Generate Instant Cash Profits in Real Estate (Chicago: Dearborn, 2001); and David Schumacher, Buy and Hold 2004-2005: 7 Steps to a Real Estate Fortune, rev. ed., (Schumacher Enterprises, 2004). Robert Irwin has written a "Tips and Traps" series of books on buying and selling real estate that I've found very practical. My all-time favorite—because it got me started—is George Bockl, How to Use Leverage to Make Money in Local Real Estate (Englewood Cliffs, N.J.: Prentice-Hall, 1965). I bought George Bockl for a buck at a library book sale, and it changed my life. I'd also advise reading Julie Garton-Good, All About Mortgages: Insider Tips to Finance or Refinance Your Home, 2nd ed. (Chicago: Dearborn, 1999); Peter G. Miller, Successful Real Estate Investing: A Practical Guide to Profits for the Small Investor (New York: HarperPerennial, 1995); William Benke and Joseph M. Fowler, All About Real Estate Investing From the Inside Out (Chicago: Irwin, 1995); Gerri Willis, The SmartMoney Guide to Real Estate Investing (New York: John Wiley & Sons, 2003); and Andrew McLean, Gary W. Eldred and Andrew James McLean, Investing in Real Estate,

3rd ed. (New York: John Wiley & Sons, 2001). All of these books focus on investing in urban/suburban real estate, a similar but different game than what you're thinking about.

I've bought rural land with no money several times. They were 100 percent lender-financed, using the value of the merchantable timber as extra security and as a near-instant pay down of the note. The lender, in other words, had my consulting forester's timber cruise showing the merchantable value that was likely to materialize within a month or two of the deal being done as well as his own sense of the land's FMV as bare dirt. The timber's sale value was projected to cover the acquisition cost, or very close to it. A client recently bought a large wooded tract for about $5.5 million. The merchantable timber cruised out at about $4 million and the sale of the compound, lake and 600 acres (about 20 percent of the entirety) would net him another $4 million. The quick sale of the timber would come close to paying off his debt on this investment. Consequently, the lender's exposure in these loans was minimal, given that most, if not all of the debt, would be repaid within a couple of months.

I would not have been able to make a self-financing timber deal work without knowing how to scope property and having a competent consultant forester estimate the timber's merchantable value as part of that scoping. Lenders in rural areas will understand how these deals work; lenders who don't have this experience will be reluctant to get their feet wet. I've uncovered a few deals where the immediate timber sale more than paid for the acquisition cost.

Self-financing timber deals are hard to find, especially for an inexperienced buyer. But deals that combine the sale of several assets—some timber, an unwanted main house, a bit of acreage to a neighbor, a hunting lease to cover the property taxes—are readily available to anyone willing to part with some assets to pay for others. For these deals to work most advantageously, you have to buy more property than you want, and those assets that you want to sell should be of the type that have a ready market. If you are a non-resident, first-time buyer with no knowledge of a particular community, don't weigh down your first "deal" by trying to buy something for nothing. Don't throw every curve-ball California-acquisition technique that you've read about at a guy whose back is bent from 50 years of honest work. That stuff will confuse the seller into not responding to your offer. Just try to protect your interests through scoping and buy at a reasonable price. Keep your mistakes small. Prudent investing in land never involves rolling the dice on anything. Make a good deal for yourself honestly. Swindling is not recommended.

The "system," though I don't call it one, that I've set forth in this book is based on learning how to ask questions about a property and its seller, obtain reasonably reliable answers and then combine the acquired information into an offer that keeps the buyer's risk to a minimum. This is the process of **dirt-smart scoping**, which will save you money in the property's acquisition, expose you to as few risks as possible and make you money on its sale. These are not tricks or schemes. I have never dazzled a seller with my negotiating wizardry or cheated anyone. Being dirt smart is simply a matter of being a good investigator who doesn't push the facts he acquires farther than they take him on their own.

The investment strategy that I advocate in this book is research: know as much as you can about the target property and the seller prior to purchase and fit your buying strategy to the property itself. Save money through knowledge and thoughtful planning.

The real-estate investment books show you how to use financial leverage, whereby a small amount of money puts into play a much larger amount of borrowed capital that is forecast to produce a large profit on the small amount with which you started the deal. If you are absolutely sure that you can cover the debt payments under all circumstances, it generally pays to borrow as much as you can, given the current tax break on interest for mortgages and investments. The more you borrow, the more highly leveraged your deal. But the key to making money is buying at the right price after you know the property's value, not the degree of leverage you are able to arrange. A no-cash purchase—a 100-percent leveraged acquisition—can go splat; I've been there once. Leverage is one tool in rural real-estate investing that can help you, but it is of less importance than property research and planning. Leverage can get you into deep trouble; research and planning keeps you out of what heady leverage can get you into.

It's easy to think that buying a house is the ordinary American's best real-estate investment, if only because it forces savings. That's certainly true when property is appreciating at ten percent a year over the term of the mortgage. But let's think about appreciation and leverage in more normal terms. On a $100,000 home, you put in ten percent—$10,000—as a cash down payment, which allows you to leverage $90,000 in mortgage money. You might have another $6,000 out of pocket in various charges and fees. You keep the house for 30 years, paying off the $90,000 in a 30-year, nine percent note in 360 identical monthly payments of $724.17, for a total of $260,701.20. You've paid $170,701.20 in interest on the $90,000 in principal. Inflation has helped you as the years went by allowing you to pay a fixed sum with dollars that are less valuable and easier to earn. (That, of course, is one reason why lenders front-load interest on mortgages. Front-loading has you paying most of the interest in more valuable dollars and most of the principal in dollars eroded by inflation.) You also get to deduct interest payments from your gross income, which means roughly that for every three to five dollars in interest paid to the lender you will pay one dollar less in federal tax. (The tax benefit varies according to your income and tax rate, year to year. There is a $100,000 cap on the interest deduction, which means that you can't deduct interest paid on a home mortgage over that amount.) Now let's assume that your home has appreciated in value over 30 years, so that you net $250,000 from its sale. How do the numbers work:

	Cash In	Cash Out
Down payment	$10,000	
Fees/charges	6,000	
Principal	90,000	
Interest	170,700	
Interest deduction		$57,000
Net Gain on Sale		250,000
Tax on Profit		0
	$276,700	$307,000

Over 30 years, you've made about $30,300 above what you paid in; that's about an 11% gain on your total cash paid over time. Looked at from a leverage perspective, you made $30,300 in profit on an initial cash investment of $16,000 over 30 years while living in your investment. If you adjust the value of these dollars over 30 years to account for inflation, you've lost money. Your $30,300 in profit won't buy what your upfront $16,000 would have bought 30 years earlier. You've also paid property taxes, insurance and maintenance. Think of that as rent—the amount of money that you have to pay for living somewhere. Keep the rent expense out of the investment analysis; if you put it in, the profit disappears. The $16,000 in upfront cash got this "investment" rolling, but your payment of interest and principal over the years reduced leveraging's benefits. The $6,000 I've allocated as a cost to get a mortgage is about what you'd pay at a big bank. As an investment, you would do better at the end of 30 years to have invested your $16,000 in CDs.

You can argue to yourself that you've leveraged $16,000 to make $307,000, but it's more honest to say that you've leveraged $276,000 to generate $307,000 after 30 years. Which is okay, but not so great. It helps that you don't have to pay tax on this amount of gain from the sale of a principal residence—at least that's the rule as of 2006.

The numbers will obviously improve if your house benefits from a much higher appreciation rate. It follows, then, that the long-term benefits of leveraging depend largely on the property's appreciation.

Now let's see how leveraging works when you invest in property for more than a year (but not much longer than that) to get the capital-gains rate on taxable gain. A one-year-plus holding period qualifies for the capital-gains rate, which is now 15 percent or less on taxable gain, depending on your income level. Investors usually try to hold for at least a year for this reason. For middle- and upper-income taxpayers, the capital-gains rate is less than the rate applied to their wage or salary (ordinary) income. A short-horizon investment strategy also limits the cascade of interest you pay over a long-term note. If you invest with leveraged money and resell after one year, you will be repaying what basically amounts to an interest-only loan. Unfortunately, the upfront cost of a one-year mortgage or a 30-year mortgage is the same. For that reason, a short-term investor in land is usually better to take a commercial loan (with a higher rate, but much smaller upfront charges, if any) than a mortgage of whatever kind.

A very short digression is in order. **Long-term capital gains** is profit made on an investment—things like real estate or stocks—that are held for more than one year. For most investors, this type of profit is now generally taxed at a lower rate than ordinary income, such as wages or salaries. The Jobs and Growth Tax Relief Reconciliation Act of 2003 lowered the long-term capital-gains tax rates from 20 percent to 15 percent, and from ten percent to 5 percent, depending on your income. The top four ordinary income rates are all higher than 15%. If you flip property in less than a year, you will pay tax at your ordinary rate, which can be ten percent, 15, 25, 28, 33 or 35, depending on your income and your filing status. With investors in the upper four ordinary-income brackets, the long-term capital-gains rate of 15 percent will save them between ten and 20 percent on federal tax owed. In many if not most situations, it is to the taxpayer's advantage to set the closing on the flip of an asset for at least a year and a day past his own closing. It can be more profitable to carry the property for the year and pay interest on the debt if it allows the taxpayer to qualify for the 15 percent capital-gains rate on profit from the sale. If, of course, you're selling the severable asset for about what you paid for it, then you will have little taxable gain and the cost of carrying for a year will exceed the break on tax rates. These capital-gains rates are set to expire in 2008, and Congress is currently debating extending them. If nothing happens, the pre-2003 rates will reappear on January 1, 2009. Extension is likely for 2009 through 2010.

There are two other long-term capital-gains rates that you should be aware of. A 25-percent rate applies to part of the gain from selling depreciated real estate. This category of real estate is known as **Section 1250 property.** (See Chapter 3 in IRS Publication 544, Sales and Other Dispositions of Assets.) You would pay 25 percent on the amount you depreciated as "recapture," then your capital-gains rate on your taxable gain. Timber sales do not involve depreciation. If you split off 15 acres from the 100 you just purchased, there is no depreciation involved. A 28-percent rate applies to gain realized from the sale of small-business stock held for more than five years after you exclude one-half of your gain from income. The 28-percent rate also applies to the sale of collectibles, such as art, antiques, gems, coins, precious metals and stamps. These rates existed before the 2003 legislation and were continued.

When planning a purchase of rural property coupled with the sale of some of its assets, you need to determine whether you net more after taxes by flipping within the first year or waiting for the long-term capital-gains rate to apply. End of digression.

Let's rework the house example to fit the purchase of a $100,000 piece of rural property that you finance at nine percent over 30 years. Nine percent is above market as I write in 2006; so the actual dollars in these examples will be lower when you plug in mortgage money at, say, six percent. Lenders may charge a higher rate when the borrower's purpose is to buy a second home in the country. And rates go up if the borrower is buying undeveloped (raw) land with no improvements. You might choose to amortize the loan over 30 years to keep your monthly payments as low as possible. The longer the amortization, the more you're leveraging a small amount of money to acquire a property. **You must be sure that your mortgage**

agreement *allows you to prepay some or all of the principal at any time without penalty.* You sell the property a year and a day after you purchased it for $110,000, a ten-percent appreciation. You don't use a broker to sell the property and you make no improvements to it. This is not considered your principal residence, and you sell it a year after buying it to get the 15 percent capital-gains rate. Here's how these numbers look:

	Cash In	Cash Out
Down Payment	$10,000	
Fees/charges	6,000	
Principal	592	
Interest	8,125 (e)	
Interest deduction		$2,681
Gain on Sale		10,000
Tax on Profit (15%)		(1,500)
	$24,717	$11,181

(I've not added certain costs to each column, such as property tax on the cash in and selling fees on the cash out. I've also not recast the loan as a no-fee/charge commercial note, which is what I would recommend doing in this example.)

You've leveraged $16,000 in cash to acquire a $100,000 property, which you sold for a $10,000 net gain after a year. Leveraging looks good this way. But let's look again.

This investment shows a loss of almost $13,536 after taxes, even though it looked like you "made" $10,000 on the flip. You had $24,717 invested over a year, and you cashed out for $11,181.

To make this investment work with borrowed money, the rate of appreciation over the time you hold the property must be much higher, or the selling price, regardless of appreciation, must be higher. It's hard to make a real profit on a short-term flip with borrowed money when appreciation is the only factor working in your favor. Leveraging alone does not produce a profit. Leveraging, on the other hand, does allow you to get in the game where profit can be made on a big-ticket item bought right and sold right. In the right circumstances, a ten percent profit on a $100,000 property purchase using $10,000 as a down payment will exceed a ten percent profit on the $10,000 invested in stocks. But you cannot assume this will occur automatically without projecting realistic numbers over the term of your investment.

How can this investor increase his profit in this example?

1. If the investor takes $100,000 out of his savings and borrows nothing, he'll make a $10,000 gross profit and pay $1,500 in capital-gains tax. That's an 8.5 percent profit on the use of his money. His Cash In is $100,000 but he saves $14,717 in fees, principal and interest. But most of us don't want to use our cash this way; and even more of us don't have the full purchase price in cash. His 8.5 percent profit is lowered by the amount of money he would have earned on the $100,000 invested for a year in something else.

2. A fully leveraged deal doesn't help. If the investor is able to borrow $100,000, his monthly payment at nine percent on a 30-year schedule is $804.63, for a total one-year P&I expense of $9,655.56. About $700 of that sum went to principal, and $8,955.56 to interest. Roughly $3,000 came back as a mortgage interest deduction. The investor still has $6,000 in buying costs. When each column is totaled, the investor loses about $3,000. Leveraging

even with a ten percent appreciation rate doesn't make the numbers work. The $6,000 cost of getting the loan and the $9,656 in P&I exceed the $3,000 in deduction plus the $10,000 in gain, less the 15 percent in tax ($1,500). Leveraging makes the short-term flip worse than the conventional loan when structured over 30 years.

Both examples above, 1 and 2, work a bit better if the investor takes a six-month or one-year adjustable-rate mortgage at 7 percent instead of nine. That would save a good bit of interest. Finding a lender that charges fewer points and fees would knock down the $6,000 loan-origination cost.

3. The two locally owned banks in my county charge higher interest rates on mortgages than the big banks, but neither charges much to originate the loan. The numbers in a short-term investment can turn positive when the cost of getting borrowed money drops to $500. Therefore, if you're looking to flip, find this type of lender. You might also check out borrowing from a local community credit union. A commercial loan for land, or even a personal loan, carries a higher rate, but avoids the front-end mortgage costs.

4. Reduce your borrowing. A short-term flip works best in generating profit to the extent that you can use cash and borrow as little as necessary. The comparison that you must do before making this investment is whether the profit you project (together with the investments risks) promises a sufficiently greater reward considering risk than leaving your cash where it is.

5. Keep carrying costs down. Holding a house for a year involves insurance, maintenance and significant property taxes. Holding unimproved rural land for a year involves paying low property taxes and perhaps nothing else. Cosmetic improvements to a home will pay for themselves and then some, but major jobs—especially hidden ones like rewiring, replumbing and fixing a foundation—won't. Cosmetic improvements to undeveloped land such as $1,000 in grading and seeding an access road or mowing the interior roads do pay for themselves and more. Flipped investments, as a rule, work best when the improvements are limited to low-dollar cosmetics. Unimproved land can often generate enough income through a hunting lease to cover the property taxes.

6. If the seller finances the purchase, you save the $6,000 in fees/charges and perhaps some interest. But you still end up losing money.

7. The real way to make this type of flip work is to **part out** the property as your investment strategy. A 100-acre property bought for $100,000 can be divided into four 25-acre parcels and sold for a total of $150,000, because smaller acreages always fetch higher per-acre prices than larger acreages. Division might require a total of $10,000 in road work and surveying. You might spend another $5,000 for marketing. But the profit rises from $10,000 to $35,000, even after these expenditures. (Of course, you need to be able to come up with the additional $15,000 to get that next $35,000 in gross profit.) Parting out automatically boosts the per-acre price of the land and allows each small parcel to gain more value even if the appreciation rate is the same. The land is not depreciated so the long-term capital-gains rate of, say, 15 percent, will apply.

You can also part out assets in advance of division. If you sell the merchantable timber for $50,000, then divide into four cutover lots that sell for a total of $125,000, you're even better off. A timber job of this sort is called a "residential cut." It leaves timber untouched around the four house sites and removes high-value species. Lopping the slash improves aesthetics before resale.

Profiting from a rural land investment usually involves combining a number of elements discussed above. Leveraging through borrowing is one. Selling merchantable timber immediately after purchase for the pre-purchase cruise value is a second. Selling some other severable assets is a third. Buying the entirety at the right price is an obvious fourth. Calculating the most tax-advantaged way of timing your sales is the fifth. Finally, holding for more years rather than fewer allows appreciation to work for you.

Buying a second home in the country or investing in rural property should be approached with an accountant's eye right from the start. A buyer's wants and emotions cannot be allowed to trump his own pocketbook. So before you scope your first acre, and even before you get in the car to spend a sunny Saturday afternoon with a real-estate agent, draft a **goals-and-money plan**. This is a document that puts in writing (don't skip this step) your generic ability to acquire property of the type you're seeking. The document becomes property-specific once you've found one that you think will work. Then it becomes a **target property**. I urge you to think of your money plan in terms of your goals. You will find that modifying goals can either increase or decrease the money you need to buy the property. For example, if you want to buy woodlands and your initial goal is to not intervene in their management in any way, you will have to pay for the tract without any help from the land itself. If, on the other hand, you want to buy woodlands and your goal is to have the timber pay for a portion of its price—after which you decide to follow a hands-off policy—your purchase will be a lot easier to manage financially but harder aesthetically in the short run.

You can brainstorm goals at whatever level that you think is operational. That can include everything from maximizing the property's contribution to fighting global warming on one hand to squeezing the last dollar out of the property as soon as possible on the other. Here are some ideas about *possible* first-draft, property-buying goals in relation to purchase money. Your job is winnow your list of goals into an internally consistent set in terms of the level of contribution, if any, you want the property to make to the purchase.

Ask: Is this goal consistent with having property help pay for itself?

	Can Property help pay for itself?		
First-draft Property Goals	Yes	No	If yes, how?
Family recreation opportunity			
Long-term appreciation as investment			
Place to relax—no work, maintenance			
Possible retirement home			
Hunting property—leave undeveloped; place for camper desirable			
Flip—turn as much profit asap and get out			
Conserve environment for specific objectives e.g., enhance bird habitat or game habitat, promote diversification of plant species, no human interference in natural processes			
Build second home			
Accrue retirement capital			

Most land-buying goals, like many aspects of buying and selling, can be combined in various ways and are subject to adaptation and balanced compromises. In this case, it's a matter of negotiating with yourself. Welcome this internal bargaining, because it's beneficial. It focuses your thinking and forces you to research your ideas in light of the property's specifics.

I started this discussion about money by asking you to think through your goals for the property. Only after you have done that, should you move into the more conventional considerations of money, such as how much cash can you put into the purchase. I've asked you to think about how the property can help pay for itself, because your answers to that question in terms of each goal directly affects how much cash you need to put into the purchase, how much money you need to borrow and for how long, what level of income the property might generate, how you might cover P&I payments and so on.

Apart from asking questions about how you will pay for the property, discussed in the following chapters, one of your initial financial questions about any land purchase is **how liquid is it**? Rural property is not illiquid, but it's far more illiquid than stocks or cash. A liquidity "analysis" will give you a sense—but no certainty—as to how long it will take you to sell the property if you have to.

If you project your cash flow to be variable or uncertain in the future, you probably don't want to buy discretionary property with substantial financing (leveraging) if you anticipate that it will take a year or more to sell at an acceptable price. The monthly mortgage payments can drain your cash and even produce a foreclosure. If the property is odd owing to location, size, shape or other factors, it's likely to be less liquid than properties comparable in price and acreage.

A **liquidity analysis** starts with determining the recent sales prices of properties that are roughly comparable to your target property. (You should be doing this anyway as part of your scoping.) This information should be available in, or calculable from, recent deeds. If not, talk with a couple of local real-estate brokers as well as the county clerk and assessor. Your task is to determine approximate selling prices as well as the amount of time each property was on the market before being sold. It's also helpful to get an idea of the spread between asking price and selling price of each comparable; asking prices for listed properties should be available from brokers. Then you want to ask the brokers their opinion as to how much time might have been shaved from the time it took to sell each comparable for each, say, five percent, off the asking price. You might find, for example, that the brokers think, as a general current rule, that a five percent discount on asking price might have produced a sale three months earlier. This is a very coarse opinion-analysis, but it's probably worth something for your purpose.

Assuming, then, that market conditions and interest rates will be roughly the same as current conditions three years into the future, you can make a few reasonable liquidity projections. Take the price you are willing to pay as FMV for the target property. Project appreciation of this FMV year by year, compounded, at what you anticipate the appreciation rate of the target property will be. The brokers can help you estimate the recent appreciation rate for properties comparable to your target property. Then take the brokers' consensus opinion about average time on the market for your type of property, say, one year, and discount your appreciated FMV projection by whatever the brokers estimate to be the local price discount-to-time ratio. If, in other words, your ratio is 5:3 (five percent discount in asking price to three fewer months on the market), you can project that a 20 percent discount in your future FMV/asking price will produce a very quick sale, a 15 percent discount will produce a sale in six months, a ten percent discount will produce a sale in nine months and a five percent discount will produce a sale in 12 months. A 20 percent discount on FMV does not mean you lose money on the sale. How much you make or not make depends on the appreciation rate you use and how quickly you need to sell. There's lots of slop in this "methodology," but it will give you a reasonable guess at how much time it will take you to sell your target property at a particular price at various points over the next year. Projecting appreciation rates and assuming steady market factors much beyond three years gets increasingly chancy.

Property values can go down. Most readers will be familiar with stories of booms and busts in urban residential real estate. Property can become illiquid in a down turn though the degree of illiquidity is driven by price. I've not seen rural property in most areas go down in price. I have seen appreciation go through periods of fast increase, slow increase and in-between increase—but the trend has always been up. The exception has been in certain West Virginia counties that have lost significant population; there, I've seen house prices weaken, but prices for undeveloped land continue to increase. The general trend in rural land has been one of appreciation—at least from what I've seen.

An owner can increase the liquidity of rural property by division. Cut a large tract into smaller parcels, each of which is priced at market. The smaller tracts are affordable to a larger market, and the total sales revenue obtained should exceed that gained from a single entirety sale. Make sure to incorporate your cost of sales—broker fees, taxes, etc.—in your calculations. Successive sales of divided land also keep your lender feeling secure to the extent that you use a portion of the net proceeds to repay proportionately your mortgage principal.

A second quick digression. I've emphasized that you consider yourself an investor in rural real estate. An investor gets the benefit of long-term capital-gains rates on property sales. If, however, the IRS classifies you as a **real-estate dealer**, your properties are considered inventory, rather than investments, and your gain is taxed at your ordinary rate. The line between investor and dealer is murky. Courts have used nine tests to determine the difference, among the most important are the purpose for which the taxpayer held the property just before its sale, the extent to which it was subdivided, how much improvement was made to the property, and the amount of time and effort the taxpayer devoted to selling the properties. Your pre-purchase investment plan should be oriented around your new property as an investment, rather than a dealer-like buy, divide and flip. Selling merchantable timber and several severable assets as a strategy for keeping the core property should not classify you as a dealer. As part of your scoping and pre-purchase planning, work with your CPA to make sure that your intentions and plan stay within the confines of investment. Your investment should be made and held for "productive use," not trade or business. (Dealers also have to pay self-employment tax and cannot do installment sales where gain is deferred until the money is received.)

You can also assume with some, but not all, rural properties that growing demand over time will increase its liquidity. But market liquidity is a function of demand, supply and price. If demand is strong and supply is adequate, a price way above FMV will produce an illiquid property. You can take comfort by knowing that you can affect your property's liquidity insofar as you set its price. You can always sell property quickly by pricing it below market, but you have to evaluate that emergency tactic in light of your need for net sale income sufficient to pay off any debt. The flexibility you have in pricing is determined by the level of debt you need to repay and the amount of equity you've built up. The lower your debt, the lower you can price the property and get it sold quickly.

Two other considerations when selling property are the direct costs of selling (broker fee, taxes, legal fees, etc.) and the amount of federal income tax you owe on your taxable gain. The first of these questions is fairly easy to project; your CPA or lawyer can estimate these costs with reasonable accuracy for three to five years, at least. You can always expect these charges to rise over time.

The tax-hit question involves the specifics of the property, your length of ownership, your applicable tax rate and how your original basis in the property has been adjusted over time. I would ask a tax accountant to work up a **tax forecast** before you agree on terms with your buyer. The tax forecast will start with your anticipated cost of acquisition (basis) and incorporate projected changes in light of your plans for the property, such as sale of assets and investment. Your CPA will have to estimate your selling price and the applicable tax rate. A tax forecast is a very small expense that can save you thousands of future tax dollars by showing you your future tax hit in light of your alternative plans for the property and form of ownership. The form of your ownership—personal property, sole proprietorship, corporation, trust, limited liability company, etc.—should fit your objectives, both toward the property and in terms of minimizing future tax obligations. Your CPA should also factor in state tax considerations where they apply.

The first steps, then, in working up a financial plan for the purchase of the property are to think through your goals, the money you will need in light of those goals, where it's going to come from consistent with those goals and, finally, a couple of likely future scenarios, involving hypothetical sales at different points in the future in different circumstances, including an emergency bail-out plan. The plan will change, and should change. Most of the issues won't.

Do Not Skip thinking about and doing something about the questions just discussed as part of your scoping. Add your own.

Do not skip writing them out as a plan!

If you are unwilling to take the time and effort to do this little bit of work, which requires a small amount of your time and perhaps a few hours of CPA and lawyer time, don't buy country land. Failure to start a land purchase right increases the risk of poor results down the road.

HOW ABOUT A TRIAL RENTAL?

For those who prefer to toe-dip before jumping in, **consider renting your target property with an option to buy**. I recommend renting for at least one year if you are hesitant to buy. (You may be able to combine this with a lease-purchase option discussed in Chapter 29.) Renting gives you the opportunity to be on the land at least a couple of times in each season for a couple of days each time. You may run into some highly informative bad weather. If you can live with the target property in miserable conditions, it should suit you at all other times. (Bad weather is also the best time to visit target properties or negotiate a purchase. Nothing beats haggling over price with a seller while standing in *his* mud, with rain blowing in *his* face.)

You will not *know* your target land after a one-year rental; that takes at least ten years. But you should know a lot more about it than when you started if only from what you learn when you take a home-made pie over to each neighbor as a way to introduce yourself. (Store-bought pies are tacky, no matter how expensive.) Consider your tenancy as a year-long engagement that may or may not lead to a wedding. Take Louis Agassiz's instruction to his students, "Look at your fish." as your own. Observe like a science student. Learn what you can. Identify what you don't know. And at the end of the year speculate knowledgeably about what it is that you don't know you don't know.

The cost of renting will depend, of course, on the target property's assets, asking price, the seller's carrying costs and your expenses outside of the lease. Farmhouses tend to rent for at least 50 percent less for the equivalent floor space than urban/suburban houses, and sometimes the rural discount is much larger. Old farmhouses are the cheapest rental deals—and serve your part-time needs. Expect quirks with old wood-frame structures—windows that rattle in the wind, possums that visit your front porch, odd noises in the attic and plumbing from a Rube-Goldberg manual. Don't expect much maintenance from your landlord if he senses that you're a buyer. Such relics are just fine for renting on a try-out basis, and you will get a first-hand lesson in what needs to be done to meet your needs as an owner. "New farmhouses" are usually brick ramblers, log cabins or second homes. If a relatively high-rent house runs with the target property, you might be able to swing a deal whereby you rent a spot for your tent/camper and allow the owner to rent the house and farmland to another party. That puts you on the property for next to nothing possibly within a lease-option contract. If he balks, consider renting the entire farm with a provision that allows you to sublet the house. The ball, on which you want to keep your eye, is big and moving slowly: **get access to the land for a while, for cheap, while postponing any sale**. Done wisely, a buyer can option a property in this fashion for far less than through a conventional option.

A seller whose only carrying costs are routine maintenance and property taxes is a likely rent-option owner as long as he does not need his equity out of the property for some pressing purpose. Offer to pay the property taxes, for starters—and that alone might be a fair rent. You can also offer to provide labor in lieu of rent. Since the seller will be far smarter than you about the **misery content of any farm labor** you are negotiating, I'd be very careful about such a swap. Do not agree, for example, to "help with the hay" in lieu of rent. The seller may quite rightly take this to mean that you will be on hand six days a week from June 15 to October 1 as needed. (You, on the other hand, are thinking that this will involve no more than two or three hours on two or three pleasant Saturday afternoons during which time you drive his tractor with a beer in hand.) "Hay help" generally gets the hard jobs. I know of one such swap that involved putting up more than 10,000 "square" bales of hay—with the tenant stacking 50-pound bales on a moving wagon and then restacking them in the barn's mow. This had him lifting and toting one million pounds of hay over several months in return for some machine work.

Assuming that you've done your pre-purchase scoping before renting, you should have a reasonably accurate idea of the seller's carrying costs and his income from the property. You can propose a straight cash rental, maybe two or three percent of the asking price for property with a livable house. On undeveloped land that is suitable for your camper/RV/tent, you might offer one year of property tax payment plus something extra. The extra might be one to four of his mortgage payments (which he will pay tax on because it's rent and you will get no interest deduction) or some percentage of his asking price, say, 3/4 to 1 1/2 percent. You can also propose a rental credit formula that kicks in if you exercise an option to buy. Obviously, the higher the credit, the more money you save. When negotiating, remember that rental income and capital gains are taxable revenues to the seller, and likely at different rates. He may pay at 30+ percent (his rate on ordinary income) on rental income and 15 percent on the long-term capital gains from the sale of the property. He will, therefore, have more money left in his after-tax pocket from a sale dollar than from a rental dollar. Accordingly, you might discount the rent a bit in return for upping the deferred sale price. Don't get too fancy with this, though. If the seller's after-tax net is important to the property's sale, he'll take you up on your flexibility. Your CPA can project alternative tax differences for the seller that will help you in your negotiations.

You may encounter a seller who agrees to **rent** to you for a year on the basis of **cash-only payments**. Such a seller may or may not declare cash income on his tax return, but probably not. He will be unlikely to agree to sign a rental agreement with you or a lease with an option to buy, because he doesn't want to create a paper trail. In return for cash, he might knock 15 percent or more off the property's fair rent. You can live without a written rental agreement, paying monthly, since you are really just trying on the property for size. But you take on many risks without a written lease—who pays for the grease-fire damage that your guest starts in the landlord's antique kitchen woodstove; do you need to pay him for the firewood you cut on his land; when the toilet backs up because the septic tank is full, who pays to empty it.

The other risk in cash deals comes from the IRS. A lot of cash transactions in the country are done to allow the person who receives the cash to avoid declaring it and paying tax on it. Since the payer—you—may be in a position to deduct certain types of expenses paid in cash, the lack of receipts may cost you additional tax dollars if you're audited and can't produce paper supporting the expense. Apart from that penalty, if you have knowledge of the seller's fraudulent purpose in requesting cash, you are aiding his tax deception. Pay by check or get a receipt, you'll sleep easier. If the seller/landlord insists on cash without receipt, find another place. And if you do pay cash, keep a record of each payment with its purpose to support a deduction. If you're set up as a land investor or business, it may be possible to deduct some, or all, of the rent to the extent that it was incurred pursuant to making an investment or business-related purchase. Clear this plan with your CPA.

Buyers/renters—you—sometimes offer to pay rent in cash to sellers/landlords. This can be perfectly innocent where, for instance, you claim no tax benefit for your rental expense. On the other hand, you may be offering cash—less than he's asking in rent—to lure him into not declaring the income on his taxes. If he accepts your low-ball, cash offer, you both gain: you by paying less, he by netting out more from cheating the government. As long as you don't collude in planning the seller's tax strategy, I suppose your cash-offer strategy is legal enough. The tax fraud rests on the seller as long as you don't know about it, or the IRS can't prove that you should have reasonably known about it. If, with the advice of your CPA or lawyer, you propose a low-ball, cash offer, withdraw it immediately if the seller starts talking about his taxes. At the level of ethics, a buyer/renter of this sort does not walk way with clean hands.

There is one other variation of the buyer's cash offer that I should mention. I've occasionally heard about land purchases where the buyer and seller agree on a low-ball official purchase price that is used in all the legal documents, with a back-door cash payment that leaves no paper trail. The cash helps the seller reduce his taxable gain. The lower price helps the buyer and reduces the hit of recordation taxes and broker commissions. In states that require deeds to include the full purchase price, this practice is fraudulent. Even where no requirement exists to include the full purchase price in the sale documents, a phony figure cheats on recordation taxes. I've found buyers of large tracts in both Virginia and Tennessee shorting the recorded number to save on taxes. A buyer who conceals part of his purchase price may run into trouble establishing his actual basis when he goes to sell. If you engage in paying back-door cash on the purchase of land, you are being foolish and, often, criminal. Don't play this game.

COUNTRY MONEY IS DIFFERENT FROM CITY MONEY

Buying rural property will differ from your experience in buying urban or suburban property. Several of these differences affect the buyer's money—how much you pay the seller; how much you borrow from and repay the lender; where you get the money; how much you pay in local property taxes; and how much tax you pay on both your annual *itemized* 1040 and on taxable gain when you sell. What you buy and how you plan for your country property directly affects the income, if any, that it generates and your tax obligations.

The two most familiar tax benefits of real-estate ownership are the mortgage-interest deduction and the tax-exclusion on the sale of a principal residence. Both carry dollar caps, above which they don't apply. Other tax breaks—expensing of business-related costs, capitalization of other costs, deferment of capital-gains tax, depreciation, conservation easements, 1031 exchange and the like—can be batched together for your benefit. Interest on a first mortgage (debt up to $1 million) is deductible; up to $100,000 in interest can be deductible on a second mortgage or home-equity line on the same property. Mortals, mere and otherwise, are not likely to know the labyrinthine ins and outs of our changing tax code. So at some point in your pre-purchase scoping, you should hire a dirt-smart CPA and a lawyer to structure your purchase, ownership and management with tax considerations in mind.

One of the first differences you are likely to encounter involves your relationship with the seller. You will in all likelihood meet directly with the rural seller either before you make an offer or soon thereafter, even when a real-estate broker is involved. It is usually in the buyer's interest to meet the seller inasmuch as a broker, no matter how willing and able, does not know as much about the land or farm as the owner. The broker representing the seller may or may not disclose relevant information to you. A buyer's broker, one who's working for the buyer exclusively, may not know the right questions to ask even though he's supposed to. When all is said and done, the buyer has to take responsibility for the quality of his pre-purchase due diligence. In almost every case, I would recommend at least two meetings with the seller.

The first is a best-behavior, get-acquainted session. Tell the seller something about yourself and your intentions for his property as a way of starting this conversation. Don't fudge. Your first words to the seller will be what he holds you to. Gently ask general questions and write down the owner's answers. Ask whether there are any boundary disputes, unrecorded agreements and claims against the property. Ask how the owner uses the land—which field is good pasture, which is best for the locally grown crop, which might be suited for something you want to do, such as plant a small fruit orchard or vineyard. Ask about water—quality and reliability—and soils. Probe for troublesome issues, such as boundary disputes, without being accusatory. Plead ignorance and ask for his help, invoking the Golden Rule. Try not to be aggressive, know-it-all, urban-neurotic, big-wordy (a sesquipedalian), urban stupid, piously Green, shocked (that a cattle-raising farmer sells his cattle to meateaters) or slippery. Don't affect a local accent; don't chew grass. Don't share your opinions about why farm animals are mistreated, guns should be beaten into plowshares and loggers should be retrained for cell-phone repair. Don't drive into the seller's front yard in the biggest, shiniest, yellowest Hummer you can buy. Similarly, don't wheel up to the seller's farmhouse in an urban trophy car that hangs up in his driveway athwart a cow flop. If you have access to a moderately old, moderately styled, moderately priced pick-up truck, drive that. Don't drop big-shot names, tell how important you are or reveal how much money you make. Don't ask where the closest "decent" wine shop is. Don't lard your conversation with any of the following: Latin legalisms (such as *per se*, *ad hominem* and *sui generis*—all of which I've heard buyers use); Yiddish (Don't ask if the neighbor is a mensch or a schmuck.); French (The seller's farmhouse may indeed have a je-ne-sais-quoi quality, but the seller may not appreciate the comment just the same because it sounds a lot like that new, pesticide-impervious Formosan termite the county extension agent told him about last week.); Valley Girl/1960s Hippie; or your office-dot-com blah blah. Be friendly, interested and bland without being condescending. Keep opinions about politics, religion, ethnicity, race, animal rights, bovine flatulence, exotic vegetables, tobacco use, guns, hunting, rednecks, hillbillies, local yokels, tacky Christmas decorations and pink-painted rooms to yourself. If the seller's house is lovingly planted in forsythia, don't yuk it up over the "vomit of spring." Ease into a conversation where the seller explains about his land and why he's selling.

The second time you meet the owner will be after you've done your scoping. Come to his house bearing normal American food—a pie is always good, or a signature item from your hometown that will be familiar to the seller. Don't give the seller a gift of booze, dope or the dish of the day, such as leaf litter from Amazonia harvested sustainably by right-on indigenous peoples. Ask specific questions about things only the owner can answer. You want to pin down answers, but you don't want to pin him. You want to obtain information in a way that doesn't threaten the owner or challenge his honesty. You want to create an atmosphere of mutual problem-solving: "I'll help pay to get the barn roof fixed by closing, if you get the well pump repaired by then, ok?" Remember that you want to buy the seller's place, not prove that you're smarter than he is. Lawyers are especially bad at this type of information-gathering.

In this second conversation, you may want to raise money issues. Doing this hypothetically—"What if I offered you $100,000 (instead of the $150,000 being asked)?"—is a common tactic, but I advise against it. Hypothetical offers are worthless to a seller because an oral agreement on real estate is not legally enforceable. You'll hear this invoked as the state's statute of frauds, which requires that certain types of contracts—such as real-estate offers, deeds and leases longer than a year—be in writing so that they can be enforced. If, in other words, the seller orally accepted your $100,000 offer—"I'll take it. We have a deal."—he, the seller, can't enforce that in court, and neither can you. You may not have a deal despite both of you agreeing that you do. (Exceptions exist to the statue of frauds.) It doesn't matter whether you shake hands or swear on Bibles. Real-estate agreements are binding when they are written, dated, reasonably specific and signed by buyer and seller. (A contract should, of course, reflect a meeting of the minds.) So the seller's reply to every oral offer should always be: "Put any offer you might want to make in writing, including dollars and all terms." Hypothetical offers are usually no more than tire-kicking—non-serious, low-ball offers from buyers who are looking for a distressed seller forced to accept humiliation. From a buyer's perspective, there's nothing wrong in being a tire kicker. But don't be surprised when a seller invites you to leave as soon as you've kicked his.

I recommend raising the set of money issues all at once, putting them on the table and watching which ones the seller is willing to work on with you and how he goes about it. Such issues beyond price and terms—seller financing, asset sales, 1031 exchange, tax implications—are discussed below.

Putting together a workable money package is no different than working a jigsaw puzzle. In both cases, it's most efficient to spread everything out. Keep in mind that every puzzle is solvable, though you may not be the solution to this seller's puzzle. Unlike a jigsaw puzzle, you may do better with certain sellers to work from a whole solution back toward troublesome parts instead of starting with the pieces that are easiest to figure. The way to do this is to discuss a possible range of prices acceptable to you, depending on how the difficult issues are resolved (that is, what is done and who pays for doing them). With other sellers, however, you may need to work in baby steps toward a deal, starting with the easiest issues.

Before you open negotiations, have in mind the elements of the deal that you want. Identify a general range of acceptable prices, terms, throw-ins, throwaways and so on. Put your whole offer on the table at once. Don't bog down fighting over price. Movement—even little agreements—creates momentum toward a deal.

An old real-estate adage goes: "I'll agree to any price the seller puts on his property, if he'll agree to my terms." If the seller's asking price of $200,000 is $50,000 over all the comparables and he knows it, propose agreeing to his price so long as he finances the entire $200,000 at one percent over 40 years, with a one-time balloon payment of the entire principal at the end of the term. Do this with a twinkle in your eye: you want the seller to know that you're kidding around because he started it. If the seller wants more than you want to pay, work down the price through terms, throw-ins and seller financing. Be ready to give up all of these negotiated advantages in return for what you really want—a lower price. If you fall into pounding one another over price, price and nothing but price, you may never get to a deal. Sellers are looking to hear something close to their number; give them an offer that will sound right with terms that favor you by a lot. See if that doesn't get things off dead center. There are times when inductive negotiating—from the particulars to the whole deal—can work, but my experience is that the buyer should approach the seller using deductive negotiating—which is based on having a general sense of your final number and final terms and then tying up loose ends as part of that general understanding.

Remember that the right price from your perspective depends partly on the nature of the deal's loose ends. Where, for instance, you have identified a specific problem, such as a neighbor claiming access to his property over the seller's land, you will need to determine the seller's position and, if possible, agree on a method of resolving the dispute. That type of problem is common. Its impact can be negligible—the neighbor uses the road a few times a year—or a daily nuisance that will drive you bonkers. Therefore, as part of spreading the deal's pieces on the table, make sure to pitch in everything that your scoping has turned up that could cost you money, time or enjoyment. Do this directly with the seller, preferably while sitting at his kitchen table.

I usually write a letter to the seller, explaining how I arrived at my offering price. I include this letter with a purchase contract. I think I am more effective in putting my arguments forward in writing than orally. A letter also allows you to get everything out, the way you want it out.

You will also notice that there is a more **informal sales process** in rural areas**.** The paperwork may be a bit simpler; fewer people and organizations are likely to be involved; everything is personal. Your new local banker might want to rent your pasture; your local lawyer might want to sell you hay. **Don't let informality substitute for scoping**, no matter how friendly your new friends are. You may be told that you don't need to worry about mineral ownership, title insurance, testing the water, etc., because "we just never do much of that out here." That's not good enough. Worry about something if you think it's necessary.

You have to determine when your scoping is legitimate as against when it crosses into compulsive nerdiness. I've seen deals blow up when buyers rag sellers on detail after detail with no judgment applied as to which detail is truly important and which is not. A real-estate broker recently told me not to worry about the fact that a 170-acre parcel was accessed by a two-mile-long road for which he knew of no recorded easement. You don't need a deeded right of way, he told me, because "you have a prescriptive easement." A prescriptive easement is not established legally simply by using a road over someone's property. It must meet state-specific tests. If use is based on permission, it is not a prescriptive easement. Permission ends with a sale or the death of either party. That means a new owner has no right to use the road. Permission can be withdrawn at any time and without cause. A prescriptive easement, finally, needs to be established in court "against" each landowner over whom the road crosses if it is challenged. A real-estate broker's opinion establishes nothing in the eyes of the law. Fortunately, an earlier deed was finally found that did provide an access easement.

The borrowing aspect of buying rural land can be, and often is, different than the elaborate process you go through in the city. There, you would shop for the best loan terms with little regard for which financial institution is closest to you, or has the most borrower-friendly board, or is most open to working with newcomers to the neighborhood. These factors, alone or in combination, may drive your decision in the country. It's useful to check out the differences in loan packages between locally owned banks (possibly state-chartered) in your target county and the local offices of the big regional banks. I discuss these alternatives below. The key point to understand is that locally owned lenders are likely to have more flexibility on mortgage terms in their communities, particularly when they keep the loan, than the big banks, which more often than not will insist on the borrower meeting rigid loan requirements that will allow them to sell the loan in the secondary market soon after it is made. Flexibility, of course, comes with a price. You may get better terms (no fees, no points, even 100 percent financing) from the local lender, but at a much higher interest rate than the big bank. Generally speaking, if you're looking to pay back the note quickly, take the local lender's terms; if you're going to keep the note for ten or more years, take the lower interest rate.

Rural property lends itself to classification as an investment or business for IRS purposes. Even if your first intentions are purely recreational for the targeted 150 acres of woodland, I urge you to discuss setting up the ownership and tax management as an investment using the timber—whatever its present value—as the door in. You will be able to write off mortgage interest, as well as expense certain costs and depreciate certain improvements. Many rural counties, especially those feeling development pressure, give a break on property taxes to farmers and others with undeveloped property called **land use**. It may be easier to qualify for this lower property tax rate if your land is set up as a farm or timberland investment. Ask if the county in which your target property lies has land-use taxation, and, if so, whether the seller's property is "currently in land use." It's far easier to continue land-use than to get your property reclassified.

If the property has a house or your intention is to build a house, consult with your local CPA before purchasing the property. As a taxpayer, you get certain tax benefits from a second home, and even more if you rent it for a minimum number of weeks each year. Rental property can also be depreciated. Depending on your plans, it may be worth considering renting out the house and buying a small trailer or RV for your own use while on site.

Every taxpayer can currently take advantage of the tax exclusion of $250,000, single filer/ $500,000, joint filer of taxable gain (profit) on the sale of his **principal residence**. Simply put, if you file a return by yourself, you don't have to pay federal income tax on the first $250,000 in profit that you make when you sell your home. If you file with a spouse, the two of you don't have to pay taxes on $500,000 from such a sale. Generally speaking, your principal residence is one where you have lived for any two out of the last five years prior to sale, spending the majority of each of those two years there. The years don't have to be consecutive. A *second home* in the country is not your principal residence. Therefore, gain on its sale is not eligible for the exclusion, nor is it eligible for a 1031 tax-deferred exchange because it is not held for investment or use in your trade or business. But you might choose to configure your life so that you meet the residency requirement and other qualifications to allow you to turn a second home into a principal residence prior to sale. The IRS would look to confirm a principal-residence claim by checking your addresses for voting registration, utility bills, driver's license and the like. I don't know how prevalent such scrutiny is. You can use this exclusion on your principal residence every two years. During a five-year period, you can, it appears, qualify two residences as a "principal residence," with both getting the big tax break. No exclusion of this sort exists on rural property that is not used as your principal residence.

You may be able to get a partial exclusion if you have to sell before you meet the two-year, principal-residence requirement. If you lived in your second home as your principal residence for just one year, you could exclude $125,000 in profit if you meet certain tests. Accordingly, if you made a $100,000 profit (taxable gain) on the sale at the end of your one year, you would owe no tax on that gain because you could legitimately exclude $125,000. Current IRS rules limit the circumstances in which you can get the partial exclusion on home sales forced by health reasons (related to a disease, illness or injury to an owner or co-owner); change in your place of employment (the new workplace has to be at least 50 miles farther from the old home than the old workplace was) or "unforeseen circumstances." The last would include circumstances involving death, divorce, job loss, change in job status that leaves the owner unable to pay the mortgage or living expenses, multiple births and condemnation of the property. These rules do not exclude other unforeseen circumstances, but you will need to make that case. The partial exclusion can be used to get a refund for prior years if your forced sale qualifies. I'd advise against using "unforeseen circumstances" to obtain the partial exclusion on your own intuition of IRS intent: run your circumstances past your CPA first. (Kenneth R. Harney, "IRS loosens rules about home sales," <u>Richmond Times-Dispatch</u>, December 29, 2002.)

While you should be aware of the tax benefits available to you in the principal-residence game, most readers will ultimately benefit the most from setting up a rural property purchase as an investment, investment business (though not as a real-estate dealer) or, possibly, as another type of business where the land purchase is a necessary part. (This need not foreclose your opportunity to use the rural house as a principal residence at some future point.) You may want to organize only some of your new property as an investment or business. The tax code is far more helpful to those purposes than to buying and using land for personal recreation. While a farm classification opens its own set of tax benefits, you need not meet the IRS farm tests to rent your open land for grazing or "organize" your woods as a timber investment or timber-investment business. Even inaccessible, undeveloped land can be rented for hunting or hiking. Crop land can always earn money. If your new property can generate income, consider the advantages of doing so in light of the tax benefits that result. As a personal playground, your rural property provides you with minimum tax benefits—mortgage interest and property taxes, mainly. The same ground organized as an investment allows you to take these items as well as all investment-related expenses (from a lock on the gate to a culvert in a road) and depreciation on existing and new improvements (from battle-scarred tractors to outbuildings). As a business, rural property losses can offset gains from other sources of income. Whether you set up your new property as a personal asset, investment or business, you can still donate or sell conservation easements on the land if that severance fits your overall plan for the property. Conservation easements, however, benefit individual taxpayers more than corporations, so that may be a factor in how you take ownership. **Your CPA will help you understand the tax implications of each ownership option and property plan during your scoping.**

Another money difference between city and country property involves the owner's annual carrying costs. You would, of course, be able to determine your annual mortgage payment, insurance and property taxes in each case with a high degree of accuracy. Rural property tax, particularly if you have land use on your rural property, should be very low, in both absolute and comparative terms. You might pay $4,000 in property tax on a modest suburban lot and its 2,400-square-foot suburban house and half that on a 150-acre farm with a similar house.

You should also price out **homeowners' insurance** and **private mortgage insurance (PMI)**. Conventional homeowner's insurance on farms—a farm policy—covers a lot of things, but probably doesn't protect against damage from floods, forest fire, electricity surges to appliances with chips, among others. You should ask whether all of the outbuildings are covered and what your liability coverage is for visitors drowning in your swimming hole, falling from your barn loft and rolling your tractor. One type of PMI protects you: you buy a policy that protects your property in the event that you are unable to make payments. The other type of PMI protects your institutional lender when you borrow more than 80 percent of the property's value.

If the property has functioning utilities, ask the seller for a year's bills so that you can project your basic service costs. Make sure that you determine how much use the seller made of the property in the winter (heat) and summer (possibly AC). If there is no electricity on the property, get a free estimate from the local power company of the cost to run a line to where you want it along with assurances from neighbors that they will agree to a utility easement across them to you. Try to negotiate the location of utility easements with the neighbor and the power-company engineers on site at the same time. Utility engineers prefer to run straight lines regardless of how they affect your neighbors who are under no requirement to agree to anything. Neighbors may only agree to an underground installation, which is usually more expensive than pole service. The three utilities with which I've dealt allow the new, remotely located homeowner to spread the installation cost over a number of years and apply some of the monthly usage charges against that sum. In the country, you should expect to pay a trash fee and local taxes on farm equipment and vehicles.

Sewerage can be a capital expense in the country whereas in places served by public systems you may be charged only a nominal amount for hooking on or opening a new account, followed by periodic usage charges. If you find yourself scoping a country house that does not pipe grey water (sink, shower, washing machine) *and* black water (toilet) into an **approved sewage system**, you may be required to install one following your purchase.

If there is no sanitarian-approved sewage treatment system in place where you need it, you may be able to install a conventional septic system (for $3,000 to $5,000) if the ground is suitable. This is determined by a water percolation test in some states or a soil-color test administered by the sanitarian or a soils engineer in others. If your dirt doesn't "perc," you can construct an engineered system for $15,000 to $20,000. In some circumstances, it may be possible to substitute a self-contained chemical or composting toilet for a drain-field-type system. If you are thinking about such alternatives, check with your county sanitarian before submitting a purchase contract to determine which, if any, alternatives are acceptable and their likely cost.

Jurisdictions differ widely over what they require in terms of wastewater treatment. One West Virginia county that I contacted recently required no sewerage system as long as the remote cabin had no inside running water. If a line from a spring was run to the kitchen sink, however, a gravel-lined ditch would need to be constructed to accept its grey water. If a shower and toilet were installed, then an approved septic system was expected. At least one state, North Carolina, now requires all residences whose waste waters are not connected to an approved system to put one in. Localities may have different rules for full-time residences and part-time hunting camps. You cannot assume that a current sewerage arrangement will be grandfathered for the new owner. The rule is: ask specific questions of the proper official during scoping. If you're going to get hit with a $20,000 sewerage-system-installation bill immediately after taking possession, you need to know that before you submit your offer.

A major difference between city and country real estate lies in routine maintenance costs. Country property can be maintenance free when you're working with undeveloped land. But even these properties can involve unanticipated expenses, such as fence replacement, aerial spraying to protect trees from insects and flood clean up. Improvements (structures, residences, facilities, roads, bridges, etc.) on country property always require upkeep, though deferring upkeep is common enough. Some upkeep can be deferred, though roof leaks and failing bridge girders cannot. Self-initiated safety investments take on more prominence in the country. In town, your investment choice might be between spending $30,000 on a prettier kitchen or a prettier bathroom. In the country, your first investments are likely to go to rewire the house for safety and rebuild the cattle guard (bridge) that gives you access to the state-maintained road. On the whole, skilled and unskilled labor is much cheaper in the country, which means that all such work is proportionately cheaper. This also holds true for excavation, tree trimming, auto mechanics, shop work and the like. Materials, if procured locally, are likely to be higher than at your suburban Home Depot.

Therefore, as part of your pre-purchase scoping it's important to gather as much information as you can about what the new place will require for safety-related improvements and then move to costing changes related to immediate other needs related to convenience and functionality. Following that, list things that are deferrable needs and discretionary expenses. Each item in the safety and immediate-need category should be a bargaining chip in your negotiations with the seller.

CHAPTER 32: BORROWING MONEY

SYSTEM OVERVIEW

Since institutional lenders, such as banks, are often involved in rural property purchases, it's useful to know some of the basic concepts, vocabulary and procedures they use. A borrower cannot avoid becoming conversant with these matters, if only because the choices each borrower must make to pick a loan require it.

Realize going in that taking out a mortgage is a process that is often opaque. It is made more impenetrable by unfamiliar words that have legal and financial meanings as well as acronyms that rival those of the Pentagon. Membership-owned credit unions are, in my experience, the most consumer-friendly mortgage lenders. They usually have the best loan packages, and they should be completely open about charges and profit spreads. Their institutional purpose is not to wrest the most profit out of each loan, so they don't try to trick and stick their borrowers. But a credit union may not be available to you in your target area.

Even with the most scrupulous lender, each borrower needs to develop at least a background familiarity with how money is borrowed—its benefits, risks, choices, standard formulas, vocabulary and procedures. I recommend the following sources: Jack Guttentag, The Mortgage Encyclopedia: An Authoritative Guide to Mortgage Programs, Practices, Prices, and Pitfalls (New York: McGraw-Hill, 2004); Randy Johnson, How to Save Thousands of Dollars on your Home Mortgage (New York: John Wiley & Sons, 1998); Julie Garton-Good, All About Mortgages: Insider Tips to Finance or Refinance Your Home, 2nd ed. (Chicago: Dearborn, 1999); www.bankrate.com; www.nfsn.com; www.hsh.com; www.mortgage-x.com; and www.mtgprofessor.com.

Figuring out the best mortgage for you is far more involved than finding the lowest interest rate. In fact, the lowest rate can be nothing more than sucker bait for a hugely disadvantageous loan package. The key question you have to answer is how long you anticipate owning the property. If you anticipate either owning it for less than five years or being able to pay down a large chunk of the principal within that time, find a mortgage with the least amount of upfront fees, points and other closing costs. Make sure your mortgage allows you to pre-pay at any time some or all of the principal without penalty. (If you pre-pay principal, make sure to note on your check the exact amount you are applying to principal pre-payment or write a separate principal-only check.) Most borrowers—some 95 percent—pay off their mortgages before the full term expires. (Johnson, Save Thousands, p. 131.) Since interest is **front-loaded**—that is, the borrower's monthly payment goes mainly for interest in his first payment and mainly for principal in his final one—and given the upfront charges you've had to pay to get the loan, the quicker your pay off, the higher the interest rate you will have paid on the borrowed money. In return, you pay far less interest (total dollars), which is a great reason to pay off debt sooner rather than later. If you plan to hold the country property over a 20- or 30-year term, you're best off shopping for the lowest *fixed* interest rate—which stays the same over the loan's entire term—even if you have to pay the lender a bit more upfront to get that rate.

In mortgage shopping, a complicated array of loan choices are available, which combine an interest-rate formula and a set of closing charges (upfront fees, points and other costs) that produce a target yield—that is, gross profit—for the lender over the term. Consumer Reports refers to these choices as a "bewildering assortment…all of them designed to help Americans get into a house with a minimal amount of cash and low monthly payments." (Consumer Reports, "Your Home: how to protect your biggest investment," May, 2005.) Rates and charges change with the length of the term, but the lender's target yield is roughly the same whatever the combination. You won't get a lender to agree to terms that drop him below his target yield, but you may be able to get him down from way above his target. Play one lender against the others to get the best deal. A lender may cut his mark up a bit to get your business, but be aware that the lender most willing to cut may have started above the others. Evaluate lender offers from your perspective, not the lender's. Every loan package you are offered should produce a profit for the lender, but the benefits of each offer from your perspective can range widely, depending on the terms you agree to and how long you hold the mortgage.

You also need to understand that benefits for you may involve high risk for you: **adjustable-rate mortgages (ARMs)** are riskier than fixed rates, and interest-only ARMs are riskier still. When risk converts to reality, you can lose your property. It's fair for your lender to make a profit on his business dealings with you. Your job is not to strip his profit out of the deal, but to estimate to the best of your ability which combination of interest rate, charges, risks and terms is likely to cost you the least and work best for you given your plans for holding the property. A win for the borrower does not require a loss for the lender.

Most property is bought in a standard format: the buyer comes up with a cash **down payment** and borrows the rest from an institutional lender, such as a bank, savings and loan or credit union. The borrowed money takes the form of a **mortgage**, which is a **lien** that uses the property as security for the debt the buyer has just taken on. The property's market value—what you just paid for it—will exceed the mortgage amount in most cases. (Loans are also made in certain circumstances that require no down payment, which means the loan covers 100 percent of the purchase price or even 125 percent. Such notes carry higher interest rates. They can make sense in markets where land prices are appreciating rapidly and the borrower has a strong income flow, but they are very risky.)

One of the many decisions a lender makes on each loan is how much of the borrower's cash it wants to be sunk in a particular property. This decision takes the form of a **loan-to-value (LTV) ratio**, which expresses as a percent the amount of money the lender will offer (loan) in terms of the property's "value." The common LTV ratios are 80 percent and 90 percent, that is, the bank lends to the borrower 80 percent of the property's current value, as the lender defines it. On large land deals, however, I've encountered banks that would lend only 50 or 60 percent of value, packaged as an interest-only commercial note. A lender might use a 90 percent LTV ratio of an appraisal value for a property with a quality improvement (usable house) and 80 percent or less for a totally unimproved property. What the lender won't lend, the borrower must produce from other sources. An 80 percent LTV ratio means the borrower must come up with 20 percent of the value—as determined by the lender—usually in addition to closing costs. The lender decides which definition of "value" he wants to use. It may be the property's appraisal number (which should be fair market value), or the contract price, or the lesser of the two. *If the appraisal price is less than your contract purchase price, an 80 percent LTV ratio based on appraisal price means that you will have to produce more than 20 percent of your purchase price from your other resources.* Lenders have historically preferred a higher percentage of borrower cash in the property, that is, a lower LTV ratio. But that's changing. Many offer 90 percent LTV loans and even 100 percent LTV loans—at higher interest rates, with higher points and a strong borrower.

Some states have lenders holding mortgage liens directly, while others use a trustee to hold the note, in which case the mortgage is called a **deed of trust**. A mortgage lien of either type is a claim by a creditor—in this case the lender from whom you've borrowed—to control the property you've just bought to meet your debt/liability. If the borrower does not make his mortgage payments, the creditor who holds the lien can seize the property and sell it. The trustees or the creditor directly hold legal title until either the debt is paid in full or a default occurs, in which case a foreclosure is declared and the property sold to benefit the lender. (See Benny L. Kass, "Housing Counsel: Deed of Trust Gives Lender Broad Power Over the Home You Buy," <u>Washington Post</u>, February 5, 2005.) While the borrower—you—possesses the property, uses it and improves it, the lender retains the power, though seldom exercised, to either prevent you from doing what you want with his **security interest** or establish certain guidelines that you must follow to do what you want.

If, for example, you want to sell a portion of the land that you've just mortgaged and put the cash in your pocket, you will need to clear it with the lender since the sale of that acreage will reduce his collateral securing the entire debt. The lender must agree to issue a **release** on the partial sale before you can sell. A lender may insist that you pay down your mortgage by a proportional amount before you put sale dollar one in your own wallet. The amount a lender will ask you to pay toward your mortgage from a partial sale will depend on how much equity you have in the root property, how much the property has appreciated since you first borrowed the money and how much of the property you will have left to secure the remaining note. The lender may also insist that you receive a minimum amount of money from the partial sale. This is known as imposing a **reserve price** on your sale. The lender will not release that portion of the property for sale unless your buyer meets the lender's reserve price. If you plan to sell either timber or a lot from the rural property you are about to purchase, discuss your idea with your lender so that you will know in advance how he will respond.

If you fail to meet the terms of your mortgage, which is called a **default**, the holder of the lien can sell your property that's serving as collateral/security in an effort to get his money. **Foreclosure** is the legal process by which the property securing borrowed money is sold to satisfy a debt. A borrower in foreclosure can be charged for the lender's expenses in cashing out the property. If the foreclosure sale does not net enough money to cover the loan principal, expenses and accrued interest, the lender may be able to get a **deficiency judgment** against the borrower to make up the difference. This will be ugly. If a foreclosure sale covers all claims, anything left goes to the borrower. Foreclosure, default and bankruptcy require a borrower to get help from a lawyer. If you have personally guaranteed the note in addition to placing the property as collateral, the lender will expect you to make up any shortfall. But mortgaged property is generally secured only by the real estate, the common exception being business deals involving property. With most real-estate mortgages, your risk is generally limited to the loss of the property serving as collateral (which includes the cash you have invested in the property), since a foreclosure sale generally produces enough income to cover most, if not all, of the debt. If you find a mortgage structured as a **recourse loan**—that is, one under which the lender can get at your other assets when a foreclosure sale does not cover your note—don't be shy in striking that language. A borrower, pinched in default, should have his lawyer try to arrange with the lender for the borrower to give a **deed in lieu of foreclosure** to the lender. The borrower loses the property and his invested cash (equity), but the lender agrees not to foreclose and take other assets. You want to avoid default and foreclosure.

The foreclosure rate historically tracked the economy. But another factor that should have driven up the foreclosure rate in the middle of the 21st Century's first decade is the willingness of lenders and borrowers to get into riskier loans with each other. For their part, lenders offered the bait of no-interest and adjustable-rate loans to get borrowers on the treadmill. Refinancing was easy. The Internet offered quick, low-interest loans, even to, or especially to, borrowers with marginal financials. And borrowers took the bait, because they saw home and property ownership as a constantly appreciating asset. In one sense, borrowers are right: property, generally, appreciates over the long term, which makes it less risky than investment alternatives. But it is the most risky investment in another sense, since three or four missed monthly payments can lead to the loss of the entire appreciated asset, including all the equity the borrower has in it, and additional costs. Michael Powell of The Washington Post reported that 63 percent of new mortgages in 2005 were interest-only or those with adjustable rates. (Michael Powell, "U.S. housing boom a bust for many," www.washingtonpost.com, May 29, 2005). One third of the home mortgages in the Washington, D.C. area and 54 percent in the District of Columbia were **interest-only** (IO) loans during the first six months of 2005. (Albert B. Crenshaw, "Interest Only, Except for the Risk," Washington Post, June 12, 2005.) Where borrowers and lenders agree to a loan that situates the borrower right at the edge of his ability to repay, both sides are hoping that his financials don't change for the worse. A spell of unemployment, an illness, car crash, any unexpected event that negatively affects the borrower's cash flow or savings—can lead to foreclosure for such individuals. Powell reported that "…more than 8 percent of homeowners spend at least half of their income on their mortgage," which is way above the standard income-to-mortgage formulas.

Having said all that, the foreclosure rate in mid-2005 was about one percent of all outstanding mortgages, compared with 1.2 percent in mid-2004 and about 1.16 percent in 1998. (Kenneth Harney, "Late-mortgage-payment data may surprise you," Richmond Times-Dispatch, September 25, 2005; 1998 percentage from the Mortgage Bankers Association.) That amounts to about 400,000 foreclosures at mid-2005 on 40 million current home loans. The nation-wide average late-mortgage-payment rate is 4.3 percent. (See also Terry Savage, "The hazards of some home-equity loans," March 12, 2003 at: http://moneycentral.msn.com/content/Banking?Homefinancing/P37886.asp.)

If risk is up, why is the foreclosure rate steady to down? Harney writes:

> Foreclosure rates in general are lower in 2005 than they have been in prior decades in part because Fannie Mae, Freddie Mac, the Federal Housing Administration and most major lenders now use sophisticated 'loss-mitigation' techniques to keep even the most seriously delinquent borrowers in their homes. The techniques include restructuring loan terms, deferring late balances to the end of the loan and sometimes even lowering interest rates.

This suggests to me that foreclosures would have increased had not these institutions found it wiser to lower the foreclosure rate by nursing along troubled loans. A more lenient set of rules disguises the real increase in penalty that borrowers bear from assuming "easy" loans of higher risk. If the old rules (less the new loss-mitigation techniques) were still being applied, the foreclosure rate would probably be rising. As it is, an apples-to-oranges comparison proves nothing save that we are looking at different fruits. My guess is that the foreclosure rate will rise if only because both lenders and borrowers are now operating under a false sense of borrower capacity to handle the riskier loans.

In April, 2006, the Wall Street Journal reported a shift in trends. Both foreclosures and delinquencies were up. Mortgage loans in some stage of foreclosure had risen by 117,000 in February, an increase of 68 percent over February, 2005. Late payments ran at about three percent for poor credit risks and at about .76 percent for better risks, both up from a year earlier. Two factors were cited as driving the shift—economic distress (unemployment) and a cooling off of home appreciation. The Midwest—Indiana, Ohio and Michigan, in particular—showed especially high rates of foreclosures and delinquencies. In December, 2006, the Journal reported that about 80,000 subprime mortgages—almost four percent of that type—were behind in payments, and "there are signs [delinquencies] are spreading to other parts of the mortgage market." (Ruth Simon and James R. Hagerty, "More Borrowers With Risky Loans Are Falling Behind," Wall Street Journal, December 5, 2006.) I've not found data on foreclosures and delinquencies on second homes or unimproved rural property, but I think it's fair to assume that most borrowers will sacrifice those assets before they'll abandon their principal home.

If you find yourself in this type of jam, approach the lender or the mortgage company that services your loan in a straight-forward manner, explain the circumstances and provide a realistic overview of your resources. Harney believes that mortgage holders are willing to help borrowers for reasons of self-interest, namely that "…they lose tens of thousands of dollars on average with every foreclosure…" and for reasons of social policy. (Kenneth Harney, "The Nation's Housing," "Many options available to head off foreclosure," Richmond Times-Dispatch, December 25, 2005.) These foreclosure-avoidance options include: "forbearance" arrangements by which the borrower is allowed to pay less each month, or even nothing; "reinstatements" that allow the borrower's account to be brought into balance at some specified future point; "repayment" plans that allow the borrower to catch up on missed payments by adding on to future monthly payments; and "loan modifications" that recast the terms of the note, e.g., converting an ARM to a fixed-rate mortgage or lengthening the term. A Freddie

Mac study in 2004 found that repayment plans—where a portion of the past-due money is tacked on to each monthly payment over a fixed time period—lowered the home-loss chances for 80 percent of all borrowers. www.freddiemac.com provides detailed information about foreclosure-avoidance options.

Many lenders will consider trying to develop a **work-out plan** with you rather than categorize your loan as **non-performing** or take back the property. With most institutional lenders, you'll have a month or two of leeway in the event that a payment is delayed. But don't expect more than 60 days, and don't expect 60 days more than once or twice. Use this time to put a plan into place; this is not a grace period that can be invoked at your discretion. Lenders are lazy. They don't want to foreclose for their money; they want placid payers and no problems. But foreclose they will; some more precipitously and self-righteously than others. The one time I found myself in this situation, the lender did nothing but demand all of the money owed immediately. Had this lender been willing to give me two or three years in a restructured note, I could have paid off all the obligations without going through a fire sale.

When a foreclosure occurs, the borrower has an **equitable right of redemption in most states**. This allows the borrower (or some other party with a legal interest in the property, such as a creditor with a junior lien) to pay off the amount in default and costs. This renews the debt under the same terms as before. Some states also have a **statutory right of redemption**, which allows the borrower a period in which to reacquire his property *after* the foreclosure sale—at great expense. If you find yourself struggling in these waters, approach the mortgage holder after getting legal advice. If you ignore your missed payments and stonewall the bank's calls, you will be foreclosed.

The point I'm making is simple: while the purchase of rural property is readily financed and should, if properly scoped, prove to be a profitable investment, no one should place himself at financial risk to acquire this asset (or any other) simply because borrowed money is available.

Most buyers find themselves involved in two types of initial money-borrowing decisions when buying rural property. The first is a decision about the **package of financing** the buyer needs to effect the purchase. The package usually involves several sources of money, though it may be as simple as the buyer withdrawing the full purchase price from his passbook savings. In this unusual case, the buyer is borrowing the full purchase price from himself—losing earned interest, but saving paid interest. If your money is sitting in a one-percent savings account, you are borrowing from yourself at a very favorable rate, that is, the one percent of taxable interest your money would have earned. Generally, a buyer looks to piece together the purchase-price package.

The package's biggest component is usually the loan that originates from an institutional lender as a **property-secured note**—the lien described above. The seller may also finance a portion of the sale in the form of a note that is in second (junior) position after the institutional lender. A **second mortgage** note can involve another institutional lender, the seller or an individual. In a foreclosure, creditors are paid in accordance with their seniority ranking.

Most of the time, the buyer is expected by the lender to pay the seller ten to 20 percent of the purchase price as a down payment. This money provides security to the lender in case of default and represents the buyer's beginning **equity**, which is at risk of loss if he defaults. A lender can adjust the down-payment percentage, up or down, depending on the mortgage terms, purchase price, appraisal value, financial position of the borrower and whether the borrower plans to sell some of the property's assets quickly to reduce his debt principal. Where the property securing the note is substantially more valuable than the loan involved in its purchase, a borrower may be able to negotiate a loan covering 100 percent of the purchase price with minimal risk. Rural property containing significant merchantable timber can be financed this way.

Down payment can also take the form of a gift (e.g., a parent gives cash on behalf of an adult child purchasing property), or land (where a lot has been owned for a long time, some lenders will allow the owner to use its appreciated value as down payment when the owner is ready to build; the difference between the appraised value of the lot plus completed house and the house's construction cost is the amount of down payment the lender will assign to land in a note secured by both lot and house), or a gift from the seller (who raises the price by the amount of the gift which lets the buyer into the deal with less cash and more debt; this must be done openly and transparently, and the appraisal value has to cover the higher purchase price) or borrower-owned securities (e.g., stocks) deposited with the lender. (See Guttentag, Mortgage Encyclopedia, pp. 51-57.) Borrowers are usually expected to contribute at least three percent of their down payment, but no down-payment loans can be gotten in the right conditions.

First-time buyers sometimes confuse the **earnest money** they submit with their purchase contract with down payment. Earnest money (security money, deposit) is the cash a buyer offers to the seller when he submits his contract. It's usually on the order of one to five percent of the offering price. Earnest money is held in escrow pending completion of the purchase. It usually is folded into the buyer's down payment at closing.

The buyer's down payment, combined with the principal he retires, combined with any additional investment he puts into the property—represents his evolving **equity** in the property. The process of paying down debt and increasing the owner's stake in the property is called **equity build up**. The more equity an owner has in his property, the more secure the institutional lender feels and the less likely he should be to pull the plug over a couple of missed payments. An unscrupulous lender with a 20 percent down payment in a property and a couple of years into the note might be very quick to foreclose on a very marketable place because of the high profit that will result. That is my fear with Internet lenders, though I have no first-hand experience to feed my suspicion.

Equity build up along with appreciation over time allows the owner to borrow additional money using the original property as security.

A **home-equity loan** borrows against the owner's increased equity and the property's appreciated value. You can borrow your down payment for country property from yourself this way as long as your overall debt-to-income ratio does not exceed the lender's standards. Such a loan is a second mortgage on your principal residence. As a **home-equity loan**, it's a fixed amount with a fixed interest rate; as a **home-equity line of credit (HELOC)**, the amount you borrow can go up to the limit set by the lender, but it is a variable-rate loan with no cap on interest rates.

You can also raise a down payment for country property by **refinancing** your principal residence. Borrowers refinance mortgages when current interest rates are at least two points lower than their mortgage rate. Large loans can benefit from refinancing with a rate reduction smaller than two points, but the question in all instances is how long it will take for the costs you incur in refinancing to be recouped in savings. If the new interest rate is a lot lower than your current rate that **break-even point** comes sooner; if the new rate is not much lower, it takes a lot longer.

A refinancing replaces your existing first mortgage on a property with a new first mortgage. You pay off the old note and take on a new one under new terms. You can replace your current lender with a different one as well.

When equity has built up and the principal residence has appreciated, a borrower can refinance at a lower interest rate and pull some cash out of the deal for down payment on country property (or anything else). The cash you extract is money on which you still pay interest.

Refinancing for a reduced interest burden involves comparing the costs of your existing mortgage over a period of time against a refinanced note (with its costs) over the same period. Guttentag's Web site—www.mtgprofessor.com—provides these comparisons. Refinancing can help a borrower or hurt him, depending on the new terms, their cost and how long he holds the property. When you refinance to get a lower interest rate, you have to weigh into your calculations the upfront costs of refinancing and the total interest that you will pay over the term of the note. The best deal for refinancing is to be able to do so without incurring any costs. You may be able to modify your existing note at not much cost with your current lender if he gets the idea that you're shopping to refinance. But where the lender only services your mortgage, rather than owns it, this can prove difficult. Guttentag suggests requesting a **payoff statement** from your current lender, which is a heads up that you're looking to refinance. It's then in your lender's interest to keep your business.

In refinancing, you also need to estimate your **break-even point**, that is, the date in the future when the costs you incur to refinance match the benefit in savings from the lower interest rate. Break-even points depend on the interest rates, term of the note and the amount of refinancing costs. Guttentag provides tables for refinancing break-even points. (Guttentag, Mortgage Encyclopedia, pp. 251 ff.) The less you have to pay in refinancing costs and the greater the spread between your existing interest rate and your lower, refinanced rate, the shorter is your break-even point. If, for example, you refinance a new loan over 30 years, with one point and pay other costs that amount to two percent of the loan amount, your break-even month is 83 (of 360) if you get a one percent interest rate reduction; month 48 for a two percent reduction and month 22 for a three percent reduction. Cutting the other costs from two percent to one percent of the loan amount lowers the break-even period to 49 months for a one percent rate reduction, 22 months for a two percent reduction, and 14 months for a three percent reduction. If you refinance at a lower rate and a shorter term, that is helpful; if you lengthen the term, you can end up paying more interest, though in smaller monthly payments. A recent study of 3,785 fixed-rate mortgages between 1996 and 2003 found that only 1.4 percent of borrowers carried their mortgages long enough to break even against their upfront points. The lesson seems to be for most of us: take the higher fixed interest rate with fewer points, because we pay off the loan early. (Ron Lieber, "Deciphering Mortgage Points," Wall Street Journal, December 23-24, 2006.)

Generally, the interest rate has to be about three points lower than your current rate for refinancing to be beneficial, but it also depends on the amount of points and costs you have to pay and the length of time you hold the property. A new rate two points lower with low costs can also work. Remember that every time you refinance, you start paying the full term on the new note with front-loaded interest. The deductibility of interest will help on your taxes, but this is not reason enough to refinance. You may also be able to rid yourself of **private mortgage insurance**, the non-deductible monthly premium charged to borrowers with less than 20 percent down payment.

Serial refinancing can pull cash out of a property, but you may find that your principal is never reduced by very much. Your equity build up in a serially refinanced property comes almost entirely from appreciation, not from principal repayment. And you turn that type of equity into cash only when you sell. If you keep refinancing for the same term (30 years) every few years, your total cost of borrowing can be more than if you had stuck with the original higher rate, owing to charges you pay each time. But whether refinancing makes sense depends on the specific loan terms you get in relation to your existing note and how long you keep the property. Weston points out that you can end up paying more total interest over your term by refinancing from 8 percent to 5.5 percent if its length is extended by ten years. (See Liz Pulliam Weston, "Beware the hidden costs of refinancing," March 12, 2003 at: http://moneycentral.msn.com/ content/Banking/Homefinancing/P42715.asp.)

Apart from thinking about a package of financing options, the buyer's second decision involves **fitting the available sources of money to his package of needs**. In its simplest form, the borrower needs to choose one lender from among many. But a dirt-smart buyer can have other sources of money available to buy rural property beyond a bank loan. Rural property, for instance, often lends itself to

partial self-financing, whereby some of the purchase price can be quickly recouped from the property itself through the sale of an asset. I discuss non-bank sources of money below.

Underwriting is the term used to describe the many-stepped process that a lender goes through with a borrower in determining how large a loan the lender will offer and on what terms. The borrower initiates the process by approaching a lender with information about himself and, eventually, a target property. The lender evaluates and investigates both the borrower and the property. The lender may decide not to extend mortgage credit at all, or offer loans whose terms range from harsh to favorable from the borrower's perspective. Once a loan is underwritten, the lender may keep it or sell it. The borrower has no say in that decision. It's worth asking the lender you're working with whether his institution plans to sell your loan. Loans that a lender sells will have to fit standard formulas; you may do better with a lender who won't sell your note. If your loan is a little out of the ordinary, ask your lender whether he can **keep it in his portfolio**; this gives the lender a bit more flexibility in making a loan that fits your circumstances.

Where your package of financing includes an institutional lender, such as a bank or savings and loan, your first step will be to **prepare your financial profile**. Your profile consists of a number of documents that you package for the lender's consideration. I discuss these below.

A key part of your financial profile is your **credit report and your credit score**. The former is a selective history of your bill paying, focusing on mortgages, car loans, credit cards and the like; the latter rates you numerically as a credit risk based on the report. You do not provide the lender with this report, though you pay for it. Your report is routinely accessed when you apply for a credit card, mortgage or loan, and with increasing frequency with rental housing, insurance and employment. The report captures all of your credit payments—credit cards, mortgages, student loans, car loans, consumer loans, etc.—and any problems you may have had, such as defaults, bankruptcies, late payments, court judgments, check bouncing, tax liens and so on. (Bankruptcies are required to be removed from your report after ten years, most other blemishes after seven.) In addition to your payment history, a credit report will assess your current borrowing capacity.

You have rights under the federal Fair and Accurate Credit Transactions Act to obtain a free copy of your credit report. The three major credit bureaus that produce reports are: **Equifax**, Disclosure Department, POB 740241, Atlanta, GA 30374, 1-800-685-1111, www.equifax.com; **Experian**, POB 2002, Allen, TX 75013, 1-888-397-3742, www.experian.com; and **TransUnion**, Consumer Disclosure Center, POB 1000, Chester, PA 19022, 1-800-916-8800, www.transunion.com.

You can theoretically access a free report from www.annualcreditreport.com; also at POB 105281, Atlanta, GA 30348; 1-877-322-8228. I found access impossible with TransUnion when I tried, because the Website demanded that I provide account numbers for accounts I do not have. TransUnion did not include my mortgage lender's account. Consumer Reports had exactly the same experience, describing the free credit report process as an "online maze...that can make it seemingly impossible to get your personal information." (Consumer Reports, "Credit Scores: What you don't know can be held against you," August, 2005.) Consumer Reports suggest that consumers go to www.myfico.com and order the $44.85 package, and then correct the errors in each of the three reports. www.bankrate.com offers a number of articles on credit reports and credit-rating scores.

Credit reports will be used in most cases to evaluate your ability to carry new debt. These reports are notoriously inaccurate, errors usually weighing against the borrower. Consumer Reports wrote that 25 percent of credit reports "...had errors serious enough to cause consumers to be turned down for a loan or a job, according to a 2004 survey by the U.S. Public Interest Research Group." The less creditworthy your report says you are, the more money you will have to pay in fees and interest rate to get a mortgage or a loan. The Consumer Federation of America reported in December, 2002 that as many as 40 million consumers are at risk of paying higher interest rates than their true circumstances merit owing to errors of missing information in their reports. (See Kenneth R. Harney, "Study shows credit scoring shortcomings," Richmond Times-Dispatch, December 22, 2002.)

What you will not find in most credit reports is your **credit-rating score**, or **FICO**. This number reflects the assessment of a computer model at Fair, Issac and Co. (FICO) as to your credit worthiness, based on your credit history involving delinquent payments, the extent to which you use credit, the length of your history (age of credit file), the number of times credit is applied for and the mix of credit you have. (See, Michael D. Larson, "Credit scores can make or break borrowers," www.bankrate.com/brm/news/pf/19981204.asp; and Pat Curry, "Consumers want access to those powerful, secret credit scores," www.bankrate.com/brm/news/mtg/20000508.asp?.)

The FICO score runs from about 300 to 850, with 660 and above, good; 620-660, a bit chancy; and below 620, rocky. Above 720 (the U.S. median) is golden; below, you won't get the absolute best deals. Credit providers and mortgage lenders use FICO scores to screen applicants and offer terms to each one based on risk and profitability. It appears that it's difficult to improve your FICO score quickly, though you should establish a record of making prompt installment payments and clean up errors on your credit report. Consumer Reports suggests carrying at least five credit cards (which gives you a lot of credit), but don't use much of it because you gain FICO points by using a small percentage of your available credit. The scoring system itself tends to most hurt young borrowers, first-timers, minorities, the elderly, folks who have errors in their credit reports and individuals who hate credit cards. Lenders, of course, have no particular interest in doing anything about this scandal, since they benefit by charging higher interest rates to worthy borrowers with less-than-worthy FICO scores.

Thirty-one percent of the Consumer Federation of America's 500,000-plus sample, cited above, showed at least a 50-point difference between credit reports, and five percent showed a variation of 100 points. A 50-point difference, Harney pointed out, could mean a difference between a 6.01 percent interest rate on a 30-year fixed note and a 7.70 percent rate, about $4,500 per year. The average variation among the reports was 43 points—enough to cost you more than $100,000 in interest over a mortgage's 30-year life. For this reason alone, **you should correct omissions of favorable information and errors on your three credit reports well before approaching an institutional lender**.

The three major credit bureaus—Equifax, Experian and TransUnion—proposed in the spring of 2006 to replace using FICO scores with a system they call, VantageScore, which is a program that unifies the scoring and makes it consistent across the bureaus. Scores now can vary from one bureau to another, and lenders may seek three bureau scores for a borrower and take the middle one. The VantageScore runs from 501 to 990, with 900 to 990 representing an A, 801 to 900 a B and so forth. The proposed system does not address the main problems with these systems, which are that they give false results if borrower information is not up to date, incorrect or missing. VantageScore was not widely used as of the beginning of 2007.

When asking for a report use a consistent identifying name. Communicate with the credit bureaus in dated writing when you have a correction or dispute; keep copies of your correspondence. Check on your credit reports before you apply for any mortgage loan. If you are rejected, ask the lender in writing for the specific reasons and then go about correcting your credit reports if that is where your problem lies.

As part of putting together your financial profile, get your three credit reports and correct in writing all errors and old information six months before you apply to an institutional lender for a mortgage. Make a paper trail. Supply each bureau with the documents needed to support your position. Keep copies of everything. Assume that it will take three or four months to straighten things out. Don't walk into a bank without having checked your credit reports, because the bank most assuredly will. In addition to reviewing your credit reports, you will be using this pre-purchase time to put together the rest of your financial profile, as discussed below. (See Dani Arthur, "5 steps to do-it-yourself credit repair," www.bankrate.com/brm/news/cc/20011008b.asp?keyword=CREDITCARDS.)

My inclination is to provide a lender with more information instead of the least I can get away with. That includes complete 1040s for the last two years, possibly a list of savings/checking accounts and information on life-insurance policies, retirement accounts, stocks, real estate and so on. I also provide the names and contact information for the professionals who've worked on the property I want to buy, such as the forester, surveyor, lawyer who's done title work on it in the past, soils consultant, appraiser familiar with the property, etc. If there's something quirky about my income for the last couple of years, I explain and offer my best guess as to my future income. Where references are requested, I'll give my CPA/tax preparer, lawyer, business associates and others who know my circumstances and financial character. The more confidence I can build with a lender, the better deal I'm likely to get.

Self-employed people often bear an extra burden with lenders if their cash flow varies from month to month, or year to year. In that case, the borrower needs to show long-term trends and substantiate current and future prospects. This can be hard. I once had a credit union turn me down for a mortgage because they would only accept 1040s as evidence of income. When I submitted cancelled checks for income received and confirming bank-deposit records in the current year (when a 1040 could not obviously exist), I was told this evidence of self-employment income proved nothing.

As you prepare your financial profile for evaluation, you will, in turn, be evaluating the institutional lenders available to you and the loan packages (rates, fees, formats and other terms) each offers. You can start your screening by comparing advertised terms that are being offered—interest rates, (packaged either as a **fixed rate** over a certain number of years or a **variable rate** that changes at predetermined times), upfront fees and charges, and other terms. You will quickly discover that you can compare one type of loan from one lender with exactly the same type of loan from other lenders, but it's very difficult to compare the cost of an adjustable-rate mortgage to a fixed-rate mortgage even when they're amortized over identical terms, because you can't anticipate what your interest charges will be on the ARM. Monthly ARM mortgage payments are fixed for certain periods of time. A fixed-rate mortgage sets the payment when the loan is originated, and it never varies. An ARM payment will change every time the interest rate is adjusted, unless the new interest rate is identical with the old one. Each monthly payment with any loan contains a changing ratio of interest to principal; your first monthly payment is almost entirely interest, and your last is almost entirely principal. The total amount of interest you will pay over the life of your loan depends on the interest rate you are charged and either the **term (length)** of the loan if you hold it for the full term or how long you keep the loan before paying it off. The lower the interest rate and the longer the term, the lower your monthly payment. But the longer the term and the longer you hold the note, the more total interest you will pay.

You should ask around locally about each lender's reputation. Banks don't differ much in their procedures and terms, but they can be quite different in their flexibility and, for lack of a better word, "warmth" toward customers. What you want is a lender who will not spring his trap door if you're late on a payment and will offer some time if you run into cash-flow trouble. Lenders don't like to repossess property, but all do. Some lenders will be very quick to foreclose, particularly on notes that are well into their terms with a lot of equity build up. The deeper into the term, the less interest is being paid, which can provide a financial incentive for foreclosure. Banks project a neighborly image, but they have the ability to pound you into the dirt. While banks suffer some financial and image damage over each foreclosure, my feeling is that they fully understand that the occasional repossession keeps the fear of their hammer right in the middle of their borrowers' brains.

As a newcomer, small rural lenders may treat you either with more deference or less than community natives. You might seek out other out-of-town folks who have bought property recently and get their opinions. I admit this is a slap-dash methodology, but you might gain the anecdotal insight you need to choose the friendliest lender. I would make a point of meeting some of the lender's board, particularly its leadership. A friend on the board even a new one can't hurt though don't count on much help if you ever need it. Banks are not social workers; helping borrowers through jams is not their nature.

Banks want to *feel* "secure" about their loans. Normally, they provide mortgage money using only the purchased property as collateral with a ten to 30 percent down payment. The amount of down payment is one of those requirements that can be negotiated if you show reasons why the lender should feel just as secure with less down payment. The greater your equity build up, the more secure your lender will feel, because his chance of losing money is decreasing. A history of regular payments doesn't count for much when your lender finds you in default. Your lender's feeling of security can be based on your last, full monthly payment. Don't expect loyalty, though lender self-interest might provide some relief by way of loss-mitigation techniques.

Most mortgage notes contain a **demand clause**, which allows the lender to call your note—that is, demand full payment of all principal and interest due—when the lender no longer feels secure. The document—a "Promissory Note"—that I've signed says a "default" occurs when, among other things, any of the following occurs:

- Borrower fails to make any payment when due under this Note.
- The death of the borrower. [Having life insurance that more than covers mortgage principal calms jittery lenders. The face amount of the insurance also improves net worth on the borrower's annual financial statement.]
- A material adverse change occurs in borrower's financial condition, or lender believes the prospect of payment or performance of this note is impaired. [Lender does not have to define what it considers to be an adverse change or tell the borrower why it believes the prospect of payment is impaired.]
- ***Lender in good faith believes itself insecure.***

If you are ever faced with a lender calling the note for reasons of insecurity, don't waste time and money fighting it. The presence of a demand clause means you will lose. Move the note to another lender as quickly as you can.

COSTS OF BORROWING

A typical mortgage loan is burdened with three types of fees/costs: 1) government-imposed fees, such as a tax (deed stamps) and recording fee; 2) lender-imposed fees, including points, loan-origination fees, processing fees, garbage fees (see below), etc.; and 3) third-party fees, for services such as an appraisal, home inspection, title search, soils report, percolation tests, termite inspection and so on. You cannot negotiate with the government to lower its fees though you may be able to negotiate with the seller as to who pays how much of them. You can negotiate with the lender on his fees/costs, and you can ask the seller to pay some portion of them. You can price-shop on third-party fees that you commission, and you can negotiate with the seller over allocation on some of them. You can also complain to the lender about third-party services he "provides" for you, particularly where the costs are jacked up. The borrower needs to understand from the start that certain charges are fair, such as those for a credit report, appraisal, title policy, recording fee and, where applicable, a state registration fee. On some of these legitimate fees, the borrower needs to be on the look-out for gratuitous inflation. On illegitimate fees—processing fee, underwriting fee, warehousing fee, loan-originating fee, document preparation fee, application review fee and the like—the borrower needs to fight tooth and nail.

Each one percent of interest is called a **point**. A borrower pays a lender cash upfront to cover each point the lender charges to make the loan. You will find that lenders use a system where they offer borrowers lower interest rates in return for more points paid at the time the loan is made. On a typical fixed-rate loan with a 30-year term, a borrower might pay 2.75 points for a 5.375 percent rate, .0125 points (1/8th) for 5.875 percent, and get a 2.0 percent rebate for 6.375 percent. (A rebate—or negative points—is cash the borrower does not have to pay to get the loan, but it means a high interest cost if you hold the loan for 30 years.) The difference between a 30-year fixed-rate loan at 5.5 percent with no points on $100,000 in principal and 6.5 percent with no points is more than $23,000 in interest over the full term. If you're going to hold the note for a long time, pay higher points in exchange for a lower fixed interest rate. But if you're going for a short term or plan to pay it off well before 30 years, pay fewer points and take a higher rate. Your key variable in this decision is how long you will hold the note. www.mrtgprofessor.com provides calculators that allow you to figure which combination of points and interest-rate costs the least, given your projected timeframe. However, no one, not even the insightful professor, can help you predict how long you will hold a note; that's up to you and your crystal ball.

The borrower usually has the ability to bargain for a lower rate by paying more points. Lenders are not required to bargain, and no federal rule exists that governs the process. But Bruss believes that for "…each one-point loan fee paid, you should receive at least a one-eighth percent reduction in your loan's interest rate for the life of the mortgage." (Robert J. Bruss, "Which Home Mortgage Fees Are Proper?," The (Staunton) News-Leader, June 18, 2006.)

Many institutional lenders tack on **points**. Some points may also be referred to as "discount points," though from the borrower's perspective they should be called "extra points" paid by the borrower. Each **discount point** represents one percent of the loan amount. This point is pre-paid interest. If you agree to pay a **one percent discount fee** (that is, one discount point) to the lender, you will receive $99,000 on a $100,000 loan, but you will pay interest on the full $100,000—thereby, increasing your effective interest rate. (In your mortgage shopping, you may also hear the term "**basis point**," which represents 1/100th of one percent of interest. Thus, a 6.75 percent mortgage interest rate represents 675 basis points.) If the lender says he is charging you "a point" to originate the loan, it is one percent of the amount he's willing to lend you. You will then pay that one percent to the lender at the time the loan is made, and it is on top of the interest you will pay each month. This $100,000 loan would cost you $1,000 cash at closing, plus all other front-loaded charges and costs. The more points of any kind that a lender forces you to pay, the more the loan costs you to start your borrowing. Paying high points can make sense if you get a very low fixed interest rate that you hold for a long time.

In most cases, the points you pay at closing are tax-deductible over the course of the loan, not in the year in which you pay them. You should check with your CPA about which of your projected loan costs are immediately deductible and which are taken over the life of the loan.

Lenders will also often charge **fees for processing your loan**. In effect, you are being charged twice to get a loan: first, the lender is charging you an upfront processing fee to process your loan application; and second, the lender is charging you a rate of interest that covers his cost of overhead and loan processing. Fight processing fees.

It is common for a lender to charge a **loan-origination fee**, which generally amounts to one to two percentage points. A fee is a set dollar amount, however; it is not a percentage of the principal. A loan-origination fee is not pre-paid interest. It is a charge to cover the costs of generating the loan, including staff salary and overhead. A loan-origination fee can be a fair charge or foul, depending on what other costs the lender is imposing. Just remember, the more money a lender squeezes from a borrower upfront, the lower the lender's risk and the more profit he's likely to make.

You may also hear about a **pre-approval fee**, which is money you are expected to pay to have the lender evaluate your credit-worthiness. Even credit card companies don't try this one.

Also be alert to a **cancellation fee**, which may be imposed at various points during the underwriting if you don't go through with the loan.

You may also encounter an **assumption fee** if you are taking over a loan from the seller. An assumption fee should be resisted since the lender has already evaluated the property for the seller who has been making payments. How much can it cost a lender to change the name on a note? The lender will get a current appraisal on your nickel so his risk in lending on the property will not increase. Nonetheless, you may get nowhere with the lender on this fee.

Don't agree to a **pre-payment fee (penalty)** that falls on you for paying off any portion of your principal or your entire note before the full term. Such fees range from one percent of the balance to "…as much as all the interest due for the first ten years of the loan." (Galaty *et al.*, Modern Real Estate Practice, p. 212.) When the federal government insures or guarantees a mortgage, pre-payment fees are prohibited. Front-loading interest means the lender makes an above-rate of return on all early pay offs during the first half or more of a mortgage's term. The lender does not lose on pre-payment; in fact, he wins—just as you do. If the seller's note has a pre-payment penalty attached, it is his obligation, not yours, to pay it. But don't be surprised if the seller's pre-payment fee, in whole or part, wanders over to the buyer's side of the settlement sheet. You are perfectly within your rights to "wander" it back where it belongs.

You may also be charged specific, line-item fees, such as for a bank-required appraisal. If you are financially strong and borrowing a lot, grumble and complain; negotiating may save you some money. If you've had an appraisal done as part of your scoping, submit that to the lender and refuse to pay for a duplicate. If your appraiser is on the lender's "approved list" of appraisers, you should win; if not, you won't. Before hiring an appraiser as part of your scoping, check with the lender you think you will use to find out whether your choice is approved. Hire an approved appraiser.

In the loan business, a distinction is drawn between institutional lenders who are considered fair in their dealings with consumers of credit and those that practice "**predatory lending**." I've always been a bit skeptical of this division, given that the good guys engage in some of the same practices as the bad guys. I won't write that all lenders are in the predation business since several have treated me fairly and decently. I've found community credit unions often offer better loan packages than banks and S&Ls.

Mortgage brokers find loans for borrowers from various lenders. They do not lend their own money. The borrower pays a fee when he accepts a loan the broker has found. The fee is usually disguised as an undisclosed mark up above what the mortgage broker has found as terms from a lender. A two percent mark up on a $150,000 loan is common; a lower mark up is applied as the loan amount increases. Mortgage brokers may find a better deal than any the borrower finds for himself, even after his fee is included. A 2005 study by Gregory Elliehausen of Georgetown University found that total costs on broker-originated first mortgages for subprime borrowers (subprime equals credit problems) were 1.13 percentage points lower than loans originated by employees of lenders, and 1.98 percentage points lower on second mortgages. (Kenneth Harney, "Brokers get some respect in new study," Richmond Times-Dispatch, April 17, 2005.) You want to make sure that the mortgage broker is not receiving a fee from the lender outside of closing. If you find the phrase—**Premium Yield Adjustment/POC**—on your settlement statement, it means the broker is expecting another fee in your deal—Paid Outside Of Closing (POC). The broker gets this fee for steering you, the borrower, into a loan with a higher interest rate than you would otherwise receive.

Since most mortgage brokers do not reveal their fees (mark ups), it's impossible for a consumer to know the size of the fees that competing brokers are charging. A more consumer-friendly system is being organized by Jack Guttentag for what he calls, "**upfront mortgage brokers**." Such brokers disclose the amount they are charging for their service before you agree to retain them. Guttentag provides a list of upfront brokers at www.mtgprofessor.com.) See also www.bankrate.com/brm/news/mortgages/20021024a.asp?prodtype=mtg; this article discusses the practices of mortgage brokers who are not upfront.

Mortgage bankers make and service loans; they also sell loans they originate. Cast your net broadly when looking for the best loan package, and remember that you will throw all your catch back into the sea, save for one.

The nature of the lender-borrower relationship is clearly one in which every dollar that is put into your lender's pocket comes directly out of yours. "Money-lending" has an off-putting quality about it, but "banking" is accorded prestige. While the definition of predatory lending is unclear because the suspect practices vary from state to state, the following are those that appear to be most commonly included:

1. Interest rates that are noticeably above others in the area.

2. Adds points to the loan without reducing the interest rate.

3. Adds fees and costs, particularly padded fees and costs.

4. Demands an upfront application fee to look at your material. Don't use a lender that demands a fee for processing your application. Such fees, ranging from about $100 to several hundred dollars, are rip-offs.

5. Requires the borrower to buy unnecessary items, such as a pre-paid, one-premium, credit-life insurance policy whose cost is sometimes added to the loan principal so that the borrower pays interest on it.

6. Offers a loan based solely on the borrower's equity in the property (e.g., a down payment) and not on the borrower's repayment capacity. If you are not asked to demonstrate your income, be suspicious. This lender is signaling that he's likely to foreclose at the first excuse.

7. Large penalty, which may be called a "fee," for pre-payment of the loan.

8. Upfront fees that total more than three percent of the loan amount. "…most lenders say the total for origination fees and closing costs shouldn't add up to more than 3% of the loan amount, not counting 'points,' assuming the borrowers have reasonably good credit." (Patrick Barta, "Swimming With the Home-Loan Sharks," Wall Street Journal Sunday in Richmond Times-Dispatch, February 9, 2003.).

9. Be very careful with loans that tag on one large "balloon payment" at the end of your term. A balloon means that you have that amount of principal still to repay. Balloons are big lump sums. If you don't have the money, you'll have to renew the note at current rates or move the note to another lender. Some mortgages refinance the remaining principal periodically at current interest rates with no danger or additional fees. But predatory lenders will add fees each time you refinance through them. Borrowers are often lured into predatory balloon loans by short-term **teaser** interest rates. Frequent balloon payments, or multiple refinancing, is also known as "flipping." Each flip is accompanied by additional fees and costs. Each refinance starts the interest front-loading fresh. The effect can be that the borrower spends his life paying a lot of interest and very little principal even when the interest rate is declining.

10. Outright falsification of loan documents. Consumer advisers say to fill in all blanks on loan applications, because blanks that have been left open have been known to have been completed by the lender—and not as a favor.

11. Promise of a guaranteed loan. A lender, credit-assistance business or mortgage broker who advertises or promises that you will get a mortgage regardless of your credit history is not your new best friend. Think about it. Why would anyone lend you money if there's a high likelihood that you will be unable to repay? Could it be that he hopes you are unable to repay? To get such a loan a borrower will have to cough up lots of upfront fees and have a lot of equity in the purchase going in. Foreclosures on such borrowers make a lot of money at the borrower's expense.

12. Closing-costs runaround. Lenders are required to give an applicant/borrower a **good-faith estimate of closing costs** no later than three business days after receiving a mortgage application. This can take the form of a single dollar amount or a range. A loan officer should be able to give a borrower a reasonably accurate estimate of the official good-faith estimate at the time the borrower orally outlines his financial profile and describes the target property. If the loan officer won't give a ballpark estimate during that interview, ask him to provide a list of the lender's standard charges. If these appear padded, be prepared to slide down a slippery slope. If you don't get the good-faith estimate by the fourth day, the lender is likely to prove slicker than the slope itself.

The federal Real Estate Settlement Procedures Act (RESPA) governs closing-cost procedures, including the good-faith estimate. But some types of mortgage lending are not covered. RESPA covers mortgage loans made by federally insured lenders, loans insured by the Federal Housing Administration (FHA) or guaranteed by the Veterans Administration, and those to be resold on the secondary mortgage market. It applies to first-position (lien) residential mortgage money applied to one- to four-family dwellings, for either investment or occupancy. RESPA does not apply to seller financing, an installment contract and a buyer's assumption of the seller's note, except where the lender charges more than $50 as an assumption fee. RESPA applies to second mortgages and home-equity lines.

13. One-stop shopping. A borrower may find himself working with a multi-faceted, real-estate firm, known as a Controlled Business Arrangement (CBA). The same company provides the borrower with a broker through whom to work, lender, title insurance provider, home inspector and so on. This is a closed loop once you're in it; closed loops can have another name as well, noose. The potential for borrower abuse is great. The borrower is supposed to be made aware of a CBA, whereupon he can contact other providers at his option. Any particular CBA can provide good service that is fairly and competitively priced, but you may benefit from additional research.

A variation on this idea is the lender who leads borrowers to a particular lawyer or appraiser. A clear conflict of interest exists when a lender steers customers to the law firm of the one lawyer on its board of directors. If you ask a lender to recommend local professionals, you should get at least two names, and preferably three. Sweetheart arrangements are indicated when you ask for the "names of some local lawyers," and are given one name. In a dispute, the odds are that the lawyer to whom you have been steered will side with the business-generating lender, not you, his one-deal client from somewhere else. A very common sweetheart arrangement is one between a real-estate brokerage and a title (insurance) agency, or a lawyer and a title agency. In such cases, as much as 80 percent of the buyer-paid title premium can go to the title agency where it is split with whoever—broker or lawyer—steered the buyer to that agency. The actual cost of the policy is 20 percent of the premium. Ask the title agency to show you how much of your premium is going to policy and how much to fees.

14. Negative amortization. This is the situation where the borrower makes monthly payments, but the loan is structured in such a way that he ends up owing more principal at the end of the note than when he started. This often happens through repeated refinancings. Make sure to get an amortization schedule

from the lender, which shows exactly where you are in terms of principal and interest for each month of your term.

15. Deals that are too good to be true, e.g., "No money down/no fee." Would you lend money to a stranger on those terms? Read the fine print. (These practices are discussed in Barta's "Swimming"; Fannie Mae Foundation, "Borrowing Basics: What You Don't Know Can Hurt You," 2001, pp. 2-3; 1-800-541-6300; www.fanniemaefoundation.org; and www.aarp.org/consumerprotect-homeloans.)

A useful legal discussion of predatory lending, including an analysis of mortgage documents, can be found in the National Consumer Law Center's, STOP Predatory Lending: A Guide for Legal Advocates, available from the NCLC, 77 Summer Street, 10th Floor, Boston, MA 02110-1006; 617-542-9595; FAX 617-542-8028; www.nclc.org/initiatives. Additional information can be found at http://twincityhomeloans.com/protect.htm and http://helpdesk.uvic.ca/technote/1998/tn98012.html. At this writing, the federal Office of the Comptroller of the Currency (OCC), which regulates federally chartered banks, is considering issuing national guidelines on predatory lending. The bank lobby favors these guidelines because several states, particularly Georgia, have enacted much tougher rules. The Georgia law allows a borrower to sue both the original underwriter and any subsequent buyer of a loan that fits the definition of predatory. Georgia places no limits on punitive damages. It appears that the banks will win this contest, which will result in weak national guidelines. (Anitha Reddy, "U.S. Advises Banks to Stop Predatory Lending," Washington Post, February 22, 2003.).

The cost to you of borrowing with a mortgage is the total amount of money you have to pay the lender, both at the start and over the time you carry the note. This will include the total of interest paid; one-time front-end points, fees and charges; penalties that you are likely to incur; and **private mortgage insurance (PMI)** premiums that you may be required to pay to protect your lender.

Lenders differ in how they combine their various bites out of a borrower's pocketbook. Locally owned banks in my very rural area don't charge any points or loan-origination fees, but always impose an interest rate higher than the lenders who do. It is typical for a major regional/national lender to have upfront points, fees, charges and costs that add three to six percent (or more) to the principal you are borrowing. Borrowers usually pay these sums, included in **closing costs** or **settlement costs,** at closing (settlement) when the buyer's package of monies is exchanged for possession of the seller's property. Closing costs may include loan-origination fees, points (sometimes called discount points or financing points), attorney fees, document-preparation fees, inspections, title and/or settlement services, transfer and recordation taxes, title insurance, survey fee, inspection fees, appraisal fee and PMI, among others. The lender gets points and origination fees. The former is charged as a percent of the loan and the latter as a fixed amount. Some, but not all, lenders charge a loan-origination fee. The Fannie Mae Foundation says that loan fees by themselves—points and origination fees together—should not exceed 5 percent of the loan amount unless you are [intentionally] paying more for a lower interest rate." (Fannie Mae Foundation, "Borrowing Basics: What You Don't Know Can Hurt You," 2001, pp. 6-7). Five percent is on the high side in my experience. Loans with reasonable interest rates—though not the rock-bottom rates—should be available with a hit of two percent or less for points and origination fee combined.

The lender may also impose other fees presented as dollar amounts on the settlement statement, such as "processing," tax service, wire transfer, document preparation, courier, postage, "lender inspection" and so on. Ask each lender you interview to give you a rough estimate of these dollar fees when you're comparing loan packages.

A **Good Faith Estimate (GFE) of settlement costs** is supposed to be given to a borrower within three days of his mortgage application. But you should ask for a general (non-binding) approximation of the lender's total settlement costs when you're shopping for the best loan package, that is, before you formally apply. A lender won't guarantee either estimate, but it's worth haggling over a cap on settlement charges during your shopping phase. Simply say that you don't want to pay more than X dollars in such settlement costs packaged with Y rate and Z terms—and then ask him to work his side to help you get there.

Aside from the fees you pay to the lender, you will pay settlement fees to third parties at closing, each of whom will have done something that is needed, such as a termite inspection or an appraisal. Some third-party fees cannot be readily predicted by lenders, such as title and settlement services, which vary with each deal.

As a rule, buyers do not borrow their closing costs from their lender, though some types of costs can be handled that way. If you pack closing costs into your loan, you increase the amount you're borrowing and the interest you will pay. There are circumstances when this is a sensible strategy. A borrower has to figure how much cash he will need at closing as part of the process of his self-evaluation of how much debt he can afford.

The last financial factor to consider on loan packages is the tax deductibility of various items. Interest and property taxes are tax deductible on home/second-home mortgages, subject to certain limits. Points and origination fees are also deductible on home mortgages, but lender fees and other settlement costs are not. If, on the other hand, you are taking out a mortgage on country property as an investment or for a business purpose, then everything should be tax-deductible. Since your mortgage's interest is front-loaded, your benefit from its deductibility is disproportionately high at the beginning of the note's term and disproportionately low at its end. The degree of your tax benefit depends on your income level and the amount of your annual interest payment. Most middle-income taxpayers will be able to deduct all the mortgage interest paid from their gross income. (See discussion below.)

My experience is that credit unions and locally owned, small rural banks impose lower closing costs than the big banks.

There is no single upfront-costs-to-interest-rate formula that is always best for every borrower in all circumstances, because the final cost of every loan to every borrower depends on the individual's circumstances and how long the loan is held. Certainly, low costs with a low interest rate is a good initial target, except when it's bait to get you into an adjustable-rate mortgage with unfavorable terms. If you start with a higher interest rate and low closing costs, you can wait for an interest-rate dip and then refinance. Closing costs are dollars lost forever. You can erode some of the pain of high interest rates by pre-paying principal as long as your lender allows pre-payment without penalty. As I write in 2006, the mortgage rate has been eight percent or less for a decade—relatively low historically. A fixed-rate mortgage for 30 years at five or six percent is a good deal, assuming, of course, you can make the payments. (A no-interest, no-cost mortgage is a bad deal if you can't.)

The interest rates offered by lenders reflect interest rates in the national economy, which are set by financial markets, speculation and politics. The mortgage interest rate—the interest on a 30-year fixed-rate mortgage—tracks the ten-year Treasury yield and the yield on 30-year Treasury bonds. The mortgage interest rate has been running about 1.4 points higher than the ten-year Treasury yield for about 18 months. In June, 2005, the ten-year Treasury yield was about 4.26 percent and the mortgage interest rate (on a 30-year fixed-rate note) was 5.65 percent. When demand increases for bonds in financial markets, their prices rise and their yields go down. In bond terms, yield represents the interest rate paid on a bond after taking purchase price into account. When yields on bonds and Treasuries fall, mortgage interest rates should rise. But in 2004 to mid-2005, this expected relationship did not materialize. In fact, the opposite occurred: the ten-year Treasury yield slid and so did the mortgage interest rate. And the mortgage rate declined at the same time the Federal Reserve was raising its Federal Funds interest rate, which, according to conventional wisdom, should have had the effect of boosting the mortgage interest rate. Countervailing factors were at work. I include this contrarian information to caution readers about trying to be too clever by half in predicting interest-rate trends. Anytime you can borrow for 30 years for less than seven percent with two points or less, that's a package worth considering.

Buyers of country property should ask lenders specifically about a **land loan**, in addition to fixed-rate mortgages and ARMs. Community-minded lenders in rural areas may offer one, because they want to encourage the purchase of unimproved land for agriculture, timber production and subsequent construction. If your target property has a house (improvement) on it, it may not qualify for a land loan. A second complicating factor is that your lender may try to shift your land-acquisition loan to a business loan (with a higher interest rate) if you are setting up the property as an investment or business. It's worth asking about land loans because their terms are usually borrower-friendly. The community credit union I belong to offered the following types of loans in May, 2005 that could be used for buying country property:

```
ARM  (1 year/80% LTV)     30 year term    4.26% (for 1 year)
ARM  (1 year-90% LTV)     30-year term    4.76% (for 1 year)
ARM  (3 year-80% LTV)     30-year term    5.51% (for 3 years)
ARM  (3 year-90% LTV)     30-year term    6.01% (for 3 years)
ARM (5/1 year-90% LTV)    30-year term    5.26% (for five years)
ARM (5/1 year-100% LTV)   30-year term    6.51% (for five years)
ARM (7/1 year-90% LTV)    30-year term    5.76% (for seven years)
Land Loan (80% LTV)       20-year term    4.51% (for 20 years)
Land Loan (90% LTV)       20-year term    5.01% (for 20 years)
```

A 5/1 ARM means that the starting interest rate is fixed for five years, after which it is adjusted at one-year intervals. All the ARMs carried a minimum interest-rate "floor" of 1.5 percent. I found it interesting that this credit union no longer offered the standard 30-year fixed-rate mortgage. The longest fixed-rate "products" were the 20-year land loans at rates between about 0.5 percent and one percent below the then-current 5.65 percent mortgage rate on a 30-year fixed bank mortgage. The credit union charged neither points nor an origination fee. Closing costs were reasonable. The land loan was my best deal, and the credit union was the best lender I found when I shopped for one.

You may also benefit during your lender shopping from asking whether each lender might make an exception or modification to its offered terms. You might, for example, ask the lender to set up a 30-year amortization schedule rather than the offered 20. If that sticks, propose a 30-year schedule for the first five years after which the monthly payment is increased to pay off the note in 20 years. Or you might propose paying an extra point or two to get a lower interest rate on a fixed-rate loan, which makes sense if you know that you will hold the note for 20 or 30 years.

No deal is any good if you can't afford it. Remember that ARMs are crapshoots. If you start an ARM when interest rates are historically low, the odds are that your rate will rise. Nonetheless, the percentage of new home loans using ARMs is now almost 50 percent. Interest-only ARMs, whose monthly payments don't include principal, are even riskier. Lenders have been willing to make borrowing easier in an appreciating real-estate market because of competition among them and because foreclosure protects their money. Every borrower needs to be alert for the scam outfits who offer *really* easy terms with payment plans that beckon from the outer limit of your ability to pay. These thieves want the borrower to default so that they can foreclose, sell the property and grab the borrower's equity as ill-gotten profit. The rip-off now has a name, **equity stripping**. Never stretch your ability to pay a mortgage to buy country property no matter how good the deal is.

Interest-only loans are increasingly popular, but they involve far more risk of borrower failure if income doesn't rise. An IO gives the borrower a fixed monthly payment for a certain period, say five years, that only pays the lender interest. With a 30-year amortization schedule, the last 25 years is set up to repay both principal and interest with a new fixed monthly payment. The rescheduled monthly payment will be higher than the first, because all of the principal will be packaged into a repayment plan set up for 25 years, rather than 30. Crenshaw provided the following example: a $300,000 loan at five percent would have a $1,250 monthly payment for its first five years and a $1,754 payment for the next 25 years. (Crenshaw, "Interest Only," Washington Post, June 15, 2005.) If the borrower's income has not risen sufficiently, default follows. An IO can work to the borrower's benefit on second-home and country property, particularly where the borrower plans to sell an asset to pay down acquisition debt or the borrower has the means to pay off the note by the end of the IO's first phase.

While you are evaluating lenders, you should already have evaluated yourself as your lender will. This self-evaluation will give you a rough idea in advance of how much additional debt the lender thinks you can carry. Use the same two guidelines a lender will apply. First, the lender will follow the rule that your monthly housing cost (mortgage, property taxes, insurance and homeowner-association fees if applicable) should not exceed 28 percent of your monthly, pre-tax gross income. Second, the lender will say that all of your long-term monthly debt (housing costs plus car payments, student loans and other installment debt) should not exceed 36 percent of your monthly, pre-tax gross income. These rules are applied to your recent income history, which may or may not predict your income prospects. If your income is going up on a predictable basis, you might consider arguing for a larger loan. If the lender is keeping the loan in his own portfolio, he may have more flexibility than if he intends to sell it. If, on the other hand, you are either self-employed or otherwise decoupled from a regular paycheck, the lender will insist on compliance with his guidelines.

TABLE 32-1 plots interest rates against income to show the loan amount an individual is likely to be offered. This TABLE assumes that the interest rate is fixed for the entire loan term and that borrower income remains the same. It was constructed using a 25 percent rule, rather than 28 percent, to account for taxes, insurance and other costs the borrower has to pay. The dollar amounts in TABLE 32-1 represent the maximum loan amount you should consider assuming at each interest rate for your income level.

TABLE 32-2 provides a quick-and-simple reference for determining a borrower's monthly payment of principal and interest for a 30-year, fixed-rate mortgage at different interest rates for various amounts of principal.

TABLE 32-1

Feasible Mortgage Amounts, By Interest Rate and Annual Income

INTEREST RATES	ANNUAL INCOME											
	$15,000	$20,000	$25,000	$30,000	$35,000	$40,000	$45,000	$50,000	$55,000	$60,000	$65,000	$70,000
5.5%	$55,000	$73,400	$91,700	$110,100	$128,400	$146,800	$165,100	$183,500	$201,800	$220,200	$238,500	$256,800
6.0%	52,100	69,500	86,900	104,200	121,600	139,000	156,400	173,700	191,100	208,500	225,900	243,200
6.5%	49,400	65,900	82,400	98,800	115,300	131,800	148,300	164,800	181,300	197,700	214,200	230,700
7.0%	47,000	62,600	78,300	93,900	109,600	125,300	140,900	156,600	172,300	187,900	203,600	219,200
7.5%	44,600	59,600	74,500	89,400	104,300	119,200	134,100	149,000	163,900	178,800	193,700	208,600
8.0%	42,600	56,700	70,900	85,100	99,300	113,500	127,700	141,900	156,100	170,300	184,500	198,700
8.5%	40,600	54,100	67,700	81,200	94,800	108,300	121,900	135,400	149,000	162,500	176,100	189,600
9.0%	38,800	51,700	64,700	77,700	90,600	103,500	116,500	129,400	142,400	155,300	168,200	181,200
9.5%	37,200	49,500	61,900	74,300	86,700	99,100	111,400	123,800	136,200	148,600	161,000	173,400

■ *Interest Rate*   □ *Annual Income*   □ *Mortgage Amount*

Assumes a 30-year, fixed-rate mortgage. This TABLE uses a 25 percent ratio of mortgage debt to income, with an additional three percent allocated for taxes and insurance. The typical lender ratio is 28 percent.

SOURCE: Fannie Mae Foundation, "Opening the Door to a Home of Your Own," 2001, p. 16.

TABLE 32-2

Monthly Mortgage Payments, By Interest Rate and Loan Amount

LOAN AMOUNT	INTEREST RATES								
	5.5%	6%	6.5%	7%	7.5%	8%	8.5%	9%	9.5%
$20,000	$114	$120	$126	$133	$140	$147	$154	$161	$168
25,000	142	150	158	166	175	183	192	201	210
30,000	170	180	190	200	210	220	231	241	252
35,000	199	210	221	233	245	257	269	282	294
40,000	227	240	253	266	280	294	308	322	336
45,000	256	270	284	299	315	330	346	362	378
50,000	284	300	316	333	350	367	384	402	420
55,000	312	330	348	366	385	404	423	443	462
60,000	341	360	380	399	420	440	461	483	505
65,000	369	390	411	432	454	477	500	523	547
70,000	397	420	442	466	489	514	538	563	589
75,000	426	450	474	499	524	550	577	603	631
80,000	454	480	506	532	559	587	615	644	673
85,000	483	510	537	566	594	624	654	684	715
90,000	511	540	569	599	629	660	692	724	757
95,000	539	570	600	632	664	697	730	764	799
100,000	568	600	632	665	699	734	769	805	841

■ Loan Amount ☐ Interest Rate ☐ Monthly Payment

Assumes a 30-year, fixed-rate mortgage. Monthly payments do not include Taxes and homeowner's insurance.

SOURCE: Fannie Mae Foundation, "Opening the Door to a Home of Your Own," 2001, p. 12.

More sophisticated **loan calculators** are available in book form and on the Internet. (See Delphi Information Sciences Corporation, The Loan Calculator: Monthly Amortization Loan Schedule [Chicago: Contemporary Books, Inc., current edition]; Robert de Heer, Realty Bluebook: Financial Tables [Chicago: Real Estate Education Company, 1995, or current edition]; www.eloan.com; www.LendingTree.com; www.mrtgprofessor.com; and www.moneycentral.com, among others.)

You can calculate monthly payment amounts for common interest rates and terms, using the mortgage factor table below.

TABLE 32-3

Monthly Mortgage Payment Estimator

How To Use This Chart

To use this chart, start by finding the appropriate interest rate. Then follow that row over to the column for the appropriate loan term. This number is the *interest rate factor* required each month to amortize a $1,000 loan. To calculate the principal and interest (PI) payment, multiply the interest rate factor by the number of 1,000s in the total loan.

For example, if the interest rate is 10 percent for a term of 30 years, the interest rate factor is 8.78. If the total loan is $100,000, the loan contains 100 1,000s. Therefore

100 × 8.78 = $878 PI only

To estimate a mortgage loan amount using the amortization chart, divide the PI payment by the appropriate interest rate factor. Using the same facts as in the first example:

$878 ÷ 8.78 = $100 1,000's, or $100,000

Rate	Term 10 Years	Term 15 Years	Term 20 Years	Term 25 Years	Term 30 Years
4	10.13	7.40	6.06	5.28	4.78
4⅛	10.19	7.46	6.13	5.35	4.85
4¼	10.25	7.53	6.20	5.42	4.92
4⅜	10.31	7.59	6.26	5.49	5.00
4½	10.37	7.65	6.33	5.56	5.07
4⅝	10.43	7.72	6.40	5.63	5.15
4¾	10.49	7.78	6.47	5.71	5.22
4⅞	10.55	7.85	6.54	5.78	5.30
5	10.61	7.91	6.60	5.85	5.37
5⅛	10.67	7.98	6.67	5.92	5.45
5¼	10.73	8.04	6.74	6.00	5.53
5⅜	10.80	8.11	6.81	6.07	5.60
5½	10.86	8.18	6.88	6.15	5.68
5⅝	10.92	8.24	6.95	6.22	5.76
5¾	10.98	8.31	7.03	6.30	5.84
5⅞	11.04	8.38	7.10	6.37	5.92
6	11.10	8.44	7.16	6.44	6.00
6⅛	11.16	8.51	7.24	6.52	6.08
6¼	11.23	8.57	7.31	6.60	6.16
6⅜	11.29	8.64	7.38	6.67	6.24
6½	11.35	8.71	7.46	6.75	6.32
6⅝	11.42	8.78	7.53	6.83	6.40
6¾	11.48	8.85	7.60	6.91	6.49
6⅞	11.55	8.92	7.68	6.99	6.57
7	11.61	8.98	7.75	7.06	6.65
7⅛	11.68	9.06	7.83	7.15	6.74
7¼	11.74	9.12	7.90	7.22	6.82
7⅜	11.81	9.20	7.98	7.31	6.91
7½	11.87	9.27	8.05	7.38	6.99
7⅝	11.94	9.34	8.13	7.47	7.08
7¾	12.00	9.41	8.20	7.55	7.16
7⅞	12.07	9.48	8.29	7.64	7.25
8	12.14	9.56	8.37	7.72	7.34
8⅛	12.20	9.63	8.45	7.81	7.43
8¼	12.27	9.71	8.53	7.89	7.52
8⅜	12.34	9.78	8.60	7.97	7.61
8½	12.40	9.85	8.68	8.06	7.69
8⅝	12.47	9.93	8.76	8.14	7.78
8¾	12.54	10.00	8.84	8.23	7.87
8⅞	12.61	10.07	8.92	8.31	7.96
9	12.67	10.15	9.00	8.40	8.05
9⅛	12.74	10.22	9.08	8.48	8.14
9¼	12.81	10.30	9.16	8.57	8.23
9⅜	12.88	10.37	9.24	8.66	8.32
9½	12.94	10.45	9.33	8.74	8.41
9⅝	13.01	10.52	9.41	8.83	8.50
9¾	13.08	10.60	9.49	8.92	8.60
9⅞	13.15	10.67	9.57	9.00	8.69
10	13.22	10.75	9.66	9.09	8.78
10⅛	13.29	10.83	9.74	9.18	8.87
10¼	13.36	10.90	9.82	9.27	8.97
10⅜	13.43	10.98	9.90	9.36	9.06
10½	13.50	11.06	9.99	9.45	9.15
10⅝	13.57	11.14	10.07	9.54	9.25
10¾	13.64	11.21	10.16	9.63	9.34

Monthly mortgage payments includes principal and interest. Does not include other expenses, such as taxes and insurance.

SOURCE: Fillmore W. Galaty, Wellington J. Allaway and Robert C. Kyle, <u>Modern Real Estate Practice</u>, 15th ed. (Chicago, IL: Dearborn Financial Publishing Co./Real Estate Education Company, 2000, p. 231.).

Remember the true cost of your loan includes closing costs; whether these costs are paid upfront or folded into your borrowing; the degree of benefit that you get from the tax deductibility of interest and other costs; and whether you will be expected to pay continuing charges, or premiums, during the term of the loan for, say, mortgage insurance. Any calculation that you use to predict your tax benefit, however, will have to make large assumptions over small to large periods of time regarding future interest rates; your income each year; the absence of economic bad fortune in your life over the term of the loan; your anticipated length of holding the note before paying it off; and federal tax policy. You can make things simple by assuming that for every three dollars in paid home-mortgage interest, you will pay one less dollar in federal income tax each year (subject to two or three dozen qualifications and exceptions that may apply) in the higher tax brackets.

Internet sites that provide mortgage calculators, loan comparisons and useful information include: www.interest.com; www.usatoday.com/money/calculator.htm; www.LendingTree.com; and www.mrtgprofessor.com.

Many loans are now set up as **adjustable-rate mortgages (ARMs)**. They offer a fixed interest rate for, say, one to five years, at which time the rate is reset according to a formula pegged to a pre-determined financial **index,** such as the interest rate on a certain type of Treasury bill (T-bill) plus the lender's **margin**, usually two to three points. At the end of each adjustment period, which can range from a month to ten years, the interest rate is recalculated in light of whatever index your loan is tracking. The lender's margin should stay the same. ARMs, thus, give you a fixed interest rate at the start for some amount of time, and then a fluctuating interest rate for the rest of the term or until you pay it off. Your monthly payment is, accordingly, fixed at the start, after which it can be changed in line with the loan's index. In effect, an ARM is a system of scheduled refinancings of the declining balance of the note at set intervals based on then-current interest rates. But an ARM "refinancing" doesn't cost you anything each time you do it, because the schedule is set up at the time you take out the loan and you pay its costs then. Like fixed-rate mortgages, you choose the length (term) of the loan with an ARM: shorter terms should, in most cases, mean higher monthly payments but less total interest paid; longer terms should have the opposite effect. Since ARMs will undoubtedly carry different interest rates over the loan's term, you cannot compare an ARM's total interest cost to the total interest cost of a fixed-rate loan (which you can calculate precisely).

ARMs always start you off at an interest rate below the typical fixed rate for a 30-year mortgage. Whether an ARM is a better deal than a fixed-rate loan depends on how long you carry the mortgage and the trend in your index. ARMs often carry very low "**teaser rates**" that last for six months to a year, whereupon they are converted to the higher "contract interest rate." A teaser rate is a baited hook, with you as the fish. But a low starting rate that is fixed for a year or two can work to your benefit in buying a rural property whose principal you pay down quickly through the sale of some of its assets. A buyer with this in mind must make sure that the ARM allows him to pre-pay some or all of the loan principal without penalty.

Borrowers should avoid ARMs where the interest rate is adjusted frequently. When an adjustment formula starts adding interest into the principal balance, the borrower ends up paying interest on interest. A financing arrangement whose loan balance is increasing rather than decreasing over the term and whose monthly payments are less than the true amortized amounts, is called **negative amortization**. ARMs can create conditions leading to negative amortization as when the interest rate adjusts more frequently than the borrower's payment or when the index rises faster than the borrower's payment. In these circumstances, the ARM's "locked in" monthly payment for the first years of the note conceals the fact that the interest rate is adjusting upwards monthly, or semi-annually or annually during that period, thus adding unpaid interest into the balance owed. In the worst case with a monthly adjustable and a rapidly rising interest rate, your monthly payment can be less than the interest due that month. Federal law requires that lenders disclose certain information regarding a loan that contains this potential. The only certain way to protect yourself against an ARM or other loan with terms that allow negative amortization is to get written assurance from the lender that it does not. Staple it to your loan documents, and don't lose it. Loan documents are dense and complicated. Don't hesitate to ask your local lawyer to explain each bank's proposal.

It is important to research lenders and their loan terms with care. Don't just compare interest rates. Dig into the details. It is often the case that a lender advertising the lowest interest rate is not the best overall deal. The lender may impose conditions on his lowest rate that only some properties and borrowers can meet. The low rate may be packaged with terms that make the deal unfavorable. The low rate may be limited to borrowers with near-perfect credit scores. The low rate may also carry an assortment of fees and charges that raise your cost of borrowing substantially. If you decide that you can handle an ARM, look at the three-, five- and seven-year packages. Your choice will be shaped by where on the interest-rate-curve the Federal Reserve is when you start the note. A fixed-rate loan always benefits a borrower with rising income, and the fixed monthly payment allows inflation to make it easier for your pocketbook to pay back the note.

If you've decided that you want a fixed interest rate for 20 or 30 years and you hope to be able to pay off the debt in 15, you might have something like the following conversation—conducted with genuine politeness—with the lenders you're interviewing. You will adapt this script to your individual circumstances and the lender's general policies, which should be available on its website.

> I'm shopping around for a loan. I plan to have a talk just like this with Banker B and Banker C this week or next. I want to get a pretty good idea of the best deal you [Banker A] can offer me.
>
> I want to borrow $100,000 for __ years at a fixed interest rate to purchase property that will be your only security. The property is located in ____ County. I'm setting this up as an investment for tax purposes. I'm doing my research on the property now, and I will share with you what I find about the value of its assets and any liabilities or uncertainties. It is ___ is not ____ unimproved land. [If it's improved, state what improvements are on the property. If it's unimproved, state the nature of its physical access and whether or not it's currently serviced by utilities.] The land is currently used for _____, and its tax-assessed value is $_____.
>
> Here is a brief overview of my financials. [Hand him a two-page, typewritten summary of your financial profile on your letterhead.]
>
>> Your name and contact information. Age. SS number. Education. [If you and spouse are applying jointly, include spouse information]
>>
>> Place of employment. Years there. Other major employment experience.
>>
>> Adjusted Gross income [Line 35] from your last two 1040s.
>>
>> Current monthly income, including sources. [Include "est." after figure]
>>
>> Short net worth statement, listing all major assets, all major debts
>>
>> Estimate of future gross income, monthly/annually for next five years
>>
>> Very short explanation of any unusual circumstances bearing on your ability to pay, such as, kids about to go to expensive college, or illness in the family
>>
>> Equally short explanation of any past payment problems.
>>
>> Credit report and FICO, if you have them.
>
> The asking price is $110,000, and I plan to make a cash down payment of ten percent of the purchase price.
>
> What is the lowest interest rate you are currently offering on a 90 percent LTV over your

longest term? What points and origination fees, if any, do you want to impose on such a loan? How much will it cost me to buy down the rate on this loan to the lowest fixed rate I can get from you?

I want you to help me get into this loan with the least cost at your lowest interest rate.

What is the longest term you routinely offer? Can I get a longer term approved, if I want it?

This property will not be my principal residence now, but it could be in the future. I'm looking for a mortgage, not a personal or business loan.

What debt-to-income requirements must I meet?

Please itemize all charges (types, not dollar amounts) that will be imposed on me. Leave nothing out.

On a $100,000 loan, give me a ballpark estimate of what these closing costs will come to. I realize that this is not a number that will bind you.

Please add up my total cost of borrowing $100,000, including all estimated closing costs, over the term of this loan.

Are you willing to offer me better terms on such a loan than Bank B and Bank C to get my business?

Would you also be interested in financing a house on this land down the road?

I want a loan that does not carry any pre-payment penalties or charges.

The script that you prepare for your initial round of lender shopping will vary according to the particulars of the property and what terms you want. Ask your local lawyer to help you prepare for this negotiation. It may even be to your benefit to have him come along with you.

I've oriented this introductory script around a fixed-rate loan rather than an ARM to encourage you to shop lenders using a comparable loan product each has. Be prepared for a response that inundates you with choices. Don't get sucked into the option miasma where confusion is supposed to govern your judgment. Keep your proposed loan as simple as possible. You will be operating on the assumption that the lender who offers you the best deal on the simplest loan will offer you (at least) a competitive deal on the riskier options. That assumption may not be true, but it's as good a starting point as any.

This script approach is the way I shop for a new Toyota truck from three Toyota dealers. Give each one the exact specifications of the vehicle you want and get each dealer to quote his best price—everything included—for that exact model. Many lenders like many car dealers may try to tack on fees (profit) after quoting you an everything-included price. Resist. When a loan officer quotes you specific loan terms, you should confirm that he is legally authorized to commit the institution. Car salesmen are not "agents" of the dealership and cannot commit the dealership to a deal. The car deal must be done with the sales manager. If you find yourself facing a loan manager renegotiating terms that you've agreed on with the loan officer, walk away from it. You're probably being hustled.

INTEREST RATES

Much of your lender shopping and lender negotiating will involve looking for the lowest **interest rate**. Lenders offer their lowest mortgage rates to borrowers willing to borrow for the shortest terms with adjustable interest. An adjustable-rate mortgage (ARM) that is adjusted every year should carry the lowest interest rate the lender offers, because the lender is offering a low starting out rate to get you into a loan where all risk of interest variability over the loan's term is shifted onto you. This can, however, be a great deal if you are able to pay off the ARM at the end of the first rate-adjustment period. ARM loans are amortized over whatever term you and the lender agree on. The rate is changed at the end of the year (or adjustment period) to reflect changes in the lender's cost of money. Remember that interest rate is only one part of *your* cost of borrowing over the time you have the loan out. If you're looking for a fixed-rate over a specific term, it's easy to compare lenders on the basis of rate and costs. ARMs can be compared on the specifics of each lender's package, but the best you can do is project hypothetical total interest costs based on different assumed future interest rates.

Interest rates vary with the amount of time you want it to be fixed. You will not get to choose how the bank computes interest—and there's the rub.

Institutional lenders say they charge "**simple interest**." Simple interest is calculated with the formula of I = PRT, where I is interest, P is principal, R is rate and T is time. Simple interest could look like this on a $50,000 loan at seven percent for one year:

I = PRT
I = $50,000 x .07 x 1
I = $3,500

This is a fair calculation if you have one payment that you make at the end of the year since you will have the bank's money for the entire 365 days. This is how a seller-held second mortgage is usually figured. If you are making monthly payments of both principal and interest, you should be paying simple interest on the declining balance of the principal. If you are not, you are paying more than seven percent. While banks charge mortgage interest on the declining balance, they rig the process in their favor by front-loading interest. This is not negotiable with your loan officer.

All institutional mortgage notes **front-load interest payments**. Front-loading means that each of your fixed-sum, monthly payments contains a changing ratio of interest to principal, with almost all of your first monthly payment being interest and almost all of your last payment being principal. FIGURE 32-1 provides an approximate trend of the changing ratio of principal to interest payment each year over a 30-year, fixed-payment (or level payment) term. Note that it's not until the 25th year, that the borrower is paying more principal than interest. If you have a 30-year term and you pre-pay the entire note after ten years, you will still owe the lender almost all of the original principal. The interest rate that you've agreed to is true only when the note is paid out over the full term. If you pay on a shortened term, you will end up paying a higher interest rate because of front-loaded interest scheduling. As it is, if you pay the note at 30 years as scheduled, you will end up paying about $3 in interest (depending on the interest rate) for every dollar in original principal. As you might expect, lenders don't feature this aspect of consumer borrowing in their advertising.

FIGURE 32-1

Front-loaded Interest Repayment Schedule

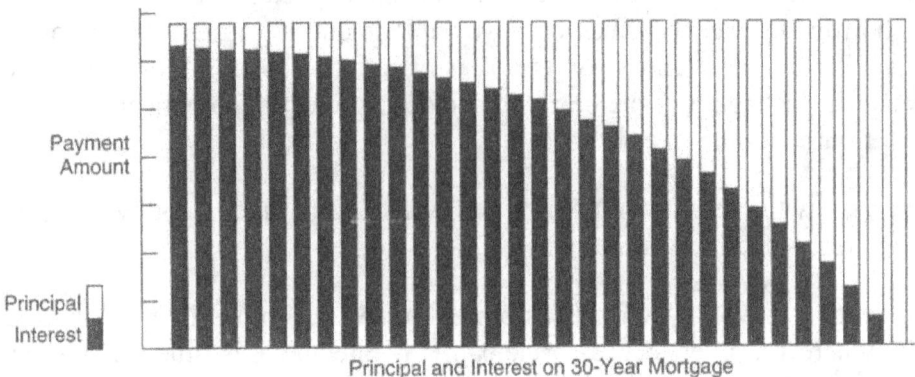

Principal and Interest on 30-Year Mortgage

Calculated on a 30-year, fixed-rate (level-payment) amortization schedule.

SOURCE: Fillmore W. Galaty, Wellington J. Allaway and Robert C. Kyle, Modern Real Estate Practice, 15th ed. (Chicago, IL: Dearborn Financial Publishing Co./Real Estate Education Company, 2000, p. 229.).

You should consider one other wrinkle with front-loaded interest: **balance owed as a ratio of original amount borrowed**. As you know, the amount of principal owed to the lender declines each year during the term of a note. But the rate of decline is faster the lower your interest rate. TABLE 32-4 shows these ratios for six interest rates on a 25-year, fixed-payment note.

TABLE 32-4

Balance Owed as a Ratio of Original Amount for Six Interest Rates on a 25-Year Note

Age (Years)	5%	6%	7%	8%	9%	10%
1	.979	.982	.985	.987	.989	.990
5	.886	.899	.911	.923	.932	.941
10	.739	.762	.786	.807	.826	.845
15	.550	.578	.608	.635	.659	.686
20	.308	.330	.356	.380	.399	.425
24	.066	.070	.080	.087	.088	.100

SOURCE: William Benke and Joseph M. Fowler, All About Real Estate Investing from the Inside Out (Chicago: Irwin, 1995, p. 190. TABLE 32-4 is excerpted from Appendix A, pp. 183-190.)

At the end of year one, the five percent borrower owes 97.9% of the principal while the ten percent borrower owes 99 percent. At the end of the 24th year, the five percent borrower owes 6.6 percent of the original principal while the ten percent borrower will pay off ten percent of the original loan amount in his last year. The lender's way of calculating front-loaded interest makes it harder for the high-interest-rate borrower to build up equity—just in case you didn't know. And as the term of a note increases, it takes the borrower longer to build up equity at every interest rate; the higher the rate, the harder it is. The borrower gets to 50 percent of principal repaid on a ten-year note at five percent in year five, at ten percent interest in year six. On a 20-year note, the five percent borrower gets to 50 percent principal repaid in year 12; the ten percent interest rate gets there in year 15. On a 30-year note, the five percent borrower gets to 50 percent principal repaid in year 20; the ten percent borrower gets there three years later. The obvious reason for borrowers to search out the lowest fixed-interest rate is to pay as little total interest as possible; now you know a couple of other reasons as well.

One interest trick that you might run into is the **add-on rate**. Some real-estate lenders use it. The lender calculates the interest due on the total principal for the entire term, then adds this sum to the principal owed for you to repay over the loan's term before calculating your fixed monthly payment. The effect of an add-on rate is to almost double the advertised simple interest rate you're being charged. Be particularly watchful for add-on rates with private mortgage companies and with home-improvement loans. Internet lenders might use it too. Lenders sucker borrowers in to add-ons with obviously low advertised rates.

Buyers should determine what is the **truer rate of interest being charged**. The truer rate of interest in my mind is the total cost of borrowing the lender's money expressed as an annual percentage rate. The truer interest rate will be higher than either the **nominal rate** or the **simple interest rate** the lender advertises. Your total cost of borrowing will include the one-time fees and charges that you pay as closing costs, on which you don't pay interest. The truer rate of interest should reflect the cost of borrowing from a lender when all fees and charges are added to the nominal rate, and recalculated as a single percentage rate. This methodology overstates your interest rate, because it includes charges on which you won't actually pay interest. But the approach should end up giving you a valid way of ranking interest-rate offers, despite the built-in inaccuracy. A lender's nominal (advertised) rate will not include the one-time, upfront fees and charges that are imposed as part of your closing costs. You may be able to get each lender to do a truer rate calculation for you, but don't be surprised if you have to do it yourself. I discuss APR (annual percentage rate) below. Your truer interest rate along with the amount of time you have the loan until it is paid off determines your total cost of borrowing.

Most borrowers start their comparison shopping for mortgages by looking at interest rates. The alternative recommended by several consumer-oriented professionals is to start by examining lender closing costs. The latter comparison is difficult at best, and "'…the good-faith estimate is often not sufficiently close to the mark so consumers know what the closing costs will actually be,'" said Allen Fishbein, director of housing policy at the Consumer Federation of America in 2004 after the U.S. Department of Housing and Urban Development refused to reform the disclosure process to provide borrowers with clear, comparable information about closing fees. (Andrea Coombes, "Closing-cost maze: You're on your own," CBS Market Watch, <u>Richmond Times-Dispatch</u>, May 30, 2004.) The good-faith estimate given three days after application is not set in stone, because some costs vary with the actual closing date. Non-lender fees, such as the recording fee and tax, vary with the selling price. Where problems arise in the title search, other costs will increase. It is unreasonable for a borrower to expect that a good-faith estimate will remain unchanged over two or three months, given the uncertainties of getting a purchase to closing. But the lender's fees that appear on the settlement statement should be reasonably close to those the lender estimated in good faith. You can use the good-faith estimate or even the preliminary estimate that lenders may give prior to application for the purpose of calculating your true interest rate.

Lenders are expected to disclose to borrowers the **annual percentage rate (APR)** of interest that they will be charged. This is a central component of a truer rate, as I'm using the idea, but it's not the complete story. One might assume that a borrower could feel confident in comparing one lender's APR with all others, secure in the knowledge that an apple is being compared with other apples. Lenders are not required to factor into their APR certain "**garbage fees**," including, but not limited to, charges for postage, courier service, review of documents, administration fee, preparation fee, notary fee and other overhead items. I've also read about a warehousing fee, sub-escrow fee, lender-review fee and "miscellaneous fee." I anxiously await a lender adding in fees for loan approval, director compensation and office Christmas party. Lenders rework their fees from time to time, changing names and adding new ones. A first-time borrower might challenge a "miscellaneous fee," but not something as important-sounding as a "sub-escrow fee." Garbage fees and phony costs cut into borrowers twice. First, they are paying for lender overhead that should already be figured into the interest rate and other fees. And second, lenders pad these fees which they shouldn't be charging in the first place. The amount of garbage fees will vary from lender to lender, which can make a decision based on an APR to APR comparison misleading. Not all lenders, of course, charge garbage fees or pad the fees they do charge.

Three federal appeals courts have ruled that the federal Department of Housing and Urban Development cannot prevent lenders, title companies, mortgage brokers, escrow agents and others that facilitate real-estate settlements from **marking up fees** far beyond their actual costs. (Kenneth R. Harney, "Another court rebuffs HUD's junk fee rules," Richmond Times-Dispatch, February 2, 2003.) The appeals courts upheld a $55 courier-service fee to the borrower that cost the lender $15; $350 for a part-computer, part-drive-by appraisal that cost less than $50; and a $65 credit-check fee that cost only $9. These anti-consumer decisions cover 15 states, and the Supreme Court is likely to uphold this line of argument unless Congress specifically empowers HUD to limit fee padding. The 15 states, as I write in mid-2005, that allow lenders to mark up loan charges without limit are Maryland, Virginia, North and South Carolina, West Virginia, Illinois, Iowa, Wisconsin, Indiana, Minnesota, Missouri, Arkansas, Nebraska and North and South Dakota. The no-mark-up states are Florida, Georgia, Alabama, New York, Connecticut, Vermont and New Jersey. The situation is in limbo in most other places until Congress or the U.S. Supreme Court decides the issue, which has split appellate courts. In the 15 no-limit states, mark-up fees can cost a borrower hundreds of dollars for nothing. The federal government's position has been that mark ups without additional services should be prohibited.

One alternative to dancing with the fee thieves is to find a so-called "**zero-cost mortgage**," in which all lender fees are bundled into the interest rate, except for title-insurance. The lender does not offer the borrower a package of lender fees, points and other costs inasmuch as the package is incorporated into the rate. This differs from the fixed-fee cost packages that Ditech.com and ABN-AMRO Mortgage Corp. offer. Bank of America is offering a zero-cost primary mortgage for home buyers; it should be arguable that its "Mortgage Rewards" program be available for rural second homes as well as rural property. If you are a Bank of America customer, you may be able to save as much 40 percent on closing costs through this program. (Kenneth Harney, "Fee simple: Mortgage giant streamlines a loan," Richmond Times-Dispatch, May 8, 2005.)

Most ripped-off borrowers grumble and pay, inasmuch as it's a one-time rip-off and the cost of suing is not worth the effort and money at issue. They walk out of their closing feeling cheated and violated, and rightly so. The individual's only chance to contain this thievery in the no-limit states (4th, 7th and 8th federal appeals circuits) is to force lenders to reveal the costs they pay for services, such as appraisals, overnighting mail, documents, credit checks, electronic house evaluations, etc., against the amounts they will charge you to pay for these services. This needs to be done when lenders are competing for your business. If these costs suggest padding, ask your friendly loan officer in a no-limit state when he is in his friendly mode (that is, when he's trying to get your business) if he has any problem with allowing you to pay the actual cost of each required service plus a ten percent mark up. A fee-padding lender will be reluctant to agree to a reduction in his padded fees, but a ten percent sweetener might work. Shame, I think, is your only realistic leverage, but don't count on it working. Ask the loan officer why the lender should pad a cost that you are fully paying. Don't personalize this discussion or be hostile. Frame your questions in terms of simply trying to learn what that lender will charge you *altogether* to borrow money, and why.

I would ask the lender for a full disclosure of **all fees and estimated settlement** costs during your first or second interview with a loan officer. Together, fees and costs averaged $3,562 on a $180,000 mortgage in 2004 according to a www.Bankrate.com survey. (Consumer Reports, "Your Home: How to protect your biggest investment," May, 2005). This is your most opportune moment to use the leverage of your potential business to free your loan from the lender's add-ons and padding. Consumer Reports recommends that a borrower "compare, haggle, challenge." Ask for the **preliminary estimate** while you're sitting in front of the loan officer; tell him you understand that it's approximate, a reasonable approximation that should be pretty close all the same. At that time, ask him to estimate your true interest rate based on all fees/costs on which you will be paying interest. Whether or not you get an answer, you will at least have put a shot across the lender's bow that you will be scrutinizing his offered loan package and shopping for the best one. More likely than not, you will end up comparing loan terms from each lender in two tiers: APR against APR, and all other costs against all other costs.

Even though most APRs don't include all costs, they are the handiest way to start comparing interest rates from various lenders. (Remember that the APR alone is only part of what determines a loan's cost to a borrower over the term and what the true interest rate is.) Each lender's APR will be a bit higher than the nominal (advertised) rate, because it includes pre-paid finance charges. These have the effect of reducing the principal that you're borrowing, which, in turns, boosts your APR over the nominal rate. But your truer rate—sometimes defined as a borrower's **effective interest rate;** the rate you actually pay—folds in all of the lender's charges that you pay to get the mortgage. That rate you have to figure yourself, from loan to loan and lender to lender.

Every APR that you are shown, in addition, is calculated over the full term of the note. If you pay off before the term, as almost all mortgage holders do, your true/effective interest rate will be higher than the stated APR. Johnson shows that a nominal interest rate of exactly ten percent with the borrower paying one percent in pre-paid finance charges amounts to a projected APR of 10.123 percent—the publicized APR—only over the full 30 years. If the borrower holds the note for five years, the effective interest rate is 10.2 percent; four years, 10.25 percent; three years, 10.33 percent; two years, 10.5 percent; and one year, 11 percent. (Johnson, Save Thousands, pp. 132-133.) If pre-paid finance charges are identical among the lenders you're interviewing, then comparing APRs is a good starting point. But APRs alone do not provide sufficient information about the cost of borrowing for valid comparisons. The true/effective interest rate of each lender's loan package (interest rate plus all costs, fees, charges, etc.), not the nominal interest rate or the APR, is what you want to calculate. And that true/effective interest rate requires that you use the number of months you expect to hold the loan, because term length changes the rate you wind up paying.

You can now see that projections are murky on both sides of the lender-borrower relationship when a borrower is trying to make a true-rate calculation to obtain the cheapest loan cost. Lenders are not likely to give you a true rate, because they don't want you to know it. The only lender whose self-interest is advanced by full disclosure and comparison shopping is the one offering the lowest true rate. All the others are higher; hence, they're likely to be less helpful. But on the borrower's side, it may be impossible to predict when you will pay off the loan. And if you can't do that, you can't figure your true rate for comparisons among lenders.

If you find yourself in this familiar muddy muddle, do the best you can. Get from each lender a reasonable estimate of all the costs of the loan, then compute your truer rate from each lender over a fixed term of your choosing. Your CPA can do these calculations for you. If you're working with an ARM or a no-interest loan, you can't project your truer interest rate, because it's impossible to predict the rates you will be charged at each adjustment period. So work up a worst-case future where your interest rate is increased one half of one percent each year over the 15 years you expect to be in the loan, a middle case where the rate goes up by one quarter of one percent each year, and an optimistic case where the rate rises one tenth of one percent each year. Your chances are greater for paying higher interest rates over an ARM's term if you start the loan when interest rates are historically low, and vice versa.

It's fair for you to ask each loan officer you interview to calculate your total cost of borrowing and your true/effective interest rate (based on that total cost) over both the full term of the note and the period that you estimate you will hold it. Don't be surprised if he says he can't—a revealing admission, if nothing else. He may say "it's against policy" to do these calculations, or that too many costs are unknown for him to project an accurate estimate. Push him a bit. Make him feel a bit guilty and defensive in hope that you can get disclosure on other information you're requesting. It will help to have had your CPA do these estimated calculations before you start interviewing lenders.

You should ask every mortgage lender to print out for you an **amortization schedule** for the **loan terms** you are considering. These would be based on the length of the term in number of months and interest rate if it is fixed. The **amortization print out** should show the break down of how each of your fixed monthly payments is divided between interest and principal. From the amortization schedule, you will be able to determine how much principal remains to be paid at any month during the term of your fixed-rate mortgage. The sooner you can pay off principal, the less interest you will pay. That is why many real-estate writers advise borrowers to make one extra principal-only payment every year if possible. (This principal-only payment must be clearly designated as "principal only," otherwise the bank may use it for interest. And your note must permit pre-payment without penalty.) Such a strategy gets you out of a 30-year mortgage at about 22 years, with a goodly saving in interest. Be aware that the amortization schedule you are handed will use an interest rate that does not include points and fees that you will be charged. Your actual cost of borrowing will be higher than the amortization schedule's interest rate. Amortize, incidentally, contains the root "mort"—familiar to us in words such as "mortality," "mortician" and "mortgage." Amortize means "to kill slowly over time." Make sure that it is your debt that is killed slowly and not you by paying more than you can afford.

Adjustable-rate mortgages (ARMs) are not generally not considered a predatory-lending practice, but they can be foreclosure traps waiting to be sprung. An adjustable-rate mortgage changes the interest rate on your remaining loan balance at scheduled times in the future. What adjusts is the amount of money that you pay during the next payment period, and the period after that. Your interest rate will be revisited at the beginning of each payment period in relationship to whichever financial benchmark your lender is using. In the worst case, the total cost of paying back your loan over its amortized term can double. Special caution must be exercised when you take out an ARM during a period of low interest rates. The up-down cycle of interest rates will be working against you; anticipate paying higher rates deeper into the term. Always insist on having the lender show you the worst case for you under his ARM—the fully indexed rate. If you cannot afford that rate, don't borrow the money.

ARMs change your interest rate according to some public economic or money-related index, such as the one- or five-year Treasury Bill (T-Bill) Rate or the Federal Reserve Discount Rate. The lender will adjust your rate periodically and automatically according to a set schedule that you choose when you first borrow the money. The months/years between resettings is called the "adjustment interval." If you are comparing ARMs among lenders, your best bet for a long-term note is to take the one whose interest rate is tied to the **slowest-moving index**, except, of course, if the starting rate is above the stratosphere. If you have to jump in at 16 percent, which some did in the early 1980s, you had to assume that rates would go down. In that case, a fast-moving index and a short adjustment interval would have helped, and a 30-year fixed rate would have been ruinous over the full term. Refinancing a high fixed-rate is the borrower's best option, but refinancing usually involves additional, upfront costs. The six-month T-bill index and the one-year Treasury securities index are the fastest roller-coasters in this park. If interest rates are high and likely to decline, you could shop for one of them on a note of a couple of years. The three-year Treasury securities index is the usual borrower choice when rates are likely to rise. The longer Treasury indexes—five and ten years—are the slowest moving; if you're getting in when interest rates are low, consider them.

The National Mortgage (NACR) Interest Rate Index moves slowly, because it is an average rate charged on previously occupied homes. The Eleventh District Cost of Funds Index and the London Interbank Offered Rate (LIBOR) also move slowly.

The lender's ARM rate will be set according to his chosen index rate plus the lender-added **margin** or "**spread**," which is a fixed percentage or ratio established at the time you agreed to borrow the money. The lender's cost of money approximates the index rate, and the margin represents the lender's business costs and profit. The formula that you are offered might be something like the "prime (interest) rate + two points." That formula covers the lender's cost of money and his spread. If prime is five percent, you will pay the lender seven percent during the next period on your principal. The smaller the lender's margin, the less you pay over the life of your loan. The lender's margin should not change during the entire term of the loan. If you take out an ARM with a 30-year amortization schedule, your index never changes; your lender's formula never changes; your formula never changes; but your monthly payment will go up and down according to the interest rate of your index when adjustments are made.

There are three types of **caps** (or ceilings) that you should look for with ARMs. A **periodic cap**, or **rate cap**, imposes a limit on the interest rate to which an ARM can rise over a period of time. A commonly used periodic cap is two percent, which means the lender can't raise your interest rate more than two percent in any one adjustment period. A **payment cap** imposes a ceiling on the amount you will be expected to pay in any one mortgage payment. A **life-time cap** means the lender can't raise your interest rate by more than a certain specified number of percentage points over the term of the loan. This is often packaged as something like a "2-and-6 cap," under which the maximum upward rate adjustment during any one period is a two percentage point increase (e.g., from a three percent interest rate to a five percent rate) and the maximum rate increase over the life of the loan is nine percent. Using these numbers, the worst case for this ARM is that you pay a nine percent rate over most of the loan. If you're planning to pay off a note quickly, look for a low interest rate ARM with as few fees and points as you can find. When considering ARMs, compare the cap packages from each lender.

Beware of **teaser interest rates** in bait-and-switch ARMs. A teaser rate is one that is two or three points below the prevailing range of rates that most lenders are offering. It is fixed for a few months or a year, then "upgrades" to an adjustable rate, often with one or more high caps. The purpose of a teaser rate is to get you into what will soon amount to a very favorable, low-risk, high-profit loan for the lender. The bait is the below-market rate for the introductory period; the switch is into a variable rate in which you bear all the risk and cost.

A final word on interest rates. Institutional lenders are smart about loan terms, particularly interest rates. It is how they make a lot of their money. They are way smarter than I am, and probably smarter about their business than you. Their objectives are to make money from each mortgage loan with as little work as possible and to strip as much risk out of their lending as they can. You can reasonably expect of yourself to weed out the worst deals. But it's difficult to find the single best deal if only because you cannot predict your own future.

You can start sorting through lenders by finding the loan packages with the fewest of your dollars required in upfront fees, points and costs. Then compare the total cost of interest over the term of the loan, if you want a fixed rate. If you're shopping for an ARM, you have more variables to compare—rates, caps, adjustment periods and so on. Make sure that the property alone is securing the loan and that no pre-payment penalty exists. Have your short list of possible lenders give you good-faith estimates of their closing costs in writing. Ask to see a **remaining balance** table, which shows how much principal remains to be paid at your rate for various years during the note's term. You can get this table for both fixed-rate loans and ARMs, but the interest you will pay on the ARM cannot be predicted. You still may not be able to compare apples with apples, but these requests will at least get you into the produce section.

When you have advanced your conversation with your top pick to the point where you ask for the **full disclosure statement** (mortgage lenders are required to provide certain disclosures within three days after application which describe closing costs, origination fees, "effective interest rate" and whether or not the lender might sell your loan), also ask for a copy of the note you will be expected to sign. Read this document. If particular language troubles you, ask the loan officer to explain how the lender applies those words. I doubt that you can get troublesome language deleted, but at least you can get a sense of how and when it is used against borrowers. You may want to have a lawyer review the loan documents if they scare you. Mortgaging your life is a scary proposition, and the risk of calamity—along with its awful pain—is on you, not the lender.

If you are proposing to have the seller finance a portion of the purchase through a second mortgage, you will need to negotiate loan terms and particularly the interest rate with him. When a seller finances all or part of a purchase, the note is often called a **purchase-money mortgage**.

Be careful that both you and the seller have the same idea about the amount of interest you will be paying. Let's say the seller agrees to take back a second mortgage at seven percent interest. What does that mean? Is it seven percent on the original principal you're borrowing from the seller, or seven percent on the declining balance? If you have three payments on a three-year $45,000 second, your schedule could look like this:

Seven Percent Interest Paid on Original Balance

Principal = $45,000
Payment 1: $15,000 plus 7 percent of $45,000 = $3,150
Payment 2: $15,000 plus 7 percent of $45,000 = $3,150
Payment 3: $15,000 plus 7 percent of $45,000 = $3,150
Total: $45,000 principal, plus $9,450 in interest = $54,450.

This format amounts to an interest payment of 21 percent of the principal.

The alternative is this:

Seven Percent Interest Paid on Declining Balance

Principal = $45,000
Payment 1: $15,000 plus 7 percent of $45,000 = $3,150
Payment 2: $15,000 plus 7 percent of $30,000 = $2,100
Payment 3: $15,000 plus 7 percent of $15,000 = $1,050
Total: $45,000 plus $6,300 in interest = $51,300.

This format amounts to an interest payment of 14 percent. Interest is usually paid on the declining balance, as in this example.

It's possible that you can negotiate a seven percent note for three years where you pay only $3,150 in interest (that is, seven percent of $45,000) at the end of three years, along with all $45,000 in principal. That would be a very good deal. You could work the same interest payment while making three equal installment payments of $15,000 each in principal.

In sum, buyers should look for a loan with the **lowest truest interest rate**, consistent with a borrower's other objectives and needs. A low interest rate that is fixed for a long time is usually best for most borrowers as long as it carries no penalty for pre-payment of principal or early pay off. A long term—20 years or more—means a low monthly payment. The longer the term, the more total interest a borrower will pay.

PITCHING AND HITTING

Once you narrow the field to a couple of lenders, you might want to submit a full **financial profile** with each loan application. This profile expands the summary that you gave the loan officer when you were interviewing. Your profile puts you in front of the lender voluntarily and in your own format. It is your first step toward having a lender **pre-approve you for the maximum amount that he is willing to lend you at a specific rate and set of terms**. The lender will probably ask you to fill out his own form. Nonetheless, you establish confidence in your application and credibility by submitting an accurate profile of your own design before being asked. Don't be obscure or dishonest. After reviewing your application, the lender will tell you the amount of mortgage for which you are pre-approved. **Pre-approval is what you ultimately seek, not pre-qualification**. Pre-approval means you will get the money; pre-qualifying is less certain. Pre-qualification gives the borrower a ballpark idea of what the lender may lend, based on the information submitted. It does not bind the lender to give a particular amount, or even anything at all. Negotiating for a pre-qualification amount is not dissimilar to negotiating with a dealer's salesperson over the price of a car—in both cases, the number may or may not mean something. In your shopping for a lender, pre-qualification gets you started, which is good enough during your lender-selection phase.

Your financial profile should set forth in sufficient detail your ability to borrow the sum you want. "Ability to borrow" means the ability to repay the note over its term. You don't want to try to borrow more than your financials show that you can feasibly repay. "Stretching" of that sort gives lenders the willies and compromises the credibility you're trying to establish. Worse, if the lender gives you more than you can handle, it puts you at a high risk of loss. Review your profile as a lender would. You want to make it easy for the lender to verify your statements. Therefore, provide copies of account statements, pay stubs, 1040s and other documents. Provide all relevant financial and employment information, including:

1. **Contact information and profile**.
   a. Name, address, phone, fax and e-mail of the applicant (s). (Be consistent in using your name. Don't be R. Frederick Balderdash, III on your SS card, Frederick Balderdash on your credit cards, and Fast Freddy Balderdash on your checks. If you have multiple names, so to speak, note them on your profile.)
   b. Social security number of applicant (s).
   c. Name, address, phone of employer. If self-employed, state place of business, nature of business and how many years so employed.
   d. Age, marital status, number and age of financially-dependent children.
   e. Brief history: place of birth, education, short employment history, military service, licenses (work-related).
   f. Credit report, FICO score, if you have them.
   g. Immigrant status and nationality, if relevant.

2. **Summary statement of your net worth** (which is all your debts subtracted from all of your assets). Group your assets and itemize them:

		Net Worth, Date		
1		2	3	(2-3)

Assets	FMV	Debt	Net Worth

Real Property
  Personal residence
  Rental property
  Non-rental Investment property

Personal Property
  Vehicles
  Boats/Planes
  Household (lump sum)
  Special stuff—artwork, jewelry

Financial resources
  Stocks/bonds/future contracts/options/CDs
  Cash
  Savings accounts
  Checking accounts
  Retirement accounts/Social Security
  Life insurance/annuities
  Receivables
  Other

Other
  Personal loans
  College loans
  Business loans
  Credit card debt (other than current)
  Tax obligations (out of the ordinary)*
  Alimony/child support
  Future income expected
    Trust fund
    Inheritance
  Don't include hoped-for winnings in the lottery.

  * If you are self-employed and have set up a dedicated tax-escrow savings account, don't count that as a liquid asset. It's obligated.

A net-worth statement for assets carrying debt is set up in three columns. The first column is Fair Market Value (FMV) of the asset. Assets should be included at their gross fair market value. On items like real estate, pencil in your best estimate of current market value. Higher values are better than lower values as long as the higher value is credible and established in a defensible way. A more conservative approach would be to use the tax-assessed values of your property, which are, generally, lower than current FMV. If you have current appraisals, include them. Don't inflate asset values, especially items such as cars that the lender can check in his Blue Book. If you have separate appraisals to show the value of discrete assets that are part of your real estate—such as a building or merchantable timber—append them.

The second column is Debts where they apply to an Asset, such as a mortgage on property, or where they are unsecured. It might also mean a reservation of interest/profit in part or all of your asset held by another.

The third column is Net Worth, that is, the difference between each asset's FMV and the amount of outstanding principal in its Debt. You do not include interest owed as part of your debt; only remaining principal. Unsecured debt, such as credit cards or personal loans, are also subtracted from your asset values. Your net worth is the sum of the third column. When your debt exceeds your asset values, you have a negative net worth—not good.

For a bank loan, you don't need to have your assets and real property professionally appraised for your net-worth statement. But you should be clear and honest. Don't fail to mention debt. Make a reasonable estimate of FMVs whose logic and basis you can defend if asked.

I suggest including other assets that are not normally requested, such as expected inheritance and money owed (receivables). They help you make your case.

3. **Last two years of your IRS 1040s**. Use more years if you are self-employed or had big fluctuations in income or adjusted gross income. Explain anomalies. Lenders like to see rising income each year.

4. **Current monthly balance sheet.** Show all income sources/gross amounts.

Income (est. for current year, not last tax year)

    Wages/salary, or self-employment earnings
    Interest
    Dividend
    Royalty
    Rent
    Pension/social security/disability
    Revenue anticipated from something big, e.g., sale of something, court award, pension start

Expenses

    Household (estimate total food, clothing, utilities, repairs)
    Current rent/mortgage payment
    Property tax
    Loan payments, e.g., car, college
    Credit card
    Tuition
    Alimony/child support
    Vehicles—gas, insurance, maintenance
    Insurance—health, life, homeowner, other
    Health care/medicines, not covered by insurance if out of the ordinary
    Other

5. **Estimated future annual gross income for next three years**.

6. **Account numbers and contact information**: Include mortgages with other lenders, credit cards, checking, savings, retirement, stocks/bonds, CDs

7. **Items of public record**, summaries of consent agreements, divorce settlements, judgments, etc. that affect your cash flow.

8. **Any other items that materially affect your ability to meet a mortgage payment,** including costs of treating serious disease, special child-related or parent-related expenses, anticipated changes in your cash flow or expenses, etc.

9. **Mortgage history with other lenders**. Include names of recent lenders, approximate dates, location of property, amount. If you don't have these records, provide a one-sentence summary of what you recall about each mortgage.

10. **Current mortgage record.** Include name of lender, amount, terms, number of the note and the amount of interest paid annually. Do not count on your current mortgage lender to provide another lender with accurate information. Do not assume that a lender will be able to figure out a mortgage interest payment from your 1040, particularly a complicated one.

11. **Your (corrected) credit report/score that you've purchased.**
(www.mifico.com for $44.85 in 2005.)

This financial profile provides more information than most lenders ask for. Even if you have a shaky financial history, it's better in my opinion to put it on the table voluntarily and in advance of your lender digging it up. Your profile allows you to inject into your conversation the ideas of future income and future financial stability—assuming, of course, that these ideas work to your advantage. (If they don't, you probably shouldn't be thinking about taking out a mortgage.) It takes some effort to pull together your financial profile, much of which you will have to do anyway as part of the lender's application that you will be required to complete.

If a conventional lender won't give you a conventional loan—fixed for at least 20 years or something like a five- to seven-year ARM on reasonable terms—for rural property, then you should forget conventionality. You're asking for more mortgage than you can handle, or your past has caught up with you. In this situation, find a property where you can sell part of it quickly, using the net proceeds to pay down the loan. You may need to arrange a release with the lender. Make sure to get a professional evaluation of the asset's value prior to purchase, which you will have to do anyway to qualify the property for a lender. To the extent that you sell post-purchase for the established value pre-purchase, you minimize taxable gain and tax owed on the immediate sale. The tax obligation shifts down the road. This **buy-whole-sell-part strategy** changes your loan request. It can reduce your mortgage principal by 10 to 90 percent depending on how much you sell. You can sell during your escrow on a contingent basis. You can assign part of your interest in the purchase to your buyer. It also changes the borrowing time frame. You now want a 100 percent LTV loan for no more than six months, after which you want a different loan for a much smaller amount over a much longer period. Many ways exist to configure this two-step borrowing plan. In both steps, the lender should feel very secure.

Institutional lenders use a cookie-cutter procedure for determining the amount of money they will lend. They focus on your historic cash flow and its reliability. They review the amount and cost of debt you're already carrying to figure how much more you can reasonably carry based mainly on your past. They also look at your assets beyond the property itself to measure your ability to meet your obligations if your normal cash flow is interrupted by unemployment or illness. Most readers who are looking for country property will already be carrying a mortgage on their principal residence. That's good; new lenders like borrowers who make payments on time to other lenders. It's evidence that "your mind is right," in the way the prison-camp boss wanted Cool Hand Luke to meet his obligations without complaint. If the cookie-cutter formulas don't quite get you into the loan that you want, ask the lender to tell you his specific concerns. Use your purchase to help buy your purchase. That helps lenders make the loan.

Banks and other institutional lenders will subject your numbers to a percentage analysis, which they often refer to as a "**qualifying ratio**." The details of this calculation are not important for this discussion, but the idea is. The lender will determine your gross monthly income and then multiply that number by a percentage that the bank has determined is the amount of debt you can handle in relation to the debt you are already carrying. On a principal residence, most lenders will allow you to borrow up to 28 percent of your monthly income for this expense; and allow 36 percent for your total long-term debt. If you have a lot of cash, or easily cashed out assets, and the rural property is a relatively minor addition to your assets, you have room to negotiate. You are particularly strong if your recent history shows steady income growth, which has the effect of lowering the percent of income you spend on debt service. A low percent is a low ratio; low ratios are good for your application since they indicate room for additional debt. Banks turn down borrowers on the basis of high ratios, not because of their concern for you, but because of their concern for their money. Lending money is not "A Wonderful Life," and your banker is not Jimmy Stewart, complete with hems and haws.

The lender assembles a picture of your financial past and present. From those patterns, the lender sort of projects your future and takes into account uncertainties. Many futures are not very predictable based on the past. You are likely to be as good a predictor of your future as any bank formula. There is always room for discussion of this type when you think your income and/or net worth are likely to increase over time.

Once the lender reviews your profile, he'll assign you a ratio and, assuming everything is okay, pre-approve you for a loan amount with terms. At that point, you need to ask whether your approved loan amount will be reduced if you modify your offer to the seller, say by decreasing your down payment (which preserves your cash) and having the seller take back a second for the difference (which increases your debt). Get such matters straight with your lender before you start negotiating with the seller. Once you have an approved loan amount, you don't need to max it out on a purchase. Carrying less debt is always easier than carrying more.

Debt is the foundation of our consumer economy. It's easy to forget that debt is neither benign nor passive. It has to be fed each month, and if you don't, it will gobble you up in one bite. I encourage middle-income readers to finance country property by selling some of its assets rather than stretching to buy with maxed-out debt. The least amount of debt in your life, the better. Mortgages are often structured over 20 to 30 years. Who can predict what will happen to you during that time? Debt assumes financial stability. But everyone is subject to illness, unemployment, financial reverses, unforeseen expenses, divorce, death and dozens of other unpredictable events that destabilize personal finances. Many, if not most, Americans, are one big illness away from financial disaster. Having been burned by debt and one such disaster, I suggest considering buying more country property than you need and quickly selling one or more assets to reduce the debt as much as you can. You will almost always sell a parted-out asset for more than you paid for it when it was part of an entire package. This strategy can reduce your debt by a significant amount while allowing you to retain the core of your target property, comfortably financed. If you want to build wealth, this is as safe a way as I know to do it.

Once you have worked up a financial profile and gotten pre-approved, the next step—after finding the target property—is to **pitch your deal to your chosen lender**.

Pitching property is no different than pitching any other proposal. You have to show how the deal will work from the bank's perspective. Get all the relevant property data that you have gathered from your pre-purchase scoping. Put them in a tabbed portfolio or loose-leaf binder. Once again, I'm proposing to give the lender more than he's likely to ask for; and again, you're doing it out of self-interest. The items will be part of what you're gathering in your scoping, so little effort is required to make copies for your lender. More information improves your pitch, which unlike in baseball, you want your lender to hit out of the park. So free your property pitch from curves and sinkers. When a borrower is asking for some exception to the lender's policies, it helps to be as forthright and comprehensive about the property—warts and all—as is consistent with the lender's attention span. Consider the following items for submission:

1. Short narrative description of the property, including the obvious—road location, acres, improvements, current uses, types of land, water resources, minerals, timber, etc.

2. Current deed into the seller.

3. Copy of any recorded easement that materially affects the value or use of the property. You don't need to include vanilla utility easements.

4. Survey if available; tax map if not.

5. Topographical map with boundaries drawn.

6. The legal description that was used to draw the boundaries on the topographical map. (Should be in the deedwork's back trail if it's not in the seller's deed.)

7. Note whether the deed's calls close and whether the acreage in the deed matches what your surveyor has calculated as that which is in the deed. Note boundary problems, if any.

8. Note any recorded items that bear on the value of the property, such as the severance of mineral

rights, life estate, reserved interest or profit in the land or timber. Also note current zoning/land-use classifications of property.

9. Tax information.

   a. Tax-assessed value of land, improvements and minerals.

   b. Annual property tax.

   c. Is the property either in land use or enrolled in a tax-break-giving timber management program with the state?

   d. Is there a conservation easement in place? This should reduce the property tax, but it reduces market value by the easement's estimated value. I recommend against buying rural land with conservation easements in place, unless the property is price discounted and the easement is what you want.

10. Photos of improvements, land, assets.

11. Cash-flow analysis if the property generates income from leases, sales, etc.

12. Your plan for purchasing the property.

    a. Amount of cash down payment.

    b. Sale of sub-asset, such as timber, minerals, acreage or improvement if that's part of your plan.

    c. Seller's second, if applicable.

    d. Other sources of money toward the purchase, such as gift from parent, sale of conservation easement

    e. Anticipated amount of lender's money you will need.

    f. Project amount of money the property will generate that you will use for mortgage repayment.

    g. Show sources of income for remainder of monthly payment.

    h. Short discussion of cash reserves available to meet payments in the event of a change in circumstances.

13. Your plan for managing the property.

    If you want to have the property generate income, explain your idea with some rough numbers. Indicate what portion of anticipated income will apply to the lender's debt service and your overall debt service. If you are buying an operating farm, you should submit a CPA-prepared set of financial projections. If you are planning to sell timber or other asset, submit a cruise or an FMV appraisal value along with an estimated net from the sale. Indicate how much of the net after-tax income you will apply to the mortgage principal.

14. Your pitch.

    Put in a short narrative paragraph about the type of loan you want; its term; amount of cash down payment you want to invest; LTV ratio you prefer, definition of "value" you prefer (appraisal value or purchase price); total amount of points, fees and other closing costs you are willing to pay; security in addition to the property and so on. Be aggressive in putting forth your opening position, but reasonably so. You can stretch a lender in several directions, but you can't break him. You want the lender to negotiate a few things with you, not run from the office when you appear. So peg your pitch to the type of loans/terms that his website indicates he offers.

Your lender will evaluate your target property to determine 1) whether the amount of the loan you want can be comfortably covered by its liquidation value, and 2) your ability to pay it off without a problem. A pre-approved amount does not mean that you can borrow that sum against any property you want to buy. The property's liquidation value has to exceed the lender's exposure (money lent to you) by whatever the lender determines is its comfort level.

APPRAISALS AND BORROWING

The lender's review of your target property starts with a buyer-paid **appraisal**, which is an estimate of its current **fair market value (FMV)** by an independent third-party, the appraiser. You may have already paid for an appraisal as part of your pre-purchase scoping; submit that and argue no need exists for you to pay for a second. (If you pay for an appraisal during scoping, make sure that it is done by an appraiser on your lender's approved list. Otherwise, it won't be accepted.) Appraisers say that an appraisal is an "estimate of value," i.e., a reasoned estimate. (William L. Ventolo, Jr. and Martha R. Williams, Fundamentals of Real Estate Appraisal, 7th Edition [Chicago: Dearborn Financial Publishing/Real Estate Education Company, 1998, p. 19.]) Robert J. Bruss, the knowledgeable real-estate columnist, believes that an "…appraisal is a guess of a property's probable market value." The process, he writes, is an art, not a science. (Robert J. Bruss, "Real Estate Mailbag," Washington Post, January 25, 2003.) When done honestly and without bias in either direction (toward buyer or the lender), my experience with rural appraisals is that they provide an FMV number that is within 15 or 20 percent of current market value, and often within ten percent. When done to satisfy the party paying for the appraisal, they can be off by 25 percent or more.

Appraisers use one of three methods for determining the FMV of real property: 1) cost method, which estimates the dollars needed to replace a property; 2) income method, which compares the net income a target property is generating for the seller with income-generating properties of the same type; and 3) comparable sales approach, or **comparables** (aka **"comps"**), which derives an FMV for the target property by finding recent sales of roughly similar properties and tweaking their characteristics to match those of the target property. The tweaking adds or subtracts dollars to account for differences between the comps and the property that is being appraised. Determining FMV using comps is the way most country property is appraised. Large, working farms might be appraised on an income basis, because they are more a business than a property purchase from the lender's perspective. Most, if not all, institutional lenders now require a third-party appraisal as one step in determining how much money they will lend to you. Local bankers will have personal experience with local property that will allow them to double-check the appraiser's FMV. Often, a lender will have financed the same property for a previous buyer. If there's a problem with access, soils or boundaries, a local banker may know about it.

Appraisals currently run about $300 and up, depending on the area. Lenders require one, and the borrower pays it as a closing fee. A lender may mark up the appraisal cost in some states and pass it through. When you're working with an existing residence, you may be able to lower the appraisal cost by insisting on a "**collateral valuation insurance**" **(CVI)**, which uses a combination of electronic databases, drive-by visual exterior inspection and insurance for the lender. CVI costs about one-half of the standard appraisal since it requires far less appraiser time. But it may not be available in your target area, and it may not be applicable to undeveloped land. A CVI is worth asking about, particularly during your scoping when you should be getting an appraisal to both inform and enhance your negotiating.

With an appraisal in hand, the lender then applies his loan-to-value (LTV) ratio, which is the amount of money he will lend to you as a percentage of either the appraisal value or your purchase price—*whichever is lowest*. You will be told that the LTV percentages are set in institutional stone. In my area, those stated percentages are a maximum loan of 90 percent on land with improvements and 75 to 80 percent on undeveloped land. But I have seen stone-set percentages fall, even vanish, in light of a property's specific characteristics, price and the borrower's plans. Lenders will give buyers more, if they're going to get a chunk of principal back reasonably soon after closing. Remember that the lender chooses the lowest of the two numbers in front of him—your purchase price or the appraisal value. Lenders force the lower number on the borrower to protect their money by levering more of the borrower's into the deal.

And so we come to the familiar buyer's crack. Your purchase-offer price of $500,000 has been accepted. You assume the local branch of Big Friendly Bank will lend you 90 percent of that price, or $450,000. This means that you have to come up with $50,000 as down payment, plus maybe $25,000 more in closing costs. Then the appraisal comes in for $450,000. The appraiser, you find out, does a lot of work for Big Friendly. The bank says it will lend you 90 percent of the appraisal value ($450,000), that is, $405,000. This means that you have to find $95,000 in down payment and $25,000, in closing costs, not $50,000 and $25,000. In the event of default, Big Friendly is in a far less risky position, because you have more cash equity in at the start. Maybe the lender's policy helps by preventing you from borrowing beyond your effective payment capacity. But maybe it leads you to stretch your resources to come up with the unexpected difference. The $25,000 in closing costs at this point in the process is a hard number; any room to negotiate with the lender is probably passed. The real-estate agents involved might help out by cutting their commissions; it's worth asking.

This is an interesting situation. The buyer has offered $500,000. Is that not ground-truth evidence of market value? Is the buyer's offer above fair market value? Alternatively, it may be that the appraiser has lowered his appraisal value to protect the lender and guarantee future business for himself. When you apply to an institutional lender for a loan and "agree" to have an appraisal done, you are forced to pay for an appraisal that is being done for the bank, not you. Banks often won't even show you the appraisal you've paid for. If you want to see it, you may have to ask for it in writing. I don't think I've ever seen a property appraisal for a bank or the Federal Land Bank, a principal lender for rural property, that came in above the buyer's offering price, though nothing prevents that from occurring. I've seen a number of appraisals that come in for less. I've drawn my own conclusion; maybe I'm wrong.

So what should you do?

Challenge the $450,000 appraisal. It is obviously quite possible that the $450,000 appraisal is a better reflection of fair market value *based on comparables* than your well-researched offer of $500,000. But if you've done your scoping and know the real value of the property, take your information and analysis to the lender and show him why your estimate of value—based on the market value of the property's assets disaggregated or whatever method you used—is a truer indication of the property's total FMV than a cookie-cutter appraisal, done by an approved appraiser who may be trying to maintain favorable relations with the bank. Explain why your offer of $500,000 is at, or below, the true FMV of the property—which it should be if you've taken my advice. Insist that the bank's appraiser redo his appraisal in light of the information you've developed on your own. You can also attack the comparability of the three properties the appraiser used as comps. If your research has turned up more relevant comps—more recent sales; closer fit; nearer to the target property—than those used by the appraiser put them in front of the lender. If you have commissioned an appraisal as part of your pre-purchase scoping that has produced a value of $500,000, or higher, submit that to the lender. I think it's a good idea to give your lender a copy of your scoping appraisal when you apply for the loan. I would not tell your appraiser which bank you're applying to. You're trying to get an appraisal that is a true FMV estimate and one that fits your needs; don't confuse the appraiser with thoughts about his own self-interest. If you have a scoping appraisal from an unapproved appraiser, then you need to demand a meeting at the bank where both appraisers appear and argue their cases. You will frequently develop information during scoping that affects FMV which an appraiser never seeks to discover. Use it now to establish the superior FMV credibility of your offering price to the appraiser's valuation. You can also offer to split the cost of a third appraisal, the result of which either, by mutual agreement, trumps the first two or is used to calculate a value that is the average of the three appraisals. While you may be incensed about having to pay for more than one appraisal, spending $1,500 for three appraisals to save $50,000 in upfront cash makes sense to me. You may also want to point out that an appraisal value is tied to past prices. In an appreciating market, comps that are even a few months old, can produce a value for your target property that is out of date.

Conventional wisdom is that appraisers and banks work more often to get borrowers into loans pegged to the property's selling price, which overvalues the property securing the note, and thereby get a borrower on the mortgage hook for more than the property is worth. I've seen this happen with cash-heavy, non-resident buyers. Early in 2003, the Federal Housing Administration proposed a plan whereby the mortgage lender would be equally responsible with the appraiser for appraisal errors. Mel R. Martinez, Secretary of Housing and Urban Development, said: "'[Some] lenders tacitly require appraisers to make the appraisal computations match the sales price to ensure that a home sale and mortgage loan closes for the appraiser to obtain additional business,' [and]...other lenders collude with appraisers, he adds, to fraudulently create property 'flips'—rapid-fire resales of homes with inflated valuations—that harm consumers and the FHA insurance fund." (Kenneth Harney, "Appraisal rules aimed at lenders," Richmond Times-Dispatch, January 19, 2003.)

In my geographically limited experience, I've sensed collusion from time to time between lender and appraiser going toward *undervaluing* the property to protect the bank by squeezing the borrower for more down payment. I had this game run on me years ago before I knew what was going on: I bridged the gap between what the lender wanted to lend based on his appraisal and the purchase price with a three-year second mortgage from the seller. Robert J. Bruss concludes that "...appraisals remain the weakest link in the home mortgage process." (Bruss, Washington Post, January 25, 2003.)

The advice to be drawn from these impressions such as they are is this: Be aware that your price expectations and the lender's expectations can influence some appraisers. If you want a "high" appraisal, let that be known. If you want an appraisal at the purchase price, let that be known. If you intend to back out of a deal if the appraisal does not meet the purchase price, let that be known.

The way to protect yourself against lender-oriented appraisers who are deliberately discounting the target property's value is to place an **appraisal contingency** in your purchase contract:

> **Buyer's offer is contingent on Buyer's lender receiving and accepting a property appraisal from a qualified appraiser approved by lender within ___ days of this Contract taking effect that establishes the fair market value of Seller's property at no less than the purchase price agreed to in this Contract.**
>
> **Buyer may void this Contract without penalty in the event that the lender's appraisal is less than the Buyer's price accepted by Seller.**

I find it useful in many instances to have the buyer commission his own appraisal in advance of approaching both the seller with an offer and the institutional lender with a pitch for a loan. Approach your appraiser after doing some of your scoping so that you can share your findings with him. Give him your expectation about the property's value and the reasons justifying it. If you've paid for a timber cruise or an independent valuation of farm assets, give these documents to the appraiser. If you want a high valuation, make sure to have him take into account all assets on the property, including the ones you've valued separately.

This **full-factor appraisal** requires a different format than the conventional comparables approach. Most of the land appraisals I've seen do not adjust the target property's value according to separate valuations of timber and other less-obvious assets. Appraisers adjust price for acreage, percent open vs. wooded, style of house, square footage of house and so on, but not for the value of certain assets, such as timber and minerals. Most appraisers don't know how to evaluate those components. Accordingly, an appraiser does not factor in the value of merchantable timber on wooded property. He sets the property's worth according to wooded comps regardless of how much or how little merchantable timber both the comps and the target property contain. This is nonsensical, since the three wooded comps might have no immediate timber value and the target property of approximately the same acreage might contain $250,000, or vice versa. Small farms and part-time farm operations might be used as comps for a target property whose real market value is much higher as a second home to an urban buyer. If a land appraiser says he can't change his comparables format, accept his position and then ask him to file an appendix to his appraisal that includes your independent valuations. You then take his appraisal and add on the values of assets the appraiser did not include. (This, of course, assumes that you're trying to get the appraisal up. If you want to lower the appraisal, share all the negatives that you've found during your scoping.)

Keep in mind that a comparables analysis involves adjusting judgments about each comp in terms of judgments about the target property. Appraisers have guidelines for making adjustments between properties for house-related items like finished area (square feet), basements, finished attics, garages and the like. But comparisons between land-related items, such as soil quality, water, topography, access, floodplain, fence condition, farm infrastructure and many other variables that actually determine land FMV, are rarely done, or done well. While it's relatively straight forward to do a comparables analysis for 500 acres of Illinois crop land, it's harder to find comparables for a 500-acre mountain farm in Virginia with 75 acres in pasture, 175 acres in bottomland and 250 acres in hardwood timber of mixed ages with a house and four significant outbuildings. While the appraiser is expected to produce a single "hard" number as his FMV for the target property, much of his approach is not "hard." This gives you a way to introduce hard evidence into his semi-subjective analysis. The appraiser should have choices among the comps he uses, what asset factors to value and by how much, and what liability factors to include as a discount. The more your target property is one of a kind, the more leeway he has in choosing his appraisal number.

The point here is an unfortunate one: appraisals can be influenced and should be in some cases. Appraisers can be corrupted by their self-interest enough to hurt a buyer. A seller can buy an inflated appraisal; a buyer can buy a deflated appraisal. And a lender can set up certain expectations for appraisers on his approved list. Given the opportunities for others in the buying process to influence appraisal value, I can only advise buyers to defend their interests.

Kenneth Harney wrote about the key role of appraisals and appraisers for sellers in a weakening market. (Kenneth Harney, "The Nation's Housing," "In a sagging market, the appraiser's word is key," <u>Richmond Times-Dispatch</u>, January 1, 2006.) He quoted Tom Berge, head of a California appraisal firm, who said that he "ignores pressure by lenders or realty agents to 'hit the number' on the sales contract." Berge's advice to sellers, buyers, lenders and realty agents about how to influence the final appraisal number ethically and legally is this: "'If you want me to adjust [the number], go out and get me better comps....'" In the best of circumstances, all parties would find the three property sales that are closest in all respects to the property being appraised—and all adjustments will be the same. But in most circumstances, the comps used are chosen somewhat subjectively, leaving room for other comps to be used with equal justification.

Your first objective in using your scoping appraisal is to bring an above-market-price seller down to earth. Your second objective is to protect yourself from a low-ball bank appraisal that seeks to wring more down payment out of you. Your third objective is to be able to offset a bogus seller's appraisal. Both the seller and the bank may want to dismiss your appraiser's FMV number. With both of them, force a discussion on the details of the process and the specifics of the property. You have nothing to lose with either party. If the seller has not paid for his own appraisal (which is likely), your appraisal is one of three pieces of fair-market-value information available for negotiations: 1) your appraisal; 2) a realtor-provided competitive market analysis (CMA), which is a comparables analysis; and 3) current tax-assessed value. Both your appraisal and the tax-assessed value should help you in your negotiations with the seller. Both will be done by a neutral, third-party professional who has no self-interest (presumably) in the results of his work. If the seller is working through a real-estate broker, the CMA can be marginalized as a self-interested exercise intended to get an above-market price.

If your scoping appraisal is substantially below the seller's asking price, share the information with the seller and use it to work him down to a more realistic price. If you can negotiate a price with the seller that's in line with the appraisal, hand the appraisal to the bank during your first meeting as part of your property-information package. If you can't get the seller to come into line with the appraisal, then ask yourself how much of a premium you're willing to pay for this particular property. You can always ask the seller to take back a second mortgage on terms that are very favorable to you: say, five years at two percent, interest-only annual payments with a balloon of principal at the end of the term. You're still overpaying, but the burden is a little lighter. If the seller's price is significantly above market and he figures that the next buyer will be no more nor less of a fool than you, he should come into line. There are, of course, sellers who deliberately price their property high above market and simply wait until someone comes along who is able and willing to pay the premium, fool or not.

On-the-ground appraisals for conventional rural property currently cost between $300 and $400 in my county. That's likely to be on the low side for many places. A **drive-by appraisal** with some comparables analysis—which is what you can get without the seller's cooperation—costs about $200. You may need to give the institutional lender an on-the-ground appraisal, but a drive-by will suffice for negotiating with the seller. Drive-bys can be combined with electronic appraisal techniques in some areas.

Look for an appraiser who is certified by the National Association of Real Estate Appraisers. If you've done some price research, tell him what you've found in terms of tax-assessed comps and asking-price comps. Give him an idea of what you think the ballpark purchase price might be if you're confident in your analysis. If not, keep quiet. Your appraiser should help you out a bit without any obvious pressure from you. If you're looking for a figure on the high side, you can give him a comparables analysis of current asking prices that a real-estate broker can run for you.

TAX BENEFITS AND MORTGAGE-INTEREST DEDUCTIBILITY

The tax benefits of owning real property are significant. The precise package of benefits available to you depends on whether the property is your primary residence, second home (that you use exclusively and personally), full-time rental property, vacation rental property (that you use no more than the IRS-allowable days), land that has usable or saleable assets (pasture, house, timber, minerals, water rights, etc.), the nature of your plans for the property—personal use, investment, business, a combination—and how you organize your plans legally and implement them subsequently. Your individual package of tax benefits arising from any particular parcel of rural land depends on how you, your lawyer and your CPA combine these various options. At the risk of sounding like a jaded taxpayer, it appears to me that tax benefits rise with the level of complexity you choose—in the property itself (the more differentiated the property's assets, the more benefits are likely to be available), your plans and your type of ownership organization.

Underlying the United States real-estate market is the **deductibility of mortgage interest**. On your principal residence, you are currently allowed to deduct the interest you pay up to $1 million in mortgage debt. You cannot deduct up to $1 million in interest; rather you can deduct the interest paid on up to $1 million in mortgage loans. To qualify for deductibility, the mortgage must be secured by the house. A mortgage from a friend, relation or seller also qualifies as long as it's so secured. The $1 million cap on mortgage debt applies to the buying, building or improvement of your principal residence and/or second home.

Mortgage interest is known as a **below-the-line deduction**, because the amount of interest is subtracted from your 1040's adjusted gross income (AGI). An **above-the-line deduction** is subtracted from your gross income and is part of the subtraction process that produces your AGI. Below-the-line deductions spare the taxpayer more in taxes than the same amount applied above the line.

Mortgage interest can be deducted for a primary residence, second home, unimproved rural land and investment/business property. (See IRS Publication 550, Investment Income and Expenses and Publication 936, Home Mortgage Interest Deduction.) But you need to set up your taxes appropriately, and you need to itemize deductions on your tax returns.

On a primary residence and *one* second home (in the country or anywhere else, including a yacht that provides basic living accommodations), mortgage interest is generally deductible, not to exceed a total of $1 million in debt each year, when the mortgage was taken out after October 13, 1987. There are some qualifications to this general statement that Publication 936 explains. Mortgage interest is deductible only when the home is collateral for the debt. If mortgage money is not used for buying, building or improving a "qualified residence," primary and secondary, you can't take the home-mortgage deduction for that interest. "Grandfathered debt," a mortgage taken out before October 13, 1987 that was secured by a qualified home, is deductible without having to meet the buy-build-improve rule. A qualified home will include all the land that goes with it. Your deduction is limited to one second home. *If you set up your rural property as an investment, you can deduct mortgage interest and other expenses only if you file an itemized return.* (Only about one-third—46 million of 130 million returns—itemize.) Unimproved land will be considered an investment property if you do not begin construction of a home/second home that you can occupy within 24 months of purchase.

Mortgage interest on home-equity loans taken against a "qualified residence" (essentially your principal residence) for the purposes cited above is deductible below the line as long as the debt does not exceed $100,000. Interest paid on a home-equity loan is deductible, up to $100,000 in debt on top of the $1 million in debt for mortgage-interest.

A second home that you rent out can qualify for the mortgage-interest deduction if you use it as a residence for either more than 14 days that year or more than ten percent of the number of rented-out days that year, whichever is longer. You don't have to live in your second home to have it qualify for the deduction.

If your second home does not qualify for the home-mortgage interest deduction, you may be able to set it up as a rental unit, investment or business and obtain the appropriate tax benefits, including depreciation. The deductibility of interest directly reduces the cost you pay to buy country property, so check with your tax adviser before borrowing for this purchase.

The simplest purchase—buying a full-time personal residence in the country—gives you the deduction of local property taxes and mortgage interest from your taxable income, subject to IRS limitations. You can deduct *all* mortgage interest you pay if you 1) took out the mortgage on or before October 13, 1987; 2) took out the mortgage after that date but these mortgages and any grandfathered debt equal $1 million or less; or 3) took out a mortgage after that date that you used for something other than buying, building or improving your home; and these mortgages totaled $100,000 or less and the mortgage total on the home does not exceed its fair market value. Those who don't fit into these categories, can deduct interest on up to $1,000,000 in mortgage debt a year. If you have a second home in the country, the interest on that mortgage debt qualifies for deductibility as long as the taxpayer's total mortgage debt does not exceed $1 million. (The IRS has exceptions to this rule if you rent your second home.)

In addition to mortgage interest, you can deduct the **real-estate tax** you pay on your rural property if you itemize. In the year of your purchase, you can deduct the share of the property's taxes you paid, as shown on your settlement statement, or HUD-1.

Finally, on your principal residence, you can deduct **points** related to your mortgage loan for the tax year in which you purchased the home. Or you can amortize these points over the term of the loan. That choice is yours. (Points may also be called loan-origination fee or loan-discount fee.) The points must be related to the buyer's purchase, construction or improvement of the qualified residence. The buyer is also generally able to deduct points that are paid by the seller on his behalf. If you refinance your principal residence, you have to amortize the points over the loan's term. With a second home or land purchase, the buyer has the same choice of deducting or amortizing points. The IRS imposes a reasonableness standard concerning the amount of points a buyer can deduct or amortize. Ten or more points are probably beyond what the IRS would consider reasonable; six or fewer is probably okay. Consult with your CPA before agreeing to five or more points, just to be certain.

The IRS imposes no interest-deductibility cap on land bought for investment or business. Mortgage interest paid on land purchased for business or investment is deducted above the line. Mortgage interest paid on rental property is similarly an above-the-line deduction.

Many of your closing costs are not deductible. The tax that you pay to record your deed—called a recordation tax, transfer tax or deed stamps—is not deductible. Neither are the cost of title insurance, credit-report fee, appraisal fee and private mortgage insurance. Your CPA or lawyer will be able to tell you in advance of closing which of your closing costs are deductible. (See Kay Bell, "First-time home buyers' guide to taxes," www.Bankrate.com, April 13, 2006.)

As I write this in 2006, the Bush Administration's tax policies, the war in Iraq and the Katrina/Rita/Wilma clean up have created record annual budget deficits. The Administration would like to cut taxes more and certainly not increase them. But doing so would enlarge the budget deficits that are being offset by increased borrowing. Reducing tax benefits may be one approach to increasing revenues without raising tax rates. (Cutting federal programs would offset some of the debt-financed spending.) A Bush-appointed panel, chaired by former Florida Senator Connie Mack, ranked the mortgage-interest deduction as the second most costly for 2006 ($76 billion est.) after the business deduction for providing employees with health benefits ($126 billion est.). The capital-gains tax break on the sale of a *principal residence* (joint filers can exclude from tax $500,000 in gain; individuals, up to $250,000; *this break does not apply to second homes*) was the third largest, $36.3 billion, and the deduction for state and local property taxes was the fourth, $14.8 billion. (The Associated Press, "Group studies tax breaks," The [Staunton] News Leader, April 25, 2005.) The President, it was reported, asked the panel—President's Advisory Panel on Federal Tax Reform—to preserve tax breaks that promoted home ownership and charitable giving.

The panel recommended in late 2005 that the mortgage-interest deduction for both a second home and a home-equity loan be eliminated. Also under consideration was the idea that the mortgage-interest deduction on a principal residence be limited up to 15 percent of interest paid with caps equal to the Federal Housing Administration's loan limits in the homeowner's area—currently $172,000 to $312,000. (David Brunori, "Bush's Tax Panel Has a Crazy Idea. Let's Go For It." Washington Post, October 23, 2005.) The elimination of second-home interest and home-equity interest will fall on many more taxpayers than putting a $300,000 interest cap on principal-residence interest. The Administration did not endorse the Mack Commission recommendations. They are, however, out there, and land buyers should keep an eye peeled for changes in interest and expenses deductibility brought into the IRS code piecemeal.

If the budget deficits continue to grow, pressure to reduce property-related tax benefits will grow. This uncertainty is yet one more reason to set up your rural property purchase as an investment or business rather than as a second home.

CHAPTER 33: SOURCES OF DIRT-SMART MONEY

Dozens of ways exist to finance real-estate purchases. Some are more risky to the buyer than others. Some involve falsification and/or concealment, both of which I advise against. The real-estate books I've mentioned in other chapters discuss many techniques that are applicable to rural land. It's worth reading several to have a general sense of what tools are available, and, more importantly, which ones you feel comfortable working into a rural land purchase.

Financing brings out greed. I've seen buyers push their financing packages beyond anything they need in pursuit of finding the last dollar of **OPM—other people's money**. That isn't necessary, and, ultimately, it's probably not in your best interest. You want a good deal, a deal that works for you by stripping risk out of the purchase through scoping and promises a healthy profit. That's enough. If you've bought at the right price in relation to the property's value, you've secured a profit for your anticipated length of ownership. Applying a house-of-cards-financing scheme to avoid putting your own cash into the purchase is more than likely to jeopardize either your deal or your financial security.

If you are a beginner at buying land follow this rule: the simpler a deal, the more likely it won't go wrong anywhere along the line from purchase to disposition. Your buyer's pitch to the seller should be clear, understandable and feasible; the same must be true of your post-purchase plan. I've seen good buys squirreled up by a many-phased, post-purchase plan that is too intricate for the buyer to implement. The more dependent each layer of profit is on the one preceding it, the more precarious the profitability of the purchase will be. Financing is, in a sense, a buyer's first step toward simplicity or complexity. I'm sure that simple deals can be based on complicated financing arrangements, but my brain is disposed toward linear consistency, from scoping through liquidation.

The money sources I discuss below include both the familiar and the not so familiar. If you are wealthy enough to buy real simplicity, put down a big cash payment and borrow the rest from the largest bank in the target property's county seat. Simplicity getting in, however, does not eliminate the risk of a flawed purchase. Usable cash does not lift the obligation you have to yourself to protect it through scoping.

13 PLACES TO START

Purchase money in one or another form can be found from one or more of the following sources, singly or in combination:

1. Your own resources
2. Sale of one or more "severable" assets from the target property
3. Neighbors
4. The seller
5. Co-investors/partners
6. Locally owned local lenders
7. Regionally owned local lenders
8. Non-local lenders
9. Life insurance companies
10. Internet

11. Government agencies
12. 1031 Like-Kind (Starker) Exchange
13. Conservation easements

All of us faced with the purchase of property must decide how much of our own kaboodle we want to put in and how much we want to borrow. The more cash in upfront, the less we need to borrow, the lower our monthly payments, the less interest we have to pay and, perhaps, the more secure we feel in light of life's pending bummers that eventually befall all of us. But it can be either hard or expensive to get cash out of property, which is one reason to borrow OPM.

For every upfront dollar invested in a down payment, the buyer incurs both a **direct cost** and an **opportunity cost**. The direct cost can be considered as the amount of his down payment plus his **transaction costs** in buying the property—points and fees charged by the lender; recordation and other taxes; scoping costs and miscellaneous professional fees. The buyer also has the direct cost over time of paying his mortgage interest and principal along with property-maintenance charges. In return, the buyer gets the use of the property and its appreciation in value.

The property buyer also incurs **opportunity costs**, which are the opportunities the buyer might have pursued with his direct-cost dollars had he not made the purchase. The dollar spent for dirt cannot be spent to buy stocks, bonds or a Ferrari. Any dollar placed in a real-estate investment can lose value over time. That goes for stocks, bonds and Ferraris as well. The possibility of loss in any investment is a risk, not a direct cost or an opportunity cost. Real-estate risk is contained, though never totally eliminated, through research, analysis and planning. The costs of buying property are contained by: 1) buying within your means, 2) understanding the true value of the property before acquiring it and 3) predicting with some reasonable accuracy its appreciation at the anticipated date of sale.

Most land buyers want to put in as little of their own cash as possible. Using Other People's Money is usually necessary. The buyer uses a little of his own cash to **leverage** the borrowing of a much larger sum. Leverage is debt, which must be repaid. It is OPM on which you pay interest. OPM is not free money. Leverage can get you into and out of a deal cleanly and profitably; it can also lead to default and bankruptcy. The Crash of 1929 wiped out my grandfather and thousands of other paper millionaires when the perceived value of his highly leveraged properties nose-dived and the banks called their notes. It took him years to pay back his creditors. He was never wealthy again, even on paper. Leverage works to your benefit as long as you can make the monthly payments on your debt. As soon as you can't, leverage starts working against you. Think of a person using a fulcrum and a lever to lift a large boulder off the ground and over his head. As long as sufficient forced is applied down, the boulder stays up. When force stops being applied, the boulder's full weight falls straight down. That is how leverage works for and against you.

Real-estate writers always advise readers to use other people's money to finance purchases. Taking out a mortgage is the simplest and most familiar form of this practice. The borrower is using the lender's money to acquire an asset that's likely to appreciate over time. Keep in mind, however, that the structure of that repayment has you, first, paying back far more than you borrowed, and, second, exposed to losing the entire asset plus whatever you've paid in interest and principal. **For those reasons, I advise to look for ways that you can use both your current assets and a portion of the rural asset you're about to buy to come up with the cash you need to buy.** I don't rule out borrowing.

If you like to live on the edge of disaster, write me off as an old fuddy-duddy. If the absolute worst that can happen in a default on a purchase of country property is the loss of the property itself and your sunk cash, that's an acceptable level of risk, assuming that the probability of default is low. If the probability is not low, don't buy. If you risk losing other significant assets, then don't get into the deal.

I offer one exception to this rule. If you are looking at rural property exclusively as an **investment flip**, you will want to narrow your search to properties with an **immediate cash-out profile and use as much OPM as possible**. You may take out an ARM or an interest-only mortgage on a 30-year term to finance the deal, but your plan is to pay off the entire note as you sell the property's assets. A successful flip, however, depends on the flip yielding more money than you have in both the front-side of the deal (purchase) and its back-side (the cost of resale, as an entirety or in parts). The danger in using OPM for flips is that the resale takes longer and you net less than you've anticipated.

I would attach four caveats to using OPM in highly leveraged purchases of rural land, and all have to do with melt-down scenarios, such as a foreclosure. First, make sure that the property alone secures your mortgage. If a **non-recourse loan** cannot be arranged, you must be very confident that any forced sale of the property will cover the note. Don't personally guarantee OPM. Second, don't tie the leveraged rural property into your core assets, such as your principal residence, with a mortgage that covers both. Third, be psychologically ready to lose the rural land to save your primary butt. Don't liquidate every cash asset you have to hold on to it if that will leave you cash poor and land rich. Finally, I would use OPM to buy rural property that did not exceed the value of my principal residence. Your first rural venture might be limited to 50 percent or less of the value of your principal residence unless you have extensive cash or other assets to see you through a pinch. This rule of thumb will allow you to sleep at night.

Buyers correctly assume that inflation and normal growth in their earnings will make it easier for them to pay off a loan with fixed terms over time. Counting on background inflation over time to help pay a long-term note works as long as macro-economic factors, such as economic growth and interest rates, are reasonably favorable. A recession/depression can catch an otherwise sound investment in a triple bind of no buyers for your property, falling values and a cash drain on all your other assets. If you can't sell your land investment when you need to, you either have to continue to carry it or lose it. Time and inflation can work against a buyer if his earnings don't rise. Buying rural land with a 30-year mortgage does not lock you into prison for 30 years. Rather, it locks you into paying back the principal borrowed and interest accrued to date, with the balance of the principal to be paid by the sale of the property itself if you can't carry it.

Buyers try put in as little of their own cash because they've read or heard that rural land and undeveloped land are **illiquid**. Is it hard to sell rural property? In my experience, rural land is illiquid in four types of circumstances: 1) where the property has one or more major negatives, such as no legally established access; 2) where the property has been dedicated and configured for an activity that is increasingly out of favor, such as farms that can grow tobacco but nothing else; 3) when it's priced above market and the seller won't budge; or 4) when it lies in a **zone of repugnance**.

This last phrase needs a bit of explanation. Cattle will not graze where they have recently fouled the grass. Beef-cattle academics call the area, under and immediately around a cow flop, "a zone of repugnance." Certain areas of our country have been either so beaten up or are so inhospitable that not many people live there and even fewer want to move there. Fairly or not, they are seen from the outside as zones of repugnance. In such places, land will be illiquid, even at knock-down prices. I should add that some old zones of repugnance, such as some played-out Western mining towns, can be turned into recreational cash cows. A "nice" community can have a zone of repugnance, such as a 5,000-head feedlot on one side of town or a noisy mill. Places for sale nearby will have a limited, illiquid market.

While I do not agree that rural land is inherently illiquid, it may not be immediately saleable at your preferred price. Average land for sale at market price should sell, though it may take six months or a year. In the best circumstances, it will take between 30 and 90 days to get to closing. And if the buyer's contingencies are not satisfied, the contract will be terminated, which means the owner must start from scratch. Land cannot be converted to cash with the same-day convenience of a drive-through ATM. If you are an absentee owner, a land sale can take longer, especially if you are selling it yourself.

Still, I think it's generally wrong to assume that an owner will have a long, hard ordeal selling run-of-the-mill rural land for current market value. The degree of liquidity, that is, the time needed to sell a property at approximately fair market value, is often determined by how much above FMV the owner sets his asking price and how determinedly he doesn't budge. While the owner may be under financial pressure to get as much for the property as possible, it remains his choice as to how to balance asking price and selling price against time on the market. The cost of holding tight to an above-market price is often not worth it when sales are slow. Fear of illiquidity is not in my opinion a good reason for limiting the amount of cash you put into the purchase of rural land.

When your circumstances are such that using OPM to buy discretionary rural property is a feasible approach subject to the caveats I've expressed, then I would advise proceeding if you are confident that the property will sell within six months at a price that will cover the note and sale expenses. A six-month time frame means you might have to sell it below FMV—and still have enough to pay your debt. These parameters change, of course, if you have sufficient cash assets to replace the income you normally will be spending to pay the country note. Go into an OPM-based purchase with a clear idea of how you will handle a worst-case scenario. (Don't cheat on the definition of "worst"; assume a real catastrophe.) A large mortgage on a property other than your primary residence can drain your cash resources in a time of financial crisis without contributing anything to getting you through the squeeze. Your worst-case planning has to include letting the rural property go before it drags you under.

Consider these sources for dirt money.

1. Your own resources.

Most lenders require at least ten percent down on rural land that has a house or other improvement and at least 20 percent on undeveloped rural land. Out-of-pocket cash need not be your first choice for this money. What other sources might be available for a required down payment?

First, sell stuff. Raise down payment by cleaning out your attic, garage and basement. Sell stocks (equities) that are losing money and which you've grown to hate. Sell one or more of your less-than-needed possessions—the Mercedes that's capable of 150 mph at one gallon per mile, the sailboat that leaks no matter how many times you pay for repair or the RV that hasn't moved since Nixon walked on the beach in wingtips.

Second, borrow some cash. Borrow from relatives. Borrow against life insurance. Borrow from a credit union or take out a personal note for the down payment. You may be able to borrow against your primary residence, but that is a sleep-loss tactic. If you borrow your down payment and transaction costs, you do not want to push your debt to the edge of your carrying capacity. Leave yourself plenty of room to muddle through the losing crapshoots of life. The best borrowing strategy is from friends or relatives who won't need a specific payback date. Borrow sensibly—not from your kid's college savings, not from a loan shark or credit card, not from your tax-escrow account, not more than you need and can pay back with no sweat. All things considered, borrowing down payment is the least preferred option.

Third, trim current expenses and save the difference to accumulate a down payment. How much do you really want this country property? Do you want it enough to eat out less, buy cheaper clothes, drive an older car?

Fourth, get money from your family. Money from family can take many forms: a formal loan, complete with signed note; an informal loan that you are expected to repay when you have it; an informal loan that you are not really expected to repay; a co-investment, whereby a family member joins in the purchase with you; an investment with family members (by way of a corporation, partnership or limited liability company) that holds title and manages the investment according to a plan that is agreed to prior to purchase; and a gift of cash, kind, income flow or saleable asset. You might propose waiving some portion of your inheritance in return for cash now if that's agreeable to parents and siblings. A gift is best, and, indeed, it was $3,500 from my mother that allowed me to buy my first piece of rural America—a half share in 60 acres about 40 minutes north of Amherst, Massachusetts in 1970.

Both the money source and recipient should check out the tax consequences of various arrangements and amounts. As of 2006, a donor can give a **gift** of $12,000 tax free each year to an individual; above that a gift tax applies, subject to other factors. (See www.irs.gov; Publication 950: Introduction to Estate and Gift Taxes.) Each parent can give $12,000 annually to a child, tax free. This exclusion may be increased in the future. The recipient pays no federal tax on the receipt of a cash gift. A loan is not a taxable event on either end. However, a loan that is never paid off and was never expected to be paid will, if examined by the IRS, be considered a gift. A **gift of property** requires that the recipient assumes the giver's adjusted cost basis in the property. (It is tax-smarter for a recipient to inherit property than have it come as a gift, because the recipient's basis in the inherited property is figured at the time of the decedent's death, not the decedent's adjusted basis from when he bought it. The recipient's basis at the time of death is known as a "**stepped-up basis**." Inheritance is not conveniently scheduled, so you may have to make do with a gift.) If you are fortunate enough to have access to gift help in one form or another, run the options through the CPA who does the giver's taxes. He can estimate the tax consequences for both donor and recipient.

Fifth, rework debt to free cash.

When interest rates are low, you can **refinance** the debt on your appreciated primary residence and use the cash—on which you will pay interest—for down payment on additional property. This is a fairly common way to find down payment. It results in a fully financed purchase of the second property, with all of the virtues and risks that entails. (See Kenneth R. Harney, "Acute Cases of Refi Fever," Washington Post, August 24, 2002.) The five features you're looking for in a refinancing are: 1) significantly lower interest rate, 2) as little refinancing cost as possible, 3) less total interest paid over term; 4) relatively short break-even point; and 5) a total debt load that you can handle in emergencies. Be careful with refis that you are not hit with both a pre-pay penalty along with upfront costs.

A typical refi with cash out might look like this. Assume that you have $100,000 remaining on your home mortgage at 8 percent fixed rate with an amortization term of 30 years. Your monthly principal and interest mortgage payment is $734. If you refinance that $100,000 at 6 percent for 20 years, your monthly P&I payment would be $716. If you refinanced $110,000 at 5.75 percent for 20 years, your monthly payment would be $703, leaving $10,000 available for a down payment. But keep in mind the risk of this strategy. Those who refinance to pull cash out of their homes default at a higher rate than those who refinance either the original principal amount or the remaining principal. The more borrowed, the greater the default likelihood. "Fannie Mae says a borrower who takes a new loan that is 20 percent larger than the balance due on the old loan is three times more likely to default than a borrower whose cash out is 3 percent or less of the old balance." (Jeff Brown, "Cash-out deals tempting many: Refinancings may lead to more debt," Richmond Times-Dispatch, November 6, 2002.)

If you are refinancing a primary residence for more than the principal so as to pull cash out for a down payment, expect to pay upfront costs. Lenders who have not sold your note on your primary residence should be able to refinance the remaining balance at low cost. But the lender who sold your note on the secondary market is collecting only a 0.25 percent fee for servicing your loan. That $250 a year on a $100,000 loan does not get the borrower much refinancing help in many lender offices. (See Robert J.

Bruss, "Real Estate Mailbag," Washington Post, August 24, 2002.)

Even where you can get a low-cost refi from the lender, be aware that state-imposed transaction costs vary from state to state, e.g., $1,207 in North Carolina to $3,001 in Florida on a $150,000 refi with a 70 percent loan-to-value (LTV) ratio, according to a Quicken-Loan Inc. study. These costs would include, where applicable, document (deed) stamps, transfer tax, title fee, among others. (See Kenneth R. Harvey, "Rates make it hard to stay out of market," Richmond Times-Dispatch, March 16, 2003.)

A second option is to use a **home-equity loan** to raise cash for a down payment. A home-equity loan is for a fixed amount, and can be used for the homeowner's choice of purpose. The loan is a lien against the property that secures it. A home-equity loan leaves the original mortgage in place. It is a new debt, secured by your primary residence. Interest is usually a variable rate, such as the **prime rate** plus two points. (A bank's prime rate is its base rate that it extends to its most creditworthy commercial customers. In practice, large banks tend toward adopting the same prime rate, which reflects their cost of borrowing short-term as set by the Federal Reserve's interest rates.) Home-equity interest rates tend to be higher than other interest rates a lender offers. If you fail to meet the payments on the home-equity loan, the lender can come after your primary residence, which is his security for the loan. (His security for the home-equity loan is not your second home in the country.) Lenders typically add fees and charges for these loans.

A third option is to establish a **home-equity line of credit (HELOC)**. A HELOC makes cash available to a homeowner at a variable interest rate, using the primary residence as security. The homeowner can choose to borrow the available money at any time. The line will be set up as a second mortgage on the primary residence. The lender will make available up to 70 or even 80 percent of the home's appraisal value, less the principal remaining on the first mortgage. HELOCs are available for as much as 125 percent of appraisal value less the value of the first mortgage, but such loans would, in the event of default, require the homeowner to come up with more than the primary residence is worth to keep it. A HELOC with the same lender can be done with low transaction costs. HELOC interest rates are lower than those on credit cards, but higher than most mortgage rates. Mortgage interest on home-equity loans and HELOCs is tax-deductible up to $100,000 for any purpose, and for over $100,000 if the money is used to buy investments (e.g., timberland, farmland) or for business reasons. (Holden Lewis, "Trading mortgage for a loan on equity," Richmond Times-Dispatch, from www.bankrate.com, March 9, 2003.)

A fourth option is take out a **second mortgage** on your principal residence. Your first mortgage is left untouched and in first position. Your second mortgage is also secured by your residence. Whoever holds the first mortgage has first claim on your house in a default. A home-equity loan is one type of second mortgage.

These sources are also discussed in Chapter 32, with an emphasis on their risks.

Sixth, try to get a rental payment upfront. Many rural properties have rentable assets—pasture for grazing; flat land for row crops; woods and fields for hunting; water for fishing; trails for horses, snowmobiles and ATVs; facilities for storage; and tenant houses for renters. To the extent you can, get as much of any rental payment upfront so that you can use it to help purchase the property. This money won't come to you prior to purchase for use as your down payment, but it might be scheduled for soon after closing so that you can repay borrowed down-payment money. You might discount the first year's rent for an upfront payment of the full year's payment. Rental income is subject to taxation.

Seventh, take advantage of an assumable mortgage. An "assumable" is a seller's mortgage obligation that allows the buyer to take the seller's place. A buyer would like to take over an assumable that has better terms than are currently being offered. The additional advantage to the buyer is that the lender's fees imposed are substantially less than those on new loans and refinancings. Loans originating with the Federal Housing Administration, Veterans Administration and some ARMs are likely candidates for assumable mortgages. The buyer will usually need to qualify with the lender to assume the seller's position. Most mortgage notes no longer allow assumption, because lenders make more money on new loans.

Assumptions help buyers. Sellers need to exercise caution in allowing a buyer to assume their notes because such mortgages usually keep the seller liable in some way for the debt. A **mortgage assignment** substitutes the buyer for the seller's obligation to pay the note. If the buyer defaults on an assigned mortgage, the seller is liable for paying the note's outstanding balance. A **"subject to"** assumption places the seller in a position of being responsible for paying both the note's balance and any deficiency following a foreclosure sale. A **novation** frees the seller from all obligations on the note the buyer has assumed.

Eighth, take over seller-owed, non-mortgage debt. The seller may be in trouble with back taxes owed, liens on the property and consumer debt. If your cash is short but your cash flow is strong and getting stronger, you may be able to persuade the seller to reduce his asking price in return for paying some portion of his debt. Creditors should welcome the idea of substituting a stronger financial profile for the seller's. You might also propose to the creditors that they write off some of the debt in return for getting you on their obligations. Talk to your lawyer and CPA about this.

2. Sell some of the property's "severable" assets

Rural property often includes one or two severable assets that can be sold without unduly diminishing the core reasons that you wanted to buy the property in the first place. I mean by "severable," an asset that can be sold generally within one year of purchase for more than you paid for it.

Severable assets can include merchantable timber, houses, mineral rights, small lots with road frontage, back acreage, agricultural equipment, personal property that came with the sale (tractors, farm machinery, tools, wood stoves, fuel tanks, materiel) and abandoned buildings (especially log cabins). I have used timber cruises to arrange 100-percent-financed purchases from a local bank on the understanding that I would use the net proceeds from the lump-sum timber sale that I would arrange soon after purchase to pay down the loan. The bank ended up with far more than the normal 20 percent in down payment and almost zero risk. I bought the properties with nothing out of pocket. You can work the same tactic with other assets. The more severable assets your target property has—things that can be sold without degrading the core asset that you want to keep—the more that property can pay for itself.

It will be to your advantage to have the value of any severable asset you're planning to sell appraised by a qualified, independent third-party prior to your purchase of the entire property. That appraisal, valuation or timber cruise can then be used to establish your original **tax basis** in the specific asset. In simple terms, your **"adjusted basis"** is what you have net in an asset when you sell it, after deductions from and additions to basis are calculated. If you immediately sell an asset for the same money as your pre-purchase valuation, you will show no taxable gain, hence no current tax obligation at your regular rate on the sale. A transaction of this sort changes the way your accountant allocates your total basis among the remaining assets. The sale of this asset decreases your basis in the remaining property. This tactic defers your tax obligation, it does not eliminate it. (If the property goes into your estate, the deferred tax may never be paid if your estate falls beneath the tax-free cap.) As a rule, the higher your basis in an asset/property when you go to sell it the better, because it means your taxable gain—the difference between what you net on the sale of the asset/property and what you have in it—is less. When you sell the remaining entirety, your basis will be lowered in proportion to and how you handled your post-purchase asset sales. The lowered basis left in your timberland as a result of the post-purchase sale of timber (which reduces basis) means that your taxable gain on your last sale—the property itself—will be higher. Estate planning, however, can protect both the tax-deferment and, by bequeathing the property to heirs rather than selling it, eliminate or reduce taxation altogether. Different types of **trusts** are also available to minimize current and future tax burdens; talk to your lawyer and CPA about these options. And, if the country property becomes your principal residence for two years out of five prior to its sale, you will be able to exclude from taxation as much as $250,000 (individual) and $500,000 (joint) of profit on its sale. Your CPA and lawyer can advise you on strategies to minimize your future tax obligations.

Another strategy that you can apply to severable assets is to arrange for their sale as part of your purchase. The seller of the target property will be selling to at least two buyers: you, the principal buyer, and the asset buyers whom you are coordinating. A lender or a seller financing the sale may count some or all of the income you receive from the immediate sale of the asset as amounting to down payment if you put it against your note. If you are working with an institutional lender, you may have to take title to the seller's entirety and then sell the asset. But this is usually not necessary. You line up your buyers with a **contingent sales contract** between you and them, then sell them the assets they want contingent on your buying the entirety from your seller. This approach involves a **simultaneous closing** by which you buy the whole from the seller and at the same time sell an asset to your buyer. I did this on a 425-acre farm, selling the house and 30 acres for just under 30 percent of the total purchase price. You can avoid paying some transaction costs, like recordation fees and property transfer taxes, to the extent that you arrange before closing to have separate deeds to you and your **piggy-back partners** for whichever assets they're buying.

A variation on this tactic is to persuade the seller to sell you only that combination of his property's assets you want. This reduces the money that you have to front and borrow as well as eliminates the risks and headaches that can be involved in selling unwanted assets. The common downside of trying to persuade a seller to part out his own property to your advantage is that he will increase the per-acre price to you for the smaller parcel. And if what you want is the choice piece, be prepared to pay top dollar. It's worth trying to persuade the seller that he will net more money by following your parting-out strategy than by selling the entirety, which means, you argue, that he doesn't need to raise your per-acre price. Most sellers don't want to bother with parting-out their property. It's been my experience that a buyer has trouble convincing a seller to sell him only what he wants. If you do buy more than what you want, I think you will find that your unwanted assets can often be sold at a profit, though it may take some time.

It's important to think through your plan to sell some assets of your newly acquired property before you buy it. First, this will help you project costs and income. Second, you need to start very low-key testing with potential buyers as you are moving toward a purchase. Your quiet marketing should be designed to avoid stimulating other entirety buyers. Once you have a signed purchase contract, you can market hard during your escrow period with the idea of scheduling a simultaneous closing. Third, you will need to make certain that any mortgage note you sign allows you to sell a portion of the collateralized property. Your note-holder needs to agree to release what you want to sell, and, in return, you will usually have to pay off a proportional part of your note. Make sure that your lender does not have a pre-pay penalty in your mortgage document, which would penalize your sale of severable assets. Fourth, you need to project the tax consequences of your parting-out strategy. How your CPA allocates original basis among the various assets will affect your tax obligations. If you can sell an asset soon after closing, but schedule the majority of your payment for one calendar year later, you will get capital-gains treatment on that delayed profit to the extent that it's not tax-deferred. Most taxpayers benefit from paying their capital-gains rate on income rather than their regular rate, when it is higher.

The other way to think about lender releases is to arrange with your lender at the start to pay off your new property, parcel by parcel. This allows you to free your core "keeper" asset (s) from debt relatively quickly. One or more of those assets can then be sold or refinanced with cash sticking in your pocket. A **partial release** allows you to pay down your debt so that you free an asset for your unencumbered use fairly quickly. Lenders should like this strategy, because their time exposure is short and the repayment is pegged largely to sales, not borrower cash flow.

Here is an example of how an entirety purchase can be paid for by the sale of severable assets. Take a 200-acre farm near, but not on, a developed lake, with the following asset mix:

1. 100 acres of merchantable timber with an immediate cash value for the standing timber and an independent value for the cutover land (bare land value);
2. 30 acres of open pasture, with road frontage and two house sites;
3. 20 acres of relatively level, tillable ground with high agricultural value. Also very developable owing to long road frontage;
4. 30 acres of marginally productive open land that is sometimes used as hayfield, sometimes as pasture, sometimes as cornfield. Has road frontage; and
5. Two-story farm house with assorted outbuildings and livestock pens, and 20 acres.

The asking price is $230,000. Proximity to the lake adds market value to the lots. The investor's objective is to have his investment pay for the 100 acres of timberland, which he wants to add to his estate. He values these five assets separately and sells them quickly. His investment strategy is: 1) sell the merchantable sawtimber 16" DBH and larger and keep the cutover land; 2) sell the 30 acres as two 15-acre lots, each with a nice house site; 3) sell the 20 acres of valuable agricultural land to a local farmer for agricultural use, or to a house builder, or as two ten-acre lots; 4) sell the 30 acres of marginally productive agricultural land to a local farmer or as a lot; and 5) sell the house, barn and 20 acres to a second-home buyer, possibly with the 30 acres of marginal land. This investor has chosen to keep the productive timberland as his core long-term investment and is flipping off all other assets to pay for that acreage. The investor could choose to follow the same strategy to retain any other asset, though the numbers will work differently. A common example for a second-home buyer is to sell most of the land to pay for the farmhouse and 20 acres.

This strategy is no different from that used in **merger and acquisitions (M&As)** to pay for corporate raider B's purchase of conglomerate A by shedding A's saleable assets and keeping those B wants. The economic logic is this: the sum of the pieces sold individually will exceed the investor's purchase price for the whole. The difference between what the investor nets after taxes on his sales and his costs for acquisition and resale is his profit. If the investor plans to part out all assets in a flip, he should borrow most, if not all, of the entire amount of the acquisition and other costs, using the pre-purchase valuations of each separate asset as security for his business plan and debt. A **parting-out strategy** will not work if your seller has priced his land to you at its "parted-out" value, and, you, the buyer, foolishly pay his retail price. Nor will it work if you overvalue the selling price of the parts. Time always has a money value in such deals, and the longer a highly leveraged investment is carried, the harder it is to make a profit. On the other hand, time usually increases the value of each country part.

Here's a simplified picture of how the numbers might work. The seller's asking price is $230,000, to which the investor/buyer agrees. Prior to placing his full-price purchase offer with the seller, he has a timber cruise in hand, along with an FMV appraisal of each asset. His plan is to sell all the assets except for the 100 acres of cutover timberland. Using the timber cruise and a two-page business plan that shows his pre-purchase asset valuations (column II, in TABLE 33-1 below), he is able to secure 100 percent financing. He pays down the note with every asset sale until it's completely retired.

The investor uses the 120 days of escrow between when his purchase contract takes effect and when he closes with the seller to complete the following tasks: 1) introduce his division plan to local authorities and revise, if necessary; 2) survey the property for division; 3) retain a consulting forester to mark the timber for a competitively bid sale to be conducted one month after the closing; 4) test the soil for perc sites; and 5) market the assets to appropriate buyers, e.g., local farmers, local residents, and non-local lot buyers. The last of these tasks can take the form of a sale contingent on the investor's purchase. Property division can be simple—or expensive, complicated and uncertain. If you're working with a difficult property, you have to insert a **division-approval contingency** in your purchase offer that makes your purchase contingent on obtaining to your satisfaction all necessary permits and approvals to implement your post-purchase plans. Your closing occurs within two weeks of obtaining the final permit or approval. The costs of applying for and securing these permits is yours, but they will be secured in the name of the seller and then conveyed along with the property. Any activity such as surveying or marking timber during escrow should be introduced to the seller as part of your offer. The buyer should have the seller agree in writing to each and every activity the buyer wants to do during escrow, none of which harm the seller's land. In many states, the buyer should be allowed to do such tasks during escrow as a matter of equitable title once contigencies are removed, but I advise buyers to notify sellers through their purchase offer of their intentions. A good part of the investor's work can be finished during the seller's ownership in this manner.

I've simplified the example by assigning a straight-through price to all land, even though the parcels of acreage to be sold will be priced differently according to their retail value in the marketplace. I've allocated values at the time of purchase as $60,000 for all improvements and $850 per acre for the land, $230,000 in all. I've also simplified the investor's costs by not including any upfront charges he incurs in scoping and purchasing the property.

TABLE 33-1

Cash-Out Investment Analysis

	I Cost	II Investor's Pre-Purchase Valuation	III Actual Net Sale Value	IV Investor's Retained Value or Cash
1. 100 acres. Sell timber	$85,000 (Land + timber)	$140,000 (Timber only)	$90,000*	$40,000 (RV)**
100 acres cutover	-	35,000		35,000 (RV)
2. 30 acres of open	25,500	75,000	65,000	39,500 (Cash)
3. 20 acres of developable land	17,000	55,000	50,000	33,000 (Cash)
4. 30 acres of marginal land	25,500	30,000	25,500	-0-
5. House/20 acres pasture.	77,000	150,000	155,000	78,000 (Cash)

$230,000 $485,000 $385,500 $75,000 RV
                                            +
                                            $150,500 Cash

* Net sale value is the buyer's remaining money after deducting his expenses in selling each part. These expenses would include attorney fees, consulting forester fee for managing the timber sale, surveying, interest, closing costs, interest, etc.

**The buyer sold a selective harvest of the standing timber at the time of purchase, say all trees with stems 16" DBH and larger. That left a number of premerchantable trees standing whose estimated present value is $40,000.

This investor finances the entire purchase of $230,000. After selling all the assets he is able to sell, he nets $385,500. He pays off his note and $25,000 in interest, a total of $255,000. His pre-tax cash in hand is $150,500 from the asset sale. He also keeps 100 acres of cutover timberland that has a retained value of $40,000 in the premerch timber less than 16" DBH and $35,000 in the land. The 100 acres is now owned free of a mortgage. On the cash, he will owe federal income tax at his regular rate or his capital-gains rate, depending on when he sold each asset. He will have deductions for interest and other costs. He can defer paying income tax on the timber sale, because he sold the timber for his pre-purchase valuation, which created no taxable event.

It was not OPM that made this deal work so well. It was, rather, the buyer's careful and accurate pre-purchase scoping that allowed him to see that the seller's wholesale price on the property was way below the retail price of its separate assets. The seller priced his property as a farm, not as a collection of assets near a lake. The advantage to this buyer of using OPM was that it left his own cash free to cover other costs, emergencies and the dollar cost of delays. This investor used his own resources—mainly his brain—to finance this purchase.

3. Neighbors

While the Old Testament instructs us not to covet our neighbor's assets, I have found such coveting is as common in the countryside as everywhere else. It's actually quite understandable. Farms—and often other types of rural land—depend on having in place an integrated system that works efficiently. The best 500 acres of Iowa dirt is not worth much if it can only be accessed by a mile-long easement that is restricted to equipment no wider than six feet. Every good property works physically, legally, environmentally and in terms of its resource mix. Where one or more components is less than optimum, the property as a whole works below its optimum. A neighbor, therefore, may need one of your seller's components more than your seller does. And for reasons that can range from rational to petty, your seller has always refused to sell this something to this neighbor. The odds are high that at least one of your neighbors both covets and has the money to buy one of the asset components that you are about to purchase. This sale alone can produce your down payment—without substantially reducing the core asset you want to keep.

You do need to be careful in distinguishing between a severable asset that does not substantially diminish the ability of your new land to do what you want it to do and an asset that does. An inexperienced buyer should not assume that he knows the difference. I would proceed cautiously, asking your seller what he thinks of the sale to the covetous neighbor; also ask the county extension agent and other neighbors. You do not want to sell your only barn or the one livestock pond on the farm. As long as the sale of the component is marginal to your use of the core property, it can be sold. The covetous neighbor will be smarter than you about the value of the asset he seeks; don't sell quickly when someone waves quick cash under your nose.

4. The Seller

The rural seller is an obvious source of cash.

When a seller fully finances a buyer's purchase, he does not reach into his pocket and give cash to the buyer the way a bank does. Rather, he retains ownership of the property and allows the buyer to pay him the agreed price over time with interest. When the buyer has paid the note completely, the seller conveys the title to him. While the buyer is paying the seller, he holds **equitable title** in the seller's property, which allows him to possess and use the property. The buyer should not be allowed under the terms of this agreement to damage the seller's property. The seller holds a first and primary mortgage in such circumstances, which means he is due his payment before any other party whose loan is secured by the property. This might also be referred to as the "seller taking back a first trust." (See Benny L. Kass,

"Housing Counsel: In Matters of Trusts, Sellers Shouldn't Make Deals on Faith," Washington Post, May 10, 2003.)

A common format for this arrangement is the **installment land contract** (also referred to as a "land contract," "land installment contract," "contract for deed" and "installment contract"). This type of purchase contract provides that the seller retains legal title to the property that you, the buyer, are allowed to possess and use. The property is the seller's security in the event that you default on the agreed payment schedule of interest and principal. The buyer receives a deed from the seller upon his last payment and the fulfillment of all other contract provisions. A seller-financed sale contract should specifically provide that the buyer is permitted to possess and use the seller's property without restriction, except for activities that reduce the value of the property as collateral. You and the seller should have a meeting of the minds about which activities will be permitted and which won't. If you want to cut timber on the property, your installment land contract should be written in such a way that you are permitted to do so. If there are rent, lease income or production royalties from minerals, the contract should reflect how these are to be handled and monies to be apportioned. The seller may insist that some or all of the proceeds be applied to your debt. If you want to build a house, you will have to make an arrangement that works for both of you; otherwise, all improvements you make to the property will run with the land in the event of your default. One way to handle this situation is to arrange with the seller that your note with him runs in two stages: the first is for, say, 25 acres, on which you build your house; the second is for the remainder of the property. In that fashion, you pay for the 25 acres first so that they and your new house are not exposed to the seller if you fail subsequently to pay for the rest of the land.

A seller-financed purchase generates money to the buyer through savings. First, the buyer is spared paying all points, fees and charges that a lender would normally impose. This alone can keep five percent of the purchase price in the buyer's pocket. Second, interest charged the buyer is not front-loaded and should be calculated on the declining balance. The interest rate should be a truer rate, lower than the same rate from a bank. A buyer should pay less total interest to a seller at any given rate than he would pay at that rate to an institutional lender over the same period. Third, a buyer may be able to get a discount on price by structuring the seller-financed payments over several years to advantage the seller's after-tax net income each year. Fourth, if you're doing a seller-financed purchase when interest rates are low, have the seller carry the note on a fixed rate rather than on an adjustable basis. Fifth, the seller may agree to a proposal that requires either no down payment or less than an institutional lender. Finally, you may be able to establish a below-market rate with a seller, something that's never possible with an institutional lender. Seller financing, obviously, is an option only with sellers who don't need to cash out the full sale price at closing.

It is essential for the buyer to record the installment land contract. Indeed, some states require recordation. The county office where this occurs might be called the Clerk's Office, Deed Registrar or County Recorder. Recordation prevents the seller from mortgaging the property or selling it out from under you.

In such a contract, nothing prevents the seller from encumbering his property with liens that can remain in place after the buyer makes his last balloon payment and title transfers. The seller must remove any existing mortgage and liens before transferring title. This requirement should be written into your seller-financing document. Better yet, your agreement should prohibit the seller from placing liens on the property during your period of equitable title.

If you are considering such a contract, make sure that you have a thorough title search and get title insurance. Your purchase contract should include language that requires the seller to prove that he has marketable title. (In reality, your lawyer may have to determine whether the seller has good title.) Don't do a land contract without having a smart lawyer reading every line *as you are negotiating*, not after.

A note between buyer and seller for all or part of the selling price is often referred to as a **purchase-money mortgage**. The seller accepts a note on his own land for all or part of the purchase price, using the property as collateral. If the buyer fails to make payments, the seller retakes possession of his property. The note may also be called a **mortgage** or a **deed of trust**.

A land contract should include a 60-day grace period that allows the buyer to cure a missed payment. If you do default, you lose all the payments you paid to the seller as **liquidated damages**; you should not owe the seller money beyond what you have paid. You will lose the property as well.

If the seller is totally financing the sale, he may ask that you provide additional collateral in addition to the property itself. This would cover his foreclosure and remarketing costs if you were to default soon after taking possession. I would resist adding collateral to the seller's land, except if he's allowing you to finance 100 percent of the purchase. If you do increase collateral, negotiate a **release schedule** that frees the add-on security when you reach and satisfy a certain scheduled payment. Make sure to record the release documents.

Why would a seller become his buyer's banker? First, this arrangement may be the only way to sell a unique property or one that is over-priced. Second, there may be tax strategies involved. The seller may want to reduce his tax hit by spreading income from the sale over several tax years. Third, holding title to his own property while a buyer makes interest-bearing payments does not put the seller at very much risk. If the buyer defaults, the seller still owns the property plus whatever improvements the buyer made. The seller keeps all the principal and interest the buyer has paid. The risk to the seller involves damage to his property or the sale of its timber that is not used to repay the note. Fourth, it's not a bad investment. The seller may figure that a note paying an interest rate above what he could get on a three-year CD and is secured by his own appreciating property is a better investment than his alternatives. Fifth, the seller may be more interested in predictable future payments than in a lump sum that he has to invest. Finally, the seller may know of some complication running with his property that, if discovered, would complicate a conventional sale. Seller financing may keep the cover on this defect or allow it to be resolved in the future.

.The major reason why sellers don't do seller-financing all the time is simple: most need to get all their cash at closing. Only sellers who don't need to cash out completely can fully finance a purchase. Sellers will weigh the risk of default buyer to buyer, and the burden of remarketing according to the individual property.

The most common form of seller-financing is for the **seller to take back a second mortgage** to help the buyer piece together a workable money package. A **seller's second** is usually for less money than the first mortgage. When a seller partly finances the buyer's purchase with a second mortgage behind a lender's first, title is held either by the lender holding the **first mortgage** or in trust. In either case, the buyer gets title (ownership) when he finishes paying both mortgages. In the event of a default, the seller is in second position—after the institutional lender—in getting his loan repaid from a sale of his property. Being in second position is also referred to as the seller agreeing to **subordinate** his loan to the one held by the primary lender. When a buyer defaults on either the first or second mortgage, foreclosure ensues. If the buyer defaults on the first mortgage, the holder of the second gets whatever is left after the first mortgage and the costs of foreclosure and resale are paid. If the buyer defaults on the second mortgage, the seller can force the sale of the property. But the holder of the first mortgage would be paid first, with anything left going to the seller. A seller with a second mortgage will not get his land back in the event of default unless he negotiates a buy-back with the lender or is the high bidder at the foreclosure sale. The seller holding a second could, therefore, wind up without the payment due him and without his property in the absolute worst case. A seller offering a second to a buyer tries to minimize his risk by carrying a note for no more than two to five years.

Institutional lenders rarely object to a seller holding a second mortgage, because they end up lending less on the property and feeling more secure about their exposure. The lender's first mortgage becomes increasingly secure as the buyer pays down his second. Once the seller's second is paid off, it will be the buyer's equity rather than the lender's principal that will be hit hardest by a default. Further, the holder of the first mortgage has no responsibility to protect the holder of the second. To the degree that the lender's risk is pushed onto the second-holding seller, the lender is in a win-win situation—a profitable loan with little, if any risk, from a default.

If you choose to work with some form of seller financing, you need to make sure that you understand who has the title to the property during the time of your indebtedness; what circumstances allow the seller to call the note, that is, payment of the entire amount; and precisely what happens once you make your last payment to the seller. On the day you complete paying off a second mortgage, you should have the seller sign a **certificate of satisfaction** and record it that day. (In states using a deed of trust or title theory of mortgage, this document is called a **deed of reconveyance**.) This document shows that you have paid your obligation to the full satisfaction of the note holder, and that his lien is removed from your property. When you pay off the first mortgage, you or the trustee holding the note, will record a similar document. Only at that point will you own the property free and clear, with the original deed and satisfied lien notes in your possession.

Seller-financed notes rarely front-load interest. But be advised that the term **"simple interest"** can have different interpretations. (See discussion under "Interest Rates" in Chapter 32.) I believe the best policy is for the buyer and seller to agree at the time the note is negotiated as to how interest is to be calculated, when exactly interest (and principal) is to be paid, how much exactly each interest payment will be, and exactly how payments will be delivered from buyer to seller. I would also insist on a **no-penalty, pre-payment option** that allows the buyer to pay off the entire note early. The seller-financing document should be drafted by a lawyer, preferably yours. It should set out what happens when the buyer is either late with a payment or misses one entirely. The parties should agree on a correction period—15 to 30 business days, for example—during which the buyer can make good a missed payment without penalty. It's also reasonable to limit the number of such no-penalty periods to no more than, say, two over a five-year term. If the buyer is late more than twice, the seller can impose a penalty. The trigger for default should be simple and unambiguous. Default procedures will depend on whether the buyer has improved the property through the construction of a house, for example or taken value from the property. I'm always inclined to work out **anticipated-catastrophe language**, such as for default, in advance when everyone is being nice as pie, or at least fairly cooperative. Most seller-financed documents I have seen, primarily seller-held seconds, leave a lot to everyone's imagination. As an out-of-town buyer, don't sign a seller-financing document without first running it by your local lawyer.

I should point out a "found-money-for-the-buyer tactic" that you might find a seller proposing. Many older rural landowners have their life's work and capital tied up in their property, buildings and equipment. Depending on their individual circumstances, a large property sale could mean a large tax payment. Where equipment and improvements (buildings, silos, farm structures, etc.) have been depreciated, a portion of that depreciation will be recaptured upon their sale, which increases the tax owed. Such a seller may advertise as a FSBO and offer you a noticeably below-market price for what he calls **"an all-cash deal."** The specifics of such a proposition will vary but its essence is that you are being asked to agree to buy his land in a fashion that will not be honestly reported on his 1040 or settlement statement and which will leave as little paper trail as possible. This may involve falsifying documents, or not recording the deed of sale, or delaying recordation of the deed until after his estate is settled, or not using a lawyer (who is required to file certain IRS forms for every property transaction), or not claiming sale expenses on your own 1040. I don't mean to suggest that all sellers, or even most sellers, in this circumstance will offer you a proposition of this sort. But someone might, and he'll call it "seller financing." **DO NOT PARTICIPATE IN SUCH CONSPIRACIES.** You will likely get caught. Sooner or later, you will have problems in your record of ownership, and that can lead to headaches in disposing of the property. Such a seller will always have something on you. You will be co-conspirators in a scheme to defraud the IRS and your local/state taxing authorities. Having said all that about a slippery seller, let me add that it is just as scummy to offer an aged, vulnerable seller a pay-in-cash deal at a low-ball price to lure him into tax fraud.

In addition to seller-financing arrangements, a buyer can propose to a seller a sale using a **wraparound purchase money mortgage** where circumstances are favorable. A "wrap" is subordinate to the seller's own mortgage, but it draws into its terms the seller's note. If the seller's mortgage includes an **acceleration clause**, which provides that the note's unpaid balance is due immediately if the seller fails to meet his payments or property taxes, then a wraparound cannot be used. The wrap's advantage to the buyer is that his down payment on the entire property is limited to the cash required for the wrap. In the right conditions a comparatively small wrap can leverage the purchase of a large property as long as the buyer can handle the monthly mortgage payment on the combined notes. Since the wrap is smaller than a primary mortgage, all the fees and points the seller would normally pay are scaled down. The buyer gets title to the property, and the seller gets cash. But the seller remains liable for payment of the original note, so buyer and seller continue to be involved with each other. A wrap, in this way, is not an **assumption**, by which the buyer takes over the responsibility for the seller's original note. A wrap allows the buyer to acquire an over-priced property on terms that make it favorable. Do not write a wrap note yourself! It requires a skillful lawyer, and it must include protections for both buyer and seller. The buyer, for example, must be protected against the seller's failure to keep up payments on the original note (for which the buyer is providing him funds each month).

A seller can help a buyer through a **buydown**. This is a seller-made, lump-sum payment to the buyer's lender to reduce the buyer's interest rate. The seller is, in effect, paying the lender a point or two to increase the lender's yield. On a 30-year note, the general guideline is that six points reduce the interest rate by one percent. A buydown does not give cash to the buyer, but it reduces his total interest cost. A note for $100,000 at ten percent for 30 years involves a monthly payment of $877.58, or a total P&I of $315,929. The same $100,000 at 9 percent for 30 years has a payment of $804.63, or $289,667. The $6,000 buydown at the beginning of the note saves the buyer $26,262 over the full term. Time-limited buydowns might be arranged where the buyer repays the seller at a future date. Rules for buydowns are set up for some programs, such as those through Fannie Mae, VA and FHA.

The seller can also pick up a greater share of the settlement costs as a way of helping a buyer reduce his need for cash. **Seller contributions** can include the payment of discount points, routine closing costs, mortgage insurance, moving costs, property tax, among others. When a seller pays certain points for a buyer, the buyer may deduct them.

The seller can also help you with a down payment by selling you certain items of personal property for you to cash out and use for that purpose. (Better yet, the seller could give you such items for resale.) You might, for example, offer to buy all of his farm equipment "for one money." This can be attractive if the farmer does not want to go through the emotional travail of watching his stuff auctioned and paying the auctioneer ten percent plus costs for doing so. If you're willing to spend the time selling the seller's assets, you may be able to generate enough after-tax cash to cover an appreciable portion of your down payment.

Finally, a seller can help you by agreeing to **reserve some asset** from his sale to you that he can sell to another party. This might be a tenant house or acreage. The idea is that the seller can sell two things—the big thing to you and the small thing to someone else—for more money than he can sell the two things together to you. You now need less down payment to buy the property that you want than before. You've also avoided the cost and hassle of selling the smaller property.

5. Co-investors and partners

Rural property lends itself to "going in on it together." One hundred acres of woods or a farmhouse and acreage are easily shared with friends, either sequentially (as in a time share) or simultaneously. A number of legal structures are available by which buyers can organize shared property ownership. The advantage of a partner to a cash-strapped buyer is that your down payment and mortgage obligations are cut in proportion to his financial contribution. There are, as you might expect, down sides to sharing. You may also persuade a partner that he should pay disproportionately more in down payment as compensation for having you find the property and do all of the scoping.

I've been involved in three joint purchases. All used **tenants (tenancy) in common**, by which there was one title to the property and each of the owners had an undivided interest in the property as a whole. If four buyers each put up 25 percent of the cash to buy a property, as tenants in common each owner would have an equal ownership interest in the entire property. Each owner's interest is inheritable, and each owner can sue for partition of the property if things don't work. Another ownership format is **joint tenants (tenancy)**, by which upon the death of one owner the other owners inherit his share in the whole. Thus, upon the death of a quarter interest, the remaining three owners automatically assume that interest with each now owning one-third of the whole. The last surviving owner gets 100 percent of the property. Joint tenants must own equal shares; tenants in common can own unequal shares. Joint tenancy avoids **probate**, which is the legal process by which a court determines the assets of the decedent's estate and who owns what. Heirs want to avoid probate because it can be lengthy and costly. But joint tenancy means that the longest lived wins the property lottery at the expense of the other joint tenants, and, more accurately, their estates and heirs.

Two of my three tenants-in-common land purchases ended sourly, mainly, I think, because of divorce, relocation and changed circumstances of all involved. In one case, I had to sell a highly-appreciated interest in land on which I did not live to a partner without much money. My partner who lived on the property wanted to preserve the status quo at best, and, alternatively, pay less than FMV to buy me out. We had a hard time agreeing on how much the property, less his improvements, had appreciated. Appraisers we hired did not estimate timber value on the 100 acres of woods. Had we not finally reached a buy-out number, my circumstances would have forced me to bring a **partition suit**, by which a court would have supervised the property's sale and the distribution of its proceeds. In the other purchase, the two remaining partners of the original four decided to sell the property together following divorces, but had a hard time determining the value of a house I had built. The third example, done 20-25 years after the first two, has been problem free, because both owners see the property as a long-term timberland investment. While I would be inclined to use this mortgage-free property in a 1031 exchange to increase the value of our shared asset, I'm not opposed to keeping it for our daughters as their joint inheritance. It helps, of course, to have paid for this property with a selective timber cut two years after purchase, with cash left over.

The lesson I draw is that partnerships among older, more settled individuals who share goals are likely to work better than partnerships among younger adults who can be more subject to changes in relationships, careers and needs. Key to making these "go-in-together deals" work are pre-existing friendships that have weathered a bump or two, shared objectives and flexibility to adapt to the inevitable changes in individual circumstances. The other factor that benefits a partnership is having each member hold sufficient net worth and represent enough financial stability to exempt the shared property from anyone's emergency need to cash it out. If one member is pinched, the partners should be able to buy his share.

The wildcard in partnering is how you and your partners behave toward each other over time. If you've ever acted selfishly in such an arrangement or had others disappoint you, you know that individuals do not always act nobly and honestly. Therefore, I advise entering any partnership with exits clearly marked and understood. Nothing helps more than a written plan signed by all partners that spells out shared objectives, how to change those objectives and what to do when the partners disagree.

For the purpose of coming up with cash for a down payment, you can consider a more business-like "partnership." Contract for the property in its entirety, then sell a piece or a share in the whole to a friend for a profit, which becomes your down payment. Do a simultaneous closing so that you can give the down payment to the seller at settlement. Calculate your tax consequences before agreeing on numbers. There should be limits to your mark up, which will be determined by the degree of closeness in your relationship, both present and anticipated. If you're selling the "partner" a piece off the entirety, you're not partners in the future, except to the extent that you socialize and borrow each other's stuff. If, on the other hand, he comes in as a tenant in common or as a joint tenant, then you want to be as fair as you can. Ten to 20 percent profit on what you sell seems reasonable if you were the one who found the property and did the legwork. You may want to give each other a **first right of refusal** if either decides to sell.

Other shared-ownership formats are available, including corporations, limited liability companies, partnerships, among others. Each offers a different set of implications for debt liability and tax obligations.

All **partnering arrangements** work better when everyone agrees at the outset on the long-term objectives of the ownership, its term and what happens when one or more of the principals wants to get out. Once everyone agrees on the objectives, put them in writing. At minimum, the group should see the rural property as an investment first rather than as an affirmation of lifestyle values. Emotions quickly get incorporated into "my land, my trees, my picnic spot, my spiritual center." It's fine to have feelings for your shared property, but try to keep those feelings secondary to a certain business-oriented objectivity. Rural land bought as an investment can be managed with collective objectivity, rather than owned as a shared family pet or an axis of psychic security. It is, however, difficult to get lifestyle oriented partners thinking this way about lifestyle property. The problem I've found with my own **lifestyle land partnerships** is that lifestyles change, attitudes about many things evolve and money becomes needed. Shared-interest partnerships—such as a group of hunters buying hunting land—seem to last better than shared lifestyle partnerships.

Parents, of course, can be the best partners a child can find for a land deal if only because they're likely to be more forgiving than other lenders. One way to pay them back for purchase cash is to promise them a **future right (reservation)**—say, a right to cut merchantable timber in 15 years when they are looking for retirement money or the right to sell a piece of the property when needed. If a parental gift exceeds the annual tax-free cap on gifts, a tax hit will follow.

An individual can gift up to $12,000 to any number of individuals each year without being bitten by the federal gift tax. Each parent, in other words, can gift $12,000 to a child and his spouse tax-free each year, for a total of $48,000. One $48,000 gift can be given in December and the next $48,000 can be gifted in January, a month later. When a taxpayer's lifetime gift cap of $1 million is exceeded, a 47 percent tax is imposed. The recipient pays no tax, however. One alternative—or supplement—to a gift is a loan. Parents can make below-market-rate loans, but the IRS will force the parents to pay tax on "imputed interest" on what is known as the applicable federal rate. If a loan is made, the child should record it so that he can deduct the interest payments to his parents. (Colleen DeBasie, "Helping a Home Buyer Can Trigger Taxes," Wall Street Journal, April 10, 2005.)

6. Locally owned local lenders

I've mentioned institutional lenders, such as banks, in discussing mortgages and interest rates. For the purpose of finding money for rural property, I'll distinguish between locally owned lenders in your target county and the local branch offices of regional/national banks.

Many rural counties still have at least one more-or-less locally owned bank along with the branch offices of larger banks. The locally owned bank may be state chartered and regulated. State banking rules are likely to be fewer and less intrusive than federal rules. Consumers/borrowers are likely to have fewer protections. In Virginia, for example, state bankers have no state code of ethics they're expected to follow.

The larger the bank the more tied to procedure and numerical measures it's likely to be in making loans. This is not necessarily harmful to a buyer's interest. Coming from a city or a suburb, you're likely to be familiar with big-bank rigmarole and their formulas. Your "**financials**" will have already been gathered and scrutinized if you've borrowed the mortgage money for your principal residence from such institutions. The high-income urban buyer looks good to rural banks of both kinds. Such individuals often benefit from the disparity between high-paying city jobs and low-paying country jobs. But if you're an out-of-county buyer with "a problem," you may find that the loan officers at the rural branch banks may not have much discretion on applications that don't fit within their cookie cutter. Their LTV ratios are probably immutable, and I would expect no negotiation on fees and points, which they will pronounce are set by policy.

Locally owned banks, in contrast, may be expected to exercise some flexibility on individual applications. Many continue to hold most home-mortgage loans in their own portfolios, which allows them to make loans that don't conform to the standards of the secondary mortgage market. They should have a good idea of the foreclosure value of your local property, even if they don't know much about you. As a stranger appearing on its doorstep asking for money, a local bank will review your financials and apply its formulas. Don't be surprised if the bank makes a few inquiries with whomever you've dealt with locally—real-estate agent, surveyor, forester, lawyer, perhaps even the waitress who served you lunch (who may be the bank president's cousin).

A local bank is likely to charge a higher interest rate than the local offices of the big banks. But I've seen four practices that offset that interest premium: 1) if the locally owned bank charges fees and points at all, they are likely to be substantially lower; 2) it's likely to accept deals where you use something on the property to help with the purchase, such as using a timber sale to generate a down payment; 3) it's not likely to sell a non-conforming note, which gives them a bit more flexibility; and 4) they push paper faster and probably require less of it. A higher interest rate with low upfront costs will work much better for a borrower who plans to pay off a long-term debt within five or so years.

One down side to using a local banker of whichever kind is that folks in the community may come to know your business. The price you paid will in most states be public record, stated in the deed or calculable from taxes paid at closing. The new tax-appraised value when it appears should reflect your purchase price. And, people talk.

After you've been around a while, you will undoubtedly have rubbed some folks the right way and others differently. Local bank boards sometimes make decisions based on personality, friendship and kinship. A bank with a mortgage wields awesome power over an individual, particularly one who's in financial trouble. If you've made the wrong enemy, don't be surprised by active pay back. Small places have large virtues, but affairs within them can be conducted on the basis of personal likes and dislikes. Some in your new community, like any other place, will view your position as a zero-sum game, with every dollar you gain as a dollar out of their pocket and every dollar you lose as a dollar they win. You may find that certain individuals in your new community are hostile to "outsiders." This attitude may or may not be reasonable and justified. You may run into individuals who don't want your business, don't want you to compete with them, don't want your advice and don't want you to succeed. You will also find local individuals with exactly the opposite views. Small places harbor a diversity of local opinions, though that may not be obvious to a newcomer. Having said all that, it is advisable to get to know the directors of the bank that holds your note. This may not help you in a crunch, but it can't hurt. (If, on the other hand, you are an insufferable, arrogant know-it-all, you might do better to apply online.)

Locally owned rural banks tend to be very profitable. The exception would be a bank in a chronically depressed area or in a place that was undercut by a cataclysmic financial disaster. Bank holding companies are always looking to buy small independents, whereupon they are made into branches even though the faces may remain the same. Banks mainly get in trouble from **insider loans** to their officers and directors that are not repaid. Both big banks and small banks are susceptible, because boards do not like to deal harshly with their own. If you pick up information that a local bank is being run as a cookie jar, avoid it. Many rural banks in farm country are susceptible to farming-related troubles affecting the bulk of their borrowers. A bank's failure, however, should not materially hurt a borrower. If stock in a well-run local bank comes up for sale, buy some. It should prove a wise investment on its own merits, as well as help you as a borrower.

The situation that you truly want to avoid is one where the self-interest of a bank's board member conflicts with your own. This can be especially troublesome when you are in a jam on the bank's loan. In my experience, board members of small, local banks do not recuse themselves from bank loans and decisions that benefit their non-bank private interests, but that may be atypical. Whether you, a newcomer and new borrower, are treated fairly in this situation depends entirely on the individual bank. I've seen local banks be helpful with their non-local borrowers as well as go out of their way to hurt those on the ropes. If you are thinking about starting a new business in town, or buying out an old one, it is critical for you to determine whether your plans run counter to the interests of those on the board of your lender.

Other local mortgage lenders include **savings institutions, credit unions** and **private mortgage brokers.**

A **savings institution** can be a savings bank, savings and loan association (S&L) or mutual savings bank. Such organizations are profit-making lenders that concentrate on long-term loans for single-family, owner-occupied housing. An application for rural undeveloped land that is some distance from your principal residence will raise a flag at an urban savings bank. Still, it's worth making a phone call. If your target county has a savings institution, pay it a visit.

Credit unions are membership-based, non-profit lenders that are specifically organized to lend money to their members. Membership is confined to a particular subset population with a common bond—employees of a specific company, residents of a particular area, members of a particular group and so on. Credit unions are organized as cooperatives and are tax exempt; some are federally chartered while others operate with state charters. Owing to their ownership structure and tax-exempt status, credit unions should be able to lend money at better rates and terms than conventional lenders. Their lending guidelines and formulas may be no different than any other lender's. But the range and type of loans is likely to be narrower than that of a bank.

In November, 2002, the National Credit Union Administration (NCUA) proposed new regulations that would expand the ability of federally regulated credit unions to operate. More people would be allowed to form and join credit unions. Banks opposed these changes. The new regulations allow credit unions to increase their presence and share of loans. You should look for a county-based or multi-county credit union as a lender. (Albert B. Crenshaw, "Cash Flow," Washington Post, December 8, 2002; see also www.ncua.gov. The NCUA charters and supervises all federal credit unions and insures savings in federal and most state-chartered credit unions.) In 2006, banks were asking Congress to remove the tax-exempt status of credit unions. Some credit unions are converting to banks. (Bernard Wysocki, Jr., "Bankers Struggle To Contain Growth Of Credit Unions," Wall Street Journal, March 7, 2006.) Credit union financial reports are publicly available.

Mortgage brokers, or mortgage companies, are private, profit-making businesses that match a borrower with a lender. They make their money by charging a fee. A mortgage broker does not hold your note; he arranges the placement of your note. Mortgage brokers work with a variety of institutional lenders. While they prefer that your loan profile fit the conventional template every bank prefers, a broker can earn his fee by finding a lender for an individual with a non-conventional financial profile. Brokers should shop your loan for the best overall deal for you, and that can be better than the package you negotiate directly with the corner bank. Mortgage brokers are actively involved in urban/suburban mortgages; I've not seen an equal presence in rural areas and on land loans. Mortgage brokers are commonly criticized for getting their clients into loans with unfavorable terms and tacking on junk fees.

7. Local lenders owned by regional/national banks

Apart from a locally owned bank, you are likely to find **branches of national or regional banks** in rural areas. Such branches make mortgage loans according to guidelines established at headquarters. Do not expect much flexibility. They may be leery of lending on unimproved land that cannot be connected to big public or private water and sewerage systems, because such properties may be hard to sell in the event of a foreclosure.

I would approach these banks with all the information they need to analyze your property and financial capabilities. The more you can focus the bank officer on your data and your forthright presentation, the easier it will be for the bank to get to know you first as an individual and then as a customer. In other words, make your financial profile—its numbers and format—fit the bank's expectations, particularly when you don't exactly. It will help if one of the lender's current customers introduces you to the the loan officer, directly or off-handedly. Approach this process as one in which both you and the loan officer want to find that common ground on which your relationship can stand. Make it easy for the loan officer's supervisor to say yes to your application.

It is always possible that you will find a loan officer hostile to your application because of who you are. The federal **Equal Credit Opportunity Act (ECOA)** prohibits lenders and others who arrange credit from discriminating against credit applicants on the basis of race, color, religion, national origin, sex, marital status, age and dependence on public assistance. If the lender doesn't like your opinions, manners, speech, grammar, regional origins, educational attainment or profession, you are not protected. The ECOA requires that lenders inform rejected applicants in writing within 30 days of the principal reasons for rejection or termination of credit. The borrower can also get a copy of the property appraisal if he's paid for it. Discrimination is difficult to prove in mortgage credit cases because it's easily disguised, and part of every application involves the subjective weighing of many factors in the applicant's presentation. If a lender wants to discriminate against an individual, he might simply offer only 70 percent of the purchase price rather than the 80 percent the applicant needs. The discrimination that I've seen is banks occasionally helping or hurting individuals based on kinship and financial interests. If you find yourself with a discrimination claim that you believe meets the test of being beyond a reasonable doubt, you can bring suit or file a complaint. Don't be surprised if your claim is hard to prove beyond a reasonable doubt. It's a bad idea to announce your presence in a new community by filing a lawsuit—even if you're dead right. Consider taking your business elsewhere and rising above the lender's slight.

8. Non-local lenders

One group of non-local lenders is the set of institutional lenders available to you in the community where you live and work. If you have a well-established relationship with one or more of these lenders, you may be able to take out a mortgage for distant property. But the further the distance, the more remote the property, the less it is developed with utilities and improvements and the more out of the ordinary it is—the more trouble you will have getting a stand-alone mortgage for it. In such cases, you can propose financing through your principal residence, using a home-equity loan, refi or line of credit. Lenders often have self-imposed geographic restrictions and property standards that eliminate some rural properties from consideration. The non-local lender may not finance a mortgage on distant property, but money may be available to help with a down payment.

An urban/suburban mortgage broker will probably be not much help on a distant country property, but it's worth a try if you've worked a mortgage through him in the past. Mortgage brokers generally work with borrowers on *residential loans in their local area* that can be sold on the secondary market to buyers, such as Federal National Mortgage Association (Fannie Mae), Government National Mortgage Association (Ginnie Mae) or Federal Home Loan Mortgage Association (Freddie Mac). Such loans must conform to certain guidelines, and are, therefore, called **conforming loans.** A loan for undeveloped land 100 miles away would not conform and would not be easily placed. But…a mortgage broker in your hometown may know a broker who knows a broker near your target property—so it's worth a local phone call. A broker in a town or city that is the financial center of a rural area may be able to work with an out-of-town buyer on country property.

9. Life-Insurance Companies

Life-insurance companies hold about 12 percent of all U.S. farm mortgage debt, covering about 14,800 loans and amounting to $11.8 billion. Although some 20 companies are involved, six—AEGON USA, Citigroup Investments AgriFinance, Lend Lease Agri-Business, Metropolitan Life, MONY Life Insurance and Prudential—account for about 90 percent of these farm mortgages. These companies finance large working farms with demonstrated cash flow sufficient to cover their payments. The Pacific Coast, Florida and Texas account for almost 57 percent of the total dollar volume in mortgages held by life-insurance companies. These companies will not lend on a rural second home or to individuals interested in purchasing undeveloped rural land for recreation. If your focus is on buying a real working farm as a business or investment, you can check with local life-insurance lenders. (USDA, Economic Research Service, "Agricultural Income and Finance: Situation and Outlook Report," AIS-76, February, 2001, p. 23; 1-800-999-6779 to order.)

Several insurance companies both lend money to large customers to buy big tracts of timberland, farmland and land suitable for development and manage such investments themselves for their own clients, such as endowments, trusts and individuals. Certain companies—including John Hancock, Travelers and Metropolitan Life—have lent money to "high-net-worth" individuals to finance the purchase of timberland for investment purposes. They will evaluate the merchantable timber and the value of the bare dirt along with the plans and creditworthiness of the borrower. Insurance companies look for an LTV of about 60 percent. (See Liane Luke, "Timberland Financing: A Relationship Business," Growth Magazine, Summer 2002.) These companies also sell large tracts from time to time, either directly or through a broker.

10. Internet

I have no first-hand experience borrowing from Internet lenders, such as www.ditech.com, the GMAC subsidiary, which advertises on television. I suppose these lenders work best with conforming loans where everything is straight-forward and saleable on the secondary market. This would, I think, rule out undeveloped land, second homes and farm businesses. The Internet loans I've heard about in my area require a residence on a lot of no more than five acres. My wife, a lawyer who does country real-estate work, has run into procedural screw ups with Internet financing on several occasions. These usually involved timing and forms. Internet lenders have a hard time getting their paperwork done in a timely fashion, which forces the closing attorney into a last-minute scramble. These lenders will e-mail a 90-page loan package to the attorney on the morning of the closing and expect everything to get sorted properly in an hour or two. The Internet lenders also seem to be hard to reach by 20th Century technology, such as the telephone.

The Internet provides a number of mortgage-information sites that do not make loans, such as www.bankrate.com and www.HSH.com. You can also find sites of individual lenders, including the largest banks, but I have found several large bank sites nearly impossible to use for as simple a task as acquiring a physical phone number and street address. The www.nolo.com article, "Online Mortgage Shopping," 2003 notes: "…any of the direct lender sites offer general consumer information, but it's impossible on the Web to compare rates among them. These lenders rarely provide complete product price information including points, fees, lock periods and the like."

Sites like www.LendingTree.com and www.RealEstate.com ask the borrower to complete an application, which is then submitted to lenders for possible bid.

A third type of site is used for comparison-shopping. Here you enter basic information on the target property and the applicant and then obtain general loan terms from a number of lenders. From those, the borrower can choose one or more and submit an application. If there are wrinkles in your financial profile or the property itself, plan on talking to the lender through something other than a keyboard.

The danger in online mortgage applications is exposing your financial data—credit card numbers, bank account numbers, etc.—to unknown individuals. This can lead to identity theft. I advise against responding in any way to a mortgage offer coming to your e-mail account as spam. This is called "**phishing**," the object of which is to get you to provide personal financial information. A known scam involves **mortgage aid**, where the e-mail scammer offers to help a troubled borrower get out of debt within 12 months, or so. The scammer may ask the victim to provide a copy of his deed or make payments directly to the scammer. Don't. The scammers keep the payments and may file for bankruptcy in the victim's name, without the victim knowing about it.

A second problem appears to be that a buyer with a pre-approval letter from an Internet lender may not actually be pre-approved for anything. Kenneth Harney reported the findings of an opinion survey of 1,717 real-estate agents and brokers across the country by Campbell Communications in which 39 percent of all pre-approvals extended by Internet lenders were either faulty or invalid. Almost 30 percent of mortgage-broker pre-approvals and about 20 percent of national-lender pre-approvals were similarly flawed. (Kenneth Harney, "The Nation's Housing," "'Preapproval' letter can deliver some headaches," Richmond Times-Dispatch, July 10, 2005.) A buyer who receives pre-approval without first submitting financial documents or without having the lender verify his credit and financial statements gets into a jam of this type. A non-verified pre-approval leads the buyer into submitting and/or signing a contract that he may not be able to finance.

The www.nolo.com article provides cautions and good advice on using Internet lending. (See http://www.nolo.com/lawcenter/ency/article.cfm/objectID/DB153289-50E8-4632- AA3CE.

Every lender—your corner bank to an e-mail lender—has the power to wreck you once he gets your financial information and then your note. Consumers cannot guarantee that the local bank teller with the nice smile is not stealing your identity. But the odds of that type of nightmare appear to me much higher on the Internet sites. A borrower has some protection with a local lender who wants to protect its reputation for community-mindedness and fair-dealing. An Internet lender has no such concerns. With an Internet lender, you could be dealing with an organization that is entirely legitimate, a total scam or anywhere in between.

11. Government agencies

The federal government is deeply involved in the lands, finances and management of rural America, including providing mortgage money and loan guarantees for the purchase of property.

Interior's Bureau of Land Management (BLM) alone owns about 264 million acres, about one-eighth of the United States. BLM sells timber, issues livestock-grazing permits and leases minerals—all of which may affect a new nearby landowner and the price he just paid. Much western ranch land is sold with deeded acreage the seller owns and BLM acreage that is leased. Where BLM has designated its land as part of its National Landscape Conservation System, traditional uses are being curtailed. A ranch buyer should be particularly concerned about water issues and overgrazing of BLM leased lands.

The National Park Service manages about 84 million acres, the U.S. Fish and Wildlife Service about 93 million acres and the U.S. Forest Service, about 192 million acres. Proximity to public land brings both benefits and liabilities to adjacent private landowners, which I've discussed in other chapters. **In-holdings**—land surrounded by public land—are prized and can usually be sold to the public agency at appraisal value depending on the availability of funds. Some states appropriate money for acquisitions of private land to add to their holdings. New York, for example, buys private land within the Adirondack Park.

The federal government plays a direct role in rural finance through its various programs of support. Certain sectors of agriculture receive direct support payments, while all of agriculture benefits from federally funded research and marketing efforts. The 1996 Farm Act provided about $15.9 billion in production flexibility payments during the 1998-2000 period. Another $5.8 billion ($5.4 billion in direct payments) was tacked on in 1998. Another $4 billion was added in 2001. Additional billions were added in these years for marketing-loss relief, disaster relief, emergency assistance, production losses, etc. In 2000, the Agricultural Risk Protection Act authorized $15.1 billion for federal farm assistance with about $6.7 billion in direct payments to farmers. Such payments in 2000 were $22.1 billion. In 1990-1997, farmers received about $8.8 billion a year in direct payments. In 1998-2001, that average rose to $17.3 billion annually. (USDA, ERS, "Agricultural Income," p. 7.) Then in 2002, Congress passed a $414 billion, multi-year farm bill. The next farm bill is scheduled for 2007. At the end of 2005, discussion was reported in the media about Washington cutting farm programs.

The economic effect of this yearly infusion of cash into farm counties is to maintain production at high levels and provide further repayment capacity for the $181 billion in farm business debt, about 54 percent of which is agricultural real estate and the remainder non-real-estate farm loans. The USDA's ERS survey reported: "Total direct government payments are expected to account for almost half of reported net farm income and about 39 percent of net cash income." (*Ibid.*, p. 30.) Owing to these payments, agricultural banks show low delinquency in farm loans, low charge offs (losses), zero failures in 2000 and good profitability despite weak farm prices and demand problems in certain sectors, such as tobacco and beef.

While farming and debt often go hand in hand, it surprised me that about 58 percent of America's 2.148 million farms reported no debt outstanding in 1999. (*Ibid.*, p. 44.) What explains almost 60 percent of U.S. farms having no debt, and the rest carrying a huge amount? My guess is that it's related to the fact that 57 percent of all farm households are classified as either retirement (297,566) or residential/lifestyle (931,561) in that year. (*Ibid.*, p. 34.) Such small farmers are likely to have paid off their mortgages with non-farm income while engaging in the small-scale agriculture associated with retirement and lifestyle.

Federal cash to farmers has another effect. It maintains the value of agricultural land in the face of real-estate market pressures. At the beginning of 2000, agricultural real estate nationally averaged $1,050 per acre. This figure compares favorably with the low-year value of $599 (not adjusted for inflation) in 1987 when overproduction and low prices devastated farmers. Average acreage price in 2000 ranged from $2,470 in the Northeast (Maryland to Maine) to $440 in the Rockies. Agricultural land continues to appreciate even in the face of weak commodity prices and chronic oversupply of agricultural products, partly related to federal payments. This type of support allows a farmer to build wealth through his land even when his farm business is marginal. The other factor, of course, that drives rural land prices is demand from second-home and relocating retirement buyers

The buyer of rural land needs to understand the political basis of some of its value and the derivative risks. If Washington reduces the flow of cash, agricultural land values can erode. Were agriculture to have its subsidies deeply curtailed for many years, many sectors of the agricultural economy would not show a net profit. A harsh consolidation would occur. Marginal farmland would erode in value as production was cut to boost prices. Non-agricultural rural land would probably erode in value too with, I think, the exception of timberland. Privately owned timberland should continue to rise in value as more and more public land is backed out of timbering and demand for wood products continues to show strength.

Buyers should also be aware that the political stability of federal payments to rural and farm sectors fluctuates. If, accordingly, crop payments come with the seller's property and that income helps secure a mortgage, you should try to obtain a general forecast regarding the reliability of these payments out to the mid-term future. I'd start with the experts at the state land-grant universities who specialize in the particular crops your target farm produces. While the farm lobbies are powerful far beyond the numbers of farmers, certain sectors, notably tobacco, have been pruned. Dwight Watson, the North Carolina farmer who stalled traffic in Washington D.C. for two days by parking himself and his John Deere tractor in a decorative pond the day before America invaded Iraq in March, 2003 to protest the halving of the tobacco subsidy, showed how dependent a farm sector can become on federal monies.

The other factor in rural land appreciation has nothing to do with agriculture. Where rural land lends itself to second homes, individually and in developments, land prices are driven by urban cash and urban demand. These buyers want mainly to live in the country for lifestyle reasons, not to work the land. USDA's ERS estimates that ten to 20 percent of U.S. farmland is "subject to" urban influences. Second-home buyers in the West are known as "amenity buyers" when local real-estate brokers are being polite.

I live about a 4 1/2-hour drive from the White House and three hours west of Richmond, Virginia in an Appalachian mountain county that has 2,500 people. Our closest direct "urban influence" is an hour's drive over four mountains to a city of 25,000 on Interstate 81. But our land market is driven almost entirely by second-home buyers from the Richmond-Baltimore corridor. In my sheep-and-cattle county, a farmer can no longer buy pasture for his stock because the lowest price—$2,000+ per acre—is too high for him to pay it off through farming. Poor pasture is now bringing $3,000 to $5,000 an acre in 20-acre lots. Consequently, lifestyle farmers have replaced make-a-living farmers as buyers for local farms. Farming as a livelihood is almost incapable of providing a reasonable living. We have more than 1,000 farms, but fewer than 25 full-time farmers, and the majority of those are contract poultry growers. The vast majority of the 1,000-plus farms are not farming dependent: they run enough livestock to keep the grass down, or lease the pasture, or are operated as part-time (after work) businesses, or maintain a barnyard that is part Old MacDonald and part California exotica. We are a rural county that's becoming ever less dependent on farming and ever more dependent on the aesthetics of "farminess." Much of our agricultural production is now done as a sideline, or out of habit, or for the tax benefits or as a matter of lifestyle. Almost all farmland purchases are by non-farmer, urban, non-residents—a mix of home-schoolers, preservationists, retirees and Big City refugees. Friends in Florida agriculture have told me that ordinary citrus land is bringing as much as $25,000 per acre if it's developable. This source of demand—people like you and me—is driving up agricultural land prices in pretty places—the Delmarva Peninsula, New England, southern Appalachia, parts of the Rockies, many parts of the South and on the West Coast.

In places where this type of market is operating, a borrower and his lender should feel very secure about the value of rural-land collateral. A higher-value market is replacing a lower-value market, which lifts every property value. Land prices continue to rise each time a property is sold. This underlying movement should help a land buyer use his current urban property to finance a rural acquisition. If you are looking for property where federal agricultural payments are a presence and urban demand is driving land prices, you're in a pretty good spot.

The three major lenders to farmers are: commercial banks with about 41.3 percent of all farm debt (real estate and non-real estate), federal **Farm Credit Administration (FCA)** with 26.1 percent, and individuals and others with 22.2 percent. Looking at real estate alone, commercial banks hold about 18 percent of the total farm debt, FCA about 17.5 percent, individuals and others about ten percent, life insurance companies about 6.5 percent and the USDA's **Farm Service Agency (FSA)** about 2 percent. The FSA holds a direct loan portfolio and also guarantees farm loans, including certain types of land acquisitions. The federal players in rural mortgage money are the FCA, also known as the **Federal Land Bank**; various programs within the FSA, which focus on loans for emergencies, beginning farmers (ten years of experience or fewer) and farmers socially disadvantaged by way of race, ethnicity or gender; and the **Rural Housing Service**, which provides loans, grants and loan guarantees to low- and moderate-income individuals.

A few federal housing programs may also fit your profile and needs, though they are not directed at rural housing. The Department of Housing and Urban Development (HUD) operates the **Federal Housing Administration (FHA)**, which promotes home-ownership through guaranteeing single-family home mortgages made through FHA-approved lending institutions. The FHA website is helpful: www.hud.gov/offices/hsg/index.cfm. FHA does not make direct mortgage loans. By insuring the loan, the FHA makes the private lender more secure, and, in effect, replaces much of the normal cash down payment. FHA helps low- and moderate-income borrowers whom private lenders would ignore. These borrowers, in turn, must jump certain qualification hurdles: an upfront premium must be paid that is usually factored into the financing; a monthly or annual premium may also be charged; the house must meet certain standards; an FHA-approved appraiser must appraise the property; among others. The lender may charge the borrower discount points on top of a loan-origination fee. A dollar cap is imposed that limits the FHA-insured loan on a single-family residence; in 2003 that cap was $154,896 in most areas though in high-cost locales, like New York/Long Island, it was $280,000.

Title II, Section 203 (b) of the National Housing Act is the most frequently used FHA program. Its purpose is to help qualifying individuals purchase or refinance a principal residence. It provides borrowers with guarantees for fixed-rate loans for ten to 30 years; the rates are competitive; and as much as 97 percent of the *FHA-appraised* value can be borrowed. FHA also operates a guarantee program for mobile homes and home improvements.

FHA has a loan-guarantee program for **Outlying Areas, Section 203 (i)**, for low- and moderate-income individuals in certain "underserved places where mortgages are hard to get." (See: www.hud.gov/progdesc/sin14121.cfm.) The guarantee can apply to the purchase of proposed, under-construction, or existing farm housing or single-family housing on 2 1/2 acres or more adjacent to an all-weather public road. This is a little-used program, but it could help folks who fit the criteria. The website above links to information and regulations.

The **Veterans Administration** (VA) provides loan guarantees to qualifying vets for the purchase of homes, farms, manufactured housing and lots; and the construction of new housing as well as improvements. You may also hear VA loans referred to as "GI loans." The VA does not make direct loans to vets. VA loans (i.e., the VA's guarantee of such a loan that is made by a private lending institution) can be made on no down-payment purchases. The lender can lend up to four times the veteran's "entitlement," which currently amounts to a loan cap of about $240,000. Both the veteran and the property must meet agency eligibility standards. The VA's appraisal process may hang a purchase to the extent that the VA insists the seller correct conditions before the loan guarantee is made. In this circumstance, the seller might pay for the repairs and then raise his price to the veteran to cover the expense. The VA's terms—competitive interest rates, low down payment and other benefits—are borrower-friendly, but there are fees imposed, both by the VA and the lender. If your rural property involves a house that you intend to occupy at least half the year, check out the VA program. Vacation homes, however, won't qualify; nor will purchase of land for investment. If the VA borrower defaults on the mortgage, the VA pays off the lender, leaving the borrower to repay the VA. Borrowers can access the VA through a private lender, real-estate agent or directly through one of nine regional loan centers. Contact information is available on the VA's website: www.homeloans.va.gov/.

If you're interested in working with either the FHA or VA programs, you can get **free pre-purchase counseling** at www.hud.gov/offices/hsg/sfh/hcc/hccprof14.cfm, or 1-800-217-6970.

You will hear about other national mortgage players—Fannie Mae (formerly the Federal National Mortgage Association or FNMA), Ginnie Mae (formerly the Government National Mortgage Association or GNMA), Freddie Mac (Federal Home Loan Mortgage Corporation or FHLMC) and Farmer Mac. These organizations are either federal agencies or quasi-governmental organizations that together make up the country's secondary mortgage market. They don't make direct loans to buyers of land or homes.

Farmer Mac refers to the Federal Agricultural Mortgage Corporation, set up in 1987 by the Agricultural Credit Act as a separate agency within the Farm Credit Administration system. (www.farmermac.com). Farmer Mac is a government-sponsored, though not government-funded, enterprise that provides a secondary market for agricultural real-estate and rural-housing loans. It also buys the guaranteed portions of farmownership and operating loans along with USDA loans made to rural businesses and communities. You and your lender may want to qualify your loan for a Farmer Mac **loan pool** whose requirements include, among others, the loan must be secured by a first lien on agricultural real estate (land, improvements affixed to land, rural housing); the loan must be less than or equal to 70 percent of the property's fair market value; the loan must be for less than $5 million when secured by more than 1,000 acres, and not greater than $22.5 million for loans secured by 1,000 acres or less; and after the loan is in place, the borrower's total assets must be at least twice his total debt. In return, a Farmer Mac loan can offer a borrower a fixed, favorable interest rate.

FCA, FSA and individual states offer programs whereby borrowers can access mortgage money for agricultural and non-agricultural rural property. Such programs provide direct loans and loan guarantees for rural land, rural housing and agricultural enterprises to qualified borrowers. FCA had long-term real-estate loans of more than $35 billion in 2000. FSA direct mortgage lending was about $250 million that year, with more than $1 billion in guarantees for funds coming from private-sector lenders.

If you're looking to buy farmland as an investment, or undeveloped rural land for recreation or appreciation, a locally owned bank and the FCA will be the institutional lenders most likely to work with you.

The Farm Credit Administration (FCA), also known as the Federal Land Bank and the Farm Credit System (FCS), provides direct loans for certain types of property purchases in rural areas. (FCA, 1501 Farm Credit Drive, McLean, Virginia, 22102-5090; 703-883-4000; www.fca.gov/; e-mail: info-line@fca.gov.) These loans are directed to: 1) individuals who want to buy and occupy a single-family residence in the country, and 2) farmers (and others engaged in agricultural production either full- or part-time) to buy farmland and farm equipment. "Farmers" are defined to include those in the timber business, commercial fishermen, ranchers, nursery operators and others who produce an agricultural product. Even if you live in Manhattan, you may be able to qualify for such a farm loan if you can show that you will operate your new farm as a business or a woodland tract for timber production.

The Land Bank will not help you finance a vacation home on rural recreation land. But, the Bank has **forestland loans** available to buy undeveloped timberland (for timber production) on which you can build a second home. The trick is to qualify the woodland as being used for the production of timber, which can be satisfied by an initial cruise and a consultant-prepared timber management plan. The value of the merchantable timber as established by the cruise acts as the Bank's collateral in addition to the land's bare-dirt value. If you don't want to cut the merchantable timber, you may want to consider working out a long-term plan with your forestry consultant who will recommend that you do little to your timber for the term of your note. As an alternative, you could undertake a **timber-stand improvement** immediately (which cuts or removes low-value trees so that the high-value trees have additional resources) and then not cut your increasingly valuable forest. The Land Bank will lend on agricultural land of all types, including producing farms that you use as a second home, referred to as multiple-use. If your second-home farm is set up as a farm (IRS Schedule F) or investment to produce some agricultural product—cattle, timber, crops, orchard products, honey and so on—you should consider the Land Bank programs. You don't have to produce the product yourself; a renter can produce the product.

FCA operates through user-owned regional cooperatives that require each borrower to buy shares in the local land bank (association), proportional to the size of the loan. The five to ten percent of your borrowing that is dedicated to stock purchase provides part of the association's loan capital. Each regional land bank is run independently. Depending on that association's financial performance, dividends may be issued on your stock. Your stock may also be awarded a "patronage refund." When you pay off the note, the balance of your stock is returned at its current value. It's hard to compare the local association's loan package with a local bank's because of the former's dividend/patronage feature and the unpredictability of those returns over time. While you may front more cash to get a Land Bank loan, you should get it back with interest in most cases.

The FCA will lend up to 85 percent of a property's appraised value. If the financing is guaranteed by another federal or state program, a borrower can get up to 97 percent financing. Most Land Bank loans are made to individuals with a net worth of less than $100,000. FCA loans make up almost a quarter of the country's farm-property loans. Get material on the Bank's programs from the local land-bank association, which may be listed in the telephone directory as either "federal land bank" or "farm credit." The county's cooperative extension agent should be able to provide local contact information. The Land Bank system is independent of the USDA's Farm Service Agency.

The USDA's Farm Service Agency (FSA) is the principal entrance into the world of federal agricultural programs (www.fsa.usda.gov). You will find FSA offices in rural areas, though a local office may cover more than one county. The Agency's website gives local office contact information. Walk through the door and start asking questions.

FSA provides direct loans for farmownership of up to $200,000 to purchase land, construct buildings and other facilities, and undertake soil and water conservation. Borrowers must meet certain eligibility requirements. The Agency also provides direct down-payment loans to beginning farmers and direct operating loans of up to $200,000. FSA also provides a loan-guarantee program for farmownership (up to $762,000, adjusted annually) and farm operation. With the direct loans, the borrower has to show that other lenders won't provide a mortgage; similarly, a borrower who wants a guarantee must show he can't obtain credit without one (See www.fsa.usda.gov/dafl/directloans.htm and www.fsa.usda.gov/dafl/Guaranteed.htm).

The other USDA portal is the **Natural Resources Conservation Service (NRCS)**, which administers an assortment of programs intended to conserve soils, water quality and supply; reduce erosion; and otherwise benefit land used for agricultural purposes. NRCS funds conservation-enhancing practices, such as tree planting and spring development, but does not provide money to purchase land. The local FSA office will put you in touch with the NRCS programs.

The **Rural Housing Service (RHS)** is the USDA agency that succeeded the Farmers Home Administration (FmHA), but it is not part of either the FSA or the NRCS. To access the RHS, which has no field staff, you have to contact the USDA's local Rural Development staff through the local FSA office. The RHS website is: www.rurdev.usda.gov/rhs/Individual/ind_splash.htm. Most of the RHS programs are directed to low- and very low-income individuals, and involve direct home-ownership loans, home-repair loans and grants, rent subsidies and other services. The RHS's Section 502 direct-loan program provided more than $1 billion in direct loans and $3 billion in loan guarantees for its target population, which is, generally, families with income below 80 percent of the median income in their communities. The Section 502 loan-guarantee program will finance 100 percent to eligible individuals.

Foreclosed USDA farms and houses can be accessed at www.resales.usda.gov.

I used my local Farm Credit Association (Land Bank/FCS) when I bought the farm where I've lived since 1983. At that time, I did not know how to shop for a loan. The appraiser chosen by the FCA came in at about $127,000 on a purchase price of $143,500. The seller eagerly agreed to take back a three-year second for $30,000 to make the deal go through, with $113,500 in FCA financing. I should have done some renegotiating with the seller over purchase price, given the gap between the lender's FMV appraisal at $127,000 and the purchase price of $143,500. But I did not have an appraisal contingency—performance on the contract being dependent on the appraisal value at least equaling the purchase price—in my contract. I've subsequently seen other FCA appraisals come in below contract prices, which forces the buyer to come up with more cash or work in a seller second. I refinanced the FCA loan with a local bank five or six years later when interest rates were considerably lower. I advance no claim that the local land bank jiggered appraisals intentionally, since I have no way of knowing what its internal policies are. I would consider FCA financing as one option of several when buying rural land. If you are working with the FCA, I'd advise that you talk with the FCA-approved appraiser before he visits your target property. You are aware that he has a business relationship with the FCA. The least you should insist on is honesty, fairness and professionalism.

Various states help low- and moderate-income individuals acquire single-family housing in rural areas. Private non-profit housing organizations also help with lot purchase and house construction. You will have to dig out the names of the programs and the agencies by interminable telephone or Internet work. For state agencies, start looking under "rural development," "housing," "farming" and "mortgage." HUD's website provides links to state programs: www.hud.gov/buying/localbuying.cfm. For private programs, start with Habitat for Humanity in the target county, the county's local economic development office and any county office with "housing," "farming" or "development" in its name. You can also learn about rural housing through the National Housing Law Project, 614 Grand Ave., Suite 320, Oakland, CA 94610; 510-251-9400; 510-451-2300 FAX; www.nhlp.org/html.

12. 1031 Like-Kind (Starker) Exchange

The Internal Revenue Code's (IRC), Section 1031, allows a taxpayer to exchange one kind of property for a **like-kind** property *of equal or greater value* without creating a taxable event. The properties need to be like in type, but not identical. You can't exchange a car for a lot, but you can exchange a rental house for undeveloped land, or an apartment building for a farm, because all four are real property. The property that the taxpayer exchanges (from) must be "held for productive use in trade or business or for investment." This excludes exchanging out of your principal residence and into a farm held as an investment, but you could exchange out of an urban rental property that you own or a vacation home that you rent out a sufficient number of days each year into timberland or undeveloped pasture held for investment. You cannot exchange out of a property that you hold primarily for sale or that you've acquired for the purpose of making a like-kind exchange. Stocks, bonds, notes and certain other securities and interests cannot be exchanged. Personal property can be exchanged for personal property, but the items have to be of the same type—a car for a car, but not a car for equipment.

This technique is often referred to as a **Starker exchange**, named for the taxpayer who exchanged title to his timberland for a contractual promise from Crown-Zellerbach to acquire like-kind property designated by him at a future date. The company paid Starker no cash at the time he conveyed title and carried its obligation to him as a credit on its books. When Crown-Zellerbach acquired the properties that Starker wanted, their titles were transferred to him. This was a delayed exchange, which the U.S. Supreme Court upheld in *T.J. Starker vs. U.S.*, 432 F. Supp 864 (D.OR. 1977) aff'd, rev'd & rem'd 602 F. 2d 1341 (9th Cir., 1979).

A like-kind exchange is not a *sale*, where you, the seller/taxpayer, walk away with a cash gain on which you pay tax. (If you do get some cash out of an exchange, you have to pay tax on it.) In an exchange, your taxable gain is retained in the like-kind property that you've exchanged into, and your tax obligation on that gain is deferred until you sell. Tax deferred is tax eroded. A dollar in tax owed today will cost you less than 50 cents in 20 years or so, owing to inflation. Like-kind exchanges protect profit. If the sale of your property won't generate taxable gain, you have no reason to do an exchange.

If the exchanged-into property passes into your estate, much, if not all, of the deferred tax obligation can be erased, depending on the size of your estate and applicable tax policy in the year of your death. The value of the exchanged-into property—as well as all other assets of the decedent—is calculated on the day of death, not the date of the property's purchase by the decedent. Heirs inherit this **stepped-up basis** in the exchanged property. **"Basis"** is the owner's financial interest in a property for IRS purposes, used to calculate gain or loss on a sale. An owner's basis starts with the property's original cost. **Adjusted basis** reflects additions and subtractions to the owner's starting basis over his term of ownership. Depreciation lowers basis; new investment increases it. A stepped-up basis through inheritance allows the heir to sell the asset with taxable gain figured on the value of the property at the time of inheritance. This can result in a tax-free, or at least a tax-diminished, sale when the heir flips this inherited exchanged property.

A 1031 exchange works for a seller who does not need cash from the sale of his property. If you sell because you need cash, don't involve yourself in an exchange. The exchanger must keep all the cash equity built up in the just-sold property going forward into the property that he acquires through the exchange. You can't cash out partially, except by a pre-exchange refinancing. Because the exchange defers tax on gain until the last exchanged-into property is sold for cash, it is an excellent way of building wealth. You buy a property, allow it to appreciate, exchange, defer tax, allow that property to appreciate, exchange, defer tax, and so on. When all is said and done, the most you will likely owe is the then-current capital-gains tax applied to taxable gain figured against your adjusted basis. You can pull cash out of exchange properties by borrowing against them. Various ways exist to soften any final tax burden, involving estates, trusts, gifts, charitable donations and the like.

1031 exchanges can be worked into your purchase of rural property. In its simplest two-party form, you would exchange an apartment building you own for rental income in Big City worth $500,000 for a 200-acre farm in Blue Sky County, also worth $500,000. No money changes hands; no taxable gain is recognized by either party.

A far more common format is a **three-party exchange** that involves a buyer for your (the taxpayer's) property and an escrow agent. Here's how it works. You, the taxpayer, sell your rental building to Mr. Buyer who deposits $500,000 into an escrow account. The holder of the escrow account, called the "qualified intermediary," is a neutral player who manages the escrow's mechanics for a fee. He will provide the paperwork, including the "exchange agreement," which spells out how everything is to work. You, the taxpayer/seller, do not get Mr. Buyer's $500,000 from the escrow account—ever. When the escrow opens, you put the deed to your rental building into it. You are conveying your deed into the escrow. Mr. Farmowner also puts his deed to the 200 acres you want into the same escrow. At that point, there are two deeds and $500,000 in the escrow pot. Then the escrow agent gives 1) $500,000 to Mr. Farmowner to complete your purchase of his 200 acres, 2) the deed to your rental goes to Mr. Buyer, and 3) the deed to Mr. Farmowner's farm comes to you. Your basis in the 200 acres starts with whatever your final adjusted basis was in the rental property you sold. But you pay no tax on any gain, because you've never realized any taxable gain on the property sold. A three-party exchange of this sort has no effect on Mr. Farmowner who gets his $500,000 or Mr. Buyer who gets your rental apartment property. Mr. Farmowner may owe tax on his gain from the sale, but the gain that you've realized over the time you've owned your rental is tax-deferred. Diagram 33-1 below shows the flow of money and paper into and out of the escrow pot.

Exchanges in real life, of course, involve complications—mortgage payoffs, unequal values of the like-kind properties being exchanged; appraisals; basis; and **boot,** which is the cash or personal property that one party puts in to bring his property up to the value of the property that he wants to exchange into. Boot is usually cash, but it can be other things that qualify under the IRS rules. If your rental is worth $450,000, you might put in $50,000 to make the exchange for the 200 acres even. You would pay no tax on the boot. You, the taxpayer/exchanger must never be in receipt of the cash from your sale, collect interest from that cash, or control the cash in the escrow. Where mortgages are involved, the party whose mortgage principal is reduced through the exchange pays tax on that reduction.

Since the exchange must comply with the federal rules, it is important to use a qualified intermediary who knows them and walks you through each step. Time limits, for instance, are critical. The taxpayer who is doing the exchange has 45 days from the date he relinquishes his property to identify the property he wants to exchange into. And the exchange must usually be completed within 180 days of the date of relinquishment. You can exchange one property for several as long as all other requirements are satisfied.

DIAGRAM 33-1

1031 Exchange Flow

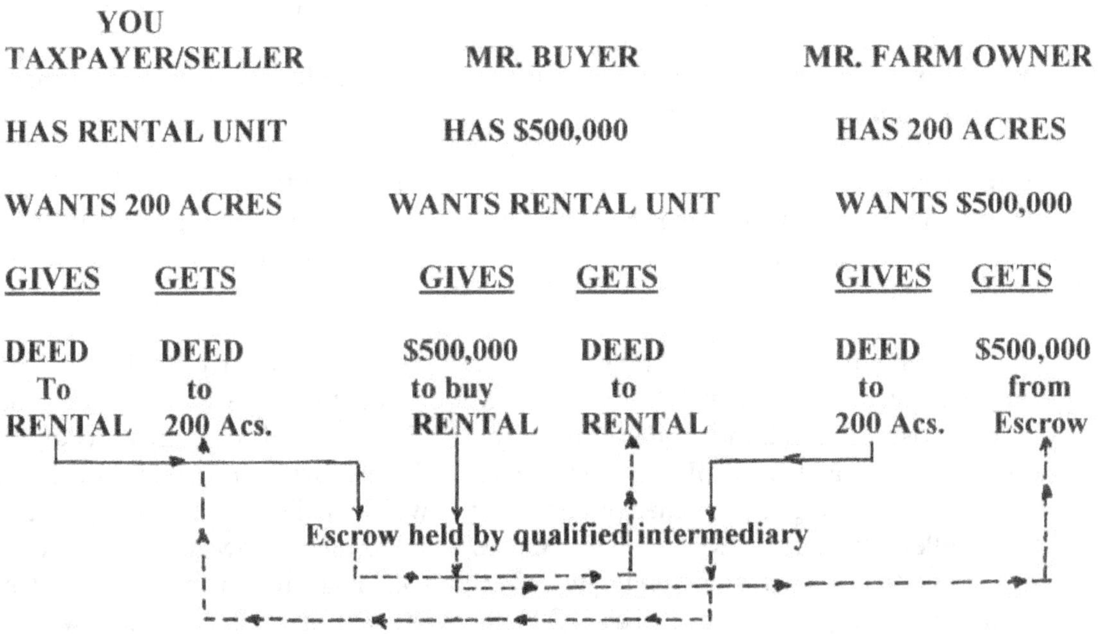

YOU TAXPAYER/SELLER		MR. BUYER		MR. FARM OWNER	
HAS RENTAL UNIT		HAS $500,000		HAS 200 ACRES	
WANTS 200 ACRES		WANTS RENTAL UNIT		WANTS $500,000	
GIVES	GETS	GIVES	GETS	GIVES	GETS
DEED To RENTAL	DEED to 200 Acs.	$500,000 to buy RENTAL	DEED to RENTAL	DEED to 200 Acs.	$500,000 from Escrow

Escrow held by qualified intermediary

A land buyer may also have occasion to consider a **reverse like-kind exchange**. In simple terms, a reverse exchange occurs when you have identified the rural property that you want to exchange into in advance of finding a buyer for the property that you want to sell and exchange out of. This situation arises when you fear the country property you want may sell before you can get your exchange lined up. In that case, you can arrange with an "accommodator" to buy the property you want and hold it for you until you find a buyer. Once you have a buyer, you transfer your property to the accommodator who sells it to the buyer. The accommodator then transfers title to the rural property to you. The IRS refers to this as a "qualified exchange accommodation arrangement." Time limits and other requirements are imposed. A reverse exchange, where the taxpayer acquires the replacement property before divesting himself of property he is selling, has not been approved by the IRS. Nonetheless, if done carefully, it appears, at least to a tax illiterate like me, to be workable. (See Max Hansen, "What is a 1031 Exchange?" www.bozeman~montana~real~estate.net/1031~exchange.htm; and "Unusual Like-Kind Exchanges," Small Business Taxes & Management, August 1, 2000; www.smbiz.com/sbw1080.html; and "FAQ The 'How To' of Real Property Exchanges," undated; http://freec.net/FAQ.html.)

Here are some general ways to weave a three-party 1031 exchange into your effort to obtain rural property:

Exchange your non-residence, second-home property for rural property;

Exchange an investment property for a rural investment property;

Exchange a business with a building/land for a farm business;

Exchange a vehicle you own for farm vehicle;

Exchange equipment you own for farm equipment;

Exchange a conservation easement for farmland or timberland; (See IRS, Letter Ruling No. 9621012, February 16, 1996.)

Exchange an urban lot for timber or mineral rights.

An experienced dirt lawyer in the county where you're buying should know how to advise you on doing an exchange. If a question arises, I would run to a CPA who knows the 1031 regs since an ounce of prevention is worth ten pounds of legal briefs in search of a cure. "Qualified intermediaries" are also found on the Internet.

13. Conservation Easements

From a buyer's perspective, a **conservation easement** that benefits the buyer is a tax break that can protect income and assets. But a conservation easement that the seller has imposed is a tax break that's already been taken and which, in many cases, will diminish the value of a target property in perpetuity.

A conservation easement separates some property right that has value from the property. The separated right is given to a certain-type of organization that owns and manages it from then on. The separated right must involve a legitimate conservation purpose. If you buy 100 acres and want to build houses on 60 acres, but leave the ugly back 40 alone, the ugly 40 won't qualify as a conservation value worthy of protection based on ugliness and your need for a tax break. If, on the other hand, the ugly 40 is important wetlands, donating a no-development/no-disturbance easement would probably qualify. The size of the tax break depends on the appraised value of the donation. It can be used to protect the gain you made from the sale of a property whose proceeds you used to buy the country place on which you placed the donated easement. You will be able to use the break against current income in future tax years until it is gone. You should also have the tax-appraised value of your country property lowered in proportion to the value of the easement that you've given away, hence a lower property-tax bill. Individual states also offer tax benefits for these easements. Finally, you can reduce the value of your estate through a conservation easement on property in your estate, thus reducing anticipated estate tax.

A conservation easement is not a free lunch. A conservation easement imposes some type of restriction on a valuable use of the owner's land usually *in perpetuity* for the purpose of promoting one or more conservation objectives. The restriction might prohibit activity, forgo an activity or require an activity. A typical easement on farmland near metropolitan areas is a full prohibition on residential and commercial development to preserve open space.

A less onerous easement—and one with proportionately less monetary value to the donor/taxpayer—is a cap on residential density. On a 1,000-acre farm near Big City, for instance, the easement might limit residential construction to no more than one home per 25 acres instead of no homes on 1,000 acres. A partial restriction of this type may be able to give the landowner the amount of tax benefits he wants while protecting his land to an acceptable level. Another type of easement might define acceptable and unacceptable uses for the land. The owner might, for example, place an easement on his land that prohibits all mineral development or all timber harvesting; or limit one or both activities in areas that are environmentally sensitive.

Each conservation easement is written to fit the particular needs of the owner and the characteristics of his land. Organizations like The Nature Conservancy (TNC) and land trusts are very interested in accepting easements on environmentally significant land, such as wetlands, the headwaters of certain watersheds and habitat for endangered species. Local and regional land trusts will work with small properties, as long as the land covered by the easement and the use-right that is donated has some conservation importance. Tax-exempt conservation organizations will not accept an easement over environmentally insignificant land. Conservation organizations emphasize different objectives, so you may find yourself talking with a state wildlife agency, a local land trust or a branch of a national organization. Informative gateway websites include The Nature Conservancy (http://nature.org/, (refers to state and local affiliates); The Conservation Fund (http://www.conservationfund.org/); The Trust for Public Land (http://www.tpl.org/); and the Land Trust Alliance (http://www.lta.org/).

While there are circumstances where a conservation organization will either buy environmentally important land or buy a conservation easement, the more widespread practice is for individual landowners to donate an easement to such an organization and take the tax benefits. Once the easement is donated, the conservation organization is responsible for managing it and assuring the landowner's compliance with its terms. The organization may charge the donor/taxpayer a one-time fee to cover the anticipated future costs of managing the easement, but this practice is more common with very large tracts. The easement is recorded and runs with the land so that all subsequent owners are bound by it. Some easements can be bought back if they are drafted with such a provision originally. Public access is not required to property bearing a conservation easement, though some form of public access to private land may be one of the elements voluntarily incorporated into an easement.

The dollar value of any particular conservation easement is determined through an appraisal by a neutral professional. What is being estimated is the current fair market value of the easement, i.e., the right in the property that the landowner is proposing to donate. If, for example, you are fortunate enough to own a 500-acre farm 15 miles from the U.S. Capitol, your **development rights** in that land are worth millions. Preserving some or all of your farm as open space or limiting development density are sound conservation objectives. An appraiser would compare your property to others of similar size and type in the area that have been sold recently to developers. Let's assume that comparables sold for $25,000 per acre and the appraiser determines that the land less all development rights with continued use as farmland is worth $4,000 per acre. Accordingly, the value of the donated development rights is $21,000 per acre, or $10.5 million.

The tax benefits to the donor vary according to the individual's circumstances. **You should have a competent CPA/lawyer who does a lot of work with conservation easements in the state where the property is located and the state where you live run the numbers for each conservation-easement option you are considering _before_ you make any choice and _before_ you make an offer to purchase.** I advise clients to have these conservation-easement options calculated as part of their property scoping so that the buyer knows in advance of purchase his range of probable tax benefits, if any.

As of 2005 in the example above, the $10.5 million value can be taken against up to 30 percent of an individual's gross income with certain adjustments (called a "contribution base") during the donation year. Any unused portion can be taken during the next five years. The landowner in this case could subtract $1.75 million a year from his gross income (with certain adjustments) for six years, as long as the amount of the deduction never exceeded 30 percent of his gross income with adjustments in any year. If the donor takes the deduction using his "adjusted basis" in the property—which is usually the case with buyers who immediately donate an easement as part of their purchase strategy and "adjusted basis" essentially amounts to the recent purchase price—the deduction can rise to 50 percent of adjusted gross income. In both cases, any unused portion of the deduction can be carried over for a maximum of five years following the donation year. The deduction benefits vary according to who is making the donation—an individual can use the 30 percent standard, but corporations can use only ten percent. This difference may determine whether a buyer organizes his ownership as an individual investment, corporation or limited liability company, among other choices. An easement's value may be deducted up to 50 percent of an individual donor's income in certain circumstances, which includes the first year following the property's purchase. Competent, seasoned professional help is required to obtain the maximum tax benefit. Even more generous time-frames and deductions were put into place in 2006, extending the carry-forward period for deductions to 15 years and raising the deduction caps.

Current information on conservation easements is available from "qualified organizations" themselves, including local, state and federal agencies along with private organizations, such as land trusts. These organizations, however, may be reluctant to provide tax counsel. To get started, read Section 170 (h) of the Internal Revenue Code along with relevant regulations. An excellent guide to this subject is: C. Timothy Linstrom, Esq., "A Simplified Guide to The Tax Benefits of Donating A Conservation Easement," October, 2001, which is available from the author at The Jackson Hole Land Trust, PO Box 2897, 555 East Broadway, Suite 228, Jackson, WY 83001; 307-733-4707; tim@jhlandtrust.org. The legal guru of conservation easements is Stephen J. Small, a lawyer who helped draft the statute and then wrote the 170 (h) regulations. He's written several books on the subject and now has a private practice specializing in conservation easements. (See Stephen J. Small, 75 Federal St., Suite 1100, Boston, MA 02110; 617-357-4012; www.stevesmall.com; e-mail stevesmall@stevesmall.com.)

States also offer varying tax benefits for donors of conservation easements. North Carolina, for example, offers a tax credit for up to 25 percent of the fair market value of the "donated property interest" (i.e., value of the easement) with a maximum credit of $250,000 for individuals and $500,000 for corporations. (See The Conservation Trust for North Carolina, www.ctnc.org.) Virginia allows its taxpayers to apply one-half of their easement's appraised value against their state income tax bill. This credit can be used over five years; it can also be sold. (Lawrence Latane, III, "Easements protect land from development," Richmond Times-Dispatch, March 16, 2003.) Tim Linstrom surveyed the tax benefits in all 50 states in "State Tax Incentives for Conservation Easements Can Benefit Everyone," Journal of MultiState Taxation and Incentives, November/December, 2002. The local "qualified organization" that would accept your donated easement can explain current state policy.

Two other tax benefits attach to a conservation easement. First, since the landowner is giving up something of value in his property, his local property-tax burden should be proportionally reduced. Localities will have different ways of discounting their tax-appraised values, so your scoping should include a visit to the local assessor to determine your likely benefit in advance once you have a good idea of the easement's appraisal value. Second, for estate purposes, a conservation easement reduces the value of the decedent's real property on which it falls, thereby enabling the estate to pay less tax. This may or may not benefit your particular estate depending on its total value, estate components, and federal and state tax policies in the year of your death. The other estate benefit is the exclusion of 40 percent of the land's value after the easement's value is subtracted. A number of qualifications and limitations apply to this "40 percent exclusion" so it's essential that you talk to a knowledgeable CPA or lawyer before assuming that your estate will enjoy the full 40 percent exclusion on a specific property.

The dirt-smart buyer should evaluate his target property for conservation-easement potential. Every easement must promote some environmental or conservation objective. Depending on the individual property, such objectives could include one or more of the following donations, among others:

- development rights to preserve open space
- partial development rights (limits residential-development density or limits development to certain portions of the property)
- rights to change current uses
- right to explore for/extract subsurface minerals
- right to cut timber, in whole or in part
- right to erect wind turbines on ridges or other sensitive areas
- right to farmland that has significant environmental values (such as, habitat for critical species)
- rights to engage in certain high-impact, industrial-type farming activities, (such as a feedlot or confined livestock facilities) or commercial activity (such as landfill)
- right to use water from critical source (such as river or aquifer) whose water is also needed to support habitat

In each case, the value of an easement right is determined by a qualified appraiser and the organization that is the intended recipient. The IRS imposes certain standards that the appraisal must fit. A common source of getting in trouble with these easements is to have a compliant appraiser inflate the value of the right being donated. While appraising a right in a property is always going to be somewhat subjective, it is not a bottomless cookie jar. A bit of puffing is likely to slip by; greed probably won't. The receiving organization does not want to have its tax-exempt status challenged on the grounds that it is being used by tax scammers.

To maximize your tax benefits and minimize future IRS problems, develop a plan for a conservation easement on a target property before submitting an offer and with the assistance of an experienced CPA and lawyer. Your easement idea must meet the IRS's standards, and you must have the numbers (of your tax benefits) run in advance of negotiating a purchase price. You need professional help to do this. (Do I need to repeat this?) The local organization should have a list of experienced appraisers, CPAs and lawyers.

Conservation easements can protect a buyer's profit in flipping a target property, as well as profit from the taxpayer's other activities. They don't directly generate money to buy, but they can increase after-tax net income. A buyer has to run sale numbers on a flip with alternative easement scenarios to see, which, if any, are of benefit. Without an easement, a buyer who flips can expect higher gross income, but less net after-tax; with an easement, there will be lower gross sale income but possibly more after tax. When buying property that carries a conservation easement, remember you are buying less than the whole package of rights. The property should be priced below how it would be priced in tact.

Life is always easier when you have cash. It certainly helps when buying land. There's nothing wrong with putting 30 percent down in cash and borrowing the rest from the first bank that gives you two balloons and a lollipop. That's easy. If you're not cash-lucky, consider some of the ways I've presented to piece together a purchase using the cash you can comfortably spare, different types of debt, the resources of the property itself and the federal tax code. Think of patching together a financing package, a technique that works as well on a $25,000 two-acre lot as on a $10 million purchase of 10,000 acres. Patching purchase money together from five or six sources takes time and persistence, but it can save you thousands of dollars. Not having cash is a problem that can almost always be solved as long as you acquire the information you need to develop a feasible plan before you submit an offer. But no plan should stretch your ability to pay off mortgage debt.

CHAPTER 34: A FINAL PLEA

As I was writing, I heard a report that 90 percent of house buyers make a yes/no decision within the first 30 minutes of their first visit. And about the same percentage of big life decisions are made on the basis of emotions, what feels right.

Given this evidence, the best advice I can offer is this: don't communicate your intention to buy to the seller or his agent during your first visit or immediately thereafter.

Take the questions and methods I've discussed and start scoping the property you've already chosen to buy. But leave yourself room for an analytical out. If your head can't solve the property's problems and issues during your scoping, buying certainly won't. Keep looking. Most problems have solutions, fortunately, but some are too expensive to consider seriously.

Scoping a property that you must have will help you in at least two ways: first, you'll know what you're getting into before you get there, which can help you negotiate solutions with the seller; and second, you'll know what you're getting into before you get there whether or not you can negotiate solutions with the seller.

Knowledge is worth the time spent and expense of acquiring it.

CHAPTER 35: AFTERWORD

I provide three types of consulting services to land buyers.

First, I provide telephone consultations charged at $125 per hour. My number is: 540-474-3297.

I do not accept credit cards. They add cost to my service and detract from the trust I promote with my clients.

Send me a check for $62.50, which covers my time in setting up your account and provides you with 30 minutes of assistance. Call me five days after putting your check in the mail. Time beyond the first 30 minutes is billed to you at my hourly rate. Payment is due at the end of each session.

Focus your questions as much as possible. Put them in writing. I am not a lawyer or a CPA, so specific questions in those fields are better directed to those practitioners. I have a network of contacts around the country, which may be useful to you.

Second, you can mail me a summary of your situation and follow it up with a phone consultation. Include your address, phone, fax and e-mail. I'll get back to you as soon as I can.

I charge a flat $50 to read your initial contact information and think about it. Enclose a check for that amount, made out to Curtis Seltzer. After that it's $125 per hour. I've found over the years that clients are best served by taking the time to put their story in writing rather than tell it to me cold. Keep your narrative to three or four pages.

Send this to:

Curtis Seltzer

1467 Wimer Mountain Road

Blue Grass, VA 24413-2307

Third, I am available to find property on a fee basis. My fee is a percentage of the gross sales price, to be paid by the settlement agent from the buyer's funds at closing. The amount of the fee depends on the size and value of the property purchased along with other factors. The larger the property, the lower the percentage. You and I will sign a contract that sets forth my duties and your obligations.

This is a finder's service. A small amount of consulting will be thrown in for free. But after that, say an hour, I will charge the hourly rate. You owe me the fee only if you buy a property that I introduce to you, but you owe me the hourly rate for discussions beyond the basic introduction.

Scoping is charged at the hourly rate. If you want me to visit the property with you, I will charge the hourly rate, plus expenses.

If you're interested in working with me as a consultant-finder, write me a short letter that outlines what you're looking for, where, why and your price range. I don't charge for reading these proposals. I'll talk with you and send a contract if we decide to work together.

I'm not a real-estate agent or broker, and I do not provide clients with brokerage services. I am paid by the buyer, not the seller.

MONEY-BACK GUARANTEE

If you feel after reading
How To Be a DIRT-SMART Buyer of Country Property
that you did not get $34.95 worth of information
or, at least, 700 pages of sleep therapy, send me the umarked copy
with your receipt and I will reimburse you.

Positive comments are welcome – especially from those who don't
owe me money and family relations with different last names.

I may post comments on my website, www.curtis-seltzer.com.

Snide, nitpicky and hateful observations will be posted on my office wall where
they will do the most good.

curtisseltzer@htcnet.org

www.ingramcontent.com/pod-product-compliance
Lightning Source LLC
Chambersburg PA
CBHW081104170526
45165CB00008B/2321